GIVING WISELY

THE ISRAEL GUIDE TO NON-PROFIT AND VOLUNTEER SOCIAL SERVICES

GIVING WISELY

THE ISRAEL GUIDE
TO
NON-PROFIT
AND
VOLUNTEER SOCIAL SERVICES

Written and edited by
PROF. ELIEZER D. JAFFE

KOREN PUBLISHERS JERUSALEM LTD

Platemakers: Agaf, Jerusalem
Press: S. Monson Ltd., Jerusalem

Printed in Israel

A DEDICATION

This book is dedicated to my parents:
Elchanan, of blessed memory;
and Sarah,
who taught me the difference between good intentions and good deeds;
to my wife, Rivka,
who is the kindest person and wisest social worker I have ever known;
and to my children, Uri, Yael, Naomi, and Ruthi, my loyal fans
and greatest comfort.

ACKNOWLEDGEMENTS

The author is indebted to Raquel (Rachel) Newman-Naymark, Alice and Morris Zipkin, and Aryeh Geiger for advice, encouragement, and professional help provided me during the work on this book. Special thanks are due to The New Israel Fund, the P.E.F. Israel Endowment Funds, Roger Herz, the American Jewish Committee, the Gimprich Foundation, The Samuel Bronfman Foundation, The Borchard Family, and the Zahavi Association for Rights of Large Families for grants which enabled the preparation and publication of the book.
And finally, my appreciation is acknowledged to the Korén Publishers and their staff for their assistance in publishing this book.

TABLE OF CONTENTS

8 SUBJECT INDEX CODES

9 INDEX OF ORGANIZATIONS

19 PREFACE

INTRODUCTION
20   Guide for the Perplexed Philanthropist
21   What About the U.J.A.?
23   A Resource Directory for Israelis

23 HOW THE GUIDE WAS PREPARED
24   Who Was Left Out
25   The Questionnaire
26   Preparation and Accuracy of the Profiles

26 HOW TO USE THE GUIDE

27 A PLEA FOR PARTNERSHIP PHILANTHROPY

29 ORGANIZATION PROFILES
   Profiles of Non-Profit Organizations
   (in alphabetical order)

656 RECOMMENDED READING

SUBJECT INDEX CODES

A — Academic and Professional Educational Institutions, Professional Associations, and Research Institutes.

B — Alcohol and Drug Addiction Prevention Services.

C — Arts, Libraries and Museums.

D — Child Welfare Services (Day Care, Abused and Orphan Children, Special Education).

E — Civil Rights Organizations and Activities.

F — Community Centers, Youth Centers, Summer Camps, and Recreation Services.

G — Community, Neighborhood, and Public Interest Groups.

H — Delinquent Youth, Prisoners and Ex-Offenders.

I — Elderly and Infirmed Persons.

J — Employment, Training and Vocational Services.

K — Family Counselling, Therapy and Psychological Services.

L — Family Planning and Pregnancy Advisory Services.

M — Financial Assistance (Foundations, Grants, Loans, Scholarships).

N — Fraternal Organizations.

O — Handicapped Persons (Physical and Mental Disability).

P — Health, Hospital and Dental Services.

Q — Homes, Shelters and Substitute Care.

R — Immigrant Absorption Services and Associations.

S — Interfaith Groups and Activities.

T — Jewish/Arab Friendship Groups and Activities.

U — Pets and Animal Protection Services.

V — Publication and Information Services.

W — Women's Social Action and Service Groups.

X — Yeshivot, Synagogues, and Religious Education.

ALPHABETICAL INDEX

OF

ORGANIZATIONS

Page	Subject Code	Name of Organization

A

Page	Subject Code	Name of Organization
29	D,Q	Achusat Sara Children's Home
31	G,O,P	Adi: The Society for Promoting Transplants in Israel
32	D,O,P	Agoudat Naschim 'Lina'
34	M	Agudat G'mach Mazkeret Dov
35	D,V,X	Agudath Israel World Organization
37	D,Q	Ahava Children and Youth Home
38	I,M	Ahavat Chesed Society
39	V,X	Aish Hatorah: College of Jewish Studies
42	A,P	Aldema Foundation
43	K,O	Alfred Adler Institute
45	D,O	Alin Mossad Abrahams — Israel Society for Crippled Children
47	B	Al-Sam Anti Drug Abuse Association
49	D,O	Alut, Israeli Society for Autistic Children
51	V,X	Amana — Institute for the Publication of Judaic Studies in Russian and Georgian
53	A,X	Amishav Organization for the Lost Tribes of Israel
55	U	Animal Protection Society, Jerusalem
56	A,D	Aptowitzer Foundation for Haifa
58	F,R	Ashdod Community Center (Neighborhood Heh)
60	A	Association for Advancement of Social Work in Israel
62	E	Association for Civil Rights in Israel
64	M,T	Association for Housing Israeli Arabs and Other Minorities in Jerusalem
65	K,R	Association for Mutual Asistance of Irgun Olei Holland
67	O,P	Association for Promoting Health Services for the Public
69	J	Association for the Promotion of Youth Technical Clubs in Israel
71	H,X	Association for the Propagation of Torah
73	M,R	Association of Americans and Canadians in Israel (AACI)
75	O,Q	Association of the Blind in Israel, Jerusalem Branch
77	M,O	Association of the Deaf in Israel
79	D,M,W	Association of Victims of Work Related Accidents and their Widows in Israel
81	I,R	Association of Yemenite Immigrants — Irgun Yotzei Teiman — Hamerkaz
83	M,O	Association to Aid the Blind and Prevention of Blindness

Page	Subject Code	Name of Organization

B

Page	Subject Code	Name of Organization
85	C,V	Bamah Association
86	M	B.A.M.B.I.—Matan Beseter
88	M,V,X	Baruch Ta'am Rabbinical College
89	X	Be'ar Maim Chaim Yeshiva
91	F	Beit Eshkol Community Center of Afula
92	F,T	Beit Kedem
94	F	Beit Miriam Community Centre
96	X	Beit Shmuel—Yeshivat Bnai Akiva, Hadera
98	A	Ben-Gurion University of the Negev
100	D,Q	Ben Shemen Youth Village
102	I,Q	Beth Avot Kiryat Sanz
104	J,X	Beth Bracha—Traditional Religious Schools for Girls
106	F,M	Beth Hanoch
108	D,K	Big Brother League of Haifa
110	I,Q	B'nai Brith Parents Home
112	J,X	B'nei Akiva Yeshiva Nachal Yitschak at Nechalim
113	S,T	Bridge, The (Hagesher)
115	M,N	Brith Rishonim Veteran Zionist Organization in Israel

C

Page	Subject Code	Name of Organization
117	X	Cave of Machpelah Yeshiva
119	V,X	Center for Torah Libraries
121	X	Central Committee for Religious Education in Israel
123	X	Central Institutions of Zvehill, Yeshivat Beth Mordechai
125	V,O	Central Library for the Blind and Visually and Physically Handicapped
127	D,M,X	Central Neshei Agudat Israel
129	D,F	Central Parents Association of Greater Tel-Aviv
131	V,X	Chamber of Holocaust Committee Inc.
133	M	Charity Organization for Israel in Memory of Yaakov Moshe Rivlin
135	X	Chaye Yehudit—Seminary for Women
137	M	Children's Memorial Fund for Children
139	F,T	C.I.S.V.—Children's International Summer Villages
141	X	Collel Bayit Began
143	G	Committe for Safeguarding Human Dignity
145	M	Committee of Honen-U-Malveh
146	A,R	Community College, Mateh Yehuda
148	O,Q	Community Residential Services for the Mentally Retarded
150	F,T	Community Center of Tamra
152	X	Congregation Mevakshei Derech
154	A,R	Council for the University of Israel
156	F	Council of Youth Movements in Israel

D

Page	Subject Code	Name of Organization
159	A	David Yellin Teachers College
161	P	Dental Volunteers for Israel (D.V.I.)

Page	Subject Code	Name of Organization
163	X	Diaspora Yeshiva Institute for Women
165	X	Diaspora Yeshiva Toras Yisrael
167	A,V	Dr. Falk Schlesinger Institute for Medical-Halachic Research of Shaare Zedek Hospital, Jerusalem
169	C,V	Dr. Samuel and Rivka Hurwich Literature Fund
171	I,Q	Dr. Zimmerman's Old Age Home for Sages

E

Page	Subject Code	Name of Organization
173	K	Edfone — Religious Help Through the Telephone
175	H,X	Education Centre, Mevasseret Zion
177	D,Q	Educational Boarding Home for Israeli Children
179	D	E.L.I. — Israeli Association for Child Protection
181	C,M	Eliezer and Bluma Gordon Fund
182	X	Emet Le'Yaakov Yeshiva
184	C	Emanuel Jaffe Museum of Jewish Education
186	O	Enosh, The Organization for the Advancement of the Mentally Disordered in Israel
188	I,O	Ezrat Holim Organization
190	M	Ezrath Torah of America in Israel

F

Page	Subject Code	Name of Organization
192	D,M	Federation of Jewish Relief Organisations in Great Britain
194	M,R	Free Loan Fund Le'Ichud Mishpachot
196	X	Friends of Converts in Israel
198	J,X	Friends of the Midrashia
201	P	Friends of the Rothschild University Hospital
203	D,O	Friends of the Home for Young Disabled in San-Simon, Katamon, Jerusalem

G

Page	Subject Code	Name of Organization
205	Q,X	Gan Yavne Youth Village — Yeshivat Achuzat Yaakov
207	F,M	Gemillut Hesed Fund of the World Council of Synagogues and the Center for Conservative Judaism
209	X	Gesher Educational Affiliates
211	D,Q	Geulah Children's Boarding Home
212	F	Gonenim Community Center
213	F,M	Greek Orthodox Community Council, Acre

H

Page	Subject Code	Name of Organization
215	D,X	Habad Ir-Ganim, Jerusalem
217	D,Q	Hafetz Haim Orphanage
218	A,V	Haktav Institute
220	J,Q,X	Hamerkaz Lechinuch Banot — Beit Bluma
222	J,O	HaMeshakem Limited
224	F	Harry Steele Community Center of Kiryat Ono
226	P	Hasharon Hospital
228	M,X	Hayal — Educating Young Jewish Boys to Torah
230	A,X	Hebrew Union College — Jewish Institute of Religion

Page	Subject Code	Name of Organization
232	A	Hebrew University of Jerusalem
235	M	Helping Hand Association: Nozer Chesed
236	M	Helping Hand Supermarket
238	R	Hitachdut Olei Australia and New Zealand
240	Q,X	Hodayot Religious Youth Village
242	A	Holocaust and Social Trauma Studies
244	I,Q	Home for the Aged
245	X	Horeb Schools of Jerusalem
247	K,M,X	Human Heart to Heart Society

I

249	G,R	I Am My Brother's Keeper (Shomer Achi Anochi)
251	F,M	Ichud Shivath Zion, Aguda Le'Umit Datit
253	M,O	Independent Living
255	A,V	Institute for Science and Halacha
257	G,N,V	Institute for the Commemoration of Galician Jewry
259	A	Institute of Research for the Temple of Jerusalem
260	T	Interns for Peace
262	M	Iraqi Jews Educational Development Fund in Israel
264	F	Irvin Green Community Center, Shlomi
266	A,G	Israel Academic Committee on the Middle East
269	A,G	Israel Association of Social Workers
271	O,P	Israel Cancer Association
273	F	Israel Corporation of Community Centers Ltd.
275	X	Israel Council of Young Israel
278	K	Israel Family Counseling Association
281	K,L	Israel Family Planning Association
284	S	Israel Interfaith Committee
286	F	Israel Leisure and Recreation Association (ILRA)
288	J,R	Israel Maritime League
290	X	Israel Movement for Progressive Judaism
292	A,M	Israel Parliamentary Affairs Association
294	B	Israel Society for the Prevention of Alcoholism
296	G	Israel Voluntary Services
298	I,N	Israel War Veterans League
300	F	Israel Youth Hostels Association
302	A,K	Israeli Association of Creative and Expressive Therapies, (ICET)
304	C,X	Italian Synagogue and Museum

J

306	X	Jerusalem Academy of Jewish Studies
309	A,X	Jerusalem College of Technology
311	O,P	Jerusalem Institute for the Prevention of Blindness
314	F	Jerusalem International Y.M.C.A.
316	A,O	Jerusalem Mental Health Center—Ezrath Nashim
318	C	Jerusalem Opera Society
320	D,M	Jerusalem Post Toy Fund

Page	Subject Code	Name of Organization
322	A	Jerusalem Society for the Advancement of Education and Culture
324	S,T	Jerusalem Society for World Fellowship
327	G,V	Josephtal Institute for Social Betterment Services

K

Page	Subject Code	Name of Organization
329	X	Kehilat Yaakov Institute of Jewish Studies
331	M	Keren Aryeh
333	M	Keren Gemach Ner Mitzvah
335	H,M	Keren Hat'shuva, Founded by Rabbi A. Hazan
337	J,X	Keren Yaldenu Tikvatenu Centers
339	O,Q	Kfar Rafael Remedial Community
341	F	Kfar Yonah Community Center
343	C	Khan Theatre Company
345	M	Kinnereth Nahari Fund
347	R,X	Kiryat HaYeshiva Knesset Yehuda
349	X	Kohav Miyaacov, Yeshivat Hagaon M'Tshebin
351	M,R,X	Kollel America Tifereth Jerusalem
353	X	Kollel Avrechim Bar-Shaul, Rechovot
354	X	Kollel Horodna Institution
356	X	Kollel Yeshiva Talmud Torah Karlin Stulin
358	M	Kupat Gemach Meor Chayim
360	M	Kupat Gemilut Chasadim in Memory of the Igell Brothers

L

Page	Subject Code	Name of Organization
361	G,K,P	La Leche League of Israel
363	H	League of Societies for the Rehabilitation of Offenders in Israel
365	K	League for Family Rights in the Courts
368	G,O	Lev-Lehan, The Association for Psychiatric Patients
370	G	Life and Environment
371	I,J,O	Life-Line for the Old
374	G,W	L.O.—Combating Violence Against Women

M

Page	Subject Code	Name of Organization
376	K,O	Maavar—Ladies Guild for the Rehabilitation of the Maladjusted Child
379	F	Maccabi World Union
381	D,M,X	Machanaim Kiryat Gat
383	X	Machon Maharshal
385	P	Magen David Adom in Israel
387	D,X	Magen Ha'Yeled Institute
389	M,P	Matan Beseter, Charity Anonymous, Haifa
391	I,O	Matav—Homemakers' Service Association
394	D,Q	Meier Shfeyah Youth Village
396	M	Memorial Fund in the Name of Micha Harel
397	X	Merkaz Yeshivot B'nei Akiva—The B'nei Akiva Yeshivot Center

Page	Subject Code	Name of Organization
399	C	Merosh Amana
401	O	Micha Society for Deaf Children, National Council
403	P	Misgav Ladach Hospital
405	X	Mishmarot Kehuna V'Beit Ulpana Torah La'am
406	G	Mitzpe Yeriho
408	M	Mivtach Oz Universal Charitable Organization for Relief and Support
410	X	Moharil Ashlag Institutions
412	X	Moreshet Avot-El Hamekorot
415	D,Q,X	Mosdot Kiryat Sanz
417	I,J,M	Moslem Women Charity Association
419	D	Mt. Zion Day Care Center

N

Page	Subject Code	Name of Organization
421	U	Naitonal Association for Welfare of Animals (NAWA)
423	G,V	Ne'emanay Torah V'Avodah
425	M	Ner Rafael Foundation
427	X	Neve-Eretz Yeshiva and Youth Village
429	G,M	New Israel Fund
431	D,O	Nitzan, Association for Children with Developmental and Learning Disabilities
433	M	Notzar Chessed

O

Page	Subject Code	Name of Organization
435	D,O	Ofarim, Organization for the Advancement of Culturally Disadvantaged Children
437	X	Ohr Elchonon Yeshiva-Meor Yerushalayim
439	H,X	Ohr-Samayach Institutions— The Joseph and Faye Tanenbaum College
442	M,X	Or Chadash Girl's Town, The Educational Center of the Galil
444	X	Or Etzion, Bnei Akiva Yeshiva High School
446	G	Organization For The Advancement of the Disadvantaged Neighborhoods
449	G,M	Organization for the Sake of Justice
450	G,X	Organization of Yeshiva Students of the Negev
452	X	Or HaCarmel College for Studies of Judaism and Yeshiva for Baalei Tshuva
454	A,V,X	Or-Hamaarav (Light of the West)
456	J	Orim Pre-Military Professional Institution
457	J	Ort Israel

P

Page	Subject Code	Name of Organization
458	M	Padam Free Loan Fund
459	T	Partnership
461	M	P.E.F. Israel Endowment Funds, Inc.
463	V,X	Petahim
465	X	Pelech, Religious Experimental High School for Girls

Page	Subject Code	Name of Organization
467	M	Pesach Matzo Fund
468	C	Pirchei Margalit
470	H	Prisoners' Aid Society (Haifa)

Q

472	V,X	Qedem — Yad Le-Yakkirenu

R

474	X	Rabbinical Seminary Ramailis Netzach Israel
476	M	Rabbi Slonim Memorial Free Loan Fund of the Chabad Synagogue, Jerusalem
478	F	Ramat Hagolan Community Center
480	P	Rambam Society
482	X	Ramot Shapira World Youth Academy
484	K,W	Rape Crisis Center in Tel Aviv
486	X	Religious Cultural Center for Kurdistan Jews in Israel
488	F,M,P	Religious Women's Union
490	A,V	Research Institute of Family Life and Family Law in Israel
492	G,M	Revacha, Organization for Families Blessed with Many Children
494	A,X	R.I.C.H.I., College for Rabbis and Research Fellows
495	G,V	Right to Live Anti-Abortion Organization (EFRAT)
497	F	Roni (Aharon) Soffer Charity Fund
499	N,P	Rotary International — District 249 — Israel

S

501	G,R	Safed Area Development Council
503	F	Samuel Rubin Cultural Center of Mitzpe Ramon
505	M	Scholarship Fund in the Name of Leon Recanati
507	M	Sela Yakov Fund
508	I,P	Services Center for the Aged in the Valleys
510	X	Shaar Ephraim and Beth Rephael Yeshiva
512	P	Shaare Zedek Medical Center
514	K,X	Shalshelet
517	I,Q	Shalva Rest and Convalescent Home
519	V,X	Shamir Association of Jewish Professionals From the Soviet Union and Eastern Europe In Israel
521	G,M	Sharal — Furniture Repair and Resale
523	M	Sharvit Hachesed Central Help Organization
524	O,Q	Shield, The Jerusalem Society for Retarded Adults
527	G,M	Shikud Used Clothing Store
529	K,L	Shilo Pregnancy Advisory Service
531	O,P	Society for Crippled Children — Alyn
534	M	Society for the Ben Golan Scholarship Memorial Fund
536	U	Society for the Prevention of Cruelty to Animals in Israel (I.S.P.C.A.)
538	U	Society for the Prevention of Cruelty to Animals in the South of Israel

Page	Subject Code	Name of Organization
540	E,G	Society for the Protection of Personal Rights
542	H	Society for the Rehabilitation of Prisoners, Tel Aviv
544	A,V	Society for Research on Jewish Communities
546	D,Q	Society for the 'Singer House'— The Home for the Child at Kefar Yeheskel
549	D,Q	Society of Orphanages, Tel Aviv
551	P,T	Spafford House
553	M	Student Scholarship Fund in Memory of Shoshana Amir
555	A	Study of Our People Institute for the Study of the Psychology of the Jewish People in Israel and Abroad
557	X	Sucath David Talmud Torah
558	N	Supreme Council (33) of Freemasons in Israel

T

Page	Subject Code	Name of Organization
559	X	Talmud Torah and Yeshiva Torat Moshe
561	X	Talmud Torah Morasha
563	K,N	Technion Faculty Wives' Club
565	S,T	Tel-Aviv-Jaffa Common Circle
567	G	Tenant's Protection Society
569	G	Tent (Ha-Ohel) Movement for Neighborhood and Community Development
571	C	Testimonium
573	C	Theatre Archives and Museum
576	X	Tifereth HaCarmel, The Great Yeshiva and College for Advanced Torah Studies
578	D,Q	Tiferet Shlomo Boys Orphanage Home
579	K,O	Tikva
581	F,X	Torah B'Zion

U

Page	Subject Code	Name of Organization
583	K,O	Unit for Consultation and Information on Development
585	I,Q	United Aged Home
587	C	United Conservatory, Yuval-Rananim

V

Page	Subject Code	Name of Organization
589	D,N,O	Variety Club of Israel

W

Page	Subject Code	Name of Organization
591	G	Widows Survivors Organization
593	M,N	Wolbrom Immigrants' Association in Israel and Abroad
595	E,G,W	Woman to Woman
597	G,W	Women's Aid Fund
599	K,W	Women for Women
602	J,O,Q,W	Women's League for Israel, Inc.
605	I,Q	Women's Social Service
607	A	W.U.J.S. Institute

16

Page	Subject Code	Name of Organization

Y

Page	Subject Code	Name of Organization
610	R	Yaakov Maimon Volunteers
612	M,X	Yad Avi Synagogue Association and Keren Eitan Free Loan Fund
614	M	Yad Eliahu Free Loan Society for Needy Young Couples
616	G,K,P	Yad Lashisha Voluntary Aid Society
618	M,O,P	Yad Sarah Organization for Lending of Medical Equipment and Rehabilitation of the Sick
620	X	Yeshivat Amaley Torah
622	X	Yeshivat Betokhakhei Yerushalayim
623	M,X	Yeshivat Chasidei Breslov—Or Hane'elam
625	M,X	Yeshivat Da'at Z'Kainim (Yeshiva for Retired Persons)
627	X	Yeshivat Elon Moreh
629	X	Yeshivat Hadarom
631	M,X	Yeshivat Hachayim Vehashalom Ve-Kollel Ateret Mordechai
633	X	Yeshivat Hakotel
636	X	Yeshivat Har Etzion
638	X	Yeshivat Harei Yehuda
639	M,X	Yeshivat Heichal HaTorah
640	X	Yeshivat Otsar Hahaim
641	X	Yeshivat Shaare Chaim
643	X	Yeshivat Shaarei Torah in Memory of the Netziv
644	J,X	Yeshiva Technicum, Technical High School, Kfar Zvi Sitrin
646	M,X	Yeshivat Tifereth Israel Talmudic College
648	M	Yismach Moshe Gemilut Chasadim Loan Fund

Z

Page	Subject Code	Name of Organization
649	D,G,W	Zahavi—The Israel Association of Large Families
652	M	Zichron Yosef Relief for B'nei Torah
654	D,Q	Zion Orphanage (Blumenthal)

17

PREFACE

In 1978, Eliezer Jaffe wrote an article on "Non-Conventional Philanthropy" which appeared in the *Jerusalem Post* and in *Moment Magazine*. The article pointed out that many laudable, grassroots efforts in Israel never got off the ground for lack of funds or lack of credibility by the Israeli welfare establishment, or simply for lack of skills in seeking out interested philanthropists abroad. The larger, better organized, and politically astute private welfare organizations in Israel have had considerable success in fund-raising, and their public relations efforts and personal contacts have made them major competitors for philanthropic funds. But there are also literally hundreds of smaller, less-known and extremely important, hard-working volunteers and welfare organizations which are also desperately in need of funds. Few philanthropists have ever heard of them and no real effort has ever been made to bring the two parties together.

From the philanthropists' point of view, the amount of reliable, systematic information available about non-profit welfare organizations in Israel is deplorable. The intelligent private philanthropist barely knows the wide range of organizations that exist in Israel, and has no mechanism for evaluating or rating them in order to decide where to give money. *Giving Wisely* responds to an increasing, expressed desire by individual donors, corporate foundations and special fund adminstrators to monitor and better evaluate the most effective use of philanthropic monies. It provides current donors and would-be philanthropists with objective, more detailed criteria by which to examine and evaluate a broad range of Israel's philanthropic organizations.

This book answers the twin dilemmas of the Israeli fund-raisers and the potential philanthropist. On the one hand, it includes detailed profiles of non-profit Israeli social service organizations, indexed both alphabetically and by the organizations' functions, and including descriptive, historical, organizational, financial, and other information about each one. It also provides frank and down-to-earth advice to philanthropists concerning how to give funds to charitable organizations, and what to look for when reviewing requests for aid.

Giving Wisely represents the first comprehensive attempt to search for and contact all known non-profit organizations in Israel and it encouraged organizations and groups to set down vital information about themselves. The book is not intended to replace personal investigation by those interested in supporting philanthropic work. It is based on the premise that a better understanding of philanthropy, will definitely provide greater personal involvement and a sense of enduring partnership. Also, *Giving Wisely* is not intended to diminish "mainstream" (e.g. UJA, Israel Bonds, Keren Hayesod, Keren Kayemet) philanthropic effort or replace it, but to open up additional innovative channels for helping Israel.

Professor Jaffe, of the Paul Baerwald School of Social Work at the Hebrew University, is superbly qualified to direct this publication effort. His understanding and contact with social services at all levels throughout Israel is brought forth in the research and vital knowledge which he has collated in this publication. His book extends the concept of philanthropy in Israel and treats the reader to a concise overview of philanthropic endeavors in the young nation. One cannot read this book without being truly impressed by the innovative efforts and accomplishments made by volunteer and non-profit organizations in Israel. It invites new response from caring people everywhere.

Raquel Newman-Naymark,
Los Altos Hills, California

Give while you have the means,
while you have the opportunity,
and while you are your own master.
(From the Talmud)

GUIDE FOR THE PERPLEXED PHILANTHROPIST

If I had a shekel for every philanthropist who wrote me, telephoned, or walked into my office at the Hebrew University's School of Social Work during the last 20 years to ask for advice about "where to contribute charity where it's really needed", I could retire in style. I promised myself that one day I would publish some personal advice about giving money in Israel so that philanthropists and friends of Israel abroad could find their way through the maze of Israeli organizations that are seeking donations.

Every time I go back for a visit to the States, my mother and relatives show me huge piles of letters they received from Israeli organizations asking for donations. The mail builds up especially towards the Passover, Rosh Hashona and Shavuot holidays. Invariably, each letter contains the familiar "P.O.B." number on an addressed return-envelope, along with a fervent plea for help.

But the philanthropist needs help too. Especially if he or she wants to do something in a personal way for Israel. They need to have more information about welfare organizations in Israel; they need some indication as to whether the organization is recognized by responsible Israeli authorities, whether donations are tax-deductible, and some knowledge about exactly who are the Israelis in charge. Ironically, instead of throwing *all* the requests for aid into the waste-basket, or sending a pittance to each of them to keep everyone happy, there is a very good chance that some of the requests may be of great interest to a potential donor and pull a specific emotional chord, answer a personal need of someone looking for a cause to support, or provide a vehicle to express that need. Who has not wanted to memorialize the loss of parents and loved-ones by undertaking a project in their name? Who has not wanted to leave some sign that we once existed here on this earth, and that we were not only out for ourselves while we were here? Who has been stirred by the miracle of Israel's rebirth and not sought to express some tangible measure of belonging and *partnership* in that magnificent enterprise? Perhaps one of those envelopes, piled high like Mount Tabor, brings the opportunity *to personalize* one's relationship with Israel and its people, and to leave your footprint on our shores, however small.

This book has been compiled as a service to Jews and non-Jews abroad who want to know more about Israeli welfare organizations and who want to be more sophisticated in their philanthropic efforts. It is an attempt to enable interested donors to follow-up their curiosity by making personal contact with the representatives of organizations listed in the *Guide*.

There is also another very important reason for writing this book, namely, to provide a vehicle and an equal opportunity for Israeli non-profit welfare organizations to describe their work, accomplishments, and needs, and to reach the ear of potential donors abroad. In the past, only the most well-oiled, sophisticated, public-relations-conscious organizations have been able to reach large foreign audiences. The smaller organizations in Israel, usually the grasssroots citizens' groups, have not used the international media or made close contacts with foreign philanthropists. Some of them wouldn't even know where or how to begin. Thus, there is a need for bringing together, for matchmaking perhaps, the non-profit and volunteer organizations with the potential philanthropists. It is a pity that some foreign Jews look upon Israel as a land of unfortunates, "shnorrers" or beggars. They harbor this stereotype in a warm, paternalistic way, proud of their own benevolence from helping out, but perhaps peering down a bit at us, nonetheless, expecting the traditional gratefulness of the poor in return.

Israelis are struggling very hard, for the most part, to make Israel work, but we see this effort as falling also upon our brothers and sisters in the rest of the world, as our *partners* in the enterprise. That is why, although we are a very proud people, reluctant to ask for handouts and ambivalent about receiving them, we do turn to Jews abroad to enlist their immigration and their philanthropic partnership. What is remarkable, and generally unsung, are the literally thousands of citizens' self-help and non-profit organizations in the fields of health, education, and welfare which have been established to improve Israeli society by private initiative. The research which went into this volume alone "discovered" over 2,000 self-help, non-profit organizations, and I would not be surprised if the actual number was at least twice that many. From miniscule, one-man, interest-free loan (*gemilut chasadim*) funds and funds for the children of deceased paratroopers, to the "big-time" educational and medical organizations, the amount of non-profit, volunteer work which is going on in Israel today is unbelievable. The same Jewish ethos of our forefathers concerning *Zedaka* (doing justice through good deeds) and pulling together to preserve Jewish life and spirit during centuries of wandering, persecution, and ghetto life, have surfaced again, from the earliest pre-State days, and are an important part of the fabric of modern Israeli society. Indeed, many of today's non-profit organizations were initiated to preserve Jewish ways of life and values often endangered by modern society, including the act of volunteering, itself.

This stream of volunteer, non-profit welfare activity in Israel seems to increase with hard times, almost as an instinctive Jewish response to hard times. Traditionally, over the centuries, and still today, Israelis have tried to link up with philanthropists abroad who could provide the financial fuel for their volunteer efforts. When these partners come together, beautiful things often occur. They happen every day, often purely by chance: The Boys' Town (Kiryat Noar) Vocational School in Jerusalem is one example of philanthropic serendipity. An American Jewish businessman, Ira Guilden, happened to share a cab to Tel Aviv with Rabbi Alex Lynchner of Jerusalem and together they launched a dream that will benefit Israeli disadvantaged youngsters for generations. This book should open a window onto the types of non-profit organizations which are active in the country, explain what their needs are, and provide access to the main figures connected with them. It shows some of Israel's human resources and strength rather than its weaknesses. It shows, simultaneously, both the empty half and the full half of our cup; what is being done and what still needs to be done. It is my hope, that this modest *Guide* will create an appetite for Jews and non-Jews abroad to get involved in organizations that interest them, and make direct, personal contact with Israelis who are genuinely seeking partnership as well as money.

WHAT ABOUT THE U.J.A.?

The publication of this *Guide* is not at all intended to downplay the importance of the United Jewish Appeal or its European counterpart, the Keren Hayesod. There is no question in my mind that the UJA is an important vehicle devised to enable Jews around the world to tax themselves and identify in some degree with Israel and the Jewish people as a whole. The funds which the UJA transfers to the Jewish Agency in Israel are utilized, for the most part, for very important projects such as Project Renewal, the crucial urban renewal program for 160 of our worst slum areas, and for imigrant absorption, land settlement, Diaspora education, housing, child welfare and other essential programs.

Nevertheless, the lack of personal, face-to-face involvement of most donors, the persistent appeal primarily to emotions rather than to intellect and the "give-and-run" philanthropic style which is the hallmark of UJA and Israel

Bonds fundraising, are simply not enough for a growing number of educated, committed, sophisticated philanthropists. These young leaders want to move beyond their regular involvement with the mainstream Jewish fund-raising apparatus and want a personal stake in Israel, a partnership relationship. They want to see how their philanthropy is spent, they want more control over it, and more accountability for its use in Israel. They want to deal with real people in Israel, counterparts whom they can trust and whose energies they can cultivate for a better Israel.

This trend of seeking "private projects" and personalization of philanthropic effort has been going on for several decades and was even institutionalized for "big givers" by setting up the Israel Education Fund for people who wanted individual projects (usually edifices), beyond their regular UJA contribution. But during the past decade, and particularly after the 1973 Yom Kippur War, a large number of younger middle-class and independently wealthy Jews and non-Jews began to seek out projects in Israel with which they could identify and experience cause-effect results from their contributions. Many of these people had visited Israel on various occasions and had been turned on by specific events and individuals. One example of this is the American and European Sephardi Zionist leadership which identified almost immediately with grassroots Jews in Israel hailing from the Moslem countries of the Middle East. Others turned to personal involvement in Israeli "private philanthropy" because of their own special interests in the communal, health, recreation, religious, or educational fields. Still others sought their own "private" projects out of disillusionment with exclusively mainstream charity; they had reached the point where writing a check for the UJA was simply not enough.

In response to this new and growing trend in American Jewish life, a network of funds, foundations and conduits were created abroad to responsibly channel private charity to Israel earmarked for specific projects. One of the most successful and reliable of these is the *P.E.F. Israel Endowment Funds, Inc.,* (see profile) located at 342 Madison Avenue, New York, N.Y. 10173. Founded in 1922 by Justice Brandeis and other prominent Americans, it has disbursed over thirty million dollars since then to Israeli institutions from private Jewish American donors. P.E.F. is a tax-exempt non-profit public charity, not a private foundation. It welcomes small and large gifts, all deductible under U.S. tax laws. Donations are sent to P.E.F. with the donors' recommendations for its use in Israel. Upon approval of the PEF Trustees remittance is made to the organization in Israel *without any deduction for administration.* This procedure usually takes up to three weeks. A potential recipient organization in Israel which is a candidate for funds from PEF must send its Articles of Association, translated into English, for review and approval by the PEF Trustees. In 1980, disbursements were made totaling over two million dollars and less than 1.5% of the total receipts were used for administration.

Another vehicle for private philanthropy, operating primarily on the West Coast, and other areas of the U.S. as well, is *The New Israel Fund* (22 Miller Avenue, Mill Valley, California 94941). The Fund was founded in 1979 as a resource for the support of community-based projects in Israel which are considered too small, too risky, or too controversial to receive funding from more traditional funding institutions or from local or national government agencies. This fund specializes in seed money grants for social action, civil rights, child welfare, women's rights, Arab-Jewish relations and a wide range of innovative volunteer social services. A highly respected and experienced Israeli Committee reviews all requests for grants and, together with the American Committee, allocates funds. In its first two years, $200,000 raised in the U.S. was allocated to over twenty new projects in Israel. The New Israel Fund is a new, unique vehicle for direct involvement and funding of non-conventional, change-oriented citizens' groups in Israel.

Many of the Israeli organizations that solicit funding abroad have also established their own "Friends" organizations in the U.S. and elsewhere which receive donations for forwarding to Israel. This is common for Israeli universities, yeshivot and social service organizations. For example, many projects in Jerusalem (parks, museums, theaters, etc.) have been funded through the Jerusalem Foundation, in which the Mayor of Jerusalem has a prominent voice. Similarly, the Zahavi Association for Rights of Large Families in Israel has a sister branch in Cleveland, Ohio, which is tax-exempt in the United States.

Some of these organizations provide for "delayed donations" in the form of bequests and life insurance policies assigned to the organization. Most insurance companies and lawyers are familiar with these arrangements and in many cases legal consultation and standard forms containing the proper legal phraseology can be obtained, without cost, from the benefitting organization.

A RESOURCE DIRECTORY FOR ISRAELIS

One of the best ways to judge whether an Israeli social worker knows his or her business is how knowledgeable they are about, and how expertly they make use of existing resources. This skill is often found in community leaders as well, and even seems to be a key variable frequently lacking among members of lower income groups. Information is indeed power. In the welfare, health and education fields there is as yet no resource listing in Israel equivalent to this book. Thus, the author hopes that the *Guide* will serve as a helpful, although partial handbook for Israeli professionals, clients, and citizens who are in need of information about resources. Unfortunately, many Israelis have little knowledge about the wide range of non-profit services available to them or whom to contact in order to apply.

If funding permits, future editions of the *Guide* will also appear in Hebrew to allow broader utilization in Israel. And judging from the number of organizations that asked to be included after the Guide went to press, the next volume will be much larger than this first edition.

HOW THE GUIDE WAS PREPARED

Since the purpose of this *Guide* was to list and objectively describe non-profit, volunteer organizations active in Israel in fields of health, education and welfare, the most crucial task involved in this effort was the compilation of a list of the organizations which answered these criteria. This was done in a very systematic way during a six-month period beginning in February, 1980, and involved two stages. In the first stage the author obtained comprehensive lists of organizations from the Ministries of Education, Health, Labor and Social Affairs, and Religious Affairs. Each of these Ministries have contact with volunteer organizations or are involved in providing these organizations with letters of reference or certification of one kind or another, and each has its own lists. We also approached the tax authorities at the Ministry of Finance, and after much delay we eventually received a list of tax-free organizations registered with the Ministry, minus addresses or phone numbers.

In the second stage we solicited lists of volunteer organizations from a large number of municipalities, some of which (Tel Aviv, Jerusalem and Haifa) had mimeographed their own directories of social services for use by social workers and citizens in general. More lists were obtained from volunteer roof-organizations such as The Israel Voluntary Services, a government-funded organization established to promote and coordinate volunteer activity. In addition to the above, we scoured the "Yellow Pages" and telephone directories of the various regions in Israel to find more non-profit organizations, and sifted through tourist guidebooks for more names. We also obtained lists from local Religious Councils, and news items in the daily papers, and from social workers in the community organization field. We contacted officials at the Ministry of Interior for permission to read the files of organizations that had been duly constituted and approved by the Ministry as Non-Profit Organizations under the "Law of Ottoman Societies" (now called "Amuta Societies"). Under that law, all organizations wishing to obtain official status as a non-profit organization must apply to the Ministry of Interior for an Ottoman Society registration number. They must also submit a copy of their By-Laws, a list of their officers, and their seal, or rubber mailing-stamp. They must then publish in an Israeli newspaper an announcement of their name, goals, address, and officers. Once the Minstry of Interior agreed to give us access to these files, we very diligently sorted through thousands of files and prepared a long list of those relevant to this *Guide*.

Finally, in order to make sure that all of the relevant organizations had an equal opportunity to be listed in the *Guide*, we published a large ad in Friday's edition (the weekend edition) of four major Israeli papers announcing the purpose of the *Guide* and asking organizations that had not yet received our questionnaire to apply for inclusion. Every possible avenue had been taken to guarantee that every organization had been given an equal chance to participate in the *Guide*.

Once lists were gathered, we prepared a central list of non-profit and volunteer organizations resulting in a comprehensive list of nearly 2,000 organizations. Every organization on that list was sent a detailed, four-page questionnaire explaining, in English and Hebrew, the purpose of the *Guide* and asking for their cooperation in filling-in the questionnaire.

WHO WAS LEFT OUT?

National and Municipal Government Agencies

In view of the fact that the *Guide* was to provide a platform for *volunteer* and *non-profit* organizations, to which private individuals abroad can donate tax-free gifts, these criteria automatically ruled out of the *Guide* all government agencies and organizations, national and municipal. Although many non-profit organizations listed in the *Guide* receive funds from government sources, they were included since they are not government-owned or operated by civil service employees. Incidentally, it is important to point out that the trend in Government spending regarding non-profit institutions and agencies has been to greatly decrease such aid in the past few years. Thus, many private organizations which once received sizeable Government or Municipal grants, are now, more than ever, dependent on local fundraising and private donations. It is also important to remember that government agencies do not provide tax-exempt status for donations from local or foreign donors.

Synagogues

We did not include in the *Guide* the thousands of synagogues which abound in Israel. For one thing, it would be technically impossible to find and list them all. Moreover, their functions (in Israel) do not fall under the general theme of "social service organizations", which is the major basis for including or excluding organizations in the *Guide*. On the other hand, if a synagogue operates a free loan fund or another type of social service, it was included in the *Guide*.

Political Parties and Labor Unions

We did not reckon political parties as "non-profit social service organizations", and they are not tax-deductible organizations for donors abroad. It will be noticed when reading the *Guide*, that some Israeli welfare organizations are supported by grants from political parties, as a service to members of the party and their families. Labor Unions were also not included in the *Guide* since these are inextricably linked to the various political parties and also benefit greatly from national and municipal government resources.

West Bank and Gaza Organizations

The *Guide* relates only to non-profit services registered in Israel proper, and does not include organizations in Judea and Samaria (i.e. the West Bank) or in the Gaza strip area.

Organizations That Opted Out of the Guide

This category refers to organizations that were included in our comprehensive list, but opted, of their own accord, not to participate in the *Guide* simply by not returning their questionnaire. We can only speculate about possible reasons for opting out. One reason (mentioned by some organizations) was a desire to maintain privacy and anonymity. Others may not be interested in mingling "outside" funds with family funds that, for example, have been contributed to a free loan fund in memory of a loved-one. That fact that we "discovered" them and sent them a questionnaire may be completely irrelevant to their particular needs and goals.

Another possible reason for opting-out of the *Guide* was the desire not to reveal financial information requested in the questionnaire. Some organizations called the Editor to "ask permission" to omit this item of information. When this was refused they may have chosen not to send the questionnaire at all. However, other organizations sent in the questionnaire, minus certain items. Laziness or sloppy administration may well have been another reason for not sending in the questionnaire, although an addressed return envelope was included with each questionnaire. Nevertheless, some organizations may have been deterred by the serious task of answering a four page detailed questionnaire. It is certain, however, that no organization was deterred from participating for financial reasons, since there was absolutely no charge for printing their profile in the *Guide*. It is very important to note that of the 2,000 questionnaires sent out, less than 30 were returned by the Postal authorities due to a wrong address. In other words, almost all of the questionnaires arrived at the proper destination and were claimed.

THE QUESTIONNAIRE

A lot of thought was invested in developing the questionnaire sent to the organizations on our list. Several versions were developed, pretested and revised before we selected the final version. Several American Jewish leaders and astute foreign philanthropists were consulted concerning the questionnaire and their advice was very helpful. The main "audience" for the *Guide*, English speaking Jews interested in Israeli social affairs, was uppermost in our minds. Primarily, we wanted the reader to obtain a brief overview of the organizations listed, including their history, organizational structure, goals, achievements, names of board members, financial situation and tax-exempt status in Israel and abroad, scope (i.e. members, branches, employees), and references abroad that can be contacted for further information.

As noted earlier, the basic purpose of the questionnaire was to gather enough information to enable interested potential donors to read about and follow-up their curiosity concerning an organization by making direct, personal contact with its officers. For this reason, we gave special importance to the listing of names, addresses, and phone numbers of the board members of each organization. We wanted a potential donor to be able to walk into the organization's office in Israel, call any of its board members by phone, or ask friends in Israel if they know or ever heard of the organization and its officers. Most important of all, we want prospective donors to be able to write directly to organizations listed in order to obtain more information and intelligently proceed to explore the possibility of granting them funds.

PREPARATION AND ACCURACY OF THE PROFILES

Upon receipt of the completed questionnaire, a Profile was carefully prepared for each organization, using uniform headings and relying only on information abstracted from the material submitted. The typescript Profile was then sent to each organization by the Publisher for written approval of the text and permission to publish. When the Profiles were returned to the Publisher, the organization's corrections were reviewed by the author and included in the Profile. Even at this stage, some organizations did not return their Profiles or written approvals for publication, and they were reluctantly omitted from the *Guide*.

HOW TO USE THE GUIDE

The essence of "partnership philanthropy", in my opinion, is information. There are smart ways and naive ways to give away money. It never ceases to amaze me how well-meaning businessmen and economy-conscious housewives will sometimes give charity to organizations or programs in Israel without the slightest demand for information, accountabilty, or credentials from the recipient organization. To encourage a more rational process, the Profiles of the non-profit organizations which follow in Part Two of this *Guide* have been carefully prepared and edited to provide information which can be helpful to potential philanthropists. The "Historical and Descriptive" material in each Profile is essentially that reported by the organization and represents what the organization wanted to communicate about itself, within the guidelines that we requested in the questionnaire. The accuracy of the Profile material is the responsibility of the reporting organization, and not a result of any investigation or office visits on our part. Many of the organizations participating in the Guide did send in their "Articles of Incorporation" and public relations literature, but we do not claim to have verified all of the information presented.

The "Financial Information" section should be of special importance to readers, especially the information concerning tax-exempt status. In Israel, anyone can get involved in volunteer work and operate a philanthropic enterprise if they desire. But Israel has also developed certain regulations for these efforts in order to protect the public and guarantee some degree of organization and accountability to donors and the Government. These regulations are particularily necessary when charitable groups request benefits from the government, such as special status regarding tax laws and official recognition as a legal entity, both of which facilitate fund-raising activity.

In the field of philanthropic work the five most important laws which regulate charitable, non-profit organizations in Israel, are the following: the Law of Ottoman Societies (1909) initiated by the Turks and replaced by the Law of Amutot (1980), the Trust Law (1979), the Value Added Tax Law (1975), and the Income Tax Ordinance (1962). Lack of space prevents us from describing these laws in detail, but suffice it to say that in general, a non-profit organization must be registered as an Amuta by law, and then must apply separately to the Ministry of Finance for tax-exempt status. In the Profiles presented here there are three numbers to watch for:

1. The Ottoman (Non-Profit) Society registration number shows that the organization has been registered with the Ministry of Interior as a non-profit group. This does *not* mean that donations are tax-exempt, in Israel or anywhere else. It does mean that the organization is legally constituted, formally recognized, and liable to government scrutiny (which is rare).

2. The tax-exempt number provided by the Israel Minstry of Finance. This means that donations in Israel are tax deductible and that the organization has been approved and reviewed by the Ministry of Finance.

3. The Internal Revenue Service (I.R.S.) number shows that American citizens can deduct donations to the organization, and that a file on the organization is availabe at the I.R.S. in Washington.

Please note that some organizations have declared in their Profile that they are an Ottoman Society or are tax-exempt in Israel and the U.S., but they have not provided the registration numbers which are issued by the government authorities upon approval of registration.

To enable the reader to make enquiries about the organizations listed in the *Guide*, we provided the "Affiliations and References" section, purposely including addresses of foreign organizations and individuals abroad, when these were given, who can serve as references and can be contacted. For the same reason, we requested and listed in each Profile the names, addresses and phone numbers of officers and board members of each organization.

A PLEA FOR PARTNERSHIP PHILANTHROPY

The choice of one's area of philanthropic interest is a matter that involves personality, cultural and religious background, financial capacity, and a host of other conscious and unconscious factors. Different people give in very different ways. The main principle, however, in giving wisely is always to take time to verify who it is you are giving your money to and follow-up on the use of your resources. If you just want to feel good for having helped someone or some organization, one can "feel good" by doling out dollar bills to as many people as possible. But the wise donor who really wants to help should feel a personal involvement and *sense of partnership* with the organization or people being helped. There should be a combination of informed, intelligent thinking as well as emotional investment in what you are doing. Perhaps most important of all, is the need for developing a *strategy* of giving. For those individuals who are seriously looking for a philanthropic partnership in Israel my advice would be not to play the whole field, but to concentrate on one or two specific organizations or areas of service and support them for several years before moving on to another project. Make a dent. Pick an organization, a person, an issue, some cause that you believe in — and leave your mark on it. The more involved you become, the more intelligently you will be able to understand issues and to help. And the more intelligent you become in your philanthropy, the sooner you will become a partner with thousands of Israelis who are trying to create a better society. This moving away from a charity and purely check-book relationship with Israel, to a partnership relationship is perhaps the best possible form of philanthropy. However, make no mistake: for us Israelis the highest form of partnership, more important than any philanthropy, is *aliya* — or immigration to Israel. For us, laymen and professional alike, even the biggest donation can never replace immigration.

I have met a lot of wealthy and not-so-wealthy Jews during their visits to Israel, but only a handful of them really understood and practised the art of giving properly. And it had nothing to do with the size of their gift. You could tell who gave a damn and who didn't, who was involved and wanted details, and who gave merely for the personal honor they got out of it. For me, the thing that separates the pros from the amateurs in philanthropy is not how much they gave, but how and why they gave what they did. Donors should always be anxious about the results and change created because of their gift. It's this style of giving that makes a difference. Most of us learned about the *importance* of giving from our parents. But how many of us really learned *how* to give? How many of us have experienced a joy in giving and the very special kinship that it bestows? And who has reached that level of kinship that enables us to give without a sense of paternalism or benevolence, or the ability to choose not to give, without feeling guilty?

The art of giving is something that has to be developed and learned. The transmission of that art, and a genuine appreciation of the Jewish tradition of brotherly involvement and partnership upon which it rests, may well be the major gifts we can make to ourselves, to our children, and to the generations that will come after us.

ACHUSAT SARA CHILDREN'S HOME

מוסד ילדים אחוזת שרה

24 Kalisher Street
Shikun H
Bnei Brak
Telephone: (03) 782578
Office hours: All hours

HISTORY AND DESCRIPTION

Achusat Sara Children's Home was founded in 1956 by Mizrachi Women from South Africa and Israel, with the purpose of accommodating 160 children, aged six to fourteen, from all countries. They were children of new immigrants, or orphans, or children whose backgrounds presented difficult social problems (divorced or ill parents, or parents with anti-social behavior).

Organizational Structure: The children are divided into small groups according to age and sex. The Home staff includes counselors, teachers and two social workers.

Goals: The Home provides an environment conducive to the healthy physical, intellectual, social and emotional development of the children, and tries to give them the "home" they are missing, instructing and inducing them to take active part in the responsibilities of running the Home. The organization tries to provide a complete education (on a religious base) which prepares the children for life as happy young people, religious and decent citizens of Israel, who can care for themselves and need not be dependent on others.

Services, Activities and Accomplishments: The children go to municipal school and in the afternoons, after preparing homework, they engage in a wider variety of extra-curricular activities, including arts and crafts (ceramics, carpentry, etc.), music, ballet and sports.

The children may visit with their families once every three weeks and on all holidays. While they may rejoin their families during the summer vacations, they have the option of remaining in the Home and of the benefit of a rich summer program of extra-curricular activities. The Home staff generally maintains a close relationship with ex-pupils, which continues even after they establish their own families.

Graduates of the Home go on to make their mark in all walks of life, achieving success as teachers, academicians, farmers, nurses, soldiers and family members; this is, it is believed, caused through the open and wide-ranged aspects of the Home's educational system.

OFFICERS

Director: Mr. Samuel Ron, 24 Kalisher St., Bnei Brak.
Educator. Tel. (03) 782578.

Board Members
(Partial list): Mrs. L. Schmidt, 4 Josef Elijahu, Tel Aviv.
Tel. (03) 287454.

Rabbanit Z. Goren, 51 King David Blvd., Tel Aviv.
Tel. (03) 222244.
Rabbanit N. Rabinowitz, 69 Shenkin, Tel Aviv.
Tel. (03) 241627.
Mrs. L. Kossovsky, 4 Shapira, Tel Aviv.
Tel. (03) 280794.
Mrs. B. Broide, 11/25 Degel Reuven, Petah-Tikva.
Tel. (03) 927074.
Mrs. H. Melamed, 10 Sutin, Tel Aviv.
Tel. (03) 227739.
Mrs. T. Sanhedrai-Goldreich,
43 Louis Marshall, Tel Aviv.
Tel. (03) 444448.
Prof. Dr. L. Bronner, 1 Killarney Park, 2nd Ave.
Killarney 2193, Rep. of South-Africa.

FINANCIAL INFORMATION

62% of the organization's income is provided through maintenance fees from the Ministry of Social Welfare, 30% comes from maintenance fees from Youth Aliyah and the remainder from donations. Last year's budget of $144,000 left the Children's Home with a deficit of $8,250. The Home employs twelve full-time staff, as well as twenty-seven part-time workers.

The organization is also registered as an Ottoman Association (Tel Aviv district, reg. no. 2317/99). Donations are tax free in Israel (reg. no. not supplied).

AFFILIATIONS/REFERENCES

Achusat Sara is affiliated with the "Emunah" Women's Religious Zionist political party in Israel.

FUNDING NEEDED

1. For installation of solar heat and hot water systems to reduce the very high fuel expenses.
2. To create additional sleeping accommodations through interior changes in the building to make room for more children who so badly need a home.
3. For renovation and thorough restoration of the building, including painting and plastering.

ADI: THE SOCIETY FOR
PROMOTING TRANSPLANTS IN ISRAEL
"אדי" אגודה לקידום השתלות בישראל

26 Katznelson Street
Petach Tikvah
Telephone: (03) 922059
Office hours: all day

HISTORY AND DESCRIPTION
Adi was a young man (28) who died because of malfunctioning kidneys.
By the time he received a transplant his heart was weak from the dialysis
treatment he underwent. He died but willed that an organization would
be formed to prevent others from suffering as he did. His family and
friends organized and started a kidney donor program in Israel which
provides donor cards upon request. ADI lectures on the subject of
kidneys, dialysis and transplant, all over the country. It has within a very
short period of time accumulated over 25,000 donor signatures from
people who now carry donor cards.
The major accomplishment of the organization until now has been to
inform the public about the need to help kidney sufferers.

OFFICERS
Shmuel Ben Dror, 26 Katznelson, Petach Tikvah.
Agriculturalist.
Yakov Marmor, 53 Brande, Petach Tikvah.
Company manager.
Dvorah Ben Dror, 26 Katznelson, Petach Tikvah.
Effie Hercky, 24 Borochov, Givatayim. Nurse.

FINANCIAL INFORMATION
Last year's annual budget was $130,000, which came from donations. It
is registered as a non-profit Ottoman Association (no. 1579). Donations
are tax-free in Israel (no number listed) but not in the United States. The
organization is staffed entirely by volunteers.

MEMBERSHIP, SCOPE, AND POLICY
There are 30,000 members in Israel.

AFFILIATIONS/REFERENCES
The organization is not affiliated with any political party in Israel. It is
in contact with Eva Gottscho of the Ruth Gottscho Kidney Foundation
of New Jersey.

FUNDING NEEDED
1. For preparing a film to be shown on television on the need to
   transplant and on the suffering of the kidney patient.
2. Transportation costs for lecturers, to all parts of the country, including kibbutzim, army camps, factories and private homes.
3. Funds to cover office equipment, stationery and postage.

AGOUDAT NASCHIM 'LINA'

אגודת נשים "לינה"

Wolfson 47
Tel Aviv
Telephone: (03) 227666
Office Hours: No set hours; services available at any time.

HISTORY AND DESCRIPTION

The 'Lina' branch of the Agoudat Naschim was founded in 1936 with the expressed intent of providing medical, financial and constructive aid to sick and needy imigrants to Israel from the Balkan countries. Today, these efforts are continued, and aid has also been extended to those recommended to the organization by the Social Welfare Department of the Tel Aviv municipality.

Activities, Accomplishments, And Funding Needed: As part of its benevolent activities, Agoudat Naschim 'Lina' is in close contact with Tel Aviv-area social welfare authorities. Through such contacts, the organization sends children of local poor families to summer recreation camp and purchases various medical appliances for disabled children. The organization works in conjunction with most Tel Aviv-area philanthropic associations, as well as with local hospitals, where its contributions of medical equipment, especially in children's wards, are numerous. The organization lists among its major accomplishments the fact that in the 44-years of its aid to needy families, the groups' funding of summer recreation camps and medical equipment has more than doubled; it has donated three oxygen tents and bed sheets to the children's ward of Tel Aviv's Rokah hospital; it has contributed cancer equipment to the Tel Hashomer hospital; and an E.K.G. apparatus has recently been supplied to the Aged Home in Rishon Le Zion. In order to continue its philanthropic efforts among Israel's sick, disabled and destitute, Agoudat Naschim 'Lina' will gratefully welcome any donations.

OFFICERS

Director:	Mrs. Shelly Alcalay, Hen 55, Tel Aviv. Tel. (03) 222337.
Treasurer:	Mrs. Violette Alcalay, Shlomo Hamelech 15, Tel Aviv. Tel. (03) 285063.
Board:	Mrs. Mazal Cohen, Herzl 59, Ramat Gan. Tel. (03) 725684.
	Mrs. Susan Hornstein, Adam Hacohen 22, Tel Aviv. Tel. (03) 227666.
	Mrs. Becky Diga, Adam Hacohen 18, Tel Aviv. Tel. (03) 240551.
	Mrs. Elsa Guershon, Weizman 19, Tel Aviv. Tel. (03) 237642.
	Zizi Haim, Toscanini 8, Tel Aviv. Tel. (03) 232680.
	Lucie Farhi, Hovevei Zion 32, Tel Aviv. Tel. (03) 282164.

FINANCIAL INFORMATION

The Agoudat Naschim 'Lina' had a last annual budget totalling $4,000. Of this total, 25% was achieved through membership dues while the remaining 75% was acquired through donations. The organization did not have a deficit for the last year. The organization has been a registered Ottoman Association since October 1936 (reg. no. 1034/99, Tel Aviv-Jaffa district office of the Ministry of the Interior). Donations to Agoudat Naschim 'Lina' are tax-free in Israel (reg. no. 4503735, Ministry of Finance), but not in the United States. There are no salaried employees in the organization. All members are volunteers.

MEMBERSHIP, SCOPE, POLICY, AND AFFILIATIONS

The 250 members of the organization are represented by its one branch in Tel Baruch. Anyone who wishes to volunteer may become a member. Decisions are made by the National Board. Agoudat Naschim 'Lina' claims no affiliation with any Israeli political party, nor with any foreign bodies.

AGUDAT GEMACH MAZKERET DOV

אגודת גמילות חסד מזכרת דוב

Kiryat Moshe St. 16, Jerusalem 96102
P.O.B. 3122, Jerusalem. 91031
Telephone: (02) 523450.
Office Hours: 9:00 A.M. to 5:00 P.M.

HISTORY AND DESCRIPTION
The organization was founded in 1976 in memory of Rabbi Dov Perla,
who was director of the Office of Holy Places in the Ministry of
Religious Affairs from 1970-1976. The purpose of this project is to
provide a free loan fund for financial assistance to needy persons, in a
variety of areas including: wedding expenses; housing; medical care;
purchase of furniture; dental treatment; clothing for the poor.

Services, Activities, and Accomplishments: The organization has helped
hundreds of people in need by supplying funds for short and long terms
without interest. Its first priority is the extending of aid to brides and
grooms, parents of poor children, young couples in need of funds for
housing, and other people who require assistance.

OFFICERS
Director: Zvi Friedman, Shikun Kiryat Moshe 9,
         Jerusalem. Retired. Tel. (02) 524965.
Treasurer: Asher Perla, Desler 12, Bnei Brak.
         Rabbi. Tel. (03) 700877.

Board or
Hanhala Members: Yehuda Perla, Kiryat Moshe 16,
         Jerusalem. Student. Tel. (02) 523450.
         Yehuda Neer, Gat 12, Jerusalem.
         A. Rubin.
         A. Carmel, Ben Zion 2, Jerusalem.

FINANCIAL INFORMATION
The organization's income is derived solely from donations. Last year's
annual budget was $400, with no deficit. Donations to the organization
are tax-free in Israel but not in the U.S.A. (no Israeli tax number
supplied). The organization is registered as a non-profit Ottoman Association with the Ministry of the Interior (reg. no. not supplied). The
organization is served by 3 volunteers.

MEMBERSHIP, SCOPE, AND POLICY
The organization has 2 branches in Israel and none abroad. There are no
members as such, and no criteria for membership. Decisions are made
mostly by the National Board.

AFFILIATIONS/REFERENCES
The organization is not affiliated with any political party in Israel nor
with any group abroad.

AGUDATH ISRAEL WORLD ORGANIZATION

אגודת ישראל עולמית

Shomer Hakotel 5
Haheruth Square
P.O.B. 326, Jerusalem
Telephone: (02) 223357
Office Hours: Sunday-Thursday, 8:30 A.M. to 2:30 P.M.

HISTORY AND DESCRIPTION

Agudath Israel World Organization was founded in Kattowitz in 1912 at a Congress of Orthodox Jewry. Preceeding World War Two, the organization was represented in various European Parliaments. Now, it is represented in the Israeli Knesset.

Organizational Structure: The organization is composed of members of national rabbinical councils responsible for Jewish matters. The International Central Council, the organization's world executive, is composed of 100 members nominated annually by affiliated organizations. The organization has consultative status with ECOSOC and UNESCO, and its members also sit as a nongovernmental organization (NGO) committee of UNICEF.

Goals: The aims of Agudath Israel are to solve problems which periodically confront the Jewish people through Orthodox Jewish efforts; to work in and for Israel; to create a Jewish press and literature inspired by Jewish tradition; to further religious education and representations of the interests of 'Torah-true' Jewish communities and of the Jewish people.

Services, Activities, and Accomplishments: Activities of Agudath Israel include religious adult and youth education, Torah education for girls, charity, special financing of yeshivot, aid to the Baalei Tshuva (Jews returning to Judaism) movement, and involvement in various other matters concerning Israel. Publications sponsored by Agudath Israel include Hamodia, an Israeli daily, as well as various weeklies and news journals in London, New York, Buenos Aires, Antwerp and Zurich. The major accomplishments of the organization include the 'Chinuch Atzmai' independent educational network of schools in Israel; various institutions for needy children, including Chazon Yehezkel and Kiryat Hayeled (Children's Town); trade schools; Boys' Village (Sedei Chemed); Free Loans Funds; and the spiritual absorption of immigrants from all over the world, especially Russia.

OFFICERS

Chairman: Rabbi Y. M. Abromowitz
General Secretary: Mr. Abraham Hirsch
Board Members: S. J. Gross

Rabbi S. Lorincz, M. K.
Rabbi M. Porush, M. K.
Mr. S. Siroka

FINANCIAL INFORMATION

Sources of income for Agudath Israel include membership dues, donations and grants (proportional figures were not supplied). Last year's budget of $2 million left the organization with a deficit of $350,000. Agudath Israel is registered as a non-profit Ottoman Association (No. 11-101) in Israel, and donations to the organization are tax-free both in Israel (No. 4501398) and in the United States (via affiliated bodies). Agudath Israel World Organization has 250 full-time and 500 volunteer employees.

MEMBERSHIP, SCOPE, AND POLICY

There are 25,000 members of the 70 Israeli branches of Agudath Israel, and some 275,000 members in 21 branches abroad. Membership is open to all those who acknowledge the superiority of the Torah laws. Decisions for the international organization are made by its World Executive Council.

AFFILIATIONS/REFERENCES

Agudath Israel World Organization is directly aligned to the Agudath Israel political movement in Israel. It is affiliated with the following international organizations:

Agudath Israel of America, 5 Beekman Street, New York,
New York, 10038, U.S.A.
Agudath Israel of Great Britain, 97 Stamford Hill,
London, N. 16, U.K.
Agudath Israel of Switzerland, 56 Pflanzschulstr,
Zurich, 8004, Switzerland
Agudath Israel of Belgium, Lamoriniere Street 67,
Antwerp, 2000, Belgium

FUNDING NEEDED

In order of priority, the following are the most outstanding funding requirements presently facing Agudath Israel World Organization:
1. Financing yeshivot and educational institutions.
2. Establishment and maintenance of the Baalei Tshuva (Jews returning to Judaism) movement.
3. Support and sponsorship of the RIAF, Russian Immigrant Aid Fund.

"AHAVAH" CHILDREN AND YOUTH HOME

בית ילדים ונוער "אהבה"

P.O.B. 4
Kiryat Bialik
Telephone: (04) 740296

HISTORY AND DESCRIPTION
Ahava is an institution for Jewish children aged 6-16 years founded to educate children in agricultural training, workshops, and domestic work. The major accomplishment of the organization has been the education of thousands of children.

OFFICERS
Director: Jechiel Dror, Jehuda 2a, Kiryat Bialik.
Board Members: Baruch Jafe-Nof.
                   Eliezer Alter.
                   Towa Ben-Dov.
                   Menasche Korn.
                   Ebel Jizhak.
                   Bodoch Gabriel.
                   Baram Baruch.
                   Hana Wafniash.

FINANCIAL INFORMATION
No details were given regarding the sources of last year's annual budget. The budget was $360,000, with a deficit of $40,000. The organization is registered as an Ottoman Association (reg. no. 61/302). Donations to the organization are tax-free in Israel (no tax number was supplied) and in the United States (tax no. 910003946). There are 50 full-time workers employed by the organization.

AFFILIATIONS/REFERENCES
The organization is not affiliated with any political party in Israel. No other information was supplied.

FUNDING NEEDED
The acquisition of tools, cooking utensils, and musical instruments.

AHAVAT CHESED SOCIETY IN MEMORY OF GITEL BEUTELMACHER

ארגון אהבת חסד ע״ש גיטל באיטלמכר

Yitzhak Prag St. 4, Jerusalem
Telephone: (02) 223095
Office Hours: 7:00 P.M. to 9:00 P.M. daily

HISTORY AND DESCRIPTION
Since Gitel Beutelmacher z"l devoted her life to charity, her friends and admirers decided to organize to continue her good deeds in the following areas: (1) hospitality and overnight lodging; (2) visiting the sick; (3) distributing food to the needy; (4) monetary help in times of distress; (5) support for the needy, including brides and Torah scholars.

OFFICERS
Director: Yisroel Fenner, Shimoni 4, Jerusalem. Merchant. Tel.: (02) 669058.

Treasurer: Miriam Grossman, Sanhedria HaMurchevet, Jerusalem. Housewife. Tel.: (02) 810393.

Board Members: Shulamit Dolgin, Ramat HaGolan 17, Jerusalem. Housewife. Tel.: (02) 811256.

Yitzchak Wechsler, Apraq St., Jerusalem. Engineer. Tel.: (02) 223095.

Abraham Gold, Sanhedria HaMurchevet 102. Employee. Tel.: (02) 811371.

FINANCIAL INFORMATION
The income of the organization is derived entirely from donations. Last year's annual budget was approximately $1,500, with no deficit recorded. Donations to the organization are tax-free in Israel (no tax number supplied), but not in the U.S.A. The organization is registered as a non-profit Ottoman Association in the Jerusalem District Office of the Ministry of the Interior (reg. no. 11/2881). Five volunteers serve the organization.

MEMBERSHIP, SCOPE, AND POLICY
Any man or woman over 18 years of age who accepts the by-laws of the Society and obligates him- or herself to participate in its activities, is eligible for membership. There are seven members in Israel and none abroad. Decisions are made mostly by the Executive Director.

AFFILIATIONS/REFERENCES
The organization is not affilated with any political party in Israel nor with any group abroad.

FUNDING NEEDED
1. To remodel the hospitality and dormitory building—$36,000.
2. To expand the present program of visiting the sick to include all Jerusalem hospitals—$16,000.
3. To provide support for needy brides and scholars—$14,000.

AISH HATORAH COLLEGE OF JEWISH STUDIES

ישיבת אש התורה

66 Chayei Olam
Jewish Quarter
Old City
Jerusalem
Telephone: (02) 284659
Office hours: Sunday-Thursday, 8:30 A.M. to 4:30 P.M.
Friday, 8:30 A.M. to 12:00 noon

HISTORY AND DESCRIPTION

Aish HaTorah was established in 1974, following the Yom Kippur War, by Rabbi Noach Weinberg, as a direct response to the spiritual and moral crisis facing the Jewish people. In the six years of the yeshiva's existence, the student body has grown from less than 10 to 200, and the physical plant from two apartments to twenty facilities. Besides the Jerusalem Center, branches in Safed and Tel Aviv have been established, as well as two Aish HaTorah Outreach Centers in America (in Los Angeles and St. Louis). Further expansion is planned for Jerusalem as well as outside of Israel.

Organizational Structure: In order to bring relevant Jewish education to masses of unaffiliated Jewish young people, an efficient international organization is being built. Presently Aish HaTorah consists of a central branch in the Old City of Jerusalem, smaller units in Israel, and two full-time branches in the United States.

Goals: Aish HaTorah College of Jewish studies is dedicated to the goal of furthering Jewish identity among Jewish young people, by showing them the importance of Israel and Jewish heritage. The crisis of assimilation, intermarriage, and cult membership, can only be met by combatting its root cause which is ignorance of Jewish values and the beauty of the Jewish way. Relevant Jewish education must be brought to the masses of our young people. To do this, courses have been developed and out-reach techniques explored which can successfully return a significant portion of this generation to their Jewish heritage. It is imperative that this work be done now to insure support of Israel and Jewish causes in the coming generation.

Services, Activities, and Accomplishments: The College has introductory courses for the recruitment of new students with basic classes in Jewish philosophy, religion and identity; an intermediate program involving in-depth study of text, out-reach and teacher training; and a Rabbinical program, ordination upon completion of required study, leadership training and placement in communities to educate others. Among the services and activities of the Aish HaTorah College are: outreach to non-affiliated young Jewish travellers; introductory Jewish identity education; advanced Jewish studies; an English/Hebrew Jewish reference library and study halls; dormitory and dining facilities; outreach branches in Israel and the United States; intermarriage crisis conference; anti-cult, anti-missionary research and publications; tape cassette library and distribution department; Bar Mitzvah program; generous student scholarships (no one is turned away for lack of funds). Since its beginning, Aish HaTorah has been at the forefront of the "Return to Judaism Movement". Over 10,000 Jewish young people have studied at the school and received a favorable and lasting impression of Jewish values. Hundreds of young men have been motivated to dedicate their energies to working for Jewish survival, both in Israel and throughout the diaspora. Programs, techniques and classes have been developed which can successfully reach this generation of Jews. These are now being applied through a continually growing network of dynamic learning institutions, and outreach projects.

OFFICERS

Director:	Rabbi Noach Weinberg. 12 Zayit Ra'anan, Jerusalem. Educator. Tel. (02) 816495.
Treasurer:	Shalom Kugelman, 2 Zayit Ra'anan, Jerusalem. Educator.
Board Members:	Shmuel Mintzberg, 10 Zayit Ra'anan, Jerusalem.
	Yitzchak Geltzer, 10 Sha'arei Torah, Jerusalem.
	Moshe Weinberg, 20 Yishayahu, Jerusalem.
	Aryeh Friedman, 3 Panim Meirot, Jerusalem.
	Boruch Gutfarb, 20 Imrei Binah, Jerusalem.

FINANCIAL INFORMATION

60% of the College's income comes from donations, 30% from Israeli Government Ministries, and 10% from tuition fees and membership dues. Last year's annual budget of $500,000 left a defecit of $140,000. The College is registered in Jerusalem as a non-profit Ottoman Association (reg. no. 11/2310). Donations in Israel, the United States and Canada are tax-free (U.S. tax no. 11-2400-877, Canada 0511279-21-13). Fifteen full-time and thirty-five part-time workers are employed by the organization as well as ten volunteers.

MEMBERSHIP, SCOPE, AND POLICY

Students must be Jewish (from mother's side), male, and have a stable psychological profile. There are 200 students in Israel and in two branches, and 100 abroad in two branches. Decisions are made by department heads.

AFFILIATIONS/REFERENCES

The College is not affiliated with any Israeli political party. It is affiliated with the following organizations in the United States:
American P'eylim, 3 W 16th Street, New York, N.Y.
Torah U'Mesorah, 229 Park Ave. S., New York, N.Y. 10003.
Hillel—Bnai Brith, 315 Lexington Ave., New York, N.Y.

FUNDING NEEDED

1. Intensive recruitment and training of Jewish leaders. To recruit 5,000 aliented and assimilated Jewish young men within a one year perid; to educate and train them to be the committed and articulate core group that can reach out to young Jewry and reverse the trend of assimilation. Total one year program — $2,493,000.

2. Building and accommodation requirements: In order to accommodate the increased enrollment resulting from intensified recruitment and real growth, additional facilities in Jerusalem are required and are available for dedication.

Addition to study hall to accommodate 500 students	$1,000,000
10 classroom facilities — each $25,000	$250,000
Dining Hall and Kitchen completely equipped accommodating 500 students	$500,000
Library facility	$150,000
Synagogue	$250,000
50 Dormitory rooms — accommodating 4 students each — $18,000 each	$900,000

3. Out-reach center in American city: To reach Jewish American youth during the influential college years it is proposed to send teams of rabbis, teachers and counselors to work in American communities. Salaries, office equipment, library, special events, etc.
   bi-annual estimate — $166,794

ALDEMA FOUNDATION

אלדמע

P.O.B. 33511
Tel Aviv
Telephone: (03) 266382
Office hours: 8:00 A.M. to 3:00 P.M.

HISTORY AND DESCRIPTION

The Aldema Foundation was established in 1977, as a non-profit organization dedicated to further the prevention, research and treatment of digestive diseases.

It has an all volunteer membership, run by a 5-member elected committee.

The Aldema Foundation supports various public health and research projects in the field of digestive diseases and coordinates its activites with the Department of Gastroenterology of the Tel Aviv Government-Municipality Hospitals (affiliated to the Tel Aviv University Sackler School). This part of its activity is meant to further the treatment of patients with various digestive disorders.

Among activities promoted by the Foundation are the following: a large-scale program for screening and early detection of colon cancer and polyps (the only one of its kind in Israel); a large scale survey of the long term effects of a high fiber diet and bran consumption on trace metals and minerals; a survey of the relation between diet and gallstones in Jews and Arabs.

The Foundation also helps in the purchase of various instruments for the Department of Gastroenterology.

OFFICERS

Chairman: Mordechai Rotenberg. Tel Aviv. Banker.

FINANCIAL INFORMATION

All of last year's annual budget was received from donations. The budget for last year was $10,000. There is no deficit. No additional information was supplied.

FUNDING NEEDED

1. The funding for additional manpower.
2. The maintenance and purchase of medical instruments.
3. The initiation of additional public health and research projects.
No cost estimations were supplied.

THE ALFRED ADLER INSTITUTE

המכון ע״ש אלפרד אדלר

Shenkin 60,
Tel Aviv
Telephone: (03) 614071
Office hours: 8:00 A.M.-1:30 P.M.

HISTORY AND DESCRIPTION
The Alfred Adler Institute in Tel Aviv was founded in 1962 by the late
Professor Rudolf Dreikurs, a pupil of Alfred Adler, together with a
group of his students who continued and developed his work.

Goals: The purpose of the Institute is threefold: to cure or alleviate
mental suffering; to prevent the development of mental malfunctioning;
and to promote, in the community, a better spirit of cooperation in all
spheres of life — family, work and community. The basis for the work is
the belief that the existing society is groping for a better and more equal
interrelationship among people and that the democratic way of life
requires new techniques of education. People who want to be free and
equal must learn to take on responsibilities as early as possible. This
general philosophical idea takes body in techniques and approaches for
changing attitudes and behaviors of individuals and groups.

Services, Activities, and Accomplishments: To achieve its three purposes,
the Institute has three Departments: a Psychotherapeutical Clinic, Parent Education Centers, and a Theoretical School, for both professional
and lay people who work with the community. Among the Institute's
accomplishments are the outstanding group-work done with war widows, bereaved parents and the disabled, and the introduction of parent
education to the underprivileged communities in development areas. In
addition, the Institute has succeeded in gaining the cooperation of the
Ministries of Defense and Education.

OFFICERS
Board Members: H. Kirschner, Ben Gurion 60, Tel Aviv.
                    Psychologist. Tel. (03) 222060.
                M. Katz, Gur 6, Tel Aviv. Psychologist.
                   Tel. (03) 261317.
                A. Fried, Habiluim 18, Ramat Gan. Counselor.
                   Tel. (03) 771277.

FINANCIAL INFORMATION
The Institute is financially self-supporting, drawing its funds from the
fees of its clients and students, and from projects undertaken for
Government and private organizations such as the Ministries of
Defense and Education, the Jewish Agency, and others. No percentage
break-down is given for these sources of income. The organization
registered in Tel Aviv as an Ottoman, non-profit Association in 1968

(no number stated). Donations in Israel are tax-free (no number provided); contributions from the U.S. are not. There are 4 full-time and 60 part-time employees.

MEMBERSHIP, SCOPE, AND POLICY
There are approximately 200 members in the Institute in Israel today. Members include professional and lay people working with the Adlerian psychology system. The Board (Hanhala) makes the decisions concerning the Institute.

AFFILIATIONS/REFERENCES
The Institute is not affiliated with any Israeli political party. It lists as references the Alfred Adler Institute, 159 N. Dearborn St., Chicago, Ill. 60601, U.S.A.; the Alfred Adler Institut, Beekstrasse 14, D-5100 Aachen, Germany; and the Greece Society of Adlerian Studies, Semitelou Str. 6, Athens 611, Greece.

FUNDING NEEDED
1. For scholarship and bursary funds.
2. To acquire educational equipment. This includes technical equipment such as videotapes, projector, films, cassettes, and library equipment and books.
3. To acquire a premises.

ALIN—ISRAEL SOCIETY FOR CRIPPLED CHILDREN MOSSAD ABRAHAMS

אגודה לעזרת ילדים נכים בישראל אלין מוסד אברהמס

Yitzhak Elchanan 2
P.O.B. 29370, Tel Aviv 61293
Telephone: (03) 653410
Office hours: Sunday-Thursday, 9:00 A.M. to 1:00 P.M.

HISTORY AND DESCRIPTION

Alin was founded in 1941 upon the initiative of the Tel Aviv-Jaffa Rotary Club. In the early 1950's, there was a polio epidemic and the limited facilities available at the time could not serve all the young invalids. Thanks to generous donations, in particular, that of Mr. Abrahams from South Africa, Mossad Abrahams was built. Later the "Tekuma" Elementary School for handicapped children was established, as well as an Audiological Institute and a swimming-pool, which is the property of the Tel-Aviv Municipality and is maintained by the municipality.

Organizational Structure: Mossad Abrahams has a day-home, kindergartens, an elementary school, workshops, an Audiological Institute, a Physiotherapy Department, and a summer camp, as well as a swimming-pool.

Goals: Alin is devoted to the care and rehabilitation of physically handicapped children.

Services, Activities and Accomplishments: Alin provides medical assistance and educational services, also for graduates of elementary school. In addition to Mossad Abrahams, the "Tekuma" Elementary School and the Audiological Institute, Alin has established a Youth Center, and is participating in the complete renovation of the former Alyn Hospital in San Simon, Jerusalem, which will be reopened as a hostel for young handicapped persons.

OFFICERS

Director: Elga Cegla, Suttin 24, Tel Aviv.
Treasurer: Stephan Auerbach, Weisel 8, Tel Aviv.
Board Members: Eva Saenger, Arlosorof 7, Tel Aviv.
Gret Cahn, Ruppin 28, Tel Aviv.
Friedl Schwartz, Bograshov 4, Tel Aviv.
Sophie Vreedenborg, Jona 23, Ramat-Gan.
Else Eisen, Lipski 8, Tel Aviv.
Dr. Akiba Hoffman, Adam Hacohen 6, Tel Aviv.
Kurt Riese, Mordechai 11, Ramat-Gan.

FINANCIAL INFORMATION

The organization depends upon donations, which are tax-free in Israel (Registration No. 4507633). Alin is registered as an Ottoman Association (Tel Aviv, reg. no. 3594/99). It employs one part-time worker; the Board Members and others are volunteers.

MEMBERSHIP, SCOPE, AND POLICY

There is one branch in Israel (number of members not supplied), and none abroad. Decisions are made by the Board.

AFFILIATIONS/REFERENCES

1. Ruth Kirzon Group for Handicapped Children Inc., 28-46 209th Place, Bayside, New York 11360, USA.
2. Jewish Child's Day, 183/9 Finchley Road, London N.W.3., England.

Alin is not affiliated to any political party in Israel.

FUNDING NEEDED

To enlarge Physiotherapy Department by adding several treatment rooms and an indoor swimming-pool.

AL-SAM, ANTI-DRUG ABUSE ASSOCIATION

אל-סם, האגודה למלחמה בסמים

Arlozoroff 112
Tel Aviv
Telephone: (03) 233951 or (03) 238587
Office hours: 8:00 A.M. to 2:00 P.M.

HISTORY AND DESCRIPTION
Al-Sam, which in Hebrew means "no drugs", was founded in 1974 by a group of concerned citizens in order to meet the ever-increasing problem of drug addiction in Israel. Its members are doctors, psychologists, public officials, Members of the Knesset, and citizens who have volunteered to advance the Association's goals.

Goals: The goals of the Association are: to work for the prevention of drug abuse, especially among adolescents and students; to assist drug addicts during their withdrawal process and rehabilitation, and to urge Government and municipal institutions to work actively for the advancement of the Association's cause.

Services, Activities, and Accomplishments: During seven years of activity, Al-Sam has taken important steps to curb the abuse of drugs. In cooperation with the Ministry of Health, it helped to establish Rehabilitation Centers in Tel Aviv - Jaffa, Jerusalem and Haifa. Al-Sam founded Israel's first Walk-in Clinic for adolescents, in Tel Aviv, and a second one in Haifa. Others are soon to be set up in Jerusalem, Rishon-Le-Zion, Beersheba and Eilat. The function of the Walk-in Clinic is to offer advice and help to wayward and problem youth who do not accept the established system and are deterred by existing institutions. Lectures are given to high-school students and to groups of parents, teachers, etc. To remedy the shortage of professional lecturers on the subject of drugs, Al-Sam provides training and tuition in this field, in cooperation with the Government Information Center.

OFFICERS
Director: Levana Zamir, Zichron Yakov 18, Tel Aviv.
      Tel. (03) 233951 or (03) 257570.
Treasurer: Amos Proshan, Idelson 2, Tel Aviv.
      Tel. (03) 656726.
Chairman: Gabriel Zifroni, Feivel 5, Tel Aviv.
      Tel. (03) 252813.
Vice-Chairman: David Yotan, Epstein 8, Tel Aviv.
      Tel. (03) 440805.
Board Members: Moshe Vidal, Ibn Givirol 104, Tel Aviv. Advocate.
      Tel. (03) 235544.
      Ada Machness, David Hamelech 55, Tel Aviv.
      Tel. (03) 225693.

Pinhas Kopel, Shaul Hamelech 35, Tel Aviv.
Tel. (03) 269165.
Dr. Michael Reiter, Psychologist.
Tel. (03) 824642 or (03) 585554.

FINANCIAL INFORMATION
50% of last year's annual budget came from donations from the public;
the balance from the Government (in particular, the Ministry of
Health). Last year's annual budget of $70,000 left Al-Sam with a deficit
of $16,000. Donations to the Association are tax-free in Israel (no
registration number supplied), and are tax-free in the United States if
channelled through the IADAF (International Anti-Drug Abuse Foundation). Al-Sam is registered as an Ottoman Association (Tel Aviv, no.
5524/99). Two full-time and ten part-time workers are employed by the
Association, as well as 100 volunteers.

MEMBERSHIP, SCOPE, AND POLICY
150 members represent four branches in Israel. There are no branches
overseas. Every citizen over the age of 18 can join the Association, upon
recommendation from an Al-Sam member. Decisions are made by the
National Board.

AFFILIATIONS/REFERENCES
The Association is affiliated with the IADAF (International Anti-Drug
Abuse Foundation) in New York. It is not affiliated with any political
party in Israel.

FUNDING NEEDED
1. To open more Walk-in Clinics so that there is at least one in every
   town.
2. To sponsor lectures and education.
3. To set up a "therapeutic community" for the rehabilitation of drug
   abusers.

ALUT, ISRAELI SOCIETY
FOR AUTISTIC CHILDREN

אלוט, אגודה לאומית לילדים אוטיסטים

6 Har-Nevo
Tel Aviv
Telephone: (03) 241067

HISTORY AND DESCRIPTION

ALUT, Israeli Society for Autistic Children was established in 1974
stemming from the need for adequate services and methods of rehabilitation and education of autistic children.

Organizational Structure: All members are invited to participate in an
annual general meeting in which the past year is reviewed, the agenda
for the coming year is decided upon and the Parents Committee is
elected. The Parents Committee consists of from ten to fifteen members
who are responsible for the Society's activities. There are three members
of the management: the head of the management, the treasurer and the
general secretary (who is not a member of the Parents Committee and
who receives a full salary) who are elected by five members from the
Parents Committee. From one to three accountants, not members of the
Parents Committee, are elected by the annual general meeting to look
after the financial and general activity of ALUT.

Goals: To establish suitable educational and rehabilitation centers for
autistic children; to train professional manpower for work in this field;
to aid families.

Service, Activities, and Accomplishments: Autistic children are educated
within the healthy community and not in the closed wards of mental
institutions. At the Yachdav School behavioral patterns and habits
required for everyday life are taught together with reading, writing and
basic arithmetic. Summer and holiday camps are organised and parents'
groups with the purpose of guiding the parents of autistic children in
suitable ways to care for their children. The Society gives financial help
to existing institutions, organizes volunteers to help in homes and
institutions and pays professional helpers to spend time with children
and adolescents in some psychiatric wards. The Society has succeeded in
increasing public awareness of the problem through the mass media
(television, radio, newspapers, etc.) and publishes a periodical distributed among the parents and friends of the Society. It is an established
"address" for families of autistic children to turn to when in need of
advice.

OFFICERS

Chairperson of
Public Comm.: Lea Rabin, 5 Harav Ashi, Tel Aviv.
          Tel. (03) 424455.

Chairpersons of	
Parents Comm.:	Batya Polnikov, 34 Nordau, Rishon Letzion.
	Tel. (03) 942182.
	Edna Mishori, 24 Rommema, Ramat Aviv.
	Tel. (03) 485199.
Treasurer:	Ami Hierstein, 21 Borochov, Givatayim.
	Tel. (03) 721781.
Secretary General:	Pirchia Shifman, 17 Bnei Moshe, Tel Aviv.
	Tel. (03) 448225.
Members of	
Public Comm.:	H.J. Zadok, D. Recanati, Y. Gafni,
	Z. Shoval, A. Katz, A. Meir,
	D. Mosheirtz, Y. Rotloi.

FINANCIAL INFORMATION

40% of last year's annual budget came from donations, 14% from Municipal authorities (Tel Aviv, Holon, etc.), 11% as income from cultural events, 2.5% from parents' fees, 1.5% from membership fees and 31% from other sources. Last year's annual budget of $31,186 left a surplus of $2,385. The Society is registered as a non-profit Ottoman Association. Donations in Israel up to $1,500 are tax-free (no. 4504424) and in the United States completely tax-free (U.S. tax no. 52-1157230). One full-time and one part-time secretaries are employed by the Society as well as five volunteers.

MEMBERSHIP, SCOPE, AND POLICY

There are approximately 150 members in Israel, in 3 branches, and one branch abroad. Most decisions are made by the Parents Public Committee.

AFFILIATIONS/REFERENCES

The Society is not affiliated with any Israel political party.

FUNDING NEEDED

1. To establish an institution for autistic adolescents — $1,000,000.
2. To continue to maintain and develop pre-vocational education which is a vital part of the Yachdav School program — $100,000.
3. To develop services for diagnosing and educating very young children and assisting their families — $50,000.

AMANA—INSTITUTE FOR THE PUBLICATION OF JUDAIC STUDIES IN RUSSIAN AND GEORGIAN

אמנה – אגודה להפצת תרבות ישראל

P.O.B. 588,
Jerusalem
Telephone: (02) 635282

HISTORY AND DESCRIPTION

The Institute was founded in 1972 by the Department of Torah Culture of the Ministry of Education and Culture, and the Ministry of Religion.

Organizational Structure: The Institute is headed by a Board of Trustees, a Management Committee, and an editorial staff. The Institute has two departments: the Publications Department, and the Translation Department (which deals with the translation and adaptation of materials relevant to the Institute's projects).

Goals: The publication of educational material to enable Russian immigrants to gain an understanding of Judaism through the study of its sources.

Services, Activities, and Accomplishments: Books have been published by the Institute, covering the following fields: Jewish literary sources; Jewish values and 'Weltanschauung'; highlights of Jewish history, biographical studies, and chapters from the history of Jewish significance; and the Jewish tradition and way of life. In addition, periodicals have been published for the study of Judaism, its values and traditions. Among the Institute's major accomplishments are "Festival Series", including ten booklets covering the entire Jewish year, and "Menorah", a quarterly, dealing with comtemporary Jewish thought.

OFFICERS

Director:	Yaakov Drori, P.O.B. 588, Jerusalem. Educator. Tel. (02) 635282.
Treasurer:	Rina Weingarten, P.O.B. 588, Jerusalem. Accountant. Tel. (02) 635282.
Board Members:	Rabbi Y. Dolgin, Ramat Hagolan 17, Jerusalem. Rabbi. Tel. (02) 811256.
	Mr. M. Barsela, Jabotinsky 36, Jerusalem. Educator. Tel. (02) 631674.
	Mr. H. Zohar, Olifant 2, Jerusalem. Diplomat. Tel. (02) 633445.
	Mr. Olshtain, Ibn Gabirol 166, Tel Aviv. Educator. Tel. (03) 444151.

FINANCIAL INFORMATION

50% of last year's annual budget came from the Ministry of Education and Culture, 15% from the Ministry of Religion, another 15% from the Memorial Foundation for Jewish Culture, and the balance from the sale of publications. Last year's annual budget of $23,500 left the Institute with a deficit of $5000. Donations to the Institute in Israel are tax-free (Israel non-profit reg. no. 11/2262). The Institute employs four part-time workers. The Institute's decisions are taken by the National Board.

AFFILIATIONS/REFERENCES

The Institute has no affiliations with any of the Israeli political parties. It is in contact with the Jewish Agency, 515 Park Avenue, New York, the Al Tidom Society, New York, and various federations in the United States.

FUNDING NEEDED

1. $15,000 — For "Jewish Literary Sources" — source books for the understanding of Judaism.
2. $12,000 — For "Highlights of Jewish History, Biographical Studies, and Chapters from the History of Jewish Culture".
3. $9,000 — For "The Land of Faith" — Historical Sights and their Judaic Significance.

AMISHAV ORGANIZATION FOR THE LOST TRIBES OF ISRAEL

עמישב — למען נדחי ישראל

24 Hida
Jerusalem
Telephone: (02) 424606
Office hours: 4:00 P.M. to 8:00 P.M.

HISTORY AND DESCRIPTION
The organization was founded in 1973, encouraged by Rabbi Zvi Yehuda Cook. Its first Chairman was the late Mrs. Rachel Yanait Ben-Zvi.

Goals: To research and make contact with the lost tribes and communities of Israel.

Services, Activities, and Accomplishments: The organization issues publications and has lectures on the subject of the lost tribes of Israel. Its delegates go out to find and meet those groups which consider themselves as belonging to the Jewish People and help them return "home". Some of them are interested in conversion, some of them in renewing their connection with the Jewish People. A lot of research is still to be done and many actions are necessary in order to spread the awareness of more circles of the lost parts of the Israeli nation. The organization keeps contacts with scholars abroad, exchanging information and knowledge, and does its best to help lost sections of the Jewish people return to their origin. In addition to the demographic problem of Israel, the country needs more and more sympathetic aid from all over the world and in India there are thousands of people willing to renew the historic contact with Judaism and Israel. The organization has published a brochure of the background and the present condition of the 10 "lost" tribes and has organized hundreds of lectures. Delegations have travelled throughout the world for purposes of research, and awareness has been intensified in Israel and abroad through the publication of newspaper articles. The organization also maintains contact with Marrano Jews in Spain and Portugal.

OFFICERS
Director: Rabbi Aliyahu Avihail, 24 Hida, Jerusalem. Tel. (02) 424606.
Treasurer: Arye Kostiner, 30 Hida, Jerusalem.
Chairman: Alfonso Sabah.
Board Members: Prof. Harold Fisch, Rabbi Dr. Nahum Rakover, Dr. Shalva Weill, Prof. Mordechai Rothenberg, Rabbi Ely Brin.

FINANCIAL INFORMATION
100% of last year's annual budget came from donations. Last year's annual budget of $11,000 left the organization with a deficit of $7,000.

The organization is registered in Jerusalem as a non-profit Ottoman Association (reg. no. 11/2459). Donations to the organization in Israel and abroad are not yet tax-free but the matter is under consideration.

MEMBERSHIP, SCOPE, AND POLICY
Membership is open to suitable persons according to decision of the organization's management. There are 200 members in Israel in 1 branch, and 1 branch abroad. Decisions are made by members of the Board.

AFFILIATIONS/REFERENCES
The organization is not affiliated with any Israeli political party. It is registered with the Memorial Foundation for Jewish Culture, N.Y., and HIAS, New York.

FUNDING NEEDED
1. To finance publications and research.
2. To send delegations to various places in the world for gathering information and material.
3. To finance actual and practical actions for bringing groups to Israel and helping the interested in conversion.

ANIMAL PROTECTION SOCIETY, JERUSALEM

האגודה להגנת בעלי חיים ירושלים

P.O. Box 4009
Jerusalem
Telephone: no phone yet
Office Hours: no office yet

HISTORY AND DESCRIPTION
The Society was founded to develop animal welfare in the Jerusalem area.

Organizational Structure: An Executive Committee comprising a President, Vice-President, Chairman, Treasurer, Secretary and additional members run the organization. All of these are volunteers serving in an honorary capacity. The Executive Committee reports to and gets directives from the Annual General Meeting of members.

Services, Activities, and Accomplishments: The activities of the Society have been educational through the school system, influencing public opinion through the press and media, dealing with individual cases of cruelty to animals, contacts with the government and municipal authorities in matters of animal welfare. The main project is the establishment of an Animal Center in the Ataroth Industrial Zone of Jerusalem which includes kennels for boarders and strays, a Clinic (being built) and a riding school.

FINANCIAL INFORMATION
The organization is a non-profit association registered as a public charitable organization. Donations to the Society are tax-free in Israel, the United States and Canada (through the Jerusalem Foundation, New York and Montreal), Britain (through the Society for Animal Welfare in Israel), and Johannesburg, South Africa.

MEMBERSHIP
Membership is open to all.

AFFILIATIONS/REFERENCES
1. The Society for Animal Welfare in Israel, (SAWI) 4 North Mews, Northington St., London WC1N 2JP, England.
2. Accredited Representative of SAWI in South Africa is:
   Mrs. Galdys Lurie, 11 Tyrwhitt Court, 13 Sturdee Ave., Rosebank, Johannesburg, Republic of South Africa.
3. The Jerusalem Foundation, 1407 Broadway, New York, N.Y. 10018.
4. The Jerusalem Foundation, 5151 Cote st. Catherine Road, Montreal, Quebec, 83 W 1N6, Canada.

FUNDING NEEDED—not supplied.

THE APTOWITZER FOUNDATION FOR HAIFA

קרן אפטוביצר למען חיפה

P.O. Box 289
Haifa
Telephone: (04) 511221; (04) 255956
Office hours: 8 A.M. to 3 P.M.

HISTORY AND DESCRIPTION

The Aptowitzer Foundation for Haifa was founded in 1975 by Willi Z. Aptowitzer, in memory of nearly all the members of this family who were victims of the Nazi regime in Europe.

Goals: The goal of the Foundation is to see the city of Haifa achieve higher standards in education, cultural activities, and better living conditions.

Services, Activities, and Accomplishments: The Foundation has distributed annually the "Haifa Municipal Prizes" for Best-Operated Districts, Best-Kept and Run Kindergartens, and Best and Cleanest Condominiums. It has also established a special foundation to activate the decision by the Board of Governors of Haifa University to create the Chair of Insurance.

OFFICERS

Director: W.Z. Aptowitzer, P.O. Box 289, Haifa.
Insurance Executive. Member of Lloyd's, London. Tel. (04) 225956, (04) 511221.

Treasurer: B. Hattis, 118 Hatishbi, Haifa. Auditor.

Board: Arieh Gurel, Mayor of Haifa.
Josef Almogi, Form. Chairman, Jewish Agency and Minister of Labour
Gershon Avner, President, Haifa University.
Eitan Avneyon, Managing Director, Hassneh Group.
B.R. Balcombe, Insurance Assessor, London.
Jack Borman, Los Angeles, Insurance Executive.
Jean Nordmann, Pres., Jewish Communities in Switzerland.
Eliezer Raphaeli, Formerly Haifa University.
Y. Shaanan, Legal Advisor to the Board.
Mrs. Manzi M. Aptowitzer.

FINANCIAL INFORMATION

The sources of income for the Foundation are primarily donations — some, from members of the board, but mainly from Mr. Aptowitzer's own sources (companies, personal, etc.). Last year's annual budget was about $5,000 and there was no deficit. The organization is registered as a

Trust Association (reg. no. 51-070527-0). Donations are tax-free in Israel (no. 4504765) but not in the U.S. There are no persons employed by the Foundation.

MEMBERSHIP, SCOPE, AND POLICY
Whoever is interested in contributing can be considered by the board for membership. At present there are ten members in one branch in Israel and three members abroad.

AFFILIATIONS/REFERENCES
The Foundation has no affiliation with political parties in Israel. Abroad, its work is known to the Friends of Haifa University, U.S.A.

FUNDING NEEDED
1. For the Chair of Insurance at Haifa University $180,000 has already been pledged; $70,000 is still in the process of being raised.
2. For improvements of kindergartens, cleaner neighborhoods, and for better-run and better-equipped condominiums.
3. For support of needy youth learning the professions, and to further musical and theatrical institutes.

THE ASHDOD (NEIGHBORHOOD HEH) COMMUNITY CENTER (MATNAS)

מרכז תרבות נוער וספורט רובע ה', אשדוד

Shmuel Hanagid St.
P.O.B. 841,
Ashdod.
Telephone: (053) 62478
Office Hours: 8.00 A.M.-1.00 P.M., 4.00-6.00 P.M.

HISTORY AND DESCRIPTION

The Center was established in 1976, in one of the suburbs of Ashdod (H. Quarter). It serves approximately 300 families. The present building measures barely 300 meters, which results in many of the activities being held outside of the building in various shelters.

Organizational Structure: The Center is one of 92 Centers belonging to The Corporation of Community Centers in Jerusalem, which is headed by Haim Zipory. The budget is financed mainly from three sources. The Corporation, the Ashdod Municipality, and Amigur. The Board consists of the Director, and representatives drawn from the general community.

Goals: The main aim of the Center is to create a pleasant environment for leisure activities, and so enrich community life in general.

Services, Activities, and Accomplishments: Although the Center operates with a very small budget, it caters to many sections of the community, including young children, youth, women at home, and senior citizens. There are also many new immigrants from Georgia, Russia, and 192 families with an average of seven children each. Hobby Shops have been established, Education, Journalism parties, Jewish holidays, are amongst the various fields of activities.
The Center feels it has created a Community Center to which the residents really feel they belong.

OFFICERS

Director: Michael Koenig. Ashdod. Teacher.
                  Tel. (055) 32576.

Executive
Committee: Avinoam Seri. Ashdod. Economist. (Chairman).
                  Tel. (055) 22311.
               Shlomo Levi. Ashdod. Director—Amigur.
               Sam Bloom. Ashdod. Director. Tel. (055) 31341.
               Shalom Adari. Kiryat Malachi. Youth Guide.
               Tova Schleifer. Ashdod. Teacher. Tel. (055) 42325.
               Yehoshua Fruchtman. Mgr. City Welfare Project.
               Judge Solomon. Neighborhood Rep.
               Yehiel Iluz. Neighborhood Rep.

FINANCIAL INFORMATION

12% of last year's annual budget came from membership dues, with 88% coming from government sources. Last year's annual budget of $33,333 left the Center with a deficit of $4,167. The Center is registered as an Ottoman Association (no no. reported). Seven full-time and seventeen part-time workers are employed by the Center.

MEMBERSHIP, SCOPE, AND POLICY

Present membership numbers around 300 families, all residents are welcome to join, the only problem being lack of space. All decisions are made by the National Board. The Headmistress of the primary school cooperates closely with the centre and is on the Committee.

AFFILIATIONS/REFERENCES

The Center itself has no direct affiliations, although the Corporation does have affiliations with many Jewish Centers in the U.S.

FUNDING NEEDED

1. To develop the present building by adding a second floor which will cost $80,000.
2. To finance staff and teacher training, for adult education at the Center, costing $10,000.
3. To expand the sports facilities, improve the lighting, and landscape gardening, and provide a more attractive environment.
   Cost: $20,000.

ASSOCIATION FOR ADVANCEMENT OF SOCIAL WORK IN ISRAEL

האגודה לקידום העבודה הסוציאלית בישראל

93 Arlosoroff
Tel Aviv
Telephone: (03) 264308
Office hours: 8:00 A.M. to 4:00 P.M.

HISTORY AND DESCRIPTION
The Association is a new organization, registration having begun only in early 1980. It intends to develop, improve and advance the Social Work profession.

Organizational Structure: A National Council of 26 members, elected for four-year terms by all social workers recognized as members of the profession, meets once yearly. An Executive Committee of 6 members chosen by the Council from its members handles the Association's affairs. A Chairman, Secretary and Treasurer are elected from the members of this Executive Committee. The Executive Committee meets at least once every two months.

Goals: To develop, improve and advance the social work profession in Israel by means of institutes, extension studies, and specialized study programs; initiating research projects; exchange programs between Israeli social workers and those of other countries; the publication of a professional journal; experimental demonstration projects; finding ways to motivate social workers to serve in distressed neighbourhoods and towns; wide efforts at public education; co-operative efforts with institutions, agencies and social workers.

OFFICERS
Director: Hava David, c/o Israel Association of
                      Social Workers, P.O.B. 303, Tel Aviv.
                      Social Worker.
                      Tel. (03) 264308.
Treasurer: Ephraim Milo, address and telephone as above.
                      Social Worker.
Board Members: Yitzhak Kadman. Social Worker.
                      Natan Lavon. Social Worker.
                      Moshe Shtepel. Social Worker.
                      Elisheva Sadan. Social Worker.
                      Shoshana Yacobey. Social Worker.

FINANCIAL INFORMATION
80% of the Association's income is derived from membership dues. Last year's annual budget was $6,000. The Association is registered as a non-profit Ottoman Association in Tel Aviv (reg. no. not supplied). Donations are tax-free only in Israel (tax no. 4507190). The Association employs three part-time workers as well as many volunteers.

MEMBERSHIP, SCOPE, AND POLICY
Membership is open to all social workers who are members of the Israel Association of Social Workers. At present, with registration only open for a few months, there are 300 members. Most decisions are made by the Executive Director.

AFFILIATIONS/REFERENCES
The Association is not affiliated with any Israeli political party. It is affiliated with the International Federation of Social Workers.

THE ASSOCIATION FOR CIVIL RIGHTS IN ISRAEL

האגודה לזכויות האזרח בישראל

P.O. Box 8273
Jerusalem
No telephone number supplied.
No office hours stated.

HISTORY AND DESCRIPTION
The Association was founded in Jerusalem in 1972.

Organizational Structure: A General Assembly of the members, which meets at least once a year, determines general policy and elects an Executive of 7-11 members. The Executive meets every 2-3 weeks.

Goals: The Association's goals are to work for the protection of human and civil rights in Israel and to promote voluntary aid in the field of civil rights.

Services, Activities, and Accomplishments: Activities undertaken by the Association are public meetings, symposiums, appeals to the Authorities, the release of press statements, the appointment of panels or sub-committees to probe a certain area and suggest remedies, and endeavors to help individual cases. Among topics dealt with in the last two years are: the Bedouin and their land; violence to detainees and suspects by the police and the security services; soldiers' rights and their implementation; forced hospitalization in mental homes; the Press Ordinance of 1927 and suggested amendments; the Wire-Tapping Case; and students' rights on campuses. One accomplishment of the Association to date has been the modification of the draft Bill on the Law Expropriating Land from Bedouin to Build an Airfield. In addition, first steps have been taken in making a wider public aware of the importance of human rights.

OFFICERS

President:	Prof. Haim Cohn, 36 Tzernichovsky St., Jerusalem. Tel. (02) 639973.
Honorary President:	Prof. Hans Klinghoffer, Hatibonim 8, Jerusalem. Tel. (02) 631574.
Chairman:	Michael J. Berger, Ramban 40, Jerusalem. Advocate. Tel. (02) 632714.
Board Members:	Yosef Dueck, Hapalmach 40, Jerualem. Advocate. Tel. (02) 634058.
	Prof. Claude Klein, Ben Zakkai 62, Jerusalem. Tel. (02) 664460.
	Dr. David Kretzmer, Beitar 15, Jerusalem. Lecturer. Tel. (02) 712324.

Amos Azubel, Azza 4, Jerusalem. Advocate.
Tel. (02) 636278.
Liora Segev, Beit Hakerem 12, Jerusalem.
Historian. Tel. (02) 532563.
Dr. Leon Shellef, Yehuda Halevi 62, Ra'anana.
Lecturer. Tel. (052) 91462.
Tsadiq Nassar, Turian. Law Clerk.
Prof. Daniel Amit, Ha'ari 8, Jerusalem. Physicist.
Tel. (02) 669332.
Dr. Ruth Gavison, Hess 6, Jerusalem. Lecturer.
Tel. (02) 241711.

FINANCIAL INFORMATION
Membership dues account for 49% of the Association's budget. Another 26% comes from donations, and the remaining 25% from interest and linkage increments. Last year's budget was $7,000 with no deficit. The Association is registered as an Ottoman non-profit organization (Jerusalem District, no number supplied). Donations are not tax-free. At present, all work is done voluntarily, except for one very part-time employee. American donations may be sent through the American Jewish Committee (for legal services in Israel).

MEMBERSHIP, SCOPE, AND POLICY
The Association lists 200 members in 4 branches in Israel, and 20 members abroad. Any adult resident of Israel can become a member; non-residents may become associate members. Decisions are made by the Board.

AFFILIATIONS/REFERENCES
The Association is not affiliated with any Israeli political party. It lists as a reference the International League for Human Rights, 236 East 46 St., New York, N.Y.

FUNDING NEEDED
1. To rent an office with telephone and hire a full-time secreatry; $1300 per month would have to be guaranteed for a substantial period. The entire nature and effect of the Association, which until now has been run by volunteers, would be transformed if an office with a full-time employee were to be established.
2. To publish and disseminate research papers in the field of human rights in Israel, at a cost of $3,000 per paper.
3. To promote research on relevant subjects by way of research grants, at $1,000 per grant.

ASSOCIATION FOR HOUSING ISRAELI ARABS AND OTHER MINORITIES IN JERUSALEM

האגודה לשיכון הערבים הישראלים
והמיעוטים האחרים בירושלים

Derech Hebron 88, P.O.B. 10384, Jerusalem
Telephone: (02) 718090
Office hours: By appointment.

HISTORY AND DESCRIPTION
The Association started in July of 1979. The purpose is to deal with housing for Israeli-Arabs and other minorities in West Jerusalem.

Goals: The aim of the Association is to establish and strengthen the peace initiative in the country between Arabs and Jews. Primarily, it works to build houses for Israeli Arabs, help support educational and cultural projects, as well as set up and operate educational and cultural institutions, charitable institutions, and free loan societies.

OFFICERS
Director: Skafi Habib, Derech Hebron 88, Jerusalem.
      Y.M.C.A.
       Tel.: (02) 718030.
Treasurer: Willian Assous, Agrov 24, Jerusalem.
      Y.M.C.A.
Board Members: Wahbeh Wahbeh
      Elias Husari
      Gabi Gashan
      Fayez Akleh
      Boutris Skafi
      Jabra Samuel

FINANCIAL INFORMATION
Information regarding annual budget and sources of income were not reported. The Association had a $10,000 deficit last year. Donations are tax-free in Israel (registration no. not reported). Eleven part-time employees and 50 volunteers are active in the organization.

MEMBERSHIP, SCOPE, AND POLICY
Most decisions are made by the Naitonal Board, and the Association has 11 members in Israel.

FUNDING NEEDED
1. For housing projects.
2. For help with education and cultural projects.
3. To improve conditions of poor families and increase membership.

ASSOCIATION FOR MUTUAL ASSISTANCE OF IRGUN OLEI HOLLAND (THE DUTCH IMMIGRANT ASSOCIATION)

אגודה לסיוע הדדי של עולי הולנד

8/3 Berdiczevsky
Tel Aviv
Telephone: (03) 234901
Office hours: Sunday-Thursday, 8:30 A.M. to 1:00 P.M.

HISTORY AND DESCRIPTION

In April 1979 a group of volunteers, members of the Dutch Immigrant Association (I.O.H.) in Israel, decided to establish a supporting service for survivors of World War II originating from a Dutch-speaking background. The decision was triggered by the fact that the Dutch Embassy stopped its follow-up and after-care service to people in Israel who had claimed financial assistance according to the Dutch Law of restitution for war victims.

Organizational Structure: An office has been established, a professional coordinator-director and part-time secretary were appointed who are responsible to the Director and the Board.

Goals: To give psycho-social assistance to Dutch-speaking survivors of World War II and to children of the survivors in need of help.

Services, Activities, and Accomplishments: Clients are received at the office or visited in their homes and given psycho-social assistance in their daily-life problems as they are often unable to handle difficulties by themselves. The service does not give financial assistance and deals only with the immaterial aspects of the lives of the survivors. The activities of the Association are in the developmental phase and more could be accomplished if wider means were available. The Association would like to extend help to the second generation, the children of survivors, whose psychological problems are highly influenced by the background of their parents. It would also like to organize research in order to help future generations and this should be accomplished soon because of the present age of the objects of research, the survivors of the holocaust. The Association is presently looking for Dutch-speaking social workers to employ on a part-time free-lance basis, in every region of the country, in order to be capable of helping the Dutch-speaking survivors as efficiently as possible, to make their life worth living. Since the foundation of the Association it has dealt with 75 clients.

OFFICERS

Director: Manfred Klafter, 8 Hagiv'ah, Savyon.
              Commercial counsellor. Tel. (03) 755773.
Treasurer: Shlomo Israeli, 1 Hevron, Bnei-Brak.

                         Bank official. Tel. (03) 787174.
Vice-chairman: Hans Noach, 35 Zabastr, Beer-Sheva.
                         Touring-guide. Tel. (057) 74697.
Board Members: Henk Nijk, 15 Achimeir, Ramat-Gan.
                         Translator. Tel. (03) 799946.
                         Nathan Dasberg, Kfar Batyah.
                         Former Director of Youth Village.
                         Tel. (052) 91247.
                         Prof. C. Dasberg, 35 Aza, Jerusalem.
                         Director of Hospital. Tel. (02) 632702.
                         Andries Hofman, 48/8 Katz, Petach-Tikva.
                         Former El Al Official. Tel. (03) 929596.
                         Mart Cohen, 75 Hofzicht, Wateringen,
                         Holland. Psychologist.

FINANCIAL INFORMATION

100% of the Association's income comes from donations. Last year's annual budget of $60,000 left the Association with a deficit of $10,000. It is registered in Tel Aviv as a non-profit Ottoman Association (reg. no. 7178/99). Donations in Israel of $200 or more are tax-free (tax no. not supplied). United States tax status information not supplied. 10 part-time workers are employed by the Association, alongside the volunteer members of the Board.

MEMBERSHIP, SCOPE, AND POLICY

Membership is open to all those interested in the well-being of survivors of the holocaust. There are 11 members in Israel and 1 abroad. Decisions are made by the National Board.

AFFILIATIONS/REFERENCES

The Association is not affiliated with any Israeli political party. It is affiliated with Joods Maatschappelijk Werk (Jewish Welfare Organisation), 145-147 de Lairessestraat, Amsterdam, the Netherlands.

FUNDING NEEDED

1. To establish a supporting-service for survivors of World War II originating from a Dutch-speaking background, in order to give them counselling and assistance in their problems.
2. To extend help to the children of survivors (the "Second Generation") whose psychological problems are highly influenced by the background of their parents.

ASSOCIATION FOR PROMOTING HEALTH SERVICES FOR THE PUBLIC

אגודה למען שירותי בריאות לציבור

2 Ben Tabai Street
Jerusalem
Telephone: (02) 638212 ext. 465 (Mr. Rony Rom)
Office hours: Sunday-Friday 8:00 A.M. to 3:00 P.M.
                 Friday until 2:00 P.M.

HISTORY AND DESCRIPTION

The Association for Promoting Health Services for the Public was established in 1972 to assist the ministry of Health in funding and promoting certain health service projects for which regular Ministry budgets are not available or are insufficient.

It includes approximately 20 registered members, who function in different areas of health service (mental health, public health, geriatrics, etc.), most of whom are on the senior staff of the Ministry of Health. These members constitute the general meeting, which chooses an executive committee of four members (chairman of the Association, treasurer, secretary and one other member). The general meeting also elects a "central" committee of three members.

The executive committee meets more frequently (about 4-6 times per year) and the general meeting at least once a year, to review activities, decide on new projects, and to confirm the annual balance sheet which is prepared by a certified accountant.

Goals: Establishing or assisting to establish hospital departments and outpatient clinics, supply of rehabilitation equipment to the disabled, rehabilitation services, medical equipment for medical facilities, promotion of studies in health care, promotion of community health services, etc. The Association receives donations and bequests from persons and agencies in Israel and abroad, most of which are specifically given for certain projects, the Association acting as an approving body and a means for channeling these contributions, with appropriate control of the funding.

The major accomplishments until now have been the promotion of hospital-based home care services; participation in the establishment of dental services for low-income persons; and participation in establishing a center to help problems in child development.

OFFICERS

Chairman: Prof. Baruch Modan, Jerusalem. Physician.
                  Tel. (02) 638212.
Board Members: Mr. Moses Horwitz, Jerusalem. Administrator.
                  Tel. (02) 638212.
                  Dr. Nahum Agos, Haifa. Physician.
                  Tel. (04) 526045.
                  Mr. Rony Rom, Jerusalem. Administrator.
                  Tel. (02) 638212.

FINANCIAL INFORMATION

The entire annual budget for last year came from donations. Details on size amounts of the budget were not supplied. The organization is registered as an Ottoman Association (reg. no. 11/1972). Donations to the organization are tax-free but the tax numbers were not supplied. There is one full-time and two part-time workers employed by the organization, in addition to ten volunteers.

MEMBERSHIP, SCOPE, AND POLICY

Most decisions are made by the National Board. There are 18 members in Israel. Any adult may become a member. In practice, all members are connected with health services in one way or another.

AFFILIATIONS/REFERENCES

The organization is not affiliated with any political party in Israel. It is in contact with the American Joint Distribution Committee, 60 East 42nd Street, New York, New York 10017.

FUNDING NEEDED

1. Assistance for persons suffering from chronic renal failure, such as providing dialysis equipment, enabling structural changes in the home for home dialysis.
2. Assistance for elderly and chronically disabled persons, such as purchasing rehabilitation equipment for personal use, e.g. electrically driven wheelchairs.

ASSOCIATION FOR THE PROMOTION OF YOUTH TECHNICAL CLUBS IN ISRAEL

אגודה לטפוח מועדונים טכניים לנוער בישראל

15 Y.L. Peretz
Haifa
Telephone: (04) 662515
Office Hours: 8:00 A.M. to 1:00 P.M. & 4:00 P.M. to 7:00 P.M.

HISTORY AND DESCRIPTION

The organization was founded in Haifa in 1948 by a few public-minded citizens to help integrate a new generation of immigrant youth into Israeli society and to prepare it for the difficult task of building and living in a modern and progressive society. The Association worked to provide facilities for the young where they could spend their spare time constructively and to help develop in them a feeling of responsibility for their fellow citizens. This is particularly important in a country where immigrants from so many varied countries have arrived.

Organizational Structure: The organization is headed by a public council which is responsible for strategy, planning, financing and controls. National government, local government, industry, banks and others are represented on this council. A Managerial Committee is responsible for the implementation of council resolutions and the day to day supervision of the staff.

Goals: The Association works to induce youngsters to benefit from an educational set-up, combining technical and professional training with social and educational activities. Another aim is to evoke and enliven the youngsters' imaginations and curiosity and to induce them to motivated actions needed for developing their individual abilities, characteristics and skills and bringing out their potential possiblities. The Association also hopes to accustom the young generation, from its earliest ages, to creative labor and to enable every youngster to choose his or her own future, according to the abilities and inclinations of each.

Services, Activities, and Accomplishments: The Society's headquarters in Haifa is responsible for the planning, training and supervision of all afternoon and day Youth Clubs, Mobil Clubs and all other activities. Models are centrally developed and instructors are trained in Haifa. There are programs working for parent-child cooperation, work groups, a Mobil Club, Day Clubs and programs for occupation of elderly people.

OFFICERS

President: Mr. Alexander Goldberg, 109 Yefe Nof, Haifa.
              Tel. (04) 81682.
Chairman: Yosef Ami, 8 Netiv Ofakim, Haifa.
              Tel. (04) 242642.

Director-General: Joseph Cohen, 67d Rothschild Ave, Kiryat Eliezer. Tel. (04) 539725.
Executive Committee: (twelve members, details not supplied.)
(Note: All members stated above, except the General Manager, are volunteers.)

FINANCIAL INFORMATION
The organization is registered in Haifa as an Ottoman Society (no. 6118-61/361). 88% of the organization's income is derived from Government allocations, 11% from membership dues, and the remainder comes from donations which are not tax-free in the United States. Donations are tax deductible in Israel (reg. no. 910009638). Thirty-two full-time and twenty-seven part-time workers are employed by the Association, as well as twelve volunteers. Last year's budget of $390,000 left the organization with a deficit of $28,850.

MEMBERSHIP, SCOPE, AND POLICY
Nine thousand members make up the fifty-six branches of the Association in Israel. The Executive Director is responsible for the implementation of decisions made by the Board as well as for supervision of overall operations. The Managerial Committee is responsible for direct implementation of policy and planning.

AFFILIATIONS/REFERENCES
The organization is connected with Jewish Child's Day, 183/9 Finchley Rd., London NW3 6LB, England.

FUNDING NEEDED
1. For financing the activities of the Association's Center of Development and Training in Haifa.
2. To add one or two more Mobile Clubs to the one in use at present along the Lebanon border.
3. To open and operate Technical Community Clubs.

ASSOCIATION FOR THE PROPAGATION OF TORAH

התנועה להפצת תורה

Belilius 10
P.O.B. 6141, Jerusalem
Telephone: (02) 232414/18
Office Hours: Daily, 8:00 A.M. to 1:00 P.M.

HISTORY AND DESCRIPTION

A result of the large influx of immigrants from North African countries has been the development of an educational and social gap in Israeli society. In the attempt to bridge this gap, the Association for the Propagation of Torah was established, and concentrates its efforts mainly in settlements heavily populated by North African immigrants.

Goals: The Association establishes Torah Centers for young men and encourages the transfer of young couples from the cities to the newer settlements (including some border settlements). These young couples endeavor to assert their influence on the North African immigrants, endowing them with religious and traditional Jewish values. In addition, the representatives of the Association attempt to care for the potentially delinquent youths of these settlements. The main goal of the Association is to establish a relationship based not only upon accepted institutional care but also through direct personal contact.

Services, Activities, and Accomplishments: Consistent with its expressed goals, the Association for the Propagation of Torah endeavours to establish educational institutions for young boys and youths who are rejected by the regular educational facilities, as well as clubs and Torah learning centers for young men. The Association also publishes educational books for religious youth.

The Association sees as its major accomplishment the fact that it has helped 'save' a large number of youth of North African origin who were potentially delinquent through an introduction to religious and social values facilitated through the Association's educational institutions.

OFFICERS

President: Rabbi Y.F. Zacks, Shatz 5, Jerusalem.
       Rabbi.
       Tel. (02) 231759.
Director: Rabbi E. Kugel, Shaarei Zedek 1, Jerusalem.
       Rabbi.
       Tel. (02) 234044.
Treasurer: Rabbi A. Ravitz, Bayit Vegan 103, Jerusalem.
       Rabbi.
       Tel. (02) 422069.
Board Members: Mr. S. Rotem, Redak 24, Jerusalem.
       Tel. (02) 634372.

Rabbi Y. Hendeles, Malahi 20, Jerusalem.
Tel. (02) 285546.
M. Wagner, Hillel 14, Jerusalem.
Lawyer.
Tel. (02) 221708.
E. Jacobs, Evan Ha'ezel 7, Jerusalem.
Tel. (02) 814859.

FINANCIAL INFORMATION
60% of the Association's income is derived through Israeli government subsidies; 25% from foreign donations; and 15% from local donations. Last years' annual budget of $300,000 left the Association with a deficit of over $80,000. The organization is registered with the Jerusalem District Office of the Ministry of the Interior as an Ottoman Association (reg. no. 11/1124). Donations to the Association are tax-free in Israel (no reg. no. supplied) but not in the United States. The Association employs 112 full-time and 17 part-time workers, as well as over 120 volunteers.

MEMBERSHIP, SCOPE, AND POLICY
Daily operating decisions for the Association are made by the president, director or treasurer, while more fundamental issues must be decided upon by the entire board. Membership is open to all those who are close to the Association's principles, although all applications for membership must be submitted to, and confirmed by, the Board. Information regarding the size of the organization or its scope was not supplied.

AFFILIATIONS/REFERENCES
The Association for the Propagation of Torah claims no affiliations with any Israeli political party, nor was information regarding foreign affiliations supplied.

FUNDING NEEDED
1. The erection of a synagogue in the settlement of Yeruham. Cost, $200,000.
2. The financing of the Torah Learning Center in Bet She'an. Monthly budget, $4,000.
3. The erection of an Educational Center in Kiriat Gat. Cost, $500,000.

ASSOCIATION OF AMERICANS AND CANADIANS IN ISRAEL (AACI)

התאחדות עולי אמריקה וקנדה בישראל

6 Beit Hashoeva Tel Aviv
Telephone: (03) 611401/5
Office hours: Sun.-Tues., Thurs.: 8:00 A.M.-4:00 P.M.;
Wed.: 8:00 A.M. to 6:00 P.M.

HISTORY AND DESCRIPTION

The Association of Americans and Canadians in Israel was established in June 1951. There are probably 50,000 Americans and Canadians residing in Israel today. Of these, 12,000 belong to this unique organization which is quite different from other immigrant associations in many respects. Its uniqueness derives from the background of its members in their communities of origin in North America where volunteerism and community concern are an integral part of Jewish life. When AACI first opened its then one-man, part-time office, with IL 9 in the kitty, it was embarking on a pioneering venture of a nature the magnitude of which none could possibly foretell. Now, in five regional offices (Jerusalem, Tel Aviv, Haifa, Netanya and Beersheva), dedicated counselors of AACI interview about 10,000 people per year to guide them through the maze of bureaucracy, rules and regulations, rights and privileges. Often just plain, "good old" American and Canadian friendly faces and voices are as important as the experienced advice in the many potentially explosive areas of the "minefield" of integration.

Goals: To provide a supportive environment for the new immigrant (oleh) from the U.S. and Canada, an environment in which his problems can be dealt with in a relaxed atmosphere by someone who understands his background, mentality, needs and expectations; to organize activities of a social and cultural nature that bring the oleh into contact with others who are facing or have faced the same difficulties and are happily settled in the country; to interpret Israel to him so that he understands it and remembers that his purpose in coming to Israel was to affirm his Jewish identity and his desire to maintain and strengthen it for himself and his children in the Jewish State; to provide advice, guidance, assistance and services required to facilitate his integration so that he may participate in the life of the country as rapidly and fully as possible; to provide him with practical help in the form of loans, second mortgages, ulpans, tours, classes in cooking, history, and Tanach.

Services, Activities, and Accomplishments: Apart from providing the services outlined in the Association's goals, the AACI has developed into an effective pressure group which, together with other immigrant associations, has brought about the creation of new facilities for new immigrants by the Jewish Agency and later by the Israeli Government. All of the following were originally ideas considered by the AACI which worked diligently until they were accepted and implemented by the authorities: family Ulpans for Hebrew studies (now known as Absorption Centers), hostels for temporary housing, summer Hebrew courses for new immigrant children, free high school and university education for new immigrant students, increased deductions in income and other taxes during the first years following aliyah, club houses for newcomers (Moadonei Olim), apartments for rent with options to buy, substantial mortgages for new immigrants, some rental housing subsidized by the Government, assistance to parents having to pay for private tutoring for their children, liberalization in customs duties and clearing procedures at ports including the elimination of customs guarantee requirements, and the equalization of rights and facilities for temporary residents and new immigrants. The AACI believes that its blend of professional staff, lay leadership independence and volunteerism is the best formula for effective absorption (klita).

OFFICERS

President:	Morton Skidelsky, P.O.B. 28, Petach Tikva. Tel. (03) 929990.
V. Presidents:	Lucille Krieger, 14/17 Hashachar, Kfar Saba. Tel. (052) 37422.
	David Stern, Kibbutz Degania Bet, D.N. Emek Hayarden. Tel. (067) 50376.
Secretary:	Jonathan Davis, 7 Ha-Irisim. Ramat Poleg, Netanya. Tel. (053) 51695.
Treasurer:	Don Edelstein, 20 Habanai St., Jerusalem. Tel. (02) 535969.
Nat. Exec. Dir.:	Joseph S. Wernik, Rechov Hahayil 31/6. French Hill, Jerusalem. Tel. (02) 813122.

FINANCIAL INFORMATION
83% of the Association's income comes from allocations, 11% from membership dues, and 6% from linkage interests. Last year's annual budget of $245,000 left the Association with a deficit of $12,375. The Association is registered as a non-profit Ottoman Association (reg. no. 9199 664/99). Donations in Israel and the United States are tax-free (tax nos. not supplied). Employees include 17 full-time and 12 part-time workers.

MEMBERSHIP, SCOPE, AND POLICY
Membership is open to anyone who resided in the U.S. or Canada for at least 5 years. There are 12,000 members in Israel, in 5 branches, and 650 members abroad. Decisions are made by the National Board.

AFFILIATIONS/REFERENCES
The AACI is not affiliated with any Israeli political party. It is affiliated with the following: NAAM, North American Aliya Movement, 515 Park Ave., New York;
APAI — Association of Parents of Americans in Israel;
JWB (Israel Program and Information Desk Project of the JWB).

FUNDING NEEDED
1. To finance second mortgage funds for new immigrants.
2. To finance small emergency loan funds.
3. To finance senior young adult and student activities, and advocacy programs.

ASSOCIATION OF THE BLIND
IN ISRAEL, JERUSALEM BRANCH

האגודה הישראלית של עוורים

P.O.B. 6010
Jerusalem
Telephone: (02) 410033, 522211
Office hours: Tuesday, 6:00 P.M. to 8:00 P.M.

DESCRIPTION
All members of the Jerusalem Association are blind. The help given by the Association is mostly advisory, as one blind person to another, and a loan fund is available to help deserving cases. The Executive negotiates with Government and Municipal offices on behalf of the blind. The Association of the Blind works in cooperation with the Association to Aid the Blind, a separate organization which includes sighted people working on behalf of the blind and to prevent blindness.

Goals: The Association aims to help the blind in every respect, to rehabilitate them and make them productive citizens.

OFFICERS
Director: Michael Peretz. Mexico 6, Jerusalem. Computer programmer. Tel.: (02) 410033.

Adviser: Moshe Gordon. Yehuda 43, Jerusalem. Engineer. Tel.: (02) 717972.

Treasurer: Meir Murad. Shaarey Zedek 3, Jerusalem. Gardener. Tel.: (02) 228052.

Secretary: Ruth Arnon, Bruria 3, Jerusalem. Housewife. Tel.: (02) 633359.

Board Members: Bechor Macluf. Derech Hebron 5, Jerusalem. Social worker. Tel.: (02) 712077.

Hava Lotham. Shikun Patt 26/28, Jerusalem. Music teacher. Tel.: (02) 420386.

FINANCIAL INFORMATION
All of last year's annual budget came from the Association to Aid the Blind. Last year's annual budget was $1,000; there was no deficit. Donations to the Israel Association of the Blind are tax-free in Israel (registration number not supplied); donations are not tax-free in the USA or in other countries outside Israel. The Association is registered as an Ottoman Association (Tel Aviv, no registration number supplied). One part-time worker is employed by the Association and there are five volunteers.

MEMBERSHIP, SCOPE, AND POLICY
There are some 250 members in Jerusalem, the main branch of the Association. Membership is open to all blind persons over the age of 18. Decisions are made by the Executive Board. The Association is not affiliated with any political party in Israel.

FUNDING NEEDED

1. For a hostel to accommodate the blind who are waiting to receive permanent accommodation, and who cannot look after themselves.
2. To acquire a building for a club and offices, to replace the present rented rooms. The plan is to be carried out in cooperation with the Association to Aid the Blind.
3. For a home for the elderly blind. Existing homes for the aged are reluctant to receive blind persons.

THE ASSOCIATION OF THE DEAF IN ISRAEL

אגודת החרשים בישראל

Yad Labanim 13, Yad Eliyahu
P.O.B. 9001
Tel Aviv
Telephone: (03) 331526, 331181
Office hours: Sunday-Thursday: 8:00 A.M.-4:00 P.M.
             Friday: 8:00 A.M.-1:00 P.M.

HISTORY AND DESCRIPTION

The Association of the Deaf in Israel is the outgrowth of a club which was organized in 1944 by a small group of deaf young men and women in Tel-Aviv who were eager for companionship and knew that the best chance of finding it would be amongst their own. Eventually a number of prominent citizens formed a public committee which adopted the club, and turned it into a dynamic national association to which almost 85% of Israel's adolescent and adult deaf belong.

Organizational Structure: The deaf members of the Association play the major role in the organization. Regulations call for an elected body of volunteers to serve for a stipulated duration. Every four years there is a National Convention, with a General Assembly of branches meeting annually, and the National Council meeting three times a year.

The National Central Committee consists of a minimum of seven members. In addition, there are the Branch Committees in the major cities and a National Control Committee.

Services, Activities, and Accomplishments: Within the special clubs, there are cultural, sporting and social activities, including classes in Hebrew and English, with attention being paid to helping new immigrants become integrated. The Association provides vocational training, social help and rehabilitation, and a mutual welfare fund. Another important aspect of the Association is the progress it has made on the development of methods of communication and familiarization with them by the deaf and those in contact with them. Further achievements are publication of the "Demama" journal, and the sponsoring of the dance group "Kol U'Demama", to promote dance and movement skills among the deaf. Also, the Hoffberger Secondary Vocational ORT School was founded, thus establishing the first vocational rehabilitation program for the deaf in Israel. The Association has promoted special television programmes about the deaf in Israel, and produced a special 16 mm. film, "Touching with Words", about the life of the deaf in Israel, as well as publishing the first dictionary of Hebrew sign-language. There are five different Funds available for member's assistance.

OFFICERS

President: Shem-Tov Moshe. Bat-Yam. Manufacturer.
Director: Issachar Goldrath. Efael. Educator. Tel.: (03) 754481.

Treasurer:	Lupo Berziano. Bat-Yam. Textiles.
Executive	
Committee:	Meir Noah. Ramat Gan. Designer.
	Abraham Kaufman. Tel-Aviv. Building worker.
	Joseph Weinstock. Jerusalem. Accountant.
	(Chairman of Jerusalem Branch.)
	Assaf Politzer. Haifa. Metal Worker.
	Zvi Moshe. Haifa. Electrician.

FINANCIAL INFORMATION
83% of last year's budget came from donations, with 15% from governmental sources, and 2% from membership dues. Last year's annual budget of $395,430 left the Association with a deficit of $41,395. Donations in Israel and the U.S. are tax-free (Israel no. 4500058, U.S. tax number not supplied). The organization is registered as an Ottoman, non-profit association (no. 411/99).
The Association employs 19 full-time and 45 part-time workers, and has 550 volunteers.

MEMBERSHIP, SCOPE, AND POLICY
2,800 members represent the 10 branches in Israel with membership open to any deaf person age 18 and over. An active interest is taken in young people, from the age of 14. Policy decisions are made by The National Central Committee.

AFFILIATIONS/REFERENCES
The Association is affiliated with the following organizations:
World Federation of the Deaf, 120 Via Gregorio V11/Rome, Italy;
International Committee of Sports For the Deaf, Hvidovre, 2650, Langaavej 41, Denmark; and the
World Organization of Jewish Deaf, c/o Mr. A. Fleischman, 9102 Edmonston Court, Greenbelt, Ma., 20770, U.S.A.

FUNDING NEEDED
1. To construct a new center for accommodating up to 140 resident pupils, which would serve as a national center for rehabilitation of the deaf—Cost $3,700,000.
2. To construct a covered sports field adjacent to the club in Haifa-—Cost: $360,000.
3. To restore the Hellen Keller Building—Cost: $40,000.

ASSOCIATION OF VICTIMS OF WORK-RELATED ACCIDENTS AND THEIR WIDOWS IN ISRAEL

ארגון נכי תאונות עבודה ואלמנות נפגעי עבודה בישראל

Halevy Eliezer 11, Kiryat-Moshe
Jerusalem
Telephone: (02) 537995
Office hours: Sunday-Thursday, 8:00 A.M. to 13:00 Noon;
Tuesday 16:00 to 18:00; Friday, 8:00 A.M. to 13:00 Noon.

HISTORY AND DESCRIPTION

The Association was established in 1954 to assist workers and their widows in three major areas: rehabilitation; ensuring that the worker and the worker's family receive their due rights; assisting in the initiation and promotion of new legislation to benefit disabled workers and their families. The Association was founded in conformity with the Israel Social Welfare Insurance Law.

Organizational Structure: The activites in the four branches (Tel Aviv, Haifa, Jerusalem, Beersheba) are run entirely by volunteers except for an administrative secretary in each branch. There is a General Governing Board consisting of volunteers elected every four years by the branches. There are also two subsidiary funds with separate governing bodies: one for loans (funded by membership dues), the other, for developing club centers for members (funded by donations).

Services, Activities, and Accomplishments: The volunteers are divided into three groups: one receives the public, another gives individual assistance to newly disabled workers in their rehabilitation and return to daily life; the third group is composed of widows who, as a group, help newly bereaved families, especially orphans, to return to daily life. Through these services, the Association assists thousands of workers and their families. The 1979 Israel Prize for the "Outstanding Volunteer of the Year" was awarded to the volunteer who heads the widows' program.

OFFICERS

Director: Joseph Tomer, Hayarden 13, Rehovot.
                   Administrator. Tel. (02) 537995.
Board Members: Max Stoppelman, Moshav Bitzaron.
                   Farmer. Tel. (055) 94264.
                   Miscka Zilberstein, Neve Sha'ana, Haifa.
                   Ex-seaman. Tel. (04) 234176
                   Esther Minz, Heller 14, Givat Mordechay,
                   Jerusalem. Widow. Tel. (02) 662044.
                   Avshalom Zohar, Hapardes 13, Ramat-Hasharon.

FINANCIAL INFORMATION

65% of last year's annual budget came from membership dues, 29% from donations, 3% from the Government, and 3% from the General Federation of Labor ("Histadrut"). Last year's annual budget was $64,000; there was no deficit, as many activities were cancelled. Donations to the Association are tax-free in Israel (registration number 4500975) but in the United States the exemption status is unclear. The organization is registered as an Ottoman Association (Jerusalem, reg. no. 11/2888).Four full-time workers are employed by the Association, and there are 100 volunteers.

MEMBERSHIP, SCOPE, AND POLICY

There are four branches in Israel, with 10,000 dues-paying members and 3,000 widows. Membership is open to any worker with a disability recognized by the authorities of the National Insurance Scheme as resulting from a work-related accident; the widow of such a worker can also become a member. Decisions are made by the National Board. There are no branches abroad.

AFFILIATIONS

The Association is not affiliated with any political party in Israel.

FUNDING NEEDED

1. To help obtain suitable premises for clubs, with meeting-rooms and other rooms for group activities.
2. To help cover the travel expenses of the groups of widows who visit newly widowed familes to give help.
3. To help set up professionally organized psychological group therapy for badly disabled workers such as quadraplegics.

ASSOCIATION OF YEMENITE IMMIGRANTS — CENTRAL OFFICE

ארגון יוצאי תימן — המרכז

19 Vardiel— Postal Code 67757
P.O.B. 33331— Postal Code 61232
Tel Aviv
Telephone: (03) 337465
Office hours: 8:00 A.M. to 12:00 noon, 4:00 P.M. to 7:00 P.M.

HISTORY AND DESCRIPTION
The Association of Yemenite Immigrants was founded in January 1977.

Goals: To establish Old People's Homes and Mutual Aid organizations.

Services, Activities, and Accomplishments: The Association is at present renovating a building in preparation for use as a Day Home for old people in Tel Aviv. When the Day Home is completed it will provide old people with lunches, refreshments, easy work, cultural and social activities, and special rooms for afternoon rests for those who wish. Furthermore, as a result of negotiations with the Rosh Haa'in Local Council the Association has been allocated an 18 dunam plot of land on a hill which is eminently suitable for the establishment of an Old Age Home. A very large information campaign has been mounted in Israel and abroad explaining the very special purpose of the organization which intends to cater for all Jews but have some of the character of Yemen Jewry. The Association has many adherents in the United States and intends to open a branch in London.

OFFICERS
Chairman: Shlomo Madmon, 52 Dalet, Kfar Shalem,
                  Tel Aviv. Clerk.
                  Tel. (03) 395881.
Treasurer: Rabbi Mordehai Izhari, 26 Hatabor, Tel Aviv.
                  Rabbi.
                  Tel. (03) 654702.
Vice-President: Joseph David Sharabi, 54 Haalonim, Tel Aviv.
                  Pensioner.
                  Tel. (03) 332361.
Secretary: Rabbi Meir Malahi, 16 Hapartizan, Tel Aviv.
                  Rabbi. Tel. (03) 252 037.
President: Rabbi Ovadia Joseph. Harishon Le-Zion,
                  Chief Rabbi of Israel.
Board Member: Rabbi Josef Tzubeyri, Chief Rabbi and
                  President of the Yemen Community in Tel Aviv.

FINANCIAL INFORMATION
70% of the Association's income comes from donations and 30% as grants from institutions. Details of last year's budget not supplied. The

organization is registered in Tel Aviv District as a non-profit Ottoman Association (reg. no. 6440/99). Donations in Israel are tax-free (tax no. not supplied) and application is being considered for tax-free status in the United States. Two part-time workers are employed at present by the Association, as well as volunteers.

MEMBERSHIP, SCOPE, AND POLICY
The Association has 2,000 members in Israel, in one branch, and 80 members abroad with one branch in the United States. Decisions are made by the Council and directory meetings.

ASSOCIATION TO AID THE BLIND AND PREVENTION OF BLINDNESS

האגודה למען העוור ומניעת עוורון

P.O.B. 7424
Jerusalem
Telephone: (02) 631690
Office hours: Daily, 8:00 A.M. to 12:00 Noon

HISTORY AND DESCRIPTION

The Association to Aid the Blind is a voluntary organization that was founded in 1950. It works together with the Israel Blind Society, two of whose members sit on the Board of the Association to Aid the Blind. The latter covers the expenses of the Jerusalem Blind Society and deals with cases recommended by it for help.

Organizational Structure: The Association is run by an Executive Committee which is elected by members. Reports are given by the Executive at the general meetings.

Goals: The purpose of the Association is to help the blind in every respect.

Services, Activities, and Accomplishments: The Association gives help to the individual in the form of interest-free loans, money grants for special occasions, and supplies such items as tapes, braille watches, canes, washing-machines, cooking-stoves, refrigerators, etc. On the educational side, the Association organizes study-courses, excursions, visits to museums and theatres, and helps the children of blind parents with their homework. Volunteers visit homes to help mothers cope better as well as learn about their needs. The Association also runs occupational therapy clubs where the blind are taught cane-work, weaving and knitting. It also operates social and cultural clubs where a variety of courses and lectures are given, and where the blind can meet over a game of chess or at a party. Through these activities, the Association has succeeded in rehabilitating many blind people, including beggars who have been taken in from the streets and taught to take pride in constructive work and be productive citizens.

OFFICERS

Chairman: O. Michaelson, Balfour 19, Jerusalem.
Housewife. Tel. (02) 631690.

Treasurer: A. Goldstein, Beit Vegan 79, Jerusalem.
Social worker. Tel. (02) 414156.

Board Members: M. Gordon, Yehuda 43, Jerusalem.
Engineer. Tel. (02) 717972.

Dr. S. Mendelbaum Hachavatzelet 9, Jerusalem.
Lawyer. Tel. (02) 232672

R. Arnon, Bruria 3, Jerusalem.
Housewife. Tel. (02) 633359.

P. Ganz, Jerusalem.
Housewife. Tel. (02) 414907.
P. Margoliot, Tchernikovsky 36, Jerusalem.
Social worker. Tel. (02) 635987.

FINANCIAL INFORMATION
50% of last year's annual budget of $25,000 came from donations, 28% from functions, 20% from membership dues, and 2% from the Municipality. There was no deficit. Donations to the Association are tax-free in Israel (no registration number supplied); they are not tax-free in the USA or in other countries outside Israel. The organization is registered as an Ottoman Association (Jerusalem, reg. no. 11/500). The Association employs two part-time workers and has many volunteers.

MEMBERSHIP, SCOPE AND POLICY
The Association has 500 members in Jerusalem. Most of the major towns in Israel have associations to aid the blind, but each of these is responsible for its own activities and fund-raising. Thus, although they carry the same name and cooperate with each other, they are not branches of the Association in Jerusalem. Membership is open to all who want to help the blind. Most decisions are made by the Executive Board of the Association. There are no branches abroad.

AFFILIATIONS/REFERENCES
The Jewish Braille Society, New York, USA.
The Association is not affiliated with any political party in Israel.

FUNDING NEEDED
1. To acquire a building for a club and offices. The present rented rooms have to be vacated soon.
2. To acquire a hostel to accommodate the blind who are waiting for permanent accommodation and are unable to look after themselves.
3. To acquire a home for the elderly blind. Existing homes for the aged are reluctant to accept the elderly blind people.

BAMAH ASSOCIATION   אגודת במה

P.O.B. 4069, Jerusalem
Telephone: (02) 631940, (02) 227566.
Office hours: Monday, Wednesday, Thursday, 9:00 A.M. to 3:00 P.M.

HISTORY AND DESCRIPTION
The Bamah Association is the formal framework of the drama quarterly, "Bamah". The quarterly was first published in Jerusalem in 1959, and is the only journal of its kind in Israel. Its character is of a theoretical, scientific, and research nature. Among the contributors to "Bamah" are lecturers in the fields of drama, theater, and literature. It is a non-profit quarterly and rarely pays authors' fees.
Services, Activities, and Accomplishments: "Bamah" has become a source of learning and research material for university and high-school students, as well as for members of the public interested in the subject. The Association's major accomplishment is the continued publication of the quarterly on a regular and non-profit basis, with minimal staff.

OFFICERS
Director: Israel Goor, Jerusalem.
                    Editor. Tel. (02) 669354.
Board Members: Shlomo Du-nour, Jerusalem.
                    Lecturer. Tel. (02) 631310.
                    Nachman Gordon, Tel Aviv.
                    Artisan. Tel. (03) 452951.
                    Binyamin Ventura, Jerusalem.
                    Clerk. Tel. (02) 661815.
                    Yitzchak Tishler, Jerusalem.
                    Journalist. Tel. (02) 632824.
                    Shlomo Sneh, Jerusalem.
                    Journalist. Tel. (02) 811813.

FINANCIAL INFORMATION
75% of last year's budget came from donations, 22% from subscriptions, and the balance from advertising. Last year's annual budget of $9000 left the Association with a deficit of about $600. Donations in Israel are tax-free (Israel non-profit reg. no. 11/1688). The Bamah Association employs one part-time worker, and one volunteer.

MEMBERSHIP, SCOPE, AND POLICY
The Bamah Association has twenty members in its two national branches. Anybody interested in the subject can join the Association. Decisions are made by the Executive Director and the National Board.

AFFILIATIONS/REFERENCES
The Bamah Association is unaffiliated with any of the political parties in Israel. It maintains contact with the Israel Matz Foundation in New York, and several university drama departments in the United States.

FUNDING NEEDED
To ensure the continued publication of the quarterly on a regular basis, which under present inflationary conditions is difficult.

B.A.M.B.I.—MATAN BESETER

מתן בסתר ב.מ.ב.י. – בסיוע למשפחות ברוכות ילדים

c/o Samuel,
Sderot HaMeiri 5,
Jerusalem
Telephone: (02) 533651, 526721
Office hours: No formal hours.

HISTORY AND DESCRIPTION

Matan Beseter was founded in 1973 just after the Yom Kippur War. The aim of the organization is to "adopt" families in distress by providing them with regular financial aid. Presently, some 150 families are being helped with a monthly allowance of $50 to $100. An additional twenty families need "one-time" help to solve an urgent financial crisis. Most of the cases receiving support are widow/ers with young children; parents suffering from a chronic illness and/or psychiatric disorder which prevents them from working to support the family; or children with cerebral palsy or mental retardation. The families are referred to the organization by rabbis in the neighborhood, heads of yeshivas, teachers, social workers and community leaders. Each family is known individually by a responsible person who attends to their needs and provides them with their monthly stipend.

Services, Activities, and Accomplishments: The organization's purpose is to help the family in need to reach a normal standard of living or to overcome periods of acute crisis. Matan Beseter is also involved in allocating special funds in emergency cases towards transporting patients out of the country, purchasing vehicles for families with handicapped children, etc. The organization is now providing the equivalent of about $9,000 a month to families in need. Last year, nearly 20 families were helped to regain a position of independence and now are no longer in need of the organization's support, thus allowing the rechannelling of resources to other needy families. Twice a year, prior to the High Holidays and Passover, an additional 600 families, who are capable of supporting themselves during the rest of the year, are provided with supplementary income to help them bear the added expenses that accrue at those times. During each of these two periods last year, approximately $45,000 in aid was extended. Currently, the organization has a list of another 20-25 poor families waiting for monthly help.

OFFICERS

Director: Joseph Meyer, Moshav Alon Shvut.
Old-Age Home Director. Tel.: (02) 742993.

Treasurer: Jacob Hertz, Eliezer Halevy 17, Jerusalem.
Salesman. Tel.: (02) 523078.

Board Members: Daniel Weinstock, Beth-El. Computers.
Henriette Samuel, Sderot HaMeiri 3, Jerusalem.
Tel.: (02) 533651.
Rachel Chalkowski, Beth Horvat, Givat Shaul,
Jerusalem. Midwife. Tel.: (02) 526721.

FINANCIAL INFORMATION

Matan Beseter's income is derived entirely from donations. Last year's annual budget was $110,000, with no deficit. Donations to the organization do not carry tax-free status in Israel or the U.S.A. The organization is registered as a non-profit Ottoman Association in the Jerusalem District Office of the Ministry of the Interior (reg. no. 11/2960). Four to five volunteers make up the staff of the organization. No part of the contributions is spent on salaries, office expenses or other administrative costs, in order to pass along all donations directly to the families.

MEMBERSHIP, SCOPE, AND POLICY

Membership is open to anyone who wants to do volunteer work. Presently, the organization has 1 branch in Israel with 10 members. There are no branches abroad. Decisions are made mostly by the National Board.

AFFILIATIONS/REFERENCES

Matan Beseter is not connected with any political party in Israel. The organization is affilated with the following:

1) "London-Jerusalem Chain", c/o I.D. Kahn, 5 Gloucester Gardens, London, NW1.
2) Agudath Israel Frauen Gruppe, Brands schenkesteig 14, Zurich, Switzerland.

BARUCH TAAM RABBINICAL COLLEGE
כולל אברכים מצוינים ברוך טעם

12 Hanna Street
P.O.B. 7341, Jerusalem
Telephone: (02) 817207
Office hours: 8:00 A.M. to 3:00 P.M.

HISTORY AND DESCRIPTION
The Rabbinical College "Baruch Taam" was founded in memory of the famous Gaon and Tzaddik, righteous scholar, Rabbi Baruch Teumim-Frankel, for outstanding married Torah-scholars, many of them with large families, who study with diligence.

The Yeshiva's major accomplishments have been the editing and publishing of various manuscripts of the Gaon "Baruch Taam".

OFFICERS
Director: B.S. Schneerson, 19 Elkana, Jerusalem. Rabbi.
Treasurer: Joshua Levy, 15 Michal, Jerusalem.
Board Members: Aron Frankel, Brooklyn, N.Y. Businessman.
                   Elchanan Halpern, London, England. Rabbi.
                   Schlomo Greenstein, 6 Panim Meirot,
                      Jerusalem. Retired.
                   Nachum Schneerson, 12 Even Haazel,
                      Jerusalem. Rabbi.

FINANCIAL INFORMATION
The sources of income are mainly from individual donors in Israel and abroad and from the Ministry of Religion. Last year's annual budget of $39,300 left the Yeshiva with a deficit of $5,700. The Yeshiva is registered as an Ottoman Association (reg. no. 11/1701). Donations to the Yeshiva are tax-free in Israel (no. 4506799) but not in the United States. The Yeshiva did not indicate any full-time or part-time employees but did not specify one volunteer working for them.

MEMBERSHIP, SCOPE, AND POLICY
No information was supplied on decision-making or membership criteria, but reference was made to the bylaws supplied to the Ministry of Interior.

AFFILIATIONS/REFERENCES
The Yeshiva is not affiliated with any political party in Israel. The Yeshiva is in contact with the Federated Council of Israel Institutions, 15 Beekman Street, New York 10038, and Esras Torah, 235 East Broadway, New York, New York 10002.

FUNDING NEEDED
1. For supporting avrechim (students) with large families.
2. Funding is needed for the publication of the manuscripts of the famous Gaon and righteous scholar, Rabbi Baruch Frankel-Teumim, known as the "Baruch Taam" who was the Chief Rabbi of Leipnick.

BE'AR MAIM CHAIM YESHIVA

באר מים חיים

20 Hazfira Street
Jerusalem
Telephone: (02) 714190
Office hours: regular business hours

HISTORY AND DESCRIPTION

This evening-yeshiva was established in 1976 in order to return children, youth and adults to Jewry. It has succeeded to lead many people back to the tradition of the Patriarchs. In addition, some youngsters who were rejected by society have become a good example for every citizen in Israel.

Goals: To open evening courses in order to teach 13 to 18 year old boys Jewry and a profession, so they can build new and good lives from both a spiritual and a material point of view.

Services, Activities, and Accomplishments: Children have been returned to Jewry. Some of them have been sent to religious institutions. People have been convinced to repent and to become religious.

OFFICERS

Director: Chaim Shirazi, 24/53 Naphtalli. Rabbi.
                     Tel. (02) 714190.
Treasurer: Baruch Sharvit, 36 Halamed Hey. Contractor.
                     Tel. (02) 661667.
Board Members: Moshe Moonir, 1 Machalkey Hamaim. Rabbi.
                     Tel. (02) 666126.
                     David Malci, 2 Hameiri. Circumciser (Mohel).
                     Shimon Rahamim, 9 Hamodai. Teacher.
                     Yosef Ben Porat, 32 Haim Ozer. Businessman.
                     Yoav Asis, 18 Naphtalli. Teacher.

FINANCIAL INFORMATION

The Yeshiva's sources of income are: membership dues, donations, and the Ministry of Religion. No breakdown of the percentages supplied by each source was given. Last year's annual budget was $6,000. The Yeshiva has no deficit. The Yeshiva is registered as an Ottoman Association (reg. no. 11/3314). Donations are not tax free. There is one full-time employee and two volunteers.

MEMBERSHIP, SCOPE, AND POLICY

Decisions are made mostly by the Executive-Director. There are seven members in Israel.

AFFILIATIONS/REFERENCES

The Yeshiva is not affiliated with any Israeli political party. The Yeshiva is in contact with individuals in several countries abroad:

Belgium: Rabbi Shimon Ben-Nizri, Brussels.
France: Rabbi Amram Ben Chano, Paris.

FUNDING NEEDED

1. The expansion of current activities ($1,000 per month).
2. The purchase of regular facilities ($500,000).
3. The contacts with officials and agencies abroad ($500).

BEIT ESHKOL COMMUNITY CENTER OF AFULA

בית אשכול – מרכזים קהילתיים עפולה

P.O.B. 1060, AFULA
Telephone: (065) 91004/5
Office hours: 8:00 A.M.-1:00 P.M.
               4:00 P.M.-8:00 P.M.

HISTORY AND DESCRIPTION
The Beit Eshkol Community Center was established in 1970 in Afula, which is a small town situated in the Jezreel Valley.

Goals: To assist the depressed suburbs of Afula, which have many pressing social needs, by means of social work, vocational training, sport, and education.

Services, Activities, and Accomplishments: The Center aims at providing activities for all ages within the community, and to integrate the social work and the cultural life of the varied population.

OFFICERS
Director: Zvi Harary, Tel.: (065) 91004/5.
Treasurer: Ovadia Azzar, Tel.: (065) 91004/5.
Executive
Committee: Ovadia Elly, Mayor of Afula.
                 Michael Nizany. Shlomo Levy. Yehuda Hindy.
                 Arie Lev. Baruch Vazan.

FINANCIAL INFORMATION
30% of the budget comes from membership dues, with 70% from Government sources. The annual budget in 1979 of $170,000 left the Center with a deficit of $20,000. Donations in Israel are tax-free (tax exemption number not supplied). There are 30 full-time and 40 part-time workers employed by the Center, as well as 60 volunteers.

MEMBERSHIP, SCOPE, AND POLICY
Membership is open to everyone living in the town, providing the membership fees are paid, and at present there are 1,300 members. Decisions are made by the Executive Director.

AFFILIATIONS/REFERENCES
The Center has no political affiliations. It does seek to establish friendships with Community Centers in other countries.

FUNDING NEEDED
1. To establish a library which would serve the whole Afula area.
2. To expand cultural activities such as forming a theater group and music group.

BEIT KEDEM   בית קדם – מרכז קהילתי ערבי-יהודי

Pincas 12
P.O.B. 295, AKKO
Telephone: (04) 910310
Office hours: 8:00 A.M.-12:00; 4:00-8:00 P.M.

HISTORY AND DESCRIPTION
Beit Kedem was founded in 1973 as an Ottoman organization, composed of a committee of 66 members, and a management of 10. Beit Kedem was founded with the initiative of the local Jewish and Arab citizens of Akko, with the aim of holding joint social and cultural activities.

Organizational Structure: The management of this community center consists of representatives from the Municipality, the Histadrut, Matnasim (Israel Corporation of Community Centers), and the general public.

Goals: The primary aim is to foster good relations between Arabs and Jews. Cultural events and folklore performances are held demonstrating the customs and traditions of both peoples. Seminars are held in Israel, and delegates from the Center are sent to conferences abroad. The Center tries to meet basic needs in the fields of community and culture, with social and educational activities for youth.

Services, Activities, and Accomplishments: Creating a service to the community, that is acknowledged by the citizens, and making contact with other organizations in Akko, to hold joint activities.

OFFICERS
Director:	Y. Zagori, Herzl 35. Teacher. Tel. (04) 912819.
Treasurer:	B. Bedoyan, Herzl 18. Bank Manager. Tel. (04) 911291.
Exec. Com.:	M. Habaishi, Ben Ami, 55. Judge. Tel. (04) 910492.
	D. Kemchi, Anelevitch 31. Histadrut.
	S. Katz, Akko Municipality. Municipality employee. Tel. (04) 912368.
	M. Abdo, Sh. Ben Yousif 10. Secretary. Tel. (04) 910605.
	T. Omari, Herzl 39. Notary. Tel. (04) 91031.
Management:	F. Falak, Ben Ami 27. Judge. Tel. (04) 910427.

FINANCIAL INFORMATION
35% of last year's annual budget came from the municipality, with 25% from "Matnasim", 20% from the Ministry of Education, and the final

20% from membership dues. Last year's annual budget of $35,840 left the Center with a deficit of $3,409. Donations to the Center, in Israel, are tax-free (tax exempt — no. not reported). The Center is a non-profit Ottoman society (no. 5854055). There are 7 full-time and 25 part-time workers employed by the Center, with 60 volunteers.

MEMBERSHIP, SCOPE, AND POLICY
The Center serves approximately 1500 people, with membership open to any person aged 18 and over. Most decisions are made by the Executive Director together with the National Board.
Recently, further branches have been established in the Old City of Akko.

AFFILIATIONS/REFERENCES
The Center is not affiliated with any political party in Israel, but is affiliated with the Political Center in Bonn.

FUNDING NEEDED
1. As new branches have been opened in the Old City, money will be required for a social worker.
2. To establish a Jewish and Arabic Dance Group.
3. To organize an Oriental Orchestra.

BEIT MIRIAM COMMUNITY CENTER

מרכז קהילתי ע״ש בית מרים

23 Haturim Street
Jerusalem
Telephone: (02) 228957
Office hours: 9:00 A.M. to 9:00 P.M.

HISTORY AND DESCRIPTION

The Community Center originated as a Ministry of Education sponsored Youth Center almost thirty years ago. Three years ago it was
decided to convert the Youth Center into a Community Center to serve
all levels of the community. It was then handed over to the sponsorship
of the Jerusalem Municipality. The Center is situated in an old neighbourhood of Jerusalem, Mekor Baruch, which comprises two major
sub-groups, the Ultra-Orthodox, and Secular, as well as Kurdish and
other ethnic groups such as Persian and Iraqi.

Organizational Structure: As a non-profit Association, the Center is run
by a Board of Governors which is comprised of: three district representatives, and one representative each from the Ministry of Education, the
Municipality, the Community Centers Corporation, the Jerusalem
Fund, as well as the Center Director, youth leaders, social workers, and
occupational leaders.

Goals: To enhance and strengthen the family unit, develop and strengthen Jewish identity, and to help create a unified society.

Services, Activities, and Accomplishments: There is an Elderly Citizens
club, with such diverse activities as gymnastics and handicrafts, social
service lectures, ulpan for improving Hebrew, and outings.
There is also a counselling service for adults provided by social workers
and community leaders, and cultural and educational activities, including lectures, dressmaking, gymnastics, Judaism and English. For the
youth there is a pre-army enlistment project to help prepare them for
army life by having meetings, outings, and lectures with army officials.
There is a counselling service for the youth, which utilizes group dynam-
ics, music, folk dancing films and discussions on Judaism. For the
younger children, the Center has creative activity corners, game rooms,
and a Kabbalat Shabbat program. Sports programmes including soccer,
basketball and gymnastics are also offered.
The Center has established a stable and devoted staff team, and helps
with the rehabilitation of wayward youth. There are also the beginnings
of a neighbourhood governing committee.

OFFICERS

Director: Uri Amedi, Ben Dor 1, Jerusalem.
             Tel. (02) 536619.
Exec. Comm.: Bentov Mizrachi, Haturim 11, Jerusalem.
             Tel. (02) 228351.

Avraham Goren, Beit Zayit 38, Jerusalem.
  Tel. (02) 522897
Yossi Fisher, Keren Hayesod 36, Jerusalem.
  Tel. (02) 666103.
Zeev Alon, King David St., Jerusalem.
  Tel. (02) 242035.
Chava Rom, Takhkemoni 26, Jerusalem.
  Tel. (02) 246245.
Shoshanna Nagy, Rashbam 15, Jerusalem.
  Tel. (02) 52242.
Yosef Middeh. Youth Representative.

FINANCIAL INFORMATION
70% of last year's budget came from the Municipality of Jerusalem combined with the Association of Community Centers, with 15% from membership dues and a further 15% from donations. Last year's annual budget of $88,000 left the Center with a deficit of $17,700. Donations to the Center in Israel and the U.S. are tax-free. (Israel and U.S. tax exempt numbers not supplied.) The Center employs 5 full time and 5 part time workers, and there are 20 volunteers.

MEMBERSHIP, SCOPE AND POLICY
Fifteen hundred members represent the two Israeli branches. Anybody living in the neighbourhood is eligible to join, as well as those having left the neighbourhood, but still maintaining strong ties.

AFFILIATIONS/REFERENCES
The Beit Miriam Community Center is not affiliated with any other organizations.

FUNDING NEEDED
1. To finance more in-depth work with families.
2. To provide auxiliary lessons for youth and children.
3. To fund special projects such as family summer camps.
4. To assist pre-Army-service youth, as well as work with youth on leave from the Army.

BEIT SHMUEL YESHIVAT
B'NEI AKIVA — HADERA

"בית שמואל" ישיבת בני עקיבא, חדרה

P.O.B. 403, Hadera
Telephone: (063) 32753
Office hours: 8:00 A.M. to 4:00 P.M.

HISTORY AND DESCRIPTION

Beit Shmuel was founded in 1962 to enable boys unable to receive an adequate education in their home setting to profit from a traditional Jewish education combined with high-school studies. The Yeshiva also provides its students with dormitory, sport and art facilities, as well as clothing.

Organizational Structure: Beit Shmuel has seven directors, coming from varying walks of life, all of whom have a concerned interest in the education of Israeli youth.

Goals: To give boys from disadvantaged homes and underdeveloped nieghborhoods the possibility to study.

Services, Activities, and Accomplishments: Beit Shmuel has educated hundreds of students in its Yeshiva high-school, many of whom have gone on to become officers in the Israel Defence Forces, rabbis, university graduates, or otherwise active in Israel society. The students are encouraged to undertake voluntary work with disadvantaged sectors of the Israeli population.

OFFICERS

Director: Rabbi M. Ofen.
Treasurer: M. Lieberman. Member of Hadera Municipality.
School Director: B. Marmor.
Board Members: M. Kostelitz. Vice-Mayor of Hadera.
                F. Diamant. Director of Central B'nei Akiva Yeshiva
                Yeshivot Organization.
                Mr. Gazit. Self-employed.
                Rabbi S. Burstin. President of Yeshiva.

FINANCIAL INFORMATION

50% of last year's annual budget came from donations, 40% from government sources, and the balance from membership dues. Last year's annual budget of $600,000 left Beit Shmuel with a deficit of $120,000. Beit Shmuel is registered as a non-profit organization (Israel reg. no. 31-671/36), and donations to it made in Israel and the United States are tax-free (no tax numbers supplied). The Yeshiva employs thirty full-time and twenty-eight part-time workers, as well as twelve volunteers.

MEMBERSHIP, SCOPE, AND POLICY
Beit Shmuel has seven members in its two national branches. Members are co-opted by the decision of the Board. The Board is also responsible for decision making in general.

AFFILIATIONS/REFERENCES
Beit Shmuel is not affiliated to any of the political parties in Israel. It is in contact with American Friends of Yeshivot B'nei Akiva, 39 Broadway, New York, N.Y. 10006.

FUNDING NEEDED
1. To provide basic salaries for teachers, food, and special activities — $15,000 monthly.
2. To provide sport facilities — $50,000.
3. To provide teaching and educational facilities — $280,000.

THE BEN-GURION UNIVERSITY OF THE NEGEV

אוניברסיטת בן־גוריון בנגב

P.O.B. 653
Beersheva
Telephone: (057) 61281 (Dept. of Public Affairs)
Office hours: 8:00 A.M. to 3:00 P.M.

HISTORY AND DESCRIPTION

Founded in 1969 by a Government decision, the Ben-Gurion University of the Negev is mandated with the vital task of spearheading the social, cultural and scientific development of the sounthern region, some 60 percent of Israel's area within the pre-1967 boundaries.

Goals: As the youngest institution of higher learning in the country, the University is acutely aware of the need to maintain the highest academic standards in its pedagogy and in its research so as to attract the best to its campuses in Beersheva and Sde Boker.

Services, Activities, and Accomplishments: The University is composed of four faculties: Humanities and Social Sciences, Natural Sciences, Technology and, the youngest faculty (founded in 1974), Health Sciences. The latter faculty's seven-year program is a unique addition to the Israeli medical scene. From the first day a student begins his medical studies, he acquires the skills needed to function effectively as a community doctor. For the Negev, with only 10 percent of Israel's population, has had difficulty in attracting the qualified and specialized medical personnel needed to create a complete health infrastructure. Because the Health Sciences Faculty is a potential model for medical education in developing countries, it has been designated by the World Health Organization as a Collaborative Institution. Its progress in this vital field is continuously monitored by the WHO.

In addition to two Beersheva-based campuses, a third campus is located at Sde Boker, 40 kilometers south of Beersheva, where David Ben-Gurion lived and found his final resting place. There the Jacob Blaustein Institute for Desert Research situated in a dramatic setting, affords the resident scientists and supporting staff a natural, outdoor laboratory in which to study all aspects of life, work and development in the desert. Also part of the University is the Research and Development Authority with an Applied Research Institute. Its scientists devote themselves exclusively to the development of new products, many of which will form the nucleus for future science-based industry and agriculture suited to the region.

In addition to scholarship, research, and regional development, the University is actively working to bridge the social and economic gap seperating Israel's diverse communities. More than 50 percent of Israel's population are of North African and Middle Eastern origin. In the Negev the figure is 70 percent. Too many of these families are economically underprivileged and blessed with numerous children but unable to provide them with proper social and educational opportunities. Over one-third of the University's enrollment, twice that of any other Israeli university, is made up of students from Sephardi backgrounds. Providing needy students with scholarships is a major priority. An extensive network of pre-academic programs — on campus and in the Negev communities — gives those lacking a matriculation certificate the opportunity to qualify and enjoy a university education. Over 1300 BGU students participate in a "one-to-one" tutorial project, in which each student takes a child under his wing, both as a tutor and as a friend, helping the child to continue his high school studies up to graduation. Others run youth clubs in Beersheva and development towns and participate in various social welfare activities. The University has made participation in social integration programs a condition for receiving a scholarship.

Another 400 students participate in a special program for Sephardi civic leaders from development towns. More than 300 students take courses in the Heritage of Oriental Jewry Program. The Faculty of Humanities and Social Sciences graduates teachers and community workers who serve throughout the region. The administration has launched a crash program for the advancement of the Negev's underprivileged sectors, marshalling as much of its resources toward this end as it possibly can.

FINANCIAL INFORMATION
Budget and financing details not supplied. Donations in Israel and the United States are tax-free (tax nos. not supplied).

AFFILIATIONS/REFERENCES
There are 18 Associate Organizations of the Ben-Gurion University of the Negev, throughout the world, in Australia, Brazil, Canada, France, Germany, Great Britain, Israel, Japan, South Africa, Switzerland, Venezuela and the U.S.A. Details can be obtained from the University.

BEN SHEMEN YOUTH VILLAGE

כפר הנוער בן שמן

Post Ben Shemen 71-910
Telephone: (054) 29111
Office hours: Sunday-Friday, 8:00 A.M. to 4:00 P.M.

HISTORY AND DESCRIPTION

The Ben Shemen Youth Village was established in 1927 by Dr. Lehman.
Today there are over 900 students in the Youth Village.

Goals: To raise children successfully from terribly disadvantaged
homes, give them back a little childhood happiness, raise them to a
higher standard of education, and prepare them for an active citizen's
life in this country.

Services, Activities, and Accomplishments: The students of the boarding
school are divided into three main sections: the children's section, the
junior high section and the youth section. Most of the children in high
school are from development towns, poor neighborhoods and from
moshavim that were established after the creation of the state of Israel.
The School strives to give them the opportunity to successfully graduate
high school in order to continue in professional and academic studies,
which for them is an advancement in society. The high school students
work three times a week in the school farm. This work is considered to
be an educational instrument in the study program. The students are
organized according to educational groups and learn to live together in
respectful relationships and with increasing self-responsibility. Rich
cultural activities involve the students such as preparations for Shabbat
celebrations and holidays, and courses in drama, dancing, and drawing.
The Youth Village has succeeded in raising children from terribly
disadvantaged homes, and given them a high standard of education.
Many of the graduates of the Youth Village continue in service professions in order to help others.

OFFICERS

Dean:	Aryeh Shiryon, Ben Shemen. Tel. (054) 29111.
Accountant:	Joseph Salpeter, Ben Shemen. Tel. (054) 29111.
Principal:	Maier Levy, Ben Shemen. Tel. (054) 29111.
Social Activities Director:	Aryeh Velovsky, Ben Shemen.
Farm Director:	Nissan Peled, Ben Shemen.

FINANCIAL INFORMATION

The Ministry of Education and the Ministry of Health finance a subsistence level of education. Their subsidies only cover the minimal basic
needs of the children, and not expenses for building, the pool, renova-

tion, etc. The Youth Village receives assistance from Youth Aliyah and sporadic private donors. Last year's annual budget of $1,250,000 left a deficit of $312,000. The Youth Village is registered in Ramle as a non-profit Ottoman Association (reg. no. 3939/462). Donations in Israel are tax-free (tax no. not supplied). Donations in the United States are tax-free if sent through Youth Aliyah/U.J.A. and stipulated to be sent to Ben Shemen Youth Village (tax no. not supplied). Donations in England are tax-free if sent via Youth Aliyah. 200 full-time workers are employed by the Youth Village as well as five volunteers.

MEMBERSHIP, SCOPE, AND POLICY
The Youth Village is not a member organization. Decisions are made by the Executive Board.

AFFILIATIONS/REFERENCES
The Youth Village is sponsored by the Ministry of Education. It is affiliated with Youth Aliyah, the Jewish Agency and the American Reform Movement.

FUNDING NEEDED
1. To finance the construction of a dormitory for 100 elementary school children and to house two additional groups of 48 children each.
2. To finance the construction of a hall for 600 people.

BETH AVOTH KIRYAT SANZ

בית אבות קרית צאנז

Rabbi Akiva Street
Kiryat Sanz
Netanya
Telephone: (053) 92483
Office hours: 8:00 A.M. to 1:30 P.M.

HISTORY AND DESCRIPTION
Beth Avoth Kiryat Sanz, an Orthodox religious Home for the Aged, was built 22 years ago under the auspices of the "Klosinburg" Rebbe as part of a small village including a yeshiva, day schools, an orphanage, and now a hospital. The Home is situated close to the shore of the Mediterranean Sea.

Goals: To try to make the last years of the old-aged Orthodox as pleasant as possible.

Services, Activities, and Accomplishments: The Home for the Aged (Beth Avoth) houses approximately 75 people. Each person, or married couple, has a room for himself and each room is equipped with a toilet, bath, shower and balcony. The Home has its own synagogue and study and has recently been furnished with central heating. Beth Avoth Kiryat Sanz accepts people other old age homes will not have and tries to make their last years as pleasant as possible.

OFFICERS
Director: M. Fishbane, Rabbi Akiva,
                       Kiryat Sanz, Netanya.
Treasurer: H.Y. Erenfeld
Board Members: J. Weizenbloom
                       J. Gevirtz
                       M. Moskowitz

FINANCIAL INFORMATION
60% of last year's budget came from residents paying whatever possible, 10% from donations, and 30% was deficit. Last year's annual budget of $65,000 left a deficit of $20,000. The organization is registered in Ramle as a non-profit Ottoman Association (reg. no. 535/1). Donations in Israel and the United States are tax-free (tax nos. not supplied. For U.S. tax information apply to Shaarit Hapleita, 3400 New York Ave., P.O.B. 373, Union City, N.J.). 16 full-time and 5 part-time workers are employed by the Home.

MEMBERSHIP, SCOPE, AND POLICY
Most decisions are made by the Executive Director. Major decisions are made together with the Board of Directors.

AFFILIATIONS/REFERENCES

Beth Avoth Kiryat Sanz is not affiliated with any Israeli political party. It is affiliated with Shaarit Hapleita, 3400 New York Ave., P.O.B. 373, Union City, N.J.

FUNDING NEEDED

1. To pay for central heating recently installed; to install an elevator; to paint and repair Home, inside and out.
2. To complete the building of a home for the chronically ill aged. Building was stopped in the middle due to lack of funds. There is a great need for institutions for the chronically ill, especially for the Orthodox. The Home started building the new wing which was planned as a two-storey building with 50 beds and other facilities.
3. To aid in the general upkeep of Beth Avoth Kiryat Sanz.

BETH BRACHA—TRADITIONAL RELIGIOUS SCHOOL FOR GIRLS

בית ברכה – בית חינוך חרדי לבנות

20 Yona Street
Jerusalem
Telephone: (02) 282506 and 271061
Office hours: 8:00 A.M. to 6:00 P.M.

DESCRIPTION

Beth Bracha was founded in 1961 in order to fill the need for orthodox institutions for girls of religious backgrounds. It has quickly attained high levels of achievement in education. There are two nursery classes, one kindergarten, two pre-school classes, eight elementary grades with parallel classes, and four classes for academic and vocational high school/seminary. There is also a girls' organization, ladies auxiliary, society for printing educational works, and a weekly magazine.

Goals: The goal of Beth Bracha is to give a well-rounded personal education to girls from poor and large families, in both secular and religious fields.

Services, Activities, and Accomplishments: Beth Bracha provides individualized education to each student; vocational education and courses for older students; extra curricular activities, including extra help for weaker students, assembly programs, trips and parent participation; printing and distribution of educational works and books, a weekly periodical and articles on special subjects. Projects in education for hundreds of students, girls from deprived families receive a full or partial scholarship, gaining a well-rounded education on a personal level. Thoses who have completed their vocational studies have found excellent skilled jobs. Many graduates have settled in married life and have begun to build their homes, a pride to the Nation.
Due to the institution's outstanding rate of growth and development, the student body has quickly outgrown its meager quarters and is presently housed in inadequate, poorly constructed and overcrowded, rented buildings. The students and teachers suffer despite the many accomplishments. In order to deal with this drastic problem, Beth Bracha purchased two school buildings which, after proper renovations will be suitable for the various departments of the school.

OFFICERS

Director &
President: Rabbi Shimon Buchspan, 70 Rashi, Jerusalem.
                 Tel. (02) 535915.
Vice President: Rabbi Chaim Y. Mizberg, 21 Berlin, Jerusalem.
                 Tel. (02) 665917.
Treasurer: Rabbi Ch. Zwebner, Shomrei Emunim B',
                 Jerusalem.
                 Tel. (02) 287048.

Principals:	Rabbi A. Eisen, 10 Elkanah, Jerusalem.
	Tel. (02) 814580.
	Rabbi S. Auerbach, 4 Baharan, Jerusalem.
	Tel. (02) 284977.
	Rabbi S. Goldhaber, 15 Gesher Hachaim,
	Jerusalem.
	Tel. (02) 526860.
Secretary:	Rabbi Y. Buchspan, 7 Yoel, Jerusalem.
	Tel. (02) 286750.

FINANCIAL INFORMATION

The sources of income for the annual budget of last year were as follows: donations, 55%; national funds, 25%; and the remaining 20% from tuition. The budget for last year was $78,000, with a deficit of $34,000. The institution is not registered as an Ottoman Association. The institution is currently in the process of obtaining a tax exempt right in Israel. Currently, donations are not tax-free. There are 17 full-time and 29 part-time workers employed with the institution, in addition to 9 volunteers.

MEMBERSHIP, SCOPE, AND POLICY

Decisions are made mostly by the Executive Director. It is not a membership organization. Every girl is admitted whose parents strive for an education as instilled by the school, with no exception as to economic or social background.

AFFILIATIONS/REFERENCES

The School is not affiliated with any politcal party in Israel. It is in contact with: Beth Sarah School for Girls, 58th Street and 16th Avenue, Brooklyn, New York; and Institutions of Karlin Stolin, 54th and 18th Avenue, Brooklyn, New York.

FUNDING NEEDED

1. Funds for day care centers, kindergarten and secondary and primary education school buildings — one million dollars.
2. Regular yearly budget, this year $155,00.
3. Redevelopment of new projects in education, approximately $33,000.

BETH HANOCH

"בית חנוך"

29 Bar-Ilan
Jerusalem
Telephone: (02) 281839, 271259
Office hours: normal office hours

HISTORY AND DESCRIPTION

Beth Hanoch was established following the Yom Kippur War, in memory of the late Hanoch Mechaber, a parachutist who fell in battle in the Sinai desert, and his parents' only son.

Goals: To perpetuate the memory of the late Hanoch Mechaber by the establishment of a Synagogue in his name with a Youth Center and library attached, and a Scholarship Fund for distinguished pupils.

Services, Activities, and Accomplishments: The organization intends to establish the Synagogue within the neighbourhood of the late Hanoch Mechaber's home, in the area where he grew up, where everybody knew him, and where his friends live. This will be accomplished by the acquisition or purchase of suitable buildings or construction on a suitable plot of land. Nothing concrete has yet resulted from discussions with the Israel Lands Authority and the Jerusalem Municipality, but, in the meantime, donations from friends and relatives are accumulating.

OFFICERS

Director: Mordechia Mechaber, 29 Bar-Ilan, Jerusalem.
Driver.
Tel. (02) 271259.

Treasurer: Nissan Mechaber, 18 Ohalei Yosef, Jerusalem.
Retired.
Tel. (02) 288959.

Board Members: Moshe Chanuka, 8 Etzel, Jerusalem.
Clerk.
Tel. (02) 816968.
Zion Guata, Rabanu Gershom, Jerusalem.
Merchant.

FINANCIAL INFORMATION

The organization's income derives from donations only. Last year's annual budget was $100. The organization is registered as a non-profit Ottoman Association (reg. no. 11-2346). Information concerning the tax status of donations not supplied.

MEMBERSHIP, SCOPE, AND POLICY

Membership is open to anyone interested and willing to help. Decisions are made by general membership meetings according to need.

AFFILIATIONS/REFERENCES

The organization is not affiliated with any Israeli political party.

FUNDING NEEDED

1. To purchase a plot of land for the construction of the Synagogue, Youth Centre and Library.
2. To finance construction of the Synagogue, Youth Centre and Library.
3. To cover operating costs of the Synagogue, Youth Centre and Library.

BIG BROTHERS LEAGUE OF HAIFA

אגודת אחים בוגרים — חיפה

10 Achad Haam
Haifa
Telephone: (04) 665644
Office hours: Monday and Thursday, 4:00-7:00 P.M.

HISTORY AND DESCRIPTION

The Big Brothers League of Haifa was originally started in 1973 as a 3-year pilot project by the Haifa Social Welfare Council, with the help and guidance of the Baltimore Jewish Big Brother League. Afterwards, the volunteers themselves took over the organization and are running it as an independent, government-recognized volunteer organization.

Organizational Structure: The Board runs the League, and it is made up of Chairman, Treasurer, heads of the various committees, and ex-officio representatives of the Government, Defense Ministry, Ministry of Welfare, and the National Insurance Institute. The various committees are: Supervision; Financial, Professional; and Publicity and Recruitment.

Goals: The League works to recruit volunteers (men) who will befriend a fatherless boy, so as to provide the child with a male image with which to identify as he is growing up. Its goal is to expand services to include every boy in Haifa needing a Big Brother (at the present time there are many waiting for the right volunteer). In addition, people have approached the League about help in setting up new leagues, or branches, in outlying districts such as Safed, Tivon, Kiryat Motzkin, Kiryat Bialik, Kfar Ata and Acre.

Services, Activities, and Accomplishments: The League provides a unique service for fatherless boys, much needed by the Ministry of Defense, National Insurance (department dealing with widows and orphans), Ministry of Welfare, and school counselling services. Widowed mothers also approach the organization for Big Brothers for their sons, on their own, without intermediaries. After a difficult beginning, the League now successfully guides some 60 Big Brother-Little Brother friendships at a time. Some of the boys have now "graduated", but most of the friendships formed will probably last a life-time.

OFFICERS

Director: Alec Mendelson, Hanassie 20A, Haifa.
                                   Capt., Port Authority. Tel. (04) 332907.
Treasurer: Josef Navon, Kiriat Sefer 17, Haifa.
                                   Financial Advisor. Tel. (04) 246490.
Board Members: Helen Golan, Sweden 13, Haifa.
                                   Teacher. Tel. (04) 244308.
                                   Benjamin Jonas, Achad Haam 45, Nahariya.
                                   Educator. Tel. (04) 921832.

Ariel Karie, Einstein 99A, Haifa.
  Sociologist. Tel. (04) 251934.
Zwi Shulman, Harofe 25, Haifa.
  Psychologist-Business. Tel. (04) 255948.
Shlomo Kopelman, Gush Halav 3A, Zur Shalom.
  Tel. (04) 712058.
Yizhak Weiss, Vered 4, Kiryat Bialik.
  Industry. Tel. (04) 710729.

FINANCIAL INFORMATION
Most funding (62%) comes from the Ministry of Defense. Another 24% of the income is provided by the Ministry of Welfare, and the rest by the Haifa Municipality. Occasional small donations come from friends in the U.S. Last year's budget of $13,920 left a deficit of $5,000. The League is an Ottoman non-profit organization (registered in Haifa, no number stated), and donations in Israel are tax-free, (number 4504766). There is no U.S. tax exemption. Three part-time employees and 2 volunteer workers make up the staff, in addition to the Board members.

MEMBERSHIP, SCOPE, AND POLICY
Those interested and willing to become Big Brothers, who have been found suitable, can join the League. At the moment there are 60 active volunteers who donate their services. Most of the League's work is done in the committees, but no major decisions are made without the consent of the Executive Board.

AFFILIATIONS/REFERENCES
The League is in contact with the Baltimore Jewish Big Brother Association, 5750 Park Heights Ave., Baltimore, Md. 21215. It is not affiliated with any Israeli political party.

FUNDING NEEDED
1. To keep the organization going, salaries are needed for the professionals (social worker, administrator, secretary — all very part-time but highly trained). Estimated cost: $10,000.
2. To increase recruitment of new Big Brothers by more publicity of the aims of the League. Estimated cost: $2,400.
3. To expand activities to surrounding communities, starting Big Brother Associations in the environs of Haifa. Estimated cost: $6,720.
4. To increase joint Big Brother-Little Brother functions such as trips, picnics, and outings, Estimated cost: $2,880.

BNAI BRITH PARENTS HOME

בית אבות בני ברית

20/22 Horev
P.O.B. 7057
Haifa
Telephone: (04) 246669
Office hours: 8:00 A.M. to 1:00 P.M.

HISTORY AND DESCRIPTION
The Bnai Brith Parents Home was founded in 1958 by Bnai Brith Lodges in Israel, partially aided by reparation money from Germany.

Organizational Structure: The shareholders of Bnai Brith Parents Home are solely Bnai Brith Lodges in Israel. Its Board of Directors works on a voluntary basis.

Goals: To care for old people lovingly and warmly.

Services, Activities, and Accomplishments: The Bnai Brith Parents Home is housed in a three-storey building with 75 single rooms and 6 double rooms for married couples. Each room has private amenities. In the sick department there are 10 beds in 5 rooms for people who are incapable of taking care of themselves. The inhabitants of Bnai Brith Parents Home are taken care of lovingly and warmly by a dedicated crew, supervised by the matron, who takes care of all their needs. Social life consists of lectures, concerts, parties, movies, etc. which are organized by a Committee of residents from the Home. There is a great demand for admittance from old people who want to live in the Home which does not have the means to build more rooms and increase its facilities.

OFFICERS
Director:	B. Winnik, 17 Moria, Haifa. Accountant. Tel. (04) 89566.
Treasurer:	W. Shelizer, 118 Hayarkon, Tel Aviv. Retired. Tel. (03) 225924.
Board Members:	L. Rassis, 5 Ayalon, Haifa. Retired. Tel. (04) 241602.
	G. Hirscson, 11 Ahad Ha'Am, Haifa. Retired. Tel. (04) 664832.
	N. Reich, 5 Zipori, Kiryat Bialik. Accountant. Tel. (04) 722294.
	Z. Schwartz, 24 Rachel, Haifa. Industry. Tel. (04) 82656.
	Z. Jasmin, 103 Einstein, Haifa. Lawyer. Tel. (04) 243326.
	E. Neeman, Hageffen, Kiryat Ata. Retired. Tel. (04) 441883.

FINANCIAL INFORMATION

78% of the Parents Home's income comes from monthly payments, 14% from admission fees, and 8% from donations from Bnai Brith members, and legacies. Last year's annual budget of $293,000 left a deficit of $29,300. The Parents Home is registered in Haifa as a non-profit Ottoman Association (reg. no. 52001940/7). Donations in Israel are not tax-free; donations in the United States, channeled through the Bnai Brith Foundation in Washington are tax-free (tax no. not supplied). 11 full-time and 39 part-time workers are employed by the Parents Home, as well as 20 volunteers.

MEMBERSHIP, SCOPE, AND POLICY

The Parents Home is not a membership organization. Decisions are made by the Board of Directors.

AFFILIATIONS/REFERENCES

The Parents Home is not affiliated with any Israeli political party. It is affiliated with the Bnai Brith Federation, 1640 Rhode Island Avenue N.W., Washington, D.C.

FUNDING NEEDED

1. To build a hall for social and cultural functions.
2. To build a new home in the vicinity of Haifa in order to help more old people seeking admittance to a Parents Home.
3. To build more homes in other parts of the country.

B'NEI AKIVA YESHIVA
NACHAL YITSCHAK AT NACHALIM

ישיבת בני עקיבא "נחל יצחק" בנחלים

Moshav Nechalim Near Petach Tikva
Telephone: (03) 915831
Office hours: 8:00 A.M. to 6:00 P.M.

HISTORY AND DESCRIPTION

The Yeshiva was founded in March 1955 in its present location with a small number of students, with the purpose of developing the network of B'nei Akiva Yeshivot in Israel. The high-school department grew rapidly over the years, and now offers a number of different courses in which the students may elect to major, including mathematices, physics, biology, computer studies and electronics. Torah studies are unprejudiced by such intensive science programs.

Services, Activities, and Accomplishments: The Yeshiva currently starts with seventh grade, with a junior high-school. From the ninth grade all students become boarders at the school's dormitories. Outside the regular curriculum, the Yeshiva provides facilities for sport, music, photography, arts and crafts, singing, and trips and hikes to enhance geographical and topographical knowledge. There are about 750 students in the school today, and there are plans for expansion. The Yeshiva has produced a large number of students and alumni and is the largest Yeshiva high-school in Israel.

OFFICERS

Director: Rabbi Yosef Bagad, Yeshivat Nechalim.
                   Tel.: (03) 915831, 910968, 905751.
Treasurer: Yaakov Shifman, Yeshivat Nechalim.
                   Tel.: (03) 915831.

FINANCIAL INFORMATION

Last year's annual budget of $1 million (the sources for which were not supplied) left the Yeshiva with a deficit of $250,000. The Yeshiva is registered as a non-profit organization (reg. no. 392-1). Donations to the Yeshiva in Israel and the United States are tax-deductible (Israel: no tax number supplied; donations in the USA, through the New York American Friends branch). The Yeshiva employs 100 full-time and 50 part-time workers. Decisions are generally made by the Executive Director.

AFFILATIONS/REFERENCES

The Yeshiva is politically unaffiliated in Israel. It is in contact with American Friends of Yeshivot B'nei Akiva, 39 Broadway, New York, N.Y. 10006.

FUNDING NEEDED

1. To provide scholarships for needy students which has become crucial due to rising costs and inflation.
2. To expand dormitory and sport facilities.
3. To develop the facilities for computer studies in the school.

THE BRIDGE (HAGESHER)   הגשר

21a Ilanoth
Haifa
Telephone: (04) 87890

HISTORY AND DESCRIPTION
The Bridge was founded in 1975 as a response to the encouraging exchange of letters between Ruth Lys and Mrs. Sadat in 1974. The Bridge is a non-political women's organization whose members originate from Israel's various ethnic and religious communities.

Organizational Structure: The organization is headed by a Committee which consists of the President, 4 Arab and 4 Jewish members, each of the members coping with a specific task.

Goals: To reach mutual understanding and mutual respect between peoples which is indispensable for a peaceful co-existence.

Services, Activities, and Accomplishments: Educational activities include arranging meetings of youths of different ages belonging to various ethnic and religious communities, often with the participation of parents. Monthly meetings are held in which given subjects are discussed (sometimes with the help of group-dynamics) or lectures attended. Outings are held and the Association organizes the 'Women's Symposium for Peace in the Middle East'. The organization has succeeded in many cases in bridging the gap between members of Israel's various ethnic and religious communities. On October 28th, the Israel Interfaith Committee presented a prize to The Bridge in acknowledgement of its endeavours.

OFFICERS
President: Ruth Lys, 21a Ilanot, Haifa. Teacher.
Tel. (04) 87890.

Chairman: Dr. Ada Aharoni, 57 Horeb, Haifa. Lecturer.
Tel. (04) 243230.

Treasurer: Lucie Farchi, 22 Radak, Haifa. Secretary.
Tel. (04) 523605.

Board Members: Michelle Cohn, 46 Hasharon, Haifa. Secretary.
Tel. (04) 523072.

Dr. Shoshana Meir, 26 Vitkin, Haifa. Lecturer.
Tel. (04) 241396.

Eugenia Klef, 16 Caesaria, Haifa. Teacher.
Tel. (04) 535464.

Magda Srugi, 21 Agnon, Haifa. Teacher.
Tel. (04) 529617.

Outef Khoury, Kfar Jassif. Teacher.
Tel. (04) 642592.

Madg Khoury, 10 Aba, Haifa. Secretary.
Tel. (04) 530864.

FINANCIAL INFORMATION
100% of last year's annual budget of $50 came from membership dues. The Bridge is registered in Haifa as a non-profit Ottoman Association (reg. no. 61/1393). Donations in Israel are tax-free (tax no. not supplied). The Bridge employs volunteers only.

MEMBERSHIP, SCOPE, AND POLICY
The Bridge has approximately 200 members in Israel in one branch, and one branch abroad. Most decisions are made by the Committee.

AFFILIATIONS/REFERENCES
The Bridge is not affiliated with any Israeli political party. It is affiliated with 'The Edinburgh Friends of Israel', Mr. & Mrs. John Eivan, 4 Afton Terrace, Edinburgh, Scotland, and the 'Friends of Israel Educational Trust', John Levy, Lyndale Avenue, London NW 2, England.

FUNDING NEEDED
To finance the organization of the "Women's Symposium for Peace in the Middle East", to cover the expenses for accommodation etc. of foreign delegates and the salaries of the lecturers.

BRITH RISHONIM VETERAN
ZIONIST ORGANIZATION IN ISRAEL

ברית ראשונים — ארגון עסקנים ציונים ותיקים

Nachmani 26
Tel Aviv
Telephone: (03) 296250
Office hours: Sunday to Thursday, 9:00 A.M. to 12:00 P.M.

HISTORY AND DESCRIPTION

Brith Rishonim was founded in 1931 by the leaders of the World Zionist Movement to serve as a social framework for veteran Zionist active workers. After the establishment of the State of Israel, Brith Rishonim took upon itself the task of explaining and spreading Zionist ideology among the general public, and especially among new immigrants.

Goals: The organization's main aim is to contribute to the successful social and cultural absorption of new immigrants in Absorption Centers throughout Israel.

Services, Activities, and Accomplishments: On every Zionist and national festival or day of mourning, activities such as lectures, cultural programs, community singing and dancing are held in the Absorption Centers. Organizations have been set up in large towns and small settlements throughout the country to provide information and renew ties between the people and Zionist ideals. Seminars are held to examine the history of Zionism and the Zionist Movement from its earliest days until now, and a symposium is held, with the participation of Zionist leaders and political leaders, which deals with modern Zionist problems. In addition, a Zionist library, for the use of research workers, journalists, students, etc., has been established. The organization runs its own loan fund (Kupat Gmilut Hachesed) which provides direct financial aid or no-interest loans to elderly Zionist workers in times of need. Social and humanitarian aid, as well as individual help, is also given.

Brith Rishonim is a completely voluntary organization whose activities have won praise from leaders of the Jewish Agency and the World Zionist Organization, and from persons active in immigration and absorption. Important personalities from all political parties serve in Brith Rishonim as Honorary Presidents, including Dr. Jochanan Bader, Yitzchak Ben-Aharon, Dr. Israel Goldstein, and many others.

OFFICERS

Director: Dr. Z. Brender, University 21, Tel Aviv.
                 Lawyer. Tel. (03) 413216.
Treasurer: N. Levanon, De Haas 26, Tel Aviv. Merchant.
                 Tel. (03) 441414.
Board Members: A. Manor, Shochat St., Tel Aviv. Author.
                 Tel. (03) 413382.

115

Dr. M. Chansin, Bartenura 4, Bnei Brak. Professor.
Dr. I.B. Frankel, Margolin 3, Tel Aviv. Rabbi.
   Tel. (03) 330411.
B. Niv, Dizengoff 144, Tel Aviv. Administrator.
   Tel. (03) 226795.
Mrs. L. Talmi, Spinoza 24, Tel Aviv. Teacher.
   Tel. (03) 229579.
Y. Canaani, Hamaagal St., Ramat Gan.

FINANCIAL INFORMATION

Brith Rishonim receives 60% of its income from a Jewish Agency donation. Another 26% comes from other donations, and the remainder from membership dues. Last year's budget amounted to $10,000, with a deficit of $4,000. The organization is registered as an Ottoman, non-profit Association (no. 58-99/1163, Tel Aviv District). Donations in Israel are tax-exempt (no number is provided). There is no tax-free status for contributions from the U.S. There is one part-time employee; members do most of the work on a volunteer basis.

MEMBERSHIP, SCOPE, AND POLICY

Brith Rishonim has 600 members in 3 Israeli branches. Members are active Zionist veterans living in Israel who once occupied important positions in the diaspora in all political parties. Most decisions are made by the National Board; only urgent matters are decided by the Director only.

AFFILIATIONS/REFERENCES

Brith Rishonim is not affiliated with any political party. It was once a World Organization whose leaders were also the leaders of the American Zionist Organization. These men, such as Dr. Israel Goldstein of Israel and Sir Barnett Janner of England, are acquainted with the work of the organization.

FUNDING NEEDED

1. To enable Brith Rishonim to increase its main enterprise in the social and cultural absorption of all new immigrants in the country's many absorption centers.
2. To expand this enterprise to include students, workers, women's organizations and youth movements.
3. To purchase books on the subject of Zionism.

CAVE OF MACHPELAH YESHIVA, HEBRON, CITY OF THE PATRIARCHS

ישיבת מערת המכפלה בעיר האבות חברון

P.O.B. 85
Kiryat Arba
Hebron
Telephone: (02) 971252
Office hours: 9:00 A.M. to 6:00 P.M.

HISTORY AND DESCRIPTION

The Yeshiva was established at the beginning of 1979 by Rabbi Shlomo Ashlag in a building adjacent to the Cave of Machpelah, the burial place of the Patriarchs and Matriarchs. This was the first Jewish institution to return to Hebron since the massacre in 1929 of 67 Jews — including women, children, Yeshiva students, and Rabbis — and it was at this time that the Jewish community of 4,000 years' standing came to an abrupt end.

Organizational Structure: The general policy is decided by the Board of Directors in accordance with the constitution and under the inspection of the supervisory committee. Educational program is determined by the Rosh Yeshiva in consultation with the staff. Regular meetings are held between the directors, staff, and students to discuss and solve problems.

Goals: The restoration of Jewish learning in the Holy City of Hebron, the teaching of Zohar and Kabbalah (Jewish mysticism), and serving the local community, Israel and world Jewry.

Services, Activities, and Accomplishments: Both staff and students serve in the army reserves and also perform civil defense duties. Training is provided for policemen studying for the police-chaplaincy and for the training of Sofrim (scribes who write holy documents). Synagogue facilities and evening classes are available for members of the community. Afternoon after-school classes are provided for both boys and girls of the community, and new immigrants from countries of oppression. The major accomplishments of the Yeshiva have been the re-establishment of Jewish learning in the center of Hebron; the training of policemen for the police-chaplaincy; and the provision of afternoon school classes for the children of the community and new immigrants. The Yeshiva has a very dedicated body of students, who continue to study there every day, despite the very difficult conditions prevailing there.

OFFICERS

Director: Rabbi S. Ashlag, 29/9 Kiryat Arba, Hebron. Rabbi (Rosh Yeshiva)

Treasurer: A. Koch, 39/5 Kiryat Arba, Hebron. Teacher.

Secretary: Rabbi Dr. C. Simons, 306/20 Kiryat Arba, Hebron. Yeshiva Director. Tel. (02) 971252.

FINANCIAL INFORMATION

75% of last year's annual budget was supplied from private donations from Israel and abroad; the remaining 25% came from government allocations. The account books are inspected and audited by a chartered Accountant, and are open to inspection at the Yeshiva office.

The Yeshiva is a registered Ottoman Association (reg. no. 11/3329).

MEMBERSHIP, SCOPE, AND POLICY

Decisions are made by the Board of Directors at their regular meetings and are implemented by the Executive.

AFFILIATIONS/REFERENCES

The Yeshiva is not affiliated with any political party in Israel.

References held by the Yeshiva include the Chief Rabbi of Israel, Rabbi Ovadia Yossef, Rabbi Simon Dolgin (formerly California), Rabbi L. Askenazi (Director of "Mayanot"—formerly Paris), and Hanan Porat (Gush Emunim).

FUNDING NEEDED

1. The establishment of a scholarship fund—to provide needy students with financial support to enable them to study. Estimated cost: $150 per month to fully support a student.
2. Building fund—construction of a building, adjacent to the Cave of Patriarchs, worthy of its proximity to this Holy Place. (A plaque in the building costs $250 to $1000, depending on the size of the plaque.)
3. Support for afternoon school classes for the children of the community. Estimated cost: $150 per month.

CENTER FOR TORAH LIBRARIES
המרכז לספריות תורניות בישראל

Panim Meiroth 13
Jerusalem
Telephone: (02) 527014
Office Hours: 8:00 P.M. to 10:00 P.M.

HISTORY AND DESCRIPTION

The Center For Torah Libraries in Israel was founded in Tel Aviv in January 1964, when it was decided to establish a center unifying all the Torah libraries throughout Israel, thereby increasing the efficiency of their services.

Organizational Structure: The Center has an Honorary President (its first was Rabbi Reuven Margolis), as well as an elected working council and secretariat.

Goals: The Center for Torah Libraries seeks to facilitate more sophisticated study of Torah in Israel, through the training of librarians in the use of a more efficient indexing and research center.

Services, Activities, and Accomplishments: Consistent with its goals, the services of the Center For Torah Libraries include: the training of Toraic librarians through intensive courses aimed at preparing candidates for their matriculation examinations; the establishment and development of a central card/catalog for Toraic literature through the Center For Public Libraries; the publication of Toraic bibliographies and guidance publications to aid Toraic librarians in dealing effectively with the demands of students of Torah; and the assistance provided to Toraic librarians with professional problems through personal visits and correspondence. Among its major achievements to date, the Center includes publication of three volumes of 'Meir Einayim' and six volumes of 'Tagim', and other guidance publications; organization of three courses for new Toraic librarians; and establishment of the Institute for cataloging Toraic literature.

OFFICERS

Director: Zvi Malachi, Achad Haam 6, Petach Tikva.
Professor of Hebrew Literature.

Treasurer: Yitzhak Yudelov, Panim Meiroth 5, Jerusalem.
Librarian.

Board Members: Meir Wunder, Panim Meiroth 13, Jerusalem.
Librarian.
Yehoshua Markowitz, Old City of Jerusalem.
Supervisor of Education.
Shlomo Yacobovitz, Yonah 22, Bnei Brak.
Rabbi.

FINANCIAL INFORMATION

Last years' annual budget of $10,000 left the Center For Torah Librarians with a deficit of $15,000. The organization is not registered as an Ottoman Association, nor are donations tax-free in either Israel or the United States. The Center has two volunteer employees.

MEMBERSHIP, SCOPE, POLICY AND AFFILIATIONS

Membership in the Center is available to any student of Toraic library science in Israel. Decisions are made by the organization's National Board. The Center For Torah Libraries is not associated with any Israeli political party, nor is it affiliated with any foreign organizations.

FUNDING NEEDED

In order of priority, the following are the most outstanding funding requirements presently facing the Center For Torah Libraries.

1. Publication of bibliographic reports on Toraic literature. Estimated cost, $25,000.
2. Organization of training courses for Toraic librarians. Estimated cost, $10,000.
3. Further support for the cataloging of Toraic literature. Cost, $5,000.

CENTRAL COMMITTEE FOR RELIGIOUS EDUCATION IN ISRAEL

מרכז לחינוך הדתי בישראל

54 King George
P.O.B. 7524,
Jerusalem 94262
Telephone: (02) 635282
Office hours: 8:00 A.M. to 3:00 P.M.

HISTORY AND DESCRIPTION

With the passing in the Knesset of the Government Education Law, the Central Committee for Religious Education was established to continue the Mizrachi Education System, originally established in 1910.

Organizational Structure: The Committee is administered by a Public Executive consisting of the leading personalities of religious education in Israel.

Goals: To establish religious kindergartens, new religious elementary schools in suburbs and development areas, to strengthen and further Torah education in schools, to organize religious youth clubs for Torah study, to develop technological education for religious pupils, to organize communal activities for parents of underprivileged youth and to award scholarships to needy students in religious secondary schools, Yeshiva High Schools and Teachers' Colleges.

Services, Activities and Accomplishments: The Committee is active in the fields outlined above and has succeeded in increasing Torah education in State Religious Schools and attracting children from traditional homes to these schools.

OFFICERS

Chairman: Baruch Duvdevani, 27 Harav Berlin, Jerusalem.
    Tel. (02) 669587.

Treasurer: Elimelech Lendner, Mann 4, Jerusalem.
    Tel. (02) 667725.

Board Members: Rabbi S.A. Dolgin, 17 Ramat Hagolan, Jerusalem.
    Tel. (02) 811256.
    Charles Bick, 52 Hechalutz, Jerusalem.
    Tel. (02) 526567.
    Jacob Drori, Kibbutz Saad, Doar Na Hanegev.
    Tel. (051) 97128.
    Danny Vermus, 29 Eliezer Jaffe, Ra'anana.
    Tel. (054) 32944.
    Raphael Ben-Nathan, Moshav Hemed.
    Aaron Kopolovitz, 8 Sokolov, Bnei Brak.
    Tel. (03) 786892.

FINANCIAL INFORMATION

50% of last year's annual budget came from Government offices, 40% from the Mizrachi—Hapoel Hamizrachi Movement, and 10% from synagogue members and personal donations. Last year's annual budget of $145,000 left the Committee with a deficit of $14,500. The Committee is registered in Jerusalem as a non-profit Ottoman Association, registration number 44190. Donations in the U.S. are tax-free (reg. no. 941087488), as are donations in Israel (no. not supplied). Eight full-time and three part-time workers are employed by the Committee, as well as fifty volunteers.

MEMBERSHIP, SCOPE, AND POLICY

Policy decisions are made by the executive director and the National Board.

AFFILIATIONS/REFERENCES

The Central Committee for Religious Education in Israel is an affiliate of the World Mizrachi—Hapoel Mizrachi Movement, and Mizrachi—Hapoel Mizrachi in Israel.

FUNDING NEEDED

1. To increase communal activities.
2. To strengthen Torah Education in all State Religious Schools, primarily in development areas.
3. Scholarships.

THE CENTRAL INSTITUTIONS OF ZVEHILL —
YESHIVAT "BETH MORDECHAI"

מרכז מוסדות זוועהיל – ישיבת בית מרדכי

Admor Rabbi Shlomo Street
P.O.B. 5088
Beth Israel Quarter, Jerusalem
Telephone: (02) 285464
Office hours: 9:00 A.M. to 1:00 P.M. and 4:00 P.M. to 7:00 P.M.

HISTORY AND DESCRIPTION

The Yeshiva was founded in 1939 by the late Grand Rabbi of Zvehill, Admor Rabbi Shlomo, who immigrated from Russia. It was then continued by his direct descendents, the Admorim, Rabbi Gedalia Moishe and Rabbi Mordechy, and now continues under the presidency of his great grandson, Rabbi Avrohom.

Organizational Structure: The institutions include a senior Yeshiva, a grade school Yeshiva, a Kollel for married men, a Talmud Torah, kindergarten, dormitory, dining rooms, youth organizations, charitable funds, and the main synagogue.

Goals: To educate youth in the footsteps of the Yeshiva's holy forefathers.

Services, Activities, and Accomplishments: Free loans, food and clothing for the needy, and a sound Jewish education for all students from the kindergarten up.
The major accomplishment of the Yeshiva has been the education acquainting of hundreds of students with Torah Judaism. At present, over 250 students of all ages from Israel and abroad are being educated in the organization's institutions.

OFFICERS

Director:	Rabbi G.M. Goldman, 3 Harav Blau, Jerusalem. Tel. (02) 811397.
Treasurer:	Rabbi S. Deutsch, 3 Harav Blau, Jerusalem. Tel. (02) 811940.
Board Members:	Rabbi M. Cohen, 22 Rapaport, Jerusalem. Educator.
	Rabbi M. Horovitz, 18 Achinoam, Jerusalem. Rabbi.
	Rabbi P. Blank, 34 Batei Hungarim, Jerusalem. Kollel Director.
	Rabbi Y. Eisenbach, 28 Tachkemoni, Jerusalem. Rabbi.
	Rabbi Y. Deutsch. 16 Imrei Binah, Jerusalem. Accountant.

FINANCIAL INFORMATION

The sources of last year's annual budget were from Israel and abroad, as well as subsidies from Israeli govermental ministries. Last year's annual budget was $350,000, with a deficit of $37,000. The Yeshiva is registered as an Ottoman Association (reg. no. 11/148). Donations to the Yeshiva are tax-free both in Israel and the United States and other countries as well. However, no tax numbers were supplied. There are 22 full-time and 17 part-time workers employed by the Yeshiva, in addition to 11 volunteers.

MEMBERSHIP, SCOPE, AND POLICY

Decisions are made by the National Board. No information was stated regarding membership.

AFFILIATIONS/REFERENCES

The Yeshiva is not affiliated with any political party in Israel. Former students of the Yeshiva represent the institution in most countries of the world.

FUNDING NEEDED

1. The completion of a new wing from the main building of the Yeshiva, at a cost of $250,000.
2. Reparation of the main building, at a cost of $140,000.
3. Construction of a children's town for the students. The cost is not yet estimated.

THE CENTRAL LIBRARY FOR THE BLIND AND VISUALLY AND PHYSICALLY HANDICAPPED

הספריה המרכזית לעוורים כבדי ראיה ומוגבלים פיזית

Histadrut 4
Netanya
Telephone: (053) 25321 or (053) 32422
Office hours: Daily, except Friday, 7:30 A.M. to 3:00 P.M.

HISTORY AND DESCRIPTION

The Central Library for the Blind and Visually and Physically Handicapped was established in 1949 and is the only library of its kind in Israel. It was started in the home of its first director, Mrs. Chaya Boehm; today it is housed in a four-storey buiding which has two main departments: Braille and "Talking Books", as well as an Arabic department.

Organizational Structure: The Library is a public institution headed by a Board of Directors. It is only partly subsidized by Government welfare and education services.

Goals: The Library produces books and magazines of all kinds — texts for schoolchildren of all grades, fiction, non-fiction, children's books, etc. — in Hebrew and other languages. The Library wishes to expand the collection of reading materials which is at present very limited, so that the blind and physically handicapped may enjoy the same books and magazines as their sighted and able-bodied friends, and so that students will have the same text-books and dictionaries as their peers at school.

Services, Activities and Accomplishments: From Netanya, the Library lends books to individuals and institutions throughout Israel, with the cooperation of the Post Office. Materials are also sent abroad. In this way, the Library meets the cultural needs of the blind and the physically handicapped.

OFFICERS

Director:	Uri Cohen, Tagor 40/2, Ramat Aviv. University degrees.
Treasurer:	Chaim Preshel, Golumb 58, Givatayim.
Board Members:	Avraham Shor, Jerusalem St. 22, Netanya.
	Moshe Shlesinger, Yehuda Hanasi 38, Ramat Aviv.
	Micha Tal, Ministry of Education, Jaffa 19, Jerusalem.
	Reuven Magen, Derech Yavne 59, Rehovot.
	Orit Evenstein, "Elan Center", Gordon 9, Tel Aviv.
	A. Sokolik, Ministry of Welfare, Yad Harutzim 10, Jerusalem.

FINANCIAL INFORMATION

70% of the annual budget comes from donations; the balance from the Government. The 1978-1979 annual budget was $46,000 approximately. Donations are tax-free in Israel and in the USA (no registration numbers supplied). The Library is registered as an Ottoman Association (Ramle, reg. no. 413/1). Eight full-time and fourteen part-time workers are employed by the Library. There are ten volunteers at the Library itself and seventy in private homes and in other towns.

MEMBERSHIP, SCOPE, AND POLICY

The Library's Talking Book Department has 1,600 members, the Braille Department 600 members. There are about 100 members abroad. Membership is open to anyone who is unable, for reason of blindness or physical disability, to read printed material; a medical certificate to this effect is required in each case. Decisions are made by the Board of Directors and the Executive Committee; when an immediate decision is required, the Director of the Library is responsible.

AFFILIATIONS/REFERENCES

1. Jewish Braille Institute of America, New York 10016, USA.
2. Jewish Blind Society, London W2 3EW, England.
3. Friends of the Central Library in Holland, Switzerland, Germany and France.

The Library is not affiliated with any political party in Israel.

FUNDING NEEDED

1. To build a recording-studio.
2. To improve the Library's services as regards supplying students with material required for their studies, and providing suitable literature for teenagers. Also, to supply more literature on Judaism and religion and more books in other languages, as well as to distribute more braille and Talking Book magazines.
4. To modernize the Library's system of producing books in braille.

CENTRAL NESHEI AGUDAT ISRAEL IN ISRAEL

מרכז נשי אגודת ישראל בישראל

Shomer Hakotel 5
Jerusalem
Telephone: (02) 244633
Office Hours: Sunday-Thursday, 10:00 A.M.-1:00 P.M.

HISTORY AND DESCRIPTION

The Neshei Agudat Israel was founded in 1945 as a religious-educational and social welfare organization. Branches are to be found throughout Israel; the central 'mother' agency being in Jerusalem since 1963.

Organizational Structure: The central branch of Neshei Agudat Israel in Jerusalem serves as the headquarters for all other branches throughout Israel — providing required services and funding to the regional associations, and serving as the distribution center for all foreign funding to the organization.

Goals: The goal of the Neshei Agudat Israel is to serve as a religious-educational and philanthropic organization within Israel. The goal of the Central Neshei Agudat Israel in Jerusalem is to initiate the opening of new branches of the organization within Israel, and to help in their activities.

Services, Activities, and Accomplishments: As part of its educational and benevolent activities, Central Neshei Agudat Israel sponsors courses and clubs for adults and girls throughout the country; free loans funds; summer camps for mothers of large families. The organization also aids needy families and needy brides, as well as dental care for some young women, actual and monetary help to the sick, and diaper service to large families in need. The organization also raises funds through a project known as the 'Committee for the Care of the Immigrant Child in Israel'. The Central Neshei Agudat Israel sees all of these activities as its major accomplishments, along with its chain of kindergartens and day nurseries throughout the country.

OFFICERS

Director: Lydia Birnbaum, Charlap 44, Jerusalem.
                   Tel. (02 632019.
Treasurer: Bettina Katz, Charlap 32, Jerusalem.
                   Tel. (02) 636586.
Board: Bertha Saritzki, Hachashmonaim 13, Jerusalem.
                   Tel. (02) 520879.
                   Channa Schlesinger, Maimon 39, Jerusalem.
                   Tel. (02) 632739.
                   Rosa Zucker, Ben Yehuda 35, Jerusalem.
                   Tel. (02) 226043.

Gella Sprung, Chafetz Chaim, 17, Jerusalem.
Tel. (02) 234065.
Channa Ordentlich-Efrati, Harav Hirsh 15,
Bnei Brak.
Tel. (03) 788869.

FINANCIAL INFORMATION

100% of last year's budget of $77,000 was achieved through donations to the Central Neshei Agudat Israel, which then distributed funds to various regional branches so as to reduce their deficits. Central Neshei Agudat Israel has been registered as an Ottoman Association since November 1972 (reg. no. 11/2025, Jerusalem District Office of the Ministry of the Interior). Donations to part of the regional branches are tax-free; each has its own registration number. The Central Neshei Agudat Israel retains two part-time employees and many volunteers.

MEMBERSHIP, SCOPE, AND POLICY

There are ten branches of the Neshei Agudat Israel in Israel, and fifteen abroad. The number of members in either the former or the latter was not listed. Membership is open to any woman accepting the organization's goals. Decisions are made concurrently by the organization's Executive Director, its National Board, and General Assembly. Information regarding the specific division of labour among these three decision-making bodies was not supplied.

AFFILIATIONS/REFERENCES

The Central Neshei Agudat Israel is formally affiliated with the Agudat Israel political movement in Israel, but operates independently in every regard. Internationally, the organization is represented in Canada and the United States by the:

Aguda Women of America, 5 Beekman Street, New York, N.Y. 10038;

and in Europe by:

Miss Melly Rothschild, Zurich 8002 Traubenstr 5, Switzerland.

FUNDING NEEDED

In order of priority, the Central Neshei Agudat Israel lists the following as its most outstanding present funding requirements:

1. The maintenance of the 'Beith Yehudah' girls' home in Rishon le Zion, home to 80 girls. Present monthly deficit of $2,000.
2. The maintenance of various welfare projects, including help for needy families, help for needy brides, summer camps for mothers of large families, a free loan fund, and aid to the sick and infirmed; courses for adults.
3. Construction of a day nursery and 2 classrooms for kindergarten in Ramot Elchanan—Bnei Brak. Outstanding funding still required for this project—$40,000.

THE CENTRAL PARENTS ASSOCIATION OF GREATER TEL AVIV

ועד ההורים המרכזי למערכת החינוך בתל-אביב-יפו

Shenkin 37, Tel Aviv
Telephone: (03) 283240
Office hours: 8:00 A.M.-2:30 P.M., daily.

HISTORY AND DESCRIPTION
The Central Parents Association of Greater Tel Aviv was established
about 40 years ago. The P.A. was the founder of the school-nurse,
school-kitchens, summer camps for children and many other programs
connected with the educational and social needs of pupils and parents.

Organizational Structure: Every school sends a representative for each
400 pupils. These representatives form the Council, which is the top
institution of the P.A. The Council chooses the Chairman, Treasurer
and the heads of the various departments: culture, education, welfare,
recreation, and mutual help.

Goals: The Parents Association aims to help fill the cultural, educational, psychological and social needs of pupils and parents.

Services, Activities, and Accomplishments:
The Association provides a variety of services. It runs recreation camps,
mainly for underprivileged children, and provides hundreds of new
school uniforms, consisting of shoes, sweaters, trousers, shirts and
blouses. Tens of thousands of children have been provided for over the
years in this way. Meetings of parents, headed by a psychologist, are
held, as well as meetings of parent-children groups. Help with homework is provided, stipends are given to gifted children of underprivileged families, and symposiums, seminars and educational performances are held. These activities all work toward the integration
of parents and children, and give cultural, educational and psychological support to parents and children.
The Parents Association owns a recreation home for children in Netaim
(near Rishon Lezion). The home has been in existence for about 34
years, and with the lapse of time the buildings have deteriorated and are
hardly fit for use. New dormitories should be built, but the necessary
funds are lacking.

OFFICERS:
Chairman:	Moshe Mizrachi, Yiftach 18, Tel Aviv.
	Ass't. Manager, Tax Dept.
	Tel. (03) 262111.
Treasurer:	Benjamin Lapidot, Ashi 8, Tel Aviv. Engineer.
	Tel. (03) 917174.
Vice-Chairman:	Mrs. Ahuva Rosenwasser, Nachmani 56, Tel Aviv.
	Tel. (03) 613372.

Board Members: Dr. Schmuel Baniel, Herzog 42, Givatayim.
Advocate. Tel. (03) 220379.
Moshe Feldman, Arlosorov 39, Bat Yam.
Accountant. Tel. (03) 219241.
Peter Frye, Zlotopolsky 19, Tel Aviv.
Film Director. Tel. (03) 229813.
Baruch Kirschenzaft,Harugei Malchut 14B,
Tel Aviv. Bank Manager. Tel. (03) 266513.
Mina Yoskovitz, Mercaz Ba'alei M'lacha 31, T.A.
Moderator of parent/teacher discussion groups.
Tel. (03) 284150.
Dr. Henry Sharon, Rahel 7, T.A.
Manager, investment Dept., T.A. Municipality.
Tel. (03) 220378.
Cila Alkoshi,Machanaim 54, T.A. Clerk.
Tel. (03) 393301.
Yaakov Eligon, Haviva Reich 3, T.A. Clerk.
Tel. (03) 262464.

FINANCIAL INFORMATION
Donations account for 43% of the Parents Association's funds. Another 37% come from ticket sales at performances for children and grown-ups, and the remaining 20% of the income comes from Sponsors' Day, which is held once a year. No budget figures are provided. The organization is a registered Ottoman, non-profit Association (no. 2904-99, Tel Aviv District). Donations in Israel are tax-free (no registration number is provided); contributions from the U.S. are not. There are one full-time and 5 part-time employees. The number of volunteers varies according to need.

MEMBERSHIP, SCOPE, AND POLICY
Every school has a branch of the Parents Association, and all parents of school children are potential members. Representatives to the Council are chosen by the school's Parents Association and/or recommended by the school administration. Decisions are made by the Executive Board.

AFFILIATIONS/REFERENCES
The Parents Association is not affiliated with any Israeli party. No references are listed.

FUNDING NEEDED
1. To erect new dormitories in Netaim — the recreation home for children. The new buildings can be dedicated to the donor or donors.
2. To build a swimming pool at the recreation home in Netaim.
3. For the purchase of standard school uniforms to be stored at the clothing depot for needy children. Budget for this purpose is $30,000.
4. For resources for educational and cultural work among parents.

CHAMBER OF HOLOCAUST
COMMITTEE INC.

מרתף השואה

P.O.B. 6426
Mt. Zion, Jerusalem
Telephone: (02) 716841
Office hours: 8:30 A.M. to 5:00 P.M.

HISTORY AND DESCRIPTION
The Chamber of the Holocaust was founded in 1949 by Rabbi Dr. S.Z.
Kahana as a monument and memorial to the atrocities of the Nazi era.
Amongst its exhibits are relics of the Holocaust, memorial plaques for
entire communities and individuals destroyed by the Nazis, and a
"Library of the Six Million".

Goals: The main purpose of the Chamber of the Holocaust is to maintain a public awareness of the horrors of the Hitler regime, and to
preserve the memory of those slaughtered.

Services, Activities, and Accomplishments: The service provided by the
Chamber of the Holocaust is three-fold: Educationally, it commemo-
rates the history of a human tragedy, invoking the horrors and inhuman-
ities of the Nazi period. By showing the public the errors of the past it
acts as a preventative, thus showing the way to hope for a brighter
future. Spiritually, the Chamber of the Holocaust provides a suitable
outlet for emotions. It contains stone plaques with the names of the
various communities and individual families destroyed during Hitler's
regime. Memorial services are frequently held. Economically, financial
contributions are requested to create public awareness for the prevention of another Holocaust. These funds also help the Diaspora Yeshiva
to maintain the Memorial and, in addition, go towards the religious
education of the Yeshiva's 160 students.

OFFICERS
Director: Rabbi Dr. M. Goldstein, Mann 5, Jerusalem.
                     Tel.: (02) 716841.
Treasurer: Rabbi D. Schultz, POB 6426, Jerusalem.
                     Tel.: (02) 716841
Board Members: Rabbi B.Z. Freid, POB 6426, Jerusalem.
                     Tel.: (02) 716841.
                     Rabbi David Rubin, Hameshorerim 1, Jerusalem.
                     Tel.: (02) 281281.

FINANCIAL INFORMATION
Last year's annual budget of $74,000 (which derived entirely from
donations) left the organization with a deficit of $58,000. The Chamber
of Holocaust Committee Inc. is registered as a non-profit organization
(Israel reg. no. 1433), to which donations in Israel, the United States,
Britain, and Canada, may be made tax-free (Israel: no. 4505097; USA —

through Diaspora Yeshiva Toras Yisrael: I.R.S. no. M-67-EO-529; Britain—through British Friends of the Diaspora: no. 277919; Canada — through La Corporation du Centre des Hautes Talmudiques du Mont Sion Inc.: no. 04201-74-4908). Two full-time and six part-time workers are employed by the organization.

MEMBERSHIP, SCOPE, AND POLICY
The Chamber of the Holocaust has 500 national members and 5000 members from abroad. Membership is open to anyone willing to pay the membership fee. Decisions for the Chamber of Holocaust Committee Inc. are made by the Executive Director.

AFFILIATIONS/REFERENCES
The Chamber of Holocaust Committee Inc. is politically unaffiliated in Israel. It is recognized by the United Jewish Appeal, 1290 Avenue of Americas, New York, N.Y. 10019, the Bnai Brith, 823 United Nations Plaza, New York, N.Y. 10017, and the Anti-Defamation League, 823 United Nations Plaza, New York, N.Y. 10017.

FUNDING NEEDED
1. To provide housing for elderly rabbis—$50,000.
2. To completely overhaul or replace electricity system—$15,000.
3. To replace doors, windows, locks and make other repairs—$7,000.

CHARITY ORGANIZATION FOR ISRAEL IN MEMORY OF YAAKOV MOSHE RIVLIN

גמ״ח למען ישראל לזכרו של יעקב משה ריבלין

Hillel Street 10
P.O.B. 466
Jerusalem
Telephone: (02) 223967, 223525
Office Hours: Sun.-Thurs.: 9:00 A.M.-1:00 P.M.; 4:00-6:00 P.M.

HISTORY AND DESCRIPTION

The Charity Organization for Israel in Memory of Yaakov Moshe Rivlin is actually a combination of an old organization operationg since the early 1950's (Charity for Israel, founded with a donation by five American women), and a new organization which was founded in 1976. Over the years, the money dwindled. Four years ago, when the son of one of the chief directors died during his military service, there was an opportunity to revive and increase the charitable activities of the organization. With government approval, an addition was made to the former name of the organization. Yaakov Moshe Rivlin z"l, after whom the organization is named, was active in the religious scouts organization in Israel, and also wrote a book entitled "The First Settlement Out of the Old City Walls", which was published after his death. Its popularity in Israel has helped to greatly increase the funds coming in to the organization.

Organizational Structure: The Committee of Directors consists of five respected members of the community who meet at least once a month. The organization has no membership. Decisions regarding loans are made jointly by the Committee, all of whose members serve on a voluntary basis. Every applicant is required to fill out a formal document and to provide guarantees that he will repay the loan within a year's time. There is no discrimination whatsoever in the allocation of loans.

Goals: In recent years, the organization has been able to respond to 60-70 applicants a month. But unfortunately, many applications must be refused due to lack of funds. The organization's main priority is to reach a stronger financial position, which would allow it to help every applicant in need and to increase the sums provided. It is also hoped that a project to help young couples can be established in the future.

OFFICERS

Director: Isaac Benjamin Rivlin, Ben Maimon 14, Jerusalem. Advertiser. Tel. (02) 639102.

Treasurer: Moshe Zalzman, Ben Maimon 29, Jerusalem. Treasurer of Bank Hapoalim. Tel. (02) 630336.

Board Members: Isaac Kariv, Gan Rehavia, Jerusalem.
Ex-mayor of Jerusalem.
Isaac Moshejoff, Balfour 7, Jerusalem.
Industrialist.
Jacob Ettinger, Peres 7, Jerusalem. Merchant.

FINANCIAL INFORMATION

All income is derived from donations. No annual budget has been provided. Application has been made for tax-free status for donations in Israel and the U.S.A. It is hoped that the approval will be received shortly. The organization is registered as a non-profit Ottoman Association (No. 11/1165).

AFFILIATIONS/REFERENCES

The organization is not affiliated with any political party in Israel nor with any group abroad.

CHAYE YEHUDIT—
SEMINARY FOR WOMEN

סמינר לבנות – חיי יהודית

127 Uziel Street—P.O. Box 16191
Bayit Vegan, Jerusalem
Telephone: (02) 550956
Office hours: 8:00 A.M. to 3:30 P.M.

HISTORY AND DESCRIPTION

The ever increasing interest of young Jewish women to learn about their heritage prompted the establishment of summer courses in 1980. The idea of the course was to determine whether there was a viable need for a Baale Tshuva seminary for women. The overwhelming response proved beyond all shadow of doubt the need for such an institution.

Organizational Structure: A national committee of seven members and an executive committee of four members are the backbone of the organization.

Goals: 1) To educate, establish, maintain and operate institutions for women in the spirit of Orthodox Judaism. 2) To inform and increase an awareness in everything connected with this education. 3) To establish local information centers emphasizing this education. 4) To train teachers and volunteers to further this education.

Services, Activities, and Accomplishments: Chaye Yehudit offers a full-time daily program, counseling, and invitations for girls to spend the Sabbath in a traditional atmosphere.
The major accomplishments of the organization until now have been a summer program in 1980 with Judaica courses in English for women. It was attended by 230 women and cost $225. In addition, there is a full-time program during the Winter of 1980-81.

OFFICERS

Director: S. Udwin, 158 Akiva, Bnei Brak.
Educator.
Tel. (03) 702327.

Treasurer: C. Cohen, 127 Uziel, Bayit Vegan, Jerusalem.
Home economist.
Tel. (02) 550956.

Board Members: E. Kugel, 1 Shaare Tzedek, Jerusalem.
Rabbi.
Tel. (02) 234044.
C. Rudner, 50 Hapisga, Jerusalem.
Accountant.
Tel. (02) 411098.

FINANCIAL INFORMATION

There is no annual budget. The organization has registered to become an Ottoman Association but is currently awaiting final confirmation. The organization depends completely on contributions. Donations are not as yet tax-free. There are 8 part-time and one full-time employees as well as 15 volunteers.

MEMBERSHIP, SCOPE, AND POLICY

There is one branch in Israel. Most decisions are made by the executive committee. There are 7 members in Israel and 8 members abroad.

AFFILIATIONS/REFERENCES

The organization is not affiliated with any political party in Israel. The organization is in contact with the following associations abroad: Friends of Chaye Yehudit, London. 43 Osbaldeston Street, N.16. Friends of Chaye Yehudit, 41 Osprey Street, Kensington, JHB R.S.A. Friends of Chaye Yehudit Ginz, 23 Walcott Avenue, New York, New York USA.

FUNDING NEEDED

1. The expansion of existing programs at the school and the inclusion of a program for tourists and uncommitted Jewish youth visiting Israel. Estimated cost—$10,000.
2. The establishment of a building fund and campus project. Estimated cost for the first stage—$1,080,000.
3. The establishment of a reach-out project to the Army, kibbutzim, moshavim, and city dwellers. Emphasis will be placed on Sephardic Jews, but it is intended to encompass all classes of Israeli society. Estimated cost—$20,000.

CHILDREN'S MEMORIAL FUND—
FOR CHILDREN

קרן לזכר ילדים – למען ילדים

5 Shiller Street, Beit Hakerem
Jerusalem
Telephone: (02) 536813
Office hours. 8:00 A.M. to 12 Noon; 17:00 to 20:00.

HISTORY AND DESCRIPTION
The Children's Memorial Fund was created by Aliza Shimoni in 1978, shortly after the terrorist attack on the coastal highway in March, 1978. She and her husband, the poet Yehuda Yannai, decided to use the IL4,000 they had saved for their holiday to start a fund to aid children. When she had IL50,000 she began with 20 children, providing them with books, visiting their homes, contacting their teachers. Now there are some 120 children being helped by the fund. This includes bus tickets and vouchers to buy clothing and school supplies at the Tamir book shop and Hamashbir Department Store, each of which has given her clients sizeable discounts.
An impressive list of public figures has agreed to be directors of the fund, but it is still very much Mrs. Shimoni's project. Most recently, Jerusalem Mayor Teddy Kollek and Knesset members have brought to her attention the children of the Ir Ganim neighborhood. A large proportion of these children leave school early, suffer neglect from parents overwhelmed by financial and social difficulties, and require intensive attention and help. The fund maintains an ongoing relationship with these children.

Goals: The fund would like to widen its scope and help the additional children who have approached it for aid.

Services, Activities, and Accomplishments: All children sponsored by the fund have progressed immensely thanks to the help they receive. None has left the educational framework. The fund has also organized the transfer of children from broken homes to boarding schools and maintains close ties with the families.

OFFICERS
Director: Mrs. Aliza Shimoni, 5 Shiller, Jerusalem.
                            Tel. (02) 536813.
Treasurer: Mrs. Shula Muskal, Lawyer.
Board Members: Mrs. Tamar Eshel, Knesset Member.
                            Dr. Miriam Rahavi.
                            Mordechai Muskal, Lawyer.
                            Frida Fogel.
                            Yehuda Yannai.
                            Avi Cassouto, Jerusalem. Ram Hotel Manager.
                            Yaffa Brender.
                            Rachel Abramzon.

FINANCIAL INFORMATION
Sources are derived from donations from private persons and industries. The fund is registered as an Ottoman Association (reg. no. not listed) and donations are tax-free both in Israel (no. 4506620) and the U.S. (no. not listed). Volunteers include a lawyer and an accountant.

MEMBERSHIP, SCOPE, AND POLICY
Anyone willing to volunteer is welcome as a member of the fund. Currently there are 10 members in Israel and 6 in Los Angeles. Decisions are made by the national board.

AFFILIATIONS/REFERENCES
The fund is not affiliated with any political parties in Israel.

FUNDING NEEDED
1. To provide stipends for secondary education, teachers' seminar and university education.
2. To aid young couples who were in the past aided by the fund.
3. To widen the fund and aid more children.

C.I.S.V. (CHILDREN'S INTERNATIONAL SUMMER VILLAGES)

"סי. איי. אס. וי." — עמים במעגל

7 Sinai, Haifa
Telephone: (04) 253050 (home of Chairperson)
Office hours: 1:00 P.M. to 11:00 P.M.

HISTORY AND DESCRIPTION

C.I.S.V. was founded by Dr. Doris Allen and started its activities in Cincinnati, Ohio, in 1951. It organizes International Summer Camps, Seminars for Youth, Youth interchanges and other activities. The Israeli National Branch has existed since 1976.

Organizational Structure: The organization is run by a board of directors comprising a president, two vice-presidents (elected every three years), a Secretary General, a treasurer (both nominated and non-voting members of the executive), one director nominated by each member National Association and two Junior representatives nominated by the Junior Branch Center and Junior Work Committee (both international). Every year in August there is an International Board Meeting combined with a Conference of plenary sessions and standing international committees, every year in another member-nation's country. Thus the work of the coming year is prepared and the work of the previous year evaluated. The international office is in Newcastle upon Tyne, England, as a permanent center.

Goals: Education for international understanding—to foster world peace in the world. The Association believes that it is important for Israeli children to create normal relationships with Arab children and Germans in the framework of healthy and true friendship internationally and to foster the popularity and understanding of the Israeli people in the whole world.

Services, Activities, and Accomplishments: The organization holds international summer camps, seminars for youth (17-18 year old); organizes youth interchanges, supports Junior Clubs, trains leaders and has permanent activities in national associations in all member nations throughout the year. The Israeli National Branch has held three villages, several interchanges and one seminar-camp. It has a group of 200 kids between the ages of 10 and 18 who learn to live together in harmony, to understand other cultures, respect them, and want to make friends with children from all over. In 1977 the National Branch brought the first group of children from Lebanon to spend a peaceful vacation in its camp.

OFFICERS

Director: Shosh Euler, 7 Sinai, Haifa.
                           Interpreter. Tel. (04) 253050.
Treasurer: Nimrod Graiver, 3 Absalom, Haifa.
                           Gas Station Owner. Tel. (04) 87147.
Vice-President: Hannah Bloch, 17 Kanders, Haifa.
                           Sports Teacher. Tel. (04) 535623.

Legal Adviser: Amiram Harlaff, 22 Oren, Haifa.
                      Lawyer. Tel. (04) 242203.
Board Members: Idit Ben-Shem, 32 Oren, Haifa.
                      Psychologist. Tel. (04) 253129.
                      Shlomo Diskin, 40 Margalit St., Haifa.
                      Biology teacher & educator. Tel. (04) 243914.

FINANCIAL INFORMATION

Each National Association runs its own budget independently. It must pay membership fees to the International Office yearly ($600 if it cannot afford holding a village that year, $300 if a village or seminar camp is held). Each Branch also pays delegation registration fees, seminar registrations, and interchange registration (which the Israeli Branch tries to collect from the participants in the summer activities). Sources of income vary from year to year, greater donations being needed in a village-holding year. 80% of last year's annual budget came from membership dues and 20% from donations. Last year's annual budget of $9,000 left a deficit of $1,000. The National Association is registered in Haifa as a non-profit Ottoman Association (reg. no. not supplied). Donations in Israel and the United States are tax-free (Israeli tax no. 4505213, US tax information can be supplied by Mrs. Hildreth Miller, 206 N. Main Street, Casstown, Ohio 45312). All of the Association's workers are volunteers: the 5 members of the National Board, all the leaders (about 10) and lecturers. All families help when needed.

MEMBERSHIP, SCOPE, AND POLICY

Membership is open to anybody from age 10 who agrees with the Association's goals and is prepared to help carrying them out. There are about 40 National Branches abroad, including several Chapters in many countries. The Israeli Branch has approximately 200-250 members. Most decisions are made by the National Board. Suggestions and decisions are also made by the Annual National Assembly.

AFFILIATIONS/REFERENCES

The Association is not affiliated with any Israeli political party. It is affiliated with the United Nations (1979's IYC non-governmental organization), UNESCO, Paris (1979's IYC non-governmental organization), and the International Counsel of Psychology, California (CISV as a standing committee).

FUNDING NEEDED

1. To hold International Summer Camps for children aged 11 every summer for at least 10 nations (delegations) at a time (cost $20,000-$25,000 per camp).
2. To hold Seminar-Camps, train future leaders and educators (cost $9,000-$10,000 per camp).
3. Follow-up work for ex-campers, educational activities throughout the year. An appropriate club is needed to hold meetings.
4. To support kids who cannot afford foreign travel.

COLLEL BAYIT VEGAN

כולל בית וגן

Collel: 49 Hapisgah Street
               Bayit Vegan, Jerusalem
Office: 86 Bayit Vegan Street
               Bayit Vegan, Jerusalem
Telephone: (02) 415743
Office hours: regular working hours

HISTORY AND DESCRIPTION

Collel Bayit Vegan is a Torah institution which was established ten years ago by Rabbi Israel B. Caplan, a graduate of Ner Israel Rabbinical College of Baltimore, Maryland, to enable young, gifted, married Torah scholars to continue their studies after completing their Yeshiva training. Collel Bayit Vegan offers post-graduate courses in advanced Talmudic studies especially geared to train teachers in advanced Yeshiva institutions, and to prepare Halachic scholars for careers as Rabbis and judges in Rabbinical courts in which broad and specialized halachic expertise is required to render the difficult decisions that arise in blending the life of a Torah true Jew with today's complex world.

Goals: To provide financial assistance to these young scholars to enable them to study, free from financial burdens, and to offer direction and assistance in furthering their educational goals.

Services, Activities, and Accomplishments: Providing teachers for various advanced Yeshivot and training Halachic scholars whose services have been utilized in the Torah community.

OFFICERS

Director: Rabbi Israel B. Caplan, 86 Bayit Vegan, Jerusalem.
                Tel. 415743.
Board Members: Louis Caplan, 6317 Park Heights Avenue,
                Baltimore, Maryland. Tel. 358-3390.
                Samuel Caplan, 3707 Menlo Drive,
                Baltimore, Maryland. Businessman.
                Tel. 578-8832.
                Alvin Gerstein, 6717 Westbook Road,
                Baltimore, Maryland. Businessman.
                Tel. 358-2639.

FINANCIAL INFORMATION

95% of last year's annual budget came from donations. The remaining 5% came from funds from various charities. Last year's annual budget of $55,800 left the Yeshiva with a deficit of $8,500. The Yeshiva is not registered as an Ottoman Association. Donations to the Yeshiva are tax-free in the United States (tax no. 23-7204516). Donations are not tax-free in Israel. The Yeshiva has five volunteers working with it.

MEMBERSHIP, SCOPE, AND POLICY

Most decisions are made by the Executive Director of the Yeshiva. The Yeshiva is recognized by the Ministry of Defense as a legitimate yeshiva and the students can be deferred from military service.

AFFILIATIONS/REFERENCES

The Yeshiva is not affiliated with any political party in Israel. The Yeshiva is in contact with Ner Israel Rabbinical College, Mt. Wilson Lane, Baltimore, Maryland and Collel Bayit Vegan, c/o Caplan, 6317 Park Heights Avenue, Baltimore, Maryland 21215.

FUNDING NEEDED

The most pressing need requiring funds is to continue to subsidize the young men and to provide special assistance to those with special problems. The present budget for providing these services is $70,000 per year.

COMMITTEE FOR SAFEGUARDING HUMAN DIGNITY

ועדה ציבורית להגנת כבוד האדם

Strauss 13
P.O.B. 5052, Jerusalem
Telephone: (02) 232851, 286087 (all hours, day or night)
Office Hours: 10:00 A.M. to 1:00 P.M., 4:00 P.M. to 6:00 P.M.

HISTORY AND DESCRIPTION

The Committee for Safeguarding Human Dignity was established in 1966 in response to the practise of 'forced' autopsy in Israel. In 1966, claims the organization, over 90% of those who died in Israeli hospitals had to undergo post-mortems, often despite it being against the patient's wishes and/or religious beliefs and despite vehement family objection. The organization seeks to protect the 'human dignity' of patients in Israeli hospitals.

Organizational Structure: The Committee consists of a non-political body including prominent community leaders, rabbis, doctors, judges and lawyers of both a religious and secular background. There is a director, a corresponding secretary, a committee of three which handles most financial matters, and a national board of eighteen.

Goals: The Committee For Safeguarding Human Dignity seeks to ensure that all post-mortems performed in Israel are authorized by the patient or his next of kin, as is the procedure in most 'enlightened' countries.

Services, Activities, and Accomplishments: The Committee seeks to alleviate the problem of unauthorized autopsies in Israel. Its representatives throughout the country provide free advice and assistance to anyone with a problem concerning the 'human dignity' of critically ill patients in Israeli hospitals. It works ceaselessly to see that patient's rights are respected and protected at all times. The organization claims that its major accomplishments to date include the assistance and advice given to thousands of patients, and the fact that the Committee has succeeded in making both the Israeli public and intelligentsia more aware of the difficulties associated with present autopsy laws in Israel.

OFFICERS

Directors: Raphael Solavachik,
Yedidyah Weiner, Strauss 13, Jerusalem. Teacher. Tel. (02) 286087.

Corresponding
Secretary: Reuven Davidowitz, Malachi 2, Jerusalem.

Overseas Secretary: Phillip Waxman, 1870 Drumgoole Rd. East, Staten Island, N.Y. 10309

143

FINANCIAL INFORMATION
A full 100% of the Committee's income is achieved through financial contributions from supporters in Israel and abroad. Donations are *not* tax-free in either Israel or the United States. The Committee is registered as an Ottoman Association (reg. no. 11/1751, Jerusalem). No information regarding the organization's last annual budget was supplied. The organization has approximately 675 volunteers.

MEMBERSHIP, SCOPE, AND POLICY
Some 500 people are members of the Committee's nine Israeli branches. There are also 175 members in eight foreign branches. The only criterion for membership is a willingness to engage in volunteer work. Decisions are made by the Committee's National Board.

AFFILIATIONS/REFERENCES
The Committee For Safeguarding Human Dignity claims no association with any Israeli political party.

FUNDING NEEDED
The Committee For Safeguarding Human Dignity requires funding in order to establish new branches throughout Israel and to expand existing offices. Funding is also required in order to impress Israeli government leaders of the serious need to close loopholes in Israeli law which permit abuses of 'human dignity', and to impress upon the medical profession and researchers the importance of taking into account the humanitarian, personal, and religious wishes of others as they relate to post-mortems performed in Israel.

COMMITTEE OF HONEN-U-MALVEH
גמילות חסד חונן ומלוה
Rechov Alfandri 21 Jerusalem
Telephone: (02) 228408
Office hours: Sunday-Thursday, 5:00 P.M. to 8:00 P.M.

HISTORY AND DESCRIPTION
The Committee of Honen-u-Malveh was founded in 1963 to supply interest-free loans to brides, grooms, large families and other worthy causes.

Organizational Structure: The organization has a 5-member volunteer board, with major authority in the hands of the Executive Director. There is no membership as such and no salaried staff. The only branch is located in Jerusalem.

Services, Activities and Accomplishments: In the period 11/30/78 to 12/31/79, the organization was able to provide a total of 205 loans, ranging in size from the equivalent of $25 to $125.

However, the majority of requests for loans had to be turned down due to lack of sufficient funds.

OFFICERS
Director: Rabbi Ezra Shaayo, HaNeviim 84b, Jerusalem.
                     Rabbi. Tel. (02) 228408.
Treasurer: Eliyahu Sasson, Givat Shaul 17, Jerusalem.
                     Gov't. Clerk. Tel. (02) 521180.
Board Members: Moshe Matalon, Alfandri 15, Jerusalem.
                     Gov't. Clerk. Tel. (02) 249936.
                     Chazan Dahan, Shmuel HaNavi, Jerusalem.
                     Gov't. Clerk. Tel. (02) 818570.
                     Mordechai Abulafia, Kotler 11, Jerusalem.
                     Tel. (02) 524275.

FINANCIAL INFORMATION
The Committee's sole source of income is donations and bequests. The annual budget for the year 1979 was $8,820. There is no accumulated deficit. Donations do not carry tax-free status either in Israel or the U.S.A. The organization is registered in Israel as a non-profit Ottoman Association in the Jerusalem District Office of the Ministry of the Interior (reg. no. 11/1178).

AFFILIATIONS/REFERENCES
The organization is not affiliated with any political party in Israel nor with any group abroad.

FUNDING NEEDED
1. To provide aid to needy brides—$12,500.
2. To provide aid to large families—$12,500.
3. To answer other requests—$7,500.

COMMUNITY COLLEGE, MATEH YEHUDA

מכללת מטה יהודה

Ein Karem
Jerusalem
Telephone: (02) 416564
Office hours: 8:00 A.M. to 3:00 P.M.

HISTORY AND DESCRIPTION
Today there are 25,000 people in settlements of all kinds in the area called the Mateh Yehuda region. Most of the settlers are Jewish immigrants from the Arab countries who came to Israel during the 50's. The leadership of the region did not have the opportunity to complete their formal education at university level and in many cases even at high school level. In 1976, therefore, the region of Mateh Yehuda started its own community college in a Learning Centre housed in a group of temporary buildings in the village of Ein Karem, west of Jerusalem.

Goals: To secure the possibility of a continuing education, academic as well as non-formal, for all the members of the leadership of the region, and for all professionals who are rendering services in the region, as well as other adults who are interested.

Services, Activities and Accomplishments: The College operates a variety of programs including an academic program (in conjunction with Rockland Community College and Empire State College — SUNY, the State University of New York), an academic program for American students, combining work and study under the auspices of Rockland Community College; a program for Community and Youth Workers, including a two-year school for full-time students combining community work in the moshavim (communal villages) and studies in the college; a centre for Ethnic Studies for the sharing of the ethnic heritage of the Oriental and Western communities living in Israel; a program for Continuing Education with vocational, complementary studies and language courses. In the previous academic year 800 students were served by the Community College.

BOARD OF GOVERNORS
Director: Baruch Kedar, 9 Zionism St.,
                  Jerusalem. Tel. (02) 411148.
Chairman: Yuval Aloni.
                  Tal Shahar, Farmer. Tel. (054) 57772.
Treasurer: Chaim Kochmeister
Board Members: Yochanan Daniel, Farmer.
                  Yitzchak Saidoff, Farmer.
                  Saadia Haddad, Farmer.
                  Shmuel Shani, Farmer.
                  Azriel Tzadok, Farmer.
                  Yaakov Malkin, Ph.D.

FINANCIAL INFORMATION

The Community College receives 80% of its funds from the Regional Council and 20% from donations, Government appropriations and tuition fees. Last year's annual budget of $700,000 left a deficit of $175,000. The Community College is registered in Jerusalem as a non-profit Ottoman Association (reg. no. 450634). Donations in Israel and the United States are tax-free. The college employs twelve full-time and a varying number of part-time staff.

MEMBERSHIP, SCOPE, AND POLICY

Policy decisions are made by the Regional Board.

AFFILIATIONS/REFERENCES

The College is not affiliated to any Israeli political party. It is affiliated with the Rockland Community College, State University of New York, and the Empire State College, State University of New York.

FUNDING NEEDED

1. To enlarge learning space and facilities.
   (Estimated cost— $1,000,000).
2. To establish a fund for building maintenance, on a matching basis between the Regional Council and donors.

COMMUNITY RESIDENTIAL SERVICES FOR THE MENTALLY RETARDED

האגודה לתכנון ולפתוח שרותי מגורים בקהילה למפגר בשכלו

P.O.B. 753
Beer Sheva 84106
Telephone: (057) 77327
Office hours: no set hours

HISTORY AND DESCRIPTION
The association was founded in April 1980 in order to establish group homes for persons with mental retardation in Beer Sheva and the area. The first home, serving eight children, opened in July 1980.

Organizational Structure: The general membership meets yearly to set general policies, elect a Board of Directors, and approve the budget. The Board of Directors meets monthly to oversee operations.

Goals: To aid in the planning and development of residential services in Beer Sheva and environs for persons with mental retardation; to co-ordinate the services of the Association with other services provided to persons with mental retardation; to manage, own and operate residential services for persons with mental retardation; to increase public support for and awareness of the needs of persons with mental retardation.

Services, Activities, and Accomplishments: The Association currently operates one group home for eight children with mental retardation and behavioral problems. The home is located in rented quarters in Beer Sheva. It is the first group residence of its kind for children in Israel. Planning activities are underway for a second residence, for teenagers and young adults.

OFFICERS
Asst. Chairperson: Dr. Marta Galkman, Hameshachririm 82, Beer Sheva. Dentist.
Treasurer: Amichi Maor, 4 Smilansky, Beer Sheva. Businessman.
Board Members: Arna Porat, 26 Haeshcolot, Kiryat Gat. Social Worker.
Dr. Philip Reiss, 27 Kotel Hamaaravi, Beer Sheva. Psychologist.
Dorit Torelli, 102 Hanasiim, Beer Sheva.
Eli Kadosh, 7 Golomb, Beer Sheva.

FINANCIAL INFORMATION
The Association receives 50% of its income from Services for the Retarded, Ministry of Labor and Social Affairs, and 50% from Yad Avi Hayishuv. This year's annual budget is $50,500 and the present deficit is

$15,000. The Association is registered as a non-profit Ottoman Association in Beer Sheva (reg. no. 7867/825 416/78). Donations in Israel are tax-free (tax no. 4507304) and an application for tax-free status in the United States is pending. One full-time and six part-time workers are employed by the organization as well as five volunteers.

MEMBERSHIP, SCOPE, AND POLICY
Membership is according to the vote of the National Board, as specified in by-laws. There are 10 members in Israel. Decisions are made by the National Board.

AFFILIATIONS/REFERENCES
The Association is not affiliated with any Israeli political party.

FUNDING NEEDED
1. To improve staff salaries (cost $15,000). Restrictions on our initial grants coupled with galloping inflation have resulted in a large budget deficit for the first year. Changes in support services also necessitate additional staff hours.

2. To purchase an appropriate home (cost $60,000). The first residence is located in rented quarters. Purchase of a house makes more economic sense over a long range.

3. To purchase and operate a second home, for teenagers and young adults (cost $115,000).

COMMUNITY CENTER OF TAMRA

המרכז הקהילתי תמרה

Tamra Village, West Galilee
Telephone: (04) 728259
Office hours: 8:00 A.M. to 12:30 P.M.
3:00 P.M. to 7:00 P.M.

HISTORY AND DESCRIPTION

The initiative for the establishment of the first community center in the Arab sector came from three sources: The Israel Corporation of Community Centers (Matnas), the Local Council, and the Ministry of Education. The Center began to function in 1973, sharing the facilities of the nearby elementary school. In 1979 the Center moved to its own separate facility, which includes a large auditorium, a nursery school, a club, and offices and rooms for different interest groups. In 1979 the Tamra Matnas was incorporated as an Ottoman Association.

Organizational Structure: The Advisory Council, composed of representatives from the local council, the Ministry of Education and the public, determines general policy and approves budgets. The Center Director is responsible to the Advisory Council. There are Supervisors of Sport, Early Childhood Education, and Youth and Cultural Activities. In addition there is a secretariat, a maintenance staff, and part-time counsellors for various interest groups.

Goals: The Center attempts to open different frameworks as a means for the community to improve the "quality of life" in the areas of social betterment, use of free time, education, cultural activities, etc. In general, the Center seeks to provide for the needs of the community.

Services, Activities, and Accomplishments: The Center provides ongoing educational, social, cultural, and sports activities. For example, there are clubs for children and youth, a club for teachers, classes in Karate, exercise for women, language training, parent-child activities, handicrafts. The Center has been responsible for establishing the first Community Theatre, and the first Community Debka (dance) Troupe. Other major accomplishments are the Adult Night School, a club for body development (which produced several national champions), a course for training young counselors, and the creation of summer camps for children and mothers.

OFFICERS

Director: Diab Mounir, Tamra Village.
                 Tel. (04) 728259.
Treasurer: Aorna Livav, Kata. Accountant.
                 Tel. (04) 442332.
Board Members: Abas Hijazi, Tamra Village. Mayor.
                 Tel. (04) 728526.
                 Victor Gabay, Tel Aviv. Inspector, Education.

Mohamed Knan, Tamra Village. Teacher.
Diab Adel, Tamra Village. Principal.
Aoae Shakib, Tamra Village. Worker.
Ab Alhija Mouin, Tamra Village. Worker.

FINANCIAL INFORMATION
Membership dues provides for 25% of the budget. The rest of the funds come from the Ministry of Education, the Municipal Authority, and the Israel Corporation of Community Centers (Matnas), i.e. 25% each. Last year's annual budget of $60,000 left the Center with a deficit of $7,000. Donations to the Center are tax-free in Israel. It is a non-profit Ottoman Association (registration no. 58-54-72/4). Nine full-time and eighty part-time workers are employed by the Center, as well as twelve volunteers.

MEMBERSHIP, SCOPE, AND POLICY
One thousand members participate in activities in two branches of the Center in the village itself. As well, services are provided for all the people (15,000) of the village. The Director is responsible for the staff, programming, and execution of planned programs. The Advisory Council determines policy.

AFFILIATIONS/REFERENCES
The Center is not affiliated with any political party in Israel. Association is maintained with Interns for Peace, an organization of Jewish and Arab volunteers committed to the betterment of Arab-Jewish relations in Israel, and the Association for the Advancement of Community Centers.

FUNDING NEEDED
1. To provide services in Early Childhood Education ($10,000).
2. To create neighborhood branch centers ($20,000).
3. To establish and promote the club and social activities for the elderly ($10,000).

CONGREGATION MEVAKSHEI DERECH

קהילת מבקשי דרך

Gymnasia Rehavia Keren Kayemet
P.O.B. 7773 Jerusalem

HISTORY AND DESCRIPTION

During Chanukah of 1962, some 70 people from cities, towns, kibbutzim and moshavim throughout Israel gathered in Jerusalem to discuss
the ethical and spiritual problems of life in Israel. As a result, study
groups were formed, a religious service emerged, and Congregation
Mevakshei Derech came into being. The Congregation regards Judaism
as an evolving religion and civilization, which adapts itself to the needs
of the day and judges contemporary behavior in the light of the most
lasting norms of Jewish tradition. It is essentially a family congregation,
with complete equality afforded to both men and women. The weekly
D'var Torah, given by members of the Congregation or by guests after
the reading of the Torah and Haftorah is followed by discussion in
which all may express their views.

Organizational Structure: There is no officiating rabbi, although the
membership includes several ordained rabbis. All officers of the Congregation are elected at an annual meeting. These include the chairman,
two vice-chairmen, a treasurer, two secretaries, two editors of the
monthly bulletin (Hebrew and English), and the members of 11 committees, including religious service, cultural activities, youth, students,
hospitality and building fund. Besides the Board, there is also an
Expanded Board which includes the 11 chairmen of the committees.

Goals: Congregation Mevakshei Derech strives to create forms of religious expression and a synagogue service steeped in tradition yet drawing from many sources of spiritual inspiration indigenous to Israel. The
study of Jewish heritage and the ethical pursuits of the Jewish people are
considered to be as important as worship. The Congregation extends a
warm welcome to Olim as well as to native-born Israelis.

Services, Activities, and Accomplishments: Congregation Mevakshei
Derech holds all required Shabbat, festival, and high holy day services,
as well as bar-mitzvahs and bat-mitzvahs. Annual events include a
'Shabbat Together' to discuss religious and ethical issues, a 'Seder Leil
Yom Ha'Atzmaut' Independence Eve seder, a Tisha B'Av tour of the
Old City Walls, as well as Chanukah and Purim parties. There are also
various voluntary activites outside the Congregation, including aid
extended to sufferers of multiple sclerosis. The Congregation lists
among its major accomplishments the conducting of a vibrant congregational life and a full range of activities, including making Olim feel at
home; convening a nationwide conference on Religious Pluralism in
Israel; creating a new meaningful way to observe Yom Ha'Atzmaut
(through the creation of a 'haggadah' for the 'seder'), and enriching the
observance of other holidays; and creating an anthology of Hebrew
poems and extracts read at services.

OFFICERS

Chairman:	Professor Meir Rigbi, Baron Hirsch 18, Jerusalem. Biochemist. Tel. (02) 523036.
Treasurer:	Herman Greenberg, Hanassi 4, Jerusalem. Insurance Agent. Tel. (02) 660288.
Deputy Chairman:	Professor Hava Lazarus-Yafeh, Ben-Labrat 11, Jerusalem. Orientalist. Tel. (02) 633653.
Deputy Chairman:	Shimon Brandeis, Ben-Maimon 13, Jerusalem. Travel Agent. Tel. (02) 664267.
Secretary:	Mrs. Bruria Hermon, Nayot 42, Jerusalem. Secretary. Tel. (02) 660878.
Secretary:	Mrs. Rachel Lurie, Ramban 23, Jerusalem. Teacher. Tel. (02) 634582.

FINANCIAL INFORMATION

For the period August 1978 to July 1979, 72.9% of the Congregation's income came from return on investments; 15.7% from donations; and 11.4% from membership dues. For the fiscal year ending on August 31, 1979 the Congregation had a budget of $2,700. There was no deficit. Congregation Mevakshei Derech is registered with the Jerusalem District as an Ottoman Association (reg. no. 58-11/2185). Donations to the organization are *not* tax-free in Israel, but are tax-free in the United States if made through either the *Jewish Reconstructionist Foundation* or the *P.E.F. 'Israel Endowment Funds, Inc.* The Congregation employs three part-time workers and about 40 volunteers.

MEMBERSHIP, SCOPE, AND POLICY

There are 155 members of the Congregation's only branch in Jerusalem. Decisions are made by the Board or by the responsible committee (s). Membership is open to any interested Jew whose candidacy is approved by the Congregation's Expanded Board, and who is willing to pay annual membership dues.

AFFILIATIONS/REFERENCES

Congregation Mevakshei Derech is not associated with any Israeli political party. The following American organizations know of its work:

> *Jewish Reconstructionist Foundation,* 432 Park Avenue South, New York, N.Y., 10016;
>
> *P.E.F. Israel Endowment Funds, Inc.,* 511 Fifth Avenue, New York, N.Y.

FUNDING NEEDED

Congregation Mevakshei Derech has been allotted a plot of land by the Jerusalem Municipality for the purpose of building a synagogue center. Acquiring contributions to its Building Fund is its number one priority at present. At present, the Congregation has approximately $60,000, whereas another $200,000 is required before construction can begin.

THE COUNCIL FOR THE UNIVERSITY OF ISRAEL

המועצה ל״אוניברסיטת ישראל״

Herzl 114/3
P.O.B. 3091
Jerusalem
No definite office hours.

HISTORY AND DESCRIPTION

The Council was founded in 1976 by seven people to encourage the consideration by Israeli and Diaspora Jewish leaderships of a comprehensive approach to attracting and serving a greater number of Diaspora students, primarily in Israel. It is essentially seen as a pressure group working on and with Israeli governmental officials, officials of the Jewish Agency, and leaders of Diaspora organizations.

Goals: Its goal is the formation of a roof organization — The University of Israel — to mobilize educational resources in the Diaspora and in Israel, and to foster Diaspora Jewish culture.

Services, Activities, and Accomplishments: In 1979 activity was begun to establish a larger informal council for the comprehensive consideration of this approach. Diaspora leaders in the U.S. are being contacted systematically about this. To date, the Council has gained positive responses from the Prime Minister, the Minister of Education, and the Department of Diaspora Education of the Jewish Agency.

OFFICERS

Director: Norman Greenwald, Herzl 114/3, Jerusalem.
Professor.
Tel. (02) 532848.
Treasurer: None, as yet.
Board Members: Simha Greenwald, Herzl 114/3, Jerusalem.
Secretary.
Lea Ben Yosef, Herzl 114/3, Jerusalem.
Professor.
Ofra Muki, Ramot 25B, Jerusalem.

FINANCIAL INFORMATION

The Council has neither budget nor income. It is registered as an Ottoman non-profit organization (no. 11/2647, Jerusalem District). Donations in Israel are tax-free (no. not stated) but contributions from the U.S. are not. The Council is run by 3 volunteer workers.

MEMBERSHIP, SCOPE, AND POLICY

Anyone who subscribes to the Council's approach can be a member. At present, 6 members in Israel are listed, none abroad. Most decisions are made by the Director.

AFFILIATIONS/REFERENCES
The Council maintains a close association with the past president of the American Association of Jewish Education, Dr. Leivy Smolar, President of the Baltimore Hebrew College, 5800 Park Heights Ave., Baltimore, Md. 21215. The Council is not affiliated with any political party in Israel.

FUNDING NEEDED
The Council does not seek funding at present. The question of funding may arise for a larger informal committee which has not yet been established.

COUNCIL OF YOUTH MOVEMENTS IN ISRAEL

מועצת תנועות הנוער בישראל

28/A Rashi Street
Tel Aviv 63265
Telephone: (03) 284098/282787
Office Hours: 8:30 A.M. to 4:00 P.M.

HISTORY AND DESCRIPTION

The Council of Youth Movements in Israel has been set up as a supreme body for all youth movements in the State of Israel, in order to deal with matters of common concern to its constituent members. Israel's youth movements have an overall membership of more than 250,000 Jewish and non-Jewish boys and girls.

Organizational Structure: The Council selects its representatives to international meetings and fosters ties with other national councils throughout the world. The Executive Directors of each of the eleven member youth movements serve as members of the National Board.

Goals: The Council constantly strives to increase the cooperation between its member movements on the basis of those things they share in common. It runs leadership training projects and carries out other information and training services in order to accomplish this end.

Services, Acitvities, and Accomplishments: The Council initiates a variety of joint activities and also assists the movements in carrying out their educational activities and in deepening and enriching their educational experience. It coordinates their activities and represents them before other organizations and public bodies within the State and overseas. It brings the message of the youth movements of Israel to the masses of youth throughout the world, and strengthens the international ties of the youth of Israel. The Council holds conventions, seminars and study courses, assists in publishing leadership manuals and gathers information about the educational experience obtained from the activities of the various movements and puts it at the disposal of all Council members. The Council sponsors activities in the area of welfare; youth volunteer work in development towns and poor sections of the big cities. Educational seminars on "Youth Movements and the Israeli Society" are sponsored as well as efforts to take care of youth who do not study or work.

The eleven member organizations are as follows:

HA'NOAR HA'OVED VE-HALOMED: founded in 1924, this is the largest organization with 100,000 members. It is affiliated with the Histadrut, the Labor Federation and the Kibbutzim Movement.

HATZOFIM: founded in 1919, this is the Israeli Boy and Girl Scout Federation. There are 55,000 members; 40,000 in the Hebrew scouts and 15,000 in five Arab associations. The organization is affiliated with the International Scout Movement.

BNEI AKIVA: founded in 1929, this organization has 30,000 members and is affiliated with the National Religious Party and its Kibbutz Movement.

HASHOMER HATZAIR: founded in 1916, this 16,000 member group is affiliated with Mapam and the Kibbutz Artzi Movement.

HANOAR HADATI HA'OVED: founded in 1951, this is the Religious Working and Studying Youth; the group has 15,000 members and is affiliated with Hapoel Hamizrachi.

HANOAR HA'LEUMI: founded in 1949, the National Working and Studying Youth organization has 10,000 members and is affiliated with the National Federation of Labor.

MACCABI HATZAIR, YOUNG MACCABI: founded in 1929, this 7,000 member group is affiliated with the Maccabi sports organization and Maccabi World Union.

DROR-HAMAHANOT HA'OLIM: founded in 1952 and with 5,000 members, this group is affiliated with the Labor Party and the Kibbutz Hameuchad Movement.

BETAR: founded in 1923, this organization with its 4,500 members is affiliated with the World Betar Movement and the Herut Party.

EZRA: founded in 1919, with 3,500 members, the organization is affiliated with Poalei Agudat Israel, the organization of Orthodox Jewish workers.

HANOAR HATZIONI: founded in 1932, this 3,000 member organization is affiliated with the Independent Liberal Party and the World Federation of the Zionist Youth.

All these groups are active in three main aspects: 1) classical scout activities, which include educational courses, hiking, pioneering and club meetings; 2) volunteer and welfare activities, in which more than three hundred and fifty clubs take part in activities in development towns and distress areas in big cities; and 3) self-fulfillment activities, including a combination of military service and kibbutz life (called Nachal), national volunteer service for Orthodox girls and voluntary service for all in development towns.

OFFICERS

Chairman:	Pini Tuchmacher, Kibbutz Nir-Eliyahu. Educator.
Treasurer:	Israel Roses. Educator.
Secretary General:	Miky Gurvitz. Public Relations.
Board members:	The Executive Directors of each of the eleven member groups.

FINANCIAL INFORMATION

The Council is registered as an Ottoman Association (Tel Aviv district, reg. no. 5948/99). 38% of the Council's funding comes from the Ministry of Education and Culture; 35% from the membership dues of the member youth movements, 5% from the Jewish Agency and the remainder from other sources. Last year's budget of $49,300 left the Council with a deficit of $8,837. Donations are tax free in Israel (reg. no. 4506954). Five full-time workers and one part-time worker are employed by the Council. The Council provides the budget for the 11 youth movements, the funding needs benefitting 250,000 youngsters.

MEMBERSHIP, SCOPE AND POLICY

Any youth movement (zionist, pioneer, etc.) with more than ten branches and 1500 members (youth aged ten to eighteen) involved in youth for youth activity and education towards self fulfillment are welcome to join the Council. The eleven member organizations have brought 250,000 youths to the Council's membership, with 1200 clubs in Israel. Decisions for the Council are made by the National Board.

AFFILIATIONS/REFERENCES

The NAJYC, the North American Jewish Youth Council, as well as most other national youth councils in the Western hemisphere, are familiar with the work of the Council in Israel.

FUNDING NEEDED

1. For educational training for youth leaders who are active in welfare projects and development areas, as well as maintenance of the three hundred clubs in poverty areas; cost, up to $250,000.
2. For building and renewing most of the clubs' facilities; cost, $500,000.
3. For promotion of educational institutions of the various movements and for establishing documentary educational center(s) in Jerusalem; cost, $400,000.
4. To maintain youth camps and to invest in new camping grounds for summer activities and for day-camps in poverty areas; cost, $140,000.

THE DAVID YELLIN
TEACHERS COLLEGE

המכללה לחינוך ע"ש דוד ילין

P.O.B. 3578
89 Herzl, Jerusalem
Telephone: (02) 523151/2
Office hours: 8:00 a.m. to 3:00 p.m.

HISTORY AND DESCRIPTION

The David Yellin Teachers College, a general teachers' training college, was founded in 1914 by David Yellin, a pioneer Jewish educator, and moved to its present campus in 1928. It was one of the first schools of higher education in Israel to use Hebrew as the language of instruction. During the early years of the Arab-Jewish conflict the College campus served as a defence post and training center for the Haganah in the Jerusalem area. There is an active group of Friends of the David Yellin Teachers College in the U.S.A.

Organizational Structure: Policy decisions are made by the College administration in consultation with the Society for the Advancement of the College and American Friends.

Goals: The College intends to continue its pioneering and innovative educational work in teacher education. It offers a Bachelor of Education degree (B.Ed.) for Junior High School teachers and three year teacher certification programs in the following areas: Early Childhood Education, Elementary School Education, Technical Handicrafts, Arab Elementary School Education, Nutrition and Home Economics. It offers a two-year teacher Education program for Teachers for Mentally Retarded Children in Residential Institutions and a post-graduate one-year program (the Rachel Shazar Institute for Teachers of Mentally Retarded Children and Children with Learning Disabilities), as well as a Pre-Academic Program, In-Service Teacher Certification Programs and re-training programs, and Programs for New Immigrants.

Services, Activities, and Accomplishments: The College has its own demonstration school on its premises with an enrollment of approximately 130 children between the ages of 4 and 8. The school provides the College with a means of testing and applying educational innovation and advanced pedagogical concepts. Apart from regular courses the College has an Arab Teacher Education program and serves as a National Center for Retardation. This year the College has added a new program for teachers of Nutrition and Home Economics, music for new immigrants, and in-service and re-training programs to raise the level of teachers in the field. The College conducts a Learning Problems Clinic as part of its Rachel Shazar Institute for Teachers of the Mentally Retarded and Children with Learning Disabilities. More than 4,000 students have graduated from the College and many of the leaders of today's educational establishment are alumni of the College.

OFFICERS

College Dean:	Dr. Norman Schanin
Chairman of the Israeli Board:	Judge Elazar Halevy
President of the Friends of the David Yellin Teachers College:	Mr. Sanford L. Batkin
	394 Grand Blvd., Scarsdale, N.Y.

FINANCIAL INFORMATION

The major part of support funds are received from the Ministry of Education. Friends of the College help through annual contributions and/or establishment of Endowment Funds and Trusts and through Scholarship assistance. Details of the annual budget were not supplied but can be obtained from the Education Ministry. Donations to the College in Israel and the United States are tax-free. The tax number is available from the Friends of the College and the New York State Board of Social Welfare, Office Tower, Empire State Plaza, Albany, N.Y. Public Relations are handled by 2 full-time and volunteer workers.

MEMBERSHIP, SCOPE, AND POLICY

There are approximately 1,000 Friends of the David Yellin Teachers College in the United States.

AFFILIATIONS/REFERENCES

The College is not affiliated with any political party in Israel. Affiliation in the United States:
The Friends of The David Yellin Teachers College, 309 Fifth Avenue, Suite 501, New York, N.Y. 10016.

FUNDING NEEDS

1. To complete a major building and renovation program including a new science wing with laboratories, and an enlarged library and instructional materials center.
2. Scholarship Aid.
3. To fund innovative projects sponsored and conducted by the College. (Specific details available upon request.)

DENTAL VOLUNTEERS FOR ISRAEL (D.V.I.)

רופאי שיניים מתנדבים לישראל (די.וי.אי.)

2 Hameyasdim Street
Jerusalem
Telephone: (02) 521628
Office hours: 8:00 A.M. to 2:00 P.M.

HISTORY AND DESCRIPTION

Dental Volunteers for Israel (D.V.I.) is a new organization which has been established as a result of the initiative of a group of dental surgeons from France, who wished to make a positive contribution to the Dental Health of Israel, and in particular to help alleviate the suffering of children of poor families whose dental needs cannot be met by their families or by the public services available.

Over 90% of children in Israel suffer from dental caries. The facilities available both in the private and public sectors are inadequate and provide care for about 20% of the children. There are insufficient funds available to materially improve this situation in the forseeable future. In the summer of 1979, a group of dentists, led by Dr. Ciepielewski of Paris, initiated this project by coming to Israel (at their own expense) and by providing free dental care for about 1200 needy children in Jerusalem. The clinic facilities were provided by the municipality while the regular dentist was on vacation.

The overwhelming success of this venture has resulted in the setting up of D.V.I. A building in Mekor Chayim, a poor neighborhood in Jerusalem, has been rented and is being converted and equipped as a modern dental center including complete dental equipment and accommodation for volunteer dentists who will come from all over the world to spend two weeks at the clinic. Two studio apartments with all accommodations and one 3-room apartment is available for the volunteers to live in.

OFFICERS

Director:	Mrs. Trudi Birger. Microbiologist. Tel. (02) 521628.
Treasurer:	Mr. Elijau Lazar. Tel. (02) 224790.
Secretary:	Yehuda Cohen. Lawyer. Tel. (02) 231029.
Head of Dental Offices in Israel:	Dr. Kelman. Tel. (02) 247173.
Head of the Nurses:	Mrs. Dana Chawer. Tel. (02) 227211.
Board Members:	Mrs. Aneise. Tel. (02) 522433.
	Mrs. Amid. Tel. (02) 227857.
Head of the Health Dept.:	Dr. Tamir. Tel. (02) 234650.

FINANCIAL INFORMATION

The sources for last year's annual budget were not specified. The annual budget for last year was $60,000. The organization is registered as tax-exempt (tax no. 4507161) in Israel. Contributions are tax-deductible in the U.S. and should be sent to the P.E.F. Israel Endowment Funds Inc., 342 Madison Avenue — Suite 1010, New York, New York, 10173. The contributor has to mention that the contribution is made for the D.V.I. Dental Volunteers for Israel — Mrs. Trudi Birger. The organization has part-time workers and volunteers.

MEMBERSHIP, SCOPE, AND POLICY
The organization has 8 members in Israel and 6 in France. Decisions are made at the monthly meetings of the Board.

AFFILIATIONS/REFERENCES
The organization is not affiliated with any political party in Israel. Dr. Ciepielewski is responsible for the project in France; 2 Ave de Ternes 17 eme Paris, France, (Tel. 3805097).

FUNDING NEEDED
Funds are urgently needed for adapting, equipping, and maintaining this center. Dental equipment, $60,000; alterations and furnishing, $20,000; maintenance (materials, electricity, water, cleaning, dental assisting, secretary, etc., per year), $35,000; long-term needs require funds to purchase the building, $300,000.

DIASPORA YESHIVA INSTITUTE FOR WOMEN

ישיבת התפוצות מכון לנשים

The Beth-El Building
The Jewish Quarter
P.O.B. 6426
Jerusalem
Telephone: (02) 716841
Office hours: 9:00 A.M. to 5:00 P.M.

HISTORY AND DESCRIPTION

The women's division was started in parallel with the Diaspora Yeshiva Men's Division, but in a separate location. The new women's school building was completed this year in the Jewish quarter in the Old City of Jerusalem.

Goals: The goal of the Women's Division of the Diaspora Yeshiva is to make Women of Valor — outstanding Torah women who are dedicated and knowledgeable leaders, capable of actualizing Torah values in the modern world.

Services, Activities, and Accomplishments: The women's program is designed to inculcate within the students a wholeness of character and personality. In keeping with the goal of maintaining the highest levels of scholarship and understanding, the school employs a unique and sophisticated method of intensive study designed to promote and sustain intellectual and emotional growth. The wonderful depth of Torah wisdom is revealed to the student through an exciting question and answer format, in which she is stimulated to search for real truth and to be responsible for her conclusions.

Tremendous effort is devoted to the acquisition of Yiras Hashem — the correct attitude towards G-d, which results in one's having the proper relationship with oneself, one's fellow man, the Almighty. Following the great Rabbis of the Mussar Movement, the school engages in a deep study of the forces within people. Women receive intensive training in the art of being master of their emotions and their feelings in accordance with Jewish values. A particular example of this training is the weekly session called the Va'ad Mussar, in which women offer and receive open constructive criticism from their friends. Great emphasis is placed on this point, because in Judaism, learning and perfection of character are inseparable.

It is the general policy of the Yeshiva to develop women who are individuals. This means giving women real responsibilities and first-hand experience in the practicalities of serving the Jewish people. Besides taking an active part in the functioning of the school itself, the students organize and carry out various community services and educational programs for the Israeli Army, colleges, high schools, kibbutzim and for thousands of youth from the Diaspora. Every woman is expected to see herself as a member of the Jewish People as a whole — to care about the needs of the Jewish people everywhere. What is most important is that the school gives the woman leeway, and shows her the way to bring out her special talents (art, music, etc.) and abilities in finding answers to Jewish problems.

The Women's Division is but a part of an integrated and organized community, consisting of a Yeshiva and a Kollel (married students' program). The young woman is invited and encouraged to partake of the warm and loving atmospohere in which the Kollel homes provide, and to make these young families her "home away from home".

The Yeshiva's major accomplishments have been: educating and inspiring many hundreds of young Jewish women, providing wives and helpmates and arranging over forty weddings for the Yeshiva's young rabbis, rebuilding and restoring the historic Beth-El building in the Jewish Quarter of the Old City of Jerusalem which houses the Institute.

OFFICERS

Director: Rabbi G. Goldstein, 47 Givat Afeka, Ashkelon.
Board Members: Reb Daniel Schultz, Jerusalem.
                Tel.: (02) 716841.
                Rebbitzen M. Goldstein, Jerusalem.
                Rabbi Dr. M. Goldstein, 5 Mann, Jerusalem.

FINANCIAL INFORMATION

The only source of income for the Yeshiva comes in the form of donations. Last year's annual budget of $200,000 left the Yeshiva with a deficit of $100,000. The organization is registered as an Ottoman Association (reg. no. 11/1433). Donations to the Yeshiva are tax-free in Israel (no number given), the United States (tax no. M-67-EO-529), England (tax no. 277919), and Canada (tax no. 04201-74-4908). Five full-time and two part-time employees work for the Yeshiva.

MEMBERSHIP, SCOPE, AND POLICY

Decisions are made mostly by the Executive Director. There are 100 members in Israel. Membership is open to Jewish women.

AFFILIATIONS/REFERENCES

The organization is not affiliated with any political party in Israel. The Yeshiva is in contact with Bnai Brith, 823 U.N. Plaza, New York, New York 10017; United Jewish Appeal, 1290 Avenue of the Americas, New York, New York 10019; and the National Council of Synagogue Youth, also in New York City.

FUNDING NEEDED

1. The purchase of furniture and school equipment. Cost: $40,000.
2. Furnishing the kitchen. Cost: $20,000.
3. Kitchen budget. Cost: $15,000 per annum.

DIASPORA YESHIVA TORAS YISRAEL

ישיבת התפוצות תורת ישראל

P.O.B. 6426
Mt. Zion, Jerusalem
Telephone: (02) 716841
Office hours: 8:00 A.M. to 7:00 P.M.

HISTORY AND DESCRIPTION
The Diaspora Yeshiva was founded in 1967 by an American, Rabbi Dr. Mordecai Goldstein, who is presently its Dean And Rosh Yeshiva. The Yeshiva has attracted assimilated young people from all over the world, bringing them to the paths of Torah-true Judaism. Today, the Yeshiva trains leaders equipped to handle the complex problems of the world Jewish community. It is possibly the only yeshiva in Israel where practical aspects of Orthodoxy, such as ritual slaughter and circumcision, are taught. The Yeshiva hopes to become the center for research and study in the fields of Torah-oriented social services and in governmental affairs.
The many diverse fields of interest have grown with the student body. Rabbi Dr. Goldstein's original motivation to found yet another yeshiva in "the land of yeshivas" was an answer to a crying need. He had met several young men who sincerely wanted to become part of the yeshiva world, but found their way blocked. They had been turned away from every other institution because they could not read Hebrew and had little or no Jewish education.

Organizational Structure: A Rosh Yeshiva who acts as Dean and Chancellor; an Executive Director and a board of directors direct the Yeshiva.

Goals: The Yeshiva's aim is to expand the community on Mount Zion from its current level of approximately 135 to 500 students, and to enlarge the Kollel from forty to 150 couples. This will constitute an elite nucleus. The community hopes to incorporate newspaper, radio and television facilities; to engage in educational book publishing; world peace; local and international law; statesmanship; adult and youth education; development of religious music; supplementary courses for leaders, politicians and professionals holding positions of influence throughout the world.
The Yeshiva seeks to create a force of 24,000 students, outside of its Mount Zion headquarters, who will be located in communities throughout Israel. These students will teach Torah and live a life of moral example for the Jewish community. They will demonstrate what G-d-fearing Jews should be—individuals above and beyond reproach.

Services, Activities, and Accomplishments: The organization's major accomplishments have been the influencing of Jewish youth; the rebuilding of Mount Zion; building a Yishuv in Jerusalem; and the arranging of over 40 weddings.

OFFICERS

Dean:	Rabbi Dr. M. Goldstein, 5 Mann, Jerusalem.
Teacher:	Reb Daniel Shultz.
Director:	Reb David Rubin, 1 Hameshorerim, Jerusalem.
Accountants:	Reb David Sackton and Reb Ben Zion Fried.
Exec. Dir.:	Rabbi Gedalia Goldstein, 47 Givat Afeka, Ashkelon.
Hon. Pres.:	Rabbi Dr. S.Z. Kahana, Jerusalem.

FINANCIAL INFORMATION
58% of last year's annual budget came from donations, 35% came from the government, and the balance of 7% came from loans. Last year's annual budget of $180,000 left the Yeshiva with an accumulated deficit of $40,000. It is registered as an Ottoman Association (reg. no. 11/1433). Donations to the Yeshiva are tax-free in Israel (tax number not supplied), the United States (tax number M-67-EO-529), England (tax number 277919), and in Canada (tax number 04201-74-4908). There are 10 full-time employees and 4 part-time employees of the Yeshiva.

MEMBERSHIP, SCOPE, AND POLICY
Decisions are made by the Executive Director. There are 200 members in the two Israeli branches.

AFFILIATIONS/REFERENCES
The Yeshiva is not affiliated with any political party in Israel. The Yeshiva is in contact with B'nei Brith, 823 U.N. Plaza, New York 10013; United Jewish Appeal, 1290 Avenue of the Americas, New York, New York 10019; and the National Council of Synagogue Youth also in New York.

FUNDING NEEDED
1. To complete a community housing project. Cost: $10 million
2. To construct a child day care center. Cost: $100,000.
3. To fund an annual kitchen budget. Cost: $50,000 per annum.

THE DR. FALK SCHLESINGER INSTI-
TUTE FOR MEDICAL-HALACHIC
RESEARCH OF SHAARE ZEDEK
HOSPITAL, JERUSALEM

מכון ע״ש ד״ר פ. שלזינגר ז״ל לחקר הרפואה עפ״י התורה ליד
בית החולים שערי צדק

P.O.B. 293
Jerusalem
Telephone: (02) 555111

HISTORY AND DESCRIPTION
The Institute was founded in 1965 to honor Dr. F. Schlesinger, then
Director of the Shaare Zedek Hospital, on his 70th birthday. The
Institute is directed by a physician. The editorial board includes rabbis,
doctors, a lawyer, and the Director of Shaare Zedek Hospital.

Goals: To encourage, promote, and publish medical-halachic research.

Activities: Publication of a quarterly, *ASSIA*; publication of books
dealing with above themes; arrangement of lectures and symposia on
these themes; and long-term research projects.

OFFICERS
Director: Dr. A. Steinberg, Jerusalem. Physician.
Chairman: Ch. Kahn, Jerusalem. Advocate.
Board Members: Prof. D. Maeir, Jerusalem. Director-General,
                          Shaare Zedek Hospital.
                     Dr. C. Halberstadt, Jerusalem. Physician.
                     Dr. Z. Jacobson, Jerusalem. Physician.
                     Dr. Z. Freier, Jerusalem. Physician.
                     Dr. A. Abraham, Jerusalem. Physician.
                     Rabbi Y. Strauss, Jerusalem. Rabbi.

FINANCIAL INFORMATION
Last year's annual budget came from the following sources: subscriptions, 30%; donations, 25%; book sales, 20%. There was a deficit of
25%. The annual budget for last year was $2,000, with a deficit of $500.
The organization is registered as an Ottoman Association. Donations
are tax-free both in Israel (no. 4500544) and in the United States (no.
98-6001091). There are two part-time employees.

MEMBERSHIP, SCOPE, AND POLICY
Decisions are mostly made by the Executive Director, with basic decisions being made by the Board. There are 500 subscriptions in Israel and
120 abroad.

AFFILIATIONS/REFERENCES

The organization is not affiliated with a political party in Israel, but is in contact with the following two institutions in the United States: Albert Einstein School of Medicine, Yeshiva University, Bronx, New York; and the American Committee for Shaare Zedek, 49 West 45th Street, New York, New York 10036.

FUNDING NEEDED

1. Regular publication of quarterly periodical.
2. Special research projects.

DR. SAMUEL AND RIVKA HURWICH LITERATURE FUND OF THE YIDDISH CULTURE ASSOCIATION OF JERUSALEM

הקרן לספרות ע"ש דר' שמואל ורבקה הורביץ — האגודה
לתרבות היידיש בירושלים

c/o David Breslau
4 Yehoash
Jerusalem
Telephone: (02) 660583

HISTORY AND DESCRIPTION

The Dr. Samuel and Rivka Hurwich Literature Fund was established by the Yiddish Culture Association of Jerusalem in memory of Dr. Hurwich, founder of the organization and a former chairman, who, together with his wife, played a leading role in Labor Zionist activity in Canada and in Yiddish culture in Jerusalem.

Organizational Structure: The Fund has a director and national board and is staffed by volunteers.

Goals: The purpose of the Fund is to encourage Yiddish writers in Israel, particularly from the Soviet Union, by providing an annual subsidy of $2,000 toward the publication of an original Yiddish work. This annual grant represents the largest repeated annual subsidy which is made available to a Yiddish or a Hebrew writer anywhere in the world today.

Services, Activities, and Accomplishments: Since 1977 the fund has provided the annual subsidy which has made possible the publication of works by the following authors: Meir Yellin (1977), Peretz Markish (posthumously) (1978), David Sfarad (1979), and Kalman Segal (1980). The assistance is in the form of a grant covering 50-70% of publication costs and is a dignified and most appreciated form of aid. In addition, the Fund, through the Yiddish Culture Association, sponsors annual public literary evenings in tribute to the author of the year—an act of great psychological reinforcement.

OFFICERS

Director: Gershon Winer, 4 Ben Tabai, Jerusalem.
              Professor.
              Tel. (02) 665810.
Treasurer: Meyer Bargteil, 4 Ben Tabai, Jerusalem.
              Businessman.
              Tel. (02) 664278.
Board: Yitzhak Wallerstein, 24 Ben Nun, Jerusalem.
              Professor.
              Tel. (02) 667673.

Mrs. Anka Shamir, 13 HaTibbonim, Jerusalem.
  Yiddish Radio Director.
Yitzhak Harkabi, World Jewish Congress.
  Diplomat.
Jacque Newman, 4 Shimoni, Publisher.
Mrs. Ethel Shaeffer, Teacher.
Mrs. Sima Skurkewitz, Business.
David Breslau, 4 Yehoshua, Jerusalem.
  Educator.
    Tel. (02) 660583.

FINANCIAL INFORMATION
Sources of income are donations through the following organizations:
Campaign in Canada and Israel — 60%; United Israel Appeal of Canada, Inc. — 20%; Abiezer Fund of the Jewish Agency — 20%. Last year's budget was $21,000. The fund has tax-free status in Israel (no. 4505701) and in the U.S. (through P.E.F. Israel Endowment Fund, N.Y.). The organization is staffed by volunteers.

MEMBERSHIP, SCOPE, AND POLICY
Membership is open to the public and there are currently 25 members in Israel, and two abroad. Decisions are made by the national board.

AFFILIATIONS/REFERENCES
The Fund is not affiliated with any political party in Israel. Abroad, its work is known to the P.E.F. Israel Endowment Fund, Inc., 511 Fifth Avenue, New York, N.Y. 10017.

FUNDING NEEDED
Out of an initial fund of $25,000, 85% has already been raised. The sum of $3,000 is required in the immediate future as well as funds for awards in the coming years.

DR. ZIMMERMAN OLD AGE HOME FOR SAGES

בית כנסת ובית זקנים לרבנים ע"ש ד"ר ש. צימרמן

58 Herzl
Raanana
Telephone: (052) 91322, public telephone: (052) 91309
Office hours: 8:00 A.M. to 1:00 P.M.

HISTORY AND DESCRIPTION

The Dr. Zimmerman Old Age Home for Sages was founded in 1963 by the late Dr. Simcha Zimmerman who was born in the United States of America. The Home is situated on four dunams of land, most of which is laid out as a garden with a splendid lawn.

Organizational Structure: Details not supplied.

Goals: To take care of old aged Rabbis and religious men and women, without payment.

Services, Activities, and Accomplishments: The Old Age Home has 44 beds, 95% of which are filled by people referred to the organization by the Service for the Aged of the Ministry of Social Welfare. Each room is furnished with its own toilet facilities, central heating and hot and cold running water. The Home organizes classes in Torah and Talmud for the men, and the women are fully occupied with knitting, handicrafts, painting, sculpture, and the like. The organization's major accomplishment is to have provided services for hundreds of people since its foundation. It also serves meals to the needy who are not residents in the Home.

OFFICERS

Director: Menachem Baum, 45 Orchaim, Bnei-Brak.
Tel. (03) 784336.

Treasurer: Moishe Orenstein, 61 Yehuda Halevi, Tel Aviv.
Advocate.
Tel. (03) 611260.

Chairman: Rabbi Shmuel Werner, 9 Desler,
Bnei-Brak. Dayan. Rosh Beit Din.
Tel. (03) 784055.

Board Members: Rabbi Yitzchok Kolitz, 30 Or-Hachaim,
Bnei-Brak. Dayan. Rosh Beth Din.
Tel. (03) 785887.

Dr. Y. Kister, 36 Metudela, Jerusalem.
Supreme Court Judge.
Tel. (02) 662244.

Rabbi David Weisbrot, 8 Ravad, Bnei-Brak.
Former Director of Jaffa Welfare Office.
Tel. (03) 781979.

Nachum Halpren, 24 Chisin, Tel Aviv.
Company Director.
Tel. (03) 292720.
Sender Bergman, 48 Chazon Aish,
Bnei-Brak. City Hall Worker.
Tel. (03) 793703.

FINANCIAL INFORMATION

Last year's annual budget of $94,000 left the organization with a deficit of $41,000. It is registered in Ramle as a non-profit Ottoman Association (reg. no. 611/1). Donations in Israel and the United States are not tax-free. Ten full-time and fifteen part-time workers are employed by the Home, as well as two volunteers.

Until now the Institution has not received grants or donations from any external bodies apart from the subsistence grants from the Ministry of Social Welfare. The organization has no connections abroad and no private donors in Israel. Efforts have been made to cover costs from the income of Funds established by the late Dr. Zimmerman, but soaring costs have led to encroachments into capital in order to continue necessary services. The institution is in danger of collapse as a result of this process.

MEMBERSHIP, SCOPE, AND POLICY

Membership is open to anyone who is willing to work and can be of use. There are 8 members in Israel. Decisions are made by the National Board.

AFFILIATIONS/REFERENCES

The Old Age Home is not affiliated with any Israeli political party.

FUNDING NEEDED

1. To finance the construction of additional facilities for 30 Old Aged People, including a Clinic, a room for doctors and nurses, and extensions to the kitchen and cultural hall. (Total Cost: $400,000.) This project was approved by the Old Aged Home and the Joint's "Eshel" organization and is planned for completion within the next five years.
2. To finance the construction of a club-room for handicrafts and cultural activities.
3. To finance expansion of the existing synagogue.

EDFONE—RELIGIOUS HELP THROUGH (VIA) THE TELEPHONE

עזרה דתית (נפשית) טלפונית — עדפון

Rosenheim 13
P.O.B. 92, Bnei Brak.
Telephone: (03) 702017
Office Hours: All hours of the day and night

HISTORY AND DESCRIPTION

The organization was founded in 1976 by Rabbi David Glazer, son of
the Chief Rabbi of Ramla City. It was established to provide spiritual
guidance according to the Torah, and general advice to people in
trouble.

Organizational Structure: Edfone is a national organization which is
available to anyone in need. It has an executive director and a number of
volunteers.

Goals: The organization's chief goal is to intervene in family problems
to bring about 'family-peace'. This is accomplished through the home
visits by the volunteers and via the telephone.

Services, Activities, and Accomplishments: Edfone provides such services
as providing tefillin to those in need, checking the validity of mezuzot
without payment and the giving of lectures to both pupils and the
public. They also talk on the telephone to troubled people, i.e. those
contemplating suicide. This is a 24-hour service. The organization has
been recognized by such well-known individuals as Prime Ministers
Yitzhak Rabin and Menachem Begin and various members of the
Knesset. Its accomplishments include: contact through letters, personal
meetings, and telephone conversations with over 20,000 people with
problems. It is known that 15 people have been saved from suicide; over
200 lectures to the public every year; 5000 people who were 'put back on
the right course'; numerous cases of 'family-peace'; and welfare 'cases'
who in turn became financially independent.

OFFICERS

Director: Shimon Yosef Wizenfeld, Rav Ami 10, Bnei Brak.
                 Collel.
Treasurer: Rabbi David Glazer, Rosenheim 13, Bnei Brak.
                 Collelnik. Tel. (03) 702017.
Board: Yaakov Tshinagel, Sokolov 10, Bnei Brak.
                 Collel.
                 Shmuel Hoffman, Beiz Hillel 12, Bnei Brak.
                 Tuvya Zonnenstein, Rabbi Akiva 118, Bnei Brak.
                 Collel.

FINANCIAL INFORMATION

Edfone states that they have no membership dues and do not have time
to solicit for funds. Some income does come from people they have

helped, but the amount was not mentioned. Their annual budget for the last year was $4,000 with a deficit of $2,000. The organization is registered in Tel Aviv with the Ministry of Interior as an Ottoman Association (reg. no. 6429/99). Presently, donations are not tax-free in either Israel or the United States. The organization employs 30 volunteers.

MEMBERSHIP, SCOPE, AND POLICY

The decisions of the organization are made mostly by an Executive Director. Criteria for membership includes anyone with a Jewish-religious education who wishes to volunteer his time to work for the organization. There are 30 members in 3 branches in Israel; in Jerusalem, Bnei Brak and Haifa. There is no involvement from abroad.

AFFILIATIONS/REFERENCES

The organization is not affiliated with any political party in Israel. There is no affiliation with any organizations abroad.

FUNDING NEEDED

1. Funds to erect permanent offices to be used 24 hours a day,
2. The printing of a guide-book on the subjects of family-peace.
3. "Family-life" funds to help cases with psychological problems.

THE EDUCATION CENTER, MEVASSERET ZION

קרית חנוך מבשרת ציון

P.O.B. 6605
Jerusalem
Telephone: (02) 536521, 528965, 534020
Office hours: 8:00 A.M. to 4:00 P.M.

HISTORY AND DESCRIPTION

The Education Center opened in 1968 in a private house, with 20 pupils. It now has five schools and almost 500 pupils, including a Junior Boys' School, Boys' Yeshiva, "Kol Mevaser", Junior Girls' School, Girls' Vocational High School, and a Teachers' Training Seminary, "Kolel Meretz".

Goals: The aims of the Center are to educate and remotivate youth from deprived backgrounds and neighborhoods, to impress the value of continued education and personal self-respect on the local settlement, and to send groups of graduates to distant places both in Israel and overseas, in order to spread Jewish values and teaching methods.

Services, Activities, and Accomplishments: The Center is working with and has recently been "adopted" by the Society for the Welfare of Israeli Talented Underprivileged Children, P.O.B. 5074, Jerusalem, telephone (02) 521088, Director: Mr. E. Zadok, M.A.

The organization's major accomplishments have been the growth in the number of students; the success in educating students to perform well on their matriculation examinations; the remotivation of boys of the potential "underworld" to perform successfully in army and civilian life; the providing of a vocation to girls who could end up on the streets; and the success of Yeshiva-sponsored groups in Kiryat Shemona, Nocham, Maalot, and in Paris.

OFFICERS

Chairman: Rabbi Shabtai Zelikovitz. Lives on campus.
                        Tel. (02) 528965.

Educational
Director: Rabbi Yosef Sarid (Stern). Lives on campus.
Dean: Rabbi Eliyahu Sofer. Lives on campus.
Head of
Kolel Meretz: Rabbi Uri Cohen. Lives on campus.

FINANCIAL INFORMATION

70% of last year's annual budget came from various Israeli government ministries, and the remaining 30% came from individual donations. Last year's annual budget of $560,000 left the Center with a deficit of $140,000. The Center is registered as an Ottoman Association (no. 7867/246). Donations in Israel are tax-free (tax exemption 4503367) and

175

donations from the United States are tax-deductible if checks are made out to Mevaseret Zion Judea Center. There are 25 full-time and 42 part-time employees at the Center.

MEMBERSHIP, SCOPE, AND POLICY
Decisions are made by the National Board. No other information was supplied.

AFFILIATIONS/REFERENCES
The Center is not affiliated with any political party in Israel. The organization is in contact with F.C.I.I., 15 Beekman Street, New York, New York 10033 and P.E.F. Israel Endowment Funds, Inc., 511 Fifth Avenue, New York, New York 10017.

FUNDING NEEDED
1. To cover general running expenses—$4,750 annually.
2. To move into the new kitchen and to complete the existing buildings—$7,500.
3. To develop plans for the new building—$66,000.

EDUCATIONAL BOARDING HOMES FOR ISRAELI CHILDREN

המפעל להכשרת ילדי ישראל

3 Wedgewood Street
German Colony
Jerusalem 93108
Telephone: (02) 663151
Office Hours: 7:30 A.M. to 3:00 P.M.

HISTORY AND DESCRIPTION

The Mifal, or the Educational Boarding Homes for Israeli Children, was created by Mrs. Recha Freier, the founder of Youth Aliyah, in 1943. Its purpose then was the gathering of street children in order to send them to kibbutzim for agricultural training. Since then, and particularly in the past few years, the organization has developed an original approach for the absorption and rehabilitation of children from destitute or broken homes, namely, family-type units within the framework of group homes and children's homes.

Goals: The organization's major goal is to absorb more children referred by various social agencies and social workers.

Services, Activities, and Accomplishments: The organization handles only mentally and physically healthy children. After careful processing, they are sent to one of the children's boarding homes where a group of about 10 children ages 6 to 14 live with "parents", a housemother and a counselor who are staff members. Five to seven such " families" constitutes a Children's Home. Today, more than a thousand children live in twelve homes, where they have been absorbed and rehabilitated.

OFFICERS

Director: Mrs. Rachel Sarfatti, Jerusalem. Inspector
                     of Education.
Executive
Director: Mr. Haim Dagan. Ministry of Education.
Board Members: Mr. Gadi Applebaum. Ministry of Education.
                     Mr. Eliezer Hatalmi. Pensioner.
                     Mr. Uri Fiksler. Ministry of Education.
                     Mrs. Hanni Ullman. Educator.

FINANCIAL INFORMATION

Most of the Boarding Homes' budget comes from the Minstry of Education; the remainder from donations. Last year's budget was $1,600,000. The organization is registered in Jerusalem as a non-profit Association (no. 11/347). Donations to the organization are tax-free in Israel (reg. no. 4500131), and in the U.S.A. through the P.E.F. Fund. One hundred full-time and one hundred part-time workers are employed in the Children's Homes.

MEMBERSHIP, SCOPE, AND POLICY
Decisions are made mostly by the Executive Director and the National Board.

AFFILIATIONS/REFERENCES
The organization is not affiliated with any political party in Israel. It is recognized by the PEF Israel Endowment Fund, 342 Madison Ave., N.Y.C. 10017.

FUNDING NEEDED
1. To build Children's Homes.
2. For upkeep of children in placement.
3. For playgrounds and sport facilities in the children's homes.

E.L.I.—ISRAELI ASSOCIATION FOR CHILD PROTECTION

אל"י – האגודה להגנת הילד

P.O.B. 33720
Tel Aviv
Telephone: (052) 70974 (Chairperson)

HISTORY AND DESCRIPTION
E.L.I. was founded in September 1979 by a group of concerned people. It was registered as an Ottoman Association in December 1979.
There are thousands of children in Israel who are helpless victims of serious abuse or neglect by their parents. E.L.I. has undertaken to create a network of volunteers to bring relief to these unfortunate children and to combat the phenomenon of child abuse.

Organizational Structure: A board of directors, with a chairperson, secretary, treasurer, and six additional board members.

Goals: The protection of children who are abused, molested, battered, neglected, or otherwise physically or emotionally endangered by their parents or custodians.

Services, Activities, and Accomplishments: (1) Providing advice and guidance to welfare workers and parents and promoting research on child abuse; (2) Offering immediate relief to abused children; (3) Collecting and distributing information to help locate and treat cases of child abuse; (4) Promoting stronger legislation in these areas.
E.L.I. cooperates with State and Municipal child welfare agencies. It is the first and only Association in Israel dealing with the problem of child abuse. Most Western countries and the U.S. have had such an association or a state agency for many years.

OFFICERS
>Dr. H. Zimrin, 60 Hameginim, Herzlia. Social Worker. Tel. (052) 70974.
>Mrs. G. Oshrat, 17 Aliya Shniya, Herzlia. Social Worker. Tel. (052) 88911.
>Mrs. M. Kerner, 17 Eshkol, Herzlia. Architect. Tel. (052) 77944.
>Mrs. M. Reizfeld, 65 Zahal, Tel Aviv. Social Worker. Tel. (03) 479637.
>Mrs. I. Eizenberg, 38 Eben Gvirol, Herzlia. Social Worker. Tel. (052) 54068.
>Mrs. H. Karo, 2/4 Mivza Kadesh, Tel Aviv. Social Worker. Tel. (03) 479942.
>Mr. I. Zimrin, 60 Hameginim, Herzlia. Architect. Tel. (052) 70974.
>Mr. N. Sinai, 11 Histadrut, Petah Tikva. Social Worker. Tel. (03) 914492.

FINANCIAL INFORMATION
98% of last year's annual budget came from donations; the remaining 2% came from membership dues. No other financial information was supplied.

MEMBERSHIP, SCOPE, AND POLICY
There are 42 members in the one branch in Israel.

FUNDING NEEDED
1. Employment of a part-time social worker, to coordinate volunteer activities, provide professional supervision and handle calls for help.
   Cost — $12,000.
2. Implementation of a reporting and inquiry system (possibly computerized) for locating abused children, including suitable advertisement to encourage reporting.
   Cost — $10,000.
3. Ongoing expenses, including office rental, insurance for volunteers, etc.
   Cost — $12,000 per year.

THE ELIEZER AND BLUMA GORDON FUND

קרן אליעזר ובלומה גורדון

P.O.B. 4069, Mesilat Yesharim, 13 Jerusalem
Telephone: (02) 631940

HISTORY AND DESCRIPTION

The Eliezer and Bluma Gordon Fund was founded in 1979 in commemoration of Eliezer and Bluma Gordon.

Goals: The fund has as its purposes the establishment of a multilanguage library for literature, the arts, society, and history; the organization of lectures, symposia, courses, as well as publications on the above subjects; and assistance to students, artists, and researchers on the above subjects through grants and prizes. The fund is in its early stages and is just beginning to function.

OFFICERS

Chairman: Shlomo Dinur, 2 Kaf-Tet B'November, Jerusalem.
Historian. Tel. (02) 631310.

Treasurer: Nachman Gordon, 19 Yishayahu, Tel Aviv.
Artisan. Tel. (03) 452951.

Members: Israel Goor, 45 Berlin, Jerusalem.
Editor. Tel. (02) 631940.
Dalia Bushy, 5 Hashoftim, Tel Aviv.
Clerk. Tel. (03) 286083.
Baruch Gordon, 49 Hanasy, Herzliya.
Interior Decorator. Tel. (03) 219358.
Binyamin Ventura, 12 Mendele Mocher Sforim,
Jerusalem. Clerk. Tel. (02) 661815.
Baruch Matzikofsky, 25 Hanegev, Holon. Industrialist.
Shlomo Sneh, 15 Etzel, Jerusalem.
Journalist. Tel. (02) 811813.

FINANCIAL INFORMATION

The income of the fund comes from donations. The organization is in its early stages and no information was supplied regarding budget. The fund is registered as an Ottoman Association (Israel reg. no. 11/3286) and donations are tax-free in Israel, but not in the U.S. The fund retains the services of two volunteers.

MEMBERSHIP, SCOPE, AND POLICY

Any interested person who puts in a special application can join. There are currently twelve members in Israel. Decisions are made by the Executive Director and National Board.

AFFILIATIONS/REFERENCES

The fund has no affiliations with political parties in Israel.

FUNDING NEEDED

Information not submitted.

EMET-LEYAAKOV YESHIVA
IN MEMORY OF THE LATE
RABBI YAAKOV LOFES

"אמת-יעקב" כולל ישיבה ע"ש הרב החסיד כמוהר"ר יעקב לופס

15 Chana Street
Jerusalem
Telephone: (02) 811317
Office hours: 1:00 P.M. to 8:00 P.M.

HISTORY AND DESCRIPTION

Yeshivat Emet LeYaakov is in memory of the late Rabbi Yaakov Lofes. The Yeshiva was founded in 1977. It is unique in that emphasis is placed on dawn prayers with study hours in early morning. Two goals are achieved: 1) Students become accustomed to prayers at dawn and to utilize the early hours of the morning for study. 2) Students are helped financially by the payment of a stipend for studying in the early hours in addition to the scholarship that they receive for their studies during the course of the day.

At first there were but a few students and the students studied in the early morning. The demand rose and today tens of students study all hours of the day. Many more wish to join our institution but must be rejected because of the limited budget.

In 1978 the Yeshiva subsidized the writing of a Torah scroll and hundreds of donators participated in this great mitzvah. After about two years, in 1980, the Torah dedication was held, and many people participated in the ceremony.

In 1980 a new branch of the Yeshiva was opened in the little town of Mevasseret Yerushalayim, near Jerusalem, so that Torah studies may be held in this community. Students travel daily to Mevasseret and some students from the vicinity have already joined the Kollel there.

There are plans to open additional branches in various parts of the country, but financial constraints have delayed the realization of these plans.

The organization's major accomplishment has been the expansion of the Yeshiva. Due to financial difficulties, the Kollel began with only a few Rabbis, but because of pressure from the public, the Yeshiva expanded these studies and now have a large Kollel.

OFFICERS

Director:
Rabbi Y. Abadi, 15 Chana, Jerusalem. Rabbi. Tel. (02) 811317.
Rabbi E. Tartner, 15 Chana, Jerusalem. Tel. (02) 813985.

President:
Rabbi S. Lofes, 22 Haavoda, Acco. The Chief Rabbi of Acco.

Board Members:
Rabbi S. Badani, 133 Rabbi Akiva, Bnei Brak.
Rabbi A. Salim, 3 Alfandri, Jerusalem.

FINANCIAL INFORMATION
65% of last year's annual budget came from donations, while the remaining 35% was aid provided by government Ministries. Last year's annual budget of $26,000 left a deficit of $4,800. Donations to the organization are tax-free in Israel (reg. no. 4505782). The Yeshiva is registered as an Ottoman Association, (reg. no. 11/2797). Donations to the Yeshiva are not tax-free in the United States. There was no indication of the number of employees.

AFFILIATIONS/REFERENCES
The Yeshiva is not affiliated with any political party in Israel. No other information was given.

FUNDING NEEDED
1. The establishment of a Building Fund to house the Yeshiva.
2. The establishment of additional branches throughout Israel.

THE EMANUEL JAFFE MUSEUM OF JEWISH EDUCATION

אגודת מוזיאון החינוך היהודי ע"ש עמנואל יפה

12 Hanassi
Jerusalem
Telephone: (02) 663131
Office hours: No fixed hours yet

HISTORY AND DESCRIPTION
The organization was founded in July 1978, after discussions and consultations with leading Israeli educators and with the Minister of Education and Culture and the Director-General of the Ministry of Education, who lent their support to the concept. It is intended to establish a Museum as soon as suitable temporary premises can be found. In the more distant future plans call for the construction of a building in Jerusalem which will be suitable for the project's purposes.

Organizational Structure: Activities are directed by the decisions adopted by the organization's Board which is composed of its founding members.

Goals: To gather, classify, catalogue, preserve and present a variety of educational materials (tools, instruments, equipment, games, books, certificates, etc.), both authentic and recreated, from the world of Jewish education in the Diaspora and in Israel throughout the generations. The organization is now looking for a temporary location in which to exhibit the collected materials.

Services, Activities, and Accomplishments: Since the establishment of the organization it has begun the collection of educational items for museum exhibits. It has also begun establishing contacts with the Israeli Teachers' Association, seminaries, universities, the Jewish Agency, and Jewish educators in the United States. When the museum is established, seminary days and conferences will be held, and the records of educational institutions, educational events, etc., will be kept there.

OFFICERS
Director: Yossef Yonai
Treasurer: Gedalia Ya'acobi
Board Members: Prof. Chava Jaffe
A. Shilon

FINANCIAL INFORMATION
The organization has received an initial grant of $1,500 from the Ministry of Education. It is registered as a non-profit Ottoman Association in Jerusalem (reg. no. 11/3056). Donations in Israel are tax-free (tax no. not supplied; information concerning tax status in USA not supplied). The organization at present employs one full-time worker as well as two volunteers.

MEMBERSHIP, SCOPE, AND POLICY
Supporters have not yet been enlisted as members. Decisions are made by the National Board.

AFFILIATIONS/REFERENCES
The organization is not affiliated with any Israeli political party nor yet with any other organization.

FUNDING NEEDED
1. To find suitable premises for the collection of materials and to hold modest exhibits (cost — $100,000).
2. To establish a working staff of experts; to travel to other countries to locate and gather material (cost — $15,000).

ENOSH — ORGANIZATION FOR THE ADVANCEMENT OF THE MENTALLY DISORDERED IN ISRAEL

"אנוש" אגודה לקידום נפגעי-נפש

P.O.B. 21672, Tel Aviv
Office hours: Daily

HISTORY AND DESCRIPTION

Enosh was founded in Tel Aviv in November 1978 by a group of families directly involved with the problem of the mentally disordered, and by professionals specializing in different aspects of the field. The inauguratory meeting was initiated by the mother of a girl who for several years had suffered from schizophrenia.

Organizational Structure: Enosh has a National Executive which meets once a month, and a National Council which meets three times a year. An annual meeting elects the bodies for the coming term. The National Executive consists of a National Chairman, Treasurer and Vice-Chairman, as well as a director of the fund-raising program, and a director of publicity; the two latter may add other members from the local branches, at their discretion. There is also a thirty-member Advisory Committee of Professionals in the different areas of this field. A Public Committee is currently being formed.

Goals: The principle goal is to alleviate the suffering of the mentally disordered and their families and dependents, by supplying facilities and services that are not provided by Goverment, local or health institutions. Enosh gives encouragement to the families and fosters mutual aid among them; it centralizes and distributes information to families and communities, and seeks to raise public awareness while erasing ignorance and prejudice, and the concomitant shame and stigma.

Services, Activities, and Accomplishments: Enosh is at present setting up an office in north Tel Aviv to serve as a National Center. For those who have been discharged from hospital, social clubs are being set up in Rehovot, Jerusalem, Ramat Gan and Ashdod, to serve as a bridge to normal society and working habits. Professionals and non-involved volunteers also organize the adoption of lonely and isolated sufferers, in or out of hospital. Enosh enables families to meet and to throw off shame and stigma; it helps them to cope with the daily strains thrust upon them, by sharing their similar burdens, and by benefitting from the guidance and inspiration of professional volunteers. Enosh helps the disordered to recover their self-respect and dignity when they return to society, and it has heightened public awareness in this respect. Seven national branches are in various stages of formation; the Club in Jerusalem is already operating (on a shoestring budget). The organization publishes a bulletin, "News of Enosh".

OFFICERS

Director: Chanita Rodney, Moshav Timorim 79-430.
              Housewife. Tel. (055) 82245.

Treasurer:	Mordechai Lavie, De Haas 10, Tel Aviv.
	Tel. (03) 448431.
Board Members:	Professor David Naor, Divrei Yerucham 2,
	Jerusalem. Tel. (02) 423256.
	Judge Moshe Duar, Sirkin 18, Givatayim.
	Tel. (03) 722842.
	Eliyahu Harel, Naveh Re'im 24, Ramat Hasharon.
	Tel. (03) 474741.
	Yosef Ross, Hamacabi 6, Ramat Gan.
	Tel. (03) 721845.
	Yehuda Pimental, David Hamelech 42a, Herzliya.
	Tel. (052) 32016.
	Marta Ramon, Harlap 52, Jerusalem.
	Tel. (02) 635826.
	Tova Feigenbaum, Glizenstein 5, Tel Aviv.
	Tel. (03) 240579.

FINANCIAL INFORMATION

7% of last year's annual budget came from membership dues ($4 per family); 7% ($200) from a Sick Fund grant; 14% ($400) from the Ministry of Welfare, and 72% from the Jerusalem Town Council, the Office of the President, the Jerusalem Foundation, Liverpool Aid to Israel, and British Friends of Enosh. Last year's annual budget for organizational activities, excluding the various projects, was $12,000. There was no deficit. Donations are tax-free in Israel, the United States and other countries (no registration numbers supplied). Enosh is registered as an Ottoman Association (Tel Aviv, reg. no. 6967/99). The organization has no full-time or part-time workers; it is staffed by tens of volunteers.

AFFILIATIONS/REFERENCES

1. National Schizophrenic Fellowship, 79 Victoria Road, Surrey, England.
2. Schizophrenia Association of Great Britain, Llanfair Hall, Carnavon, Wales.
3. Ontario Friends of Schizophrenics, Room 2016, 1001 Queen Street, W. Toronto, Ontario, Canada.
4. "Mind", Mental Health Association, 22 Harley Street, London, England.
   Enosh is not affiliated with any political party in Israel.

FUNDING NEEDED

1. To establish a National Center and a Tel Aviv branch office, with a half-time paid secretary and telephone: $300 per month. Printing and postage: $100 per month.
2. To cover the printing and mailing ($1,600) of the quarterly publication "News of Enosh". So far, 1,500 mailing addresses are listed.
3. To operate Social Clubs for those in the process of rehabilitation, whether before or after discharge from hospital. The Clubs serve as a bridge to regular social and working habits. The sum needed by each Club, per month is $600.

EZRAT HOLIM (AID FOR THE SICK) ORGANIZATION, REHOVOT

ארגון עזרת חולים – רחובות

P.O.B. 1233
Rehovot
Telephone: (054) 57544
Office hours: Not specified. Held at the secretary's home,
Eliyahu Yeret, Rechov Ezra 36B, Rehovot.

HISTORY AND DESCRIPTION
The Ezrat Holim Organization was founded in 1973. All members of the organization are volunteers, including doctors and others of the medical professions. The Organization helps the sick in every possible way:
1) Visits to hospitals, convalescent homes, and private homes. Members give financial and spiritual support to sick or recuperating people.
2) Blood donations for members' benefit or individuals in need.
3) Courses for members and others in first aid and other medical subjects.
4) Establishment of medical institutions.
5) Support of activities to aid sick and recuperating patients either financially or by volunteer work in institutions and private homes.
6) Provision of medical appliances and equipment, which is given free to the sick for the period needed.
7) Nurses and other medical staff are sent by the organization with or without payment. Poor patients' needs are handled according to case.

The annual budget does not reflect the scope of activities since most of the medical equipment loaned to the sick has been donated and all members are volunteers. The office of the organization is the secretary's home, no rent is paid, there are no office expenses, and the place where the medical appliances are kept costs nothing. Members handle lending of equipment, drive patients to treatment, and all other activities are also performed by volunteers.

OFFICERS
Director: Rabbi S. Cook, 4 Shimony Rehovot. Chief Rabbi. Tel.: (054) 52993.
Treasurer: F. Glovinski, 50 Ezra, Rehovot. Merchant.
Board Members: S. Cohen, 48 Ezra, Rehovot. Accountant.
B. Polak, 6 Nordau, Rehovot. Principal.
Y. Zilberberg, 48 Ezra, Rehovot. Bookkeeper.
Secretary: E. Yeret, 36 Ezra, Rehovot. Secretary.

FINANCIAL INFORMATION
The annual budget for last year was received from the following sources: membership dues, 50%; donations, 30%; public institutions, 15%; and from special events, 5%. Last year's annual budget was $10,000, with no deficit. The organization is registered as an Ottoman Association, but

no number was supplied. Donations to the organization are not tax-free. There are no employees of the organization. However, there are 200 volunteers.

MEMBERSHIP, SCOPE, AND POLICY
There are 200 members in Israel, with no members or branches abroad. Decisions are made by the Board.

AFFILIATIONS/REFERENCES
The organization is not affiliated with any political party in Israel, and has no connections abroad.

FUNDING NEEDED
1. The construction of a recovery home for mother and baby when leaving the maternity hospital. Estimated cost: $60,000.
2. Dental clinic for the poor. Estimated cost: $70,000.
3. Funds for loans to sick and poor people in need of medical treatment for chronic illnesses.

EZRATH TORAH OF AMERICA, IN ISRAEL

עזרת תורה דאמריקה בישראל

Sanhedria Murchevet
P.O.B. 6228, Jerusalem
Telephone: (02) 810714/7
Office Hours: Sunday to Thursday, 8:00 A.M. to 5:00 P.M.
                Friday, 8:00 A.M. to 12:00 noon

HISTORY AND DESCRIPTION

Ezrath Torah, the Fortress of Torah charity, was established by leaders of the American Rabbinate in 1915 with the goal of extending help to thousands of Jewish refugees who fled from Eastern Europe during World War One. Through the efforts of various European religious leaders, aid found its way to remote places such as Siberia and the Ukraine, thereby helping thousands of Jews to escape and save their families. Ezrath Torah continued its efforts during the inter-war period by supporting the settlement of many needy Jewish families throughout Europe and the United States, and during the Second World War, it endeavoured to save Jewish lives through settlement in the United States and in Israel. During the last decade, the organization has shifted most of its activities toward the assistance of needy yeshiva students and rabbis throughout Israel.

Goals: The aim of Ezrath Torah of America is to provide assistance to tens of thousands of needy religious families throughout Israel, mostly through the efforts of its Jerusalem Center (opened in 1970).

Services, Activities, and Accomplishments: Ezrath Torah currently provides assistance to tens of thousands of indigent families for a variety of needs, usually through the granting of marriage, birth, holiday and medical expenses grants. These grants are given to all needy yeshiva students and their families. The organization includes among its major accomplishments the building of 800 apartments in Jerusalem and Bnei Brak, plus the completion of another 1200 apartments within the next three years; 950 dwelling loans granted to needy yeshiva students, and over 6000 regular loans granted to needy families totaling approximately $1 million; and the granting of marriage expenses to more than 20,000 young couples over the last decade. The organization also maintains the Ezrath Torah Interest-Free Loan Fund, compsed of more than 350 individual funds carrying the names of donors who contributed to their establishment.

OFFICERS

Chairman of
the Board: Mr. A. Werdiger, Sorotzkin 16, Jerusalem.
                    Party Secretary. Tel. (02) 535187.
                 Rabbi A. J. Dolgin, Ramat Hagolan 17, Jerusalem.
                    Rabbi. Tel. (02) 811256.

Treasurer: Rabbi E.C. Shapiro, Yehuda Hamacabi, Jerusalem.
               Rabbi. Tel. (02) 524878.
               Mr. J. Halperin, Bayit Vegan 99, Jerusalem.
               Banker. Tel. (02) 410777.
               Rabbi Baruch Siniak, Even Haezel 3, Jerusalem.
               Director. Tel. (02) 812611.

FINANCIAL INFORMATION
80% of Ezrath Torah's income is achieved through donations; the balance from governmental sources in Israel. There are no membership dues. Last year's annual budget of $441,522 left the organization with a deficit of $90,992. Donations to Ezrath Torah of America are tax-free both in Israel and in the United States, if made under the name of Torah Relief Society (Israel reg. no. 4502595; no IRS number reported). Ezrath Torah is registered as an Ottoman Association (reg. no. 11/1712, Jerusalem). The organization employs 4 full-time and 3 part-time workers, as well as 3 volunteers.

MEMBERSHIP, SCOPE, AND POLICY
Decisions regarding the operation of Ezrath Torah are made by its National Board. Information regarding membership, branches, and criteria for membership was not supplied.

AFFILIATIONS/REFERENCES
Ezrath Torah of America in Israel is not aligned with any Israeli political party. It is affiliated with Rabbinical organizations and congregations in the United States.

FUNDING NEEDED
1. Establishment of additional loan funds. A fund is established by contributing $1,000 or more;
2. Financial help toward the building of apartments to aid young couples in purchasing their first home. Donations of $500 or more are accepted;
3. Contributions toward grants provided to married yeshiva students for marriage, birth, holiday and medical expenses.

FEDERATION OF JEWISH RELIEF ORGANISATIONS IN GREAT BRITAIN

הפדרציה לארגוני עזרה יהודיים בבריטניה

47 Rothschild
Tel Aviv
Telephone: (03) 299711, 291711
Office hours: 9:00 A.M. to 3:00 P.M.

HISTORY AND DESCRIPTION
The organization is based on the Federation of Jewish Relief Organizations of Great Britain, which was established many years ago, and registered as a charity. It has been active in Israel for over 25 years. The main activity in the past was contributing to the upkeeping of children in various nurseries throughout the country. The organization also built the Bikirei Haitim Youth Centre in Tel Aviv in the sixties.

Goals: To contribute to education, culture and welfare in Israel.

Services, Activities, and Accomplishments: Since 1970 the organization has branched out and its main activity in the past decade has been the building of day care nurseries in the Lachish and Shafir areas, youth centres in Beer Sheba, Naharia, Tel Aviv, and libraries in Kiriat Bialik and Naharia. The Federation is now about to begin with contributions for the establishment of computer systems in classes in schools beginning with Lachish which will be attached to the computer in Ben Gurion University. In addition the organization maintains a warehouse where used clothing received from England is distributed to the children in the various nurseries and welfare recipients. Major accomplishments of the Federation have been the establishment of thirteen nurseries in the Lachish and Shafir area, and of the Tel Aviv Youth Centre.

OFFICERS
Director:
: V. Hazan, 47 Rothschild, Tel Aviv.
  Advocate.
  Tel. (03) 291711.

Board Members:
: Doris Gruszka, 4 Shalom Aleichem, Honorary Secretary, Tel Aviv. Housewife.
  L. Questle, London and Tel Aviv.

FINANCIAL INFORMATION
100% of the organization's income comes from donations from the Federation of Jewish Relief Organisations. Last year's annual budget of $65,000 left the Federation with a balanced budget. The Federation is registered in Tel Aviv as a non-profit Ottoman Association (reg. no. 1248/99). Donations in Israel and in Great Britain are tax-free (Tax nos. not supplied). Four full-time and one part-time workers are employed by the Federation, as well as two volunteers.

MEMBERSHIP, SCOPE, AND POLICY

Membership is restricted in Israel, being mainly in England. There are 10 members in Israel, in one branch, and over 50 abroad, in one branch. Decisions are made after consultations with authorities of the F.J.R.O. in Great Britain and are subject to London's approval.

AFFILIATION/REFERENCES

The Federation is not affiliated with any Israeli political party. It has contacts with the Chief Rabbi of England.

FUNDING NEEDED

1. Lachish Schools—$35,000.
2. Naharia Library—$137,000.
3. Margulies Youth Centre in Beer Sheba—$40,000.

FREE LOAN FUND
LE'ICHUD MISHPACHOT

קרן גמילות חסד לאיחוד משפחות

Panim Meirot St. 5, Entrance 3,
Jerusalem
Telephone: (02) 531791

HISTORY AND DESCRIPTION

The Free Loan Fund "Le'ichud Mishpachot" founded in 1970, is a non-profit organization with an elected council. It operates several funds in the names of various benefactors. Thousands of needy have been aided by the organization.

Services, Activities, and Accomplishments: The Fund provides grants and interest-free loans to new immigrants from the Soviet Union and other countries. It helps them with their initial expenses in setting up homes in Israel and in providing suitable Torah-education for their children. In addition, the Fund provides advisory and counselling services to immigrants in the areas of family relations, educational opportunities, vocational training and financial planning. The various charitable funds operated by the organization distributed approximately $30,000 in the last year, and provided free counselling services to hundreds of immigrants. The organization was instrumental in helping many families from the Soviet Union settle in religious communities in Israel and send their youngsters to yeshivot. The Fund also works closely with "Yeshivat HaNegev" in Netivot in operating a special department in the Yeshiva for Russian youngsters and married pupils. Besides the free loans, the Fund is active in organizing the sending of packages and money to needy families in Russia—in particular to candidates for Aliya.

OFFICERS

Director: Rabbi Chaim Meir Kahana, Panim Meirot 5, Jerusalem. Rabbi. Tel. (02) 531791.

Treasurer: Dr. P. Weisberg, Mapu 6, J-m. Orthodontist. Tel. (02) 231350.

Board Members: M. Stern, Aza 48, J-m.
J. Halperin, B. Hirsh 16, J-m.
M. Wagner, Metudela 36, J-m. Rabbi.
Rabbi D.M. Luria, Panim Meirot 9, J-m.
M. Aviv, Ben Gurion 51, Tel Aviv.

FINANCIAL INFORMATION

The organization's sole source of income is from donations. Last year's annual budget was $42,500, with no deficit recorded for that period. Donations to the organization in Israel are not tax-free. Donations from the U.S.A. have been directed through "EZER" Inc., located in Brooklyn, N.Y. Contributions to "EZER" Inc. are tax-free (I.R.S. number not supplied). The Fund in Israel is registered as a non-profit Ottoman Association in the Jerusalem District Office of the Ministry of the Interior (reg. no. 11/1800). Three volunteers serve the organization.

MEMBERSHIP, SCOPE, AND POLICY
Membership is open to anyone. The organization currently has 1 branch operating in Israel. Decisions are made mostly at committee meetings.

AFFILIATIONS/REFERENCES
The organization is affiliated with "EZER" Inc., 1137-53rd Street, Brooklyn, N.Y. 11219. It is not connected with any political party in Israel.

FRIENDS OF CONVERTS IN ISRAEL
ברית ידידי הגר בישראל

P.O.B. 3333, Tel Aviv—Telephone: (03) 479786, (03) 225853
P.O.B. 6431, Haifa—Telephone: (04) 81050
P.O.B. 618, Beersheva—Telephone: (057) 78787
P.O.B. 1172, Netanya—Telephone: (053) 24110
Office hours: available on request

HISTORY AND DESCRIPTION

Friends of Converts in Israel was established in 1972 and serves every candidate for conversion to Judaism according to Jewish law, through training, counselling and encouragement.

Goals: The goal of the organization is to ease the way for those sincerely interested in converting to Judaism in Israel.

Services, Activities, and Accomplishments: Every petitioner to the Friends of Converts in Israel receives an individual response containing general and specified explanations regarding the procedure for conversion in the State of Israel. The Society makes use of contacts with all Rabbinical Courts and other authorized institutions for conversion in Israel and abroad, with teachers, lawyers, and all individuals who might be able to help the convert. If necessary, members of the organization will plead for the applicant before the Court, or, upon request, teach the prospective convert about the principles and laws of Judaism. Sometimes, the organization will take care of the applicant's expenses during the waiting period prior to examination before the Rabbinical Court. The Friends of Converts regards as its single major accomplishment the role which it has played in the successful completion of conversion applications.

OFFICERS

Director: Moshe Dothan, Ophir 23a, Tel Aviv.
                    Engineer. Tel. (03) 479786.

Treasurer: Abba Minin, Shulamit 3, Tel Aviv.
                    Merchant. Tel. (03) 232908.

Board: Dr. S.Z. Zeitlin, Amsterdam 7, Tel Aviv.
                    Physician. Tel. (03) 225853.
                    Abraham Erlichman, Nanege 7, Netanya.
                    Official. Tel. (053) 24110.
                    Noa Krauze, Ben-Yehuda 142, Tel Aviv.
                    Lawyer. Tel. (03) 222303.
                    Lea Aloufy, Rothschild 123, Tel Aviv.
                    Housewife. Tel. (03) 224652.
                    Ilan Hameiri, Azar 3, Bnei Brak.
                    Programmer. Tel. (03) 798016.

FINANCIAL INFORMATION
Membership dues and donations each account for approximately 50% of the income of the Friends of Converts in Israel. For the last year, the organization had neither a formal budget nor a deficit. The society is registered as an Ottoman Association (reg. no. 5548/99). Based upon the information supplied, it is not certain whether or not donations to the Friends of Converts are tax-free in either Israel or the United States. There are no paid employees in the organization; only volunteers.

MEMBERSHIP, SCOPE, AND POLICY
An estimated 200 "informal" members are represented by the organization's 5 Israeli branches. There are no formal branches outside of Israel. Membership is open to anyone prepared to contribute to the society's purpose. Decisions are taken by members present at meetings.

AFFILIATIONS/REFERENCES
The Friends of Converts in Israel is not associated with any Israeli political party. It is in contact with the *United Israel World Union,* 507 5th Avenue, New York City, New York.

FUNDING NEEDED
1. Increasing the number of actual, true converts out of all the applicants for conversion. Funding for education materials and lessons.
2. Reducing the difficulties of applicants during the mandatory waiting period, by providing maintenance and support.
3. Providing for the performance of conversions according to the principles of religious law.

THE FRIENDS OF THE MIDRASHIA

חוג ידידי המדרשיה בישראל

Head Office:
3 Achuzat Bait Street,
Tel Aviv
Telephone: (03) 652637/8
Office hours: 9:00 A.M. to 4:00 P.M.

HISTORY AND DESCRIPTION

The Friends of the Midrashia is the public backbone and financial instrument of the Midrashia institutions:

a) Midrashiat Noam, a Yeshiva High School founded in 1945 at Pardess Hannah, mid-way between Tel Aviv and Haifa, is the first of its kind in Israel. It has nearly 500 pupils, all housed in a dormitory.

b) Kiryat Yaacov Herzog, a junior high school, founded in 1972, at Kfar Saba, with about 320 pupils most of whom are housed in a dormitory.

c) For the school year of 1979/80 a new institution was established at Kfar Saba — Neot Yaacov — a higher academy for training teachers in Talmud and other Jewish subjects, who will teach at the institutions of Midrashiat Noam.

Goals: To provide gifted boys with a first-class education, harmoniously combining secular studies which lead to the matriculation examinations, with a solid Jewish religious learning and character training. This education can enable them to successfully fill key positions in the intellectual, social and economic life of Israel. Students from abroad are very welcome. Both schools enjoy the full recognition and supervision of the Ministry of Education and Culture, which has repeatedly expressed its high appreciation of their performance and achievements. Admission is based on merit and ability only and not on the financial means of parents. Nearly 50% of the boys belong to Oriental communities.

Services, Activities, and Accomplishments: The establishment of two large educational institutions at Pardess Hannah and Kfar Saba, with synagogues, school buildings, dormitories, libraries, dining halls and kitchens, gymnasium and sporting grounds, laboratories and the Computer Science Unit.

Midrashia believes that Israel's superiority over its enemies depends on the moral, intellectual and technological quality of its leadership and its boys. It provides a religiously motivated intelligentsia. Of the 4,500 and more graduates, many hold leading and highly responsible posts in Israel's religious and academic life, in its economy and professions, in its army and Civil Service.

OFFICERS

Director General: Israel Sadan.
Chairman: Yechiel Sugarman.

| Co-Treasurers: | Yaacov Lesloi, Aaron Meir. |
| Board Members: | Bernard Hochstein, Beno Gitter, Rabbi Israel Law, Meir Silverstone L.L.B., Israel Azrieli L.L.B., Shlomo Ein Chai, Rabbi Dr. Alexander Carlebach, Yehoshua Neeman L.L.B., Shalom Aberdam, Menachem Waldner, Eli Hartman, A. Pollack. |

FINANCIAL INFORMATION

The budget is divided as follows: 25% from the parents of the students (maintenance fees); 10% from donations of private individuals; 30% from the Israeli government; 20% from scholarship funds and public organizations. The remaining 15% is a deficit. Efforts are made to cover the deficit by donations from private people, scholarship funds and public causes. Last year's annual budget was $2 million. The Yeshiva has an accumulated deficit to date of $400,000. It is registered as an Ottoman Association in Tel Aviv (No. 503/99). Donations to the Yeshiva are tax-free in Israel, the United States, and Switzerland (no numbers were supplied). There are 115 full-time and 95 part-time employees of the Yeshiva.

Large accumulated and current deficits are a cause of concern, in addition to a necessary development program. The Friends of the Midrashia in Israel and the Diaspora have built the campuses, and remain responsible for the full development, and they are involved with current budget problems.

MEMBERSHIP, SCOPE, AND POLICY

There are 3000 members in Israel and approximately 1000 members abroad with three branches in Israel and six branches abroad. Most decisions are made by the National Board and by sub-committees elected by the Board.

AFFILIATIONS/REFERENCES

The Midrashia is not affiliated with any political party in Israel. The following organizations abroad know of the work of the Midrashia:

England:	Mr. Andrew Braude, Acting Chairman of The Friends of the Midrashia Central House, 32-66 High Street, London E 15 2PD.
U.S.A.:	American Friends of the Midrashia, c/o Mr. Bernard Hochstein, President; Mr. Joachim Rudoler — Treasurer, H.W.R. Corporation, 1895 Federal Street, Camden, N.J. 08105; The Federated Council of Israel Institutions Inc., 15 Beekman Street, New York, N.Y. 10038; The P.E.F. Israel Endowment Funds Inc., 511 Fifth Avenue, New York, N.Y. 10017.
Switzerland:	Mr. Michael J. Floersheim, Chairman, Friends of the Midrashia, Susenbergstrasse 153, 8044 Zurich; Dr. David Lifshitz, Secretary General, 33 Solomon Vogelin Str., Zurich 8038.

Representative in Geneve: Prof. Jean E. Halperin, 55
Route de Florissande, 1206 Geneve.

South Africa: Rabbi B. Casper, Chief Rabbi, President of The
Friends of the Midrashia, P.O. Box, 2183 Johannesburg.

FUNDING NEEDED

1. A special Scholarship Fund bearing the name of the donor may be established at a minimum donation of $10,000.
2. An additional wing to the school building at Kiryat Yaacov Herzog, Kfar Saba, and an auditorium. Cost $750,000.
3. Swimming pools at both institutions. ($1,000,000)
4. Establishment of a Micro-Computer trend which is a combination of Electronics and Computer trends. The minimum investment needed is $100,000.

FRIENDS OF THE ROTHSCHILD UNIVERSITY HOSPITAL

אגודת ידידי בית חולים רוטשילד, חיפה

43 Golomb
P.O.B. 4940
Haifa
Telephone: (04) 671693
Office hours: 8:00 A.M. to 12:00 noon

HISTORY AND DESCRIPTION
The Friends Association of the Rothschild University Hospital was founded in 1960 in order to assist the Hospital in performing as a quality center for medical care in Haifa and throughout northern Israel.

Goals: The patients' welfare is of prime concern, determining the form which the support of the Friends Association will take. The association is dedicated, as well, to developing a public awareness of the Hospital's problems, thereby hoping to alleviate them.

Services, Activities, and Accomplishments: Helping to acquire new and sophisticated diagnostic (treatment and) equipment ranks high on the list of services, as does the advancement of medical research. The association has assisted in financing medical equipment and improving the standard of hospitalization for the benefit of the patient.

OFFICERS
Chairman: Mr. Zvi Herrer, Former Mayor of Kiryat Ata.
                Tel. (04) 671693.
Treasurer: Mr. Mordechai Katz, Bank Director.
                Tel. (04) 671693.
Board Members: Mr. Reuven Ben-Zvi, Journalist.
                Tel. (04) 674674.
                Mrs. Rivka Davidas, Housewife.
                Tel. (04) 671693.
                Dr. Shimon Kedar, M.D.
                Prof. Ludwig Podoshin, M.D.
                Mr. Yoel Sagi, Manager Haifa Auditorium.
                Tel. (04) 80013.
                Dr. Dov T. Golan, M.D., Hospital Director.

FINANCIAL INFORMATION
The Friends of the Rothschild University Hospital finances its services through donations and volunteer fund-raising activities. 63.7% of last year's budget came from donations, 0.5% from membership dues, 28.8% as allocations from various institutions, and 7% from other sources. Last year's annual budget of $180,000 left the Association with an accumulated deficit of $600,000, expected to reach $1,000,000 for 1980-1981. The organization is registered as a non-profit Ottoman

Association (reg. no. 61/635). Donations to the Friends in Israel and the United States are tax-free (Israeli tax no. 4503642, USA no. not supplied). Three part-time workers are employed by the Friends as well as thirty volunteers.

MEMBERSHIP, SCOPE, AND POLICY
Membership is open to everybody who is willing to pay membership fees and is accepted by the Board of Directors. There are approximately 500 members with one branch in Israel and one branch in the United States. Decisions are made by the National Board.

AFFILIATIONS/REFERENCES
Friends of the Rothschild University Hospital,
c/o Leon Angel, 48 Prospect Park S.W., Brooklyn, N.Y. 11215
Tel. (212) 499-6200, Telex 422719

PEF, Israel Endowment Funds Inc.,
342 Madison Ave., N.Y., 10173
Tel. (212) 687-2400

FUNDING NEEDED
1. To complete the new 11-floor West Wing of the Rothschild University Hospital. Early in 1980, a high level decision was reached by the Minister of Health, the Mayor of Haifa, and the Chairman of the Friends of Rothschild University Hospital, necessitated by the ever-worsening economic squeeze. A plea for assistance would be made to the Diaspora community. By the end of 1982, when the centennial of modern Haifa and the 60th anniversary of Rothschild University Hospital will be celebrated, the Friends of the Hospital vowed to raise a minimum of $5,000,000 to complete and equip the new West Wing. This sum represents approximately 50% of the $10,000,000 which is needed. The total cost of the entire project is approximately $28,000,000, $18,000,000 of which has already been spent in building the new West Wing.
2. To assist in purchasing new medical equipment.
3. To assist in the advancement of medical research.
4. To improve standards of hospitalization for the patients' benefit.

FRIENDS OF THE HOME FOR YOUNG DISABLED IN SAN-SIMON, KATAMON, JERUSALEM

אגודת ידידי מעון לנכים בסן־סימון, קטמון, ירושלים

Katamon,
Jerusalem
Telephone: (02) 668517

HISTORY AND DESCRIPTION
Different public figures, interested in general in the welfare and fate of invalids, and in particular in the welfare and fate of invalids in the Home For Young Disabled in San-Simon, were active individually over a long period of time and volunteered to help the Home. It was subsequently decided to join forces in creating one organization. At the meeting which took place in May, 1979, the Friends of the Home for Young Disabled in San-Simon was established, a constitution was agreed upon, and officers were elected.

Organizational Structure: The Annual General Meeting is the organization's supreme body and elects its officers: Chairman, Vice-Chairman, Secretary, Treasurer, and Control Committee. The Committee directs operations and oversees funds.

Goals: To advance the invalids of the San-Simon Home for Young Disabled, socially, culturally, and medically; to improve the conditions of life in the Home; to collect grants and donations for these purposes.

Services, Activities, and Accomplishments: The Association helps the crippled children in the Home in general, and tries to satisfy individual needs, especially those of invalids who move into apartments of their own following the process of rehabilitation, helping them to seek independence within the healthy community.

OFFICERS
Chairman: Dr. Baruch Zvi Ophir
Vice-Chairman: Ursul Liebshtetter
Treasurer: David Bar-Levi
Secretary: Michelle Rosenberg
Board Member: Dorit Weiler

FINANCIAL INFORMATION
100% of the Association's incomes comes from donations. As it has only recently been established the Association has not yet fixed an annual budget. It is registered in Jerusalem as a non-profit Ottoman Association (reg. no. 11/3250). Donations in Israel are tax-free (tax no. 4507086); donations in the United States are not tax-free. The Association does not employ any workers.

MEMBERSHIP, SCOPE, AND POLICY
Membership is open to anyone interested and willing to help. There are at present 10 members in Israel. Decisions are made by the Committee.

AFFILIATIONS/REFERENCES
The Association is not affiliated with any Israeli political party.

FUNDING NEEDED
In 1979 the San-Simon Home for Young Disabled commenced a fundamental renovation of the building. As a result of inflation, costs have risen far above the means of the various partners in the project. Construction and renovation is in danger of being curtailed if the Friends organization is not successful in raising the necessary funds for completion of the project in the near future.

GAN YAVNE YOUTH VILLAGE—
YESHIVAT ACHUZAT YAAKOV

ישיבת אחוזת יעקב — קרית נוער גן יבנה

P.O.B. 31, Gan Yavne
Telephone: (055) 94328, (055) 94414
Office hours: 8:30 A.M. to 4:30 P.M.

HISTORY AND DESCRIPTION

The Gan Yavne Youth Village, Yeshivat Achuzat Yaakov, was founded in 1962 by the Rabbinical Council of America. It makes available to its 250 students a full program of Judaic and general high-school studies, and provides them with vocational training in electronics, mechanics or woodwork. The Youth Village, which also provides dining and dormitory facilities, is under the supervision of Israel's Ministry of Education and Culture, and receives guidance for the technical programs from ORT. A junior high-school division has recently been inaugurated.

Goals: The education of boys from intellectually and socially disadvantaged backgrounds, and providing them with vocational training which enables them to find work as skilled craftsmen and contribute to Israel's economy.

Services, Activities, and Accomplishments: The student body of the Gan Yavne Youth Village comprises a wide spectrum of Israeli youth from varied North African and Asian backgrounds. Becuase of the social problems which many of these youngsters face in their home environment and the frustration they experience in their elementary education, the future they can anticipate is a bleak one. By inculcating a pride in their heritage and by preparing them to become accomplished craftsmen and skilled technicians, the Youth Village promotes its students' self-esteem and self-confidence. They are directed into productive roles in society and are enabled to raise their economic and social level, breaking out of the cycle of poverty and despair. At the same time, Israel is provided with important skills needed to further the technological development of the country.

The past five years have been a period of very rapid development for the Youth Village. There has been a significant increase in the number of students, and new facilities have been built, including a technological center (1976) and a dining hall (1979) and carpentry workshop building (1979). A dormitory financed by the Agency for International Development is currently under construction.

OFFICERS

Director:	Rabbi Moshe Furst, Rechovot. Administrator. Tel. (054) 72497.
Chairman:	Rabbi Israel Tabak, Jerusalem. Rabbi. Tel. (02) 420979.
Dean:	Rabbi Moshe Z. Galinsky, Gan Yavne. Educator. Tel. (055) 94328.

Treasurer:	Yosef Gibraltar, Moshav Hemed. Administrator. Tel. (03) 944159.
Hon. Chairmen:	Rabbi M. Solomon, Jerusalem. Tel. (02) 811218.
	Rabbi M. Lewittes, Jerusalem. Tel. (02) 667195.
Treasurer:	Rabbi L. Oschry, Jerusalem. Tel. (02) 637182.
Vice-Chairmen:	Rabbi Fred Hollander, Jerusalem. Tel. .(02) 810253.
	Rabbi B. Morgenstern, Jerusalem. Tel. (02) 638460.
Board Members:	Rabbi Emanuel Rackman. Tel. (03) 752115.
	Rabbi Louis Bernstein, New York City. Chairman of Committee in the United States.

FINANCIAL INFORMATION

35% of last year's annual budget came from Youth Aliyah and the Welfare Ministry, 30% from the Ministry of Education and Culture, 20% from donations, 10% from the Ministry of Religion, and the balance from miscellaneous sources (Joint, Local Council, etc.). Last year's annual budget of $700,000 left Gan Yavne with a deficit of $120,000. The Gan Yavne Youth Village is a recognized non-profit organization (Israel reg.: under Yeshivat Achuzat Yaakov, no. 682/1; under Kiryat Noar Gan Yavne, no. 685/1). Donations to the Youth Village in Israel and the United States may be made tax-free (no tax numbers supplied). The Gan Yavne Youth Village employs sixty-three full-time and thirteen part-time workers on a permanent basis.

MEMBERSHIP, SCOPE, AND POLICY

The Gan Yavne Youth Village has 100 members in Israel. Membership is open to anyone, and members of the Rabbinical Council of America in Israel are automatic members. Policy decisions for the Youth Village are made by the Board, and are implemented by the Director and educational officers.

AFFILIATIONS/REFERENCES

The Gan Yavne Youth Village has no political affiliations in Israel. It maintains contact with: American Friends of Gan Yavne Youth Village — Yeshivath Achuzat Yaakov, 1250 Broadway, New York City, N.Y. 10001; the Rabbinical Council of America, 1250 Broadway, New York City, N.Y. 10001; and the Canadian Friends of Hadarom Schools, c/o Seymour Brudner, Leo Wynberg and Associates, 1183 Finch Avenue West, Ste. 500, Downsview, Ontario, Canada.

FUNDING NEEDED

1. To cover the growing maintenance deficit by providing scholarships (full scholarship $1000, half scholarship $500).
2. $350,000 — To complete new dormitory currently under construction.
3. $1,500,000 — To build a recreation-science building and swimming pool.

GEMILLUT HESED FUND OF THE WORLD COUNCIL OF SYNAGOGUES AND THE CENTER FOR CONSERVATIVE JUDAISM

קרן גמילות חסד של המועצה העולמית
לבתי כנסת קונסרבטיבים

Agron Street 2
P.O.B. 7456, Jerusalem
Telephone: (02) 226386, 227463
Office hours: Sunday-Thursday: 8:00 A.M. to 3:00 P.M.
Fridays and holiday eves., 8:00 to 12 noon.

HISTORY AND DESCRIPTION

Following the Yom Kippur War, funds were directed to the Jerusalem office of the World Council of Synagogues and the Center for Conservative Judaism by members and friends abroad who were anxious to help many dislocated families in need. These monies, which were distributed in trust funds to the families, became the basis of the permanent Gemillut Hesed Fund of the organization.

Goals: The organization has set as its goal the personalized servicing of needy individuals, families and groups. Contributions are also made to scholarship funds and special projects of philanthropic organizations, based on proper screening by authorized professionals. The objective is to minimize bureaucratic processes, and, wherever possible, to achieve the ideal of being an anonymous donor.

Services, Activities and Accomplishments: The organization and Center have been successful in filling a genuine need and reaching out to those who, for various reasons, have not been assisted by other institutions. In addition, they have been able to provide assistance to their own scholarship fund for underprivileged children who attend their Jerusalem Day Camp under the auspices of Camp Ramah and the Center for Conservative Judaism. They have also provided aid to their Women's League volunteers in their braille and tape projects for the blind.

OFFICERS

Director: Dr. P. Schindler, P.O.B. 7456, Jerusalem.
                Academician. Tel. (02) 226386/227463.

Treasurer: Dr. Y. Green, P.O.B. 7456, Jerusalem.
                Rabbi. Tel. (02) 223539.

Board Members: Rabbi B. Segal, Shimoni 4, Jerusalem.
                Retired. Tel. (02) 668718.
                Mr. M. Bargteil, Ben Tabbai 4, Jerusalem.
                Retired. Tel. (02) 664278.
                Mr. Yitzhak Jacobson, P.O.B. 7456, Jerusalem.
                Educator. Tel. (02) 226386, 227463.
                Dr. Aaron Singer, Efrata 28, Jerusalem.
                Academician. Tel. (02) 713419.

FINANCIAL INFORMATION

100% of last year's annual budget came from non-solicited sources in the form of donations. The annual budget for last year came to $3,000, with no deficit. Donations to the Fund in both the U.S.A. and Israel are tax-free (I.R.S. Number: ID13-2892341; Israel number not supplied). The Fund is registered as a non-profit Ottoman Association in the Jerusalem District Office of the Ministry of the Interior (reg. no. 11/2630). Six full-time and four part-time workers are employed by the organization, along with 55 volunteers. Decisions are made mostly by the Executive Director and the Treasurer.

AFFILIATIONS/REFERENCES

The organization is not affiliated with any political party in Israel. The following organizations abroad are affiliated with the Fund:

1. United Synagogue of America, 155 Fifth Ave., New York, N.Y. 10010.
2. World Council of Synagogues, 155 Fifth Ave., New York, N.Y. 10010.
3. Women's League for Conservative Judaism, 48 East 74th St., N.Y., N.Y. 10021.

FUNDING NEEDED

1. To provide high school scholarships for the underprivileged at $250 per child per year (June 1980 level).
2. To provide day camp scholarships for the underprivileged at $62.50 per child per 3-week semester.
3. To replenish the general fund at approximately $3,000 per year, which has been the extent of yearly outlay.

GESHER EDUCATIONAL AFFILIATES

Havatzelet 9, Jerusalem
Bialik 32, Ramat Gan
Beit Gesher, Mt. Canaan, Safed
Telephone: Jerusalem (02) 241015
Office hours: 8:00 A.M.-5:00 P.M.

HISTORY AND DESCRIPTION
Gesher was founded in 1969.

Goals: Gesher is devoted to the promotion of tolerance and understanding among various segments of Israeli society, especially between the religious and non-religious factions. It also strives to promote a deeper sense of Jewish and Zionist identity among all Israelis.

Services, Activities, and Accomplishments: Gesher makes use of a wide variety of programs to change attitudes and foster identity, ranging from seminars for almost 50,000 Israeli teenagers a year, to curricula development for Israeli schools and the development of a T.V. series to promote its goals. It has developed a network of eighteen campuses across the country for its seminars on Judaism/Zionism. Pioneers of informal education in Israel, Gesher has also developed totally original new curricula for the Israeli school system which have gained dramatic acceptance from teachers and students. It has gained trust as an apolitical movement to which people can turn in a highly politicized society. Since its founding, Gesher has grown into the largest organization of its kind, affecting almost all segments of the society and functioning in every region of the country. Gesher's newest project is the development of computer games which are enjoyable, exciting and teach Jewish values.

OFFICERS
Director: Avraham Infeld
Treasurer: C. Billet. Businessman
Hon. Chairman: Prof. E. Katzir. Former President of Israel.
Chairman: A. Schoen. Vice-President, Tenneco.
Board Members: M. Stern. Banker.
                  E. Shmueli. Director-General, Min. of Education.
                  Dr. D. Tropper. Special Advisor,
                    Minister of Education.
                  Prof. S. Fox. Director, School of Education,
                  Hebrew University.
                  Mrs. T. Lichtenstein. Psychologist.
                  E. Forman. Rabbi.
                  M. Bar-On. Former Chief Education Officer
                  at Israel Armed Forces.
                  U. Marom. Treasurer, Ministry of Education.

FINANCIAL INFORMATION

Gesher's income derives from three sources: 60% comes from contracts for educational services; 25% from donations and grants; and the remaining 15% from participation fees. Its projected annual budget for the year September 1981-August 1982 amounts to $2,700,000.-, and leaves a deficit of $350,000.-. Gesher is a registered Ottoman/non-profit organization (no. 11/1730, registered in Jerusalem), and donations are tax-free in Israel, and also in the U.S. and Canada (exemption numbers not provided). There are 130 full-time employees, 20 part-time workers, and 108 volunteers.

MEMBERSHIP, SCOPE, AND POLICY

Gesher, a non-membership organization, operates 23 branches in Israel. It lists 5 branches abroad, with 3,000 members. Decisions are made by the Executive Director.

AFFILIATIONS/REFERENCES

Gesher is a strictly apolitical, non-affiliated organization. No references are listed.

FUNDING NEEDED

1. For the development of a new television series to promote Jewish values. The program will be of entertainment commercial quality, to be broadcast weekly on prime-time T.V. A Diaspora option is also being developed. Required to complete a $1 million budget: $400,000.-.
2. For the 3-4 day seminars which 90% of all Israeli high-school youngsters attend. The seminars are dramatically effective in forcing youngsters to reevaluate their identity, especially before the army. Required to finance effective follow-up programming: $150,000.-.
3. For the development of seminars for adults, especially for key opinion-makers in the society, such as journalists, school principals, lawyers, army officers, etc. Cost: $220,000.-.

GEULAH CHILDREN'S BOARDING HOME

מעון ילדים גאולה

Geulah 5
Haifa
Telephone: (04) 662227
Office Hours: 7:00 A.M. to 4:00 P.M.

HISTORY AND DESCRIPTION
'Geulah' Children's Boarding Home was established in response to a perceived lack of facilities to care for children of a tender age whose mothers work and whose fathers, for the most part, are yeshiva students.

Services, Activities, and Accomplishments: The age of the children kept at 'Geulah' ranges from 6 months to 3 years. In recent years, the services of the Home have become so well used that its facilities are being taxed to the limit. As the demand for services has increased, the organization has sought to increase the present accommodating capacity of the Home.

OFFICERS
Director: Zahavah Shapira, Pewsner 37, Haifa.
                      Tel. (04) 665970.
Treasurer: Moshe Benyamini, Nahalal 6, Bat-Galim, Haifa.
                      Pensioner.
Board Member: Zvi Boimel, Hanassi 100, Haifa.
                      Indepently employed.

FINANCIAL INFORMATION
45% of Geulah's income is acquired through donations; 35% through membership dues and 20% through miscellaneous sources. Last year's budget of $58,000 left the organization with a deficit of $940. Donations to the Home are *not* tax-free in either Israel or the United States. The organization is registered with the Haifa District Office of the Ministry of the Interior as an Ottoman Association (reg. no. 61/614). Geulah Children's Home employs 31 full-time and 3 volunteer workers.

MEMBERSHIP, SCOPE, POLICY, AND AFFILIATIONS
44 members are represented by the one Haifa branch of Geulah. There are no foreign members, and it has no affiliations with any foreign organization nor with any Israeli political party. Operating decisions are made by the Committee of the Home.

FUNDING NEEDED
Construction of additional space to accommodate further numbers of children at Geulah would cost an estimated $50,000. Renovation and repair of the present building would cost $40,000.

GONENIM COMMUNITY CENTER

מרכז קהילתי גוננים

4 Elazar Hagadol St.
Katamonim, Jerusalem
Telephone: (02) 633074 — 781831
Office Hours: 8:00 A.M. to 8:00 P.M.

HISTORY AND DESCRIPTION
The Center was officially opened in August 1979, serving 40,000 residents in the area of Katamonim (Gonen) and its nearby neighbourhoods, Pat and San Simon.

Goals: Provision of a physical structure in which to meet the needs of and provide improvement for the quality of life of the serviced community. The staff of the Center works hard to involve local residents more and more in the activities, aiming for a situation where the residents themselves will be in charge of decisions concerning policy and activities provided. Existing services in the community were researched in order to avoid duplication. The population served is primarily adults, elderly, and pre-school; children and youth are offered courses in specific areas only — in order to avoid overlapping with the work of local youth clubs. The Center attempts to work side by side with other local institutions.

Services, Activities, and Accomplishments: The Center has a Morning School for Women who barely know how to read or write (200 women participate), a babysitter service, ethnic dance groups (from local talent), a Community Theatre Group comprised of local "street" youth, and a club for the elderly with some 250 active members. The Center has organized summer camps for women, trips, lectures, a wide variety of courses in the Arts, and large-scale holiday celebrations. The organization of neighborhood committees, and the residents' acting to improve their own "quality of life" are seen as major accomplishments.

OFFICERS
Director: Joseph Teitelbaum

FINANCIAL INFORMATION
Donations to the Center are tax-free in Israel and in the United States. (Israel registration no. and U.S. State I.R.S. no. not supplied.)

MEMBERSHIP, SCOPE, AND POLICY
Any inhabitant of Katamonim, San Simon, and Pat may join. At present, there are 4,500 members.

AFFILIATIONS/REFERENCES
The Center is not affiliated with any political party in Israel.

FUNDING NEEDED
(Information not supplied)

THE GREEK ORTHODOX COMMUNITY COUNCIL, ACRE

מועצת העדה האורטודוקסית, עכו

P.O. Box 1010, Acre
Telephone: (04) 912192 — office; (04) 910037 — home
Office hours: 9:00 A.M. to 1:00 P.M.
Home hours: 4:00 P.M. to 6:00 P.M.

HISTORY AND DESCRIPTION
The Council was established in 1964 as an Ottoman Society, although its origins go back to 1914 when it was a benevolent society to serve the needs of the Greek Orthodox community of Acre.

Organizational Structure: The Council is composed of 7 members, citizens from various walks of life and professions.

Goals: To help the Community remain good order socially and financially, to help boys and girls from needy families to continue higher education and professions, to assist cultural centers for the younger generation, to maintain religious buildings and cemeteries in good condition.

Services, Activities, and Accomplishments: The Council established boys' and girls' scout groups, summer camping, and weekly social evenings for youths in the cultural center.

OFFICERS
Director: Emil Asfour, Acre-Old City. Accountant.
   Tel. (04) 910037.
Treasurer: Fareed Khammar, Acre-New City.
   Sub-manager, Barclays Bank. Tel. (04) 911077.
Board Members: Naseef Menassa, Acre-New City.
   Insurance Agent. Tel. (04) 910731.
   Elias Suliman, Acre-New City.
   Building Contractor. Tel. (04) 910784.
   Michel Otaki, Acre-New City.
   Mechanic. Tel. (04) 910736.
   Nicola Khoury, Acre-New City.
   Teacher. Tel. (04) 910606.
   Shafic Matta, Acre-Old City.
   Grocer. Tel. (04) 915095.

FINANCIAL INFORMATION
50% of the Council's income comes from rent of Council buildings, 30% from donations and 20% membership dues. Last year's annual budget was $2,200, leaving no deficit.

Donations are tax-free in Israel (registration no. 4501423) and the Council is registered in Nazareth as an Ottoman society (no. 3/250). Seven active volunteers assist in the activities of the organization.

MEMBERSHIP, SCOPE, AND POLICY
Executive members of the Board make most of the decisions. People may be elected members once every five years. There are 200 members in Israel.

FUNDING NEEDED
1. Major renovations on the church — over $20,000.
2. Promotion of cultural centers — $10,000.
3. Higher education and professions for needy students — $10,000.
4. Cemetery maintenance — $3,000.

HABAD IR-GANIM, JERUSALEM

אגודת חב"ד עיר-גנים, ירושלים

15 Chile Street
P.O.B. 465, Jerusalem
Telephone: (02) 417680
Office hours: Daily, 8:00 A.M. to 1:00 P.M.
Tuesday, 4:00 to 6:00 P.M.

HISTORY AND DESCRIPTION

The organization was founded together with the Jerusalem suburb of Ir-Ganim in 1959. With the arrival of many children of Moroccan origin, who had been educated in Habad institutions in Morocco, a school and a kindergarten were opened for them by Habad Ir-Ganim. Today there are three Habad primary schools and twenty-one kindergartens and day-nurseries. Some of today's teachers are those same immigrants of twenty years ago mentioned above. Instead of living off welfare aid, hundreds of mothers now go out to work and earn a salary. The organization is proud of its devoted staff, whose day-to-day endeavors have helped broken and disadvantaged families, and given them a new outlook on life.

OFFICERS

Director:	A.M. Silberstrom, Dr. Avigdori 6, Jerusalem. School Principal. Tel. (02) 233070.
Treasurer:	J.G. Lipkin, Averbuch 1, Jerusalem. Orphanage Director. Tel. (02) 522271.
Board Members:	S.D. Slonim, Haneviim 74, Jerusalem. District Rabbi. Tel. (02) 226555.
	A.Z. Cohen, Warshaw 37, Jerusalem. Head of Kollel. Tel. (02) 282740.
	M. Weber, Zefania 37, Jerusalem. Tel (02) 287754.
	D. Schlesinger, Baharan 5, Jerusalem. Girls' Orphanage Director. Tel. (02) 523291.
	M. Kubitshek, Bate Hun. 133, Jerusalem. Employee.

FINANCIAL INFORMATION

35% of last year's annual budget came from government sources (Ministries of Education and Welfare), 30% from tuition fees, 30% from donations, and the balance from the Jewish Agency, etc. Last year's annual budget of $170,000 left the organization with a deficit of $18,000. Habad Ir-Ganim is a recognized non-profit organization (Israel reg. no. 11/977), to which donations in Israel are tax-free (Israel: tax. no. 4502000). Fifty full-time and fifteen part-time workers are employed by the organization, aided by all members of the Board and the Ladies Auxiliary who serve on a voluntary basis.

MEMBERSHIP, SCOPE, AND POLICY

Anyone of the Jewish faith interested in the advancement of child welfare can join the organization. Decisions on everyday matters are made by the Executive Director. Directives and general planning policies are decided upon by the Board. Ministry inspectors usually make the decisions on pedagogical matters.

AFFILIATIONS/REFERENCES
Habad Ir-Ganim is politically unaffiliated in Israel. It maintains contact with Lubavitch Headquarters, 770 Eastern Parkway, Brooklyn, New York.

FUNDING NEEDED
1. After 15-20 years of wear and tear, three day-nurseries need to be renovated. Three sets of architectural plans have been submitted, with respective costs estimated as: $40,000, $50,000, and $80,000.
2. $30,000 — To renew equipment and furniture in five day-nurseries.

HAFETZ HAIM ORPHANAGE

בית היתומים "חפץ חיים" ירושלים

20 Bar Ilan Street
Jerusalem
Telephone: (02) 287668
Office Hours: Almost the entire day

HISTORY AND DESCRIPTION
The Hafetz Haim Orphanage works towards saving the lives of Jewish orphans as well as their education; deprived children are also taken care of by the organization.

OFFICERS
Director: Mr. Dov Stein.

FINANCIAL INFORMATION
The Orphanage is registered as an Ottoman Association (Jerusalem district, reg. no. not supplied).
Donations to the orphanage are tax-free both in Israel and in the United States (reg. no. for Israel and USA not supplied).

HAKTAV INSTITUTE

מכון הכתב

26 Haye Adam Street
P.O.B. 6040
Jerusalem
Telephone: (02) 817662
Office hours: 8:00 A.M. to 1:00 P.M. and 3:00 P.M. to 9:00 P.M. daily

DESCRIPTION
"Machon Haktav" helps rabbis carry out independent scholarly projects in a field of Jewish specialization which will make a significant contribution to the understanding, preservation, enhancement or transmission of all fields of Jewish literature.
It has published very important books and magazines in all areas of Judaism.

OFFICERS
Director:	Rabbi M. Eliahu, Jerusalem.
	Member High Court.
	Tel. (02) 521010.
Treasurer:	Rabbi S. Mizrachi, Jerusalem.
	Member, High Court.
Board Members:	Rabbi Ezra Basri, Ashdod.
	Head Court of Justice.
	Tel. (02) 817662.
	Rabbi Moshe Malka, Petah Tikva.
	Chief Rabbi of Petah Tikva.
	Tel. (03) 908346.
	Rabbi Yosef Sharvit, Ashkelon.
	Chief Rabbi of Ashkelon.
	Tel. (051) 23549.
	Rabbi Refael Saban, Netivot.
	Chief Rabbi of Netivot.
	Rabbi Yona Porat. Rabbi of Revaha.
	Tel. (051) 91483.

FINANCIAL INFORMATION
85% of last year's annual budget came from donations; 5% came from membership dues; and the remaining 10% came from government assistance. Last year's annual budget was $25,000, and the deficit was $4,000. The organization is registered as an Ottoman Association (reg. no. 11/2963). The Institute has a tax-free status in Israel (tax no. 4507052), however, donations are not tax-free in the United States. Three full-time and seven part-time workers are employed by the Institute, as well as ten volunteers.

MEMBERSHIP, SCOPE, AND POLICY
There are 4,000 members in Israel and 2,000 members abroad. There are seven Israeli branches and four foreign branches. Decisions are made by

the National Board. Any Jew with a worthwhile goal and/or contribution is entitled to join.

AFFILIATIONS/REFERENCES
The Institute is not affiliated with any political party in Israel. It is in contact with Rabbi Abraham Hecht, Union of Rabbis, 2030 Ocean Parkway, Brooklyn, New York.

FUNDING NEEDED
1. To prepare guidance books which will help people live with mutual understanding.
2. To help rabbis publish their research.
3. To publish old manuscripts.

HAMERKAZ LECHINUCH BANOT
—BEIT BLUMA

המרכז לחינוך בנות – בית בלומה

Kfar Avraham
P.O.B. 3370
Petah Tikva
Telephone: (03) 265773
Office Hours: 8:00 A.M. to 4:00 P.M.

HISTORY AND DESCRIPTION
The institution was established in 1955 for the purpose of educating girls from broken homes and orphaned girls. Another aim was to provide a trade or vocation for these girls, and to see that their future is placed on a firm basis. The institute has earned for itself a fine name and has merited recognition of governmental bodies and public institutions which have granted their approval and backing.

Organizational Structure: The institution is run by a Managerial Council which consists of nine members, three of whom are American citizens and all of whom are educators and public personalities and act in an honorary capacity. There is also an Actions Committee of four members and a supervisory committee of four members of which two are Managerial Council members and two are public dignitaries. The Chairman of the Pedagogic Council is one of the members of the Managerial Council and there is also an active Pedagogic Committee.

Goals: This institution is about to develop from a vocational residential high school with a four-year program to a vocational residential high school with a six-year program serving five hundred pupils. Some one hundred and fifty girls will study at the preparatory section—junior high school—and three hundred and fifty at the senior high school. The main emphasis is to ensure the progress and the future of the girls from the lower echelons of Israel's society, orphan girls and those from broken homes.

Services, Activities and Accomplishments: To date, the institution has successfully educated hundreds of pupils who have subsequently married and established fine families. The Pedagogic Council maintains contact with graduates up to the time of their marriage and is always available for counselling. During the past year, the institution acquired twenty-five dunams and commenced erecting a dining hall, kitchen and dormitory for ninety-six girls. As the first stage in the plan, the current number of pupils is being doubled.

OFFICERS
Director: Moshe Zvi Neria, Kfar Haroeh. Rabbi.
Treasurer: Ezra Hartman, Petah Tikva.
                 Tel. (03) 929315.

FINANCIAL INFORMATION

Beit Bluma is registered in Ramle as an Ottoman society (no. 1483/1). The institution receives 90% of its income from donations and the remainder from governmental bodies and public institutions. Last year's budget of $300,000 left the organization with a deficit of $17,300. Donations to the organization are tax-free, both in Israel and in the United States (Israel reg. no. 4506403, USA State I.R.S. no. 52-6080692-New York). Thirty full-time and fifteen part-time workers are employed by the institution, as well as all nine board members working as volunteers.

MEMBERSHIP, SCOPE, AND POLICY

Membership is open to all those who wish to aid the aims of developing the school for the future of the girls. Most decisions are made either by the Managerial Council or the Actions Committee, Pedagogic Council or Pedagogic Actions Committee.

AFFILIATIONS/REFERENCES

Mention was made of American sponsors, but no names or addresses were listed.

FUNDING NEEDED

1. to purchase equipment for the dormitory, kitchen and dining hall.
2. For garden maintenance and landscaping.
3. To erect another dormitory block for ninety-six girls.

HAMESHAKEM LIMITED חברת המשקם

138 Allenby
Tel Aviv
Telephone: (03) 614548
Office hours: Sunday-Thursday, 7.30 A.M. to 3.30 P.M.
Friday, 7.30 A.M. to 12.30 P.M.

HISTORY AND DESCRIPTION

HaMeshakem was founded in the mid-fifties to deal primarily with the problem of employment of elderly immigrants who had arrived in Israel since 1948 and thereafter with little or no education or professional training. Since that time the organization has developed into the country's foremost employer of handicapped, infirm and elderly workers.

Organizational Structure: Branch offices in 38 towns are divided for administrative purposes into 11 geographic areas. Area Managers are responsible to the Executive Director of Organization at the Tel Aviv-based Head Office. The Executive Director is responsible to the Board of Directors. It is a joint Jewish Agency-government organization.

Goals: The purpose of the Organization is to provide employment for citizens who, because of disability, mental or physical, are unable to work in a normal capacity.

Services, Activities, and Accomplishments: HaMeshakem employs individuals who are referred by official institutions (The Ministry of Labour and Social Welfare, the National Insurance Institute, the Employment Offices, etc.) and employs them either in its own facotries or workshops, or "services" organized by HaMeshakem, or in outside factories and institutions which HaMeshakem bills for the work it performs whilst the Meshakem workers remain on the Meshakem payroll. All workers work a five-hour day. The organization has 20 factories and workshops manufacturing a very wide range of products including office files, rolls for adding machines, toys, clothes, paper tissues and sanitary towels. Services, in which work is done under the direct supervision of Meshakem's staff foreman, include gardening (and nurseries), cleaning and messenger services. The Organization's major accomplishment has been to provide employment for over 6,000 handicapped, infirm and elderly people each year since its foundation 23 years ago.

OFFICERS

Board Chairman: Mr. Y. Schiff, Head of the Department of
Rehabilitation, Ministry of Labour & Social
Welfare, Jerusalem.
Tel. (02) 661141.
Board Members: Mr. I. Tessler, HaMeshakem Limited,
138 Allenby, Tel Aviv.
Tel. (03) 614548.

Mr. H. Haklai, Director-General of the
Employment Services, Ministry of Labour &
Social Welfare, Jerusalem. Tel. (02) 661141.
Mr. Sh. Weissman, The Jewish Agency for Israel,
68 Chernichovsky, Jerusalem. Accountant.
Tel. (02) 669328.
Mr. Y. Landau, Amigor Limited, 56 Maza,
Tel Aviv. General Manager.
Tel. (03) 624345.
Mr. D. Kohavi, 33 Emek Bracha, Tel Aviv.
Teacher and former Director of the Employment
Services of the Ministry of Labour & Social
Welfare. Tel. (03) 252531.

FINANCIAL INFORMATION

About 65% of HaMeshakem's income comes from the sale of goods and
services, about 20% from the Ministry of Labour and Social Welfare,
and 15% from donations and from the Jewish Agency for Israel. The
annual budget for 1978/79 of $4,000,000 left a deficit of $1,500,000.
HaMeshakem is not registered as a non-profit Ottoman Association
and donations in Israel are not tax-free. 200 full-time workers are
employed by the organization.

MEMBERSHIP, SCOPE, AND POLICY

Membership is mainly organizations but individuals may also join.
There are 38 branches in Israel. Most decisions are made by the Executive Director based on policy decisions made by the Board of Directors.

AFFILIATIONS/REFERENCES

HaMeshakem is not affiliated with any Israeli political party.

FUNDING NEEDED

To purchase machinery for HaMeshakem's factories. Without machinery the organization cannot employ the large number of disabled
people waiting throughout the country for a place of work. Investments
could be from about $2,000 for a small press to about $50,000 for a line
of machinery providing permanent work for 30/40 people.

THE HARRY STEELE COMMUNITY CENTER, KIRYAT ONO

המרכז הקילתי ע"ש הרי סטיל — קרית אונו

106 Zahal Street
P.O.B. 365
Kiron, Kiryat Ono
Telephone: (03) 752472
Office hours: 8:00 A.M. to 1:30 P.M. and 3:00 P.M. to 7:00 P.M., daily

HISTORY AND DESCRIPTION

The Harry Steele Community Center was established in 1973 with a grant from the Steele family, through Keren Hayesod. It is a center for leisure and cultural activities and has a board of directors, a professional staff, and citizens' committees. The goal of the Center is to enrich the cultural life of the town and to work with the other services and the citizens.

The major accomplishment of the Center until now has been the developing of activities for children, adults and senior citizens in the Center as well as taking the first steps to develop activities in two other neighborhoods in Kiryat Ono and with a different population and geographical distance.

OFFICERS

Center Director: Irit Fried. Community Center, Kiryat Ono.
       Tel. (03) 752472.

Board Chairman: Asher Dar. Mayor.
       Tel. (03) 753444.

Board of Directors: Arie Achidov. Treasurer.
       Tel. (03) 753444.
       Zadok Tov. Businessman.
       Eli Shalom. Accountant.
       Zvi Meitar. Lawyer.
       Greenstein. Ministry of Education.
       Nachshon. Minstry of Education.

The same address was listed for all above members — P.O.B. 365, Kiryat Ono.

FINANCIAL INFORMATION

The annual budget for 1980 came from the following sources: membership dues, 35%; local municipality, 35%; and governmental offices, 30% and totalled $150,000; there was no deficit. The organization is tax-free, but no numbers were supplied. There are 25 full-time, 50 part-time employees and 100 volunteers.

MEMBERSHIP, SCOPE, AND POLICY

There are 20,000 participants, in the three branches in Israel.

AFFILIATIONS/REFERENCES
The organization is not affiliated with any political party in Israel. It is in contact with the Jewish Welfare Board, New York, and the Community Center of North Miami, Florida.

FUNDING NEEDED
1. Neighborhood block work in the Rassco quarter.
2. Developing branches in old Kiryat Ono and in Rassco for children, youth, adults and senior citizens.
3. Setting up sport facilities and a swimming pool.

HASHARON HOSPITAL —
PETACH-TIKVA

בית־חולים "השרון" פתח־תקוה

7 Keren Kayemet Street
P.O.B. 121
Petach-Tikva
Telephone: (03) 928111
Office hours: 7:30 A.M. to 3:30 P.M.

HISTORY AND DESCRIPTION

Hasharon Hospital operates in several buildings at 7 Keren Kayemet Street, in the south-western area of Petach-Tikva. Hasharon Hospital was established in 1942, as Section B of the Beilinson Hospital, and has since grown continuously. It is now a district general hospital, supplying medical services to Petach-Tikva, Rosh Ha'ain, and the adjacent Arab villages, and to the moshavim and kibbutzim of the neighborhood, an area of approximately 200,000 people. The hospital has several buildings all located in south-west Petach-Tikva.

The hospital has about 400 beds, with two surgical departments, 3 internal medicine departments, an orthopedic department, and departments of obstetrics and gynecology, urology, otorhinolaryngology, nephrology, geriatrics, ophthalmology and pediatrics. There are 8 operating rooms, emergency rooms, cardiology and physiotherapy. In addition, the isotope institute will begin its activity soon. There are laboratories, equipped with modern instuments, research laboratories, and outpatient clinics.

A nursing school operates in cooperation with the kibbutzim.

Many of the physicians in Hasharon Hospital are members of the teaching staff of Tel Aviv University Medical School, and some wards are affiliated to it. During the academic year many students learn in the hospital. There are also special courses for newly immigrated physicians who are helped in their first steps in Israel.

The hospital belongs to both Kupat Holim (Sick Fund) of the histadrut, and to the Municipality of Petach-Tikva. Thus, both members of Kupat Holim and other Petach-Tikva inhabitants have the right to be hospitalized in Hasharon Hospital.

Volunteer Activities: There are seven non-profit, volunteer organizations which are affiliated with Hasharon Hospital, as follows: Yael—"Lending a Hand to Patients" Organization, From Heart to Heart Society, Aid for Kidney Patients, Aid for Asthma Patients, Aid for Cystofibrosis Patients, Aid for Rheumatic Patients, and Aid for Infant-Asthma Patients.

Donations can be made directly to the hospital, or to each of the above organizations, individually, for special projects.

OFFICERS
Director: Dr. Jacob Hart. 7 Keren Kayemet, (POB 121),
              Petach-Tikva. Physician. Tel. (03) 921752.

Treasurer: Nachman Lederman.
Board Members: Israel Schwartz.
                  Administrator.
                  Tel. (03) 921752.
                  Shimon Waks.
                  Administrator.
                  Tel. (03) 922099.

FINANCIAL INFORMATION

The sources of income for the last year's budget were as follows: Central Sick Fund offices, 95%; Local Sick Fund offices, 4%; donations, 1%. Last year's annual budget was $11 million, with a deficit of $3 million. The hospital will soon be registered as an Ottoman Association. Donations to the hospital are tax-free in Israel and America (tax numbers were not supplied). There are 800 full-time and 400 part-time workers employed by the hospital, in addition to 250 volunteers.

MEMBERSHIP, SCOPE, AND POLICY

Decisions are made mostly by the Executive Director. The rest of the information does not apply.

AFFILIATIONS/REFERENCES

The hospital is not affiliated with any political party in Israel. The hospital is in contact with the Friends of Sharon Hospital, Munich, Germany.

FUNDING NEEDED

1. The construction of outpatient clinics. Estimated cost: $2 million.
2. Workshops and supply depot buildings. Estimated cost: $200,000.
3. Medical equipment: a scanner, X-ray, laser apparatus, audiometer and computer for infants, EEG-EMG, and various other medical appliances.

HAYAL—EDUCATING YOUNG JEWISH BOYS TO TORAH

ארגון חיי"ל — חינוך ילדי ישראל לתורה

P.O.B. 9465
Jerusalem
Telephone: (02) 710177 and 631282
Office hours: evenings

HISTORY AND DESCRIPTION
In 1975 Hayal was established to give assistance to youth in distress. The Hayal organization, established by Rabbi Elisha Levi, cares for 600 boys and girls.

Goals: To educate and guide boys and girls of underprivileged neighborhoods with love and friendship.

Services, Activities, and Accomplishments: There are 20 groups of boys and girls centered in Jerusalem for a total of 600 children. They come to study, play, and to receive help with their homework. Holiday camps are organized in which the dedicated instructors, in cooperation with parents and teachers, offer their assistance. The organization has a charity fund which grants loans to the children and organizes Shabbat receptions, to establish contact among the children belonging to the organization.

OFFICERS
Director and
Treasurer: Rabbi Elisha Levi, 273/13 East Talpiot, Jerusalem. Teacher. Tel. (02) 710177.
Board Members: Rabbi Naftali Rot, 18 Sorotzkin, Jerusalem. School Principal. Tel. (02) 534744.
Elana Gabbai, 10 Aviad, Jerusalem. Teacher. Tel. (02) 631282.
Zion Gabbai, 5 Pinkas, Jerusalem. School Principal. Tel. (02) 668834.
Rabbi Shaul Gabbai, 10 Aviad, Jerusalem. Rabbi. Tel. (02) 631282.
Yitzhak Ben Rumo, Sanhedria Murchevet, Jerusalem.
Rut Weisskot (Batat), 2 Hashomer, Jerusalem. Teacher. Tel. (02) 421707.

FINANCIAL INFORMATION
100% of the organization's income comes from private donations. Last year's annual budget of $10,000 left a deficit of $3,000. The organization is registered in Jerusalem as a non-profit Ottoman Association (reg. no. 11/2988). Donations in Israel are tax-free (tax number not supplied). Four full-time and seven part-time workers are employed by the organization, as well as twelve volunteers.

MEMBERSHIP, SCOPE, AND POLICY
Decisions are made by the Executive Director and the National Board.

AFFILIATIONS/REFERENCES
The organization is not affiliated with any Israeli political party. It receives help from the following people abroad: Rabbi J. Elyachar, 5 Impasse St. Gilles, Troyes 1000, France; and Shelley Berliner, 18/19 Saddle River Road, Fair Lawn, New Jersey 07410, U.S.A.

FUNDING NEEDED
1. To acquire a building which will operate as a center in which children can study and play during their free time. This building would replace the small synagogue rooms in which the organization operates at present.
2. To increase the activities of the organization, and to organize additional groups in other neighborhoods and for other age-groups (minimum cost $1,000 per month).
3. To establish a children's educational library and an educational games center (approximate cost $2,400).

HEBREW UNION COLLEGE-JEWISH INSTITUTE OF RELIGION

היברו יוניון קולג' — מכון למדעי היהדות

13 King David Street
Jerusalem
Telephone: (02) 232444
Office hours: 8:00 A.M. to 5:00 P.M.

HISTORY AND DESCRIPTION

Since its inception in Cincinnati in 1875, the Hebrew Union College-Jewish Institute of Religion, which is the institute of higher learning in Reform Judaism, has dedicated itself to the study and advancement of Judaism. At its four campuses in Cincinnati, New York, Los Angeles and Jerusalem, the College-Institute prepares rabbis, educators, cantors, communal workers and scholars to serve Judaism and the Jewish community. It also maintains extensive libraries, archives and a museum which treasure the Jewish heritage of the past, preserve the accomplishments of the present and ensure a legacy for the future.

The Jerusalem School of HUC-JIR opened in 1963. Under its auspices, the Nelson Glueck School of Biblical Archaeology has made valuable contrubutions through intensive excavations of historical sites in Israel. Since 1969, the College-Institute has required that all rabbinic and Jewish education students spend their first year at the Jerusalem School deepening their knowledge of the Hebrew language and gaining a comprehensive understanding of Israel's history and culture.

A special program for the training of rabbis for the growing Israel Reform movement was inaugurated in 1972.

Professor Alfred Gotteschalk is President of Hebrew Union College-Jewish Institute of Religion. HUC-JIR is under the patronage of the Union of American Hebrew Congregations.

OFFICERS

President: Dr. Alfred Gotteschalk.
Chairman, Board
of Governors: Dr. Jules Bachman.
Executive
Vice President: Dr. Uri D. Herscher.
Executive
Dean for
Acad. Affairs: Dr. Eugene Mihaly.
Dean, Jerus.
School: Dr. Michael L. Klein, Jerusalem.
Tel. (02) 638774.

FINANCIAL INFORMATION

Last year's annual budget came from the following sources: Reform Congregational Dues, 40%; tuition, 15%; endowment income, 15%; and annual contributions, 30%. Last year's annual budget was $865,000 for the Jerusalem School and $8,000,000 for the College-Institute. There is a deficit of $300,000 for the College-Institute. The organization is registered as an Ottoman Association (reg. no. 58-11/0772). Donations are tax-deductible both in Israel and the United States, (no tax numbers were supplied). There are 23 full-time and 15 part-time workers employed by the Jerusalem School.

MEMBERSHIP, SCOPE, AND POLICY
Decisions are made by the HUC-JIR President and Board of Governors. In order to be accepted as a student, applicants must possess a B.A. degree and other academic credentials. There are 100 students in the one branch in Israel, and 400 students in the three branches abroad.

AFFILIATIONS/REFERENCES
The organization is not affiliated with any political party in Israel. It does have the following accreditations: by the Middle States Association of Colleges and Secondary Schools, the North Central Association of Colleges and Secondary Schools, and the Western Association of Schools and Colleges, to confer M.A. and Ph.D. degrees.
Further information can be obtained from (and earmarked donations can be sent to) The Hebrew Union College-Jewish Institute of Religion, 3101 Clifton Avenue, Cincinnati, Ohio.

FUNDING NEEDED
1. The establishment of student scholarships, financing Israel Orientation lectures, programs and field trips.
2. The development of new archaelological workshops—financing archaeological excavations at Tel Dan and Tel Aroer, new archaeological display area.
3. The erection of a new library, with a 60,000 volume capacity.

THE HEBREW UNIVERSITY
OF JERUSALEM

האוניברסיטה העברית בירושלים

Mount Scopus
Jerusalem
Telephone: (02) 882111
Office hours: 8:00 A.M. to 3:00 P.M. (Office of Information & Public Affairs)

HISTORY AND DESCRIPTION
The Hebrew University opened in 1925, the realization of a dream by Chaim Weizmann and other Zionist leaders to create a center of higher learning in the Jewish homeland. From a nucleus of three research institutes—Jewish studies, chemistry and microbiology—the University grew to become a large multidisciplinary institution located on four campuses, granting degrees, training professionals, and becoming a focus of study and research for all of Israel and for the Jewish people worldwide.

Organizational Structure: The Hebrew University of Jerusalem is governed by an International Board of Governors, which elects the President. The supreme academic body is the Senate, which elects the Rector.

Goals: To serve the Jewish people as a center of culture and scholarship; to serve Israel by helping shape its national culture, training professional manpower and furthering its development through scientific research; and to serve the progress of humanity by advancing the frontiers of knowledge.

Services, Activities, and Accomplishments: The University comprises seven Faculties: Humanities, Social Sciences, Science, Law, Medicine, Dental Medicine and Agriculture; eleven Schools: Education, Social Work, Pharmacy, Nursing, Occupational Therapy, Public Health, Business Administration, Applied Science and Technology, Library and Archive Studies, Nutritional and Domestic Sciences, and a School for Overseas Students. The University has awarded over 45,000 Bachelor's, Master's and Doctoral degrees and at present over 2,500 research projects are in progress. Apart from its contribution to higher education and research, the University is a service to the community and to Jewish life. Some of its accomplishments have been to help eradicate endemic diseases in Israel, to help make agriculture a multimillion dollar export industry based on scientific research, to train the leadership of modern Israel, to make Jerusalem a world center of Jewish scholarship, offering accredited study programs for thousands of Jewish youth from all over the world each year.

OFFICERS
President: Avraham Harman.
Tel. (02) 882111

Rector:	Prof. Raphael Mechoulam
	Tel. (02) 882111
Board Chairman:	Robert Smith, Washington D.C.
Vice Presidents:	Bernard Cherrick
	Tel. (02) 882111
	Simcha Dinitz
	Tel. (02) 882111
	Prof. Michael Schlesinger
	Tel. (02) 630241
	Prof. Alex Keynan
	Tel. (02) 585111
	Prof. Yoash Vaadia
	Tel. (02) 882111

FINANCIAL INFORMATION

70% of the University's income comes from a Government allocation, 22% from donations and income from endowments, and 8% from tuition fees. Last year's annual budget was $60,000,000. There was no deficit as the University operates on a balanced budget. It is registered as a non-profit Ottoman Association, was formed as an Association in 1925, recognized as a body corporate in Israel under the Council for Higher Education Law in 1958. The present Constitution was adopted in 1965 and published in the official gazette, Reshumot, on Dec. 9, 1965. Donations in Israel and the United States are tax-free (tax nos. not supplied). The Hebrew University has 2,235 Faculty members.

MEMBERSHIP, SCOPE, AND POLICY

Not a member organization. Decisions are made by the International Board of Governors and its Executive Committee.

AFFILIATIONS/REFERENCES

The Hebrew University is not affiliated with any Israeli political party. It has Friends' offices in 30 countries, among them: —
American Friends of the H.U., Head Office, 11 E. 69 St., N.Y., N.Y.
Canadian Friends of the H.U., National Office, Yorkdale Plaza, Suite 208, 1 Yorkdale Rd., Toronto, Ont. Canada.
Friends of the H.U. of Jerusalem, 3 St. John's Wood Rd., London NW8 8 RB, U.K.
South African Friends, POB 4316, Johannesburg, South Africa.
Australian Friends, 584 St. Kilda Rd., Melbourne, Australia.

FUNDING NEEDED

1. Scholarships and student welfare. Because the Hebrew University is a national, not a local, institution, most of its students (75%) come from outside Jerusalem, making the problems of student welfare especially acute in Jerusalem where housing costs are especially high and student jobs scarce. The University is also desperately looking for aid to foster its many social service programs such as: legal aid to the needy, student "big brother" programs to coach youngsters in deprived neighborhoods, educational intervention programs for

preschool disadvantaged children devised by the School of Education, field training of social work students involving them in casework and community action, and many kinds of student volunteer activites and social action research in which the Hebrew University is deeply involved.

The standard unit for a scholarship donation is $2,500.

2. To purchase books and equipment.
3. To fund senior fellowships and junior faculty positions.

HELPING HAND ASSOCIATION "NOTZER CHESED" IN THE NAME OF ZVI AND RIVKA ZACHARIA

קופת גמ"ח "נוצר חסד" ע"ש צבי ורבקה זכריה

Pinsker St. 22, Jerusalem.
Telephone: (02) 667395 and 233141, ask for Haim Erenberg.
Office Hours: 8:30 A.M. to 14:00 P.M.

HISTORY AND DESCRIPTION
The Helping Hand Association is an organization which provides interest-free loans to the poor. The Association was founded in 1962 by Mrs. Rivka Zacharia in the name of her late husband Zvi. Mrs. Zacharia saved her own money for this purpose for more than 10 years. She was 68 years old when she founded the Gemach (free loan society). Poor people came to her house and always received a loan. She administered the Association single-handedly until the very end of her life, when she died in her home at 80 years of age. Afterwards, her son Shabtai performed this work, which is now shared by his son-in-law, Haim Erenberg. Loans are provided to people who request them, especially *olim* (new immigrants) and scholars. Unfortunately, some requests have had to be turned down due to lack of funds.

OFFICERS
Director:	Shabtai Zacharia. 12A Shamai St., J-m. Advocate. Tel. (02) 667395, (02) 246660.
Treasurer:	Haim Erenberg, "Bank Igud", Yaffo 34, J-m. Bank clerk. Tel. (02) 233141.
Board Members:	Margalith Zacharia, Pinsker 22, J-m. Librarian. Reuven Zacharia, Pinsker 22, J-m. Scholar. Daniel Zacharia, Pinsker 22, J-m. Scholar.

FINANCIAL INFORMATION
95% of the Association's income is provided by its 5-member board (all members of the Zacharia family), with the remaining 5% being derived from donations from other sources. Figures for the annual budget were not supplied. Donations to the organization do not carry tax-free status in either Israel or the U.S.A. The organization is registered as a non-profit Ottoman Association in the Jerusalem District Office of the Ministry of the Interior (reg. no. 11/2207).

MEMBERSHIP, SCOPE, AND POLICY
Membership is open to any Jew who is 18 years old, although at present the only members are the 5 relatives of the original founder, who also make up the volunteer staff and the board of the organization.

AFFILIATIONS/REFERENCES
The organization is not affiliated with any political party in Israel nor with any group abroad.

HELPING HAND SUPERMARKET יד - עדוד

Yudit 4
P.O.B. 513,
Jerusalem
Telephone: (02) 241959
Office Hours: 8:00 A.M. - 9:00 P.M.

HISTORY AND DESCRIPTION
The Helping Hand Supermarket was formed in 1979.

Goals: Its purpose is to provide food, housewares and clothing to
eligible families at cost price, thereby enabling the families to purchase
otherwise unaffordable items. This is done in a dignified manner,
through the operation of a supermarket chain.

Services, Activities, and Accomplishments: The service is provided to
families who meet the criteria of eligibility, which include those with
income up to a specific maximum amount and families which are
blessed with many children. The purchaser is provided with an eligibility
card, which he presents when paying for discounted goods. At present,
approximately 800 families blessed with children are able to cut their
food budget by about 30% per month, making the difference between
bare survival and dignity.

OFFICERS

Director:	M. Porush,	Pines 2, Jerusalem. Knesset Member. Tel. (02) 222287.
Treasurer:	Y. Pollak,	Haturim 9, Jerusalem. Rabbinical Lawyer. Tel. (02) 245917.
Board Members:	M. Heftler,	Frank 31, Jerusalem. Hotel Manager. Tel. (02) 414684.
	C. Geffner,	Haor 2, Jerusalem Secretary.
	D. Auerbach,	Hapisga 45, Jerusalem. Professor. Tel. (02) 412343.

FINANCIAL INFORMATION
Donations account for 90% of the organization's income; the remaining
10% comes from a Government stipend. Last year's budget was
$80,000, with a deficit of $60,000. The project is an Ottoman non-profit
association (registration no. 11/3066, Jerusalem District), and donations are tax-free both in Israel (no no. given) and in the U.S. (I.R.S. no.
given is 237237778). Work is done by 4 full-time employees, 4 part-time
employees, and 4 volunteers.

MEMBERSHIP, SCOPE, AND POLICY
The Ministry of Welfare sets the standards for participation in the
project. Eligibility is limited to large families with income not exceeding
a certain amount. There are 2,000 participants in Israel, in 8 branches of
the project. Decisions are made by the Board.

AFFILIATIONS/REFERENCES
The project is not affiliated with any political party in Israel. No references are listed.

FUNDING NEEDED
1. To purchase stock before inflation makes it impossible, and to enable bulk purchases at lowerer rates. Needed: $200,000.
2. To open additional branches in other Israeli cities. Estimated needs: $80,000 plus stock.
3. To establish a mobile supermarket to visit small towns. Cost: $30,000.

HITACHDUT OLEI AUSTRALIA & NEW ZEALAND

התאחדות עולי אוסטרליה וניו זילנד

5/1 Ophira, Sanhedria
Jerusalem
Telephone: (02) 818003
Office hours: Sunday-Thursday, 8:00 A.M. to 3:00 P.M.

HISTORY AND DESCRIPTION
Hitachdut Olei Australia & New Zealand (Association of Immigrants from Australia & New Zealand) was founded in 1956 to help new immigrants from Australia and New Zealand settle in Israel.

Organizational Structure: An Executive Committee of 6 persons runs and controls the activities of the organization. The Executive is elected every two years and it directs several separate committees such as publications, special events, and absorption (klita).

Goals: To aid the settling process of new immigrants from Australia and New Zealand, and provide social, cultural and ethnic support to those Australians and New Zealanders settled in Israel.

Services, Activities, and Accomplishments: The Association provides a personal absorption service, giving help to new immigrants with advice concerning their problems and bureaucratic traumas. An active network of volunteers visit Absorption Centres and aid the absorption of new immigrants, helping them to overcome their initial traumas and problems. The organization also provides a social framework for cultural activities, which include an annual Independence Day western picnic, film nights, social gatherings and Shabbat walks.

OFFICERS
Director: Dr. Stefen Sattler, 5/1 Ophira, Jerusalem.
                  Tel.: (02) 818003.
Treasurer: Norman Tarsis, 111/1 Uziel, Jerusalem.
Board Members: Dr. Gabbi Engel, 76 Bayit Vegan, Jerusalem.
                  Tel.: (02) 420917.
                  Dr. Mike Levin, 104/12 Ramot, Jerusalem.
                  Tel.: (02) 863361.

FINANCIAL INFORMATION
50% of the Association's income comes from membership dues, 20% from donations, 20% as grants from the Ministry of Absorption, and 10% as proceeds from activities. Last year's annual budget of $2,000 left the Association with a balanced budget. The Association is not registered as a non-profit Association and donations in Israel and the United States are not tax-free. Twenty volunteers are the only staff employed by the Association.

MEMBERSHIP, SCOPE, AND POLICY
Membership is open to any Australian or New Zealand settler. There are 650 members in Israel, in one branch, and one branch abroad with 35 members. Decisions are made by the National Board.

AFFILIATIONS/REFERENCES
The Association is not affiliated with any Israeli political party. It is affiliated with the Zionist Federation of Australia & New Zealand, 543 St. Kilda Rd., Melbourne, Australia, and the Israel Office of the British, Australian & New Zealand Zionist Federations, 13 Ben Maimon, Rehavia, Jerusalem.

FUNDING NEEDED
1. To establish clubs (moadonim) for new Western immigrants in the main cities such as Jerusalem, Tel Aviv, Haifa, and Beersheva — $30,000.

HODAYOT RELIGIOUS YOUTH VILLAGE

הודיות

M.P. Lower Galilee
Telephone: (067) 20791
Office hours: 8:00 A.M. to 3:00 P.M.

HISTORY AND DESCRIPTION

Hodayot Religious Youth Village was started by Youth Aliya in 1950 near Kibbutz Lavi in the Lower Galilee with a nucleus of thirty-four needy young Jews from India. These gave Hodayot its name: Hodu, in Hebrew means "India" and "Give thanks to the Lord". Today, in an atmosphere of religious observance, Hodayot provides a secondary school education in religious, general, and technical subjects for Youth Aliya wards, Israelis and new immigrants.

Goals: Within a religious environment, religious studies and a general education are combined to teach pupils coming from varied backgrounds the art of living together, the skills required in a modern competitive world, and to give content to leisure time.

Services, Activities, and Accomplishments: Students are divided into five groups, each with its own madrich, housemother, and clubroom. Community activities revolve around the madrich, who is friend-cum-counselor and initiates group activities. The housemother supervises clothing, hygiene, diet, and lends a motherly ear to youthful confidences. Free time at Hodayot may be spent browsing in the reference library or reading room, writing for the school newspaper, singing in the choir, painting, modeling, playing basketball or football, and even taking a dip in nearby Kibbutz Lavi's swimming pool on warm days. Students' councils elected and run by pupils meet weekly, deal with student affairs, and publish their own newspaper. A social worker is on hand to help the individual students when necessary. Intensive Hebrew courses are provided for new immigrants who need to be able to absorb enough of the language in a short while to enable them to join regular classes. The youngsters spend a few hours every week working on the farm or garden, or doing a stint in the kitchen.

OFFICERS

Director: David BetAreyeh, Kibbutz Yavne.
Board Members: Avraham Halperin, Ramat Gan. Lecturer.
Ovadia Chenzion, Ramat Gan. Administrator.
Norman Oster, Ramat Gan. Lawyer.
Rivka Cohen, Ramat Ha-Golan.
Director Social Services.
Itzak Flanzer, Kibbutz Lavi.
Yacov Koplowitz, Hodayot. Administrator.

FINANCIAL INFORMATION
Last year's annual budget of $200,000, of which 2% came from donations, left Hodayot with a deficit of $25,020. Although it is not registered as a non-profit organization, donations to Hodayot in Israel, the United States, and Canada may be made tax-free (no tax numbers supplied, but donations can be made through the Mizrachi movement in all of these countries). Hodayot employs thirty full-time and twenty part-time workers, as well as six volunteers.

MEMBERSHIP, SCOPE, AND POLICY
Hodayot has eight ex-officio Board members, which makes most of the decisions.

AFFILIATIONS/REFERENCES
Hodayot is affiliated to the National Religious Party in Israel, and is a beneficiary of the Youth Aliya Department of the Jewish Agency.

1. $320,000 — School building.
2. $60,000 — New kitchen.
3. $10,000 — Furniture for new three-room Moadon.

HOLOCAUST AND
SOCIAL TRAUMA STUDIES

חקר השואה וטראומה חברתית

"SHALVATA" Mental Health Center
P.O.B. 94
45100 Hod Hasharon
Telephone: (052) 32602
Office hours: 8:00 A.M. to 3:00 P.M.

HISTORY AND DESCRIPTION

The Holocaust and Social Trauma Studies program was founded by Professor Shamai Davidson, in the 1970's as a special project of the non-profit Shalvata Mental Health Center in Hod Hasharon. It is operated in conjunction with the Bar Ilan University School of Social Work. Shalvata is a subsidiary of the Histadrut Kupat Holim medical network, but the Holocaust studies program is funded entirely by donations outside the Histadrut.

Goals: The study of the long-term consequences of massive psychological trauma on different groups of people is a developing area of research of considerable importance in its implications and applications for the understanding, prevention and treatment of individual and social patterns of adjustment. Because of the large number of traumatized people who settled in Israel and the frequency of major stressful events, Israel constitutes a rich laboratory for the study of the long-term effects of traumatization on human behavior.

Services, Activities, and Accomplishments: Research projects include longitudinal follow-up studies during the life-cycles of survivors of the Holocaust, their families, children and grandchildren. The emphasis is on patterns of adaptation and protective integrative factors rather than clinical phenomena and maladaptive vulnerability. In addition, the program is working on a study of the transmission of the effects of traumatization from parents through the parent-child interaction to their children, and possibly to future generations, as well as the protective factors allowing healthy child-rearing despite massive traumatization in the parent.

A course of lectures and seminars on the Holocaust and Social Trauma is held in the Bar Ilan University School of Social Work, throughout one academic year of the M.A. program. Shorter courses are held for medical students (Tel Aviv University Medical School) and for psychiatrists as part of their specialist training in the Postgraduate Training Program (Tel Aviv University Medical School).

A counselling service for survivors and their families is available free of charge at the Bar Ilan University School of Social Work and in the Raanana Community Mental Health Unit.

An increasing number of Holocaust survivors require counselling and guidance in the later years of their lives. It is vitally important to deepen our understanding of their needs and to create additional therapeutic and counselling services in relationship to this high-risk population and their children in Israel.

In addition, the program operates a resource center on the effects of traumatization on different groups. This data is available for intramural research as well as for outside scholars. Scientific meetings are organized for interchange between investigators from different countries.

It is important to emphasize that many of the issues involved are applicable to victims of recent major traumatic events such as terrorist attacks.

OFFICERS

Prof. Shamai Davidson, "Shalvata" Mental Health Center, P.O.B. 94 Hod Hasharon 41500.
Psychiatrist.
Tel. (052) 32602.

FINANCIAL INFORMATION

All of the funds for the annual budget come from P.E.F. Israel Endowment Funds, Inc., 342 Madison Ave., New York. Last year $12,000 was received. The organization is not registered as an Ottoman Association. Donations are tax-free although no number was supplied. There is one part-time employee as well as two volunteers in addition to the director (Prof. Davidson) who is unsalaried.

AFFILIATIONS/REFERENCES

The organization is not affiliated with any political party in Israel.

FUNDING NEEDED

The employment of additional researchers for the studies of the resouces used in overcoming the effects of massive trauma on the lives of survivors and their offspring.

Amount needed—$58,000 per annum.

HOME FOR THE AGED

בית מושב זקנים וזקנות, פתח תקוה

32 Montefiori Street
Petah Tikva
Telephone: (03) 911853
Office hours: 9:00 A.M. to 1:00 P.M.

HISTORY AND DESCRIPTION
Beit Moshav Zkenim VeZkenot was established 45 years ago as a charity institute in order to help old people of scarce means to spend their old age in a home atmosphere and to fulfill their needs. There are 75 people living in the Home. Activities include Bible classes for the men, and handicrafts for the women. In addition there are lectures, films, trips, and artists' performances.

OFFICERS
Rabbi Shimon Katz, 25 Ben Zion, Jerusalem. Retired.
Ephraim Lerer, 16 Bar Kochba, Petah Tikva. Retired.
Moshe Sarid, 26 Brande, Petah Tikva. Retired.
Yechezkel Feldman, 29 Harav Bloy, Petah Tikva.
  Manufacturer.
Yaacov Linzer, 27 Montefiori, Petah Tikva. Manufacturer.
Rabbi Yitzhak Braverman, 6 Motzkin, Petah Tikva. Shochet.
Shlomo Alban, Shikun Poel Mizrachi, Petah Tikva.
  Bank clerk.
Moshe Shwalb, 7 Ahad Ha'Am, Petah Tikva. Manufacturer.

FINANCIAL INFORMATION
Last year's budget came from the following sources: token payment for boarding rates, participation of Welfare Office, and contributions. The amount of last year's budget was not stated. The organization is registered as an Ottoman Association but the number was not supplied. It was not indicated whether or not donations are tax-free. There are 22 full time and 7 part time employees.

MEMBERSHIP, SCOPE, AND POLICY
Decisions are made at Board meetings. Residents of Petah Tikva are eligible for membership. There are 16 members in Israel.

AFFILIATIONS/REFERENCES
The Home is not affiliated with any political party in Israel.

FUNDING NEEDED
1. Elevator, $12,000.
2. Painting and whitewashing, $1,000.
3. Occupational therapy rooms, $750.
4. Installation of solar heating system, $8,000.

HOREB SCHOOLS OF JERUSALEM
חוג בית ספר חורב ירושלים

Rehov Kovshei Katamon
Jerusalem
Telephone: (02) 635274
Office hours: 8:00 A.M. to 3:00 P.M.

HISTORY AND DESCRIPTION

The Horeb School System was founded in 1933 by immigrants from Western Europe—mainly Germany. The philosophical foundations were based on "Torah Im Derech Eretz"—teaching and advocating a life based on Torah and Halacha while at the same time preparing its students with a complete secular education which will allow them to meet the needs of a citizen in modern society.

Today the system has a student body of nearly 1800 students, including an elementary school (grades 1-6), which has separate divisions for boys and girls, a girls' high school (grades 7-12), and a Yeshiva high school for boys (grades 7-12).

The school system is unaffiliated with any political, municipal or governmental body, but all divisions are recognized by the Ministry of Education. The school board is an active committee of volunteer citizens rooted in the school's philosophy—most are graduates of the system. Each division has its own principal and directorate who make overall school policy.

The school's major accomplishment has been the education of thousands of students to a productive life based on Torah teachings and the fulfillment of mitzvot. It has been doing this for the past 50 years.

OFFICERS

Chairman: Eliezer Hochster, 8 Gidud Haivri, Jerusalem.
                          Civil Service Commission. Tel. (02) 633528.

Treasurer: Chaim Kahn, Gan Rehavia, Jerusalem. Lawyer.
                          Tel. (02) 224883.

Board Members: Tuvia Bier, 60 Ben Maimon, Jerusalem.
                          Real Estate Agent. Tel. (02) 632640.
                          Rabbi Yaakov Pollack, 5 Panim Meirot, Jerusalem.
                          Principal, Elementary School. Tel. (02) 521988.
                          Rabbi S. Cohen, 3 Panim Meirot, Jerusalem.
                          Rosh Yeshiva. Tel. (02) 522663.
                          Rabbi H. Leibovitz. Menahel Yeshiva.
                          Tel. (02) 531665.
                          Shlomo Merzel, 85 Bayit Vegan, Jerusalem.
                          Principal Girls' High School. Tel. (02) 421136.
                          Meir Farkash, 5b Joshua Ben Gamla, Jerusalem.
                          Lawyer. Tel. (02) 631432.

FINANCIAL INFORMATION

65% of last year's annual budget came from tuition payments; the remaining 35% from donations. The budget for last year was $750,000, with a deficit of $175,000. The school is registered as an Ottoman Association (no. 11/713). Donations are tax-free in Israel (for donations of over 10,000 shekel) and in the United States (under the New York office name, Society for the Promotion of Jewish Education, 1980 Blue Book — page 102), and in Canada via the Mizrachi Organization of Canada. There are 60 full-time employees and 100 part-time employees (teachers).

MEMBERSHIP, SCOPE, AND POLICY
Decisions are made mostly by the school principals and directorate.

AFFILIATIONS/REFERENCES
The school is not affiliated with any political party in Israel. It is affiliated with the Society for the Promotion of Jewish Education in New York City.

FUNDING NEEDED
1. The construction of a new campus for the Yeshiva high school.
   Cost — $1,000,000.
2. The erection of a library and lecture hall-synagogue for the girls' high school.
   Cost — $250,000 for each structure.
3. The construction of a dining hall-kitchen for the girls' high school.
   Cost — $350,000.

HUMAN HEART-TO-HEART SOCIETY

אגודת לב־אדם לאדם

HaPisga Street 50,
Bayit Vegan, Jerusalem OR
P.O.B. 16191,
Jerusalem.
Telephone: (02) 411098.
Office Hours: 7:00 A.M. to 8:00 A.M.; 2:00 P.M. to 6:00 P.M.;
                  9:00 P.M. to 11:00 P.M.

HISTORY AND DESCRIPTION

The Human Heart-to-Heart Society was founded to promote spiritual
and material assistance to baalei teshuva (those who return to observance of Jewish law) and to the Torah world at large. The founder of the
organization, a baal teshuva himself, runs the Society as essentially a
one-man operation. The organization provides financial aid to needy
families, devoting special interest to brides and grooms by arranging
gifts and free loans to help them set up their homes.

Organizational Structure: The by-laws of the organization stipulate that
a general meeting is to be held once a year, at which time the Board of
the Society is elected and a report on the organization's activities and its
current financial status is presented. Decisions of the meeting are taken
by a majority vote. The Board is made up of a Chairman, Vice-
Chairman, Secretary and 5 members, who meet at least once a month. A
Control Committee of not less than 3 members oversees all activities of
the Society.

Services, Activities, and Accomplishments: The Society gathers information from government programs and charitable groups, and then distributes this information to the yeshivas. It runs a free loan society
which welcomes even the smallest sums put at its disposal in order to
give more Jews the opportunity of sharing this great mitzvah. The
organization also offers a Tefillin Loan Service. New students at yeshivas for baalei teshuva must be able to borrow Tefillin until they are
committed enough to Yiddishkeit to go out and buy a pair of their own.
Torah scholars as well must borrow Tefillin when they give away their
own pair to be checked and repaired. The organization owns 14 pairs of
Tefillin and has another 4 on loan. Among its other activities, the
Society also conducts evening summer courses in Judaism for women,
and has established a location in Jerusalem for burial of "Divrei Kedu-
sha" (sacred objects), which will fulfill the needs of Jerusalem for many
years to come. In May 1980, the Society founded an organization known
as "The Ark" in response to the plight of divorcees and widows and
their children, who often find themselves suddenly without shelter,
food, advice or assistance. "The Ark's" basic goal is to provide financial
and professional advice and assistance to both mother and children
during the initial period when the need is greatest and the wheels of
bureaucracy are at their slowest. The group's professional staff provides

a wide range of services, and includes lawyers, financial advisors, a dentist, a psychologist, a rabbi, a nurse and several diagnosticians.

OFFICERS

Director:	Chaim Rudner, HaPisga 50, J-m. Accountant. Tel. (02) 411098.
Treasurer:	Mordechai Perl, HaPisga 50, J-m. Economist.
Board Members:	Michael Liani, Rav Frank 2, J-m. Rabbi. Tel. (02) 413711. Zvi Cohen, Kibbutz Lavi. Farmer. Tel. (067) 21478. Shabtai Koben, HaPisga 60, J-m. Student. Abraham Kugel, Eliezer 5, B'nei Brak. Student. Tel. (03) 708247. Kalman Packouz, Sorotzkin 18, J-m. Rabbi-Author. Shmuel Ben Abraham, Bartenura 4, B'nei Brak. Clerk.

FINANCIAL INFORMATION
The Society's income is derived entirely from donations. Last year's annual budget was $4,000, with no deficit. The organization is in the process of securing tax-free status for donations. It is registered as a non-profit Ottoman Association in the Jerusalem District Office of the Ministry of the Interior (reg. no. 11/3163). The organization is staffed by 15 volunteers.

MEMBERSHIP, SCOPE, AND POLICY
Membership is open to any Torah-observant Jew who agrees to support and promote the goals of the Society. The organization has 3 branches in Israel consisting of 7 members. There are no branches abroad.

AFFILIATIONS/REFERENCES
The organization is not affiliated with any political party in Israel nor with any group abroad.

FUNDING NEEDED
1. To support the activities of "The Ark" — $25,000.
2. To support a girls' school for baalot teshuva — $10,000.
3. To provide aid to students to continue their studies for the rabbinate — $5,000.

"I AM MY BROTHER'S KEEPER"

"שומר אחי אנוכי"

P.O.B. 9, Jerusalem
Telephone: (02) 536369
Office Hours: Twenty-four hours a day

HISTORY AND DESCRIPTION

'I Am My Brother's Keeper' ('Shomer Achi Anochi') was established following the March 1977 accusation and arrest of Anatoly Scharansky. The founders of the organization include Scharansky's wife Avital, his brother-in-law Michael Shtieglitz, and a handful of Sabras who felt that not enough was being done in Israel on behalf of 'Prisoners of Zion' and the three and one-half million Jews of the Soviet Union.

Goals: The organization seeks to arouse awareness in Israel and throughout the world to the plight of Soviet Jewry, and encourage and keep in contact with Jewish brethren in the Soviet Union.

Services, Activities, and Accomplishments: The organization has two major areas of activity. It publishes bulletins and pamphlets and distributes to the Israeli and international media any information received regarding the plight of Soviet Jewry. It attempts to bolster the spirit and resolve of Soviet Jews by establishing and maintaining contacts through correspondence, the sending of food packages for Purim, fruit for Tu Beshvat, calendars for the Hebrew New Year, and books. Among the organization's major accomplishments include the maintenance of constant communication with aliyah activists in the Soviet Union; the repeal of the verdict in the Scharansky case; and increased awareness in Israel and all over the world of the plight of Prisoners of Zion.

OFFICERS

Director: Michael Stieglitz, Jerusalem. Archaeologist.
Tel. (02) 660301.

Treasurer: Michael Baron, Eben Gbirol 190, Tel Aviv.
Teacher.
Tel. (03) 446885.

Board Members: Avital Scharansky, Ben Zakai 70, Jerusalem.
Tel. (02) 667222.
Ilana Ben-Yosef, Ben-Zakai 70, Jerusalem.
Tel. (02) 667222.
Benyamin Ben-Yosef, Ben-Zakai 70, Jerusalem.
Physicist.
Tel. (02) 667222.
Yaacov Shternberg, Yeshivat Yamit, Yamit.
Teacher.
Benyamin Eizner, Ben Zion 20, Jerusalem. Rabbi.
Tel. (02) 531473.
Eliezer Sadan, Ben Dor 18, Jerusalem.
Yeshiva student. Tel. (02) 531618.

FINANCIAL INFORMATION

Last year's annual budget of $60,000 left 'I Am My Brother's Keeper' with a deficit of $20,000. All funding to the organization is through contributions from private individuals. At present, donations are tax-free in Israel (reg. no. 450774), but not in the United States, although steps are being taken to rectify this. The organization is registered with the Jerusalem District Offiee of the Ministry of the Interior as an Ottoman Association (reg. no. 11/2820). The organization employs one full-time and one part-time worker, plus ten regular volunteers and between twenty and forty volunteers for special programs.

MEMBERSHIP, SCOPE, AND POLICY

Fifty national members of the organization are represented by its two Israeli branches. There are no foreign members or branches. Decisions are made by members of the Board (Hanhala) as well as those active in the field of Soviet Jewry and Prisoners of Zion. The only criterion for membership is good will and a devotion to the cause.

AFFILIATIONS/REFERENCES

The organization is not aligned with any Israeli political party. It has affiliations with the following international bodies:

35's Women's Campaign for Soviet Jewry, 148 Granville Road, London, England;

SSSJ, 200 West 72nd Street, Suites 30-31, New York, N.Y. 10023;

Comite des 15, 64 Ave. Henri Martin, Paris, 75016, France.

FUNDING NEEDED

The organization lists, in order of priority, the following as its most outstanding funding requirements:

1. Rental of an apartment that will serve as headquarters, plus continuation of regular activities. Estimated cost, $300/month;
2. Publication of a new booklet on 'Correspondence with Soviet Jews';
3. Establishment of an all-encompassing educational information program to be run in Israeli schools and youth organizations outlining the problems of Soviet Jewry's immigration and absorption into Israeli society.

ICHUD SHIVATH ZION,
AGUDA LEUMIT DATIT

אחוד שיבת ציון, אגודה לאומית דתית

Frishman 12
Tel Aviv
Telephone: (03) 224047
Office Hours: 8:30 A.M. to 1:00 P.M., 4:30 P.M. to 7:00 P.M. (except Friday).

HISTORY AND DESCRIPTION
Ichud Shivath Zion was founded in 1938, mainly by refugees from Hitlerism. Today, members come from many countries and number about 100.

Organizational Structure: The organization has an executive board which is elected every two years by a general assembly.

Goals: The organization strives to provide religious and social activities to many different groups in the community in a number of languages.

Services, Activities, and Accomplishments: The society is active in many areas, both religious and social/secular. These include: prayer and Torah classes; preparation courses for Bar Mitzvahs; lectures and study-days on topics relating to Judaism and Israeli culture; providing food and clothing for the poor; organizing a Golden Age Club; organizing summer camps for children from large families; and creating Oneg Shabbats each Friday night in English (which have had over 30,000 participants since the program began). The organization's greatest accomplishment to date was the establishment of a new building (synagogue and community center), built from 1967 to 1971 at Ben Yehuda 86, in Tel Aviv. The center contains two synagogues, two libraries, a modern mikva-pool and a number of class/lecture/activity rooms.

OFFICERS
Director: Dr. Shimon Bamira, Tel Aviv.
                   Director of Co. Tel. (03) 233080.
Treasurer: Eliezer Amster, Tel Aviv.
                   Accountant. Tel. (03) 221950.
Board Members: Kalman Wagner, Tel Aviv.
                   Pensioner. Tel. (03) 230669.
                   Ludwig Mittwoch, Tel Aviv.
                   Director of Co. Tel. (03) 281151.

FINANCIAL INFORMATION
The income of Ichud Shivath Zion comes from a number of sources. Membership fees and the sale of synagogue seats amounts to 8% of the total; donations, 35%; fees paid for marriages and Bar Mitzvahs, 38%; with the remaining 19% coming from legacies, interest on investments, dividiends and sundry items. The organization's 1978 budget was

$64,272. There are costs for additional initiatives and various obligations which could not be met. The organization is registered with the Tel Aviv District Office of the Ministry of the Interior as an Ottoman Association (reg. no. 37/99). Donations are tax-free in Israel (reg. no. not supplied), but not in the United States. There are 15 full-time and 12 part-time employees, as well as 10 volunteers.

MEMBERSHIP, SCOPE, AND POLICY
Decision are made by an Executive Board of members, which is elected by a general assembly. Every Jew, except those living in mixed marriages, is eligible for membership in Ichud Shivath Zion. Presently, there are 950 members in Israel, and approximately 50 abroad. There are two branches in Israel and none abroad.

AFFILIATIONS/REFERENCES
The organization is not aligned with any Israeli political party. It is affiliated with many different congregations, tourists and visitors, and the Jewish Agency abroad. The Center invites all to attend its programs, which are conducted in numberous languages.

FUNDING NEEDED
The organization has a number of outstanding present funding needs. In order of priority, these include the following:
1. Construction of an emergency exit from upper stories of the building, to facilitate easy evacuation of elderly participants in case of emergency;
2. Installation of an emergency generator for lighting and security purposes in times of power/electrical shortages;
3. Construction of additional lecture halls to replace existing open patios.

INDEPENDENT LIVING—SELF-HELP ORGANIZATION FOR THE PHYSICALLY DISABLED

חיים עצמאיים

Harav Uziel 129/10
Bayit Vegan, Jerusalem 96431
Telephone: (02) 422293
Office hours: 8:00 A.M. to 5:00 P.M.

HISTORY AND DESCRIPTION
Independent Living was founded in July 1980 by Trevor Gurewitz, formerly of Melbourne, Australia, who is himself a paraplegic and "made aliya (immigrated to Israel) in a wheelchair".

Services and Activities: Independent Living helps the physically disabled to help themselves. This, by assisting people with special needs in obtaining suitable equipment with interest-free loans, by disseminating information on technical aids, and by working to overcome architectural barriers.

OFFICERS
Director: Trevor Israel Gurewitz, Harav Uziel 129/10, Jerusalem. Businessman. Tel. (02) 422293.

Treasurer: Chaim Pearl, Harav Uziel 129/16, Jerusalem. Rabbi. Tel. (02) 422605.

Board Members: Tirza Ilan, Bayit Vegan 53, Jerusalem. Social worker. Tel. (02) 421512.

Ruth Seligman, Yosef Zvi 55, Ramat Gan. Journalist. Tel. (03) 740065.

Michael Bourke, Yosef Zvi 61, Ramat Gan. Medical practitioner. Tel. (03) 743408.

Carmella Bourke, Yosef Zvi 61, Ramat Gan. Psychologist. Tel. (03) 743408.

Lee Waldman, Matmon 10, Tel Aviv. Architect. Tel. (03) 266418.

FINANCIAL INFORMATION
(No information regarding budget was available since the newly-founded organization had not commenced operations when this entry was submitted.)

Donations to Independent Living are tax-free in Israel (reg. no. 4507509). The organization is registered as an Ottoman Association (Jerusalem, reg. no. 11/3479). The staff consists of seven volunteers.

MEMBERSHIP, SCOPE, AND POLICY
Membership (no figure supplied) is open to all, upon payment of $20 per annum to be a "Friend of Independent Living". Most decisions are taken by the Executive Director. The organization is not affiliated with any political party in Israel.

FUNDING NEEDED

1. To provide equipment for handicapped persons which they cannot afford, and for which financial help is not obtainable from the Government.
2. To disseminate information on technical aids.
3. To overcome architectural barriers which effect the disabled by campaigning for the construction of facilities suitable for invalids and by publicizing what has already been done in other countries.

INSTITUTE FOR SCIENCE AND HALACHA

מכון מדעי טכנולוגי לבעיות הלכה

Hapisga, 1
Bayit Vegan Jerusalem.
Telephone: (02) 424880
Office Hours: 8:00 A.M. to 4:00 P.M.

HISTORY AND DESCRIPTION
The Institute For Science and Halacha was established in 1966 as a research center dealing with the classification and solution of problems arising out of the advance of modern science and technology confronting the Torah-observant individual, the Jewish community and the Jewish state.

Organizational Structure: The Institute consists of Association members, and Executive Committee and a Directorate.

Goals: The Institute seeks to facilitate in all fields of human endeavour the meticulous compliance with the Halacha, to the full utilization and enjoyment of all the benefits derived through scientific and technological advances.

Services, Activities, and Accomplishments: Members of the Institute deal with a wide range of topics, including organising and preparing layouts of systems facilitating the proper functioning and full observance of Shabbat, Yom Tov and Kashrut for such institutions as hospitals, industrial plants and agricultural settlements (kibbutzim). The Institute has published seven important works in various areas of science and Halacha and has in preparation eight additional volumes. This literature constitutes the basis of the Institute's progress in the above activities. Among the major achievements of the Institute, are aid provided to organizations and institutions by giving them practical tools to facilitate observance of the Halacha, and assistance provided to manufacturers towards the production of equipment and components for institutions and individuals designed to facilitate observance of the Halacha.

OFFICERS
Prof. B. S. Fraenkel — Chairman of the Board. Hapalmach 26, J'm.
Rabbi Dr. S. R. Weiss — Chairman, Vaad Hapoel.
Rabbi L. Y. Halperin — Head of Halacha Division.

FINANCIAL INFORMATION
Various governmental agencies provide 30% and non governmental sources and donations account for the remaining 70% of the Institute's income. Last year's budget of $263,000 left the organization with a deficit of $34,000. The Institute is registered as a non-profit Ottoman Association, but no registration number was supplied. Donations to the organization in Israel are tax-free.

The Institute has 21 full-time and 5 part-time employees, as well as 28 volunteers.

MEMBERSHIP, SCOPE, AND POLICY

There are 99 founding members of the Institute. Membership is open to those who are approved by the Institutes' General Assembly. Decisions are made at the operative level by the Institute's Board of Directors.

AFFILIATIONS/REFERENCES

The Institute For Science and Halacha is not associated with any Israeli political party. It is affiliated with the Association of Orthodox Jewish Scientists in the United States, France and Great Britain. Mr. Aharon Haimowitz (3 West 16 Street N.Y.C.) is the chairman of the American section.

FUNDING NEEDED

1. To continue to research, publish books, and train personnel towards solving technological problems confronting the proper observance of Shabbat, Yom Tov, Kashrut and other elements of the Halacha.
2. To build permanent offices and a laboratory center which will include a rabbinical research center, electronics laboratory and workshops, costing a total of $50 million.

INSTITUTE FOR THE COMMEMORA-
TION OF GALICIAN JEWRY

המכון להנצחת יהדות גליציה

13 Panim Meirot
Jerusalem
Telephone: (02) 527014
Office hours: 8:00 P.M. to 10:00 P.M.

HISTORY AND DESCRIPTION

The Institute was founded in 1978 by a group of individuals who had a singular desire to memorialize Galician Jewry.

Organizational Structure: The original group of founders now serves as the administration of the Institute.

Goals: To develop the legacy of Galician Jewry and to memorialize it for future generations; to gather, classify and preserve documentary material on Galician Jewry; to encourage young scholars to research and write on Galician personalities and communities; to publish and distribute published works on Galician Jewry.

Services, Activities, and Accomplishments: Initially the Institute gathered important material from libraries and archives as well as from private sources. Memories of old people were taped and all the material was classified. The Institute provides in-depth information about families and communities in response to enquiries from all over the world. The findings of the Institute are published in books and periodicals. At present the Institute's prime activity is the publication of the wide-ranging "Encyclopedia of Galician Scholars" which includes, in addition to the biographical articles, many geneaological tables, portraits, and facsimiles, as well as indexes and biographical source material. Volume I of the Encyclopedia has already been published and further volumes have been prepared. In addition to this achievement the Institute has had many research articles published in periodicals.

OFFICERS

Director: Meir Wunder, 13 Panim Meirot, Jerusalem. Librarian. Tel. (02) 527014.

Treasurer: Zadok Sonnenblick, 16 Gordon, Netanya. Clerk. Tel. (053) 39169.

Board Members: Baruch M. Cohen, 1 Alefandri, Jerusalem. Bibliographer.

Akiva Doron, 1A Palmach, Jerusalem. Teacher. Tel. (02) 662059.

Avram J. Bombach, 12 Bet Shammai, Bnei-Brak. Rabbi. Tel. (03) 236885.

FINANCIAL INFORMATION

The Institute's income derives from private donations, Government support and the sale of publications. Last year's annual budget of

$10,000 left the Institute with an accumulated deficit of $15,000. The Institute is registered in Jerusalem as a non-profit Ottoman Association (reg. no. 11/3089). Donations in Israel and the United States are tax-free (tax nos. not supplied). Two volunteer-workers are employed by the Institute.

AFFILIATIONS/REFERENCES
The Institute is not affiliated with any Israeli political party. It is affiliated with the following organizations:

Research Institute of Religious Jewry, c/o Dr. Isaac Lewin, 258 Riverside Drive, N.Y.

Jewish Geneaological Society, c/o Dr. Neil Rosenstein, 185 Shelley Ave., Elizabeth, N.J.

FUNDING NEEDED
1. To finance the publication of a five-volume encyclopedic work on Galician scholars (cost approx. $100,000).
2. To finance research of relevant material at home and abroad (cost $25,000).

THE INSTITUTE OF RESEARCH FOR THE TEMPLE OF JERUSALEM

המכון לחקר בית המקדש

P.O.B. 17001, Jerusalem
Telephone: (02) 710467

HISTORY AND DESCRIPTION
The Institute was established in October 1980 in order to collect any already published work about the Temple in any field of research; to promote new research on the subject, and to then publish and circulate the amassed material and organize seminars and meetings concerning the subject. Voluntary contributions are sought from the scholars involved. It is expected that scholarships will be offered from time to time. The overall goal of the organization is to arouse new interest in the Temple on the part of non-scholars through the renewed research of academics.

FINANCIAL INFORMATION
As the Institute has only recently been established, no annual budget had been determined at the time of printing. However, donations will be responsible for 100% of income. Donations in the U.S. are tax-deductible (I.R.S. No. 51-086442-4). Donations in Israel are also tax-free, and recently the Institute petitioned for non-profit Ottoman society status (specific information and registration numbers were not provided).

MEMBERSHIP, SCOPE, AND POLICY
There is no formal membership. Rather, the Institute will accept practically any kind of work relating to the Temple. Decisions are made by founder-director Dr. Edoardo Recanati (Caspi 12, Jerusalem; writer), and a board of academics is to be formed.

FUNDING NEEDED
The Institute needs funds to publicize itself world-wide and to search for materials on the Temple and to publish them. Funds are needed to organize seminars and congresses in Jerusalem on Temple research.

INTERNS FOR PEACE

Shmuel Hanagid Street 16, Jerusalem
Telephone: (02) 246195 or 246196
Office Hours: 9:00 A.M. to 5:00 P.M.

HISTORY AND DESCRIPTION

Founded in 1977, Interns for Peace places teams of Israeli Jews, Israeli Arabs, and Diaspora Jews to live and work in Arab and Jewish communities for two years. The interns serve as community workers, bringing groups of Arabs and Jews together in cooperative activites.

Organizational Structure: The structure for decision-making consists of: the National Israeli Advisory Committee, which meets annually; the Steering Committee, which meets monthly in Jewish and Arab communities; and Local Advisory Committees, consisting of community members of each Jewish and Arab community in which interns work. The professional staff consists of a director, a field coordinator, community work supervisors, a recruitment officer and an administrator. There is also an evaluation team, funded by a Ford Foundation grant.

Goals: To train professional community workers in the field of Jewish-Arab cooperation and to build cooperative activities between Jews and Arabs by means of community work principles.

Services, Activities and Accomplishments: Within the Arab sector, community development projects have included: Learning centers for mothers and children; nursery schools; teenage volunteer corps; establishment of neighborhood public parks and clean-up drives; and establishment and/or strengthening of youth and community centers. Projects of cooperation between neighboring paired Jewish and Arab communities included: Summer camps; mixed sport teams; social and educational clubs for high school drop-outs; social and cultural club for young families; seminars for teachers and principals on joint curriculum and cross-cultural experiences for their students; and establishing infrastructure for regional cooperative industry.
An exchange program for Israeli (Jews and Arabs) and Egyptian teenagers is also being explored.
Interns for Peace operates as a non-political, independently funded program. As such, it has received acceptance and active involvement from both the Jewish and Arab sectors in Israel.

OFFICERS

Director: Rabbi Bruce M. Cohen, Kibbutz Barkai,
                      D.N. Menashe.
                      Tel. (063) 78586.

Assistant
Director: Farhat Agbaria, Mus Mus.
Chairman: Rabbi Henry F. Skirball, 16 Shmuel Hanagid,
                      Jerusalem. Tel. (02) 246195.

Secretary:	Muhammed Masarweh, Esq., Kfar Kara.
Treasurer:	Dov Eron, Kibbutz Barkai, D.N. Menashe.
	Tel. (063) 78586.
Board Members:	Chanan Cohen, Kibbutz Ein Hashofet.
	Munir Diab, Director of Tamra Community
Center.	
	Eli Rechess, Tel Aviv University.
	Benjamin Yanuv, School of Social Work,
	Bar-Ilan University. Lecturer.
	Mahmud Yunis, Ar-Ara. Histadrut Official.

FINANCIAL INFORMATION

Interns for Peace is supported totally by donations from North America, the communities in which the interns live and Israeli organizations such as the Histadrut. The annual budget for 1979-1980 was $140,000. Ottoman Registration in Israel is pending. Contributions are tax-exempt in the U.S. (no. 132910157) and application has been made in Israel and Canada. The professional staff in Israel consists of one full-time and 4 part-time members and fifteen interns.

MEMBERSHIP, SCOPE, AND POLICY

Israeli interns are Jews and Arabs, with a B.A. or equivalent degree. Interns from outside Israel are Jewish college graduates with an intermediate level of Hebrew and a previous six-month living experience in Israel. All candidates must have experience in community work and skills in areas such as agriculture, industry, sports, education, health, youth leadership and art.

Policy is decided by the Steering Committee. In addition, there is an Advisory Board, which consists of 200 members in Israel and 1,500 abroad. There are also 3,000 friends of Interns For Peace, located primarily in 6 communities throughout Israel.

AFFILIATIONS/REFERENCES

Interns for Peace, 150 Fifth Avenue (Room 1002), New York, N.Y. 10011.
American Jewish Committee, Rabbi Marc Tanenbaum, 165 E. 56th Street, New York, N.Y.
World Jewish Congress, Dr. Israel Singer, 1 Park Avenue, New York, N.Y.

FUNDING NEEDED

Over the next five years, the program seeks to recruit, train, place, supervise and evaluate 100 interns in order to have direct contact with at least 20% of Israel's Jewish and Arab population. The budget for 1980-1985 is $2,000,000.

IRAQI JEWS EDUCATIONAL DEVELOPMENT FUND IN ISRAEL LTD.

קרן לקידום החינוך ליוצאי עיראק בישראל בערבון מוגבל

13A Brenner St.
P.O.B. 4087, Tel Aviv
Telephone: (03) 285434
Office hours: 8:30 A.M. to 15:30 P.M.

HISTORY AND DESCRIPTION

The Iraqi Jews Educational Development Fund in Israel Ltd. was founded in the 1950's by the late Shlomo Noah and the late Dr. Ezra Korine. The fund constitutes one of Israel's main resources for aiding Iraqi students in their educational pursuits. For the Jews of Iraq and other dispossessed Jews from Arab countries the help provided by the State and other institutions was insufficient. While Sephardi Jews formed over 55% of the population, their percentage in secondary school was just over 20% and in the universities, 11 per cent. The situation is only slightly improved today, and the need for the Educational Fund is still urgent.

Organizational Structure: The fund, controlled by its Board of Trustees constituting 75 members, meets once a year to review the activities of the past year and set new goals for the future. The Board of Directors constituting 13 members, play an active role in the various committees: Scholarships, Finance, Research and Publications, Schoolwork Assistance, Public Relations, Control. They also take part in implementing the daily work of the fund.

Goals: The fund's major goal is to bridge the educational gap, to create a better image for the Iraqi community in Israel and abroad, and to promote various aspects of education.

Services, Activities, and Accomplishments: During its years of existence the fund has distributed 9,400 scholarships given as interest-free loans, refundable at the student's convenience. One million dollars have thus been distributed to students majoring in different fields of study at the various institutions for higher education in Israel and abroad. Every scholarship is seen as a contribution toward helping yet one more member of the community to cross the bridge toward social-economic security.

The fund also sponsors afternoon assistance classes in thirteen schools in all parts of the country.

OFFICERS

Board of
Directors: Ezra Gabbay, 8 Ben Zakkai, Tel Aviv. C.P.A.
              Tel. (03) 293575.
              Edward Mandelawi, 8 Kadman, Holon. C.P.A.

Oved Ben-Ozer, 1 Gluskin, Tel Aviv.
Company Director.
Arie Shemesh, 30 Ugarit, Tel Baruch, Tel Aviv.
Company Director.
Edmond Yitzahyek, 11 Hashalom, Raanana.
Dr. Nissim Nissim, 25 Pnei Hagivah, Ramat Gan.
Member, Municipal Council, Ramat Gan.
Dr. Meir Sasson, 26 Helsinki, Tel Aviv. Physician.
Amos Aslan, 121 Wingate, Herzliya. C.P.A.
Selim Shamash, 93 Krinitzi, Ramat Gan. Merchant.
Jacob Darzi, 13 Faibel, Tel Aviv.
Professor Sasson Somekh, 39 Tagor, Tel Aviv.
Tel Aviv University.
Shlomo Iny, 12 Huberman, Tel Aviv.
Company Director.
Jimmy Barhoum, 36 Hagilgal, Ramat Gan. C.P.A.

FINANCIAL INFORMATION

The fund's income is derived mainly from private contributions made periodically and also at the Annual Ball held by the fund, as well as the income derived from Donors' Trust Funds set up for this purpose. The refunds by students who were aided by the fund also constitute a small part of the income. The 1980-81 budget was $200,000. The fund is registered as a Public Company under the Israel Trust Law (reg. no. 52-1872). Contributions are tax-free in Israel (no. 4500047) and in the U.S. through the PEF Israel Endowment Fund, Inc. The fund retains one part-time and two full-time workers, as well as five volunteers.

MEMBERSHIP, SCOPE, AND POLICY

Any person of high qualification who can devote of his time is considered for membership. There are 40 members in one branch in Israel, and 20 members in one branch in the U.K. (through a separate Trust Fund). Decisions are made by the Board of Directors.

AFFILIATIONS/REFERENCES

The fund has no political affiliation in Israel. The work of the fund is known abroad to the PEF Israel Endowment Fund, Inc., 342 Madison Ave., Suite 1010, New York, New York, 10173.

FUNDING NEEDED

1. To provide scholarships to students from secondary schools through doctoral programs.
2. To maintain afternoon assistance programs and lessons for elementary schools.
   Both projects receive the same priority.

THE IRVIN GREEN COMMUNITY CENTER, SHLOMI

המרכז הקהילתי ע"ש אירווין גרין, שלומי

P.O.B. 1
Shlomi
Office hours: 8:00 A.M. to 1:00 P.M., 4:00 P.M. to 8:00 P.M.

HISTORY AND DESCRIPTION
The town of Shlomi has a population of 3,000 inhabitants, among them 1,000 youth under the age of 18. The Community Center is the only organization in Shlomi catering for sports and social and cultural activities. Most of the population of the town originates from Morocco and the average standard of education is very low. About 40 of the town's young people are studying in higher education institutions, and 200 in high schools and boarding schools.

Goals: To provide a sports, social and cultural center for the population of the town of Shlomi, including youth, adults and the old aged.

Services, Activities, and Accomplishments: The Community Center organizes social activities, tours, camps and sports competitions for the town's youth, an Old Age Club, a Young Couples Club, a variety of social, cultural, and artistic activities, and study-groups. Sports include football, basketball, tennis, gymnastics and swimming. The Community Center is the only cinema in town and hopes to acquire a large 35 mm. film projector. It has a large library to which a large number of new books are added each year. The settlement is small and situated in an agricultural area and this involves the organization in considerable transportation expenses. Because of difficult budget problems the organization has been forced to reduce its staff and to curtail many cultural activities and study-groups. The organization's major accomplishment has been the concentrated services it offers to underprivileged youth, provided them with an organized social framework, follow-up of their achievements and attempts to develop their potentialities.

OFFICERS
Director: Abraham Ben Yedidia.
            Tel. 968487.
Treasurer: Nisim Rewach.
            Tel. 968351.
Board Members: David Hasam
            Kalaman Hadad
            Moshe Biton

FINANCIAL INFORMATION
60% of the Community Center's income comes from Government sources, 30% from the Regional Council, and 10% from membership dues. Last year's annual budget of $100,000 left the organization with a deficit of $20,000. It is registered in Haifa as a non-profit Ottoman

Association (reg. no. not supplied). Donations in Israel and the United States are tax-free (details can be obtained from the Educational Fund of the Jewish Agency, 17 Kaplan, Tel Aviv). 6 full-time and 25 part-time workers are employed by the organization, as well as 17 volunteers.

MEMBERSHIP, SCOPE, AND POLICY
Membership is open to anyone. The Community Center services the entire population of Shlomi without limitations. There are 3,000 members and the organization has four youth branches in the town. Decisions are made by the Board.

AFFILIATIONS/REFERENCES
The organization is not affiliated with any Israeli political party. It is affiliated with the following organizations:
Union of American Hebrew Congregations, 838 Fifth Avenue, New York, U.S.A.
Memphis Jewish Community Center, 6560 Popla Ave., Memphis, Tennessee 38138, U.S.A.

FUNDING NEEDED
1. To purchase a bus for children's transportation services (cost $50,000-$100,000).
2. To purchase books for the library (in foreign languages, especially English), (cost $5,000-$10,000).
3. To purchase games and sports equipment for the Youth Clubs (cost $5,000-$10,000).

ISRAEL ACADEMIC COMMITTEE ON THE MIDDLE EAST

ועד אקדמי ישראלי לבעיות המזרח התיכון

Office No. 745, Clal Centre
97 Jaffa Road
Jerusalem, 94342
or P.O. Box 2192, Jerusalem
Telephone: (02) 241288
Office hours: Sunday-Thursday, 9:00 A.M.-3:00 P.M.

HISTORY AND DESCRIPTION

Towards the end of 1969, the Israel Academic Committe on the Middle East launched an information program to serve some 500 visiting academics and their families who come to Israel annually, from many different countries, for a full or partial sabbatical year. In 1972, the Committee decided to invite new immigrant academics to participate as well in its activities, during their first year in the country.

Organizational Structure: The governing body of the organization is composed of representatives of Israel's institutions of higher learning. It meets three to four times a year to make policy decisions. The professional staff is headed by an Executive Director, assisted by an Organizing Secretary and a small technical staff.

Goals: Since viewing Israel in person is the best method of understanding what is really happening in the country in particular, and in the region in general, the IAC exploits the fact that large numbers of academics (representing an influential public) come to Israel for a relatively long period annually, on their own initiative, at their own or their university's expense, and most of them come with their families. The IAC endeavors to relate to Israel within the context of the attachment to the land that is part of the ethos of the Jewish people for over more than three millennia. This gives added meaning to present developments in such areas as agriculture, industry, desert reclamation, and the absorption of immigrants from East and West. The IAC therefore provides facilities for the visiting academics to experience personal encounters in towns, villages, homes, industrial plants, and institutions throughout the country, as well as organising lecture and discussion forums. During the past 11 years, the IAC has established contacts throughout Israel representative of the country's heterogeneous and developing society, its problems and progress and the effect of both on the Israel-Arab conflict. Through the established pattern of the "open forum", the visitor is exposed to a variety of opinions, enabling him to question them and express his own ideas. As a result, the majority of the thousands of participants return to their home countries ready to work for Israel's cause, both on their campuses and in their communities through Zionist or other bodies.

Services, Activities, and Accomplishments: The IAC organizes many activities for visiting and new immigrant academics, and their families. The program includes study trips; seminars of 1-2 days' duration and discussion evenings in private homes; meetings with Israeli leaders, including an annual reception by, and discussion with, the President of Israel, and Knesset panels comprised of Knesset Members from different parties. The Committee also prints as many new publications as budget permits, to supplement the oral program. It provides answers to questions posed by academics who have returned and are working for Israel overseas. Seminars providing information for academics wishing to come on aliya were recently added to the program. The IAC has also been active on behalf of the rights of Jews from Arab countries and the struggle for Syrian Jewry and in fact provided the first roof in Israel for the World Organization of Jews from Arab Countries (WOJAC) after it was founded in Paris in 1975. In addition, the IAC has been responsible for bringing together immigrant academics from the Soviet Union with visitors from the West, many of whom were afterwards active in the struggle for Soviet Jewry. With little publicity and an absurdly small budget, the IAC has nevertheless become the largest organization for disseminating Zionist information among the overseas academic community. Since the IAC relates to the whole family it has succeeded in reaching out to thousands of Jews and non-Jews visiting Israel, who have returned overseas better equipped to help take up the cudgels of Israel's cause and to serve their own communities.

OFFICERS

Director:	Malka Hillel Shulewitz, Nayot 26, Jerusalem. Journalist. Tel. (02) 662558.
Assistant Director:	Hazel Dobrin, Hanerd 49A, Jerusalem. Tel. (02) 422347.
Chairman of the Board:	Bernard Cherrick, Vice President, Hebrew University, Jerusalem.
Board Members:	Simon Herman, Hebrew Univ. Jerusalem.
	Shulamith Nardi
	Ronald Nettler
	Moshe Maoz
	David Brandon, Haifa Technion.
	Avner Yaniv, Haifa University.
	Shlomo Bar-Noon, B.G. Univ. of the Negev.
	Yehuda Grados
	Maurice Roumani
	Zvi Lipkin, Weizmann Inst. of Science.
	Nechemia Meyers, Weizmann Inst. of Science.
	Harel Fisch, Bar-Ilan Univ., Ramat Gan.
	Amiel Unger.

FINANCIAL INFORMATION

The Israel Ministry of Foreign Affairs last year provided 40% of the IAC's income. Twenty percent came from donations, and 5% from

Israel's institutions of higher learning. The remaining 35% was secured through visitors' participation in the cost of activities. (For the first time, because of budget difficulties, study trips were run on a semi-commercial basis, instead of being subsidized, as in previous years. However, this causes hardship for visitors living on an Israeli salary.) Last year's budget amounted to $25,000, with a deficit of $1,520. The IAC is an Ottoman, non-profit Association (registration no. 11/1614, Jerusalem District);

Donations to the IAC in Israel are tax-free (tax deduction no. 4503103). Donations from the U.S. are tax-free through the PEF-Israel Endowment Funds, 342 Madison Avenue, Suite 1010, New York, N.Y. 10173 (earmarked for the Israel Academic Committee).

In Canada tax-free donations can be sent through the Canadian Friends of the Hebrew University, Att: Mr. J. Livny, Yorkdale Place, Suite 208, Yorkdale Road, Toronto, Ontario 416-7892633.

STAFF comprises one full-time and three part-time employees. Several volunteers also work for the IAC.

MEMBERSHIP, SCOPE, AND POLICY

IAC is not a membership organization. Participation in the program is open to all visiting and new immigrant academics. Other visitors to Israel are also welcome to take part. The beginnings of a network of "American Friends of the IAC" was laid this year, mainly comprising former participants in the IAC program. Publications can be obtained through an annual subscription. The Executive Director makes most decisions, but the National Board determines matters of policy.

AFFILIATIONS/REFERENCES

The IAC maintains political independence so that it will not undermine its credibility or the wide scope of its program. Organizations abroad familiar with the IAC's work are the National Committee for Jews in Arab Lands of the Canadian Jewish Congress; American Friends of the Hebrew University, the American Jewish Committee; Doopsgezinde Vredesgemeente in Nederland, Mariaweg 8, Osterbek, Holland. Friends of Israel Educational Trust, 25 Lyndale Avenue, London, N.W.2, England, and Lionel Bloch, Honorary Legal Advisor to the State of Israel, 9 Wimpole Street, London, W.1., England.

FUNDING NEEDED

1. To asssure the smooth-running of the program, its further development and the involvement of its participants on their return overseas as well as the publication of material transcribed from seminars and study trips: $30,000 annually. Individual pamphlets or special events, e.g. seminars or study days, can be dedicated in the name of the donor or in memory of a member of family for $500 up.
2. For essential office equipment, including computerization of the names of thousands of academics who have participated in the program. Cost: $20,000.
3. To acquire a mini-bus that would facilitate and cheapen the cost of the study trips, which could then be extended to other visitors outside the academic community. Cost: $40,000 and can be dedicated in the name of the donor (s).

ISRAEL ASSOCIATION OF
SOCIAL WORKERS

איגוד העובדים הסוציאליים בישראל

Arllosoroff 93, Tel Aviv
Telephone: (03) 261111
Office hours: 8:00 A.M.-4:00 P.M.

HISTORY AND DESCRIPTION
The Israel Association of Social Workers, founded in the 1940's, is the representative body of professional social workers in Israel. The "Union" (Association) is unique in that it functions both as a trade union and professional association at the same time.

Organizational Structure: The Association consists of several institutions: the Secretariat, the Governing Body, and regional branches. There are national committees in the following areas: professional advancement, public relations, social policy, manpower force, professional standards, international relations, work conditions, pensions, etc.

Goals: The Association deals mainly in 3 areas: Trade union activity, which includes negotiations on salary and working conditions for social workers; professional activities which are primarily concerned with professional ethics and principles, professional policy, definition of roles, post-graduate courses; and activities related to the Association's role as "social warner" which involves influencing social policy-making, developing research published in the form of "social reports", and the formulation of proposals for policy changes in the overall process of problem-solving. The IASW uses social action as a legitimate method in causing social change and influencing social policy in Israel.

Services, Activities, and Accomplishments: In its role as a professional association, the IASW has worked for the advancement of social legislation, as well as developing a "Code of Ethics" and a "Social Workers Law" (for determining accreditation). It convenes an annual National Social Workers Conference and puts out a bi-monthly newspaper for social workers. To its credit is the development of post-graduate courses, as well as an information-counselling center for social workers interested in professional advancement. One of the Association's accomplishments is in improving the image of the social work profession in Israeli society. The Association has become very involved with the "international family" of social workers, and in so doing has established "exchange" programs and professional trips to other countries in order to learn from others' experiences, as well as to maintain relations with other social work Associations abroad. As an advocate of better social services, the Association has recently declared a struggle for the "saving of the social welfare services", due to the budget cutbacks in municipal departments of social services. It has helped the recipients of the social services to organize, and has created situations in which social workers lobby alongside their clients in common struggles for social policy changes. Throughout its many activities, the Association has succeeded in developing positive public opinion concerning the development of social services and the needs of welfare clients and the socially disadvantaged.

OFFICERS

Director:	Yitzhak Kadman, Histadrut Bldg., Arllosoroff 93, T.A. Social Worker. Tel. (03) 264308.
Board Members: (Partial List)	Moshe Shteple, Histadrut Bldg., Haifa. Social Worker.
	Natan Lavon, Histadrut Bldg., Jerusalem. Social Worker. Tel. (02) 521683.
	Elisheva Sadan, Social Worker. Tel. (03) 720997.
	Rachel Levi, Social Worker.

FINANCIAL INFORMATION

The Association is financed totally from the Histadrut budget. Last year's budget amounted to $34,880; no deficit was recorded. The IASW is not registered as an Ottoman, non-profit association. Donations in Israel are tax-free (no number provided); no information is given regarding U.S. contributions. There are 2 full-time and 2 part-time employees, as well as many volunteers.

MEMBERSHIP, SCOPE, AND POLICY

The 4 Israeli branches of the Association have altogether 4,000 members. Certified Social Workers, i.e. graduates of schools of social work which are recognized by the "National Committee for Determining Social Workers' Status", can join the Association. Decisions are made by the Board.

AFFILIATIONS/REFERENCES

The IASW is not affiliated with any Israeli political party. Organizations abroad familiar with the Association's work are the National Association of Social Workers, 1425 H St. NW, Washington, D.C., U.S.A.; and the International Federation of S.W. (IFSW), 33, rue de l'Athene, Geneve 1206, Switzerland.

FUNDING NEEDED

1. For the development of professional manpower through the means of professional training programs and additional post-graduate education courses.
2. For the development of public awareness concerning social welfare problems in Israel and the creation of positive public opinion towards the development of social services.
3. For the development of social services that are not yet offered by government or volunteer agencies, and to demonstrate and initiate new services.

ISRAEL CANCER ASSOCIATION
האגודה למלחמה בסרטן בישראל
91 Hachashmonaim Street
P.O.B. 7065
Tel Aviv
Telephone: (03) 250361
Office hours: Sunday through Thursday 7:30 A.M. to 4:00 P.M.
              July and August 7:30 A.M. to 3:00 P.M.
              Friday 7:30 A.M. to 1:00 P.M.

HISTORY AND DESCRIPTION
The Israel Cancer Association (ICA) was founded in 1952 by a small group of medical doctors and scientists, interested in the problem of cancer. In 1962, the first national fundraising campaign was conducted.

Organizational Structure: The patron of the ICA is His Excellency Yitzhak Navon, President of the State of Israel. It has a management board composed of medical, scientific and public figures, an executive committee, professional committees, and 59 branches throughout the country. The work of these bodies is carried out by volunteers.

Goals: The prevention, detection, and improved treatment of cancer, financing of research and increasing its scope, assisting the patient and his family, providing rehabilitation services for mastectomees, laryngectomees, and ostomates, initiating and guiding anti-cancer activities in cooperation with the Government, the Sick Funds and the medical and para-medical community, and providing funds for fighting cancer, in addition to those made available thorugh the national budget.

Services, Activities, and Accomplishments: Cancer detection and diagnosis; support to oncology departments in hospitals and clinics; acquisition of radiotherapy and other equipment; awards of research and study grants; professional education; public education and information; material aid to cancer patients and their families; cancer-patient rehabilitation, and support of cancer registration and follow-up.
The major accomplishments have been the introduction of the day hospital concept, thus relieving pressure on hospital units; introduction of home care service, complete equipping of Tel Hashomer Oncology Institute; providing Rambam Hospital and Tel Hashomer with linear accelarators; building the Clore Hostel for out-of-town patients; building Beilinson Hospital's Pediatric Oncology Wing; and provision of funds for research fellowships at five of Israel's universities.

FINANCIAL INFORMATION
The entire source of income is obtained from donations, legacies and "Door Knock" Campaigns. Last year's annual budget was $902,000, with a deficit of $113,400. The organization is registered as an Ottoman Association (number not supplied). Donations to the organization are tax-free both in Israel and in the United States, but the tax numbers were

not supplied. There are 30 full-time and 135 part-time workers, in addition to 1200 permanent or semi-permanent volunteers and 35,000 volunteers for the "Door Knock" Campaign.

MEMBERSHIP, SCOPE, AND POLICY
Decisions are made by the Management Board. There are 5000 members in Israel. There are 59 branches in Israel and groups of Friends of the ICA in several countries. Every Israeli above 21 years of age can join.

AFFILIATIONS/REFERENCES
The Israel Cancer Associaiton is not affiliated with any political party in Israel. It is in contact with the following organizations: The International Union Against Cancer (UICC), 3, rue du Conseil General, 1205 Geneva, Switzerland, and the American Cancer Society, 777 Third Avenue, New York, New York 10017.

FUNDING NEEDED
1. The provision of improved physical facilities for the Oncology Department in Rambam Hospital. Estimated cost: $720,000.
2. The acquisition of equipment for an intensive care unit for children with cancer in Beilinson Hospital. Estimated cost: $20,000.
3. Other requests for building and acquisition of equipment are now being considered.

THE ISRAEL CORPORATION OF COMMUNITY CENTERS Ltd.

החברה למרכזי תרבות וספורט (לנוער ולמבוגרים) בע״מ

MATNASSIM
Joint Hill
Givat Ram,
Jerusalem.
Telephone: (02) 661261
Office hours: Sunday - Friday 8:00 A.M. - 7:00 P.M.

HISTORY AND DESCRIPTION

The Corporation was founded in 1969 by the Ministry of Education and Culture and registered as a government corporation by cabinet decision in 1971. The Corporation has engaged in the establishment of community centers and their operation, training and instruction of staff, the development and instruction of staff, and introduction of action programmes, in co-operation with state, local and public bodies in Israel and overseas for the sake of the promotion and functioning of community centers in Israel.

Organizational Structure: The Corporation has a 25 member board of directors representing local and state authorities, universities and public institutions, such as: the Joint, the Jewish Agency, the Federations and the Center of Municipal Authorities. There is also a 7 member managerial board and local and administrative committees, including the Manpower Committee, Community Services Committee, Committee for Early Childhood, Committee for Judaism and Tradition, External Relations Committee. The operational staff includes a director-general and his bureau. Staff responsibilities break down into two categories:
Staff A — Regional instructors and heads of divisions of instruction, finance, development and public relations.
Staff B — Community services personnel including experts on early childhood, community work, the elderly, arts, adult education, vacation and camping, programs in the field of Judaism and Tradition.
The Corporation screens and employs the directors of the community centers, and is a partner with the local authorities in the running of the Community Centers and financial support of their operation according to a contract between them, operates the instructional facilities of the Corporation in conjunction with the instructional facilities of the professional units in the Ministry of Education and Culture, and other ministries. The Corporation determines procedures and work methods, salary scales and employment contracts, for the whole community center network and operates a computer which reduces individual centers financial budgetary overheads. The Corporation also implements experiments, research evaluations and annual statistical review of data for the whole network.

Services, Activities, and Accomplishments: The Corporation has constructed and established a network in 111 communities, has established

273

local co-operation between all the welfare bodies in the state, and developed a concept of self-administration and involvement of the residents and decentralization of the community center facilites.

OFFICERS

Director: Chaim Zipori, Shahar 5, Jerusalem. Director.
Tel. (02) 524602.
Treasurer: Richard Ben-Haim, 233/8 Gilo, Jerusalem.
Economist.
Assistant General
Director: Shaul Lilach, Tchernikovski 43, Jerusalem.
Tel. (02) 660861.

FINANCIAL INFORMATION

33% of last year's annual budget came from residents and contributions, with 30% from local authorities, 28% from the Ministry of Education and Culture, plus the Matnass Corporation, and 9% from miscellaneous public and government bodies. Last year's annual budget for the whole network of Community Centers in Israel, was $21,000,000, which left the Matnassim (Centers) with a combined deficit of $3,000,000. The budget for the Corporation alone was $5,500,000, with no deficit. The Corporation is registered as a Limited Liability Corporation, and maintains ties with the Joint Distribution Committee which is registered as an Ottoman Association. Contributions in Israel are not exempt from tax, but in the U.S. are tax-free. (I.R.S. number not supplied).

The whole network together, employs 1280 full-time, and 1860 workers, with the actual Corporation employing 151 workers which includes the directors of the centers.

MEMBERSHIP, SCOPE, AND POLICY

Membership is open to all residents and citizens of Israel. Within the entire network of 111 community centers, there are 223,000 members, with three branches established in Rome for the benefit of Jewish emigrants in transit from Russia.

Most decisions are made by the Executive Director.

AFFILIATIONS/REFERENCES

The Corporation is affiliated with the American Joint Distribution Committee, 60 E. 42nd St., N.Y., N.Y., The Jewish Welfare Board, 15 E. 26th St., N.Y., N.Y., and the World Confederation of Jewish Community Centers, 15 E. 26th St., N.Y., N.Y.

FUNDING NEEDED

1. To reinforce the activities and programmes for population groups who are disadvantaged economically, socio-culturally and in employment.
2. To develop new action programmes for involvement of the population, for comprehensive rehabilitation of the elderly and for treating problematical youth and particularly weak population groups.
3. To promote professional and para-professional staff development.

THE ISRAEL COUNCIL OF YOUNG ISRAEL

מועצת ישראל הצעיר בישראל

28 Shmuel Hanagid Street
Yeshurun Library Building
P.O.B. 7722, Jerusalem
Telephone: (02) 669781
Office hours: Sunday-Thursday, 8:00 A.M. to 3:30 P.M.
                Friday, 8:00 A.M. to 12:00 Noon

HISTORY AND DESCRIPTION
The Israel Council of Young Israel synagogues was established in November 1974. Members of Young Israel synagogues from the United States who settled in Israel recognized the need to develop a congregational life around the synagogue, similar to that with which they were familiar in the States. It would become a community center, catering to the spiritual, cultural, educational, recreational, and social needs of the neighborhood, yet offering these services within the setting of the traditional synagogue.

Organizational Structure: The Constitution stipulates that elections are to be held annually for President, Vice-Presidents, Treasurer, and Executive Committee. The President appoints Charimen of subcommittees for Youth and Education, Aliyah, New Branches, Newspaper, and the Free Loan (Gemilut Chassadim) Fund. There is also a Delegate Body with two representatives from each synagogue. This body meets twice annually to consider general policy and to hear reports from the Executive Committee.

Goals: As of March 1981, there are 32 Young Israel branches throughout Israel, and new applications are considered regularly. The criteria for acceptance primarily include an identification with the aims of the Young Israel movement as outlined above, and a willingness to be responsible for youth activity for the entire neighborhood, thus helping to bridge the gap between the secular and the religious sections of the community.

Services, Activities, and Accomplishments: The Israel Council is recognized by a number of governmental agencies as the spokesman for the entire group of Young Israel synagogues. Assistance is granted to branches of the Young Israel in Israel by both the National (U.S.) Council of Young Israel and by Young Israel synagogues in the United States, via the Israel Council of Young Israel. This is achieved by various means, including an adoption program by which Young Israel synagogues in the States are "twinned" with those in Israel. A full-time youth director co-ordinates youth activities within the branches and organizes youth activities on the national level. These activities include trips, tours, and day camps for children. A part-time officer specifically handles the Young Israel youth program in Katamon Tet, a depressed neighborhood in Southern Jerusalem. A newspaper reflects activities at national and local levels, and projects the Young Israel movement in wider circles. Accomplishments include the establishment of 32 branches, several of them serviced by congregational rabbis, with modern premises catering to all sections of the local neighborhood. The branches are located in Jerusalem, Petach Tikva, Tel Aviv, Rehovot, Krinitzi (Ramat Gan), Kiron, Haifa, Beersheva, Ramat Poleg, Omer, Kiryat Arba, Herzlia, Raanana, Rishon LeZion, Hod Hasharon, Ramat Hasharon, Netanya, Maalot, Elon Moreh, Chispin, Ganei Tal, Givataim and Acco.

OFFICERS

Director: Moshe Rose, P.O.B. 5324, Jerusalem.
                        Tel. (02) 812859.
Treasurer: Yehuda Azrieli, 20 Hashnayim, Givataim.
                        Journalist.
President: Aaron Krumbein, 22 Pinsker, Jerusalem.
                        Lecturer.
                        Tel. (03) 729523.
Past President: Ruby Davidman, 113 East Talpiot, Jerusalem.
                        Educationist.
Past President: Marty Saffer, 20 Chen, Petach Tikva.
                        Businessman.
                        Tel (03) 929270.
Executive
Committee: Shimon Reem, 26 Maimon, Haifa.
                        Civil Servant.
                        Tel. (04) 223423.
                        Haim Mageni, Building 9, Apartment 2,
                        Kiryat Arba. Tour Operator.
                        Tel. (02) 971015.
                        Laurie Meyer, 67 Mendes, Krinitzi.
                        Civil Servant.
                        Tel. (03) 751564.

FINANCIAL INFORMATION

75% of last year's annual budget came from donations from Young Israel sources in the United States; the balance from governmental sources in Israel. Last year's annual budget of $150,000 left the Council with a deficit of $14,000. Donations to the Council in Israel and the United States are tax-free (Israel reg. no. 11/2536; USA number not supplied). Three full-time and one part-time workers are employed by the Council, as well as twelve volunteers.

MEMBERSHIP, SCOPE, AND POLICY

Synagogues which subscribe to the aims of the Constitution, as well as individuals can join the Council. Most decisions are made by the Executive Director and officers. There are 120 branches of the National Council of the Young Israel in the United States.

AFFILIATIONS/REFERENCES

The Council's Constitution forbids affiliation with Israeli political parties. The National Council is a member of the President's Conference of Major American Jewish Organizations, and the World Conference of Synagogues and Kehillot.

FUNDING NEEDED

1. To establish a synagogue and community center in Katamon Tet. Currently, an air raid shelter under one of the tenement buildings is used for this purpose.
2. To complete current construction operations to establish Young Israel centers in Haifa, Raanana, Maalot, Herzliah, and Rishon Letzion.
3. To establish suitable National offices in Jerusalem, with facilities for the Young Adult activities as well. These have been operating successfully during the past year in the synagogue premises and under the joint sponsorship of the Yeshurun Synagogue.

ISRAEL FAMILY COUNSELING ASSOCIATION

אגודה ישראלית להדרכה בחיי המשפחה

12 Ruth Street
Tel Aviv
Telephone: (03) 238780
Office Hours: Sunday, Tuesday, Thursday: 8:00 A.M. to 1:00 P.M.,
3:30 to 7:30 P.M.
Monday, Wednesday: 3:30 P.M. to 7:30 P.M.

HISTORY AND DESCRIPTION

The Israel Family Counseling Association was established in 1954, when a small group of social workers and physicians started a pilot project on their own intiative. The professional staff worked on a voluntary basis except for a part-time secretary whose salary was covered by clients' fees. The service continued to operate in this fashion for more than ten years. An ever-increasing number of applications and insufficient staff to cope with them convinced the group that the needs could not be met by volunteer workers, and that the continuation of the service would require a substantial financial base in order to be able to employ a paid staff.

Irregular symbolic financial contributions were received from the Ministry of Welfare, the Kupat Holim Minicipality of Tel Aviv, and others. In 1973, the National Council of Jewish Women of Canada undertook to sponsor the organization. This made it possible to rent space and furnish modest offices.

Organizational Structure: In addition to the professional staff employed by the organization, an advisory board exists to deal with most of the major decisions. On this advisory board are seated representatives from the Ministry of Labor and Social Affairs, University of Tel Aviv School of Social Work, Health Committte of the Kibbutz Movement, and other individuals not representing specific agencies.

Goals: The organization is working for treatment of family problems such as incompatibility, separation, sexual problems and parent-child relationships. Prevention of these difficulties through counseling is a priority, as is public education regarding family and marital problems. Another goal is the establishment of a training center for social work students and the training and supervision of social workers from the community as a whole.

Services, Activities, and Accomplishments: The organization runs clinics in both Tel Aviv and Petah Tikva (the latter in participation with the Petah Tikva Municipality and the Ministry of Welfare), which serve clients from all over the country. Social work students from different universities and social workers from the community receive training in specific courses as well as in service. Family life education programs are developed by training professionals; another project under development is a special counseling service for retarded young people and their families, in cooperation with the Ministry of Welfare. A professional library is also available to provide information in various specific fields. Presently, these services have become more difficult to provide, due to serious budget problems. The absence of a solid funding throughout these years has caused limitations which restricted any long-range planning. In spite of the opening of a number of public welfare and municipal clinics in Marriage Counseling during the last two years, the demand for a specific service and project planning is strong. An added element is the national economic crisis, with its extremely high inflation, which means that the government's contribution to the budget is even more limited than ever before.

The major objective and most desired goal at this stage is to receive substantial sums that could be the basis for a fund which would provide the group with a permanent yearly income.

Since 1954, the organization has helped more than 9,473 clients to solve marital and family problems, to achieve better understanding in the family and to prevent family breakdowns. The Israel Family Counseling Association works mostly with families. However, a great part of the effort has been invested toward creating awareness for such services, and toward training a great number of social workers in the field of marriage counseling.

OFFICERS

Chairperson of Board:	Carol Slater, Kfar Neter. Tel. (053) 97326.
Treasurer:	Emanuel Kidron. Banker. Tel. (03) 652521.
Secretary:	Sara Melzer, 44 Jabotinsky, Tel Aviv. Tel. (03) 231439.
Board Members:	Helga Karo, Tel Aviv. Social Worker. Tel. (03) 479942.
	Ilse Scherzer, Social Worker. Tel. (03) 442022.
	Mrs. London-Yari, rep. of Ministry of Welfare.
	Mrs. Edna Gross, rep. of Ministry of Welfare.
	Dr. Aviram, rep. of Tel Aviv University, School of Social Work.

FINANCIAL INFORMATION

The National Council of Jewish Women of Canada provides 33% of the annual income. Clients' fees contribute another 33% and 10% comes from the Ministry of Work and Welfare. The remainder comes from other, non-specified sources. Last year's annual budget of $39,350 left the Association with a deficit of $2,406. The Association is registered as an Ottoman Association (reg. on. 4503210). Donations to the Israel Family Counseling Association are tax-free in Israel. Two full-time, seven part-time and five volunteer workers are employed by the Association.

MEMBERSHIP, SCOPE, AND POLICY
Decisions are made by the Advisory Board.

AFFILIATIONS/REFERENCES
The National Council of Jewish Women of Canada can serve as a primary reference concerning the work of the Association.

FUNDING NEEDED
1. To obtain eight-room housing in a residential central area of Tel Aviv.
2. To purchase training aids: audio visual equipment, $15,000; one-way screen $10,000.
3. To create a fund which will enable the organization to use its interest to support the group and encourage development on a more stable financial basis.

ISRAEL FAMILY PLANNING ASSOCIATION

האגודה הישראלית לתכנון המשפחה

3 Zvi Shapira Street
Tel Aviv
Telephone: (03) 280482
Office Hours: Sunday-Thursday, 8:00 A.M. to 4:00 P.M.

HISTORY AND DESCRIPTION
The Israel Family Planning Association was founded in 1965 and registered as an Ottoman Association in 1972. An office and staff was set up in January 1975.

Organizational Structure: A central office in Tel Aviv is staffed by two full-time and two part-time workers, with four other branch offices staffed by part-time secretaries in Tel Aviv, Haifa, Jerusalem and Beersheba. A National Board (made up of 21 volunteers) is elected bi-annually by a General Assembly of all the members. This Board elects nine of its own members to serve as an Executive Committee. Each branch has a local committee (of volunteers, usually between ten to thirteen members). The Beersheba and Haifa branches have their own offices at present; the Tel Aviv branch uses the Central Office.

Goals: The Association aims to promote development of comprehensive advisory and clinical services. One of the goals of the group is to increase the awareness of the importance of family life and family planning among all areas of the population; all ages and sectors. Coordination between various organizations at the policy and service levels is seen as an important item of interest, as is the inclusion of family life and sex education within the context of informal as well as formal gatherings. The Association also encourages inclusion of family life research and sex education in the training of physicians, nurses, social workers and educators, as well as the research in all fields of family planning as a whole.

Services, Activities, and Accomplishments: The Association publishes educational and informational materials for the public and professionals. Training courses and seminars are organized for professionals, and loans of films and audio-visual materials are available. There are reference libraries in both Tel Aviv and Beersheba. The Association publishes a quarterly journal, as well as provides catalyst funding to government and other national organizations for staffing of services and training courses. The organization has developed a multi-disciplinary approach through training and has generally increased the public awareness of the importance of family planning as a health and social measure, in the context of the social and demographic realities.

OFFICERS

Hon. President:	Prof. V. Insler, 11 Keren Hayesod St., Ramat Ilan. Ob/Gyn. Tel. (03) 758840.
Hon. Treasurer:	Mrs. S. Magidor, 18 Neve Shaanan St., Jerusalem. FP Counselor. Tel. (02) 524133.
Board Members:	Prof. J. Zackler, 5 HaRav Uziel St., Tel Aviv. Ob/Gyn. Tel. (03) 440480.
	Dr. U. Levi, District MO, Ministry of Health, Tiberias. Pediatrician. Tel. (067) 50856.
	Mr. Y. Kadman, Histadrut Exec. HQ, Arlozorov St., Tel Aviv. Social Worker. Tel. (03) 261111.
	Mrs. G. Karp, 11 Einstein St., Haifa. Lecturer, Social Worker. Tel. (04) 247930.
	Dr. E. Sabatello, 17A Beitar St., Jerusalem. Demographer. Tel. (02) 712230.
	Dr. R. Shtarkshall, Meyersdorf Bldg., Hebrew U. Mt. Scopus. Sex Educator. Tel. (02) 882690.
	Dr. M. Zaltsberger, 8 Ben Labrat St., Jerusalem. Ob/Gyn. Tel. (02) 632161.
Exec. Director:	Dr. K. Tsafrir, 16 Tsahal St., Petah Tikva. Geneticist. Tel. (03) 929097.

FINANCIAL INFORMATION

94% of the Association's budget is provided by allocations from the International Planned Parenthood Federation; the balance from membership dues, donations from local governments/municipalities, and the sale of educational materials. Last year's budget of $124,785 left the Association with no deficit. The organization is registered in Ramle as an Ottoman Association (no no. provided). Donations to the Association in Israel and the United States are tax-free (Israel no. 4505222 and U.S. I.R.S. no. 1301179); the International Planned Parenthood Federation (the parent organization) is a registered charity in England (reg. no. 229476). The Association employs two full-time and six part-time workers, in addition to some 50 volunteers on the National Board and on Ad Hoc basis on various committees.

MEMBERSHIP, SCOPE, AND POLICY

In Israel some nine hundred members represent the Association in its four branches in the country. Anyone who identifies with the aims and objectives of the Association, and wishes to assist in realizing them, is welcome to join. Decisions on fund allocations are made by the Executive Committee on the recommendation of the Grants or Publications Subcommittees.

AFFILIATIONS/REFERENCES

The Association is affiliated with the International Planned Parenthood Federation, 18-20 Lower Regent St., London SW 1Y 4PW, England.

FUNDING NEEDED

1. To develop advisory and counselling services for adolescents, run by professionals on a volunteer basis; cost, approx. $5,000 annually for each center.
2. For publication of the quarterly journal; cost, approx. $7,500 annually.
3. For publication of information and education materials for adolescents and adults (including repeat printings of existing publications); cost, approx. $30,000.

For the past five years, the Association has operated on an annual budget granted by the IPPF for the implementation of a one-year work programme which is barely balanced by the gain on the dollar exchange, but so far each year has ended with a credit balance.

The IPPF has already advised that the organization may not expect more in 1981 than it was granted in 1980 ($90,000) and that, in general, it has been pointed out to all grant-receiving Associations that they should work towards decreasing their reliance on the IPPF. So even if the 1981 allocation is received, it is obvious that this may not last indefinitely and as the administrative budget increases through inflation the organization will have less money available for activities in the field and assistance to special projects.

THE ISRAEL INTERFAITH COMMITTEE
הועד הבינדתי בישראל

P.O.B. 2028
12A Koresh Street
Jerusalem
Telephone: (02) 222493 or 231566
Office hours: 9:00 A.M. to 5:00 P.M.

HISTORY AND DESCRIPTION
Founded in 1959 by a group of Israeli scholars, public leaders, and intellectuals of various communities, this association was formed to promote interfaith and intergroup understanding and cooperation.

Organizational Structure: The association has an Honorary Presidium, a Council, an Executive Committee, and various subcommittees, all of which are comprised of religious and educational leaders, clergy and lay people from the Jewish, Christian, Muslim and Druze communities.

Goals: To promote a spirit of understanding, friendship and brotherhood without prejudice to the integrity and identity of any religious group; to be alert to any infringements of human rights on account of one's faith or way of life; to take part in inter-religious and interfaith activities all over the world; and maintain contacts with corresponding organizations in and outside the country.

Services, Activities, and Accomplishments: The Committee sponsors a range of educational and social projects, public seminars, lectures, conferences and field trips to Arab villages and Jewish communities; formal study programs for visitors from abroad; and supports other organizations that are actively engaged in improving the quality of Israeli life by reconciling the segregated communities and cultures. Accomplishments include successful educational and intercommunity projects in Israel and abroad, and several interventions in public affairs, making establishments aware of the problems in the area of interfaith relations and helping to find solutions.

OFFICERS
Exec. Dir.:   Joseph Emanuel, P.O.B. 2276, Jerusalem. Editor/Educator. Tel. (02) 222493.

Treasurer: Chanan H. Cidor, Hameyasdim St. 16, Jerusalem. Diplomat. Tel. (02) 521869.

Board Members: Dr. Zvi Werblowsky, Ha'arazim St. 4, Jerusalem. Professor. Tel. (02) 523503.

Dr. A Chouraqui, Ein Rogel St. 8, Jerusalem. Writer. Tel. (02) 715387.

Dr. Shemaryahu Talmon, Jan Smuts St. 5, Jerusalem. Professor. Tel. (02) 668893.

Sheik Muhamad Hubeishi, Ben Ami St. 55, Acco. Tel. (04) 910492.

Dr. Marcel J. Dubois, Agron St. 20, Jerusalem.
Tel. (02) 231763.
Dr. Wesley Brown, P.O.B. 19556, Jerusalem.
Tel. (02) 713451.

FINANCIAL INFORMATION
97% of the income of the association is from donations, and 3% from membership dues. Last year's annual budget was $150,000. The organization is registered in Jerusalem as an Ottoman Association (number 11/852). Donations are tax-exempt in Israel (number not reported) and in the U.S.A. (I.R.S. number 23 734 6101). The association is run by 2 full-time employees, 5 part-time and 2 volunteers.

MEMBERSHIP, SCOPE, AND POLICY
Any adult is eligible to join, subject to the decision of the Executive Committee. As of now there are about 500 members, and 5 branches, in Israel. Most decisions are made by the Executive Director and National Board.

FUNDING NEEDED
1. Funds for educational programs for Jewish and Arab educators, public educators, public leaders and students on the subject of education for peace, including special studies of the relations with Arab Christian groups and the Moslem community. $150,000.
2. Interfaith study programs for clergy and seminarians, theologians, spiritual leaders and intellectuals from all over the world on Judaism and Israel in their historical and religious perspectives, with special emphasis on people from the Third World and the relationship with Islam. $100,000.
3. Establishment and development of an International Interfaith Study and Conference Center in Jerusalem. $250,000.

ISRAEL LEISURE AND RECREATION ASSOCIATION (ILRA)

האגודה הישראלית לתרבות הפנאי והנופש

P.O. Box 3220
Jerusalem
Telephone: (02) 667894
Office hours: Sun.-Thurs. 10:00-14:00

HISTORY AND DESCRIPTION

The Association was established in May, 1978.

Goals: The goals of the Association are to help shape policy regarding use of leisure time in Israel, to support proper planning of leisure time facilities and resources, and to organize meetings, gatherings and exhibitions on leisure time activity.

Services, Activities, and Accomplishments. To this end, the Association helps to create advisory committees and documentation resources on leisure time subjects, and supports research related to leisure time issues. It also works to develop better training standards for manpower administering leisure time facilities, and helps in the exchange of information and ideas in this area. It publishes material for the public and finances various projects. To date, the Association's accomplishments have been the establishment of relationships with policy-making bodies in Israel and abroad; and the preparation of an exhibition on Leisure and Recreation in Israel.

OFFICERS

Chairman:	Dr. Hillel Ruskin, P.O. Box 3220, Jerusalem. Teacher. Tel. (02) 526752.
Treasurer:	Yaacov Nechushtan. Banker.
Secretary:	Zvi Dagan. Community worker.
Board Members:	Haim Dagan. Educator. Dr. Yardena Harpaz. Educator. Shalom Hermon. Teacher. Dr. Zvi Fein. Social Worker. Dr. Boaz Shamir. Teacher.

FINANCIAL INFORMATION

All the Association's income is derived from donations, which are received for individual projects. For this reason, there are no budget figures given for last year. The Association is an Ottoman non-profit organization (Israel registration no. 11/3115, Jerusalem District), and donations are tax-free both in Israel (No. 4507122), and in the U.S. (no I.R.S. no. stated). There is no salaried staff.

MEMBERSHIP, SCOPE, AND POLICY

There are 26 members in the Association in Israel, and no branches abroad. Members include the Founders of the Association and others approved by them. Decisions are made by the Director and the National Board.

AFFILIATIONS/REFERENCES
The Association is affiliated with the World Leisure and Recreation Association, 345 E. 46 St., New York, N.Y. 10017, U.S.A., and with the European Leisure and Recreation Association, Postfach Ct.—8022 Zurich, Switzerland.

FUNDING NEEDED
1. To organize a series of workshops, for policy-making bodies (Government, labor, community, outdoor recreation, planning).
2. To publish the proceedings of national and international meetings.
3. To publish a quarterly on leisure and recreational issues in Israel and abroad.
4. To support research on leisure and recreation issues in Israel.

ISRAEL MARITIME LEAGUE

חבל ימי לישראל

Neemanim 8
Haifa
Telephone: 529818, 537766
Office hours: 8:00 A.M.-1:00 P.M.

HISTORY AND DESCRIPTION
The Israel Maritime League (I.M.L.) was founded in 1936, and since its inception has actively promoted sea consciousness among the public in Israel. It has been active in, and partners to, the great maritime achievements of the past 44 years. Its Board of Directors is composed of members who are prominent personalities in sea-faring circles.

Goals: The I.M.L. concentrates its efforts on the absorption of new immigrants into the Merchant Marine fleet, helping in the integration of hundreds of immigrant seamen into the Israel Merchant Marine. It also works to promote the interest of Israeli youth in the sea as a career.

Services, Activities, and Accomplishments: In carrying out its activities, the League cooperates with the Immigration and Absorption Authorities, the Education Ministry, and Israeli shipping companies. It publishes literature and magazines, helps youth organizations, provides scholarships for outstanding and needy students to attend Nautical Schools, and for the past 31 years has been operating the Marine & Economic Club in Haifa. The I.M.L. has established a Scholarship Fund; a Fund for assisting new seamen; a Fund to enable the publication of books on sea subjects, technical works, maritime histories and general sea literature; and a Fund for the publication of a magazine, "The Young Seaman."

OFFICERS
Director: Zadok Eshel, Neemanim 8, Haifa.
                      Tel. (04) 529818, (04) 537766.
Chairman: Moshe Ben Pomrock
Board Members: Capt. Moshe Abramski
                      Adm. Shmuel Tankus
                      Eliezer Akabas
                      Zvi Herman
                      Eliezer Molk

FINANCIAL INFORMATION
The financial operations of the I.M.L. are made possible by grants supplied by the Friends of the League, both in Israel and countries abroad, as well as from various organizations connected with the shipping industry in Israel. No information concerning last year's budget is given. The League is registered as an Ottoman non-profit organization (number and District not stated). Donations are tax-free in Israel (no no. stated) and in the U.S. (tax no. 65 EO 481). There are 7 full-time employees, as well as 21 volunteers.

MEMBERSHIP, SCOPE, AND POLICY

There are 350 members in the 2 Israeli branches of the Maritime & Economic Club, the members being those approved by the Management. Six branches of the League and its Friends operate abroad. Decisions are made by the Board of Directors.

AFFILIATIONS/REFERENCES

The League is not affiliated with any political party. Organizations familiar with the League's work are: Federation of Jewish Relief Organizations, 131 Elgin Avenue, London W9 1JH, England; and Scholarships for Israeli Youth, Brooklyn Women's Division, 216 Corbin Place, Manhattan Beach, Brooklyn, N.Y. 11235.

FUNDING NEEDED

1. To provide scholarships for needy students in Nautical Schools. The amount required per scholarship is $500.
2. To assist the Nautical School at Acre.
3. To assist new immigrants while they learn Hebrew and train to become officers in the Merchant Marine.
4. To erect the new International Maritime Center in Haifa where foreign seamen will also receive every possible attention, regardless of color, race or religion.

THE ISRAEL MOVEMENT FOR PROGRESSIVE JUDAISM

13 King David Street
Jerusalem
Telephone: (02) 232444 and (02) 234748
Office hours: 8:00 A.M. to 3:30 P.M., daily

HISTORY AND DESCRIPTION

The Movement for Progressive Judaism in Israel is a national, non-partisan movement. Nonetheless, it takes a stand on public issues whenever its principles warrant such action.

In 1958 the first synagogue was founded in Jerusalem by Mr. Shalom Ben Chorin and others. In 1960 the first full-time rabbi, Rabbi Jerome Unger, was employed by the World Union for Progressive Judaism in Israel. In 1965 the MARAM (Moetzet Rabbanim Mitkadmim) or Association of Progressive Rabbis in Israel, was founded. Then in 1972, the World Headquarters of the WUPJ moved from New York to Jerusalem, under the direction of Rabbi Richard G. Hirsch, Executive Director. In 1974 a Rabbinic Department for Israeli Students at Hebrew Union College was founded in Jerusalem under the direction of Dean Ezra Spicehandler, and the first Garin Nahal—"Telem" of Israel Progressive Movement was begun as well. In 1976, the first Progressive kibbutz, "Yahel" was dedicated in the Arava.

Organizational Structure: A Chairperson is elected every two years by representatives of related organization. The Executive Board is headed by a chairperson, vicechairperson, a coordinator of the Movement, two more representatives, and the Executive of World Union for Progressive Judaism. The Coordinator of the Movement is appointed by the Executive Board. There are also a Council of Congregations and the Board of Reform rabbis, called by the Hebrew acronym, MARAM.

Goals: The Movement for Progressive Judaism in Israel aspires to strengthen the commitment and loyalty of Jews to their Jewish heritage, and to shape life in the State of Israel in light of the moral principles for individual and collective behavior prescribed by Judaism. The Movement strives to cultivate among Jews in Israel and elsewhere a Jewish way of life that is imbued with love for their people, and with a creativeness that draws from the wellspring of Judaism.

Accomplishments: Major accomplishments until now have been the establishment of 16 Reform congregations; the establishment of Kibbutz Yahel; the promotion of the Leo Baeck Educational Institution in Haifa, and the Reform Youth Movement.

OFFICERS

Nissim Eliad, 28 Lilienblum, Tel Aviv.
Tel. (03) 655467.

Meir Shafir, 30 Carmel, Nahariya.
  Tel. (04) 716204.
Dr. Hanoch Jacobsen, 76 Abass, Haifa.
  Tel. (04) 292449.
Mr. David Rigler, 23A Shoshanat Hacarmel, Haifa.
  Tel. (04) 82861.
Rabbi Richard G. Hirsch, Exec. Dir. WUPJ,
  13 King David, Jerusalem.
  Tel. (02) 234748.
Shmuel Bahagon, Coordinator,
  13 King David, Jerusalem.
  Tel. (02) 234748.

FINANCIAL INFORMATION
No information supplied. Donations are tax-free but no numbers were supplied. There are 2 full-time employees and rabbis and youth supervisors who work part time, as well as several hundred volunteers.

MEMBERSHIP, SCOPE, AND POLICY
Decisions are made collectively. There are 5000 members in Israel and about 2 million abroad. There are 16 branches in Israel and hundreds abroad.

AFFILIATIONS/REFERENCES
The Movement is not affiliated with any political party in Israel.

FUNDING NEEDED
1. The development of congregations.
2. The presentation of information to the public.
3. The maintenance of salaries for rabbis.

THE ISRAEL PARLIAMENTARY AFFAIRS ASSOCIATION

האגודה הישראלית לבעיות הפרלמנטריזם

The Knesset,
Telephone: (02) 554111
No office hours stated.

HISTORY AND DESCRIPTION
The Association was established in 1971, on the initiative of the former Knesset Speaker, the late Reuven Barkatt.

Organizational Structure: The General Meeting of the Association, whose membership may not exceed 150, elects an Executive Committee, a Membership Committee, and an Audit Committee, and determines their respective powers and duties. The Executive Committee, subject to the decisions of the General Meeting, directs the activities of the Association, fixes its budget and membership fees. The Speaker of the Knesset is the Chairman of the Association and of its Executive Committee, and he presides over the General Meeting.

Goals: The Association's aim is the advancement of parliamentary government and the improvement of the awareness and understanding of parliamentary democracy.

Services, Activities, and Accomplishments: The Association carries out its goals through the observation and study of parliamentary developments in Israel and in other countries, and the conduct of research into relevant problems. It fosters relations between academic and scientific institutions and the Knesset, and holds lectures and symposia on parliamentary subjects.

OFFICERS
Chairman: Yitzhak Berman, Ex-Speaker of the Knesset.
Tel. (02) 554333.
Treasurer: J. Lemberger, Knesset Accountant.
Tel. (02) 554511.
Board Members: There are 15 members, not listed individually.
Secretary: I. Eliasoff
Tel. (02) 554337.

FINANCIAL INFORMATION
Nearly 90% of the Association's funds come from donations, with the remainig 10% from grants from the Knesset budget. Last year, the budget totalled $3,000; there was no deficit. The Association is registered as an Ottoman, non-profit Association (no. 11/1945, Jerusalem District). Donations from Israel and the U.S. are not tax-exempt. Two volunteer workers run the Association's affairs.

MEMBERSHIP, SCOPE, AND POLICY

Membership is open to Members of the Knesset, scholars and public servants who are interested in the advancement of the Association's aims, and who have been invited by the Membership Committee to join the Association. There are now 120 members in Israel. Decisions are made by the Executive Committee.

AFFILIATIONS/REFERENCES

The Parliamentary Association is not affiliated with any political party in Israel. No references are listed.

FUNDING NEEDED

1. For annual study days.
2. For the award of prizes and bursaries for studies of parliamentary subjects.
3. To assist with the publication of books on the history and procedure of the Knesset, on comparative parliamentary studies, and on related subjects.

ISRAEL SOCIETY FOR THE PREVENTION OF ALCOHOLISM

האגודה למניעת אלכוהוליזם בישראל

10 Yad Haharutzim
Jerusalem
Telephone: (02) 717559
Office hours: 8:00 A.M. to 2:00 P.M.

HISTORY AND DESCRIPTION
The Israel Society for the Prevention of Alcoholism was legally registered in January, 1976.

Organizational Structure: The Society is governed by a Board of Directors of not less than five members, among them the Secretary, the Treasurer, the Chairman, and the Deputy-Chairman, and three National Committees, the Information Committee, the Legal Committee, and the Ad Hoc Committee. There are several regional branches throughout Israel, each with its own Chairman and committees.

Goals: To promote public action aimed at increasing the community's awareness both of the danger to the individual, the family and the community arising from excessive drinking, and also of the possibilities of treatment for alcoholics within the framework of the Ministry of Labour and Social Affairs' Centres for the Treatment of Alcoholism; to promote research on the effects of alcohol on the individual and his environment, including the testing of methods of prevention and treatment of addiction to alcohol; to develop medical treatment and social work programs including programs aimed at rehabilitating the alcoholic and his family; to initiate and promote legislation aimed at the mitigation and prevention of alcoholism; to encourage association and exchange of information with similar organizations abroad.

Services, Activities, and Accomplishments: Services and activities revolve around the achievement of the Society's goals. An information campaign has been initiated, reaching Israel's entire population, carried on through the media and by means of letters, pamphlets, bulletins and posters. The Society is involved in a continuing dialogue with the public and governmental institutions to encourage the promotion of the Society's aims within these frameworks. This involves the planning of training programs and in-service training for professionals such as physicians, social workers and members of the police force, and courses for concerned citizens, schools and youth movements. The Society also organizes fund-raising activities. Since the emergence of alcoholism as an issue of public concern in Israel, the Society has succeeded in raising public and professional awareness to the extent of the problem of alcoholism and the practical possibilities of its reduction.

OFFICERS

Chairman:	Y. Jacques Amir, P.O.B. 1, Dimona.
	Knesset Member, Mayor of Dimona.
	Tel. (057) 53391.
Treasurer:	Meir Sinai, Bialik 5, Tel Aviv.
Deputy	
Chairperson:	Pnina Eldar, 125 East Talpiot, Jerusalem.
	Social Worker.
Secretary:	Ilana Even-Ezra, Kommemiut 28, Neveh Raasco.
	Ramat Hasharon.

FINANCIAL INFORMATION

97% of the Society's income comes from donations, and 3% from membership dues. Last year's annual budget of $8,163 left the Society with a balanced budget. The Society is registered in Jerusalem as a non-profit Ottoman Association (reg. no. 11/2534). Donations in Israel are tax-free (tax no. 4507427), U.S. tax status information not supplied. One part-time worker is employed by the Society.

MEMBERSHIP, SCOPE, AND POLICY

Anyone can be a member of the Society with the exception of minors and the mentally ill. There are 300 members in Israel, in five branches. Decisions are made by the National Board.

AFFILIATIONS/REFERENCES

The Society is not affiliated with any Israeli political party. It is affiliated with the following organizations:

International Commission for the Prevention of Alcoholism, 6830 Laurel Street, N.W. Washington D.C. 20012.

P.E.F. Israel Endowment Funds Inc., 342 Madison Avenue, N.Y., N.Y.

FUNDING NEEDED

1. To establish a National Clinic for the hospitalization of alcoholics.
2. To obtain further media exposure by broadcasting public service messages and short documentaries on television.
3. To finance seminars and in-service training covering methods of prevention and treatment of alcoholism in Israel, for professionals working in the field as well as the general public.

THE ISRAEL VOLUNTARY SERVICES

המרכז לשרותי התנדבות

4 Hanevi'im Street
Tel Aviv
Telephone: (03) 293452-3-4
Office hours: 8:00 A.M. to 2:00 P.M.

HISTORY AND DESCRIPTION

The Israel Voluntary Services was established as an agency in 1972 on the recommendation of the Prime Minister's Committee for Underprivileged Children and Youth, in order to ensure and extend utmost utilization of the great potential of volunteers in Israel. The Israel Voluntary Services serves as an information and service link between ministries, the Jewish Agency, the municipalities, local councils and various types of volunteers. It is an independent public agency, registered as a non-profit organization, and budgeted by a government grant. The management board is composed of public figures and representatives of public and government agencies, research institutions, and voluntary organizations.

Goals: (1) To initiate, foster and accelerate volunteer activities in the service of society, in spheres where such activity would enrich statutory service. (2) To increase public recognition of voluntarism as an educational and social value. (3) To enhance the status of volunteers by appropriate legislation; involvement on an equal basis with statutory services in which, or with which, they are functioning; enabling volunteers and voluntary organizations to influence policy making. (4) To assist voluntary organizations in activating volunteers to meet existing needs, in accordance with their own statutes and purposes. (5) To increase the effectiveness of volunteers by research, training, seminars, guidance programs, as well as by the introduction of new programs and ideas through pilot projects. (6) To establish and maintain contacts with similar organizations in other countries.

To achieve these aims, the Israel Voluntary Services strives to increase public awareness of potentials of volunteer activity and to suggest practical ways for inclusion of volunteers in the work of government and municipal departments. Follow-up studies will show how well they were absorbed into Israeli cultural life and how clients and services benefitted by their contribution.

The major accomplishments of the organization has been to increase volunteering, to accept voluntary organizations, and to initiate legislation.

OFFICERS

Director: Sara Meltzer, 44 Jabotinsky, Tel Aviv.
Tel. (03) 231439.

Treasurer: Abraham Sucher, 91 Hachashmonaim, Tel Aviv.
Tel. (03) 267241.

(33 members of the board, Academic representatives,

voluntary organizations' representatives, representatives of voluntary organizations and of the establishment.)

FINANCIAL INFORMATION
The only source of income for the organization is from the Prime Minster's Office, which provides 100% of the budget. Last year's budget was not indicated, nor was the deficit, if any. The organization is registered as an Ottoman Association (reg. no. 5497/99). It was not stated whether or not the donations to the organization are tax-free. There are 3 full-time and 2 part-time workers employed by the organization, in addition to 3 volunteers.

MEMBERSHIP, SCOPE, AND POLICY
Decisions are made by the executive board. National organizations are eligible to join. There are 150 members. There was no mention of branches abroad.

AFFILIATIONS/REFERENCES
The organization is not affiliated with any political party in Israel. It has the following contacts abroad: The Volunteer Centre, 29 Lower King's Road, Berkhamsted, Herts HP4 2AB, England; Association of Voluntary Action Scholars, The Pennsylvania State University, University Park, PA 16802, U.S.A.

FUNDING NEEDED
1. The training of volunteers.
2. Providing incentive and support to volunteers.
3. Printing publications, and increasing public awareness.

ISRAEL WAR VETERANS LEAGUE

איגוד החיילים המשוחררים בישראל

Manne 11,
Tel Aviv
Telephone: (03) 261517
Office Hours: Sunday, Tuesday, Thursday: 2:30 P.M.-7:30 P.M.
              Monday and Wednesday: 8:30 A.M.-1:30 P.M.

HISTORY AND DESCRIPTION

The League was founded after World War II by volunteers who had joined the British Army. Absorbing other organizations of ex-soldiers (British Legion and "Tsevet", Israel Defense Force veterans), the League had more than 30,000 members in its initial stage.

Organizational Structure: The Executive Council (Mazkirut) consists of 25 members, who are representatives of each former military unit. There are committees of volunteers for each special project: parents home; volunteers forest; world assembly of Jewish veterans, etc. Elections to the convention ("V'ida") are held every four years. The Convention elects the Chairman and the President.

Goals: The League's goals are to maintain the comradeship-in-arms of its members; to erect and maintain memorial projects; to assist members of the League in need of aid, to give grants, scholarships and prizes; and to cooperate with other organizations of released soldiers, Jewish and non-Jewish, in other countries. In addition, the League strives to continue the tradition of volunteerism and to foster values of volunteerism and transmit them to the younger generations, in Israel and abroad. It promotes comradeship-in-arms among world Jewry on behalf of the State of Israel.

Services, Activities, and Accomplishments: The League is involved in organizing the first Veterans Parents Home, as well as assisting aged members in existing homes and providing welfare activities for members. It has founded the Volunteers Forest and Memorial (30,000 trees), which is located on the Ramle-Latrun road. The first volume of a History of the Israel Volunteers in the British Army (World War II) has been published by the League. It has organized two World Assemblies of Jewish War Veterans, in addition to regular get-togethers of former units in the British Army. The League also participates in the activities of the World Federation of Veterans, and serves as a liaison with similar Jewish organizations abroad.

OFFICERS

President: Lt. Gen. (Res.) Haim Laskov
Chairman: Yohanan Peltz, Ganei Yehuda.
              Engineer.
              Tel. 751833.

Treasurer: Yaacov Schlezinger, Tel Aviv.
Banker.
Tel. (03) 445950.

FINANCIAL INFORMATION
Interest from invested funds provide 80% of the League's income. Another 8% comes from membership dues, 5% from the Ministry of Defense, and the remainder from miscellaneous sources. The budget for 1979/80 totalled $25,000, with no deficit. The League is a non-profit organization, but no details concerning registration are provided. Donations in Israel are tax-free (no no. given); contributions from the U.S. are not tax-free in U.S.A. The League employs one full-time worker, 3 part-time workers, and has approximately 300 volunteers.

MEMBERSHIP, SCOPE, AND POLICY
There are 2,000 active and 8,000 non-paying members in Israel. Membership is limited to volunteers to the British Army in the Second World War. Decisions are made by the Executive Council.

AFFILIATIONS/REFERENCES
The League is in contact with other Jewish War Vetarans organizations around the world: AJEX, Association of Jewish Ex-Servicemen, 5 East Bank, Staford Hill, London, England; Jewish War Veterans of the U.S.A., 1712 New Hampshire Ave., Washington, D.C., U.S.A.; South African Jewish Ex-Service League, 110 Commissioner St., Johannesburg, P.O.B. 7309, S.A.; Jewish War Veterans of Canada, 27 Bathurst St., 210 Toronto, Ontario, Canada; and Jewish and Non-Jewish Veterans Organization, Australia.
The League is not affiliated with any Israeli political party.

FUNDING NEEDED
1. For parents home, to be built in the Tel Aviv area. Estimated cost: $3 million.
2. To publish additional volumes of the History of the Israel Volunteers in the British Army (W.W.II), and to translate the first volume, already published, into English. Estimated cost: $50,000.
3. To provide funds for a welfare fund for members.

ISRAEL YOUTH HOSTELS
ASSOCIATION אגודת אכסניות נוער בישראל (אנ"א)

3 Dorot Rishonim Street
P.O.B. 1075, Jerusalem
Telephone: (02) 222073; 222706; 225925
Office hours: Sun.-Thurs. 8:00 A.M. to 2:00 P.M.;
　　　　　　　Fri., 8:00 A.M. to 12:00 noon.

HISTORY AND DESCRIPTION
The Israel Youth Hostels Association was founded in 1937 and is a
non-profit organization chartered under the laws of Israel. It enjoys the
cooperation of the Ministry of Education and of central and local
authorities and public institutions interested in youth hostelling.

Organizational Structure: These public institutions are represented on
the National Council which authorizes the annual budget , and elects the
Executive Committee. The Executive Committee chooses the Chairman, his Deputy, and two members who, together with the Executive
Director, constitute the Board.

Goals: The IYHA aims to give youth a knowledge of the physical Israel,
of the Israel of the Bible; of ancient and modern Israel; and to bring to
them the essence and the spirit of the country, providing a common
meeting place where the youth of all races, creeds and ethnic origins may
learn to know one another.

Services, Activities and Accomplishments: The IYHA provides lodging
accommodation, meals, transportation and guides at nominal prices to
touring and travelling youth. Each of the thirty-two hostels conve-
niently spaced throughout the country is under the supervision of a
resident counselor; there are separate accommodations for boys and
girls. Each of these hostels has been made self-sustaining. Providing
three quarters of a million bednights annually, the hostels have received
youth from seventy different foreign countries. Some 40% of youths
who come to the hostels are from these countries. For the young, the
hostels have become a mainspring of informal (out-of-school) education; for the nature lovers, especially parents with children, they are
facilities for enjoying leisure time and the countryside. Israel has
acquired many new friends through hostelling.

OFFICERS

President:	Dr. Walter Katz, Jerusalem.
	Honorary President YHA. Tel. (02) 633377.
Vice-President:	Rachel Schwarz, Jerusalem.
	Honorary Vice-President YHA. Tel. (02) 632741.
Chairman:	Yehuda Gaulan, Jerusalem. Advocate.
	Tel. (02) 633544.
Executive Director:	Zvi Sarig, Jerusalem. Tel. (02) 818374.

FINANCIAL INFORMATION

The Association is registered in Jerusalem as an Ottoman Society (no. 11/604). Approximately 93% of the Association's budget comes from the income produced by services rendered; membership dues comprise another 3% and the remainder is provided by donations. Last year's budget of $1,030,000 left a deficit of $35,000. Donations to the Association are tax free both in Israel and in the United States (in Israel, Treasury no. 4500143/Administrator General: Hekdesh 120; in the U.S.A., via the P.E.F. Israel Endowment Fund, c/o Sidney Musher, 342 Madison Avenue, New York City, New York). Two hundred and forty full-time and thirty part-time workers are employed by the Association, in addition to one hundred and ten volunteers.

MEMBERSHIP, SCOPE AND POLICY

Every citizen who subscribes to the Association's aims and goals, and pays his dues, is welcome to join. There is also collective membership, for schools, kibbutzim, educational institutions, and the like. Decisions are made by the Executive Committee. In Israel, there are 14,600 individual members; collective memberships are not specified.

AFFILIATIONS/REFERENCES

The Israel Youth Hostels Association is not affiliated with any political party. The following organizations abroad are familiar with the work of the Association:
1. International Youth Hostel Federation, Welwyn Garden City AL8 6Bt England.
2. American Jewish Congress, New York.
3. P.E.F. Israel Endowment Fund, c/o Mrs. Eli Ginsberg, 30 Broadway, New York.
4. National Youth Hostels Association in nearly fifty other countries.

FUNDING NEEDED

1. For an additional youth hostel in Jerusalem/Ein Karem, with a capacity of at least another one hundred and fifty beds and facilities; cost, estimated $1,430,000.
2. For an additional building in Tel Aviv, with two hundred more beds; cost, estimated $2,000,000.
3. To build a new youth hostel in Eilat, with up to three hundred beds; cost, estimated $3,000,000.

THE ISRAELI ASSOCIATION OF CREATIVE AND EXPRESSIVE THERAPIES (ICET)

האגוד הישראלי לתראפיה ביצירה והבעה — י.ה.ת.

c/o Sekeles
Hatayassim 32
Jerusalem

Telephone: (02) 633891
Office hours: Evenings: 7-10 P.M.; Fridays: 8-2 P.M.

HISTORY AND DESCRIPTION
The ICET was founded in 1971. It encompasses the following fields: Music Therapy, Dance and Movement Therapy, Drama Therapy and Psychodrama, and Visual Art Therapy. In recent years there has been a growing interest in the use of the arts (dance, music, drama and visual arts) as a therapeutic medium. Introductory courses are offered by ICET members in Israel's teaching colleges and principal universities.

Goals: ICET's purpose is to offer therapists the opportunity to exchange ideas, to create in hospitals and institutions for special education an atmosphere that is conducive to the development of creative therapies, and to advance training and research in the field. ICET also helps immigrant therapists to continue their careers in Israel and encourages professional contacts with similar associations abroad.

Services, Activities and Accomplishments: In the three active branches of ICET, in Jerusalem, Tel Aviv and Haifa, there are fortnightly workshops, seminars and lectures for members, in addition to an annual two-day conference and several intensive courses lasting three to seven days. ICET provides a supportive framework for professionals in the field as well as offering complementary studies.

OFFICERS
Chairman:	Chava Sekeles, Hatayassim 32, Jerusalem. Music therapist. Tel. (02) 633891.
Treasurer:	Samuel Spitzer, Arazim 8, Jerusalem. Music therapist. Tel. (02) 532719.
Gen'l. Sec'y.:	Yona Shahar Levi, Boaz 22, Haifa. Dance therapist. Tel. (04) 81271.
Haifa Branch Organizer:	Graziela Zandbank, Boaz 7, Haifa. Music therapist. Tel. (04) 256006.

FINANCIAL INFORMATION
All of last year's annual budget came from membership dues ($4 per person in 1980). Donations to ICET are tax-free in Israel (no registration number supplied). ICET is registered as an Ottoman Association (Jerusalem, reg. no. 11/1926). All of the ICET staff are volunteers.

MEMBERSHIP, SCOPE AND POLICY

There are three branches in Israel (none overseas) with 250 members in the country and ten abroad. Active membership is open to professionals only; persons from correlated professions (psychology, special education, para-medical studies, neurology, psychiatry, etc.) can become associate members. Decisions are taken by the National Board and, in the branches, by the local committees.

AFFILIATIONS/REFERENCES

1. NAMT (National Association of Music Therapy), Kansas University, Lawrence, Kansas 66044, U.S.A.
2. ADATA (American Dance Therapy Association), 2000 Century Plaza, Colombia, Maryland 21044, U.S.A.
3. United Public Health Service, Dr. B.S. Brown, Washington, D.C. 20201, U.S.A.

Also other associations in America and Europe.
ICET is not affiliated with any political party in Israel.

FUNDING NEEDED

1. To subsidize a two-year course in the four art therapy fields mentioned (music, dance and movement, drama and psychodrama, visual arts) in order to establish an Israeli program that will remove the need for Israelis to study abroad. ($10,000 for initial equipment).
2. To set up a professional library. ($2,000).
3. For research projects.

ITALIAN SYNAGOGUE AND MUSEUM
בית הכנסת האיטלקי והמוזיאון, ירושלים

Hillel 27, Jerusalem.
Telephone: (02) 241610
Office Hours: Available on Request

HISTORY AND DESCRIPTION
Italian Synagogue and Museum was founded on Rosh Hashanah 1940 as a spiritual center for Jews coming from Italy. The organization is concerned with preserving its fine and valuable collection of Jewish Italian art dedicated to its founder Dr. U.S. Nahon. These are arranged next to the Old Synagogue which was brought from Conegliano Veneto, and is still being used by the Italian Congregation in Jerusalem.

Organizational Structure: There are two separate managing boards for the synagogue and the museum, under one chairman. The two boards make up the trustee board. A general assembly takes place at an unspecified time and consists of all members of the Cultural Society of Italian Jews.

Goals: The goals of the organization include: instituting the ancient Italian rite (Minhag Bnei Roma); creating a spiritual center for Jews coming from Italy; and preserving and documenting Jewish art objects, books, and manuscripts from Italy in a museum open to the general public two days a week.

Services, Activities, and Accomplishments: Activities include the synagogue's use by the Italian Congregation of Jerusalem. The collection of Jewish art from Italy and a library are being catalogued and organized. The organization's major accomplishments to date include the rescuing of Judaica objects from disappearing Italian communities, the removal of an ancient synagogue and preserving the ancient rite in a "living" synagogue and spiritual center, and organizing and cataloguing both the collection of Judaica objects and the library.

OFFICERS
Director: David Cassuto, Ein Guedi 20, Jerusalem.
                    Architect.
                    Tel. (02) 711438.

Treasurer: Th. Dishon, Keren Kayemet 37, Jerusalem.
                    Prof. of Bacteriology.
                    Tel. (02) 631939.

Board: B. Sermoneta, Nahshon 8, Jerusalem.
                    Prof. of Philosophy.
                    Tel. (02) 717927.
           Dan Segre-Avni, Ben Yehuda 1, Jerusalem.
                    Prof. of Communication.
                    Tel. (02) 225782.

B. Lazar, Mevo Yoram 7, Jerusalem.
Lawyer.
Tel. (02) 668465.
S. Della Pergola, Habanai 29, Jerusalem.
Demographer.
Tel. (02) 527867.
D. Patsi. Educator.

FINANCIAL INFORMATION
The organization receives its income from two sources: donations accounting for 75% of the organization's income, and the remaining 25% through membership dues. Last year the organization's annual budget was $8,000 and the deficit $1,600. Italian Synagogue and Museum is registered as an Ottoman Association (reg. no. not supplied). Its donations are tax-free in Israel (reg. no. not supplied) and also in the United States (I.R.S. no. not supplied). The organization employs 3 part-time staff and 7 volunteers.

MEMBERSHIP, SCOPE, AND POLICY
Decisions in the organization are made mostly by an Executive Director. Any person of Italian or non-Italian origin sympathizing with the Italian Jewish culture is eligible to join. There are presently 100 members in Israel in one branch (no members or branches abroad).

AFFILIATIONS/REFERENCES
The organization is not affiliated with any political party in Israel. Internationally it is affiliated with the following:
P.E.F. Israel Endowment Funds, Inc., 342 Madison Ave. (Suite 1010), New York.
Memorial Foundation for Jewish Culture, New York, and the *Unione delle Comunita*, Rome.

FUNDING NEEDED
The organization's most outstanding present needs include:
1. Publishing a well-documented and well-illustrated catalogue which will provide detailed information on each item of the museum's collection. Estimated cost $38,000.
2. The re-organizing of the Museums' display to simplify the display and facilitate the visit. Estimated cost: $12,000.
3. The acquisition of equipment and furniture for a reading room. Estimated cost $10,000.

THE JERUSALEM ACADEMY
OF JEWISH STUDIES
(DVAR YERUSHALAYIM)

ישיבת דבר ירושלים

8 Hayeshivah Street
P.O.B. 5454
Jerusalem
Telephone: (02) 288645 or 287858; students' campus number 271900
Office hours: 8:00 A.M. to 6:00 P.M.

HISTORY AND DESCRIPTION
Yeshivat Dvar Yerushalayim was established in 1970 by Rabbi B. Horovitz, M.A., who, as University Chaplain in Manchester, England, became aware of the spiritual deterioration of Jewish youth through assimilation and intermarriage. The Academy soon attracted young men with minimal background in Jewish learning, who received a unique, sophisticated introduction to the scholarly source-material of Judaism, in order to facilitate their successful study.
The inital campus in Sanhedria, Jerusalem, soon proved to be too small, and was converted to a Women's Seminary three years ago. The present campus, in Geulah, Jerusalem, caters to some 200 students.
Plans for a new enlarged campus, to house our expanding student body, are being drawn up at present.

Organizational Structure: The Yeshiva caters to a college level and post-college level student body — professionals, graduates and intellectually oriented, serious, searching young men and women.
The faculty consists of some 20 experienced, devoted teachers, who are sensitive to the individuality of the students.
Introductory courses for our students who come form all parts of the world are conducted in Hebrew, English, French, Spanish, and Russian. There is a bi-lingual department for Russian students, some of whom are advanced scientists now only beginning their Jewish learning.
A wide range of academic study extends from beginners' classes to advanced Kollel research programs. Individual progress is often quite rapid: students entering the Yeshiva with only a minimal background can reach high levels of learning within brief periods of time.
Branches operate in Ashkelon, Israel; London, England; and New York. Courses are accredited by U.S. colleges.

Services, Activities, and Accomplishments: A particular educational feature is the annual summer program, especially designed for those who cannot manage long term study. A Hebrew ulpan helps the students to become acquainted with the Hebrew language. A Women's Seminary has over 30 students. Dormitory facilities are available. There is a Teachers' Training Course.
Lectures and study courses are conducted in kibbutzim, immigrant absorption centers, university campuses, and in conjunction with Israeli

Defense Forces, in army camps, in order to imbue officers with a sense of religious awareness.

There are seminars for Jewish Agency youth groups.

Suitable individuals are trained as ritual slaughterers, Torah scribes and the rabbinate.

Productions: Publications, a bi-annual magazine with a worldwide circulation of 5000, audio-visual programs and musical groups.

Hundreds of the Yeshiva's students have learned Jewish values, history, and Torah, and they have become devoted Jews. Most students remain in Israel, marry Jewish girls and build their new homes in the Jewish tradition. Those who return to their countries of origin become leaders and teach Judaism to other Jewish youths.

There is also a Committee "Jerusalem Academy Trust" in England and "Friends of the Jerusalem Academy" in New York, as well as in other countries.

OFFICERS

Dean: Rabbi Baruch Horovitz, 18 Blau, Jerusalem. Dean.
Tel. (02) 819640.

Rabbi M. Farber, 31 Bayit Vegan, Jerusalem. Lecturer.
Tel. (02) 418526.

Rabbi Shlomo Wolbe, P.O.B. 3, Be'er Ya'akov.
Lecturer and author.
Tel. (02) 524955.

Rabbi I.S. Wolfson, Simtat Hagiva, Savyon. Lecturer.
Tel. (03) 759984.

Rabbi Aryeh Carmell, Rechov Bayit Vegan 94, Jerusalem.
Vice-Principal and Lecturer.
Tel. (02) 420454.

Mr. Jack Freedman, Giloh 62/37, Jerusalem. Secretary.
Tel. (02) 716360.

Rabbi Yechiel Sitzman, Panim Meirot 13, Jerusalem.
Lecturer.
Tel. (02) 534656.

FINANCIAL INFORMATION

Income for last year's budget came from the following sources: membership dues, 5%; donations, 55%; and the remaining 40% from government grants. Last year's annual budget was $180,000, with a deficit of $44,000. The organization is registered as an Ottoman Association (reg. no. 11/1902). Donations to the organization are tax-free in Israel (tax no. 4504989), the United States (tax no. M72-EO-1713), and England (tax no. 262716). There are 18 full-time and 40 part-time workers employed by the organization, in addition to some volunteers.

MEMBERSHIP, SCOPE, AND POLICY

Most decisions are made by the Executive Director and the Dean, while some administrative matters are handled by the National Board. Membership in Israel includes approximately 500 members, and another 6000 members abroad.

AFFILIATIONS/REFERENCES

The organization is not affiliated with any political party. It is in contact with the following: Hillel Organization, Bnei Brith, 1640 Rhode Island Avenue N.W., Washington, D.C.; Bnei Brith Hillel Organizations, 1/2 Endsleigh Street, London WC1H ODS; Chief Rabbi's Office, Adler House, Tavistock Square, London WC1; Conference of European Rabbis, Woburn House, Upper Woburn Place, London WC1H OEP; American Office of Jewish Agency, 515 Park Avenue, New York, New York 10022; Rabbinical Council of America, 220 Park Avenue South, New York, New York 10003.

American Office of the Jerusalem Academy, 26 Court Street, Suite 2410, New York, 11201, USA. Tel. (212) 852-2024.

London Office of the Jerusalem Academy, 1007 Finchley Road, London NW11 7HB. Tel: (01) 458 8563.

FUNDING NEEDED

1. Covering the deficit and expanding the running projects, which will cost $500,000. Then, campus project in Lifta (North West Jerusalem). Cost of total project: $20 million. Cost of first stage: $2 million.
2. Expanding the program of productions: Jerusalem Academy Publications in a number of languages; an Audio Visual Program; videotapes; films; musical productions; and research projects. The cost is $500,000.
3. A world-wide annual campus tour; groups of lecturers and musicians from Dvar will visit every university campus where there are Jewish students and attract them to Judaism and Israel, including multi-media presentation. Estimated cost: $150,000 per annum.

JERUSALEM COLLEGE OF TECHNOLOGY

בית ספר גבוה לטכנולוגיה ירושלים

Havaad Haleumi 21
P.O.B. 16031, Jerusalem
Telephone: (02) 423131
Office Hours: Sunday-Thursday, 8:30 A.M. to 4:30 P.M.
Friday and Holiday Eves, 8:30 A.M. to 11:30 A.M.

HISTORY AND DESCRIPTION

The Jerusalem College of Technology was established in 1969 by a group of religious Jewish scientists as a fully accredited technical college and yeshiva to enable religious young men who have completed their army service to continue their yeshiva studies while also studying toward a profession.

Organizational Structure: The yeshiva segment of the college is headed by a Rosh Yeshiva, a director of Beit Midrash and several teaching rabbis. The various academic/secular departments each have a departmental director and a staff of teachers.

Goals: The Jerusalem College of Technology seeks to educate young men in Jewish moral values, traditions and advanced Talmudic study while also enabling them to study for an academic degree in practical engineering. Upon earning their degrees, students of the College can seek employment in industry, teach, establish their own enterprises or continue toward advanced degrees.

Services, Activities, and Accomplishments: The Jerusalem College of Technology provides programs in the fields of electro-optics, electronics, computer science, metallurgy, teacher education and mathematics, in addition to the religious study offered through its yeshiva. In addition to the regular academic program, special courses and programs are conducted for the army and other groups. Consistent with its goal of providing the student with a maximum degree of practical experience, the College requires that each student conduct an independent research project, often contracted by industry, during his third year of study. The College sees as its greatest achievement to date the fact that it has received accreditation from the Council of Higher Education as the first technical college in Israel to combine a full yeshiva program with the pursuit of a B.Sc. degree in practical engineering.

OFFICERS

Director: Professor W. Z. Low, Sheshet Hayamim 34,
Jerusalem. Physicist.
Tel. (02) 814196.

Treasurer: Mr. J. Kiel, Hahida 9, Jerusalem.
Businessman, Tel. (02) 233386.

Board Members: Mr. M. Stern, Ben Yehuda 2, Jerusalem.
Banker.
Tel. (02) 234331.
Mr. A. Verdiger, Sorotzkin 16, Jerusalem.
Educator.
Tel. (02) 535187.
Professor A. Engelberg, Ben Tabai 4, Jerusalem.
Educator.
Tel. (02) 667740.
Professor J. Bodenheimer, Mishmar Ha'am 12,
Jerusalem. Educator.
Tel. (02) 635596.
Mr. Z. Weinberger, Yehoshua Ben Nun 24,
Jerusalem. Educator.
Tel. (02) 534515.
Rabbi N. Bar-Haim, Hapisga 61, Jerusalem.
Educator.
Tel. (02) 419525.

FINANCIAL INFORMATION

50% of the College's income is acquired through donations; the other 50% through Israeli governmental sources. Last year's budget of $800,000 left the College with a deficit of $100,000. The organization is registered with the Jerusalem District as an Ottoman Association (reg. no. 11/1720). Donations are tax-free in both Israel (reg. no. 941082083) and the United States (reg. no. not supplied). The College is also a registered charity in both England (reg. no. 263003) and in Canada (reg. no. 0414557-23-13). The College employs 40 full-time, 10 part-time, and 20 volunteer workers.

MEMBERSHIP, SCOPE, POLICY, AND AFFILIATIONS

Decisions for the Jerusalem College of Technology are made by its International Board of Governors (Executive Council). There are four branches of the College outside of Israel (foreign affiliations and their addresses not supplied). The College is not affiliated with any Israeli political party.

FUNDING NEEDED

1. The building of a single students' dormitory. Estimated cost is between $450,000 and $1 million (part of this sum has already been collected).
2. An Endowment Fund for a Senior Lecturer Chair. Cost, $150,000.
3. Contributions to existing Full Perpetual Scholarships. Cost $25,000.

THE JERUSALEM INSTITUTE FOR THE PREVENTION OF BLINDNESS

המכון הירושלמי למניעת עוורון

Straus Health Center
Straus 24
P.O.B. 499, Jerusalem
Telephone: (02) 227552 or (02) 226458
Office hours: 8:00 a.m.-1:00 p.m. daily

HISTORY AND DESCRIPTION

The Jerusalem Institute for the Prevention of Blindness was founded in 1974 as a consequence of experience and motivation regarding the prevention of blindness that was acquired by a group of senior Israeli ophthalmologists. During the past 20 years, the contributions of Israeli ophthalmologists to the prevention of blindness have become well-recognized in both underdeveloped and developed countries. At the First International Conference on the Prevention of Blindness, held in Jerusalem in 1971, Israeli ophthalmologists reported on their work in Africa, and on Israel's ten-year national cooperative research on the prevention of retinal detachment. The acclaim given to the Conference led to in the founding of the Jerusalem Institute for the Prevention of Blindness.

The Institute is housed in the Straus Health Center in the heart of Jerusalem. It occupies about 500 square metres.

Goals: The Institute aims to demonstrate that many instances of blindness are preventable. Its purpose is also to show, by example, that each medical speciality in each country, however small, can organize preventive services and research in that speciality, and find the necessary support.

Services, Activities and Accomplishments: The Institute runs a low-vision clinic for children. It has been shown that, given proper optical aid, many children with severe eye diseases can be educated at an ordinary school and not have to attend a special school for the blind. The Institute also has a genetic counselling clinic for the prevention of hereditary eye diseases, and a follow-up clinic for premature infants whose care had required incubation. In association with the Ministry of Social Welfare, the Institute participates, in an advisory capacity, in the national registration of the blind. The Institute also provides instruction for undergraduates and graduate ophthalmologists in the prevention of eye diseases. Information on the prevention of eye diseases is supplied periodically to the media for dissemination to the general public.

Much of the research conducted by the Institute is concerned with the blinding diseases of childhood, such as retrolental fibroplasia and hereditary disorders, and with such age-related diseases as glaucoma, macular disease, diabetes and retinal detachment. These diseases are common, and as they are frequently bilateral, they can result in blindness.

Junior members of the Institute staff receive part of their professional training at the National Institute of Health in Washington. Nearly all of the chairmen of the 24 eye departments and eye institutions in Israel received their training in ophthalmology under the direction of the present staff of the Institute. The Institute has formed a team of co-workers in the fields of ophthalmology, sociology, optometry, psychology and epidemiology. Programs for research in these disciplines have been planned; some have already begun where funds were available. Annual progress reports have been issued by the Institute since its inception. In 1977, the Director of the Institute, Prof. I.C. Michaelson, was awarded the Israel Prize for Medicine.

OFFICERS
Director: I.C. Michaelson, Balfour 19, Jerusalem.
                 Ophthalmologist.
                 Tel. (02) 631690.
Treasurer: Mr. Yehuda Bar-Nahum. Hadassah Medical
                 Organization. Ein Kerem. Jerusalem.
                 Tel. (02) 427427.

FINANCIAL INFORMATION
All of last year's annual budget ($40,000) came from donations; there was no deficit. Donations to the Institute are tax-free in Israel (registration number not supplied) and in the USA (the IRS tax number is that of Hadassah, the Women's Zionist Organization of America, Inc., 50 West 58th Street, New, York, N.Y. 10019, USA). The Institute is registered as an Ottoman Association (Jerusalem, reg. no. 11/2162). One full-time worker and nine part-time workers are employed by the Institute; there are also several volunteers.

MEMBERSHIP, SCOPE, AND POLICY
There is no public membership of the Institute. Most decisions are made by the Executive Director, in consultation with his principle associates at the Institute: Prof. I. Nawratzki, Prof. I.H. Abramson, Dr. L. Yanko. Prior to decisions on any national research, the Institute consults the Committee for Inter-Departmental Research in Israel. The Institute has no branches abroad.

AFFILIATIONS/REFERENCES
1. Hadassah, The Women's Zionist Organization of America, Inc., 50 West 58th Street, New York, N.Y. 10019, USA.
2. Dr. Carl Kupfer, Director, National Eye Institute, Bethesda, Maryland 20014, USA.
3. Sir John Wilson, President, International Agency for the Prevention of Blindness, Commonwealth House, Haywards Heath, West Sussex RH16 3AZ, England.
The Institute is not affiliated with any political party in Israel.

FUNDING NEEDED

1. For research on the prevention of age-related causes of blindness at all ages in the developed countries and the underdeveloped countries.
2. For research on the prevention of blindness in childhood. Retrolental fibroplasia is the cause of about 50% of blindness in childhood.
3. For the formation of an endowment fund which will make it possible to improve long-term planning, especially for research.

JERUSALEM INTERNATIONAL Y.M.C.A.

י.מ.ק.א. הבינלאומית ירושלים

P.O. Box 294
Telephone: (02) 227111
Office Hours: Monday through Friday 9:00 A.M. to 1:00 P.M. and 3:00 P.M. to 7:00 P.M.

HISTORY AND DESCRIPTION
Started in January 1878, the Jerusalem International Y.M.C.A. offers its members over 60 different ways to participate in its activites, including sports, games, art and music. The Jerusalem Y.M.C.A. has come a long way since the idea of an Association in the Holy City was first conceived over a hundred years ago.

Organizational Structure: Governed by an executive board comprised of elected officers, individuals who represent a cross section of religions and nationalities; and senior staff members who head the divisions of Youth, Culture, Sport and Membership.

Goals: In its programs and services, the YMCA assists its members to achieve the following goals: 1) the development of self-confidence and self-respect and an appreciation of every person's worth as an individual, 2) the development and strengthening of spiritual and moral convictions, 3) to grow as responsible members of families and citizens of the community, 4) to appreciate that health of mind and body is a sacred gift and that physical fitness and mental well-being are worthy objectives, 5) to work for the furtherance of interfaith, interracial and intergroup understanding, 6) the development of a sense of worldmindedness and to work for worldwide understanding, 7) the development of capacities for leadership and the use of these in groups and community life.
Services, Activites and accomplishments: Sports—tennis, swimming, football, gymnastics, squash, breathing and excercising programs; Youth—day camps, movies, organized games, handicraft, dancing, special events; Programs for Women—gym classes, swimming, tennis, ping-pong, karate, jogging; Culture—concerts, language programs, ceramics, choral organization, music lessons. The major accomplishment of the Jerusalem Y.M.C.A. has been that it is the number one community-serving agency in Israel catering to people of all races, faiths and sexes without distinction.

OFFICERS
Chairman:	Pinchas Rabinovitch, Lawyer.
Vice Chairman:	William Ayers, Director ICI.
Vice Chairman:	Gordon Primrose, Banker.
	James L. Rhoads, General Director.

FINANCIAL INFORMATION
50% of the income comes from the hotel and restaurant, 38% from membership dues, 7% from the International Division of Y.M.C.A.

—U.S.A., and 5% from donations. Last year's annual budget was $1,000,000 and the deficit of $10,000. The organization is registered in Jerusalem as an Ottoman Association and donations are tax-free in both the U.S. and Israel (number not provided). There are 76 full-time employees, 110 part-time and 36 volunteers.

MEMBERSHIP, SCOPE, AND POLICY
Anyone from age 6 and over can become a member. There are 5,000 members in Israel and 20,000,000 abroad. Decisions are made by the National Board and Local Board of directors. The Jerusalem Y.M.C.A. has 2 branches in Israel and there are 10,000 Y.M.C.A. centers abroad.

AFFILIATIONS/REFERENCES
National Council of Y.M.C.A.'s of U.S.A., 291 Broadway, New York, New York.

FUNDING NEEDED
1. Modernization of youth facilities.
2. Restoration of the 4 manual Austin Organs.
3. Modernization of the auditorium and endowment of cultural activites.

JERUSALEM MENTAL HEALTH CENTER — EZRATH NASHIM

P.O.B. 140
Givat Shaul
Jerusalem
Telephone: (02) 521231
Office hours: Sunday-Thursday 8:00 A.M. to 3:00 P.M.
Friday 8:00 A.M. to 12:00 Noon

HISTORY AND DESCRIPTION

Ezrath Nashim was founded in 1895 and is the only non-profit voluntary psychiatric institution in Israel. It is managed by an unpaid Board of Directors which is elected annually. It provides 150 psychiatric beds at the main Center in Givat Shaul, in addition to an extensive outreach program based in the community clinic in the Sanhedria district, serving an area of 120,000 people. The hospital is affiliated with the Hebrew University-Hadassah Medical School and is a major center for teaching and research. The Yaacov Herzog Research Division has achieved world-wide recognition for its publications and contributions to international psychiatric research.

In 1976 a non-psychiatric Geriatric Division was established which now provides 60 beds for the treatment of the aged.

The major accomplishments of the Health Center are that it pioneered community psychiatry in Israel and that it established Israel's foremost and internationally recognized psychiatric research center.

OFFICERS

President: Mrs. Mildred Devor.
Board Members: Irwin Gordon.
Nathan Silver.
Judge Yehuda Cohen.
Moshe Mann.
Dr. T. Fink.
M. Lockman.
Arie Ginossar.

FINANCIAL INFORMATION

25% of last year's annual budget came from membership dues and donations; the remaining 75% came from the Ministry of Health. Last year's annual budget was $1.6 million, leaving the Center with an accumulated deficit of $91,000. The Center is registered as an Ottoman Association (reg. no. 11/304). Donations to the Center are tax-free in Israel (tax no. 4500122), the United States (tax no. 8408), Britain (tax no. X91507A), and Canada (tax no. 0507814-11-13). There are 110 full-time and 75 part-time workers employed by the Center in addition to 50 active volunteers in and out of hospital.

MEMBERSHIP, SCOPE, AND POLICY

Decisions are made by the National Board. There are 850 members in

Israel and 2000 members abroad. Any person making an annual contribution to the hospital becomes a member.

AFFILIATIONS/REFERENCES
The Hospital is not affiliated with any political party in Israel. It has the following connections abroad: American Friends of JMHC, 10 East 40th Street, New York, New York 10016; Canadian Friends of JMHC, 825 Eglinton Avenue West, Toronto, Ont. M5N 1E7 Canada; British Aid Committee 15 Wildwood Road, London NW 11 6UL, England; recognized by Board of Deputies of British Jews; recognized by South African Meshullochim Board; Dublin Friends, Dublin, Ireland.

FUNDING NEEDED
General maintenance is required as a result of reduced support from the Ministry of Health. Annual support required to balance the hospital's budget — $500,000.

THE JERUSALEM OPERA SOCIETY

אגודת האופרה הירושלמית

Jasmin Street — Shwil 1/6
Mevaseret Zion
or: P.O.B. 2269, Jerusalem
Telephone: (02) 538273

HISTORY AND DESCRIPTION
The Jerusalem Opera Society was founded in 1977 by a group of American immigrants and Jacob Roden, Israeli international opera star and the head of the Voice Department of the Rubin Academy of Music in Jerusalem.

Goals: The purpose of the Society was to develop an opera company which would employ the artists presently living in Israel, in their respective fields, and encourage the return of the hundreds of gifted Israelis currently living and working abroad.

Services, Activities, and Accomplishments: In 1978 the Jerusalem Opera Society chorus of sixty-eight members began work on the first showcase production of Verdi's "Otello" and the grass-roots membership of the Society grew to 250 members. Talented children from each of Jerusalem's schools were chosen to sing in the children's choir. With the help of the Ministry of Absorption, the Ministry of Education and Culture, the Zionist Federation, the Aviezer Foundation, the Jewish Agency, and the Rubin Academy, in addition to the funds raised by the Society, all costs for the "showcase" production were met. The production was staged in 1979 with 250 performers. In the same year the Society made a co-production with the Rubin Academy of Mozart's "The Magic Flute", which was video-taped for schools and also produced for the Jerusalem school system. In 1980 the Society produced "The Beggar's Opera" with the Rubin Academy and the Jerusalem Khan Theater, and staged performances in Tel Aviv and Jerusalem. The 1980-81 project is designed to fill a void in the educational system. The Society has opened a professional studio to accommodate the many professional singers who wish to prepare roles for their future careers and acquire the necessary experience of routine performances. In addition, the J.O.S. has opened a training center for young artists. At the Y.M.C.A. Scenes and Acts of this year's productions will be brought to schools, hospitals, clubs for the aged and community centers. Two major productions will be mounted, one in Hebrew, which will travel around the country.

OFFICERS
Director: Jacob Roden, Shwil 1/6, Mevaseret Zion.
               Teacher.
               Tel. (02) 538273.
Treasurer: Jack Valencia.
               Tel. (02) 815804.

Board Members:	Mark Feiner.
	Gene Lowenthal, Sheshet Hayamin 22, Jerusalem. Emissary (shaliach). Tel. (02) 818695.
	Edward Marmelstein, Sderot Eshkol 18, Jerusalem. Technician. Tel. (02) 810962.
Accountant:	Serigiu Engel, Accountant. Tel. (02) 416436.
Legal Advisor:	Moshe Argov, Rambam 23, Jerusalem. Lawyer. Tel. (02) 630259.

FINANCIAL INFORMATION

25% of last year's annual budget came from membership dues and 25% from the Jerusalem Foundation and the Jerusalem Municipality; the balance derived from government sources (Ministries of Education and Culture, Tourism, and Absorption), and ticket sales. Last year's annual budget of $18,000 left the Society with a deficit (of taxes owed to the State) of $4,800. Donations to the Society in Israel and the United States are tax-free (Israel reg. no. 11/2742), and should be transferred through the Jerusalem Foundation (USA no. 156, Israel no. 56). Eighty-five part-time workers are employed by the Society, as well as 250 volunteers.

MEMBERSHIP, SCOPE, AND POLICY

The Jerusalem Opera Society is represented by 257 national members and 45 members from abroad. The membership fee is $10, and anyone may join. Decisions are taken by majority vote of committee members and Board members.

AFFILIATIONS/REFERENCES

The Jerusalem Opera Society has no affiliations with any of the political parties in Israel. It maintains contact with the New York Branch of the Jerusalem Foundation, and the America-Israel Cultural Foundation, 4 East 54 Street, N.Y. 10022.

FUNDING NEEDED

1. To hire professional staff, buy a piano, blackboard, and video cassettes for use in the workshops, for the training center.
2. To provide scholarships to cover tuition fees for potential singers. As the training center offers no secondary academic degree, it does not qualify for assistance from the Student Authority, so that the students are required to cover their own costs.
3. To provide a subsidy for production costs, and expenses of transportation to schools, hospitals, etc. Each full production costs $60,000; this includes sets, costumes, make-up, theater rental, transportation, and lighting.

THE JERUSALEM POST TOY FUND

מפעל הצעצועים של הג׳רוסלם פוסט

Jerusalem Post Building, Romema
P.O.B. 81, Jerusalem
Telephone: (02) 528181
Office hours: 9-1 daily throughout the year
all day during the drive, November through January

HISTORY AND DESCRIPTION

The Jerusalem Post Toy Fund began its work 31 years ago, to bring Hanukka happiness to children of the Ma'abarot (early transient immigrant settlements). A partner in those early days was the late Marion Hoofien who, through an organization called Sa'ad, had been giving layettes to needy mothers for many years before the establishment of the State. The first year was a bleak beginning, but the drive caught on and by the following Hanukka there were cash contributions and many gifts in kind, as children were asked to share their toys. Contributions continued all through the year from faithful donors.

In the early days the Israel Police assumed the job of distribution and in the two days before the holiday succeeded in bringing toys to every Ma'abara and immigrant village on the map. Dr. Sophie Rogolsky, chief social worker in the Children and Youth Section of the Ministry of Social Affairs, was instrumental in locating children in distress and she remained a constant guide, even after she retired. At her initiative a Special Fund was inaugurated in 1978, to provide for teenage children brought up in foster homes. An original glass Hanukka top was specially designed for the project and to date 8,000 have been sold to raise funds. At present the ministry's liaison officer is Elisheva Shalev.

Services, Activities, and Accomplishments: The fund has been carrying out its program fully for the past 31 years. The Jerusalem Post newspaper carries most of the running expenses of the fund and all who work for it are staff members, who volunteer their services. The Post's Certified Public Accountants, Somekh Chaikin Citron & Co., give their services free of charge and Israel Discount Bank debits the fund with minor bank charges.

For the Special Fund, the Jerusalem Post pays for the tops, boxes, dispatch, and postage. Ten special gifts were given in 1979 and at the moment $3,600 makes up the trust fund for future use.

An unusual feature of the Toy Fund is that every gift is acknowledged in the Toy Fund list, published daily. Donors are permitted to run any legend they choose. Also, four donors have set up trust funds for the benefit of the Toy Fund.

OFFICERS

Executive Director: Helen Rossi, 9 Abarbanel, Jerusalem.
Journalist. Tel. (02) 639089.
Directors: Shalom Weiss, 34 Hapalmach, Jerusalem.
Accountant. Tel. (02) 631077.

Erwin Frenkel, Ha'arazim, Motza.
Editor, Jerusalem Post. Tel. (02) 539911.
Avraham Levin, 5 Ha'arazim, Jerusalem.
Advert. Manager. Tel. (02) 526693.
Yehoshua Levy, 28 Haportzim, Jerusalem.
Press Manager. Tel. (02) 664896.
Moshe Pinto, 23 Eliezer Halevi, Jerusalem.
Circulat. Mgr. Tel. (02) 523521.
Ari Rath, 24 Harav Berlin, Jerusalem.
Editor, Jerusalem Post. Tel. (02) 665270.
Elisheva Shalev, Ramat Motza.
Chief Inspector Child and Youth Division,
Ministry of Labour and Social Affairs.
Tel. (02) 531698.

FINANCIAL INFORMATION

Last year's annual budget was $26,975, all from donations. Total income for the Special Fund was $16,837. The fund is registered as an Ottoman Association (Israel reg. no. 11/732) but donations are not tax-free, neither in Israel nor in the U.S. All workers for the fund are volunteers from The Jerusalem Post staff.

MEMBERSHIP, SCOPE, AND POLICY

It may be said that anyone who contributes to the fund is a "member". Decisions are made mostly by the Executive Director and by Elisheva Shalev.

AFFILIATIONS/REFERENCES

The fund has no party affiliation in Israel. Abroad, the fund is known through the appeal made to readers of The Jerusalem Post and The Jerusalem Post International Edition.

FUNDING NEEDED

1. To distribute the Hanukka gifts country-wide to all foster children. This is directed by the municipalities and the national and district offices of the Ministry of Labor and Social Affairs.
2. To distribute gifts to all government and some private institutions for children, including those under the Youth Protection Service.
3. To provide watches for children becoming Bar and Bat Mitzvah, as recommended by social workers.
4. To offer help to Christian and Moslem institutions which have been recommended by the Ministry of Religion and the Ministry of Labor and Social Affairs.

THE JERUSALEM SOCIETY FOR THE ADVANCEMENT OF EDUCATION AND CULTURE

האגודה הירושלמית לקידום חינוך ותרבות

P.O.B. 18095
5 Hevra Hadasha Street — Apt. 1
Tel Aviv 62998
Telephone: (03) 253958
Office hours: 8:00 A.M. to 2:00 P.M.

HISTORY AND DESCRIPTION

The Jerusalem Society for the Advancement of Education and Culture was founded as a non-profit society, in 1977, by Herbert Friedman, former executive vice president of the U.J.A., and Hertzel Fishman, advisor to the Israel Ministry of Education and Culture. Through its American Friends, it enjoys an IRS tax-exempt status in the United States. The principle purpose of the Jerusalem Society is to establish the Jerusalem Academy, on 480 dunams in the Judean Hills, 25 minutes from Jerusalem, near Tzur Hadassah. This secondary school, with residential facilities, will be devoted to the education of gifted Jewish youth from Israel and abroad. The future of Judaism and the Jewish people rests largely on the calibre of its leadership, and the aim of the Jerusalem Academy is to train its outstanding students for leadership roles in Jewish life as well as in the life of the general community. The school's curriculum will incorporate strong liberal arts and science components and a distinctive Judaic element; it will have small classes, and will encourage independent study and dialogue with teachers and peers.

Accomplishments: The approval of architectural plans by zoning authorities, receipt of building permit, lease of land from Israel Land Authorities, organization of American Friends of the Jerusalem Society for the Advancement of Education and Culture, raising of initial seed money, construction pledges of $3.6 million, and the writing of the first draft of the school's curriculum.

OFFICERS

Board Chairman: Herbert Friedman, 75 East 55th Street, New York, New York 10022. Rabbi. Tel. (212) 688-7979.

Stanley Sloane, New York, N.Y.
Chairman of American Friends.

Board Members: Hertzel Fishman, 10 Shimoni, Jerusalem. Educator. Tel. (02) 664582.

Avraham Agmon, Aluf Simhoni, Jerusalem. Director General, Delek Oil Company.

Walter Eytan, Jerusalem. Former Director General, Ministry of Foreign Affairs.

Yuval Aloni, Chairman, Local Council,
Mateh Yehuda.
Erwin Frankel. *The Jerusalem Post*. Editor.
Alex Grass, Harrisburg, Penna.
Robert Hecht, Houston, Texas.
Teddy Kollek, Mayor of Jerusalem.
Haim Laskov, Einstein, Tel Aviv.
Army ombudsman.
Israel Pollack, Nachlat Benyamin, Tel Aviv.
President, Polgat Corp.
Aharon Yariv, Nahalal. Director,
Strategic Studies, Tel Aviv University.
Avraham Avihai, Keren Hayesod, Jerusalem.
Chairman.
Ayala Zaks Abramov, Jerusalem. Governor,
International Museum.
Leonard Strelitz, Norfolk, Virginia.
Eliezer Shavit. UJA Education Fund, Jerusalem.
Israel Representative.

FINANCIAL INFORMATION

The Jerusalem Society's budget is derived only from donations. Last
year's annual budget was $250,000. There was no deficit. The organiza-
tion is registered as an Ottoman Association (reg. no. 11/2759). Donations are tax-free in both Israel and the United States. Two full-time and
one part-time workers are employed by the Society.

AFFILIATIONS/REFERENCES

The Jerusalem Society is not affiliated with any political party in Israel.
The Society is in contact with American Friends of the Jerusalem
Academy, Herbert Friedman, President, 75 East 55th Street, New York,
New York 10022.

FUNDING NEEDED

1. To obtain seed money for architectural fees, engineering costs, and
   administrative expenses. Estimated cost: $250,000.
2. To begin the first stage of building. Estimated cost: $10 million.

THE JERUSALEM SOCIETY FOR WORLD FELLOWSHIP

האגודה הירושלמית לאחווה בינלאומית

10 Shimoni Street—Apt. 8
Jerusalem 92 623
Telephone: (02) 664582
Office hours: 7:00 A.M. to 10:00 A.M. and 4:00 P.M. to 6:00 P.M.

HISTORY AND DESCRIPTION

The Jerusalem Society for World Fellowship is an ecumenical body organized in 1978 by 80 distinguished Israeli Jews, Christians, Muslims and Druze, as a non-profit (Ottoman) society. Its chairman is Erwin Frankel, editor of the Jerusalem Post. The purposes of the Jerusalem Society are: (a) to promote the fellowship of Arabs and Jews in Israel; (b) to offer programs to the many tourists who visit Israel annually, to enable them to find inspiration and new insight into their own spiritual origins, as well as to share in a common fellowship; and (c) to promote among Israeli Jewish families a heightened sense of civic responsibility, while deepening their Jewish knowledge and fulfillment. The Jerusalem Society has begun to implement these goals by day-long seminars in Israel, with Jewish and Arab participants. The central project of the Jerusalem Society is to establish and operate its World Fellowship Center in the Judean Hills, at Kibbutz Ma'aleh Hahamisha, ten minutes from the center of Jerusalem.

The Jerusalem Society for World Fellowship claims to be the first comprehensive ecumenical organizational attempt to make the Holy Land relevant to people of various monotheist faiths. Despite the strife and contention marring Israel's recent history, its eternal place in the hearts and minds of men and women everywhere continues to motivate them to "seek the peace of Jerusalem" and to transform the image of the Holy Land into one of conciliation and fellowship. By concentrating on non-political topics of human concern, Jewish and Arab citizens of Israel are beginning to realize that they are able to relate to one another on meaningful levels of mutual respect and social intercourse. By focusing on common personal and family concerns, the Jerusalem Society hopes to make a significant contribution toward easing communal tensions in the Holy Land and furthering the basic mutual interests of its inhabitants.

In 1981, Kibbutz Ma'aleh HaHamishah placed its lovely guest house, dining quarters, meeting rooms, and swimming pool (which is open during the summer months) at the convenience of the Jerusalem Society, to serve as the nucleus of the projected World Fellowship Center. The kibbutz will continue to own and operate the facilities, but the Jerusalem Society will enjoy preferential treatment for accommodating its sponsored groups and will be responsible for the programs and activities of the Center, and plan for its physical development.

Activities at the World Fellowship Center will include both cognitive and affective programs. At the cognitive level—popular lectures, seminars and mini-courses on the Bible, New Testament, Dead Sea scrolls, archaeology of the Holy Land, history of the Holy Land, comparative religions, Near Eastern cultures and societies, Arab and Jewish communities in Israel, etc. At the affective level — the Center will feature concerts, choral groups, dance performances, art exhibits, etc. It will organize international festivals of sacred music, folk-dance and folklore, with the participation of troupes from around the world.

Services, Activities, and Accomplishments: A series of all-day seminars for Arab and Jewish couples, on non-political topics of mutual concern: i.e., education of children, problems of the aged, employer-worker relationships, and civic initiatives and responsibilities. The Jerusalem YMCA has played a supportive role in these activities. In addition, a tax-exempt American Friends of the Jerusalem Society for World Fellowship has been organized in the United States.

OFFICERS
Board Chairman: Erwin Frankel, The Jerusalem Post. Editor.
Board Members: Hertzel Fishman, 10 Shimoni, Jerusalem.
    Educator. Tel. (02) 664582.
    Ziadan Atshi, Ussafiya. Member of Knesset.
    Walter Eytan, Jerusalem. Retired diplomat.
    Netanel Lorch, Jerusalem. Secretary of Knesset.
    Bernard Resnikoff, Jerusalem. Rep.
    American Jewish Committee.
    James Rhoads, YMCA, Jerusalem.
    Executive Director.
    Moshe Sharon, Hebrew University. Orientalist.
    Sheikh Wajdi Faud Tabari, Jaffa. Muslim Kadi.

FINANCIAL INFORMATION
The Jerusalem Society's budget comes exclusively from contributions. Last year's annual budget was $4,500. There was no deficit. The Society is registered as an Ottoman Association (reg. no. 11/3140). It is tax-free in Israel (tax. no. 4506554) and in the United States (tax no. 13-3014382). There is one part-time employee and three professional volunteers.

MEMBERSHIP, SCOPE, AND POLICY
Decisions are made by the National Executive Committee. The Jerusalem-Society is not currently a membership organization.

AFFILIATIONS/REFERENCES
The Society is not affiliated with any political party in Israel. The organization is in contact with the following: American Friends of the Jerusalem Society for World Fellowship, Dr. Oscar Remick, President, Alma College, Alma, Michigan 48801; American Jewish Committee, Bertram Gold, Executive Vice President, 165 East 56 Street, New York, New York 10022; Synagogue Council of America, Dr. Bernard Mandelbaum, Executive Vice President, 432 Park Avenue South, New York, New York 10006.

FUNDING NEEDED
1. Annual administrative budget—$25,000.
2. Year-round subsidized programs of a civic, cultural and social nature, for Jews and Arabs in Israel—$50,000 annually. Each monthly program costs $5,000.
3. Year-round subsidized programs of a pluralistic religious and cultural nature, for the many tourists who visit Israel—$75,000. Each program costs $3500.

THE JOSEPHTAL INSTITUTE FOR SOCIAL BETTERMENT SERVICES

המכון ע"ש גיורא יוספטל לשרותי רווחה חברתית

Beth Giora,
Kiriat Hayovel,
Jerusalem
Telephone: (02) 415820
Office hours: Sunday-Thursday, 7:45 A.M.-1:45 P.M.

HISTORY AND DESCRIPTION
The Institute was founded in 1964, to honor the memory of Giora Josephtal, by the Jewish Agency, the American Joint Distribution Committee, and the Israel Government, "to further the progress of Israeli society through training, tutoring and seminars towards self-help and reciprocal help at the community level." The Institute is governed by a public Board.

Goals: The Institute works towards the reduction of social gaps — between communities, generations, providers-recipients of services, and ethnic entities. Its main efforts are concentrated in slum neighborhoods and development towns.

Services, Activities, and Accomplishments: The Institute provides a variety of services in 3 main areas: adult education, community work, and group work. It runs dozens of training courses throughout the country, in addition to scores of workshops and one-day study sessions, in order to train indigenous leaders, especially at the grass-roots level, and to train paraprofessional indigenous workers in human services. It provides assistance to Project Renewal, and gives on-the-job training for public servants. The Institute also renders consultant services to institutions and services. Each of the Institute's programs is specially tailored to the requirements of the population and its services; it is led by a suitable professional, in charge of all its stages; and it is reviewed and evaluated by an independent professional. The programs are financed by local and national public funds and occasional special seed-money contributions. Five handbooks have been published by the Institute, as well as issues of a quarterly on Community Work ("Baavoda Kehilatit").

OFFICERS
Director: Dov Ancona, Shoeva 43, Hare Yehuda. Educator. Tel. (02) 538267.

Treasurer: Israel Shaham, Sheshet Hayamim 5, Jerusalem. Economist. Tel. (02) 816604.

Board Members: Shlomo Hillel, Ramat Denya, Jerusalem. Knesset Member. Tel. (02) 411416.

327

Mordechai Winter, Ramot, Jerusalem.
Social Worker.
Tel. (02) 862159.
Ariel Weinstein, Ramat Hagolan St., Jerusalem.
Journalist.
Tel. (02) 816848.
Greta Fisher, Hapalmach 18, Jerusalem.
Social Worker.
Tel. (02) 662259.
David Harman, S. Levin 53, Jerusalem.
Educator.
Tel. (02) 414487.
Natan Labon, Ben Zion 2, Jerusalem.
Social Worker.
Tel. (02) 521683.

FINANCIAL INFORMATION
Public sources provide 80% of the Institute's income, in the form of payments for services rendered. Another 20% comes from *ad hoc* donations, as seed money for programs. The 1980 budget totalled $47,000 with a deficit of $1,500. The Institute is not an Ottoman association; rather, it is a non-profit society (Finance Ministry no. 941073785), registered as a Public Benefit Company (Trust no. 52/002971-1). As such, donations in Israel are tax-free. Donations from the U.S. have no tax-exemption. The six full-time staff are the director-general, the manpower manager, three program organizers, and the secretary. Another 25 professionals are employed as required by the Institute's programs. There are 11 volunteer workers.

MEMBERSHIP, SCOPE, AND POLICY
The Institute has 11 members, all in Israel. Members are selected by decision of the Board. Most decisions are made by the director-general and his team, but the Board has the final authority.

AFFILIATIONS/REFERENCES
The Institute is not affiliated with any political party in Israel. No foreign references are listed.

FUNDING NEEDED
1. To provide seed money for innovative programs.
2. For the publication of additional handbooks for indigenous leaders and para-professional workers.
3. To resume publication of the quarterly on Community Work.

KEHILAT YAAKOV INSTITUTE OF JEWISH STUDIES

מכון לתודעה יהודית, ובית מדרש קהילת יעקב

12 Zayit Ra'anan
Jerusalem
Telephone: (02) 819676
Office hours: 8:00 A.M. to 3:00 P.M.

HISTORY AND DESCRIPTION

The Kehilat Yaakov Institute of Jewish Studies is an institute for families who come from a background which did not have the benefit of a Jewish heritage. For a period of two years it supports families, allowing them to learn of their roots and study the Torah, and returns them to their profession as religious Jews living in today's society. There are daily lectures for the men in Talmud, Mishna, Halacha, and Ethics. For the women there is a weekly class in Torah and Ethics. The goal is to give Jews who didn't have the opportunity to learn of their roots, ample opportunity in order to fulfill the Torah and its commandments as G-d wants.

After taking notice of Jews the world over and of an intermarriage rate of over 50%, and seeing over half a million Israelis in America, as well as over 70% of the Russian Jews who arrive in Israel leave for other countries, as well as the rise of crime, Kehilat Yaakov Institute of Jewish Studies concluded that it is a direct result of the lack of Torah knowledge. Therefore, it opened an institute to tackle this problem, the future of our children and nation.

The major accomplishment has been that over the past two years Kehilat Yaakov Institute of Jewish Studies has enabled more than 100 families to learn of their roots, to become G-d fearing Jews, and to establish a vibrant Jewish community in development towns.

OFFICERS

Director: Nissim Yagen, 12 Zait Ra'anan, Jerusalem.
Tel. (02) 819676.

Treasurer: Eliahu Attias, 28 Imrei Bina, Jerusalem.
Tel. (02) 816404.

Board Members: Amiel Ben-Mashiah, 66-48 Saunders St.,
Rego Park, New York 11374.
Tel. (212) 897-3428.
Edmond Tannenhaus, 7 Hana Lane,
Monsey, New York 10952.
Tel. (914) 356-3214.
Alexander Domenitz, 43 Osbaldeston Road,
London N.16. Tel. 8063199.

FINANCIAL INFORMATION

90% of the income for last year's annual budget came from donations from Israel and abroad, while the remaining 10% came from the Ministry of Religion. The budget for last year was $70,000, with a deficit of

$30,000. The organization is registered as an Ottoman Association (reg. no. 11/3077). Donations to the organization are tax-free in Israel (reg. no. 4506424), the United States (tax no. 11-2496130), and Canada (tax. no. 0536995-21-13). There are 6 volunteer workers connected with the organization.

MEMBERSHIP, SCOPE, AND POLICY
Decisions are made by the Board at their meetings. Anyone who is serious and willing to devote time to study is eligible to join. There are 100 members in Israel and one branch in Israel.

AFFILIATIONS/REFERENCES
The organization is not affiliated with any political party in Israel. It does have the following contacts abroad: Kenneth Spetner, 83-60 Balson Stret, University City, St. Louis, Missouri; Amiel Ben-Mashiah, 66-48 Saunders Street, Rego Park, New York, 11374; and Shmuel Ben-Ari, 20 West 47th Street, Room 501, New York, New York, 10036.

FUNDING NEEDED
1. The establishment of student scholarships. Each scholarship is $2,000 per year.
2. The maintenance and rental of the temporary premises. Estimated cost: $18,000 per year.
3. The purchase of land for building. Estimated cost: $100,000.

KEREN ARYEH

קרן אריה

21 HaVaad Haleumi
P.O.B. 16031, Jerusalem
Telephone: (02) 423131
Office hours: 8:30 A.M. to 1:00 P.M.

HISTORY AND DESCRIPTION

Keren Aryeh is a charitable organization founded in 1978 by a survivor of one of the bunkers which bore the brunt of the Egyptian offense in the Yom Kippur War of 1973. His experience in those few tense days convinced him that young men ought to be encouraged to continue their studies of the Jewish heritage while preparing themselves for professional careers.

Goals: To instill reverence for the great Jewish heritage and provide an advanced technological education which can produce people who will contribute to the spiritual, cultural and economic life of the country.

Services, Activities, and Accomplishments: As its first task, Keren Aryeh, named in memory of the Jerusalem Brigade's Yom Kippur War heroes, decided to extend interest-free loans to students engaged in both Torah study and technological training. These loans have enabled many students to complete four years of study and earn a B.Sc. degree. Many have also been aided in establishing a home. All the loans granted thus far have been repaid in full. Cognizant of their responsibility to help others as they themselves have been helped, many students have begun contributing to the fund on their own after graduation.

OFFICERS

Director: Rabbi N. Hazenfratz, 61 Hapisgah, Jerusalem.
         Rabbi.
         Tel. (02) 419525.
Treasurer: Ephraim Holland, 48 Eshkol, Jerusalem.
         Food Caterer.
         Tel. (02) 812946.
Board Members: Rabbi M.A. Slodz, 16 Blau, Jerusalem. Educator.
         Tel. (02) 271645.
         J. Willenberg. Engineer.
         Rabbi J. Gal-Ezer, 43 Sorotzkin, Jerusalem.
         Dean of Students.
         Tel. (02) 813681.
         H. Kurztag. Engineer.
         Mrs. H. Hovav, 12 Hillel, Jerusalem. Lawyer.

FINANCIAL INFORMATION

Last year's annual budget was $3,250, 70% of which came from donations, and 30% from the return of loans. There was no deficit. Keren

Aryeh is registered as an Ottoman Association (Israel reg. no. 11/3235); donations are tax-free. The Keren has two volunteers.

MEMBERSHIP, SCOPE, AND POLICY
At present the Keren is comprised of seven members. Decisions are made by the Director and Treasurer.

AFFILIATIONS/REFERENCES
The Keren has no affiliation with any political party in Israel.

FUNDING NEEDED
For those students who have expressed the desire to continue their Jewish studies a few nights a week within the framework of the Jerusalem College of Technology, the directors of the fund feel that providing such an opportunity would be a natural extension of the Keren's purposes. Funds are needed so that the Beit Midrash of the Jerusalem College of Technology can be kept open in the evenings for all who wish to use it. Evening classes could be conducted for graduates and anyone else interested. This would provide an opportunity for the dissemination of Jewish knowledge as well as a meeting ground for young men steeped in their heritage with others lacking such training. The interaction of these types can of itself be of benefit to the country as a whole.

KEREN GEMACH NER MITZVAH

קרן גמ"ח נר מצוה

c/o Mr. Reuben M. Nana
103 Agrippas
Jerusalem
Telephone: (02) 222649
Office hours: 8:00 A.M.-1:00 P.M.; 3:30 P.M.-6:00 P.M.

HISTORY AND DESCRIPTION
Keren Gemach Ner Mitzvah, a free-loan fund, was established in 1972.

Goals: To grant interest-free loans to the needy, young couples, Yeshiva students and Talmidei Hachamim (Torah scholars).

Services, Activities, and Accomplishments: The Keren Gemach Ner Mitzvah, a voluntary organization, grants interest-free loans to the needy without the normal burdensome formalities. Applicants are not asked for costly promissory notes, but only for the signatures of two guarantors, and they repay the loans by means of ten monthly cheques. Since its foundation the organization has granted loans to six hundred families for a total amounting to $15,000. Unfortunately, due to the rising cost-of-living and inflation the number of applicants for loans is increasing daily and sufficient funds are not available to satisfy all applicants, as the organization would wish.

OFFICERS
Hon. Pres.:	Rabbi Mordechai Ben Eliyahu, 2, Ben Sion. Jerusalem. Dayan. Tel. (02) 521010.
Director:	Reuben Nana, 68 Herzel, Jerusalem. Merchant. Tel. (02) 222649.
Treasurer:	Aron Tawil, 11 Hehalutz, Jerusalem. Vice Manager of Kupat Holim. Tel. (02) 526644.
Board Members:	Rabbi Abraham Shalom David, 11 Aron Koter. Jerusalem. Rabbi. Tel. (02) 522678.
	Shlomo Maron, 6 Eliezer Halevi. Jerusalem. Clerk. Tel. (02) 522838.
	Reuben Levi, 11 Rav Tsair, Jerusalem. Building Manager. Tel. (02) 534384.
	Abraham Sheweky, 14 Meiri, Jerusalem. Tourist Agent. Tel. (02) 523388.

FINANCIAL INFORMATION
100% of the organization's income comes from private donations and donations from banks. Last year's annual budget of $3,200 left the organization without a deficit. The Keren is registered in Jerusalem as a non-profit Ottoman Association (reg. no. 11/2046). Donations in Israel are tax-free (tax no. 4503766). U.S. tax status information not supplied. One full-time worker is employed by the organization, as well as seven volunteers.

MEMBERSHIP, SCOPE, AND POLICY
Membership is open to anyone who is willing to help honourably. There are seven members in Israel, in one branch. Decisions are made by the Board.

AFFILIATIONS/REFERENCES
The Keren is not affiliated with any Israeli political party, nor to any other organization.

FUNDING NEEDED
To increase the loan fund in order for the organization to satisfy a greater number of applicants.

KEREN HA'TSHUVA

קרן התשובה מיסודו של הרב א. חזן

19 Bethlehem Road
Jerusalem
Telephone: (02) 714743, 244044
Office hours: 7 A.M. to 7 P.M.

HISTORY AND DESCRIPTION

Keren Hat'shuva was founded in 1978 by the Rabbis of the Police and Prisons in Israel, together with a number of lawyers, with the aim of giving grants to young people, between the ages of 15 and 35, who have decided, while still in prison, to repent and go back to G-d and society. After their release they want to be absorbed into Yeshivot which exist especially for this purpose now in Israel.

Goals: Not content with giving grants and following the development of the recipient, the more distant goal of the project is to accumulate experience in order to present the result to the Establishment for recognition as an alternative direction for the rehabilitation of prisoners.

Services, Activities, and Accomplishments: Each ex-delinquent has a rabbi or one of the members of the Committee who follows-up on his development, behavior, and progress. The grant is renewed every three months, depending on the report. Thus far, 35 ex-prisoners have been rehabilitated.

OFFICERS

Director: Rabbi A. Hazan, 19 Bethlehem, Jerusalem. General Chief Rabbi of Police and Prisons. Tel. (02) 714743.

Treasurer: Rabbi S. Neeman, Shikun Habad, Jerusalem. Rabbi, Frontier Police. Tel. (02) 814693.

Board: M. Assulin, 64 Hapisgah, Jerusalem. Lawyer. Tel. (02) 664314.

Rabbi Meyer Cohen, 8 Hachayal Ha'almoni, Reshon Letzion. Rabbi, Prisons. Tel. 244044.

Pierre Daniel, Hamatmid, Old City, Jerusalem. Lawyer. Tel. (02) 818810.

Abraham Toretzky, Panim Meirot, Jerusalem. Rabbi of Police. Tel. (02) 534425.

FINANCIAL INFORMATION

Funds are made up totally from donations. Last year the budget was $50,000. The fund is registered as an Ottoman Association (reg. no. 11/3295) and donations are tax-free in Israel (no. 4507129). Every grant is for $120 per month, $1440 per year. The fund maintains twelve volunteers.

MEMBERSHIP, SCOPE, AND POLICY

Membership is open to any volunteer who thinks he can contribute something to the project. Decisions are made mostly by the national board. At present there are 12 members in one branch in Israel.

AFFILIATIONS/REFERENCES

The work of the Fund is known to the following organizations abroad: Siona, 52 Rue Richer, Paris, 75009, France; and the World Sephardic Federation, 10 Groix Rouge, Geneve, Switzerland.

FUNDING NEEDED

1. To provide for 50 additional grants—$12,000.
2. To create a capital fund to insure the continuation of the project—$500,000.

KEREN YALDENU—OUR CHILD'S FUND—TIKVATENU CENTERS

קרן ילדינו – מרכזי תקוותנו

5 Mem Gimmel Street, P.O. Box 819
Jerusalem 91007
Telephone: (02) 527728, (02) 527729, (02) 521825.
Office Hours: 8:00 A.M. to 3:00 P.M.

HISTORY AND DESCRIPTION

The first youth club was opened by the organization in Musrara (in Jerusalem) in 1953, with the object of providing food, shelter and educational help to needy children after school. Gradually the work expanded into such places as Beth Shean, Ramle, Kiryat Shemona, Beersheba, Jerusalem, Haifa and Rehovot. Today there are twenty-two centers with some eight thousand children attending weekly.

Organizational Structure: Keren Yaldenu is recognized by and receives support from the Ministry of Labor and Social Welfare, as well as being under the inspection of the Ministry of Education. There is an Executive Council as well as a National Council, which convenes a general meeting of the Association once a year. The National Council chooses one of its members to act as its Chairman and also as Chairman of the Association. Another member is chosen as Vice-Chairman and Treasurer. The Executive is composed of the Chairman and Vice-Chairman of the Association and three additional members.

Goals: The Association aims to encourage children to think logically, to foster their desire to learn and to realize their own potential. Programs in these and other areas are also designed to give the youngsters knowledge and appreciation of their Jewish heritage and values.

Services, Activities, and Accomplishments: There are courses in electronics, computer operation, chemistry, mathematics, English, arts and crafts, Jewish studies and sports at the Association's centers. Regular inter-club functions are held and integration of children from different backgrounds, fostering teamwork and a feeling of responsibility for others in need, all remain high priorities. A staff of social workers exists to deal with problems among the children and in their homes as well. A light meal is served to the children each day, and help with clothing problems is given discreetly.

Children from difficult family backgrounds who have attended the clubs are today found in all trades and professions, playing a valuable and important part in the life of the country.

OFFICERS

Chairman: J. Sklan, Jerusalem.
Treasurer: Prof. Z. Falk, Jerusalem.
              Law Faculty, Hebrew University.

Board Members:	Dr. Z. Wahrhaftig, Jerusalem. Knesset Member.
	A. Langerman, Jerusalem. Social Welfare.
	Dr. M. Kurtz, Jerusalem. Researcher.
	O. Cohen. Director, Dept. of Youth,
	Ministry of Education, Jerusalem.
	S. Freedman. Director of Family Welfare,
	Ministry of Welfare, Jerusalem.
	R. Weil, Jerusalem. Lawyer.
	D. Knofu, Ministry of Religions, Jerusalem.
Director-General:	M. Luzann, 5 Mem Gimmel Street, Jerusalem.
	Tel. 527728.

FINANCIAL INFORMATION

Keren Yaldenu is registered in Jerusalem as an Ottoman society (no. 11/407). 55% of the Association's income is derived from donations, government grants provide another 44.5% and membership dues the remainder. Last year's budget of $600,000 left the Association with a deficit of $45,000. Donations are tax-free both in Israel and abroad (USA through Youth Centers of Israel, Inc. 51 East 42nd St., New York City, NY 10017, and England, tax. no. XN 16690). Forty full-time and two hundred part-time workers are employed by the Association, in addition to forty volunteers.

MEMBERSHIP, SCOPE, AND POLICY

Any person aged eighteen or older, who identifies with the aims of the group and is invited by the Membership Sub-Committee, is eligible for membership in the Association. Decisions are made mostly by the National Board. Some forty members represent the Association's six Israeli and thirteen international branches.

AFFILIATIONS/REFERENCES

The Association is connected with the following orgnizations:
1. Youth Centers of Israel, 51 East 42nd St., New York City, NY 10017 USA.
2. P.E.F. Israel Endowment Funds, Inc. 511 Fifth Ave., New York City, NY 10017 USA.
3. Van Leer Foundation Koninginnegracht 52 2508 CP The Hague.

FUNDING NEEDED

1. To build a new building in Haifa for six hundred children. The site and architects' fees are given free by the city; cost, approx. $450,000.
2. To purchase new furniture and equipment and to .enable redecoration of the club in Ashdod; cost, approx. $30,000.
3. To build a sports ground and dressing room in the Romema area of Jerusalem on a site adjacent to an existing club for 1,500 children; cost, approx. $50,000.

KFAR RAPHAEL — REMEDIAL COMMUNITY

כפר רפאל, קהילה שיקומית לזכר לואי והרמן פולק

P.O.B. 425
Beersheba
Telephone: (057) 31202
Office hours: 8:00 A.M. to 2:30 P.M.

HISTORY AND DESCRIPTION

The Kfar Raphael Association was established in July 1973 upon the initiative of the Anthroposophical Society in Israel and representatives of the Parents' Committee of the Bet Eliyahu Institution in Beersheba. Its aim is to build and run a village where the retarded adult can work and live together with an adoptive family.

Organizational Structure: The Association is run by an elected Directorate and members, including parents of the residents and volunteers who work for the Association. Members are accepted after confirmation at Association meetings and the executive is elected from these members.

Goals: The Association aims to create a village where it will be possible for the sheltered residents to express their talents and live full, harmonious lives. To this end, sheltered work places have been planned: workshops, gardening agriculture, animal husbandry, work in services, etc. The family format gives emotional protection and security. By the final stage of the plan, there will be a population of between 60 and 80 protected residents giving a total of 150 persons, including families, children and workers.

Services, Activities and Accomplishments: The Association has leased some 25 acres of land northwest of Beersheba, of which 10 acres were alloted for building, the rest for agriculture. To date, three family units have been built for 18 to 24 villagers; the construction of a fourth unit has been frozen due to lack of funds. An approach-road has been paved and electricity and heating installations have been started. On the agricultural site, 900 fruit trees have been planted on 4 acres of land. The village is recognized by the Ministry of Welfare, and members are accepted in cooperation with the Ministry, which will also share in the maintenance costs. Keren Hayesod, the financial arm of the World Zionist Organization, has declared the village one of its recognized projects.

OFFICERS

Director: J. Asscher, Sokolov 8c, Beersheba.
              Tel. (057) 71731.
Treasurer: M. Levy, Hanasi 6, Jerusalem.
              Tel. (02) 633165.

Board Members: M. Friedman, Nehemia 7, Bnei Brak.
Dr. Hovav, "Hasherut Lamefager" (Service
  to the Retarded), Ministry of Welfare, Jerusalem.
E. Tal, Zabar 18, Beersheba.
Z. Mader, P.O.B. 425, Beersheba.
  Tel. (057) 31202.

FINANCIAL INFORMATION

The Association depends entirely on donations for its income. The village was inaugurated in May 1981 and the annual financial shortage is estimated at IS 312,000. Donations to the Association are tax-free in Israel, and also in the U.S.A. as a "Fund for Higher Education" (1500 Broadway, Suite 1900, New York 10036). Israeli donations over IS 10,000 are 50 percent tax exempt. The Kfar is registered as an Ottoman Association (Beersheba, reg. no. 7867/437).

MEMBERSHIP, SCOPE AND POLICY

There are currently 18 members and membership is open to all who are ready to be of help. Decisions are made by the Board.

AFFILIATIONS/REFERENCES

1. The Anthroposophical Society, Hanassi 6, Jerusalem.
2. Mahle Stiftung, Stuttgart, Germany.
3. Keren Hayesod, 22 Johannes Vermeerstr., Amsterdam, Holland.
The Association is not affiliated with any political party in Israel.

FUNDING NEEDED

1. To finance the completion of the second building—$120,000.
2. To finance the building of workshops—$170,000.
3. To finance the building of the third house for the inmates — $431,750.

THE KFAR YONAH
COMMUNITY CENTER

מרכז קהילתי, כפר יונה

Matnas, Kfar Yonah
Telephone: (053) 95111
Office hours: Sunday-Thursday, 8:00 A.M. to 3:00 P.M.
Friday, 8:00 A.M. to 1:00 P.M.

HISTORY AND DESCRIPTION

The town of Kfar Yonah, with a population of 3,500, and located about 6 miles east of the coastal city, Netanya, was established in 1932 by immigrants from Eastern Europe. The Kfar Yonah Community Center was founded in 1976 and became a member of the Israel Corporation of Community Centers in 1978. It serves a diverse population, ranging from immigrants from Kurdistan and Tripoli, to immigrants coming from Russia, Hungary, and Romania. As of May, 1980, the Center has been operating as an independent organization, no longer as a subsidiary of the Local Municipality. Its premises are a former Absorption Center.

Organizational Structure: The Center is headed by an eleven-member Board of Directors. The Executive Director of the Center manages a staff composed of a Community Worker, a Director of Child and Youth Activities, a Child Psychologist, a Director of the Mother-Infant Education Program (with a staff of six indigenous para-professionals), a Pensioner's Club Director, Youth Workers, and Special Activities Instructors, as well as a complete office managerial staff.

Goals: To provide a comprehensive program of cultural, educational, social, and recreational activities for the community. This is to be accomplished by enlisting the direct involvement of the residents in the formulation of the Center's activities, with the view to strengthening local leadership. It is hoped that the population will be encouraged to take on responsibility for, and control of the decisions for the improvement of the "quality of life" of the community.

Services, Activities, and Accomplishments: An educational program ("Ha'etgar") for mothers of children aged 4-6, offers enrichment for the development of pre-school children. After-school activities for elementary school pupils include arts and crafts, ballet, folk-dancing, drama, music, sports and social clubs. The youth programs offer clubs, sports, a discotheque, films, and a sex-education course run by psychologists. Summer camps are provided for children. Adults attend English classes, folk-dancing, sports, educational trips, and may participate in a theatre subscription series. The establishment of the Pensioner's Club is seen as a major accomplishment. It provides arts and crafts, Hebrew courses, a social club, a workshop which operates in co-operation with local industry, special holiday programs, trips, and a monthly program with the Brookdale Institute of Gerontology. The Community Center prepares special activities for the whole town for holiday celebrations. There is a psychological service for children from 18 months to 5 years old. Effort is made to co-ordinate work with the local social-service workers, and the establishment of Housing Committees and Neighborhood Councils is considered another major accomplishment.

OFFICERS

Director: Yossi Feldman, Ussishkin 38, Netanya. Director. Tel. (053) 22810.

Board Members: Ephraim Daray, Kfar Yonah "Bet". Mayor. Tel. (053) 98579.

Eli Avraham, Kfar Yonah "Aleph". Electronic Engineer.

Shlomo Yitzchaki, Kfar Yonah "Aleph". Animal Food Industry.

Moshe Elisha, Eli Cohen St., Kfar Yonah. Diamond Industry. Tel. (053) 95402.

Yitzchak Haroni, Eli Cohen St., Kfar Yonah. Flower Grower. Tel. (053) 98064.

Yitzchak Ventura, Eli Cohen St., Kfar Yonah. Postman. Tel. (053) 98216.

FINANCIAL INFORMATION
70% of the budget is made up of funds from the Local Municipality, 20% comes from the Israel Corporation of Community Centers, and 10% is collected from membership dues. Last year's annual budget was $84,000. Donations to the Center are tax-free in Israel and the United States (Israel registration no. and I.R.S. no. pending). Eight full-time and fourteen part-time workers are employed by the Center.

MEMBERSHIP, SCOPE, AND POLICY
Any resident of Kfar Yonah may join and participate in all activities. At present there are 3,500 members. Decisions are made mostly by the Executive Director.

AFFILIATIONS/REFERENCES
The Center has no affiliation with any political party in Israel. Contact is maintained with Mr. Joe Greenstein, Executive Director, YM/YWHA of Borough Park, Brooklyn, New York, 11219, and the National Jewish Welfare Board, New York, New York.

FUNDING NEEDED
To build a Community Center Complex — including classrooms, offices, auditorium, and sport facilities (indoor and outdoor) ($2,500,000).

THE KAHN THEATER COMPANY

תיאטרון החאן

2 Remez Square
Jerusalem 93541
Telephone: (02) 718281/2
Office hours: 8:30 A.M. to 8:30 P.M.

HISTORY AND DESCRIPTION

The Khan Theater Company was established in 1972 as Jerusalem's only repertory theater company. The Company works as an ensemble dedicated to the production of theatrical pieces expressing its attitude towards current events and social processes, in addition to productions which have won world-wide acclaim as classical repertory.

Organizational Structure: The Company has a Board of Directors and a General Manager, under whom function an Artistic Director, the Repertory Committee, stage directors and actors, a Technical Manager and department, and administration.

Services, Activities, and Accomplishments: Beyond its artistic activities, the Company also runs three special educational programs: a program designed for dedicated theatergoers, dealing with the process of creativity and creating a production; a program designed for high-school teachers and students, enabling them to meet actors and directors, and discuss the production from various aspects; and a program specifically designed for the residents of deprived neighborhoods, in an attempt to bridge the cultural gap between them and the theater. Since its foundation eight years ago, the Khan Theater Company has staged over fifty productions, including original plays, adaptations of well-known literary works, and international premieres. The Khan Theatre Company has presented about 450 performances annually, two-thirds of which are in communities remote from the cultural centers. In addition, the Company has afforded many artists the chance to work within the framework of a repertory theater, including more than twenty actors, four directors, three scenery designers, and three composers. The Khan Theater Company is the only professional public repertory theater company in Jerusalem.

OFFICERS

Chairman of
the Board: Zeev Scherf, Shmaryahu Levin 25, Jerusalem.
                Former minister of housing and of finance.
                Tel. (02) 417255.
Treasurer: Harry Sapir, Hatayasim 24, Jerusalem.
                Bank manager. Tel. (02) 665073.
Executive Board: Abbi Ben-Ari, Ramat Denia 7, Jerusalem.
                Partner in P.R. and mass communication office.
                Tel. (02) 418336.

343

Dan Ronnen, Neve Granot 2, Jerusalem.
Department manager in Ministry of
Education and Culture. Tel. (02) 662827.
Yossi Fisher, c/o Jerusalem Foundation, Jerusalem.
Vice-manager of the Jerusalem Foundation.
Tel. (02) 666103/4.
Yaacov Manhaim, Hatomer 10, Jerusalem.
Department manager in Electricity Co.
Tel. (02) 526623.
Yoseph Sharon, Jabotinsky 12, Jerusalem.
Construction manager. Tel. (02) 669902.
Daniel Shalem, Hatayasim 34, Jerusalem.
General manager of The Khan Theater Co.
Tel. (02) 635858.

FINANCIAL INFORMATION

40% of the Company's budget derives from self-income (ticket sales and subscriptions), another 25% from the Ministry of Education, 15% from the Jerusalem Foundation, and another 10% from private sources; the remaning 10% remains as deficit. The 1978-1979 annual budget of $227,096 left the Company with a deficit for last year of $79,690, and an accumulated deficit of $144,230. Donations to The Khan Theater Company in Israel and the United States are tax-free (in Israel, funds must be transferred via the Jerusalem Foundation for the Khan — Israel reg. no. 11/1492; USA I.R.S. no. 941-07666/3). Thirty-five full-time and fifteen part-time workers are employed by the Company, as well as six or seven volunteers.

MEMBERSHIP, SCOPE, AND POLICY

The Khan Theater Company currently has seventeen members. New members are recommended either by other members, and/or the Jerusalem Foundation, and/or the Ministry of Education and Culture, and are confirmed by the Mayor of Jerusalem. Members usually serve on the Board of Directors, which is responsible for most of the policy and budgetary decisions, decisions on current affairs generally being made by the General Manager.

AFFILIATIONS/REFERENCES

The Khan Theater Company is not affiliated with any political party in Israel. It has contacts with the Jerusalem Foundation Inc., c/o Ms. K. Unger, 40 West 57th Street, New York, N.Y. 10019.

FUNDING NEEDED

1. $30,000 — To supplement the budget for the current activities of the Company for the budgetary year commencing October 1980.
2. About $50,000 — To purchase a sophisticated truck designed for out-of-town and open-air productions in communities far away from the cultural centers.
3. To purchase video-tape, cameras, and monitor for rehearsals and the documentation of productions.

THE KINNERETH NAHARI FUND

אגודת קרן כנרת נהרי ז"ל

Moshav Tarom, D.N. Shimshon
Telephone: (02) 913048
Office hours: 7:30 to 12:00 Noon.

HISTORY AND DESCRIPTION

The Kinnereth Nahari Fund was started in June 1978, on the initiative of the parents of the late Kinnereth Nahari, who was killed in a traffic accident. Eliezer and Sara Nahari contributed their National Insurance compensation (comparable to Social Security in the U.S.) to start the fund, and equal amounts were then donated by Tarom, the agricultural settlement in which they live, and by the Regional Council. The originally invested sum of $1,800 has now reached $5,000.

Organizational Structure: Eliezer Nahari acts as Chairman, Sara Nahari as Secretary, and five members of the settlement as Managing Board of the Fund.

Goals: The Fund aims to further the educational and cultural development of the settlement of Tarom. Grants are needed to help students in their advanced education and to provide special resources for gifted children. Also, the new Cultural Centre requires furnishing in order to make it a true center of intellectual and social life in the area.

Services, Activities, and Accomplishments: As this is a new organization, there are not yet sufficient funds to begin carrying out all the projects planned.

OFFICERS

Director: Eliezer Nahari, Tarom, D.N. Shimshon.
            Agriculture.
            Tel. (02) 911969.
Treasurer: Sara Nahari, Tarom, D.N. Shimshon.
            Agriculture.
            Tel. (02) 911969.
Board: Shalom Kahati, Tarom, D.N. Shimshon.
            Agriculture.
            Azriel Zadok, Tarom, D.N. Shimshon.
            Agriculture.
            Uzeri Yosef, Tarom, D.N. Shimshon.
            Agriculture.

FINANCIAL INFORMATION

Sources of income are as follows: 34% from the family; 33% from the moshav; 33% from the regional council. The Fund is registered as an Ottoman Association (reg. no. 11/3006) and donations are tax-free both in Israel (no. 4506288) and the U.S. (number not supplied). The Fund retains two volunteers.

MEMBERSHIP, SCOPE, AND POLICY

Membership is open to all who would like to assist in expanding the Fund to create educational opportunities for the children of Tarom. Decisions for the Fund are made by the board. Currently there are seven members in Israel.

AFFILIATIONS/REFERENCES

The Fund has no political affiliations with any party in Israel.

FUNDING NEEDED

The Board of Directors estimates that a minimum of $20,000 is needed to continue work on the following projects:
1. Finish the cultural center;
2. Provide scholarships for students;
3. Allocate grants for gifted children.

KIRYAT HAYESHIVA KNESSET YEHUDA

קרית הישיבה כנסת יהודה

Sanhedria Hamurchevet
P.O.B. 15040, Jerusalem
Telephone: (02) 818397
Office hours: 9:00 A.M. to 3:00 P.M.

HISTORY AND DESCRIPTION
Kiryat Hayeshiva Knesset Yehuda was first established in Washington
D.C. after World War II by Rabbis Meir and Nechamia Malin. After
their immigration (aliya) to Israel the Yeshiva was reestablished in 1969
in the Jerusalem suburb of Sanhedria Hamurchevet.

Goals: To attract students from abroad and train them as future spiritual leaders — rabbis, pedagogues, dayanim — not only in Israel but also
in the Diaspora.

Services, Activities, and Accomplishments: The Kiryat Hayeshiva
Knesset Yehuda consists of a Yeshiva, Kollel, Talmud Torah, kindergarten, the "Tossafot Yom Tov Institute", and the "Rabbi Kirschblum
Library". Up to now the Kirya (i.e. community) has constructed two
housing units, consisting of seventy-four apartments, mainly for new
immigrants from the United States and Russia. The Kiryah was a
pioneer in developing the Sanhedria Hamurchevet neighborhood which
was built up after the Six-Day War.

OFFICERS
Director: Rabbi Meir Malin, Jerusalem. Rosh Yeshiva.
Board Members: Rabbi Mordecai Kirschblum, Jerusalem.
                   Shlomo Zalman Shragai, Jerusalem.
                   Dr. Jerome Sisselman, Jerusalem.
                   Nachman Grynzstein, N.A.
                   Rabbi Nechemia Malin, Jerusalem.
                   Harry Levi, New York.
                   Robert Kaplan, Washington D.C.

FINANCIAL INFORMATION
90% of last year's annual budget came from donations and government
sources, the balance being provided by membership dues. Last year's
annual budget of $240,000 left the Kiryah with a deficit of $42,000.
Kiryat Hayeshiva Knesset Yehuda is a recognized non-profit organization (Israel reg. no. 11/1622), to which donations in Israel, the United
States, and Canada may be made tax-free (Israel: no. 4503013; USA:
I.R.S. no. M:71:EO:531; Canada: no. 0434977-25-08). Ten full-time and
three part-time workers are employed by the Kiryah, as well as three
volunteers.

MEMBERSHIP, SCOPE, AND POLICY
Any observant Jew over the age of 20 may join the Kiryah, by the

decision of the Board—which also makes any other decisions necessary.

AFFILIATIONS/REFERENCES
Kiryat Hayeshiva Knesset Yehuda is not affiliated with any of the political parties in Israel. It is in contact with: the Union of Orthodox Rabbis in New York; the Agudat Israel Organization in New York; the Mizrachi Organization in New York; the Young Israel Council in New York; and the Rabbinical Court of England in London.

FUNDING NEEDED
1. $1 million—To complete the dormitory building.
2. $1 million—To erect the campus synagogue.
2. $1 million—To build a housing unit for 50 young married couples.

KOHAV MIYAACOV — YESHIVAT HAGAON M'TSHEBIN

ישיבת הגאון מטשעבין "כוכב מיעקב"

12 Chana Street
P.O.B. 7037
Jerusalem
Telephone: (02) 817207
Office hours: 8:00 A.M. to 3:00 P.M.

HISTORY AND DESCRIPTION

When the Holocaust of the Second World War destroyed the Jewish communities of Europe, one of the most outstanding Torah personalities of the day, Rabbi Dov Berish Weidenfeld, the rabbi of Tshebiner, escaped destruction to ultimately arrive in Jerusalem. There he succeeded in re-establishing the Yeshiva "Tshebin-Kohav Miyaacov" originally founded by his world-renowned father, Rav Yaacov of Rimilov, in the Jewish year 5623 (corresponding to the English year 1863). Do to the untiring efforts of the Rabbi of Tshebiner, the Yeshiva grew each year, and today the six-floor building houses more than 200 students. The Yeshiva devotes as much care to the students' practical daily needs as it does to their spiritual and academic demands. The ultra-modern kitchen, the dining rooms, and the spacious dormitories serve as eloquent testimony to this fact. Students come from Israel, Europe, the United States, South America and Australia.

A major accomplishment of the Yeshiva is that many of its students serve as Yeshiva heads and distinguished lecturers and teachers, after their marriages.

OFFICERS

Director: B.S. Schneerson, 19 Elkana, Jerusalem. Rabbi. Tel.: (02) 813298.

Treasurer: Nachum Schneerson, 12 Even Haazel, Jerusalem. Rabbi.

Board Members: Joshua Levy, 15 Michal, Jerusalem.
Isaac Kister, 34 Metudela, Jerusalem. Supreme Court Judge (retired).
Aaron Frankel, Brooklyn, New York. Businessman.
Simon Geldwerth, Brooklyn, New York. Businessman.
Isaac Laufer, Brooklyn, New York. Businessman.
A.S. Stub, 35 Ramban, Jerusalem. Businessman.

FINANCIAL INFORMATION

The percentage breakdown of the sources of income was not supplied. The annual budget for last year was $700,000 and left the Yeshiva with a deficit of $200,000. The organization is registered as an Ottoman Association (reg. no. 11/474). Donations are tax-free in both Israel and the United States, but the tax numbers were not supplied. There are 24 full-time employees at the Yeshiva and two volunteers.

MEMBERSHIP, SCOPE, AND POLICY
Decisions are made by the Board. No other information was supplied.

FUNDING NEEDED
For finishing building an additional four-storey dormitory building in order to accept the many new students who wish to study in the Yeshiva. Estimated cost: $750,000.

KOLLEL AMERICA
TIFERETH JERUSALEM,
RABBI MEYER BAAL HANESS
IN JERUSALEM
כולל אמריקה תפארת ירושלים הרב מאיר בעל הנס בירושלים

8 Mea Shearim Street, Jerusalem
Telephone: (02) 285950
Office hours: Most mornings

HISTORY AND DESCRIPTION

Kollel America Tifereth Jerusalem was founded in 1897 by the then
Rabbi of Jerusalem, Rabbi Yehoshuah Leib Diskin, to help the Jews
who came to settle in Jerusalem from North America. It has, since its
inception, given financial aid and encouragement to the community that
came from America to the material poverty of Jerusalem. Since the
establishment of the State and more so, since 1967, there has been a
significant Aliya from the United States. The Kollel aids many of these
immigrants to pursue their Talmudic studies and Judaic research. It also
gives stipends on a monthly basis plus an extra important grant prior to
the holidays.

Services, Activities, and Accomplishments: The Kollel has its own
Yeshiva where students study daily. Kollel America operates a free-loan
society and a special marriage fund, which is available to its members
and also to others who may apply. More than 1000 Jerusalemites and
Israelis from all over the country have benefited from the Kollel prior to
their financial independence. A Synagogue and Yeshiva have been built
and maintained. The Kollel does vital work in filling the void of services
facing American and Canadian religious immigrants even today, serving needs unmet by government agencies. Scores of American immigrants, for example, are without family in Israel, and often marry
Israelis after having forfeited official immigrant rights. In the latter
category are large numbers of Baalei Tshuva (the newly-orthodox
young men and women), who turn to the services of the Kollel for aid. In
addition, the Kollel continues to serve all Americans and Canadians and
their descendants, no matter what their original country of origin. This
remains a distinguishing characteristic of the Kollel America.

OFFICERS

President:	Rabbi Dr. N.D. Herman. Rabbi. Tel. (02) 531415.
Treasurer:	Rabbi Ben Zion Rabinovitz. Student.
Board of Directors:	Rabbi Shimon Naftalis. Rosh Yeshiva. Rabbi Avraham Barg. Student. Rabbi Yeshua Shkol. Ritual slaughterer (shochet). Mr. Naftali Levinstein. Retired. Rabbi Simha Kaufman. Student. Mr. Moshe Kahan. Administrator. Rabbi Simha Kaufman. Student. Mr. Moshe Kahan. Administrator.

FINANCIAL INFORMATION

All of last year's annual budget came from donations (USA—80%, Israel—10%, other sources abroad—10%). Lat year's budget of $20,000 left the Kollel with a deficit of $1000. The Kollel is a non-profit Ottoman organization (no registration number supplied). Donations to the Kollel in Israel and the United States are tax-free (Israel: no tax number supplied; USA: I.R.S. no. T:R:EO:1 AWP). The Kollel employs seven volunteers.

MEMBERSHIP, SCOPE, AND POLICY

The Kollel America has one branch in Jerusalem and an office in New York. Americans, Canadians, and their descendants may become members. The Kollel's decisions are made by the Board. The Kollel is politically unaffiliated in Israel.

FUNDING NEEDED

1. Grants and loans for the needy, to be distributed regularly and on special occasions.
2. To help maintain Yeshiva students.
3. To facilitate the absorption of new immigrants from the United States who come to the Kollel for aid, particularly with housing problems.

KOLLEL AVRECHIM BAR-SHAUL, REHOVOT

כולל אברכים ע"ש בר-שאול, רחובות

8 Hatikva Street, Rehovot
Telephone: (054) 71885

HISTORY AND DESCRIPTION

The Kollel was established in 1963 by the Chief Rabbi of Rehovot, the late Rabbi Bar-Shaul. In addition to being Rabbi of Rehovot, Rabbi Bar-Shaul was one of the most outstanding and important Israeli rabbis, who brought people closer to Judaism. The Kollel was named in his honor after his death in 1964, and the local rabbis continued to serve as heads and presidents of the Kollel. Today's President of the Kollel is Rabbi S. Hacohen Kook, the Chief Rabbi of Rehovot. Rabbi Kook is well-known in Israel and abroad for his erudition and outstanding scholarship.

Services, Activities, and Accomplishments: Under Rabbi Kook's guidance the Kollel has expanded to include more than fifty students, and a new building has been constructed which is a beacon of Torah for all in this area. The Kollel has attracted many religious people to settle in Rehovot, thus helping the religious development of the town.

OFFICERS

Chairman: Moshe Stern, Yavetz 10, Rehovot.
                         Tel. (054) 71885.
Secretary: Nachman Fogel, Hatikva 8, Rehovot.
President: Rabbi S. Kook. Chief Rabbi of Rehovot.
Board Members: Rabbi Z. Graz. Chief Justice, Rabbinical Court, Rehovot.
                         Rabbi Shieber. Rabbinical Court Justice, Rehovot.
                         Rabbi Lanel. Rabbinical Court Member, Rehovot.
Administrator: Zvi Boimel, Ezra 7, Rehovot.
Dean: Rabbi Yosef Yisraelzon, Chazon Ish 5, Bnei Brak.
                         Tel. (03) 701549.
                         Rabbi Moshe Pines, Miltzer 16, Bnei Brak.

FINANCIAL INFORMATION

The Kollel had a budget of $600,000 last year (the sources for this and the financial situation of the Kollel were not supplied). The Kollel is recognized as a non-profit organization (no Israeli registration number supplied), to which donations in Israel may be made tax-free (no tax number supplied). The Kollel is served by eight volunteers. The decisions are made by the Board. Kollel Avrechim Bar-Shaul is unaffiliated with any of the political parties in Israel.

FUNDING NEEDED

1. The new building for the Kollel is in the final stages of construction. Cost — $160,000.
2. To provide continuous support and grants for the fifty students and their families.

KOLLEL HORODNA INSTITUTIONS

מוסדות כולל הורדנא

Batei Horodna
53 David Yellin Street
P.O.B. 6742
Jerusalem
Telephone: (02) 535842
Office hours: Monday and Wednesday, 12:00 P.M. to 1:00 P.M.

HISTORY AND DESCRIPTION
Kollel Horodna provides housing for the poor people of Kollel
Horodna. These houses were built years ago in order to provide needy
young men with rent-free apartments. Among those were many Torah
scholars who otherwise would have no place to live. The Kollel also
provides general aid to young brides. Special free loan funds were
established to help hundreds of needy Kollel families, among them
many excellent Torah scholars with large families and no other income.
Many widows with large families also have been rehabilitated with the
help of this Institution. The Kollel regularly helps those people and
before the Holidays they also receive special allocations. In cases of
sickness, the Kollel helps with medical expenses.
There is also a special education fund. Many children have been placed
in schools and Talmudei Torah with the Kollel's help.
Large sums have been allocated to help young husbands and brides
build their new life. A special fund was established to provide non-
interest bearing loans to needy people.
The major accomplishments of the Kollel have been in helping the needy
in every possible way.

OFFICERS
Director: Rabbi Moshe A. Rosental. Rabbi.
                     Tel. (02) 535842.
Board Members: Rabbi Aaron Bialustosky.
                     Mr. Yitzchak Glick.

FINANCIAL INFORMATION
Details of the sources of income were not supplied. Last year's annual
budget was $30,000, with a deficit of $9,500. The Kollel is registered as
an Ottoman Association (reg. no. 11/20). At the moment donations to
the Kollel are not tax-free, neither in Israel nor the United States,
although they have applied for tax-free donation status in Israel. There
is one full-time and two part-time workers employed by the Kollel.

MEMBERSHIP, SCOPE, AND POLICY
Anyone from the cities of Horodna is entitled to join the Kollel. There
are 300 families connected with the Kollel, in the one branch in Israel.
Decisions are made by the National Board.

AFFILIATIONS/REFERENCES
The Kollel is not affiliated with any political party in Israel, and has no contacts abroad.

FUNDING NEEDED
To enlarge all the funds, since prices have risen greatly. The money will help the hundreds of families who come to ask for aid.

KOLLEL, YESHIVA, TALMUD TORAH KARLIN-STULIN OF BNEI BRAK

כולל וישיבה, ותלמוד תורה קרלין־סטולין דבני ברק

19 Chabakuk Street
Bnei Brak
Telephone: (03) 703670
Office hours: 8:00 A.M. to 4:00 P.M.

HISTORY AND DESCRIPTION

Ever since its inception in the later part of the eighteenth century, the Karlin-Stulin movement has been a landmark for instilling leadership qualities in its educational systems. In the dark days of the Polish pogroms and during the pre-war Stalinistic reign of terror, Jews turned to the elders of Karlin-Stulin for guidance and direction. After a village was burnt by marauding peasants, it was always an emissary from Karlin-Stulin that organized the relief and the rebuilding of the town. Since the destruction of European Jewry, Karlin-Stulin brought its unique social and educational strength to the cities of the Holy Land, Bnei Brak being one of them.

In order to produce leaders imbued with initiative, authority and effectiveness, it is important to start this training from pre-kindergarten and follow it through without interruption through post-graduate school. Karlin-Stulin began this awesome program, with a select group of kindergarten children. Their curriculum and play time were geared to instill skill and foresight. As successful program followed successful program, the Yeshiva advanced through grade school age and launched a high school program that was a break-through in Torah education. Students (12 and 13 years old) were challenged with social problems and they had to have the motivation to turn these problems into workable projects. Instead of just learning jurisprudence, real civil courts were established, cases heard, witnesses accepted and rulings passed. With this approach, law became a living force, to be studied, practiced and upheld.

History and heritage was actualized by introducing various eras of our past, by use of role-play, into the lifestyle of the school. The roles of great Jewish leaders were distributed among the students who had to study their "namesakes" and they had to parallel their lives after these "great" personalities, until they were able to see modern day problems in the light of their newly acquired insight.

Debates were conducted on current issues, such as the growing Arab influence and acceptance on college campuses world over. The debaters were Moses, the Baal Shem Tov, and King David. Each one presented his views and method of solution as gleaned from their writings and deeds.

OFFICERS

Director: Grand Rabbi B. Sochet, 26 Ezra, Jerusalem.
                   Grand Rabbi. Tel. (02) 284022.

Dean:	Yehuda Ackerman, 40 Ezra, Bnei Brak.
	Tel. (03) 787806.
Board Members:	Shlomo Levine, 4 Hirsh, Bnei Brak.
	Tel. (03) 707335.
	Shlomo Levy, 54 Ezra, Bnei Brak.
	Tel. (03) 705842.
	David Auerbach, 4 Shimon Hatzadik, Bnei Brak.
	Tel. (03) 788672.

FINANCIAL INFORMATION

The sources of income for the Yeshiva are broken down as follows: local city allocations, 15%; donations, 25%; government allocations, 40%; and tuition, 20%. Last year's budget of $275,000 left the Yeshiva with a deficit of $85,000. The Yeshiva is registered as an Ottoman Association (reg. no. 6729/99). Donations to the Yeshiva are tax-free in Israel (reg. no. 450 7025) and in the United States (802 T:S:802 CFH). There are 12 full-time employees and 9 volunteers as well as 32 Kollel members connected with the Yeshiva.

MEMBERSHIP, SCOPE, AND POLICY

Decisions are made by the Grand Rabbi of Karlin Stulin and the Board members. Information regarding the membership and the number of branches was not supplied.

AFFILIATIONS/REFERENCES

The Yeshiva is not affiliated with any political party in Israel. The following organizations are aware of the Yeshiva's work: Agudat Israel, 5 Beekman Street, New York (Rabbi M. Sherer); Torah Umesora, New York, New York (Rabbi Millman and Rabbi J. Kaminetzky); and the Union of Orthodox Rabbis of the United States and Canada (Rabbi Moshe Feinstein).

KUPAT GEMACH MEOR CHAYIM

קופת גמ"ח מאור חיים

Sanhedria HaMurchevet 115/7,
Jerusalem   OR
P.O.B. 6588
Jerusalem.
Telephone: (02) 817702
Office Hours: 9:00 A.M. to 1:00 P.M., 4:00 P.M. to 7:00 P.M.

HISTORY AND DESCRIPTION

Services, Activities and Accomplishments: In 1974, a new neighborhood called Sanhedria HaMurchevet was established in northern Jerusalem. Perhaps the most pressing problem of the new community was the need of families to secure loans in order to meet financial obligations. As bank loans in Israel are difficult to receive and extremely expensive, a group of concerned rabbis, led by Rabbi Moshe Ernster, founded the Kupat Gemach "Meor Chayim".

Goals: The Gemach's aim is to help alleviate the severe financial burden that besets many families in Israel and to help them through difficult periods. The organization's first priority is to provide assistance to young married couples setting up a new home. The exorbitant cost of housing and basic appliances make it necessary for many to rely on the Gemach to help them get started. In addition, the Gemach helps families with many children, who must cope with the high cost of living and price rises in basic foods such as milk, bread, etc. Loans are also provided in special circumstances such as medical emergencies. The Gemach provides loans absolutely free of charge, for specific sums and time periods, depending on the individual circumstances and the ability of the Gemach. Over the past few years, the organization has extended loans to many people in the categories mentioned above. It has established itself as a well-known, respected organization in Sanhedria HaMurchevet, which people know they can approach for financial assistance. Due to the financial situation in Israel today, many more families have been forced to turn to the Gemach just to keep up with the constant price rises in basic needs. Unfortunately, however, the value of the organization's capital is being constantly eroded between loans as a result of the 150% annual inflation rate. The Gemach is limited in what it can accomplish only by its limited financial resources.

OFFICERS

Director: Rabbi M. Ernster, Sanhedria HaMurchevet 116,
                Jerusalem.
                Tel. (02) 814825.

Treasurer: Rabbi S. Feldman, Sanhedria HaMurchevet 115,
                Jerusalem.
                Tel. (02) 817702.

Board: Rabbi M. Heilbrun, Sanhedria HaMurchevet 116,
                Jerusalem.

Rabbi Z. Ernster, Sanhedria HaMurchevet 115,
Jerusalem.
Rabbi Y. Adler, Sanhedria HaMurchevet 116,
Jerusalem.
Rabbi A. Heller, Sanhedria HaMurchevet 116,
Jerusalem.
Rabbi E. Fishman, Sanhedria HaMurchevet 115,
Jerusalem.

FINANCIAL INFORMATION

"Meor Chayim"'s income is derived entirely from donations. No figures
were provided for the annnual budget. Donations to the organization are
tax-free in both Israel and the U.S.A. (Israel tax number 4505096;
American number not supplied). The organization is registered as a
non-profit Ottoman Association in the Jerusalem District Office of the
Ministry of the Interior (reg. no. 11/2728). Three volunteers staff the
organization. Decisions are made by majority rule of the Board members.

AFFILIATIONS/REFERENCES

The organization is not affiliated with any political party in Israel nor
with any group abroad.

KUPAT GEMILUT CHASADIM IN MEMORY OF THE IGELL BROTHERS

קופת גמילות חסדים ע"ש האחים איגל

Ktav Sofer St. 18,
P.O.B. 6298, Jerusalem.
Telephone: (02) 526512.
Office Hours: 7:00 P.M. to 9:00 P.M.

HISTORY AND DESCRIPTION

This free loan fund was established in memory of the two Igell brothers who were killed in the Golan Heights during the Yom Kippur War. The aim of the fund is to help people in their time of need, especially young couples who are beginning to set up a home. The loans are given for longer terms and are paid back in installments. The funds are constantly in use, and there is often a long waiting list of applicants for loans.
Goals: The organization requires substantial funds in order to expand its activities. The amount of applications for loans is increasing rapidly, and the organization is unable to give more than a very limited number of loans.

OFFICERS

Director:
    Mr. Nissen Igell, Ktav Sofer 18, Jerusalem. Teacher. Tel. (02) 526512.

Treasurer:
    Rabbi Yitchok Cohen, Ktav Sofer 20, Jerusalem. Executive Secretary. Tel. (02) 524135.

Board Members:
    Rabbi Abraham Eliashiv, Ktav Sofer 20, Jerusalem. Rabbinical student. Tel. (02) 534569.

    Rabbi Moshe Chalkovski, Horvet Hse., Givat Shaul, Jerusalem. Lecturer. Tel. (02) 526721.

    Rabbi M.S. Weintrob, Ktav Sofer 20b, Jerusalem. Rosh yeshiva. Tel. (02) 537270.

    Rabbi Zvi Shapiro, Givat Shaul 9, Jerusalem. Rosh kollel. No telephone.

    Rabbi Jechiel Bamberger, Givat Shaul 13, Jerusalem. Lecturer. Tel. (02) 535743.

FINANCIAL INFORMATION

The organization's income is derived entirely from donations. Tax-free status for donations to the organization in Israel is pending. Donations to the fund in the U.S.A. are not tax-free. The organization is registered as a non-profit Ottoman Association in the Jerusalem District Office of the Ministry of the Interior (reg. no. 11/2525). Three volunteers serve the organization. Decisions are made by majority rule of the Board members.

AFFILIATIONS/REFERENCES

The organization is not affiliated with any political party in Israel nor with any group abroad.

LA LECHE LEAGUE OF ISRAEL

ארגון לה-לצ׳ה

c/o Jane Abramowitz,
Kfar Pines
Telephone: (063) 79588
Office hours: 24-hour phone counseling and information

HISTORY AND DESCRIPTION

The Israel branch of La Leche League International has been active since 1971. It has been growing steadily and quickly, particularly over the last 4 years. The parent organization was founded 25 years ago; its literature states the belief that "breastfeeding is the ideal way to initiate good mother-child relationships and strengthen family ties", in addition to providing the "most appropriate and successful nutritional solution for the harmonious development of the child.".

Organizational Structure: The League is based on individual groups, run by leaders certified through La Leche League International in America. Each group has its own treasurer, secretary, library, holds a series of 4 monthly meetings.

Goals: The League's general aim is to help mothers and babies reach the goal of "good mothering through breastfeeding". In addition, the League strives to make the public aware of the advantages of breastfeeding to both the physical and emotional health of babies, and the importance of this for the future of the country.

Services, Activities, and Accomplishments: The League helps women who want to breastfeed through support groups, 24-hour phone counseling, information sheets and reading material (in several languages), and encouragement on a one-to-one, mother-to-mother basis. In addition, certified leaders give lectures to students, doctors, nurses, in mother-child clinics, and at monthly group meetings. Members provide advisory help in hospital maternity wards and on house visits to nursing mothers. Special meetings are held for couples and older children about breastfeeding. Training programs and continuing education conferences are also run. The Israel branch of La Leche has had a great impact on the rise of successful breastfeeding in the country, and it is slowly being recognized and consulted professionally. It participated in and helped organize the International Symposium on Breastfeeding held in February 1980, in Tel Aviv.

OFFICERS:

District
Advisor: Jane Abramowitz, Kfar Pines. Mother,
                   La Leche League Leader, childbirth instructor.
                   Tel. (063) 79588.

District
Treasurer: Shira Salzberg, P.O.B. 3349, Jerusalem.
                   Mother, La Leche Leader.

There are 12 certified group leaders, not listed individually.

FINANCIAL INFORMATION

Both the local groups and the district branch of the La Leche League in Israel are run wholly on donations and memberhsip dues. Financial needs of the local groups and the district, such as phone calls, transportation, printing, etc., are budgeted according to the dues locally collected; for this reason, no national budget figures are provided. Often, personal funds are used. The organization is not registered as an Ottoman, non-profit association, and no information is provided as to tax-free status in Israel. Contributions in the U.S. are tax-exempt through La Leche League International, 9616 Minneapolis Ave., Franklin Park, Illinois, U.S.A.; no tax-exempt number is stated. All work is done on a volunteer basis, the number of volunteers changing constantly.

MEMBERSHIP, SCOPE, AND POLICY

There are 10 local groups in Israel, each group numbering about between 20-50 members at any given series. Leaders, who are certified by La Leche League International after specific courses and guidance, number 12. Abroad, there are over 4,000 branches with over 12,000 leaders and an unknown number of members. General membership is open to any woman, whether she is pregnant, breastfeeding, or not, who is interested in information about the League's aims. Decisions are made by local leaders concerning their groups, or by agreement of all leaders on district questions, after approval of Area Coordinator in USA.

AFFILIATIONS/REFERENCES

The mother organization of La Leche in Israel is La Leche League International, with headquarters at 9616 Minneapolis Ave., Franklin Park, Illinois 60131, U.S.A. The League is known by most medical organizations, childbirth groups, and parent-child groups. The organization is not affiliated with any political party in Israel.

FUNDING NEEDED

1. For printing of breastfeeding manual, which has already been translated into Hebrew by volunteers. Cost: approx. $8,000.
2. For further translations, and continual printing and distribution of reprints.
3. To send one or more delegates to the LLLI Conference in the U.S. Cost: Air fare.

THE LEAGUE OF SOCIETIES FOR THE REHABILITATION OF OFFENDERS IN ISRAEL

חבר האגודות לשיקום האסיר והעבריין בישראל

Melchet 35
Tel Aviv
Telephone: (03) 291406
Office hours: 9:00 A.M. to 2:00 P.M.

HISTORY AND DESCRIPTION

The League was established in 1961 as a roof organization for local and regional Societies for the Rehabilitation of Offenders. Today, all of the six existing regional and local Societies — in Jerusalem, Tel Aviv, Haifa, Beersheba, Netanya and Hadera — are affiliated with the League.

Services, Activities and Accomplishments: The League acts as a guiding and coordinating body and is the recognized representative of all the rehabilitation services for ex-prisoners. It receives Government grants which are then distributed to the various Societies according to their needs. The actual work of rehabilitation is carried out by the respective Societies, each in its own area, with the help of local citizen volunteers and, when necessary, by qualified social workers. Nearly all of the laymen who are appointed as Visiting Justices in the current system of prison inspection, come from the ranks of the Societies' members. The Societies have achieved considerable success in the rehabilitation of ex-prisoners with the help of volunteers and with very limited financial means.

OFFICERS

Director: Y. Eisenberg, Tel Aviv.
Chairman: Z. Berinson, Jerusalem. Judge.
Vice-Chairman: Dr. M. Rubin, Tel Aviv.
Board Members: J. Azulai, Haifa.
                 A. Sharon, Hadera.
                 E. Kaplan, Netanya.
                 Y. Lavy, Beersheba.

FINANCIAL INFORMATION

Last year's annual budget of $35,000 came entirely from donations. There was no deficit. Donations to the League are tax-free in Israel (registration number not supplied). The League is registered as an Ottoman Association (reg. no. 11/1011). Two part-time workers are employed by the League, as well as tens of volunteers.

MEMBERSHIP, SCOPE, AND POLICY

The League has six Societies in Israel (number of members not supplied). All who are prepared to volunteer their services in the aid of released prisoners can join the Societies. Decisions are made by the National Board. The League has no branches overseas.

AFFILIATIONS/REFERENCES

The League is a member of the International Prisoners' Aid Association. It is not affiliated with any political party in Israel.

FUNDING NEEDED

1. To provide busineeses or jobs for ex-prisoners.
2. To provide residential facilities for homeless ex-prisoners.
3. To launch a public campaign aimed at enlisting more volunteers in service of the organization.

LEAGUE FOR FAMILY RIGHTS IN THE COURTS, MIZVAH

משפט צדק ושלמות המשפחה,
ליגה לזכויות האשה בבתי משפט

P.O. Box 506
Netanya
Telephone: 053-44413
Office Hours: Daily, except Shabbat

HISTORY AND DESCRIPTION

The League for Family's Rights in the Courts was established in 1975 in response to the need for an alternative to the perceived unethical and costly present method of gaining a divorce in Israel. Among the contributors to the organization are rabbis, scholars and legalists. To date, branches of the League have been established in Netanya, Tel Aviv, Raanana, Jerusalem, Safed and Nahariya; with potential future branches in Haifa and Ramat Gan.

Goals: The goals of the League are to educate and strengthen women against the present marital-divorce procedures in Israel, and to make the general public aware that it is unnecessary to seek a divorce through lawyers and complex litigation in the courts. The League also attempts to influence the Knesset and the Rabbinate to introduce a pre-marital agreement as part of the legal marriage procedure.

Services, Activities, and Accomplishments: The League for Family's Rights in the Courts contends that, according to Jewish law, the only requirement for divorce is an agreement (Heskem) between husband and wife. Consequently, the League has established its own Domestic Tribunal (Beth Din Zedek), with a professor of law presiding. The tribunal has its own standard agreement, and once completed—with regard to the division of property and custody—the concerned couple, with signed divorce contract in hand, is ready for a divorce date before the divorce department of the Rabbinical Court; thus avoiding long, expensive and often painful civil court proceedings. The League is presently training counsellors to help married couples solve their domestic problems—either through voluntary reconciliation or at least painless divorce. The League also publishes a newsletter—'Aishet Chayil'—and published a book entitled *Tears in the Israeli Courts*. An annual conference on related topics is sponsored by the organization. The League considers among its major accomplishments to date the following:

—publicising the injustices of divorce litigation;
—helping women through self-help to improve their personal status;
—the establishment of the League's own 'domestic tribunal' (Beth Din Zedek), which provides for a painless divorce procedure, and has also served to *reconcile* some couples;
—the constant monitoring by League reps. of the Rabbinical divorce courts, and the League's direct relations to the Ministry of Religion.

365

OFFICERS

Director: Sylvia Mandelbaum, P.O.B. 378, Safed.
Professional Organizer.
Tel. (067) 71384.

National
President: Pnina Peli, Brenner 9, Jerusalem. Writer.
Tel. (02) 631638.

National
Treasurer: Anne Helbon, Ben Yehuda 50/12, Netanya. Teacher.

Board: Doranne Weber, Hashiva 16, Netanya.
Social Worker.
Tel. (053) 32125.
Professor Zeev W. Falk, Rav Berlin 10, Jerusalem.
Professor of Law.
Tel. (02) 32155.
Professor Alice Shalvi, Birchiyahu 11, Jerusalem.
High School Principal.
Tel. (02) 528057.
Jacob Felton, Hatayasim 17, Jerusalem.
Writer/Scholar.
Tel. (02) 666844.
Professor Judith Ben Zion, Ben Zion 12, Jerusalem.
Educator.
Tel. (02) 524886.
Dr. Alice Naumoff, Shai Agnon 46/23, Nahariya.
Social Worker.
Tel. (04) 926956.
Tmima Bar Ilan, Azir 3, Holon. Teacher.
Tel. (03) 844952.
Dr. Stanley Levin, Ben Yehuda 10, Petach Tikva.
Lawyer.
Tel. (03) 923118.
Arthur Rosenstein, 24 Dizengoff, Netanya. Lawyer.
Tel. (053) 44413.

FINANCIAL INFORMATION

Income for the League is generated through the following sources: 50% through membership dues — $2.00, and sale of the League's *Tears in the Israeli Courts* publication — $2.50; cash donations and contributions, 15%; volunteer fund-raising, 5%; and periodic lectures given by the Director, 30%. The League for Family Rights in the Courts is an Ottoman Association (reg. no. 1282/1, Netanya/Ramla Ministry of the Interior district office), and donations are tax-free both in Israel and in the United States (although the League did not list an I.R.S. number, or its Israeli registration number).

The League has no paid employees; all staff members are volunteers. Exact figures for the last annual budget were not supplied.

MEMBERSHIP, SCOPE, AND POLICY

Eight Israeli branches of the League represent approximately one thousand members. There are also some 100 members abroad. The League accepts as members all men and women of every persuasion, on the premise that all are subject to the same laws of marriage and divorce. Decisions are made mostly by the Executive Director. There is also a National Board responsible for basic policy-making, and a Board of Governors composed of rabbis, scholars and legalists.

AFFILIATIONS/REFERENCES
The League has no formal relations with any Israeli political party. In the United States, it is affiliated with:

> *The Jewish Press*, 338-3rd Avenue, Brooklyn, New York, 11215;
>
> *Rabbi Mitchell Kornspan*, 290 S. Franklin Street, Wilkes Barre, Pennsylvania;
>
> *Rabbi Dworken*, 16-05 Orchard Terrace, Linden, New Jersey.

FUNDING NEEDED
In order of priority, the League for Women's Rights in the Courts lists the following as its most outstanding funding requirements:

1. Telephone, travelling expenses and stationery supplies and postage for League's bulletin. Estimated cost — $8,000 annually;
2. Office with good typewriter, mimeographer, 2 desks, 2 filing cabinets and miscellaneous office equipment, plus rent and electricity. Estimated cost — $7,000;
3. Full-time executive secretary, $5,000 annual salary.

LEV-LAHAN—THE ASSOCIATION FOR PSYCHIATRIC PATIENTS

לב לח"ן – למען חולי נפש

Hanoter St. 47a,
Kiryat-Haim. OR
P.O.B. 1013,
Kiryat-Motzkin.
Telephone: (04) 729706.
Office Hours: Year-round: Sunday, 5:00 P.M. to 9:00 P.M.
                        Thursday, 4:00 P.M. to 8:00 P.M.
              July-Aug.: 8:00 A.M.-2:00 P.M., 4:00 P.M.-7:00 P.M.

HISTORY AND DESCRIPTION
Lev-Lahan was founded in December 1976, and was recognized by the government as a non-profit organization in July 1977. It adopted its present name in June 1980.

Services, Activities, and Accomplishments: The organization arranges discussions and cultural activities for the membership and their families. Lev-Lahan attaches great importance to maintaining contact with the men and women who need its services. Other ongoing priorities include achieving greater rights for the psychiatric patient and changing public opinion on the subject of mental illness (via television, newspapers and public meetings). The organization hopes to be able in the future to acquire more room for administration and for cultural activities, and to expand into separate sections for men and women who are outside the hospital.

OFFICERS
Director: Israel Litman, Kiryat-Haim. Anthropologist.
                 Tel. (04) 729706.
Treasurer: Sara Karol, Haifa. Teacher.
                 Tel. (04) 532241.
Board Member: Joseph Kabiri, Haifa. Insurance adviser.
                 Tel. (04) 286810.

FINANCIAL INFORMATION
98% of the organization's income is derived from donations, with the remaining 2% coming from membership dues. Last year's annual budget was $600. The deficit for this period was $500. Information on the tax-free status of donations was not supplied. The organization is registered as a non-profit Ottoman Association in the Haifa District Office of the Ministry of the Interior (reg. no. 61/1361). Three volunteers serve the organization.

MEMBERSHIP, SCOPE, AND POLICY
The Association has 7 branches in Israel, with a total of 210 members. Those who support the goals of the organization, who accept its by-

laws, and who maintain confidentiality regarding the situations of the members are eligible for membership. Most decisions are made by the National Board, consisting of the Director, Secretary-Treasurer and elected members.

AFFILIATIONS/REFERENCES
The organization is not affiliated with any political party in Israel nor with any group abroad.

LIFE AND ENVIRONMENT

חיים וסביבה

Heftman Street 3, Tel Aviv, 64737
P.O.B.: 20040
Telephone: (03) 257216.
Office Hours: 8:00 A.M.-14:30 P.M.

HISTORY AND DESCRIPTION
Founded in 1977, this is an umbrella organization of non-government organizations. It was formed to promote the quality of life and environment in Israel.

OFFICERS
Chairman: Josef Tamir, Member of Knesset.
                        Tel. (03) 223785.
Treasurer: Gideon Lev, P.O.B. 20040, Tel Aviv.

FINANCIAL INFORMATION
The Ministry of Interior and Ministry of Health are the sources of income for the organization. Last year's annual budget was $2,000. It is registered in Tel Aviv as an Ottoman Association (reg. no. 6394/99). All office services granted by the Union of Local Authorities.

MEMBERSHIP, SCOPE, AND POLICY
Most decisions are made by the National Board and there are 13 members in Israel.

AFFILIATIONS/REFERENCES
U.N.E.P., Nairobe Kenya and the Sierra Club, U.S.A. were listed as references.

FUNDING NEEDED—not supplied.

LIFE-LINE FOR THE OLD   יד לקשיש

14 Shivtei Israel
Musrara
Jerusalem
Telephone: (02) 289737, 287829, 287831
Office hours: 8:30 A.M. to 12:00 noon

HISTORY AND DESCRIPTION
Life-Line for the Old was established over 20 years ago and developed from a single workshop into an entire complex serving 450 people in 13 sheltered workshops.

Organizational Structure: Life-Line for the Old is operated by a General Council consisting of volunteers, a Board of Directors elected by the Council, and a Chairman of the Board elected annually who is responsible for all the activities of the organization.

Goals: To rehabilitate old and disabled persons, irrespctive of ethnic, religious or language differences; to train them in light crafts which enable them to be gainfully occupied for four hours daily; to avoid institutionalizing old people by developing their creative skills and gaining them a sense of dignity and independence.

Services, Activities, and Accomplishments: The organization operates 13 sheltered workshops which are involved in the following occupations: book binding, file making, ceramic jewellery, pottery, box making, enamelled metalwork, children's wear, toys, picture framing, embroidery, macrame bags, machine and hand knitting, and a special workshop for people on wheelchairs. It also has a training center as a nucleus of the Home Industry for those who cannot work on the organization's premises; a special program for the house-bound; a meals-on-wheels service for 200 people; and the Elder Craftsman Gift Shop which sells the items made by Life-Line for the Old. The organization's Day Centre has the following services: laundry, shower facilites, optometric service, chiropodist service, carpentry, hair-dressing service, shoe repairs, choir and dancing group, a luncheon club for those who cannot cook for themselves but who are able to come to the premises for their meals, and a special transportation service for those on wheelchairs. The dental service has been discontinued due to lack of funds. Life-Line to the Old has been a pioneer organization in services to the old. It played a major role in achieving free medical care for uninsured old people and in the introduction in 1960 of special reduced bus fares for the old. It also pioneered a Meals-on-Wheels service, built a specially designed workshop for those on wheelchairs, has served as a pilot project in the rehabilitation of the old, and has succeeded in educating the young towards their responsibilities to the old and disabled.

OFFICERS

Director:	Miriam Mendilow, 34 Hehalutz St. Jerusalem. Teacher. Tel. (02) 525615.
Hon. Treasurer:	Akiva A. Prout, P.O.B. 35, Jerusalem 91000. Pensioner.
Members of the Board:	Shlomo Farkash, Ministry of Labor and Welfare, Yad-Harutzim St., Talpiot. Helena Gabrilowitz, Kibbutz Member, Shuval. Dvora Goldhamer, 20 Eliezer Halevi, Jerusalem. Tel. (02) 525004. Rivka Stoyanowsky, 44 Hehalutz, Jerusalem. Tel. (02) 526686. Luba Uveeler, Bnei Betera 10, San Simon, Jerusalem. Professor. Tel. (02) 667780.

FINANCIAL INFORMATION

45-50% of the organization's income comes from the sale of workshop products, 35-45% from donations, and 10% from the Ministry of Labour. Last year's annual budget of $300,000 left a deficit of $50,000. The organization is registered in Jerusalem as a non-profit Ottoman Association (reg. no. 11/907). Donations in Israel, the United States and Great Britain are tax-free (tax nos. not supplied). Fifty part-time workers are employed by the organization, as well as 65 volunteers.

MEMBERSHIP, SCOPE, AND POLICY

Membership is open to anyone willing to help by ideas, work, or financial contribution. There are about 40 members in Israel, about 50 members of the British Friends organization, and 1,500 members of the American Friends organization. Decisions are made by the Board of Directors and its Chairman.

AFFILIATIONS/REFERENCES

Life-Line to the Old is not affiliated with any Israeli political party. It is affiliated with the following: American Friends of Life-Line for the Old, 1 State Street Plaza, New York, N.Y. 10004.
British Friends of Life-Line for the Old, 33 Tavistock Terrace, London N. 19 4BZ, England.

FUNDING NEEDED

1. The organization's major problem is that of maintenance. Hitherto it has survived from hand to mouth but inflation and the reduction in real terms of donations and governmental assistance are endangering the continuation of its activities. The cost of equipment and repairs has risen steeply, as have the remunerations which are given to the old workers. Life-Line to the Old has already discontinued its dental service and closed two of its workshops. Without more help it may have to further reduce the scope of its activities. It must be

remembered that the organization's workshops are sheltered workshops and not self-supporting.

Immediate aid is needed to enable Life-Line for the Old to continue its essential work.

2. To establish a dental care unit for artificial dentures.
3. To establish a carpentry shop for furniture repairs.
4. To increase laundry facilities.
5. To promote handicraft training for the housebound.

L.O. (NO)—COMBATING VIOLENCE AGAINST WOMEN

Sokolov 58 Herzlia   לא — לחימה באלימות נגד נשים
Telephone: (052) 83856
Office Hours: Daily, 8:30 A.M.-12:30 P.M.
                 4:30 P.M.-6:30 P.M. (often evenings)

HISTORY AND DESCRIPTION

LO—Combating Violence Against Women was established in September 1977 in response to the need for protection against increased incidents of wife-beating in the Herzlia area. In April 1978 the organization opened the Carmela Nakash Women's Aid Center in Herzlia, serving primarily as a shelter for battered women and their children. Some 296 women and 334 children have lived in the 3-room building, which has occasionally housed as many as 32 persons. Over 1,000 non-resident women have also contacted "LO" for guidance and advice.

Organizational Structure: LO has a chairperson, secretary, treasurer and committee members. The Women's Aid Center is operated with a skeleton staff comprised of 4 part-time workers; director, social worker, housemother and secretary/bookkeeper; as well as several volunteers.

Goals: The organization lists among its goals the desire to investigate the extent of all forms of violence against women, and to establish contacts with women's groups, police and governmental authorities in an attempt to combat such crimes. The attempt is also made to pressure the media into publicising the extent and meaning of wife-abuse murders, as well as exposing the correlation between wife abuse and female suicides and attempted suicides, miscarriages, births of defective children and incidents of child abuse.

Services, Activities, and Accomplishments: The Combating Violence Against Women organization gives counsel, guidance and suport to all women in distress who request such help. Some women who require physical shelter remain at the organization's refuge anywhere from 24 hours to 10 months—those who remain at the hostel the longest are the most determined to separate from their husbands, and are awaiting legal proceedings and appropriate housing. All of the organization's activities are channelled towards increasing public consciousness of the issue of wife abuse. It is the success of this effort—through the establishment of a Knesset commission investigating wife assault, and subsequent altered attitudes on the part of police and social workers—of which the organization is most pleased. It also sees the Carmela Nakash Women's Aid Center in Herzlia as one of its major accomplishments to date.

OFFICERS

Director: Ruth Rasnic, Hashachar 17b, Herzlia.
                 Translator and poet.
                 Tel. (052) 83856.
Treasurer: Shelia Prag, David Hamelech 44, Herzlia. Executive.
                 Tel. (052) 72836.

Board: Judith Bachar, Hanadiv 12, Herzlia. Teacher.
           Tel. (052) 81208.
          Bina Weiler, Hadar 10, Herzlia.
           Criminology student.
          Carla Kalo, Hanadiv 59, Herzlia. Accountant.
           Tel. (052) 88728.
          Medi Shachaf, Hashachar 17, Herzlia. Secretary.

FINANCIAL INFORMATION

The Combating Violence Against Women organization had a budget of $20,000 for the fiscal period extending from April 1979 to March 31, 1980. 60% of this total came through the participation of the Israeli Minstry of Welfare, 20% was acquired through assorted donations and the remaining 20% from women's participation from welfare funding. The organization did not register a deficit for the last budgeting period. LO is registered with the Tel Aviv district office of the Ministry of the Interior as an Ottoman Association (reg. no. 6718/99). Donations are tax-free in Israel (exemption no. 4506181), but not in the United States. The organization has 4 part-time employees, and the number of volunteers fluctuates between 10 and 25.

MEMBERSHIP, SCOPE, AND POLICY

There is one Israeli branch of the organization, representing 9 official members. All active volunters are invited to join the organization's Board. Decisions at the operational level are made by the groups' Executive Director, while issues relating to policy are for the most dealt with by the National Board.

AFFILIATIONS/REFERENCES

LO is not connected with any Israeli political party. It is affiliated with two American organizations:

Women to Women— US/Israel, c/o Virginia L. Snitow, 81 Walworth Avenue, Scarsdale, New York, 10583;

The New Israel Fund, 22 Miller Avenue, Mill Valley, California, 94941.

FUNDING NEEDED

In order of priority, the following are felt to be the most outstanding funding requirements presently facing the organization.

1. Permanent and larger housing for the Carmela Nakash Women's Aid Center. Approximate cost—$500,000.
2. Second-stage communal (2 or 3 small families) housing for women determined to stay away from their husbands. The approximate cost of 10 such apartments, at $150 rent/month, would be $1,800 per apartment.
3. Funding for additional staff, including a housemother, a marriage-guidance counsellor (available 3 times a week), and a child-care worker. Estimated costs—$1,850 for monthly salaries.

MAAVAR—LADIES GUILD FOR THE RE-HABILITATION OF THE MALADJUSTED CHILD מעבר" חוג למען הילד קשה ההסתגלות"

c/o Rachel Bendel
10 Megido Street
Haifa
Telephone: (04) 82738

HISTORY AND DESCRIPTION

In the early fifties, a group of non-political and non-affiliated civic-minded women became aware of the existence of a special school for truant and potentially delinquent children from a slum area of Haifa. These women formed a committee according to the requirements of the Ottoman Law and began to collect funds through membership dues (later annulled), bazaars, lotteries and the like.

Organizational Structure: The Committee consists of thirteen volunteer workers, whose members have been more or less the same for the last thirty years. Chairmanship rotates; during the thirty years of the group's existence, there were only two honorary treasurers and one honorary secretary. A certified accountant donates his unpaid services.

Goals: MAAVAR represents parents of school children in dealings with the municipal governmental education offices. The group also works to make parents aware of the need for proper schooling and bring them into closer contact with their children's teachers; all this being necessary due to the lack of interest displayed by the parents toward the school. There has been no active P.T.A. group in the school, and the organization has been working through the years to fill this vital gap. Finally, the group endeavors to provide the school with the educational equipment not provided by the authorities.

Services, Activities, and Accomplishments: Until eight years ago, the Committee paid a qualified social worker until the Haifa Municipality could be persuaded to take over. During all the years of its existence, the Committee has provided the fees for a part-time psychiatrist or psychologist. Furthermore, the Committee allocates funds for excursions, festivities for the Jewish holidays, school prizes at the end of the year, occupational toys and material for the workshop. Members of the Committee visit the school regularly to assist the teachers and give personal attention and lessons to children in need of help, such as drawing lessons, arithmetic and reading lessons. Until 1974, the organization cared mainly for emotionally disturbed children from broken homes, most of whom were slowly integrated into the regular school system in special classes, according to governmental decisions. Generally, only very disturbed and maladjusted children with a low IQ remained in the Committee's school. However, in 1974, the group was asked to serve also as a Committee for a school for brain-damaged and autistic children. Thus, MAAVAR now provides for two schools:

"Orim" (formerly "Nizanim") and "Gil". Children who do not remain in these schools, and who are not transferred to regular schools, are placed as apprentices in industry or workshops.

Those who have supported the organization financially have, through all the years, recognized the importance of preventive education and have never been approached in vain. Recognition and cooperation from the education authorities has also been constant, as far as moral support is concerned. In addition, the school has served as a pilot plan for similar groups.

OFFICERS

Director:	Mildred Teicher, 43 Panorama Rd., Haifa. Housewife. Tel. (04) 331393.
Treasurer:	Jenny Ye'ari, 9 Sport St., Haifa. Clerk. Tel. (04) 82698.
Committee Members:	Helen Golan, 13 Shwedia St., Haifa. Teacher. Tel. (04) 244308.
	Ahuva Cantoni, 12 Kadima St., Haifa. Librarian. Tel. (04) 82684.
	Batya Bechar, 81a Moria St., Haifa. Housewife. Tel. (04) 242666.
	Ester Ehrlich, 27a Horeb St., Haifa. Social Worker. Tel. (04) 243551.
	Sara Van-Gelder, 36 Liberia St., Haifa. Teacher. Tel. (04) 252888.
	Julia Slonim, 27 Horeb St., Haifa. Teacher. Tel. (04) 242977.
Hon. Secretary:	Rachel Bendel, 10 Megido St., Haifa. Housewife. Tel. (04) 82738.
Committee Members:	R.B. Markan, 33 Givat Dauns, Haifa. Housewife. Tel. (04) 251717.
	Channa Oren, 17 Litanis St., Haifa, Housewife. Tel. (04) 246242.

FINANCIAL INFORMATION
50% of the annual budget comes from the Committee's lottery, another 30% comes from the annual bazaar, and the remainder from donations. Last year's budget came to $900. In Israel, donations to MAAVAR are tax-free (Israel reg. no. 4501956), however, such is not the case in the United States. The organization is a registered Ottoman Association (Haifa district, reg. no. 61/512/628). Twenty volunteers work for the organization.

MEMBERSHIP, SCOPE AND POLICY
Any person who has the same aims and conceptions as the members of the group, and has been elected by a majority vote, can join. There are presently thirteen members in the Committee. Decisions are made at Committee meetings. Recruiting new and younger active members has become a problem, in addition to the difficulty of collecting funds.

AFFILIATIONS/REFERENCES
MAAVAR is not affiliated with any political party in Israel.

FUNDING NEEDED
1. To expand the existing school building. "Orim" is housed in a small building with no sports hall, no rooms for a library, for the psychologist or the social worker. A building project for expansion was curtailed because of the financial situation in the country.
2. "Gil" requires a kiln for ceramics; also a washing machine because of the incontinence of the children.
3. For playground equipment for "Gil".

MACCABI WORLD UNION

ההסתדרות העולמית מכבי

Kfar Hamaccabiah,
Ramat Gan
Telephone: (03) 778111/2/3/4 Telex: 33319 macab il
Office hours: Sunday-Thursday: 8:00 A.M.-6:00 P.M.
                       Friday: 8:00 A.M.-12:00 noon

HISTORY AND DESCRIPTION
The Maccabi World Union, founded in 1921, is a non-political and non-party affiliated youth and sports movement.

Organizational Structure: A Maccabi Congress is held every four years. An Executive, which meets monthly, numbers some 45 members, representatives of Maccabi Territorial Organizations the world over, including Israel.

Goals: The Maccabi World Union promotes the ideals of Zionism and Israel through sport and cultural activities in clubs throughout the world. The Movement is a full member of the World Zionist Organization and subscribes to all its aims and ideals.

Services, Activities, and Accomplishments: The Maccabiah Games, held every four years, is a means of bringing Jewish youngsters from all over the world to Israel. It is considered a great honor to be a participating member of any National team. Eventually, many of these sportsmen — who are visiting Israel for the first time — return to Israel and settle. The World Union has to date set up 34 Territorial Organizations (there were originally 45, but 11 that were in Eastern Europe have ceased to exist).

OFFICERS
Chairman of the
M.W.U.
Executive: Dr. Israel Peled, Mayor of Ramat-Gan.
                         There are 45 members from all over the world,
                         representing the Maccabi Territorial Organizations.

FINANCIAL INFORMATION
Membership subscriptions and other grants provide all the Union's income. No budget figures are provided. The Union is not an Ottoman, non-profit Association. Donations in Israel are not tax-free, but contributions from the U.S. are tax-exempt (no I.R.S. number given). There are 10 full-time, and 5 part-time, employees, as well as 10-20 volunteers.

MEMBERSHIP, SCOPE, AND POLICY
Any Jew, regardless of age or other criteria, can be a member of the Union. To date, there are 25,000 members in 30 Israeli branches, and 250,000 members in over 300 branches abroad. Decisions are made by the Executive at its monthly meetings, or by the Maccabi Congress, held every four years.

AFFILIATIONS/REFERENCES
The Maccabi World Union lists as references the World Zionist Organization of America, in New York; the South African Zionist Federation, in Johannesburg; the Australian Zionist Federation; and Zionist Federations in South America, North America, Canada, etc., as well as other Jewish youth organizations.

FUNDING NEEDED
For the 12th Maccabiah Games, which are to be held in Israel in July, 1984, and for establishing a World Educational Center.

MACHANAIM KIRYAT GAT   "מחנים" קרית גת

P.O.B. 25, Kiryat Gat
Telephone: (051) 82493
Office hours: 8:00 A.M. to 2:00 P.M., 4:00 P.M. to 7:30 P.M.

HISTORY AND DESCRIPTION
The arrival of a small number of young rabbis belonging to the Lubavitch Movement in the southern town of Kiryat Gat a few years ago
effected a spiritual revolution in the town itself and its vicinity. Today
there are hundreds of pupils in the Machanaim institutions in Kiryat
Gat, and the spirit of Torah pervades the city.

Goals: To bring a Jewish education to Jewish children so that they will
grow up knowing what Judaism is, and the true inner peace it affords.
Educating youth to appreciate that religion is a complete way of life.

Services, Activities, and Accomplishments: Machanaim Kiryat Gat provides 20 kindergartens and day-nurseries for 700 children; a day school
for 40 children; youth centers for 500 children; a Yeshiva High School
with a dormitory for 200 students; summer camps in the Negev area;
Talmud Torah "cheder" classes for boys; evening Sheurei Torah for
teenagers and adults; financial and material help for needy families; and
a central library for the distribution and loan of Hebrew religious
books.

OFFICERS
Director: Shalom Dov Wolpo, Kiryat Gat. Rabbi.
                   Tel. (051) 82268.
Treasurer: Avshalom Shalelashvily, Kiryat Gat.
Board Members: Gershon Levin, Kiryat Gat.
                   Moshe Mavlin, Kiryat Gat. Rabbi.
                   Eli Swisa, Kiryat Gat.

FINANCIAL INFORMATION
70% of last year's annual budget came from government bodies, 20%
from donations, the balance coming from various sources. Last year's
annual budget of $300,000 left the organization with an accumulated
deficit of $180,000. Machanaim Kiryat Gat is a recognized non-profit
organization (Israel registration number 7867/325). Donations in
Israel, the United States and Canada, are tax-free (Israel number
4505277, U.S. number EO-7301). Canada — through the Rabbi S. Cass
Memorial Foundation: no tax number supplied. The organization
employs ninety full-time and 30 part-time workers. Decisions are made
by the Board.

AFFILIATIONS/REFERENCES
Machanaim Kiryat Gat is not affiliated to any of the political parties in
Israel. It maintains contact with Lubavitch, 770 Eastern Parkway,

Brooklyn, New York; Lubavitch, 109 Stamford Hill, London N.16; and the Rabbi Samuel Cass Memorial Fund, 79 Old Forest Hill Road, Toronto, Ontario.

FUNDING NEEDED
1. $120,000 — To complete Yeshiva building.
2. $260,000 — To construct nursery.
3. $150,000 — To construct two new kindergartens.
4. $50,000 — To purchase a bus for transportation.

MACHON MAHARSHAL — NEVE-SHALOM SEMINARY

מכון מהרש"ל

Herzl 14
P.O.B. 5166
Kiriat Moshe
Jerusalem
Telephone: (02) 632607
Office Hours: 9:00 A.M. to 1:00 P.M. and 4:00 P.M. to 6:00 P.M.

HISTORY AND DESCRIPTION
Machon Maharshal was founded in Jerusalem in 1950 as an offshoot of the Yavne Jewish Theological Seminary in New York.

Goals: The aim and purpose of the organization is to train Torah scholars to become Rabbis, educators and spiritual leaders.

Services, Activities, and Accomplishments: Since its establishment, more than 500 scholars have completed their training at the Machon and are presently engaged in the capacities of Rabbis, Dayyanim, Roshey Yeshiva, Principals, teachers and educators throughout Israel and the Diaspora. The Machon also maintains a Department for Research and Publication in the fields of Halakha (Jewish Law) and Midoth (Jewish Ethics). Much preparatory work has been done in collecting and classifying material from biblical, Talmudic and post-Talmudic sources for an extensive project in the latter field. To this date, four volumes of the *Compendium Responsarum* (study in Halakha) have been published; the fifth is now in print. Because of the great efforts and financial resources required for the completion of these projects, the organization was obliged to curtail some of its other activities, including its Rabbinical Seminary and the Psycho-Religious Institute. The Machon continues to maintain evening courses in Talmud and Judaism for college students. The Machon sees as its most important accomplishments to date the graduation of over 500 students who are presently active in the rabbinical and educational fields; the publications of the Compendium Responsarum and the 'Yalkut Sinai'; and its ongoing Torah research.

OFFICERS
Director: Rabbi M.N. Shapiro, Jabotinsky 36, Jerusalem. Tel. (02) 632607.

Board Members: Rabbi-Dayyan Abraham Shapiro, Jerusalem.
Rabbi Solomon K. Shapiro, 510 Dahill Road, Brooklyn, New York, USA.
Rabbi Jacob Kleinman, Jerusalem.
Rabbi A. Zimmerman, Jerusalem.
Prof. Eli Shapiro, Columbia University, New York City, New York.
Rabbi S. Friedman, Jerusalem.

FINANCIAL INFORMATION
Sources of income for Machon Maharshal include the following: membership dues, 10%; donations, 20%; grants, 25%; trust funds, 25%; and sale of books, 20%. Last year's budget of $40,000 left the organization with a deficit of $10,000. The organization has been registered in Jerusalem since 1953 as an Ottoman Association (reg. no. 11/355). Donations are tax-free in the United States (IRS no. 1771939N). Sufficient information was not supplied to ascertain whether or not donations to the organization are also tax-free in Israel. Machon Maharshal employs 2 full-time, 5 part-time and 3 volunteer workers.

MEMBERSHIP, SCOPE, AND POLICY
One Israeli branch of the organization represents its 200 members. There are also 150 members of one branch outside of Israel. All orthodox Jews over the age of 20 who uphold the aims of the organization are invited to join. Decisions are made by the organization's National Board.

AFFILIATIONS/REFERENCES
The Machon Maharshal Seminary is not associated with any Israeli political party. Internationally, it is affiliated with the *Congregation and Yeshivath Yavne* and the *Rabbinical Conference* of America, both of 510 Dahill Road, Brooklyn, New York.

FUNDING NEEDED
1. The completion and publication of the forthcoming volumes of the 'Otzar Hasheelot U'Teshuboth'.
2. A building project to erect a central building of the Machon, to serve as a research center, lecture halls and library.
3. Extension of the present library facilities, including the acquisition of equipment needed for the seminary's vast research and archival material.

MAGEN-DAVID-ADOM IN ISRAEL

מגן דוד אדום בישראל

60 Giborei Israel Street
Tel Aviv
Telephone: (03) 336222
Office hours: 8:00 A.M. to 3:00 P.M.
   Friday and Eves of Holidays 8:00 A.M. to 1:00 P.M.

HISTORY AND DESCRIPTION

Magen David Adom ("Red Shield of David"), a volunteer organization founded in 1930 provides first aid, ambulance and blood bank services for the entire country, deals with national emergencies ranging from natural disasters to terrorist attacks and war, and it carries out the functions assigned by the Geneva Conventions to national societies of the Red Cross or other volunteer aid societies authorized by their governments. Thus, Magen-David-Adom—though its emblem is the Red Shield of David and not the Red Cross—carries out all the functions of a national Red Cross Society.

The major accomplishments of the organization until now have been the establishment of 61 first aid stations and sub-stations; a national emergency ambulance fleet based on 600 regular ambulances and about 50 special and sophisticated emergency vehicles; a central blood bank; first aid instruction school; headquarters with a national communication center.

OFFICERS

President: Prof. Arie Harell. Physician.
Board Member: Advocate Mordechai Degani.
Chairman, Exec.
Com.:   Amizur Kfir. Army General (Res.)
Treasurer: Yehiel Hami.

FINANCIAL INFORMATION

Last year's annual budget came from the following sources: from abroad and Israel, 25%; services income, 50%; government suport and support from local authorities, 25%. Last year's annual budget was $12,500,000 with no deficit. The organization is not registered as an Ottoman Association. It was founded as a result of a law of Knesset ("The Magen David Adom Law"—1950). It was not indicated whether or not donations were tax-free. There are 800 full-time workers employed by the organization, in addition to 5000 volunteers.

MEMBERSHIP, SCOPE, AND POLICY

The operational decisions are made mostly by the Executive Director while the National Board makes the policy-making decisions. There are 5000 members in Israel in the 61 branches. There are branches abroad in the following countries: U.S., Great Britain, South Africa, Australia, France, Germany, Belgium, Italy, Mexico, Venezuela, Argentina, Colombia and Canada. The following are the criteria for joining the organization: age 17 and above; medical check-up; graduated from first aid course; two recommendations; signed commitment for a year's work at least; practical work and half a year of experience.

AFFILIATIONS/REFERENCES

The organization is not affiliated with any political party in Israel. It is in contact with the following: American Red Magen David for Israel ("ARMDI"), 888 Seventh Avenue, Suite 403, New York, New York 10019; Friends of M.D.A. in Great Britain, 100 Gloucester Place, London W1H 3DA; and Magen David Adom in South Africa, Highland House, 173 Louis Botha Avenue, Orange Grove, Johannesburg 2192.

FUNDING NEEDED

1. The construction of a new blood bank national center and a countrywide "mobile intensive care unit" system.
2. The construction of new first aid stations at Rishon Le'Zion, Tivon, Lod/Ramle and Yeruham.

MAGEN HAYELED INSTITUTE

מתיבתא "מגן הילד"

3 Brandshtater Street
P.O.B. 1526
Bnei Brak
Telephone: (03) 781857
Office hours: 8:00 A.M. to 7:00 P.M.

DESCRIPTION
Magen Hayeled Institute was founded in August 1973 in an old building
that was previously used for offices and classrooms. In a short while it
outgrew the classrooms and was forced to move to larger quarters.
Although the new building was not large enough, it accepted 70 children. Before long another 30 children were accepted, and a small
building was rented for those children.
The Institute was established to spark a love of Judaism in the hearts of
young children. The basic educational foundation that the Institute has
instilled in the children has helped them overcome the negative influences of the society.
The Institute is in desperate need for a new building so that it can house
all its 150-200 children under one roof. In that way the children can be
provided with the physical and emotional care they require.

OFFICERS
Director: Rabbi Yaakov Kochi, 10 Breslev, Bnei Brak.
                   Tel. (03) 787372.
Treasurer: Rabbi Michael Hazan, 13 Kotler, Bnei Brak.
Board Members: Rabbi Yakne Yichael, 8 Sorotzkin, Bnei Brak.
                   Secretary.
                   Rabbi Shimshon David, Hai Gaon, Bnei Brak.
                   Kitchen manager.

FINANCIAL INFORMATION
The sources of last year's annual budget were as follows: welfare grants,
30%; youth allotment fund, 60%; Ministry of Religious Affairs, 8%;
donations, 2%. Last year's annual budget was $35,000 and the debt-
deficit is $40,000. The Institute is registered as an Ottoman Association
(number not supplied). Donations to Magen Hayeled Institute are
tax-free in Israel (tax number not supplied) but not tax-free in the
United States or in other countries. There are 15 full-time and 5 part-
time workers employed by the Institute, in addition to 15 volunteers.

MEMBERSHIP, SCOPE, AND POLICY
Decisions are made by the National Board. There are seven members in
the one Israeli branch.

AFFILIATIONS/REFERENCES
The Institute is not affiliated with any political party in Israel, and has
no contacts abroad.

FUNDING NEEDED

The immediate problem is the acquisition of a building to house the institution. Since all the existing buildings are rented, Magen Hayeled Institute can be asked to leave at any time. In order to start building it has to buy a plot at an estimated cost of $300,000. Construction costs will then be approximately $900,000. After the building is constructed, it will be necessary to furnish the kitchen and dining room facilities, the library, the synagogue and the dormitory.

MATAN BESETER—
CHARITY ANONYMOUS, HAIFA

מתן בסתר, אגודה לצדקה

Zvi Feigin St. 7, Haifa 34574
Telephone: (04) 81923
Office Hours: 8:00 A.M. to 11:00 A.M., and by appointment.

HISTORY AND DESCRIPTION

"Matan Beseter" (Haifa) was founded in 1970 by public-spirited retired persons. It gives assistance anonymously to needy Jews, regardless of their country of origin or their political or religious views. The organization directs its assistance to those too sensitive or proud to ask for help from official agencies; the poor; the old; the sick and families with many children. In addition, it helps soldiers, both male and female, to embark on a career at the completion of their military service. This is accomplished by paying for their professional education, supporting them until they receive their first salary, and sometimes even supporting and finding homes for their ailing relatives.

Goals: One of the organization's major priorities with regard to future funding is the dental clinic which it has established in Kiryat-Yam (near Haifa). The purpose of this clinic is to provide needy old people with dentures and other dental necessities. Other important goals of the organization include helping demobilized soldiers from disadvantaged social classes to find a profession and a home, as well as helping young couples to establish and equip their first home in Israel.

Services, Activities and Accomplishments: The organization is involved with many diverse types of services. Each week, it distributes funds to families in distress, gives assistance with monthly rents; provides quick one-time aid in cases of need; pays for a patient's stay in a convalescent home after an operation; and provides interest-free loans to trustworthy people who require this type of support. A special "Family Assistance" fund, which is supported by bequests and other large contributions, enables the organization to help young couples in need. The organization also collects and supplies furniture, refrigerators, washing machines and other appliances; clothing for every age group; linens; toys; and household and kitchen equipment. Among the group's major accomplishments has been the establishment of the dental clinic mentioned above; the setting up of store-rooms for second-hand clothing in several areas in the north of Israel; and aiding the Kiryat Shemona project for demobilized soldiers.

OFFICERS
Director: E. Bein, Zvi Feigin 7, Haifa. Retired.
                 Tel. (04) 81923.
Board Members: M. Naumburg, Smolenskin 24, Haifa. Retired.
                 Tel. (04) 244398.

S. Markowicz, Derech Hayam 59a, Haifa. Retired.
  Tel.: (04) 85103
Mrs. Jona Porat, Sd. Wingate 17, Haifa. Retired.
  Tel. (04) 663605.

FINANCIAL INFORMATION
The organization's sole source of income is from donations. Last year's annual budget was $28,000 (cash turnover), plus approximately $20,000 worth of furniture, electrical appliances and clothing. Donations to the organization are tax-free in Israel, but not in the U.S.A. (Israel tax number 4503889). The organization is registered as a non-profit Ottoman Association in the Tel Aviv District Office of the Ministry of the Interior (no. 2542/99). The staff of the organization is composed of volunteers only.

MEMBERSHIP, SCOPE AND POLICY
All donors to the organization are considered to be members. There are currently 1000 members (i.e. donors) in Israel and 20 abroad. Decisions are made by the Board.

AFFILIATIONS/REFERENCES
The organization is not affiliated with any political party in Israel nor with any group abroad.

FUNDING NEEDED
More funds are needed for continuing the programs already in progress.

MATAV—HOMEMAKERS' SERVICE ASSOCIATION

מט"ב — אגודה לשרות מטפלות בית

17 Spinoza Street
Tel Aviv
Telephone: (03) 244707 and (03) 235987
Office hours: Sunday - Friday, 8:00 A.M. to 1:00 P.M.
Monday, 4:00 P.M. to 6:00 P.M.

HISTORY AND DESCRIPTION

Matav, The Israel Homemaker Service, was established in June 1958. It now has branches all over the country. Matav is a voluntary agency governed by a Board of Directors, each branch having its own Board of Directors.

Organizational Structure: To carry out its program, Matav recruits, trains and employs a staff of homemakers who are supervised by social workers and trained nurses. The homemakers' functions are to serve as mother surrogate, home economist and counselor. Matav employs the homemakers on a part-time basis. The services of the branches are developing according to local needs. The number of the homemakers is growing steadily.

It is supported by the Ministry of Welfare, Ministry of Health, the Workers' Sick Fund and by a few other agencies. The local authorities give some support to the local branches. Requests for new branches come in from different areas of the country.

Goals: Matav's program is based on the principle that a crisis in the home should, if possible, be resolved by dealing with the core problem in the home, rather than by resorting to hospitalization or institutional care. This policy keeps families from becoming welfare cases and thus helps them preserve their self-esteem.

Services, Activities and Accomplishments: Matav's homemakers render a large variety of services to crisis-ridden families as a result of many conditions including death or absence of parent, acute or chronic illness, mental or physical incapacity of the mother to assume her responsibilities, immobility or retardation of a member of the family, infirmity of an aged member of the family, or multi-problem families. Its charges to the recipients of its service depend upon the individual's ability to pay. Matav does not turn away any person because of his inability to pay. On the contrary, where there happens to be a shortage of staff, Matav gives preference to those who cannot pay for the service. The welfare and health agencies pay for the service to families referred to Matav. The organization's major accomplishments until now have been the establishment of 12 regional centers and the training of 500 homemakers, giving over 400,000 service-hours per annum. In 1980, about 1250 families were assisted each month.

OFFICERS

Administrative
Director: H. Arvay, 6 Yaldei Teheran Street, Givatayim.
Tel. (03) 315819.

Treasurer: Y. Reifen, National Insurance Office, Rehovot.
Tel. (054) 57681.

Board Members: K. Kalir, Ministry of Law, (Acting Chairman),
Tel Aviv.
Tel. (03) 216111.

S. Baron, Union of Local Authorities, Tel Aviv.
Tel. (03) 267212.

Mrs. R. Boritzer, 5 Washington Street, Jerusalem.
Tel. (02) 224605.

Mrs. H. Cohen, Ministry of Health, Jerusalem.
Tel. (02) 638212.

Mrs. Y. Livnat, 8 Pinkas Street, Tel Aviv.
Tel. (03) 450120.

Mrs. J. London-Yaari, Ministry of Welfare,
Jerusalem.
Tel. (02) 719081.

Prof. Z. Zakler, Kupat Holim Center, Tel Aviv.
Tel. (03) 262211.

FINANCIAL INFORMATION

Less than one percent of the annual budget comes from the G. Wurzweiler Foundation, Inc. in New York. There are no membership dues. The difference in income between the cost of service hours and payments from recipients of service, is partly refunded to Matav by the Ministry of Labor and Social Welfare, the Ministry of Health, Kupat Holim, Custodian of Absentee Property, and the Jewish Agency. Last year's annual budget was $1.5 million, and left a deficit of $205,000. The organization is registered as an Ottoman Association in Tel Aviv (no. 2044). Donations are tax-free in Israel (no number supplied). There are 540 part-time employees as well as 150 volunteers.

MEMBERSHIP, SCOPE, AND POLICY

There are 12 branches in Israel, but no membership. Decisions are made by the National Board.

AFFILIATIONS/REFERENCES

The organization is not affiliated with any political party. It is affiliated with the International Council of Homehelp Services, in the Netherlands.

FUNDING NEEDED

1. For the establishment of four new centers in Kiryat Shmona and Tiberias (for the Northern Galilee), Ramle-Lod (combined center) and Dimona (for the northern Negev).
2. For the establishment of a fund to help families who cannot pay the full charges.

3. For the expansion of existing centers and services by financing the employment of more professional workers, particularly in development areas.

In connection with the urgent need to set up additional centers, more homemakers' training courses are required. Each course for 15 candidates costs (currently) $3,500 (approx.).

The growing need for homemakers' services, which help the family and also relieve the pressure from hospitals for the chronically ill, homes for the aged, etc. (which are costly institutions), is increasing Matav's financial problems. This is highlighted by a deficit budget. The ever-increasing cost of services could best be met by large and regular donations, and by setting up support foundations and groups of "Friends of Matav".

MEIER SHFEYAH YOUTH VILLAGE
(Agricultural School)

Post Meier Shfeyah 30996   כפר הנוער מאיר שפיה
Telephone: (063) 90750-1
Office hours: 8:00 A.M. to 16:00 P.M.

HISTORY AND DESCRIPTION

The Meier Shfeyah (from the Arabic word for watering place) Youth Village was originally established as a farm in honor of Meier Anshel Rothschild, the head of the Rothschild family. It is located near Zichron Yaacov. In 1924 it became an institution for orphan girls. In 1925, Junior Hadassah, the youth group of Hadassah, the Women's Zionist Organization of America, took over the Village and was responsible for it until 1958, when it became the responsibility of the Government of the State of Israel, first under the aegis of the Agricultural Ministry and later under the Ministry of Education, the Division of Agricultural Settlement. In the early years it was populated by orphan girls, many of them of Yemenite descent; in later years it became a co-educational school. In the 30's, Henrietta Szold, as Head of Youth Aliyah, commenced sending youth from Youth Aliyah.

Organizational Structure: Meier Shfeyah's property is owned by Hadassah. The main responsibility for its operation is held by the Ministry of Education, through its Division of Agricultural Settlement. The Ministry and Youth Aliyah provide regular inspection.

Services, Activities, and Accomplishments: The Village is a 6-year school catering for grades 7 to 12. The Senior High School provides two-stream, academic-agricultural educations and its graduates take matriculation and course-completion examinations. Studies include vocational training courses in the operation of agricultural equipment and integrated home economics. Pupils work 10-15 hours per week on the farm, the boys operating farm machinery two days a week, the girls working the same amount of time in services and agriculture.
Meier Shfeyah has trained thousands of young people to become useful citizens of the Yishuv and the State of Israel. Many graduates have gone on to form and join existing kibbutzim; others have entered professions in the Arts and Education. Among the graduates of the Youth Village are Bracha Zefira, Sara Levy Tannai and Itamar Siani, Israelis who are well-known in their fields.

OFFICERS

Director: Hagi Meged, Meir Shfeyah. Educator.
Chairman of
the Board: Avner Yisraeli, Alharizi 3, Jerusalem.
Co-Chairwoman
of the Board: Annabelle Yuval, 13 Balfour, Jerusalem.

FINANCIAL INFORMATION

The school is supported by the Israeli Government, with Youth Aliyah and the Ministry of Education contributing to its budget. Development funds come from a variety of sources, including the Government, Hadassah, Youth Aliyah, IKA, etc. (Previous year's budget not supplied.) The school is registered as a non-profit Ottoman Association (Haifa District Office of Ministry of Interior—registration number not supplied). Donations in the United States, channelled through Hadassah, the Women's Zionist Organization of America, are tax-deductible.

AFFILIATIONS/REFERENCES

The Youth Village is not affiliated with any Israeli political party.

FUNDING NEEDED

1. Dormitory for students—cost $250,000.
2. Improvements in staff residences—cost $100,000.
3. Agricultural equipment—cost $125,000.

MEMORIAL FUND IN THE NAME OF OFFICER MICHA HAREL

הקרן לזכרו של סגן מיכאל הראל פרייברג ז"ל

41 Hagdud HaIvri
Haifa
Telephone: (04) 721565

HISTORY AND DESCRIPTION

The Memorial Fund in the Name of Officer Micha Harel (Frieberg) was established after the the 1973 War, in which Micha was killed. At the time he was a second year student at the Technion, Haifa.

Organizational Structure: The Fund has a director and governing board, all volunteers.

Goals: To memorialize Micha, his friends established the Fund to provide scholarships for needy students.

Services, Activities, and Accomplishments: Every year five scholarships are presented in Micha's memory. The Fund has published a book on Micha's life and at the scholarship ceremony passages are read.

OFFICERS

Director:	Baruch Reches, 7 Oren, Haifa.
Treasurer:	Ihiel Frieberg, Nisenbaum,
	12/26 Neve Shaanan St. Haifa.
Board:	Lea Wohlbrum, 9 Oren St. Haifa.
	Leon Zandberg, 31 Abas, Haifa.
Secretary:	Nitza Harel, 41 Hagdud HaIvri, Kiryat Haim,
	Haifa.

FINANCIAL INFORMATION

Sources of income are entirely from donations. Last year's wealth was $4,600 with a $400 scholarship. The Fund is registered as an Ottoman Association (no number supplied) and donations are tax-free in Israel (no. 450460). There are no salaried employees—all are volunteers.

MEMBERSHIP, SCOPE, AND POLICY

Membership is open to all who wish to know about Micha Harel and who wish to contribute to the Fund. Decisions are made mostly by the director, and the committee. At present there are twenty-five members in Israel and five abroad.

AFFILIATIONS/REFERENCES

The Fund has no affiliation with any political party in Israel.

FUNDING NEEDED

Since the scholarships are provided from the interest of the donations to the Fund, we would like to increase the capital in order to keep up with inflation.

MERKAZ YESHIVOT B'NEI AKIVA— THE B'NEI AKIVA YESHIVOT CENTER

מרכז ישיבות בני־עקיבא בישראל

7 Dubnov Street
P.O.B. 40025, Tel Aviv
Telephone: (03) 265773, (03) 258804, (03) 216011
Office hours: 8:00 A.M. to 4:00 P.M.

HISTORY AND DESCRIPTION

This organization, established in 1960, is the umbrella headquarters of B'nei Akiva yeshivot and ulpanot religious high-schools in Israel, guiding youngsters towards upholding their heritage in the modern State of Israel. Originally functioning as a department of the B'nei Akiva religious Zionist youth movement, it developed into an independent educational body under a governmental and public aegis, serving: one yeshiva junior high-school; fourteen yeshiva high-schools; two yeshiva vocational high-schools; five higher yeshivot hesder; ten girls' ulpana high-schools; and one women's college—totalling thirty-three religious educational establishments, all with dormitory facilities, responsible for the education of more than 10,000 pupils including some 1000 day-pupils.

Organizational Structure: This comprises an Executive Council of principals and managers of all constituent schools; an Administrative Committee of fifteen members, with an internal Actions Committee of five.

Services, Activities, and Accomplishments: State of Israel High-school Graduation Examinations or State Vocational Examinations are mandatory in all the high-schools belonging to this organization. Yeshivot Hesder students play an important role in national security, combining military training and courses with yeshiva studies. The Hesder program includes Teacher Training Institutes, under whose aegis students who have completed 4 to 5 years of service are eligible to take the teacher certification examinations. Successful students are awarded a Certificate of Education recognized by the Ministry of Education, permitting them to teach in high-school. Hesder students make time to seek out those less fortunate in background or education, lending a helping hand. Combining defense training with yeshiva studies, soldier/students enlist for a minimum of four years instead of the three years obligatory service, not "opting-out" of duty as is legally permissible for theological students. Terminating this four- or five-year stint, the Hesder student takes his place in the academic field or in the economy of the country. Yeshiva high-school curricula provide 73 lesson-periods per week and extra-curricula activities include sports, crafts, and social groups. The Ministry of Education finances some 53 hours' general lessons weekly, but the remaining budget must be covered by tuition fees and external charitable contributions. Maintaining one pupil under full boarding facilities and subsidizing educational expenses not covered by governmental or other official bodies reaches $1600 a year. Thousands of Israeli youth have been educated in institutions belonging to this organization and have been provided with a solid foundation for their future lives and careers. The educational establishments of Merkaz Yeshivot B'nei Akiva educate students from all over the country and prepare them in such a way that they return home bringing a very positive personality to their home environment. Their contribution to Israeli society projects over the wide spectrum of positions occupied by the graduates, such as urban mayors, senior officials in public institutions, school principals, and leaders in all facets of Israeli life. Overall development of each individual institution has not yet been accomplished. Each institution under the aegis of the Merkaz is independently managed, but receives guidance in financial and developmental matters from the Merkaz.

OFFICERS

Directors:
    Rabbi Joseph Bagad, Petach Tikva.
    Rabbi Arieh Binah, Jerusalem.
    Avraham Dimant, Givataim.
    Rabbi Haim Druckman, Lachish Zafon.
    Yaakov Drori, Kibbutz Saad.
    Avraham Marmorstein, Petach Tikva.
    Rabbi M.Z. Neria, Kfar Haroeh.
    Rabbi Avraham Zuckerman, Kfar Haroeh.

FINANCIAL INFORMATION

50% of last year's annual budget (figure not supplied) came from donations, and 50% from government sources and public bodies. Funds are mobilized and distributed to the constituent institutions, balanced out according to the funding available and the specific financial problems of each institution. The Merkaz is a recognized non-profit organization (Israel reg. no. 2479/99), to which donations in Israel and the United States may be made tax-free (Israel: no. 4501990; USA—through American Friends of Yeshivot B'nei Akiva, New York: I.R.S. no. 52-6080692). The Merkaz employs four full-time and five part-time workers, as well as a great number of volunteers. Decisions are made by the Executive Committee, the Administrative Committee, and the Actions Committee—in that order.

AFFILIATIONS/REFERENCES

Merkaz Yeshivot B'nei Akiva is affiliated to HaPoel HaMizrachi, a faction of the Israeli National Religious Party. It is in contact with: American Friends of Yeshivot B'nei Akiva, 39 Broadway, New York, N.Y. 10006; HaPoel HaMizrachi organizations throughout the world; and B'nei Akiva religious Jewish Youth Movement throughout the world.

FUNDING NEEDED

1. To develop dormitory facilities in the girls' high-school in Arad.
2. To develop dormitory facilities in the vocational high-school in Meron, catering to pupils from northern border villages.
3. To complete the central assembly block, dining hall, and kitchen in Tikvat Yaakov High-school, Emek Yezreel.

MEROSH AMANA

מראש אמנה

32 Alfassi Street
Jerusalem
Telephone: (02) 661840

HISTORY AND DESCRIPTION

Merosh Amana was founded in 1980 to increase religious artistic activity by developing and promoting original Jewish art in music, painting, and poetry.

Goals: The association hopes to attract non-religious artists seeking the roots of Judaism, and to help them fulfill their endeavors. The preparation of serious and high-leveled family and public entertainment is planned. Possibilities awaiting realization include the adaptation for stage of the narrative and philosophical stories of R. Nachman of Brazlav, Ramhal, Maharal, and R. Kook.

Services, Activities, and Accomplishments: A contribution to the integration of the different art forms is the organization of combined artistic evenings, where people can listen to original Jewish music inspired by the "Mishnayot", poetry, and look at colorful slide compositions based on Hassidism, Maharal of Prague and R. Kook. Thus, musicians and painters can enjoy poetry, while poets can experience original Jewish music and fine arts—the combination of which creates an original, perfect Jewish art based on the beauty of holy purity. Such performances have been held in Jerusalem, Tel Aviv, Haifa, Netanya, Kfar-Saba, Kfar-Etzion, and Kiriat-Arba.

OFFICERS

Director: Zvi Grundman, Alfassi 32, Jerusalem. Artist. Tel.: (02) 661840.

Treasurer: Efraim Safrai, Haeelooy 8, Jerusalem. Encounter. Tel.: (02) 526011.

Board Members: André Neher, Ussishkin 16, Jerusalem. Philosopher. Tel: (02) 665873.

André Heidu, Emek Refaim 66, Jerusalem. Musician. Tel.: (02) 669011.

Zelda Mishkovsky, Hakalir 9, Jerusalem. Poet. Tel: (02) 666530.

Ellen Sternfeld. Hahagana 9, Jerusalem. Musician. Tel.: (02) 816125.

Yehoshua Rochman, Yordei Hassira 2, Jerusalem. Musician. Tel.: (02) 633998.

FINANCIAL INFORMATION

The association is presently in the developmental stage. It has received donations from the Ministry of Education, and the Municipalities of Jerusalem, Tel Aviv, Haifa, Netanya, and Kfar-Saba. Donations to Merosh Amana in Israel are tax-free (Israel non-profit no. 11/3233).

MEMBERSHIP, SCOPE, AND POLICY
The association has seven national members in its one branch. Any person accepting the principles of the association can become a member. Decisions are generally made by the National Board.

AFFILIATIONS/REFERENCES
Merosh Amana is politically unaffiliated in Israel. It has contacts with the Yeshiva University and The Jewish Museum, Both in New York.

FUNDING NEEDED
1. For the organization of performances of combined Jewish art in twenty settlements ($800 each performance)—$16,000.
2. For the preparation of an improved model of a Jewish wedding, in cooperation with an artist, a musician, and a writer—$1,500.
3. For the stage adaptation of stories written by Agnon, R. Nachman of Brazlav, and Ramhal—$6,000.

MICHA SOCIETY FOR DEAF CHILDREN, NATIONAL COUNCIL

מיח"א — מחנכי ילדים חרשים, מועצה ארצית

23 Reading
Ramat Aviv
Tel Aviv
Telephone: (03) 415146
Office hours: Sunday-Friday, 8:30 A.M. to 1:30 P.M.

HISTORY AND DESCRIPTION
The Tel Aviv branch of the MICHA Society for Deaf Children was founded in 1953 by the late Dr. Ezra Korine to fulfill an urgent need for special education and training for preschool deaf children. The MICHA chain of centers and kindergartens are located throughout Israel and, throughout the years, branches have been established in Jerusalem, Haifa and Beer Sheva.

Organizational Structure: Each MICHA branch operates independently. The National Council was established on March 26, 1979, with two representatives from each branch.

Goals: To prepare small deaf children for integration into the hearing society, so that they can take their place in later life as normal, self-supporting and productive citizens of Israel.

Services, Activities, and Accomplishments: The MICHA centers take care of about 350 small deaf children from the age of 7 months to 7 years, with a special counselling project for the parents. At the Micha Centers, the special educational curriculum comprises individual and group tutoring by a highly qualified professional staff with the help of up-to-date electronic equipment and hearing aids and audiologic tests. Accomplishments include the realization of early diagnosis and treatment for small deaf children, the setting up of integrated kindergartens, parent counselling and home care programs. 70% of the graduates of MICHA centers and kindergartens study in normal schools with their hearing peers. To date, almost every deaf child in Israel is and has been cared for through the MICHA program, from the first months of his life which is the most critical period.

OFFICERS
Chairman of the National Council:
      Mrs. Chana Yardeni, 55 Zahal, Kiron.
        Tel. (03) 759876.

FINANCIAL INFORMATION
70% of the income of the Council and MICHA branches comes from donations, 20% as subsidies from the Government of Israel and the municipalities, and 10% from membership dues and parents' payments.

Last year's annual budget, including all the branches, was $208,142. The National Council is registered in Tel Aviv as a non-profit Ottoman Association (reg. no. 7542199). Donations in Israel and the United States are tax-free. Apart from professional help in administrative and educational capacities, the organization is assisted by volunteers from all walks of life. It employs over 40 full-time or part-time staff.

MEMBERSHIP, SCOPE, AND POLICY
Membership is open to any Israeli who volunteers and pays annual membership dues. There are approximately 400 members with 4 branches in Israel and 1 abroad. Decisions are made by the National Board.

AFFILIATIONS/REFERENCES
The Council is not affiliated to any political party in Israel.

FUNDING NEEDED
The most outstanding present needs are for funds.
1. To maintain highly qualified professional staff.
2. To purchase equipment — individual hearing aids, tutoring individual hearing aids and group tutoring aids.
3. To purchase educational toys and games.

MISGAV LADACH HOSPITAL

בית חולים משגב לדך

7 Kovshei Katamon Street
P.O.B. 90
Jerusalem
Telephone: (02) 662925 and 633356
Office hours: 8:00 A.M. to 1:30 P.M.

HISTORY AND DESCRIPTION

Misgav Ladach General Jewish Hospital is the oldest Jewish hospital in the country. It began as a general hospital in the Old City of Jerusalem in the second half of the 19th century, was destroyed by the Arab Legion in 1948, and has since been housed in cramped, temporary quarters in the Katamon section of Jerusalem. The hospital now has gynecological and obstetric departments and clinics, as well as a number of other outpatient clinics, including: pediatrics, nutrition, early cancer detection, migraine.

Misgav Ladach is now building a new hospital in which it is planned to provide additional outpatient services in various spheres, including: juvenile diabetes, dental care, ophthalmy, etc. The emphasis will be placed on mother-and-child care and preventive medicine.

Despite the fact that the medical staff has had to work under difficult physical conditions, in a building not planned as a hospital, its high standards and devotion have become famed even beyond Israel's borders. This has been made possible through the help of friends throughout the world, who have enabled it to purchase the most up-to-date medical equipment. It is essential that it continue to renew the equipment.

Work has now commenced on the construction of the much needed new hospital in southern Jerusalem. This will be the only hospital in the area, which includes one of Jerusalem's most distressed neighborhoods. At current prices, it is estimated that the construction of the new hospital will cost $6 million. There are special fund-raising campaigns in Israel and abroad and by Committees of Friends in various communities, the most veteran of which are in London and New York. Additional Committees are now being formed, and there are groups of Christian friends in Denmark and Finland.

The major accomplishments until now have been providing modern, first-class medical care under difficult physical conditions. Important research has been done on diabetes and pre-diabetes in pregnancy and fetal wastage, with a grant from the U.S. Government. In addition, the medical staff give free public lectures on preventive medicine.

OFFICERS

Administration: Reuven Kashani, 6 Reines, Jerusalem.
                  Tel. (02) 524680.
Medical Director: Dr. M. Salzberger, 6 Ben Labrat, Jerusalem.
                  Gynecologist. Tel. (02) 632160.

Chairman, Board of Governors:	David Sitton, 7 Itamar Ben Avi, Jerusalem. Journalist, retired. Tel. (02) 632132.
Treasurer:	I. Askenazi, 13 Shimoni, Jerusalem. Tel. (02) 633066.
Chairman, Building Fund:	Yehezkel Shemesh, 11a Ussishkin, Jerusalem. Restauranteur. Tel. (02) 222418.
Chairman, Building Committee:	Shlomo Seruya, 4 Tchernichovsky Street, Jerusalem. Vice-President, Jerusalem Sephardi Council. Tel. (02) 632407.
Chairman, Committees of Friends:	Prof. Shmuel Moreh, Jasmin St., Mevo a/3, Mevasseret Jerusalem.
Chairman, Women's Committees:	Mrs. Bathsheva Kukia, 4 Alharizi, Jerusalem. Tel. (02) 632103.

FINANCIAL INFORMATION

Income for 1979 came mostly from patient and clinic fees (88%), Ministry of Health (7%), and other sources (5%), amounting to a total of approximately $170,000.

The hospital is registered as an Ottoman Association (reg. no. 11/125). Donations to the hospital are tax-free both in Israel, the United States and England. Tax-free donations in England can be sent to Friends of Misgav Ladach, 2 Ashworth Road, London W9 (tax exemption number 264398); in the U.S. to American Friends of Misgav Ladach, c/o Ms Ruth Wreschner, 10 W. 74th Street, New York, N.Y. 10023.

There are 70 part-time employees in addition to the volunteers.

MEMBERSHIP, SCOPE, AND POLICY

The hospital is governed by a 35-member General Council which meets twice a year; a 14-member Board of Governors and a 7-member Executive Committee and a 3-member Medical Committee. Most decisions are made by the Board and the Administrative Director and Medical Committee. There are Committees of Friends in the United States and England. Committees are in formation in South Africa, Australia, Thailand, and Europe and there are individual friends in many other countries.

MISHMAROT KEHUNA V'BEIT ULPANA TORAH LA'AM

משמרות כהונה ובית אולפנא לעם

40 Zonenfeld Street
P.O.B. 5555 Jerusalem
Telephone: (02) 272675
Office hours: 9:00 A.M. to 1:00 P.M. and 4:00 P.M. to 7:00 P.M.

HISTORY AND DESCRIPTION

The idea for a yeshiva was conceived in 1972, when a number of youths organized themselves after army service in order to study and master the Torah.

Goals: To teach a basic knowledge of Judaism and Jewish sources, including the Talmud and its commentaries, to those who did not have the opportunity to learn these in their childhood. To spiritually rehabilitate alienated youth and to help them find their way to life and to build their lives according to Jewish tradition. To provide afternoon Torah classes for youngsters in poor neighborhoods; to help them with their school homework in order to raise their level of achievement, and ensure that they do not drop out from school. To educate talented Yeshiva graduates to become community rabbis and teachers of Torah.

Services, Activities and Accomplishments: The Yeshiva supports students and grants them loans when needed in order to study Torah. Supplementary classes are given to children from poor neighborhoods. Older youth are rehabilitated.

During the past 8 years the Yeshiva has helped hundreds of youngsters with supplementary classes and has directed them to Torah institutions, including Yeshivot of a high level. It has also helped older youth (about 80-90) after army service, who were unable to adjust to society and set themselves up in life.

OFFICERS

Head of Yeshiva: Rabbi Ariel Cohen, 42 Yehezkel, Jerusalem. Rabbi. Tel. (02) 272675.

Board Members: Mr. Yosef Ben Porat, Haim Ozer, Jerusalem. Businessman.

Mr. Yitzchak Elasri, Admon, Jerusalem. Male nurse.

Mr. Meir Kapah, 17 Reichman, Mea Shearim, Jerusalem. Laboratory assistant.

Mr. Ezra Efraim Jano, 300/5, Kiryat Hayovel, J-m.

Mr. Moshe Chai Kashani, 17 Kiryat Zanz, J-m.

Mr. Shalom Daniel, 23 Zefania, Jerusalem.

FUNDING NEEDED

1. To rent or purchase a residence for students from other towns, mainly from development areas.
2. Due to inflation, funds are required for basic maintenance and for teachers' salaries.

MITZPE YERIHO

מצפה יריחו

Mitzpe Yeriho, Doar Nah Bikak, Yeriho
Telephone: (02) 226530
Office Hours: 8:00 A.M. to 1:00 P.M.

HISTORY AND DESCRIPTION
Mitzpe Yeriho is a settlement 20 miles outside of Jerusalem on the way
to Jericho. It was established in mid-1978 and now has a population of
forty families.

Organizational Structure: In a new concept, every family works for
itself, with a common agreement as to how the society should be built. It
is a religious settlement with all the required facilities. At present, the
settlement is temporary, with the permanent settlement to be completed
within the next year.

Goals: Mitzpe Yeriho is aiming for 250 families at its final stage of
development. The settlement will include facilities to serve industry,
agriculture, and tourism (for both foreigners and orthodox families
from Jerusalem). Planned industries include telecommunications,
chemistry, and electro-optics. The settlement also plans to heat the
whole area with solar energy.

Services, Activities, and Accomplishments: The organization has to this
point developed a bare landscape into a settlement worthy of human
inhabitation. Primary planning for the solar energy project has begun.

OFFICERS
Director: J. Klein, Mitzpe Yeriho.
                     Electro-optics Engineer.
                     Tel. (02) 226530.
Treasurer: David Feldman, Mitzpe Yeriho. Accountant.
                     Tel. (02) 226530.
Board Members: Haim Cohen, Mitzpe Yeriho. Offset printer.
                     Tel. (02) 226530.
                     Raphael Francis, Mitzpe Yeriho.
                     Director, Post Office Bank.
                     Tel. (02) 226530.
                     Moshe Rubaha, Mitzpe Yeriho. Social Worker.
                     Tel. (02) 226530.

FINANCIAL INFORMATION
Income for this organization comes from two main sources. Membership dues, which range from $50 to $100 per month comprise 5% of the
settlement's total income, with the remaining 95% coming from the
Jewish Agency. Last years' budget was $10,000, and there was also a
deficit of $10,000. Donations are tax-free in the United States (IRS
number not supplied). Information was not provided as to the taxation

status of donations to the organization from within Israel. Mitzpe Yeriho has four full-time and two part-time workers, plus 15 volunteers.

MEMBERSHIP, SCOPE, POLICY, AND AFFILIATIONS
Decisions are made mostly by the Executive Director. Criteria for membership is dependent on being accepted as a settler by both the settlement and the Jewish Agency. There are presently 25 members in Israel and one branch. There is no direct affiliation from abroad, nor is Mitzpe Yeriho affiliated with any Israeli political party.

FUNDING NEEDED
The community's most outstanding present needs include the following:
1. The planning, designing, and development of a solar energy power station. Approximate cost, $2.5-$4 million.
2. A sports facility, beginning with a basketball court ($20,000), and working up to a full sports complex to include tennis courts, swimming pool and various other sports facilities. Approximate cost, $1 million.
3. A public hall (Beit Am) for meetings, conferences, films and live theatre shows. Approximate cost, $500,000.

MIVTACH OZ — A UNIVERSAL CHARITABLE ORGANIZATION FOR RELIEF AND SUPPORT

מבטח עוז, אגודת פעילים עולמית לעזר וסעד

Bal Shem Tov St. 7 (P.O.B. 5645)
Jerusalem.
Telephone: (02) 271267.
Office Hours: Monday, 4:00 P.M. to 5:00 P.M.

HISTORY AND DESCRIPTION

After a great deal of consultation and thought, a group of leading community-minded social workers concluded that there was a need for a central fund-raising organization. The lack of coordination has led to a situation where one movement overlaps the other, resulting in concentrated help to certain sectors with virtually no aid to others. Organizations (often small in nature) which would be able to work charitable wonders if given larger sums of money, are frequently left stranded. Wealthier movements, which often find themselves with surplus funds that are not immediately in demand, would be able to help rectify the situation if they could be made aware of it. The missing link is — once again — a central, universal organization. This concern brought the founders of "Mivtach Oz" to establish their organization and to gather experienced charity activists to form this essential liaison, which serves the best interests of numerous charitable organizations and the recipients of their aid. But still more important is that the donor knows that his charity, wherever directed, is utilized to the utmost. The lack of such an essential service until now has been a tragic oversight. Immediately upon establishment of "Mivtach Oz", the organization was approached by the needy for financial aid.

OFFICERS

Director: Salman Brizel, Jona 15, Jerusalem. Rabbi.
Treasurer: J. Karishefski, Sanhedria HaMurchevet 114/28, Jerusalem. Rabbi.
Board Members: S. Grossman, Yisa Bracha 39, Jerusalem. Rabbi.
S. Schaffer, Bal Shem Tov 7, Jerusalem. Rabbi.

FINANCIAL INFORMATION

The organization's sole source of income is donations. No figures were provided for last year's annual budget. Donations to the organization do not have tax-free status. "Mivtach Oz" is registered as a non-profit Ottoman Association in the Jerusalem District Office of the Ministry of the Interior (reg. no. 11/2773). The organization is staffed by 5 volunteers.

MEMBERSHIP, SCOPE, AND POLICY
The organization has no membership as such. There is one branch in Israel and one abroad. Decisions are made mostly by the Executive Director.

AFFILIATIONS/REFERENCES
The organization is not connected with any political party in Israel. Its American affiliate is also called "Mivtach Oz" and is located in Monsey. N.Y. (address: 10 Romon Blvd., Monsey, N.Y. 10952).

MOHARIL ASHLAG INSTITUTIONS

מוסדות מוהר"ל אשלג

4 Shadal
P.O.B. 316
Bnei Brak 51100
Telephone: (03) 792088
Office hours: 9:00 A.M. to 1:00 P.M.

HISTORY AND DESCRIPTION

Yeshivat Moharil Ashlag is a spiritual continuation of "Beth Ulpana Rabata Itur Rabanim" the Yeshiva that the late Yehuda Leib Ashlag founded in 1925 with the aid and consent of the most eminent late rabbis. Grand Rabbi Shlomo Binyamin, the son of the Grand Rabbi Yehuda Leib Ashlag, is today the heir and successor.

The founders decided to call the Yeshiva after the Gaon, the Genius of the Torah Secrets, Moharil Ashlag, so that his name, his ideas, and his holiness would guide it. He was a hidden Zadik and a giant whom only a few people had the privilege to know, for he did not want many people and students to come to him, but his many monumental books on the Kabalah and Zohar especially the "SULAM" made him popular, as only once in many generations is there somebody equivalent to him.

The name of the Yeshiva witnesses its goal: Realization of the aim of Rabbi Yehuda Leib Ashlag, who used to say that the internal contents of the Torah, and especially the explanations of the Ari scriptures, as well as the books of the Zohar, will be widely spread when they will be taught in the Yeshivot by his adherents. The study of the Zohar is included in the program of the Yeshiva as one of the most basic and needed studies. Students are educated to become judges, leaders, and to be loyal to Eretz Israel.

In Jerusalem, Yeshivas Ashlag mainains an evening Kollel to which the Rebbe frequently lectures. Yeshivas Ashlag also mainains a girls' school in Kiryat Arba. However, the dearest and most treasured of the Ashlag institutions is their "Cave of the Machpelah" Yeshiva in Hebron.

Services, Activities, and Accomplishments: Rabbis that have been trained are presently serving the holy needs of the nation. The Yeshiva has elevated the public to a high standard of intelligence and continues this task. It has established branches all over Israel and published literature and textbooks on Kabalah for the public.

OFFICERS

Grand Rabbi Shlomo B. Ashlag, 4 Shadal, Bnei Brak.
  Tel. (03) 792088.
Rabbi Akiva Orzez, 27 Hashlosha, Bnei Brak.
  Tel. (03) 705688.
Yisrael Pecker, 51 Yerushalayim, Bnei Brak.
  Retired.
Rabbi Yechezkal Ashlag, 7 Perl, Bnei Brak.
  Tel. (03) 791803.

Avraham Borgen, Yerushalayim, Bnei Brak.
   Retired.
Shmuel Leiberman, Yerushalayim, Bnei Brak.
   Retired.

FINANCIAL INFORMATION
50% of last year's annual budget came form donations; 15% came from membership dues; and the remaining 35% came from the Israeli Government. Last year's annual budget was $80,000, which brought the deficit up to $160,000. The Yeshiva is registered as an Ottoman Association (reg. no. 6576/99) and is applying for tax-free status in Israel and the U.S.A. The Yeshiva has applied for tax-free status in the United States. Six full-time and three part-time workers are employed by the Yeshiva, as well as six volunteers.

MEMBERSHIP, SCOPE, AND POLICY
Decisions are made mostly by the Executive Director and the national board. There are 400 members in Israel and 200 abroad. There are nine branches in Israel and are in the process of forming branches throughout the world.

AFFILIATIONS/REFERENCES
The Yeshiva is not affiliated with any political party in Israel. The Yeshiva is in contact with the Mizrachi Organization of America, 25 West 26th Street, New York, New York; and the Mizrachi Organization of Canada, 5497A Victoria Avenue, Suite 101, Montreal, Canada.

FUNDING NEEDED
1. Funding for food for the students, salary for the teachers and staff, support for the rabbis and students, salary for the workers, kitchen help, maintenance, and for facilities, including the pruchase of furniture, books, and bookshelves. Estimated cost: $80,000.
2. The completion of the building; the addition of another two floors (in addition to the three existing ones), Mikve (ritual bath), dormitory, rooms for lectures and lessons, library. Estimated cost: $230,000.

MORESHET AVOT—EL HAMEKOROT

מורשת אבות (אל המקורות) להחדרת ערכי התורה בישראל

22 Vilkomirrer Street (corner 30 Chazon Ish)
P.O.B. 363
Bnei Brak
Telephone: (03) 707336, 786624, 783186
Office hours:
   Sunday-Thursday: 8:00 A.M. to 1:00 P.M.
   Friday: 8:00 A.M. to 12:00 P.M.
   Sunday, Tuesday, Wednesday evenings: 6:00 P.M. to 10:00 P.M.

HISTORY AND DESCRIPTION

Moreshet Avot was established in the wake of the spiritual revival following the Six Day War in 1967. A small group of dedicated and idealistic volunteers undertook the task of further strengthening the spiritual arousal among Israeli youth and of returning them to their true heritage.

Organizational Structure: Directed by a tiny staff, Moreshet Avot functions are executed throughout the country by a corps of over 700 competent and devoted volunteers, inlcuding veteran educators, businessmen, young Rabbis, housewives and professionals who give generously of their time and energy to teach, befriend and guide estranged brethren. The scope of activities and achievements of the movement has surpassed all initial expectations and continues to grow daily.

Requests for activities coming from all parts of the country and all segments of the population can only be responded to in part, since the Moreshet Avot budget simply does not match the great volume of requests that continues to arrive.

Goals: Moreshet Avot conducts activities in over 100 high schools. In the last year 957 lectures were delivered in schools throughout the nation. Regional study days are coordinated for up to 500 pupils each. 18,000 students participated in study days in 1979.

Numerous lectures are arranged by Moreshet Avot throughout the country, in local community centers, and in private homes, providing participants with background knowledge and guidance.

Coupled with a program of speakers and discussions coordinated by Moreshet Avot, the guests are able to grasp the rich fabric of observant life through this unique experience. Over 4,000 youngsters were hosted for Shabbath this past year.

High school students, army officers, and soldiers, and members of nonreligious settlements and kibbutzim are graciously hosted for Shabbath in the warm atmosphere of religious homes in Jerusalem, Bnei Brak and Yeshivot Hesder, arranged by Moreshet Avot.

Moreshet Avot—El Hamekorot conducts a wide range of activities geared for military personnel, in the Israeli army. Study days, lectures and discussions are conducted on the army bases for servicemen from both religious and secular backgrounds.

"Machshevet", a monthly magazine, is received free of charge by thousands of soldiers. "B'Shaarei Zahal" the indispensible handbook on how to be a truly Jewish soldier, has been distributed to over 20,000 recruits.

The Adult Jewish Studies Program of Moreshet Avot is geared to young adults from all walks of life and backgrounds who are seeking guidance and wish to learn about their heritage. Classes are held each week in the Moreshet Avot in Bnei Brak and in several other branches. These intensive courses, along with individual guidance serve for many as the bridge away from secularism and back to their religious roots.

Three two-week sessions for nearly 500 high school students are held each summer in an outdoor setting with a warm holiday atmosphere. The program includes an intense learning curriculum coupled with recreational activities, a powerful and lasting impact on all participants. Nearly 70 volunteer lecturers are transported regularly in private cars to towns and villages throughout the central region to deliver "shiurim" (Torah discourses) each week.

Accomplishments: Moreshet Avot — El Ham'korot has acquainted tens of thousands of young adults with their Jewish heritage and identity, and thus guided them to observant Judaism.

OFFICERS

Aaron N. Miletsky, Bnei Brak. Rabbi.
Azariah Hildesheimer, Petach Tikvah. Lecturer.
Jacob Berlowitz, Bnei Brak. Import/Export.
Aryeh Carmel, Jerusalem. Dean, Dvar Jerusalem.
Chaim Friedlander, Bnei Brak. Dean, Ponevez.
Yaakov Gluskinos, Bnei Brak. Teacher.
Zvi Heber, Bnei Brak. Manufacturer.
Moshe Reiss, Bnei Brak. Textiles.
Ben Zion Leitner, Bnei Brak. Rabbi.

FINANCIAL INFORMATION

The sources of income for the last budget year was as follows: Government grants, 60%; and personal contributions, 40%. Last year's annual budget was $250,000, with a deficit of $80,000. The organization is registered as an Ottoman Association (reg. no. 5009/99). Donations to the organization are tax-free in Israel (no tax number supplied), the United States (tax no. 52-1182321), and Great Britain (tax no. 262707). There are 8 full-time and 15 part-time workers in addition to more than seven hundred volunteers.

MEMBERSHIP, SCOPE, AND POLICY

There are six branches in Israel and five abroad. Decisions are made by the National Board.

AFFILIATIONS/REFERENCES

The organization is not affiliated with any political party in Israel. It has the following contacts abroad: Moreshet Avot, 21 Albert Drive, Monsey, New York 10952 and Moreshet Avot 35 Paget Road, London, N16 5 ND England.

FUNDING NEEDED

1. Organizing study assembly days for high school students. Estimated cost: $30,000.
2. Organizing summer camp seminars. Estimated cost: $25,000.
3. The publication of printed material, including *"Mach'shevet"* magazine, weekly *Sabbath Digest, To the Sources,* V. 1 & 2, *Guide for Jewish Soldiers, Life Stories of Repenters,* and others. Estimated cost: $70,000.

MOSDOT KIRYAT SANZ מוסדות קרית צאנז

5 Divrei Chaim
Kiryat Sanz, Netanya
Telephone: (053) 32886
Office hours: 8:00 A.M. to 4:00 P.M.

HISTORY AND DESCRIPTION
Kiryat Sanz was founded in 1955 by the world reknowned chassidic leader, the Admor of Klausenburg—Harav Yekutiel Halberstam. The Kiryah is a self-contained village of over 300 families.

Organizational Structure: In order to fulfill the needs of his organization the Rebbe has established a network of schools in Kiryat Sanz, Jerusalem, Tel Aviv, Haifa, Bnei Brak, and Safed. Education begins at age 3 and the Rebbe is especially interested and involved in his post-graduate schools of higher learning (Kollel).

Goals: The philosophy of Kiryat Sanz is based on the observance and study of the Torah, together with the idea of servicing the physical needs of the entire Israeli people.

Services, Activities, and Accomplishments: The Rebbe has established a number of institutions to serve the general public. These include Laniado Hospital, the only hospital in the town of Netanya and serves the needs of a population of 140,000. There are also a children's orphanage, old age home, free loan funds, free apartments for poor families, synagogues, and a mikvah.
The Rebbe also established a school to train registered nurses, and construction has now begun on a new home to serve the needs of those who cannot care for themselves.
The organization's major accomplishments until now have been the establishment of a network of religious schools and the construction of Laniado Hospital.

OFFICERS
President: Rabbi Tzvi Elimelech Halberstam.
                       Kiryat Sanz, Netanya.
                       Rabbi. Tel. (053) 32887.
Treasurer: Gershon Lieder, 10 Divrei Chaim,
                       Kiryat Sanz, Netanya.
                       Officer. Tel. (053) 32887.
Board Members: Shia Weitzenblum, 1 Divrei Chaim,
                       Kiryat Sanz, Netanya. Tel. (053) 39241.
                       Yehuda Gevirts, Zais Ranan,
                       Kiryat Sanz, Jerusalem. Tel. (02) 816730.

FINANCIAL INFORMATION
10% of last year's annual budget came from membership dues, 40% came from donations, and the remaining 50% came from the Israeli

government. Last year's annual budget was $3 million. Donations to the institutions are tax-free both in Israel and the United States, but the numbers were not supplied. It was also not indicated whether the organization was registered as an Ottoman Association. There are 250 full-time employees and 125 volunteers.

MEMBERSHIP, SCOPE, AND POLICY
The organization is not affiliated with any political party in Israel, and is not in contact with any organizations abroad.

FUNDING NEEDED
1. The construction of a home for the chronically ill. Cost: $1 million.
2. The construction of a new dormitory for boys. Cost: $600,000.
3. The construction of a major new synagogue in Jerusalem.
   Cost: $1 million.

MOSLEM WOMEN CHARITY ORGANIZATION

אגודת הצדקה לנשים מוסלמיות

Nazareth, Eastern Quarter, Street Number 708.
No Telephone.
Office hours: 2:00 P.M. to 6:00 P.M. daily, except Sundays.

HISTORY AND DESCRIPTIONS
Founded in 1974, this organization was set up by a group of women who felt the need for a self-help effort for Moslem women in Nazareth.

Organizational Structure: The Board consists of fifteen members, five of those elected directly by members.

Goals: Educational, cultural, social and religious activities to give women a chance to meet each other and to offer their services to the community, each according to her abilities.

Services, Activities, and Accomplishments: The association helps poor families by donations or buying school books and clothes for children who cannot afford to have them, passes out food to poor families in feastive seasons, organizes a club for youths between 12 and 18, plans trips for relief and pleasure and education of housewives, and gives courses in handicrafts and languages. Future plans call for a home for the elderly, a club for youth, and nursery school, depending on finances.

OFFICERS
Director:	Aniseh Daher, 21/604 P.O. Box 283. Housewife. Tel. (065) 55180.
Treasurer:	Raoofe Zubi, 201, Private house. Tel. (065) 55696.
Board Members:	Kamle Natour, P.O.B. 122. Housewife. Tel. (065) 54797.
	Afaf Saadi, 21/1001. Housewife. Tel. (065) 54797.
	Moudi Zubi, 46/604. Housewife. Tel. (065) 54382.
	Zahida Abed, Eastern quarter. Teacher.
	Kair Zubi, 202 Private house. Teacher.

FINANCIAL INFORMATION
77% of the income comes from donations and 23% from membership dues. The annual budget last year for the association was $520. One full-time employee and ten volunteers work there. The association is registered in Nazareth as an Ottoman Association (number 415/3). Donations are tax-free in Israel.

MEMBERSHIP, SCOPE, AND POLICY
Membership is open to any woman over age 18. There are 250 members in Israel. Decisions are made by a Board majority vote.

FUNDING NEEDED

1. To acquire an apartment or build one, for the organization where more and more services could take place.
2. To obtain a steady monthly income of $200 for expenses and activities.
3. To pay qualified teachers for various activities.

MOUNT ZION DAY CARE CENTER

מעון יום לילדים – הר ציון

P.O.B. 6426
Mt. Zion, Jerusalem
Telephone: (02) 716841
Office hours: 7:30 A.M. to 2:00 P.M.

HISTORY AND DESCRIPTION
The Mt. Zion Day Care Center commenced activities in 1979 in stone rooms on Mt. Zion and is now in the process of being relocated in a separate building.

Organizational Structure: The Center has a Rosh Yeshiva who acts as spiritual leader, an Executive Director, and a staff of trained nursery teachers and assistants.

Goals: To provide first-class facilities for the care of children of young married families, mainly living in the Jewish Quarter of the Old City of Jerusalem.

Services, Activities, and Accomplishments: The present facilities provide for twenty-five children, and the completion of the new building will enable a further fifty children to enjoy the Center's facilities.

OFFICERS
Director: Rabbi Dr. M. Goldstein.
　　　　　Tel. (02) 716841.
Treasurer: Rabbi Daniel Schultz.
Board Members: Reb David Rubin, Hameshorerim 1, Jerusalem.
　　　　　Tel. (02) 281281.
　　　　　Reb David Sackton.
　　　　　Reb Ben Zion Freid.
　　　　　Reb Gedalia Goldstein, Givat Afeka, Ashkelon.
　　　　　Rabbi Dr. S.Z. Kahana, Givat Afeka 47, Ashkelon.

FINANCIAL INFORMATION
50% of last year's annual budget came from donations, and 25% from government sources, the balance deriving from membership dues. Last year's annual budget of $55,000 left the Center with a deficit of $5,500. The Mt. Zion Day Care Center is a recognized non-profit organization (Israel reg. no. 11/1433). Donations to the Center in Israel, the United States, Britain, and Canada are tax-free (Israel: no tax number supplied; USA: I.R.S. no. M-67-EO-529; Britain: no. 277919; Canada: no. 04201-74-4908). Six full-time and four part-time workers are employed by the Center.

MEMBERSHIP, SCOPE, AND POLICY
In its two branches the Mt. Zion Day Care Center has fifty members, membership being extended to children up to the age of three. The Center's decisions are taken mostly by the Executive Director.

AFFILIATIONS/REFERENCES

The Mt. Zion Day Care Center is politically unaffiliated in Israel. It maintains contact with Bnai Brith, 823 U.N. Plaza, New York, N.Y. 10017, U.J.A., 1290 Avenue of Americas, New York, N.Y. 10019, and N.C.S.Y., in New York City.

FUNDING NEEDED

1. To rebuild the existing premises—$60,000.
2. To provide fittings and furnishings—$20,000.
3. To remodel the kitchen—$10,000.

NATIONAL ASSOCIATION FOR WELFARE OF ANIMALS (NAWA)

אגודה לאומית לבריאות חיות (אלבח)

Kaf Tet Be November 30/15
Ramat Hannassi, Bat Yam
Telephone: (03) 594857 or (03) 860730 for messages
Office Hours: by arrangement

HISTORY AND DESCRIPTION

The reason for setting up this organization is because the present facilities for animal welfare are inadequate for the needs of the country. These facilities are operated by a variety of independent groups. The object of this society is to set up an organization similar to those found in modern European countries, with a central main administrative and training unit staffed by professionally-trained people. This Association will serve as an "umbrella" for a national network for local units and to provide training for local managers, instructors, inspectors, etc., and to provide central organization, technical assistance.

The Association will also direct a national education programme to raise and maintain standards in all aspects of animal welfare.

OFFICERS

President: R.E. Lapidus, Kaf Tet Be November 30/15, Ramat Hannassi, Bat Yam. Accountant and Security Consultant. Tel. (03) 594857.

Secretary: S. Carmi, Rehov Eilat 40, Holon. Housewife. Tel. (03) 847247.

Treasurer: B. Lerner, Rehov Amir 19, Ramat Gan. Insurance Agent. Tel. (03) 743024.

Members: R. Seigne, Kaf Tet Be November 30/15, Ramat Hannassi, Bat Yam. Accounting Clerk and former Manager S.P.C.A. Tel Aviv.

Y. Simon, Rehov Wolfson 5, Holon. Cabinet-maker. Tel. (03) 878233.

G. Bengigi, Kaf Tet Be November 30/16, Ramat Hannassi, Bat Yam. Business Proprietor. Tel. (03) 590906.

L. Sachs, Rehov Amir 31, Romema, Haifa. Clerk. Tel. (04) 251210.

FINANCIAL INFORMATION

No budget or deficit figures were supplied. At the moment the organization has applied for non-profit Ottoman Association status and for a permit for donations to be tax-free. At the present time, all the work of the Association is being done by the President in an attempt to bring the society into existence.

MEMBERSHIP, SCOPE, AND POLICY

Anyone interested can join. Major decisions are made by the Executive Director on a daily basis and by the National Board for ratification of major decisions.

FUNDING NEEDED

1. To establish a central administration/training unit.
2. To provide mobile training/education unit.
3. To send instructors on professional training courses outside Israel.

N'EMANAY TORAH V'AVODAH

נאמני תורה ועבודה

c/o Dr. Yehezkiel Cohen
6/B Beth She'arim Street
Kiryat Moshe, Jerusalem
Telephone: (02) 531032
Office hours: 5:00 P.M. to 8:00 P.M.

HISTORY AND DESCRIPTION

The National Religious community has in the past few years become influenced by outlooks and life styles originating in the Agudat Yisrael religious camp. These influences are mostly felt among the youth, and we feel that they are mainly expressed by the following tendencies: (1) To return the Jewish woman to her previous status, i.e. to her domestic role and all that follows; (2) to erect a society of separate realms for men and women; (3) to restrict secular studies in the schools (sciences, non-Jewish culture, etc.) to a minimum so that the study of Torah becomes practically the sole academic discipline; (4) to place the study of Torah before all else—including societal problems and compulsory army service; (5) to emphasize the importance of those commandments between man and G-d at the expense of interpersonal commandments. We feel that if this philosophy will spread, the National Religious community will regress from a society that seeks to build a State based upon Torah principles to a religious sect that concentrates its energies solely upon the study of Torah. This ideology has already been somewhat successful on the National Religious scene. These concepts conflict with the original philosophy of religious Zionism, whose bywords were Torah V'Avodah (Torah and Labor) and Torah Im Derech Eretz, which does not rule out secular knowledge. The authentic, original religious Zionism sought to build a religious society based upon Torah principles, in which the Jewish woman's status was respected, its sons occupied themselves in the various pursuits of building a Jewish State and studied Torah as well, and in which concern for one's fellow man, in the spirit of the interpersonal commandments, occupied a central role. The goal of N'emanay Torah V'Avodah is to buttress the position of religious Zionism's original postulates through dissemination of oral and written information and through an organization which will identify members as a united force.

Services, Activities, and Accomplishments: The organization has been successful in bringing the dangers that lie ahead to the attention of a portion of the National Religious community. We have encouraged their continued awareness to developments on the religious and national scenes and have supported their resolve and adherence to basic National Religious ideology.

OFFICERS
Director: Dr. Y. Cohen, 6/B Beth She'arim, Jerusalem.
Tel. 531032.

Treasurer:	Mrs. H. Safrai, 14 Avshalom Haviv, Jerusalem. Instructor, Bar Ilan University.
Board Members:	Dr. A. Nuriel, 80 Midbar Sinai, Jerusalem. Instructor, Bar Ilan University.
	Mr. E. Ben-Naeh, 50 Hapalmach, Jerusalem. Supervisor, Ministry of Education.
	Mr. S. Rosner, 15 Midbar Sinai, Jerusalem. Israel Government Information Office.
	Mr. Z. Gamliel, 18 Hapalmach, Jerusalem. Ministry of Social Welfare.
	Dr. A. Laslo, 5 Mavo Hamavak, Jerusalem. Instructor, Bar Ilan University.
	Rabbi M. Nehorai, 12 Baal Hash'iltot, Jerusalem. Instructor, Bar Ilan University.

FINANCIAL INFORMATION

75% of last year's annual budget came from membership dues, the remaining 25% came from donations. Last year's annual budget was $11,500 with no deficit since the activities were restricted to budgetary capabilities. The organization is not registered as an Ottoman Association. Donations to the organization are not tax-free, neither in Israel nor in the United States. There is one part-time worker employed by the organization, plus 22 volunteers.

MEMBERSHIP, SCOPE, AND POLICY

Decisions are made mostly by the Executive Director. There are 980 members in five branches in Israel; there are none abroad. Any and every Jew, whether in Israel or the diaspora, who professes allegiance to and observes the Torah and Mitzvot (commandments), may join N'emanay Torah V'Avodah.

AFFILIATIONS/REFERENCES

While N'emanay Torah V'Avodah is an apolitical organization, some of its members who are also members of the National Religious Party (Mafdal) together with the Religious Kibbutz Movement have formed a faction within the NRP.

FUNDING NEEDED

1. To raise funds for projects (printing of informational pamphlets, booklets, etc., transportation of speakers, and postage fees).
2. To secure personnel for written and oral public relations and informational productions.
3. To secure personnel for organizational technical purposes.

NER RAFAEL FOUNDATION קרן נר רפאל

Sde Chemed St. 25,
Jerusalem.
Telephone: (02) 281793.
Office Hours: 9:00 A.M. to 1:00 P.M., 3:00 P.M. to 7:00 P.M.

HISTORY AND DESCRIPTION
Ner Rafael Foundation was founded by a Jerusalem resident who wanted to distribute money to the needy. He approached his relatives and requested that they give him their *ma'asser* money (the 10% of his income which a Jew is obligated to donate to charity). They told their friends and gradually, as word spread, he began to receive relatively large sums of money to give to poor families. Today, a group of prominent rabbis is in charge of distributing the funds received.

Services, Activities and Accomplishments: Primarily, the organization gives relatively large amounts on a one-time basis, for such purposes as weddings, the establishment of a home, operations and other medical expenses. Hoewever, a percentage of the needy who are served by the organization receive a regular monthly stipend. In addition, Ner Rafael distributes money to needy families before each Yom Tov (holiday). Other services of the organization include helping people become religious; awarding prizes to youngsters to encourage them to study Torah; and helping the needy to purchase or rent apartments.

OFFICERS
Director: Rabbi Yehuda Tzadka, Yoel 9, J-m.
                        Rosh Yeshiva. No Telephone.
Treasurer: Rabbi Chaim Yitzhak Aryeh. Sde Chemed 25,
                        Jerusalem. Retired.
                        Tel. (02) 424377.
Board Members: Rabbi Avdul Aziz Sasoon, Haggai 10, Jerusalem.
                        Retired.
                        Benin Benin, Horkaniyah 22, Jerusalem.
                        Accountant.
                        Tel. (02) 635098.
                        Rabbi Moshe Chaim Aryeh, Sde Chemed 25,
                        Jerusalem. Rabbi.
                        Tel. (02) 281793.
                        Dr. Simai, Smilanski 68, Netanya. Gynecologist.
                        Rafael Aryeh, New York City. Urban Development.

FINANCIAL INFORMATION
The organization's income is derived solely from donations. Last year's annual budget was $4,000, with a deficit of $2,000 for the period. Donations to the organization in Israel are tax-free (no tax number supplied). In the U.S.A., tax-free status is pending. The organization is registered as a non-profit Ottoman Association in the Jerusalem District Office of the Ministry of the Interior (reg. no. 11/3227). Ten volunteers make up the staff of the organization.

MEMBERSHIP, SCOPE, AND POLICY
Anyone who will offer help is approved by the Board for membership in the Foundation. Currently, there is one branch in Israel with 7 members. A branch is being organized abroad which currently includes 3 members. Decisions concerning the organization in Israel are made mostly by the National Board.

AFFILIATIONS/REFERENCES
The organization is not connected with any political party in Israel. It is affiliated with the Ohr HaEmet organization in Toronto, Canada.

FUNDING NEEDED
1. To aid young Torah scholars who need money to get married—at least $200,000.
2. To provide assistance to poor families—at least $100,000.

NEVE ERETZ YESHIVA AND YOUTH VILLAGE

Jabotinsky Street   ישיבת נוה ארץ וחטיבת ביניים
P.O.B. 28
Be'er Yaacov
Telephone: (054) 24144 and 24199
Office hours: 8:30 A.M. to 6:00 P.M.

HISTORY AND DESCRIPTION

The Neve Eretz school was founded in 1967 in Be'er Ya'acov, in order to restore to the Sephardi community its former splendor and glory. Be'er Ya'acov, a small township outside Tel Aviv, became the location of a Yeshiva which would create a reservoir from which would emerge a new generation of spiritual leaders and teachers for Sephardi communities all over the world.

Goal: Neve Eretz was founded to provide a comprehensive Jewish education and to imbue each student with a sense of pride in his Oriental background and heritage. The most modern methods of instruction were adapted to ensure individual attention and combined with a high academic level.

The Six-Day War brought a new wave of immigration from North-African countries. Neve Eretz, sensitive to the needs of the Sephardi community, was ready to help and care for these immigrant youths to ensure that they continue in the sacred path of their parents and grandparents.

In its first decade Neve Eretz had already graduated hundreds of students. The majority have continued their education in higher schools of learning, and many will surely become prominent Rabbis and spiritual leaders. The high level of education acquired at Neve Eretz, together with the great stress on character and building of personality gives each student a solid basis for any path in life which he chooses. Neve Eretz specializes in personal instruction and in a qualified and devoted staff which maintains close ties with students even after they have left the school.

Services, Activities, and Accomplishments: The accomplishments of the organization are the hundreds of graduates, who today hold important positions in Israeli social life.

OFFICERS

Director: Rabbi E. Rafoul, Be'er Ya'acov. Rabbi.
                    Tel. (03) 780329.
Treasurer: Rabbi Z. Taunsky, Be'er Ya'acov.
                    Tel. (03) 784075.
Board Members: Mr. J. Zayat, 8 Rabbi Ami St., B'nei Brak.
                    Mr. Y. Ades, 14 Hazayit St., Jerusalem.
                    Mr. S. Rafoul, 26 David Yelin St., Jerusalem.
                    Mr. M. Grilak, 20 Yehuda Halevy St., Tel Aviv.
                    Dr. Pacifici, Kfar Haroeh.

FINANCIAL INFORMATION
Half of last year's annual budget came from donations and half came from various government Ministries. Last year's annual budget of $480,000 left the Yeshiva with a deficit of $160,000. It is registered as an Ottoman Association (registration number 11-818). Donations to the Yeshiva are tax-free in Israel (number 4502858) and in the U.S.A. (No. M-73-E-1377). There are 36 full-time and 28 part-time employees connected with the Yeshiva.

MEMBERSHIP, SCOPE, AND POLICY
Most decisions are made by the Executive Director. There are two branches of the Yeshiva.

AFFILIATIONS
The Yeshiva is not affiliated with an Israeli political party.

FUNDING NEEDED
1. An auditorium and synagogue, at an estimated cost of $200,000.
2. An additional dormitory building, at an estimated cost of $150,000.
3. A gymnasium, at an estimated cost of $100,000.
4. Scholarship funds.

THE NEW ISRAEL FUND

הקרן החדשה לישראל

52 Charlap St., P.O.B. 4156
Jerusalem
Telephone: (02) 635826
Office hours: Mondays and Thursdays, 9:00 A.M. to 1:00 P.M.

HISTORY AND DESCRIPTION

The New Israel Fund was established by a group of young American friends of Israel in 1979 in California as a Public Charity under Section 510 (c) 3 509 (a) 1 of the U.S. Internal Revenue Code and registered in Israel as a foreign, non-profit institution. Simultaneously a group of veteran Israeli social activists were invited to establish the Israeli committee.

Organizational Structure: The fund is administered by a Board of Trustees in the U.S. and a parallel Board of Israelis. The U.S. Board is responsible for development of policy, fund raising and educational outreach. The Israeli committee shares responsibility for the development of policy, and constitutes the distribution and review committee for the fund. The Israeli committee receives and reviews all requests for grants, giving priority to proposals from grass-roots organizations which have organized to influence social policy and better their lot in Israeli society. It follows-up on grants made by the fund to determine whether projects approved have been carried out according to the original proposal. The fund is an innovative mechanism for funding non-conventional social welfare and community organization programs.

Goals: The fund seeks to provide financial support for community-based programs attempting to affect the quality of life in Israel. Main areas of interest are: Community Organization, Civil Liberties, Women's Rights, Environment, Arab-Jewish Relations, Information and Networking.

Services, Activities, and Accomplishments: In the first funding cycle (April, 1980) 22 grants ranging from $1,000 to $5,000 were awarded to projects in the following categories: Social Action, Civil Rights, Innovative Services, Women's Projects, Arab-Jewish Relations.

OFFICERS
Israeli Board

Members:	Avner Amiel, Jerusalem. Community Worker.
	Rabbi Zefania Drori, Kiryat Shmona. Rabbi.
	Miriam Eytan, Coordinator, New Israel Fund.
	Ruth Raznick, Director, Herzliya Women's Shelter.
	Lotte Salzberger, Jerusalem. Member, City Council.
(Chairman):	Prof. Eliezer D. Jaffe, School of Social Work, Hebrew University.

	Dr. Naomi Kies, Social Science Faculty, Hebrew University.
	Dov Koler, Member, Association for Civil Liberties.
	Dr. David Kretzmer, Law Faculty, Hebrew University.
	Niva Lanir, Journalist, "Davar".
(Director):	Marta Ramon.

FINANCIAL INFORMATION

The sources of income for the fund are made up of donations. The budget for the first half of 1980 was $85,000. The fund is registered as a non-profit foreign company operating in Israel and donations in the U.S. are tax-free (I.R.S. Number 94-2607722). The fund is staffed by one part-time worker and twelve volunteers.

MEMBERSHIP, SCOPE, AND POLICY

The New Israel Fund is not a membership organization.

Decisions are made by the Israeli and American Committees. The fund operates only in Israel and awards grants of up to $10,000 to non-profit and non-governmental groups only.

AFFILIATIONS/REFERENCES

The Fund has no affiliations with political parties in Israel. Affiliation abroad is with the New Israel Fund, 22 Miller Ave., Mill Valley, CA. 94941.

FUNDING NEEDED

1. To answer more requests for funding, especially of demonstration programs.
2. To provide capital expenses, including facilities and administrative costs of various volunteer groups whose project proposals have been approved by the Israeli Committee.
3. For a part-time field worker to review and provide feedback on projects supported by the Fund.

NITZAN—ASSOCIATION FOR CHILDREN WITH DEVELOPMENTAL AND LEARNING DISABILITIES

ניצן, אגודה לקידום ילדים לקויי למידה והסתגלות

Peretz Hiot Street 5
Tel Aviv
Telephone: (03) 281143
Office hours: Sunday-Thursday, 8:00 A.M. to 1:00 P.M.

HISTORY AND DESCRIPTION

Nitzan was founded by volunteers in 1963 with the aim of helping children who suffer from developmental and learning disabilities, and their parents. The problems of these children show up in two basic areas: behaviour, and learning (reading, writing and arithmetic). The first special school was opened after pressure from Nitzan in the 1960's. Today there are four such schools in the country, and 300 special classes in regular schools. In addition, special kindergartens are being opened.

Services, Activities, and Accomplishments: Nitzan gives financial assistance for various treatments, eg. speech therapy, physiotherapy, psychotherapy, and play, dance and music therapy. The organization also subsidizes private school lessons. Nitzan organizes volunteers to help parents and children and arrange summer camps for children. Afternoon youth clubs have been set up to help in the "social integration" of these children. Nitzan organizes sessions of instruction for parents where they can receive professional guidance. The organization represents these children's needs to all Government agencies, and is a member of a group pressing for new laws to guarantee the future education and rehabilitation of the children. Nitzan set up a Pedagogical Center where specialists in this field can obtain professional literature and such items as games, toys, diagnostic tests, etc., for the educational institutions at which they work. Nitzan's major accomplishments have been the opening of two special schools in Tel Aviv, and of special classes in regular schools, in addition to special afternoon youth clubs. It has also increased public awareness of the problems of these children.

OFFICERS

Director: Moshe Drori, Remez 34, Tel Aviv.
Builder/contractor.
Tel. (03) 448331.

Treasurer: Jehudit Tamir, Frenkel 8, Tel Aviv.
Tel. (03) 412093.
Fany Tané, Stricker 42, Tel Aviv. Housewife.
Tel. (03) 456530.

FINANCIAL INFORMATION

20% of last year's annual budget came from donations, 60% from the City Council (Tel Aviv Municipality), 5% from the Municipality's

Welfare Department, and 15% from fund-raising activities (bazaars, etc.). Last year's annual budget was $46,000; there was no deficit. Donations in Israel are tax-free (registration number 4504670), but not in the United States. The Association is registered as an Ottoman Association (Tel Aviv, reg. no. 3622/99). Three part-time workers are employed by Nitzan and there are 150 volunteers.

MEMBERSHIP, SCOPE, AND POLICY
There are five branches in Israel, but no official members since the people needing Nitzan's help vary from year to year. Nitzan has groups of "friends", many of them parents of the children in question, who help with fund-raising. Many parents are unwilling to become involved with Nitzan through fear of the stigma that may be attached to their child for being "different". Most children with learning disabilities are not immediately distinguishable from ordinary children, and parents often hide the fact of the child's disability even though they may be receiving help of some kind from Nitzan. Statistics show that up to 10% of all children suffer from some kind of learning disability. Any person over the age of 18 years can join. Decisions are made by the National Board. The organization is not affiliated with any political party in Israel.

FUNDING NEEDED
1. To establish a Diagnostic and Treatment Center, with facilities for testing and helping children, physiotherapy, remedial teaching, speech therapy, handicraft and play therapy, as well as counselling for parents and children.
2. To fund a scholarship for helping children on an individual basis. Each lesson costs about $8 and the child needs two to three lessons a week during most of the school year.
3. To set up a special fund for information services to mother-and-child clinics, kindergarten teachers, etc., so as to make the public more aware of these children and make early diagnoses possible.

NOTZAR CHESSED

מפעל סיוע מרכזי נוצר חסד

Batei Ungarin 201
P.O.B. 5619, Jerusalem.
Telephone: (02) 280214.
Office Hours: 10:00 A.M. to 1:00 P.M., 4:00 P.M. to 7:00 P.M.

HISTORY AND DESCRIPTION
Notzar Chessed was founded in 1973. Among its activities is the free
distribution of food to over 2,000 poor and needy families daily, and
especially before Shabbos and Yom-Tovim (holidays); and the sale of
grocery products, fruit and vegetables to low-income families at specially reduced prices.

Goals: The organization's first priority is to pay its bills for Passover
supplies purchased from the Tnuva Co. in Israel ($50,000). Another
important goal is to raise money for the purchase of tables, chairs and
dishes to be loaned to poor families for wedding celebrations, etc. The
organization also hopes to gather enough funds to establish a hospitality center which would provide food and sleeping accommodations for
the many people who visit the holy places in Meron (near Safed),
especially the burial place of Rabbi Shimon Bar Yochai.

Services, Activities and Accomplishments: Every Passover since the
organization's founding 7 years ago, approximately 2,000 families have
received free supplies of food and other needed items. Free daily distribution of food, grocery supplies and Sabbath needs has been established
and maintained. A store has been set up to sell household goods and
food at lower prices to poor families. The organization also manages a
storehouse of tables, chairs and dishes which are loaned out to needy
families for simchas (celebrations), without any charge.

OFFICERS
Director: Rabbi Meir Grossman, Batei Ungarin 201, Jerusalem.
                    Rabbi.

Board
Members: Rabbi David Neuhaus, Malchei Yisrael 4, Jerusalem.
                    Rabbi Yitzhak Shisha, Batei Ungarin 162, Jerusalem.
                    Rabbi Dov Valler, HaCheresh 5, Jerusalem.
                    Rabbi Chaim Lederman, Salant ,15, Jerusalem.
                    Rabbi Menachem Deutsch, Chagi 12, Jerusalem.
                    Rabbi Ze'ev Greenberger, Beis Yisrael, Jerusalem.

FINANCIAL INFORMATION
The organization's sole source of income is from donations. Last year's
annual budget was $50,000. Deficit for the same period came to $20,000.
Donations to the organization in the United States are tax-free (I.R.S.
no. 13733300-EO). The organization is registered as a non profit Ottoman Association in the Jerusalem District Office of the Ministry of the

Interior (reg. no. 11/2301). Eight full-time and four part-time workers are employed by the organization, along with 4 volunteers.

MEMBERSHIP, SCOPE, AND POLICY
Notzar Chessed has no dues-paying members as such, but encompasses 3,000 recipients of aid and 2,300 contributors (300 in Israel and 2,00 abroad). Most decisions are made by the 7-member national board, including the approval of candidates for aid. There is 1 branch of the organization in Israel and 1 branch abroad.

AFFILIATIONS/REFERENCES
Notzar Chessed is affiliated with the Agudas Israel Organization in New York City (address: 5 Beekman St., New York, N.Y. 10038). It has no affiliation with any political party in Israel.

FUNDING NEEDED
1. To build apartments (low-cost rental units) for poor families in Jerusalem— $2 million.
2. To build a yeshiva for Baalei Teshuva (rehabilitation of convicts, "society dropouts", and those wishing to return to Judaism)—$2 million.
3. To maintain on-going projects: $50 will provide support for one family for one month; $100 will provide Passover food for one family; $1,000 can establish a fund in the name of the donor for dishes, tables and chairs to be loaned to poor families for their simchas.

THE OFARIM ORGANIZATION FOR THE ADVANCEMENT OF CULTURALLY DISADVANTAGED CHILDREN

אגודת עופרים – לקידום הילד הטעון טיפוח

3 Bar Tenura Street
Jerusalem
Telephone: (02) 638485
Office Hours: 8:00 P.M. to 10:00 P.M.

HISTORY AND DESCRIPTION

The program was born out of a general examination of the failings of education and instruction resulting from weakness in the language ability of the children, particularly those from disadvantaged homes; it was also clear that the poverty of language and expression did not further the general learning processes of children. A growing number of educators felt that the routine methods of language teaching did not contribute adequately to the creation of the linguistic tools required for the various subjects to be learned.

The initiator of the project therefore considered ways of rehabilitating the language of the learner by non-conventional means, work in psycho-drama and other psycho-linguistic applications. Volunteer teams created model lessons, models of teacher training such as language games, courses, teaching manuals of various kinds for the use of hundreds of teachers, and above all, workbooks for the pupils and teacher. The country was divided for training purposes into thirty areas in which hundreds of teachers would gather to observe lessons, to analyze their presentation, and then embark on their work of rehabilitation.

The experience of years has shown that the children with language disabilities come mainly from disadvantaged families or from Special Education schools and therefore have made progress because of their contact with "graduate" teachers of the Ofarim program.

Organizational Structure: OFARIM requires courses for teachers to be given in the various centers by a panel of academic (pedagogical) teachers. Considerable educational resources required for publishing psycho-pedagogical material for teachers were gathered, as well as supplementary supportive material for the children. The organization operates with a limited team on a daily basis, mornings and afternoons; despite the limitations, the Ministry of Education and Culture has examined this educational instrument and found it extremely efficient. However, due to its budgetary difficulties, the Ministry of Education allocates only a limited sum to the organization.

Goals: The organization is working to print publications for pupils and teachers, and aims to develop instructions and lecture courses for teachers.

Services, Activities, and Accomplishments: The organization has seen a substantial improvement in the language skills of children at different age groups, in their ability to express themselves in their thought processes.

OFFICERS

Director:	Z. Korech, 3 Bartenura St., Jerusalem. Educator. Tel.: (02) 638485.
Treasurer:	M. Nesher, 16 Radak St.
Board Members:	S. Lerer, Deputy Director, Ministry of Transport. E. Ranel, 4 Sheshet Haymim.St. Accountant.

FINANCIAL INFORMATION

100% of the organization's budget comes from the Ministry of Education; last year's budget totalled $21,000. OFARIM is registered as an Ottoman Society (reg. no. not supplied). Donations to OFARIM are tax-free in Israel (reg. no. not supplied). Three part-time workers are employed by the organization, in addition to thirty-five volunteers.

MEMBERSHIP, SCOPE, AND POLICY

Decisions are made by the Committee for Primary Education in the Ministry of Education; however, anyone who wishes to join the organization is welcome to become a member.

FUNDING NEEDED

1. To print publications for teachers and pupils.
2. To develop and produce instructions and lecture courses for teachers.
3. To employ a larger number of excellent teachers available to participate in the Ofarim program.

OHR ELCHONON YESHIVA—
MEOR YERUSHALAYIM

ישיבת "אור אלחנן" – מאור ירושלים

OFFICE:
18 Even Haezel Street,
Jerusalem
Telephone: (02) 813666
Office hours: 8:30 A.M. to 2:00 P.M.

BEIS MEDRASH:
16, Ezrat Torah,
P.O.B. 5662
Jerusalem

HISTORY AND DESCRIPTION
Yeshiva Ohr Elchonon was founded in 1977 by Rabbi Meir Chodosh, of
the Chevron Yeshiva, together with Rabbi Simcha Wasserman in
memory of Rav Elchonon Wasserman, who perished during the Holocaust in the Kovno Ghetto. The Yeshiva now has an enrollment of 80
boys, aged 17-24 as well as 20 married men who continue their Torah
studies.

Goals: To use progressive educational methods, to train the students to
become leaders of world Jewry. The boys receive devoted attention
from the members of the staff, and are encouraged to cultivate their
potential for the benefit of their nation.

Services, Activities, and Accomplishments: The services and activities of
the Yeshiva serve the neighboring communities as well. Lessons in
Talmud, daily prayer services and lectures on topics of general interest
are open to the public.
Plans are now being made to construct an Ohr Elchonon Village. This
educational complex will include academic and residential facilities,
which will be available to new immigrants.
The Yeshiva has produced top rate students who have continued their
studies in institutes of higher learning.

OFFICERS:
Director: Rabbi Meir Chodosh, 25 Chagai Jerusalem
                   Rabbi Simcha Wasserman, 15 Panim Meirot,
                      Jerusalem.
                   Rabbi Moshe Chodosh, 12 Nechemiyah,
                      Jerusalem. Dean.
                      Tel. (02) 286549.
Treasurer: Rabbi Avezer Piltz, 4 Haerez, Jerusalem.
Board Members: Rabbi Mordechai Krashinsky, 24 Kiryat Zanz,
                      Jerusalem.
                      Tel. (02) 815696.
                   Rabbi Shemaryah Grossnass, 14 Elkanah,
                      Jerusalem.
                      Tel. (02) 817271.

FINANCIAL INFORMATION
The sources of last year's annual budget were as follows: government funds, 25%; donations, 50%; miscellaneous, 25%. The annual budget for last year was $180,000, with a deficit of $45,000. The Yeshiva is registered as an Ottoman Association (reg. no. 11/ 2943), and is registered as a tax-free charity in the United States (no. 13026109EO) and in U.K. (no. 281540). There are 6 full-time and two part-time workers employed by the Yeshiva.

MEMBERSHIP, SCOPE, AND POLICY
There are seven members in Israel, none abroad. There are two branches abroad and one in Israel. Decisions are made by the National Board.

AFFILIATIONS/REFERENCES
The Yeshiva is not affiliated with any political party in Israel. It has the following contacts abroad: Yeshiva Gedolah of Lakewood, Lakewood, New Jersey, Rabbi S. Kotler, Dean; Gateshead Yeshiva, Rabbi L. Gurewicz, Gateshead, England; and West Coast Talmudical Seminary, Kings Road, Los Angeles, California.

FUNDING NEEDED
1. To construct new dormitories to house additional students.
2. To cover the various expenses incurred in the purchase of the present living quarters and dining room.
3. The construction of Kiryat Ohr Elchonon.

OHR SOMAYACH INSTITUTIONS —
THE JOSEPH AND FAYE
TANENBAUM COLLEGE

מוסדות אור שמח

Shimon Hatzadik Street 22-24
P.O.B. 18103
Ma'alot Dafna, Jerusalem
Office hours: 8:30 A.M. to 6:30 P.M.
Telephone: (02) 810315

HISTORY AND DESCRIPTION

Ohr Somayach was founded in 1972, in borrowed facilities, with a dozen students. A year later, the institution moved to its own facilities, and in 1977 the present campus was completed. Beginning with the Womens' branch in 1975, the institution has set up an additional 8 branches and regional centers, including Israeli branches for men and women, an American branch in Monsey, New York, a Canadian branch in Toronto, regional centers throughout Israel, and a community for immigrants in Zichron Yaakov.

Organizational Structure: The Central Directorship of Directors and Deans has authority over the operation of the institution.
Branches and departments are semi-autonomous, but over-all budget and policy is set by the Central Directorship.

Goals: Ohr Somayach is attempting to reverse the trend of alienation and assimilation among Jewish youth both in Israel and in the Diaspora, through intensive but personal programs in Jewish studies. It also actively encourages immigration to Israel, both by making students aware of the unique importance of Israel to the Jewish people and by actively supporting communities for the settlement of immigrants.

Services, Activities, and Accomplishments: Ohr Somayach has over 800 full-time students engaged in the study of Jewish history, philosophy, ethics, Talmud, law, and Hebrew language. There are also a number of outreach programs in Israel and the United States. Special seminars and lectures in Jewish studies are provided for officers of the Israel Defense Forces. There is a program to reach young Israeli kibbutz members through seminars, informal gatherings, and Shabbat programs. Special programs are provided in Israel, the U.S.A., Canada, England and South Africa for the summer and midyear college intercessions.
The school's major accomplishments until now have been the reaching of over 10,000 students from abroad with programs which range from one day to several years, over 15,000 Israelis, through seminars in branches throughout Israel and the publication of books, prize-winning magazines and other educational materials. Hundreds of its graduates have elected to settle in Israel.

OFFICERS

Director:	Rabbi Nota Schiller, Jerusalem. Educator. Tel. (02) 531051.
Board Members:	Rabbi Yaacov Rosenberg, Jerusalem. Educator. Tel. (02) 534094.
	Rabbi Dov Schwartzman, Jerusalem. Educator. Tel. (02) 816685.
	Rabbi Mendel Weinbach, Jerusalem. Educator. Tel. (02) 532003.
	Rabbi Yehoshua Kaplan, Jerusalem. Educator. Tel. (02) 523914.
	Mr. Joseph Tanenbaum, Toronto. Businessman.
	Mr. Bernard Hochstein, Jerusalem. Businessman. Tel. (02) 666026.

FINANCIAL INFORMATION

Fifty-five percent of last year's annual budget came from donations; forty percent came from Israel Government, Jewish Agency and organizational subsidies; and only five percent came from tuition. Last year's annual budget was $1 million and left the school with a deficit of $300,000. The institution is registered as an Ottoman Association (reg. no. 11/1331). Donations to the institution are tax-free in Israel, the United States, Canada and other countries (the numbers were not supplied). There are 48 full-time and 40 part-time employees, in addition to 26 volunteers.

MEMBERSHIP, SCOPE, AND POLICY

Members of the institution's Board are educators and businessmen concerned with Jewish education. The scope is an international one, reflecting the institution's policy of establishing programs in every community where it can elicit interest in serious Jewish learning and in immigration to Israel.

AFFILIATIONS/REFERENCES

The institution is not affiliated with any political party in Israel. It enjoys the support and encouragement of a number of Israel Government ministries and the Jewish Agency. Its activities in South Africa are in coordination with the Zionist Federation there and the Chief Rabbi's Office.

FUNDING NEEDED

1. The development of a program to reach 25,000 university students throughout the world who will study and settle in Israel. Cost: $10 million.
2. The construction of a Midrasha for seminars in Jewish studies for members of kibbutzim, and other groups who are part of Israel's secular society. Cost: $1 million.
3. Spanish, French, and Russian language departments, together with the existing English and Hebrew departments, in order to prepare religious educational leadership for the millions of Jews speaking those languages. Cost: $2 million.

4. Establishment of a settlement in Israel for graduates of the school who will apply their skills and professions to developing a self-sufficient community. Cost: $7.5 million.
5. The development of a Prison Rehabilitation Program, including expansion of the current educational activities in prisons throughout Israel and study days for prisoners at Ohr Somayach. The ultimate stage of this program will be the creation, in conjunction with the prison authorities, a special program for prisoners in the last phase of their prison life which will be conducted at the institution and geared towards maximizing rehabilitation and minimizing recidivism. Cost: $3 million.
6. The construction of an Audio-Visual Center to provide multi-media educational materials both for participants in the institution's international programs and for interested outsiders. Cost: $4 million.

OR CHADASH GIRLS' TOWN—THE EDUCATIONAL CENTER OF THE GALIL

אור חדש — מרכז חינוכי בגליל

P.O.B. 8, Kfar Chassidim/Rechasim
Telephone: (04) 952511/2/3/4
Office hours: 8:00 A.M. to 4:00 P.M.

HISTORY AND DESCRIPTION

Or Chadash was founded in 1965 to deal with the specific problems of Sephardic girls. The student body is drawn from development towns and immigrant villages from all over northern Israel. Academic and vocational programs are offered on a junior high- and high-school level, and graduates are awarded a certificate of matriculation. In 1972 a boys junior high-school was opened on an adjacent campus. This was followed by the opening of a yeshiva high-school in 1975.

Services, Activities, and Accomplishments: Today, 450 full-time students are enrolled in the various divisions. The school presently occupies a 40 acre rolling campus with ultra-modern facilities constructed with the help of the United States government and friends throughout the world. In order to reach out to more of Israel's disadvantaged youth, Or Chadash has created a network of after-school youth centers known as Karnei Or. There are currently twenty-five of these centers operating with close to 1000 children taking part in activities. Or Chadash also administers a number of free-loan funds to help graduates and poor families make ends meet. In the last calendar year, loans of $12,000 were made and another $10,000 was disbursed as outright grants. Graduates have gone on to further study in teachers' seminaries and universities and, because they were given a chance, have been able to assume constructive roles in Israeli society. Some of the graduates have returned as teachers in the organization's schools, and others have returned in similar capacities to their home communities.

OFFICERS

Directors:
Rabbi Moshe Tanami. Rabbi of Rechasim.
Tel. (04) 952266.
Rabbi Yehuda Melamed. Dean of the schools.
Tel. (04) 952323.

Treasurer:
Tzvi Deutscher.
Tel. (04) 640757.

Chairman of
the Board:
Chief Rabbi Ovadia Yosef.

Board Members:
Dr. Yehuda Ben Meir, M.K.
Aaron Uzan. President, Israeli Sephardic Federation.

FINANCIAL INFORMATION

50% of last year's anual budget came from various government bodies and Youth Aliya; the other 50% came from donations. Last year's operational budget was $650,000, which left the organization with a deficit of $160,000. Or Chadash is registered as a non-profit organization (Israel reg. no. 61/865). Donations in Israel, the United States, and Canada may be made tax-free (no tax number supplied). Or Chadash employs forty-three full-time and sixty-eight part-time workers, as well as forty volunteers (including Rabbi Tanami). Decisions are taken in weekly meetings of the Executive Committee.

AFFILIATIONS/REFERENCES
Or Chadash is politically unaffiliated in Israel. It maintains contact with the Agency for International Development, U.S. Department of State, Washington, D.C.; Young Men's Philanthropic League, 4 E. 80th Street, New York; and Or Chadash Girls' Town, 1114 Avenue J., Brooklyn, N.Y. 11230.

FUNDING NEEDED
1. To complete the combied clinic/library building on the girls' campus.
2. To complete the classroom building for the boys' junior high, which will include a central assembly hall for activities of Karnei Or youth centers.
3. To construct a physical education center and swimming pool for use by all divisions, as well as participants in summer camp programs.

OR-ETZION, B'NEI AKIVA YESHIVA HIGH-SCHOOL

ישיבת בני עקיבא, אור־עציון

Merkaz Shapira 79411
Telephone: (055) 82201
Office hours: 7:30 A.M. to 3:30 P.M.

HISTORY AND DESCRIPTION

The B'nei Akiva Yeshiva High-school "Or-Etzion" was founded in 1960 by the Regional Council of Shafir to perpetuate the memory of the fallen members of the Etzion Block settlements captured by the Jordan Legion in 1948. The Yeshiva educates its students in the spirit of the late Chief Rabbi Kook, towards a life of Torah study and observance.

Goals: The Yeshiva teaches its students to love the Jewish people as a whole, developing within them a dedication to the State of Israel, and encouraging them to fulfill pioneering tasks in the building and development of the State, with the builders and defenders of Etzion serving as their example.

Services, Activities, and Accomplishments: Almost four hundred students, from grade seven through twelve, study at the Yeshiva. Over one-third of the Yeshiva's students come from Sephardic communities living in development towns and immigrant villages in the southern parts of the country. Educationally and personally their integration within the school is complete. Two special seventh and eighth grade classes have an amplified Torah study program. Their secular studies follow the normal junior high-school program. A Yeshivat Hesder (combined military-academic program) was established three years ago, wherein military service and Yeshiva studies are combined in a five-year course. The school curriculum is standard in all the B'nei Akiva Yeshivot, and is certified by the Ministry of Education. The subjects studied are: Talmud on Yeshiva level, Bible, laws and customs, Jewish thought, Hebrew, mathematics, physics, chemistry, biology, geography, general and Jewish history, citizenship, and English. In addition to the school's program there are many extra-curricular educational and social activities provided through participation in the B'nei Akiva branches in the southern region of the country, and several branches were even founded by the Yeshiva's students. The group leaders are active in their branches throughout the year, spend Shabbat in their neighborhoods, and organize special activities, camp programs, and hikes during the various holidays. Much time and energy is devoted by the Rosh Yeshiva, Rabbi Chaim Druckman, towards reaching non-observant youths. Within the framework of these efforts, hundreds of teenagers from non-religious settlements and secular high-schools come to spend Shabbat at the Yeshiva.

OFFICERS

Head of the Yeshiva: Rabbi Chaim Druckman, Mercaz Shapira. Tel. (055) 82201.

Deputy Head of Yeshiva: Rabbi Jossef Kfir, Mercaz Shapira.
Tel. (055) 82003.
Principal of High-School: Rabbi Jacob Ne-tiv, Mercaz Shapira.
Administrative Director: Mr. Chaim Bar-Yesha, Mercaz Shapira.
Tel. (055) 84543.

FINANCIAL INFORMATION
40% of last year's annual budget came from government sources, a further 40% from tuition fees, the balance deriving from donations. Last year's annual budget of $375,000 left Or-Etzion with a deficit of $70,000. Decisions are mostly taken by the Director. Donations are not tax exempt, but can be channelled through the Friends organization in New York and through the B'nei Akiva Yeshivot Center in Israel.

AFFILIATIONS/REFERENCES
Or-Etzion is politically unaffiliated in Israel. It is in contact with Friends of Yeshivot B'nei Akiva in New York, and Shaarei Shamaim Synagogue, Montreal, Canada (Rabbi Shochat).

FUNDING NEEDED
1. To renovate the central study hall.
2. To renovate and repair dormitory buildings.
3. To renew furniture and equipment in the dormitories.

THE ORGANIZATION FOR THE ADVANCEMENT OF THE DISADVANTAGED NEIGHOURHOODS (JERUSALEM)

הארגון לקידום השכונות

P.O.Box 9086
Jerusalem
Telephone: (02) 520123
Office hours: 6:00-9:00 P.M.

HISTORY AND DESCRIPTION

In November 1976, three community organizers began working with a group consisting primarily of housewives protesting against the cancellation of government subsidies for basic necessities. The following year, the nucleus of the original group was joined by another 40 families who had been relocated from their homes into another of Jerusalem's underprivileged neighborhoods without adequate compensation. After a two-year fight, the organization succeeded in winning from local and governmental bodies partial compensation for the evacuees in the form of ownership of their new apartments. Since 1978, the organization has been fighting primarily for decent housing for the poor — large families and young couples — both on the local and national levels.

Organizational Structure: The organization is run by a Secretariat of 11 members. The Secretariat is elected by a General Assembly which is composed of activists and members representing all neighborhoods in Jerusalem.

Goals: The primary aim is to aid in the process of community self-organization in order to fight the causes of social deprivation. This can be done by a network of local self-help groups operating throughout the country. To this end, the organization's efforts are directed towards: a) raising the consciousness of local people so that they may understand their situation by themselves (individually and collectively); b) helping them define clearly their own needs and interests; and c) encouraging them to enter into community activities of a social, cultural and political nature. Through the raising of consciousness, citizens learn to get rid of paternalistic attitudes and leadership, and of habits of manipulation.

Services, Activities, and Accomplishments: The organization has fought against the governmental and municipal agencies' condescending attitude toward neighborhood people on the housing issue, and tries to influence housing policy. Methods used include press conferences, petitions, meetings with officials, public and private meetings in neighborhoods, demonstrations and rallies, leaflets and wall placards. Activity in Jerusalem is seen as a first step towards a nation-wide organization. Other groups, such as "Housing Now," have sprung up in the wake of this organization's efforts, and *ad hoc* groups in other cities joined with the Jerusalem group in 1979 to form the National Headquarters of Citizens in Housing Distress to work on housing issues only. To date, the organization has consolidated a strong group of voluntary activists in the neighborhoods and has instilled a sense of consciousness among them to their situation. Housing problems are kept in the forefront of the public consciousness as a national issue, and strong pressure has been maintained on official agencies to provide housing solutions. The next issue which the organization plans to concentrate on is education, from the point of view of neighborhood residents (e.g. more quality programs, greater public expenses, teachers, facilities, etc.).

OFFICERS

Director:	Catherine Hirsch, Elkabetz 48, Jerusalem. Teacher. Tel. (02) 520123.
Treasurer:	Gaby Wexler, Nabarta 5, J'm. Translator.
Board Members:	Michael Machpuda, Derech Hebron 113, Jerusalem. Employee.
	Carmela Assor, Rashbag 42, J'lm. Housewife.
	Mashiah Zargari, Derech Hebron 9, Jerusalem. Storekeeper.
	Esther Amar, Shmuel Hanavi 109, J'lem. Housewife.
	Shimon Izincor, Reuven 6, J'lm. Employee.
	Rachel Aiden, Holtsvanger 115, J'lm. Housewife. Tel. (02) 422507.
	Reuven Eini, Tuvia 4, J'lm. Driver. Tel. (02) 690666.
	Eli Davidian, Rashbag 17, J'lm. Employee.

FINANCIAL INFORMATION

Fifty percent of the Organization's funds last year came from membership dues; the other half was provided by donations from individuals and The New Israel Fund. Last year's budget of $3,600 left no deficit. The Organization is an Ottoman, non-profit Association, (registration no. 11/2871, Jerusalem District). Donations are stated to be tax-free both in Israel and in the U.S., (no exemption numbers were provided). There are no salaried staff; work is carried out by 50 volunteer workers.

MEMBERSHIP, SCOPE, AND POLICY

Today there are 50 active members from a number of underprivileged neighborhoods in Jerusalem, and about 900 non-active members. Any Israeli citizen who adopts the Organization's goals accepts its structure and joins its activities can be a member. Decisions are made by the 11-member Secretariat.

AFFILIATIONS/REFERENCES

Political activities or affiliations are strictly forbidden. A reference listed by the Organization is The New Israel Fund, 22 Miller Avenue, Mill Valley, California 94491 (address in Israel: P.O.B. 4156, Jerusalem; Tel. 02-635826).

FUNDING NEEDED

1. For rent money for a headquarters with enough room for 20-30 people to meet, $4,000.
2. For running expenses (maintenance, phone, electricity, postage), $1,000.
3. For publishing a monthly newspaper (typewriter, mimeograph, paper), $2,500.
4. To cover budget for public events (e.g., meetings, demonstrations, rallies), $2,000.

The basis for the figures is a 1-year budget.

ORGANIZATION FOR THE SAKE OF JUSTICE

הארגון למען הצדק

18 Harav Berlin Street Jerusalem
Telephone: (02) 630655 — (02) 699397
Office hours: 1:00 P.M. to 7:00 P.M., and by appointment.

HISTORY AND DESCRIPTION

The Organization for the Sake of Justice was organized in 1977 as a non-political, non-profit organization. It promotes moral principles in Israel, including an honest day's work, lower inflation, a rejection of extravagant living standards, and respect for one's fellow-man.

The organization also operates a non-profit matchmaking service, distributes used clothing and lobbies against social ills.

The major accomplishment of the organization until now has been its positive influence on important people, in and out of government service.

OFFICERS

Charles Katriel Pam, 18 Berlin, Jerusalem. Tel. (02) 630655.
Tova Gelbart, 18 Charlap, Jerusalem. Tel. (02) 668632.
Rabbi Aaron Rakeffet, 18 Berlin, Jerusalem. Tel. (02) 660941.
Rabbi Mendell Lewittes, 18 Berlin, Jerusalem. Tel. (02) 667195.
Prof. Abraham Goldberg, 35 Berlin, Jerusalem. Tel. (02) 634259.
Rabbi Zev K. Nelson, 8 Brodie, Jerusalem. Tel. (02) 630621.
Rabbi David Shisgal, 303/5 Kiryat Arba. Tel. (02) 971538.

FINANCIAL INFORMATION

10% of last year's annual budget came from membership dues, and the remaining 90% came from donations. The budget for last year was $5,000. The organization is registered as an Ottoman Association (no. 11/2782). Donations to the organization are tax-free in Israel (no. 4506304) but not in the United States. There are ten volunteers at the organization.

MEMBERSHIP, SCOPE, AND POLICY

There are over 300 members in the one Israeli branch. Decisions are made by the national board.

AFFILIATIONS/REFERENCES

The organization is not affiliated with any political party in Israel.

FUNDING NEEDED

1. The establishment of public meetings and lectures to further the positive aims. Estimated cost $6,000.
2. The establishment of additional branches in Haifa and Tel Aviv. Estimated cost — $6,000.
3. The expansion of the services to include free used clothing for the needy, interest free loans, and free matrimonial services (shiduchim). Estimated cost — $6,000.

ORGANIZATION OF YESHIVA STUDENTS OF THE NEGEV

התאחדות בני הישיבות בנגב

c/o Yeshivat Ofakim
P.O.B. 92
Ofakim
Telephone: none listed
Office hours: 9:00 A.M. to 1:00 P.M. and 3:00 P.M. to 7:00 P.M. during school vacations.

HISTORY AND DESCRIPTION
History and Organization: More than five years ago, Israel had a very serious problem: after every school holiday there was a drop-out rate of 40% of religious pupils from public schools who joined non-religious public schools or who left school altogether. Most of these children were from development towns, where the families are typically large, and where the parents themselves, having had little formal education, were not equipped to encourage and support the continuation of their studies. Many of the children who dropped out came from broken homes, and after spending school holidays on the street, they would be disinclined to resume studies in religious schools. Therefore, a branch operates in every city in the south during vacation periods.

Goals: To occupy and strengthen the students during the vacation, and to give them the proper environment, in order to bridge the gap between school terms; and to attract new students into religious schools.

Services, Activities, and Accomplishments: In the vacation atmosphere: outings, educational films, musical activities (choir, orchestra), lectures from important rabbis, Melave Malka, holiday parties and lessons; every participating pupil receives a prize of a book (this is a great incentive for the pupil to decide to enroll). 95% return during the following school vacation. One thousand students take part from the south of Israel.

The dropout rate of students from religious schools is virtually eliminated in areas of the organization's operation. Many new students were attracted to study in religious schools after participating in these programs.

OFFICERS
Board Members: Reuven Bitton, Ofakim. Yeshiva student.
    Tel. (02) 813303 (for messages).
Joseph Glick, Ofakim, Yeshiva student.
Moshe Gafni, Ofakim. Head of a Kollel.
Joseph Peretz, Ofakim. Teacher.
Yehuda Aboaziz, Ofakim. Yeshiva student.

FINANCIAL INFORMATION
The sources for last year's annual budget were as follows: religious schools, 23%; donations, 25% and loans, 42%. Last year's annual

budget of $50,000 left a deficit of $20,000. The organization is registered as an Ottoman Association (reg. no. 58-7-0). Donations to the organization are not tax-free. Twenty full-time and ten part-time workers are employed by the organization, as well as 15 volunteers.

MEMBERSHIP, SCOPE, AND POLICY
Decisions are made by the national board. There are 45 members (working and organizing) and eleven branches in Israel.

AFFILIATIONS/REFERENCES
The organization is not affiliated with any political party in Israel. They are in contact with P'eylim, New York.

FUNDING NEEDED
1. To open more branches in order to allow more students to participate. Estimated cost: $10,000.
2. To open and start similar activities, or activities with the similar purposes for girls. The number of girls eligible would be approximately 3,000. Estimated cost: $200,000.
3. To open branches in the north and center of Israel. Estimated cost: $100,000.

OR HACARMEL
COLLEGE FOR STUDIES OF JUDAISM
AND YESHIVA FOR BAALEI TSCHUVA

ישיבת אור הכרמל

88 Hatishbi Street
Mount Carmel
Haifa
Telephone: (04) 82500 or 84044
Office hours: 8:00 A.M. to 7:00 P.M.

HISTORY AND DESCRIPTION
The Yeshiva is a college for Judaic studies designed for repentant sinners, i.e. those who had not been religious and are now interested in learning the principles of Judaism, in order to observe the precepts of the Torah and the tradition of Israel.

The section for repentant sinners has a Yeshiva for young repentant sinners, who live at a boarding school adjacent to the Yeshiva, where they are provided with all their needs. The section for married students and family men has small housing units which are put at their disposal, to enable them to study for a relatively short period (a year or up to several years), and learn matters that are often studied by observant Jews, during childhood. Their maintenance and accommodations are handled by the Yeshiva.

The Yeshiva also has external students, and clubs for repentant sinners meet every evening of the week. These clubs are for both men and women (meeting separately), who are interested in religion, wish to know more about Judaism, and to come closer to a religious and traditional life. The clubs deal with the conception of Israel, the Halacha and the Talmud.

Services, Activities, and Accomplishments: The training of many couples and hundreds of students, who are now religious Jews and useful citizens, and who educate their children to follow a religious way of life as well.

OFFICERS
Director: Rabbi Raphael Shapira, 37 Pewsner, Haifa.
Dean.
Tel. (04) 665970.

Board Members: Yehuda Rosenberg, 4 Hermon, Haifa.
Wage earner.
Tel. (04) 641024.

Yehoshua Farkash, 33 Nordau, Haifa.
Independent.

Zeev Lassman, 64 Pewsner, Haifa.
Pensioner.

FINANCIAL INFORMATION
47% of last year's annual budget came from donations, 35% came from allocations from various institutions, 6% came from membership dues, and 12% came from miscellaneous sources. Last year's annual budget of $650,000 left the Yeshiva with a deficit of $3,400. The Yeshiva is registered as an Ottoman Association (reg. no. 61/613). Donations to the Yeshiva are tax-free in Israel (no. 455/532) and in the United States (no number supplied). There are 16 full-time employees at the Yeshiva and five volunteers.

MEMBERSHIP, SCOPE, AND POLICY
Decisions are made by the management of the association or by its director. There are 28 members and one branch in Israel.

AFFILIATIONS/REFERENCES
The organization is not affiliated with any political party in Israel. The Yeshiva is not in contact with any organizations abroad.

FUNDING NEEDED
1. The construction of a second boarding school for students. Cost: $200,000.
2. The construction of small housing units for married couples.
3. The expansion and reconditioning of the existing buildings.

OR-HAMAARAV—LIGHT OF THE WEST

אור המערב

Hoshea 11
P.O.B. 6657, Jerusalem
Telephone: (02) 284955
Office hours: Sunday to Thursday, 5:00 P.M. to 9:00 P.M.

HISTORY AND DESCRIPTION

'Light of the West' was established in September 1973 by young Rabbis from North Africa in order to publicize the contribution of Middle Eastern and North African Jews to contemporary Judaism, and to make Jews of Middle Eastern origin more aware of their heritage.

Goals: Consistent with its interests, the organization seeks: to recover ancient handwritten manuscripts and books by Rabbis and prominent Jews of North African countries including Tunisia, Morocco, Algeria and Spain; to decipher and study these; to provide financial aid and encouragement to students of these works and to have them published; to distribute these publications to Yeshivas, rabbis and libraries at minimal charge in order to ensure their publicization; and to produce and distribute monthly or yearly pamphlets by Jewish youth on a variety of topics pertaining to Halacha and especially the contributions of Middle Eastern Jews.

Services, Activities, and Accomplishments: 'Light of the West' has published three important books on the laws and customs of North African Jews, and is now producing a fourth. The organization has enabled and encouraged authors to publish their works on such topics and has aided in their distribution.

OFFICERS

Director: Rabbi Amram Edery, Hoshea 11, Jerusalem.
Tel. (02) 284955.
Treasurer: Rav Shaul Edery, Yoel 16, Jerusalem. Professor.
Tel. (02) 289955.
Board: Simon Elbaz, Bank Hapoalim
(Kiryat Malakhi), Sub-Director.
Rabbi Eli Barsheshet, Shahal 19, Jerusalem.
Professor. Tel. (02) 666846.

FINANCIAL INFORMATION

Donations account for 80% of the organization's income, the remaining 20% is achieved through the sale of books. Last year's budget of $3,000 left 'Light of the West' with a deficit of $2,000. The organization is registered as an Ottoman Association (reg. no. 7867/400). Donations to the organization are tax-free in Israel, but no registration number was supplied. The organization has 3 volunteer employees.

MEMBERSHIP, SCOPE, AND POLICY

5 members of the organization are represented by its 1 Israeli branch. There are no members in foreign countries. Any student of Middle Eastern and/or North African Jewish heritage is invited to join 'Light of the West'.

AFFILIATIONS/REFERENCES

'Light of the West' is not associated with any Israeli political party, and it does not list any foreign affiliations.

FUNDING NEEDS

In order of priority, 'Light of the West' lists the following as its outstanding present funding requirements.

1. Publication of ancient Middle Eastern and North African Jewish books and manuscripts.
2. To find and encourage authors willing to research and to write about the history, customs and contributions of North African Jews.

ORIM: PRE-MILITARY PROFESSIONAL INSTITUTION

מרכז הכשרה מקצועית קדם צבאית — אורים

62 Hakarmil
Kiryat Tivon
Telephone: (04) 931180
Office hours: Sunday-Friday, 8:00 A.M. to 4:00 P.M.

HISTORY AND DESCRIPTION

The institution was established 15 years ago. In the beginning it served as an institution for children between the ages of 3 and 12, but for the past seven years it has functioned as a pre-military professional institution, accepting youth between the ages of 15 and 18, and training them in the field of machinery, machine electricty, naval machinery, general electricity and others.

Goals: The Institution attempts to provide underprivileged and difficult youth with maximum guidance for a fruitful life and to train them in professional skills.

Services, Activities, and Accomplishments: Seven, 140-member, classes have graduated from the Institution.

OFFICERS

Director:	Yoel Cohen, Orim, Kiryat Tivon. Teacher. Tel. (04) 931180.
Board Member:	Arieh Ben Zion, Ramat Shaul, Orifus 23/1 Haifa. Teacher. Tel. (04) 332640.

FINANCIAL INFORMATION

Last year's annual budget of $960,000 left the Institute with a deficit of $90,000. The Institute is not registered as a non-profit Ottoman Association and has not previously received donations. It employs 64 full-time and 9 part-time workers.

MEMBERSHIP, SCOPE, AND POICY

Local decisions are made by the Board of Directors and high policy decisions are made by the Mishan center organization.

AFFILIATIONS/REFERENCES

The Institute is affiliated to the Israeli Labour Party (Maarach) and to the Mishan organization of the Histadrut.

FUNDING NEEDED

1. To build a swimming pool—cost $500,000.
2. To purchase furniture for social club-rooms (moadonim) and for the institution—cost $140,000.
3. To purchase a color television set (cost—$2,000) and 16 mm. film projector (cost—$2,000).

ORT ISRAEL

אורט־ישראל

39 David Hamelech Boulevard, Tel Aviv
Telephone: (03) 233231
Office hours: 8:00 A.M. to 3:30 P.M.; Friday 8:00 A.M. to 1:00 P.M.

HISTORY AND DESCRIPTION

ORT, the Organization for Rehabilitation through Training, was founded in St. Petersburg, Czarist Russia, 100 years ago, by a small group of Russian Jews who wanted to give the Jews a possibility to learn a trade and thus be able to earn a better living.

The organization gradually expanded to other countries, including Lithuania, and Poland. During the Holocaust, it operated in the ghettos, and later in the D.P. (Displaced Persons) camps. ORT had thousands of different courses.

In 1948, the first ORT school was founded in Old Jaffa.

ORT now maintains a comprehensive network of 97 technical and vocational schools, all over the country, with courses in areas from carpentry and sewing to practical engineering and technology.

Elections are held annually for the Board of Directors and the Executive Committee, as well as for the President and the Chairman of the Board and his deputies.

OFFICERS (Most details not supplied.)

Director General: Michael Avitzour.
President: Chaim Herzog.
Chairman of the Board: Uzi Steinberg.
Vice President: Dr. Moshe Ezioni.
Deputy Chairman: Zalman Shalev.

FINANCIAL INFORMATION

Last year's annual budget was $20 million, with a deficit of $2 million. No other information was supplied. Donations to the organization are tax-free in Israel (public organization no. 1724) and in the United States (number not supplied). There are 4000 full and part-time workers employed by the organization in addition to 4000 volunteers in Israel.

MEMBERSHIP, SCOPE, POLICY

Decisions are made by the Executive Committee. There are 4000 members in ten branches in Israel and approximately 200,000 members abroad.

AFFILIATIONS/REFERENCES

The organization is not affiliated with any political party in Israel. ORT has contacts with the following: World ORT Union; Women's American ORT/American ORT Federation; Women's Israel ORT; and worldwide ORT.

FUNDING NEEDED

Nothing specified.

PADAM — FREE LOAN FUND

קרן גמ״ח פד״ם ליד בית הכנסת המרכזי אוהל רבקה

Rechov Harlap 17
Kiryat Shmuel, Jerusalem.
Telephone: (02) 638078.
Office Hours: By appointment, through Moshe Paritzky at above number.

HISTORY AND DESCRIPTION

The PADAM Free Loan Fund was founded in 1977 by Rabbi and Mrs. Henoch Millen in honor of Rabbi Millen's parents, *P*inchas and *D*evorah *M*illen (PaDaM). The organization provides interest-free loans to those in need for medical, educational and housing needs. In addition, it gives outright charity for various purposes, as well as material and other aid to Torah scholars and to the needy.

OFFICERS

Director: Yitzchak Wolpe, Even Ezra 13, Jerusalem. Bank manager.
Deputy Director: Rabbi Moshe Katznelbogen, Ha'ari 21, J-m. Tel. (02) 665572.
Treasurer: Avraham Kempe, Itamar Ben Avi 9, J-m. Tel. (02) 636306.
Secretary: Azriel Hildesheimer, Ha'ari 16, Jerusalem.
Board Members: Dr. Israel Zeiderman, Brodi 20, Jerusalem. Tel. (02) 636247.
Dov Froman, Herzog 19. Lawyer. (Fund's legal adviser).
Moshe Prince. (Fund's comptroller).
Rebbetzin Fayge Tropper.
Rabbi Aaron Batt.
Lippe Gross.
Moshe Paritzky.

FINANCIAL INFORMATION

The organization's income is derived solely from donations. No figures were provided for the annual budget. Donations to the organization are tax-free in the U.S.A. (I.R.S. tax-exemption number in U.S.A., for American Friends of PADAM, 38-2292480). The organization is registered as a non-profit Ottoman Association in the Jerusalem District Office of the Ministry of the Interior (under No. 11/3340).

MEMBERSHIP, SCOPE AND POLICY

The organization has 1 branch in Israel with 11 members and an affiliated branch in the U.S.A. with 5 members. Decisions are made by the Executive Director together with the National Board.

AFFILIATIONS/REFERENCES

The organization is not affiliated with any political party in Israel. PADAM's sister organization in the U.S.A. is The American Friends of PADAM, 24651 Sussex, Oak Park, Michigan 48237.

PARTNERSHIP   שותפות

c/o Moshav Rishpon, Israel
Telephone: (052) 70329
Office hours: Monday through Thursday, mornings and evenings.

HISTORY AND DESCRIPTION
Founded in March of 1977, Partnership is a registered voluntary association for creating conditions of partnership between Arabs and Jews in Israel. It was started in an Arab village, Tira, and set up a formal office in July of 1978.

Organizational Structure: Partnership is directed by a national council, an evaluation committee, and active members.

Goals: It aims to initiate and suggest solutions to concrete and psychological problems which will improve relationships between Arabs and Jews as individuals, through organizations and by means of involvement of the general public. Emphasis is on developing trust between people and working together on matters of common interest.

Services, Activities and Accomplishments: Various activities include youth and adult institutes, conferences of Arab and Jewish educators, mixed summer camps, community education lectures, inter-community workshops, training courses for group leaders, cooperative work with Youth Department of the Kibbutz movement and municipalities of Kiryat Ata and Herzliya, various publications and reports and development of a peace-studies curriculum. A major accomplishment has been to demonstrate that Jews and Arabs of Israel can find a common interest, develop mutual trust, and work together as equal partners.

OFFICERS
Co-chair.:   Benyamin Yanoov, Herzliya. Professor of Social Work.
             Tel. (052) 52485.
Co-chair.:   Nimr Ismir, Haifa. Educator. Tel. (04) 527828.
Treasurer: Avraham Lisod, Rishpon. Retired Accountant.
             Tel. (052) 70329.
Secretary: B'shara B'sharat, Yaffia. Physician. Tel. (065) 54567.
Members: Olek Ne'tzer, Ra'anana. Social Psychologist.
             Tel. (052) 28765.
             Fu'az el-Chaz, Ibalin. Teacher.
             Rachel Bat Adam, Tel Aviv. Teacher.
             Daniel Padnes, Haifa. Social Worker. Tel. (04) 530401.
             Ibrahim Sim'an, Haifa. Baptist Minister.
             Tel. (04) 522433.

FINANCIAL INFORMATION
95% of the income comes from donations, and 5% from membership dues, fees and sales. Last year's annual budget was $35,000, leaving no

deficit. The organization is registered in Haifa as an Ottoman Association (number 61/1380). Donations are tax-free in Israel, and tax-exempt status has been applied for in the U.S.A. Two part-time workers are employed.

MEMBERSHIP, SCOPE, AND POLICY
Any Jew or Arab, teen or adult, can join, provided they are willing to be involved up to 5 hours a week. As of now, there are 120 members in Israel, 60 abroad, and about 2,000 supporters. There are four branches in Israel. Most decisions are made by the National Board, and any member can bring an issue to them for decision.

AFFILIATIONS/REFERENCES
Fellowship in Israel for Arab-Jewish Youth, 39 Fayerweather St., Cambridge, Mass.
Brot Für die Welt, Stafflenberg Street. 76, D-700 Stuttgart 1. Germany.
Gereformeerde Kerken in Nederland, POB 2211, Leusden, Holland.

FUNDING NEEDED
1. Public education and public relations — $30,000.
2. Arab-Jewish summer camps — $8,000.
3. Leadership and staff training — $8,000.
4. Salaries and administration — $30,000.

P.E.F. ISRAEL ENDOWMENT FUNDS, INC.

c/o Philip Goodman
63 Shahal
Givat Mordecai
93721 Jerusalem
Telephone: (02) 635668

In U.S.:
342 Madison Avenue
New York, New York 10017
Telephone: (212) 599-1260

Office hours: 9:00 A.M. to 1:00 P.M., 4:00 P.M.-6:00 P.M.

HISTORY AND DESCRIPTION

PEF was established in 1922 by Justice Brandeis and a group of distinguished Americans as a U.S. tax exempt agency. It also has tax exempt status in Israel. Over $30,000,000 has been transmitted to Israel by the PEF since its inception. In 1980, PEF had an income of over $3.5 million, and transmitted $2,000,000 to 172 charitable organizations. Its total assets exceed $10,000,000. No officer or trustee of PEF receives compensation, and it does not do fund raising. Contributions are received from American donors with a recommendation that they be transferred to a specific institution or function in Israel. No deductions are made from any contribution for administrative purposes. Administrative costs in 1980 were 1.6% of receipts and were absorbed by the PEF. PEF's goal is to service Israeli institutions by helping contributors obtain U.S. tax exemption. It investigates Israeli institutions before sending grants. In Israel, a volunteer group of 5 persons headed by Philip Goodman of Jerusalem supervises PEF activities.

Charitable institutions in Israel may establish contact with its representatives who will give full information on its method of operation.

Institutions in Israel may refer donors to PEF with a recommendation that the contribution go to that institution. There is no deduction for administrative expense. PEF also advises prospective donors and recommends institutions which it has approved. As typical examples, in 1980, PEF granted $372,406 to Hebrew University, $229,774 for secondary school scholarships, $42,375 to Yad Sarah for medical equipment, $131,705 to Association for Welfare of Soldiers. Grants of $57,836 were given to 82 institutions of under $2,000 each.

Services, Activities, and Accomplishments: PEF provides American donors with an agency through which they can make charitable gifts to Israeli institutions without paying for overhead. PEF also provides objective advice to prospective donors.

OFFICERS

President: Sidney Musher, 342 Madison Avenue, New York, N.Y. 10017.
Tel. (212) 599-1260.

Trustee: Philip Goodman, 63 Shahal, 93721, Jerusalem, Israel.
Tel. (02) 635668.

FINANCIAL INFORMATION

80% of last year's annual budget came from donations; while the balance came from the income on investments. Last year's annual budget was $4,000,000 leaving the organization with no deficit. For the first 7 months of 1981, the organization received over $3,500,000 and transmitted to about 150 institutions in Israel over $2,300,000. The organization is not registered as an Ottoman Association. Donations to the organization are tax free in Israel (exemption no. 4500079) and in the United States (exemption no. 13-6104086). One full time and two part time workers are employed by the organizations, in addition to 10 volunteers and 34 trustees.

MEMBERSHIP, SCOPE, AND POLICY

Decisions are made by the National Board of Trustees. Membership is determined by decision of the Board. There are 5 associates in Israel and 40 abroad. There are 4 branches in Israel and one abroad.

AFFILIATIONS/REFERENCES

The organization is not affiliated with any political party in Israel. Over 250 organizations know of PEF. Examples of three of them are: The Hebrew University, the Association for Welfare of Soldiers, and the Israel Exploration Society.

FUNDING NEEDED

Priorities cover a wide range of educational, health and social services throughout Israel. Organizations must first be recognized as charitable by Israel government authorities.

PETAHIM

פתחים

6 Rashba Street
Jerusalem
Telephone: (02) 632048
Office hours: 8:00 A.M. to 12:00 Noon

HISTORY AND DESCRIPTION

PETAHIM was founded in 1967, shortly after the Six-Day War, as the result of a long-felt need to clarify the problems of religion in the modern world, and in Israel in particular. After the Six-Day War there was a thirst for understanding and faith, for which this quarterly journal seeks to provide.

Goals: The proclaimed intention of PETAHIM is the encouragement of religious thought and practice through the promotion of free expression and discussion of the values of Judaism, thus contributing to the revival of faith in Israel.

Services, Activities, and Accomplishments: Each issue of PETAHIM is devoted primarily to one main topic, but there are also articles on other subjects, discussions, book reviews, surveys of activities, etc.
Contributors present a variety of views for discussion, so that the reader can weigh one against the other and form freely his own outlook. Plans for reorganization provide for PETAHIM to be published in English as well as Hebrew. PETAHIM regards the future destinies of Israel and the Diaspora as inter-related; one being unable to survive without the other. This reorganization will necessitate an enlarged Editorial Board and the co-option of Jewish thinkers in the Diaspora as contributing Editors, as well as a much enlarged budget. PETAHIM is now in its fourteenth year of publication. It has had some influence on education in Israel, and has contributed to the growing public opinion that Judaism is not an Orthodox monopoly, but has to find its expression, not only in ritual, but in the conduct of the Jewish State.

OFFICERS

President: Jack J. Cohen, HaGedud He'Ivri 7, Jerusalem.
                     Director Beit Hillel. Tel. (02) 638896.

Editor: Joseph S. Bentwich, Rashba 6, Jerusalem.
                     Teacher, Lecturer. Tel. (02) 632048.

Editorial
Board: Avraham Aderet, Aaron Appelfeld, Raphael Arzt, Mordecai Bar-On, Alexander Barzel, Joseph S. Bentwich, Eliezer Berkowitz, Jack J. Cohen, Joseph Emmanuel, Zeev Falk, Theodore Friedman, David Hartman, Richard Hirsch, Abba Kobner, Hava Lazarus-Yafeh, Pinhas Peli, Michael Rosnak, Eliezer Schweid, Zvi Tsammeret, Moses Cyrus Weiler.

FINANCIAL INFORMATION
60% of last year's annual budget came from public grants; the balance derived from membership dues. Last year's annual budget of $7000 left PETAHIM with a deficit of $2300. Donations to the journal in Israel and the United States are tax-free (Israel non-profit reg. no. 11/1487; USA—through P.E.F.). The journal employs one full-time honorary (unpaid) Editor and two part-time secretaries.

MEMBERSHIP, SCOPE, AND POLICY
PETAHIM has twenty national members. These members are co-opted by the Board. Decisions on matters of principle are taken by the National Board. Day-to-day decisions are taken by the Editor in consultation with the President.

AFFILIATIONS/REFERENCES
PETAHIM is politically unaffiliated in Israel. It is in contact with the Jewish Theological Seminary, (Dr. Gerson Cohen), 3080 Broadway, N.Y., P.E.F. (Sidney Musher), 511 Fifth Avenue, New York, and the Department of Education of the Zionist Organization, 515 Park Avenue, New York.

FUNDING NEEDED
1. $4000 — To maintain the journal during 1980/81 in face of rising costs unmatched by a corresponding rise in public grants.
2. $20,000 — To cover initial expenses for the publication of an English edition.

PELECH, RELIGIOUS EXPERIMENTAL HIGH SCHOOL FOR GIRLS

פלך, בית ספר תיכון נסוי לבנות, ירושלים

Gideon 14
Jerusalem
Telephone: (02) 711282
Office Hours: 8:00 A.M. to 2:00 P.M.

HISTORY AND DESCRIPTION
Pelech was founded in 1967 to fill a perceived need for a girls' high school that would combine both Jewish studies at a high school level with a wide range of secular studies. It has been recognized since 1976 as an experimental school, both in its devising of new programs of study and the development of progressive teaching methods.

Goals: Pelech strives to provide an alternative method of education in Israel. It also attempts to provide disadvantaged girls with the opportunity to study in both religious and secular fields at a higher level, and to provide them with the opportunity to continue their education.

Services, Activities, and Accomplishments: Presently, the school educates some 200 pupils in grades 9 to 12 and also runs an 'adoption' (tutorial) service for selected 7th and 8th graders from socio-economically disadvantaged neighbourhoods in an effort to enable these girls to qualify for admission into Pelech and other prestigious high schools. Pelech's major accomplishments to date include the pioneering of educational programs which serve other institutions as well, and helping to educate a cadre of outstanding young women with leadership potential.

OFFICERS
Director: Alice Shalvi, Berechyahu 11, Jerusalem.
Professor of English. Tel. (02) 528057.
Treasurer: Moshe Mann, Dubnow 9, Jerusalem.
Bank Director. Tel. (02) 631245.
Board Members: Hanna Urbach, Hatibonim 22, Jerusalem.
Tel. (02) 632874.
Harry Sapir, Hatayasim 24, Jerusalem.
Bank Director. Tel. (02) 665073.
David Hartman, Graetz 7, Jerusalem. Lecturer.
Tel. (02) 668258.
Yona Frankel, Arlosorof 5, Jerusalem.
Professor of Hebrew Literature.
Tel. (02) 663207.

FINANCIAL INFORMATION
Pelech's income is derived from various sources. Parents' donations amount to 15% of the income; donations from abroad 25%; government aid (including fees) 50%; and the remaining 10% is derived from grants from independent foundations. No figures were given regarding annual

budgets and deficits. The organization is registerd as an Ottoman Association (reg. no. 11/1439, Jerusalem). Donations to the organization are tax-free in Israel (no reg. no. supplied), as well as in the United States (if channelled through the P.E.F. Israel Endowment Fund), and the United Kingdom (if channelled through the Jerusalem Foundation). The organization has 15 full-time and 25 part-time employees.

MEMBERSHIP, SCOPE, AND POLICY
30 national members are represented by the one branch of Pelech. There are also 3 members in foreign countries. Decisions are for the most part made by the Executive Director, although often in conjunction with the Board, staff and pupils.

AFFILIATIONS/REFERENCES
Pelech is not associated with any Israeli political party. Internationally, Pelech is affiliated with *P.E.F. Israel Endowment Fund, Inc.*, 342 Madison Ave., New York, New York, 10017, and the *Jerusalem Foundation*, 90 Paisner, London. U.K.

FUNDING NEEDED
1. Scholarships for needy pupils.
2. Donation to help cover the schools' considerable annual losses.
3. Library acquisitions. The school needs approximately 3,000 additional volumes to facilitate individual study.
4. Building addition.

PESACH MATZO FUND OF THE CHIEF RABBINATE OF JERUSALEM

מפעל קמחא דפסחא של הרבנות הראשית לירושלים

Hachavatzelet 12
P.O.B. 13
Jerusalem
Telephone: (02) 234361
Office Hours: 8:00 A.M. to 2:00 P.M.

HISTORY AND DESCRIPTION
The Pesach Matzo Fund was established to follow the tradition in Jerusalem, by the Chief Rabbis and offices of the Jerusalem Religious Councils, to help families in need each year before Passover.

Services, Activities, and Accomplishments: Each year over 700 families are serviced by the Pesach Matzo Fund, in an attempt to make each family's Pesach a little more enjoyable.

OFFICERS
The Pesach Matzo Fund lists as its directors the Chief Rabbis of Jerusalem. In addition there is a Public Committee under the directership of the Chief Rabbinate of Jerusalem.

FINANCIAL INFORMATION
The majority of the organization's income comes from donations and the remainder from the Jerusalem Religious Council. Letters are sent to 'friends' of the Fund each year. The organization's budget for last year was $20,000 and the fund had a deficit of $2,000. The organization is registered with the Jerusalem District Office of the Ministry of the Interior as a non-profit Ottoman Association, (registration number 11/2984). Donations to the organization are tax-free in Israel (reg. no. 4506141). The Fund has no paid employees, but ony part-time volunteers.

AFFILIATIONS/REFERENCES
The Pesach Matzo Fund is not associated with any Israeli political party. It is affiliated with the Rabbinical Council of America and Young Israel of New York City.

PIRCHEI MARGALIT   פרחי מרגלית

c/o Shalom Daniel
5 Zefania
Jerusalem
Telephone: (02) 283716
Office hours: Sunday-Thursday, 7:00 to 9:00 P.M.

HISTORY AND DESCRIPTION
Pirchei Margalit was established in 1978. It arose out of an educational motivation to promote traditional Sephardic music (particularly that of Babylonian Jewry) amongst school children and youth.

Goals: It is the organization's hope that the promotion of traditional Sephardic music will lead to its integration with Western music, the outcome of which will be an authentic Israeli music.

Services, Activities, and Accomplishments: Two children's choirs have been established, one in the Tel Aviv area (Or-Yehuda), and one in Jerusalem, and two ensembles have been formed, of singers and instrumentalists playing traditional Sephardic musical instruments. The ensembles introduce, explain, and perform traditional Sephardic music in schools. A special booklet containing traditional Sephardic songs and descriptions of Sephardic customs will shortly be published by the organization. Other activities planned, but not yet begun for lack of funding, are: 1) special courses of Sephardic cantoral music (Hazanut) and Bible recitation for youth; and 2) a Sephardic Conservatory where youngsters will be able to learn how to play the various musical instruments and also receive lessons in theory. Activities for the past year were limited to the available budget, but considerable funding will be required for their continuity and expansion.

OFFICERS
Director: Moshe Gabbay, Ben Eliezer 23/22, Gilo, Jerusalem. Teacher. Tel. (02) 781125.

Treasurer: Shalom Daniel, Zefania 5, Jerusalem. Technician. Tel. (02) 283716.

Board Members: Ezra Amit, Balfour 17, Beer-Sheva. Chemist. Tel. (057) 64782.

                 Judith Kaplan, Ramat Sharet 2, Jerusalem. Librarian. Tel. (02) 423148.

                 Nilly Landau, Mevo Ketzia 1, Gilo, Jerusalem. Teacher. Tel. (02) 713020.

Trustee: David Bergman, Ovadia 3, Jerusalem. Deputy Mayor of Jerusalem. Tel. (02) 286766.

FINANCIAL INFORMATION
80% of last year's annual budget (which amounted to $1000) came from donations, the balance being provided by self-income from performan-

ces. Donations to Pirchei Margalit in Israel are tax-free (No. 4507705). Eleven part-time workers are employed by the organization, as well as nine volunteers.

MEMBERSHIP, SCOPE, AND POLICY
About one hundred members represent the two Israeli branches. Anyone who identifies with the goals of the organization and is approved by the Board can be accepted as a member. Most decisions are made by the National Board. Pirchei Margalit also has twenty members in the United States.

AFFILIATIONS/REFERENCES
Pirchei Margalit is unaffiliated with any political party in Israel. It maintains contact with the American Sephardi Federation, 521 Fifth Avenue, Suite 1404, New York, N.Y. 10017.

FUNDING NEEDED
1. To maintain choirs and ensembles (including salaries for instrumentalists, director, and secretary.
2. To establish a Conservatory of Sephardic Music, necessitating teachers' salaries, and the purchase of musical instruments.
3. To establish additional children's choirs in other towns.

PRISONERS' AID SOCIETY (HAIFA)

האגודה למען האסיר

Y.L. Peretz 18
P.O.B. 4078, Haifa
Telephone: (04) 644385
Office hours: Sunday-Friday, 9:30 A.M. to 1:30 P.M.

HISTORY AND DESCRIPTION
The Society was founded in 1950, and was the first of its kind in Israel.

Organizational Structure: Members come together at the Annual General Meeting where the Chairman's report on activities and financial matters is thoroughly debated. A Chairman, Treasurer and Secretary are then elected, as well as members of financial, administrative and other committees which will implement the programs of the Society. The minutes of the Annual General Meeting are sent to the District Commissioner in Haifa.

Goals: The primary goal is to help the prisoner in his rehabilitation and his return to normal life and social relations, etc.

Services, Activities, and Accomplishments: The Society's Chairman and Social Worker are available every day to answer the many persons who apply to the organization. It is not easy in these times for the social services to cope with all the needs of such persons. The Society has extended help to every ex-prisoner referred to it by the Prison Social Service staff. The Society's members visit prisoners still serving their term; they correspond with the prisoners and keep in contact with their families. Official visiting members report on their meetings with prisoners and prison staff. Released prisoners are given assistance in finding employment, and contact is maintained with them.

OFFICERS
Director: Y. Azoulai, David (Pinsky) 20, Haifa. Retired judge, former President of District Court. Tel. (04) 81086 or (04) 644385.

Treasurer: I.Rosenberg, Shoshanat Carmel 104A, Haifa. Tel. (04) 87924.

Board Members: J. Kushnir, Kassel 2, Haifa. Lawyer. Tel. (04) 661038.

Amiram Harlaff, Oren 22, Haifa. Lawyer. Tel. (04) 522336.

Abraham Ben-Shahar, Hayam 139, Haifa. Reporter. Tel. (04) 87085.

Eni Lederer, Probation Social Service for Adults, Jaffa 145, Haifa. Probation officer. Tel. (04) 53046.

Sh. Shwarz, Geulle 10, Haifa. Auditor. Tel. (04) 640531.

FINANCIAL INFORMATION

The greater part of last year's annual budget came from allocations made by the Labor and Social Service Ministry; the balance, from the Municipality. The Society receives practically no donations and its membership dues do not contribute a significant amount to the budget. Last year's annual budget was $4,000; there was no deficit. Donations to the Society are tax-free in Israel (registration number not supplied). The Society is registered as an Ottoman Association (registration number not supplied). Two part-time workers (a social worker and a secretary) are employed by the Society; the other members, including the Chairman, are volunteers.

MEMBERSHIP, SCOPE, AND POLICY

There are 20 active members in Haifa, the sole branch of the Society. Anyone who is willing to devote time and work voluntarily can become a member. Most decisions are taken by the Executive Director in accordance with the Society's Constitution; when necessary, it is the National Board which takes decisions.

AFFILIATIONS/REFERENCES

1. The Administrative Office of the United States Courts, Washington D.C. 20544, USA.
2. The Society is a member of the League of Societies for the Rehabilitation of Offenders in Israel. The Society's Director is a senior officer of the League.
3. Through the League, the Society is a member of the International Prisoners' Aid Association.

The Society is not affiliated with any political party in Israel.

FUNDING NEEDED

1. For housing aid for offenders and their family.
2. To combat drug addiction and alcoholism, and to provide medical aid facilities.
3. To solve problems of unemployment.

QEDEM—YAD LE-YAKKIRENU

קדם – יד ליקירינו

Jerusalem
Telephone: (02) 634682
Postal Address: c/o Salzmann, Hizkiahu Hamelech 16, Jerusalem

HISTORY AND DESCRIPTION
Qedem—Yad Le-Yakkirenu was founded in 1974 by the descendants of
the late Moshe David U. Cassuto, the well-known scholar of biblical,
Jewish and oriental studies, as a mechanism by which to encourage and
provide funding for further studies in such areas.

Organizational Structure: The organization has a directorate (Hanhala)
and a Board of Members, all of whom are volunteers.

Goals: Qedem seeks to encourage research on Jewish matters or related
topics, and to publish them; and to honor, by these means, the memory
of Moshe David U. Cassuto and other members of the family who
disappeared in the European Holocaust or in fighting in and for the
State of Israel and other persons proposed by the directorate.

Services, Activities, and Accomplishments: The organization endeavours
to finance, by means of scholarships and the like, research on Jewish
studies, and to publish and distribute them. The organization includes
among its major accomplishments the creation of a $200 scholarship to
support the study of an Italian Jewish manuscript of the 18th Century,
and the publication of a volume to honor the memory of a young soldier
fallen in the defence of his homeland.

OFFICERS
Director: David Cassuto, Ramban 33, Jerusalem. Architect.
                      Tel. (02) 634682.
Treasurer: Lea Rocca, Korot Haittim 6, Jerusalem.
                      Accountant.
                      Tel. (02) 525015.
Secretary: Milka Cassuto Salzmann, Hizkiahu Hamelech 16,
                      Jerusalem. Librarian.
                      Tel. (02) 664217.
Board Members: E. Avital, Kevuzat Yavneh.
                      F. Benzimra, Saadiah Gaon 4, Jerusalem. Judge.
                      M. Cohn, Harlap 26, Jerusalem. School Director.
                      S. Goldschmidt, Yael 8, Jerusalem.
                      High school teacher.

FINANCIAL INFORMATION
99.9% of the organization's income is generated through royalties from
books of M.D.U. Cassuto, and only 0.1% through donations. The
organization's last annual budget totalled $867. There was no deficit.
Qedem is registered with the Jerusalem District Office of the Ministry of

the Interior as a non-profit Ottoman Association (reg. no. 11/2273). Donations to the organization are tax-free in Israel (numbers not supplied). There are 3 volunteer employees.

MEMBERSHIP, SCOPE, POLICY, AND AFFILIATIONS
There are seven members of Qedem in Israel. There are no members abroad. Decisions for the organization are made by the Executive Director. The organization is not affiliated with any Israeli political party nor with any foreign organizations.

FUNDING NEEDED
1. To publish, within three years, an English translation of a fundamental and very important, though not yet well known Italian book (U. Cassuto, *La Questione della Genesi*, Firenze 1934). Approximate cost, $25,000.
2. To prepare a volume on various Jewish topics to be published in commemeration of the centennial anniversary of the birth of M.D.U. Cassuto born in 1883. Approximate cost, $20,000.
3. To prepare a volume on Jewish history to honor the memory of members of the Cassuto family who disappeared in the European Holocaust or in Israeli wars. To be published within five years at an estimated cost of $20,000.

RABBINICAL SEMINARY RAMAILIS NETZACH ISRAEL

ישיבת רמייליס נצח ישראל

22 Even Ezra Street
Rechavia, Jerusalem
Telephone: (02) 639917
Office hours: 9:00 A.M. to 4:00 P.M.

HISTORY AND DESCRIPTION

The Ramailis Yeshiva was founded in Vilna, Lithuania, 160 years ago, and was expanded in 1840. Situated on Reb Mailis Street in Vilna, the name of the Yeshiva soon evolved to "Ramailis". Every year the Yeshiva produced young scholars who served as Rabbis, Dayanim and Roshei Yeshiva in the cities throughout Lithuania, Poland, and the neighboring countries. Physically, the Vilna of that Torah age is no more: its yeshivas, shuls, scholars, and citizens were destroyed in the Holocaust. Spiritually, however, the Vilna of yesterday lives. From the Jerusalem of Lithuania to Jerusalem, Israel—"Ir HaKodesh". For Yeshiva Ramailis, this was the beginning of a new age of Torah. A beautiful site, in the heart of Rechavia in central Jerusalem, was purchased through the backing of generous friends and admirers. The building was renovated to serve the needs of the Yeshiva. A Kollel section was added to support the spiritual and material needs of the married students. The Yeshiva's presence has boosted the religious climate of Rechavia, Talbia, Kiryat Shmuel, and the surrounding area, for it has encouraged religious individuals and institutions to move to the area.

Services, Activities, and Accomplishments: Over the past twenty-five years, since the Seminary's rebirth from the ashes of the Holocaust in Vilna to its establishment in the United States and, finally, in Israel, the Seminary has produced hundreds of rabbis, teachers, and high-caliber seminary lecturers, scholars of repute who enrich Jewish communities the world over. The Seminary is known and endorsed by leading figures of world Jewry, such as the Chief Rabbi of Israel, Chief Rabbis of Jerusalem, deans of leading world seminaries, etc.

OFFICERS

Rosh Yeshiva: Rabbi I. Gustman. Tel. (02) 668437.
Treasurer: Mr. Yosef Weiss.
Dean: Rabbi M. Berniker.
Assistant Dean: Rabbi M. Lipka.
Student Advisor: Rabbi N. Weinberg.
Building and Trust
Fund Coordinator: Rabbi Y. Lebovits.

FINANCIAL INFORMATION

60% of last year's annual budget came from donations, 20% from government sources, and 20% from membership dues. Last year's annual budget of $450,000 left the Seminary with a deficit of $59,000. The Seminary is registered as a non-profit organization, and donations in Israel and the United States may be made tax-free (Israel exemption no. 4502484; U.S. exemption no. 11-603-9894, New York City exemption no. 131164). The Ramailis Seminary employs fifteen full-time and six part-time workers, as well as twenty volunteers.

MEMBERSHIP, SCOPE, AND POLICY

The Rabbinical Seminary Ramailis Netzach Israel, with its one Israeli branch, has 200 national members. Anybody who's interested in the growth and dissemination of Torah in the world may join. Decisions are made mostly by the Executive Board. The Ramailis Seminary has one branch abroad, with 100 members.

AFFILIATIONS/REFERENCES

The Seminary is politically unaffiliated, limiting itself solely to the spiritual growth and development of its students. It is endorsed by the Union of Orthodox Rabbis of the United States and Canada, the Rabbinical Council of America in New York City; and the Rabbinical Alliance of America in New York City.

FUNDING NEEDED

1. $3 million — To create a Building Fund for the expansion of crowded quarters to meet the needs of a continually growing student body from all parts of the world.
2. $500,000 — To create a Trust Fund for the post-graduate section of the Seminary (Kollel), made up of an elite and gifted group of married students. At present these students receive a stipend which, unfortunately, is below living standard due to a lack of funding sources to cover the project cost by the Seminary. In order for graduate students to achieve the high level of scholarship necessary, over a period of five to ten years, to be lecturers of Talmud and codes in Rabbinical Seminaries all over the world, it is important for the students and their families to have peace of mind, and to be able to study without the undue hardship of a constantly precarious financial position.

RABBI SLONIM MEMORIAL FREE-LOAN FUND OF THE CHABAD SYNAGOGUE, JERUSALEM

קרן גמ"ח ע"ש הרה"ת ר' ע.ז. סלונים,
ליד ביהכ"נס שבשכון חב"ד, ירושלים

c/o Rabbi Avraham Eizen
Shikun Chabad
10 Elkana Street
Jerusalem
Telephone: (02) 814580
Office hours: 9:00 P.M. to 10:00 P.M.

HISTORY AND DESCRIPTION
The Rabbi Slonim Memorial Free-Loan Fund of the Chabad Synagogue grants loans to the needy. Loans are now given for three months to be repaid after this period. Borrowers pay no interest or other charges.

OFFICERS
Director: Rabbi Yehosef Ralbag, 2 Shmaryahu Levin, Jerusalem. Tel. (02) 411206.

Sec'y.-Treas.:   Rabbi Abraham Eizen, Shikun Chabad, Jerusalem. Tel. (02) 814580.

Board Members: Rabbi Yitzchak Wolf, 13 Even Ezra, Jerusalem. Tel. (02) 668349.

Rabbi Chaim Moshe Teichtel, 12 Elkana, Jerusalem. Tel. (02) 816382.

Rabbi Chaim Mendel Rosenberg, 14 Elkana, Jerusalem. Tel. (02) 814570.

FINANCIAL INFORMATION
The sources of last year's annual budget were membership dues, 60%; and from donations, 40%. Last year's annual budget was $3,000. The Fund has no deficit. The Fund is listed as being registered as an Ottoman Association but the number was not supplied. Information regarding the tax-free status of the Fund was not listed. There are three volunteers working for the Fund.

MEMBERSHIP, SCOPE, AND POLICY
Most decisions are made by the three volunteers. Any religious Jew over the age of 20 can join the Fund.

AFFILIATIONS/REFERENCES
The Fund is not affiliated with any political party in Israel. The Fund is in contact with Chabad-Lubavitch, 770 Eastern Parkway, Brooklyn, New York.

FUNDING NEEDED

1. To develop additional funds in order to expand the activities to grant larger loans for a more lengthy period of time.
2. To develop the means to develop charitable institutions such as storehouses of clothes and food supplies, to be sold to the needy at a token price.

RAMAT HAGOLAN COMMUNITY CENTER

מרכז קהילתי רמת הגולן

Bnai Yehudah, Ramat Hagolan, 12484
Telephone: (067) 63667
Office hours: 6:30 A.M. to 9:30 P.M.

HISTORY AND DESCRIPTION

The Ramat Hagolan Community Center was founded in October 1977, with the aim of improving social, sport and cultural interrelations among the twenty-five agricultural settlements of the Golan Heights. In addition, the community center undertakes the organization of youth activities in the Golan.

Services, Activities, and Accomplishments: The center organizes and manages youth activities, organizes regional festivals for such holidays as Independance Day, Feast of Weeks (Shavuot), Simchat Torah celebrations (Hakafot Shniot). A sports center has been built at Hisfin and operated by the Center.

OFFICERS

Director: Aharon Davidi—Bnei Yehuda, 12484.
Tel. (067) 63826.

Treasurer: Itzhak Schwartz, Hisfin. Schoolmaster.
Tel. (067) 63153.

Executive
Committee: Eitan Lis, Ramot. Head of Regional Council.
Tel. (067) 63181.
Zippora Harel, Merom Golan. Agriculture.
Tel. (067) 71641.
Yehuda Hindi, Hadera. Educator.
Moshe Ari, Zefat. Supervisor of
centers of the Israel Corporation
of Community Centers.
Itzhak Yeshurun, Afik. Agriculture.
Haya Feuer, Ramat Magshimim. Functionary
of the Regional Council.

FINANCIAL INFORMATION

40% of the center's income is derived from the Regional Council, 35% comes from membership dues, and 25% from various government agencies. Last year's annual budget was $185,000, with an added $10,000 for development. Donations to the Center are tax-free (Israel registration no. not supplied), and it is registered as an Ottoman society (no. 3/542). Two full-time and five part-time workers are employed by the Center, as well as forty volunteers.

MEMBERSHIP, SCOPE, AND POLICY

Membership is open to any inhabitants of the Golan participating through their settlements. The present population of 5000 comes from ten kibbutzim, six religious moshavim, eight moshavim, and one rural center. This population extends over an area 90 km. long and 20 km. wide. Most decisions are made by the Executive Director.

AFFILIATIONS/REFERENCES

The Center is not affiliated with any political party in Israel.

FUNDING NEEDED

1. To build three swimming pools ($240,000).
2. To upgrade local basketball fields so that they will serve as tennis courts as well ($50,000).
3. To acquire 25 kayak boats at $240 each and 3 kayak transporters at $1,000 each.

THE RAMBAM SOCIETY

אגודת רמב״ם

Rambam Medical Center
P.O.B. 9616
Haifa
Telephone: (04) 520670
Office hours: 8:00 A.M. to 3:00 P.M.

HISTORY AND DESCRIPTION

The Rambam Society was founded in January 1963 with the aim of encouraging the development and advancement of medical research in the Rambam Hospital. The essential needs of the hospital increased with the expansion of the hospital and its becoming a University Hospital and Medical Center and, since then, emphasis has been placed on raising the medical standards and physical conditions of hospitalization by the purchase of sophisticated equipment for diagnosis and treatment, building and renovating existing departments and the establishment of new departments. The Rambam Society has registered branches in New York and London.

Goals: To help the Rambam Hospital to raise the medical standards and physical conditions of hospitalization by encouraging research, purchasing medical equipment, building and renovating existing departments and establishing new departments.

Services, Activities, and Accomplishments: The Rambam Society has supported work in the field of research in the hospital, encouraging publication of articles in professional journals in Israel and abroad, and acquiring professional books for the various departments. In view of the shortage of nurses, the Society established in the Yohanna Hana Schal Fund to assist in training nurses. The Occupational Therapy Rehabilitation Center, the Sylvia and Barnett Shine Physiotherapy Department, and the Mordecai and Zippora Schreiber Hematology Outpatient Clinic, were built and equipped with the help of the Rambam Society, and the Scheinwald Cardiology Rehabilitation Center, the Elaine and Neville Blond Plastic Surgery Department and Burn Unit, and the Children's Surgery Department, were renovated with the help of the Rambam Society. The Society has also acquired a great deal of medical equipment for existing departments, laboratories and institutes, and for the treatment and rehabilitation of wounded soldiers. Equipment acquired for the Rambam Hospital by the Rambam Society includes the following: the first Skin Bank in Israel, a sterile operating theatre, equipment for the Children's Surgical Department, equipment for the Premature Baby Unit, equipment for the Gastroenterology Department, the first mobile pressure chamber in Israel, artificial kidneys, microscopes for operations, mobile X-ray machines, ultrasound equipment for the X-ray Department and labor rooms, monitors, microscopes, centrifuges, airconditioners, etc.

OFFICERS

President:	Prof. D. Erlik, 57 Pinsky, Haifa. Surgeon. Tel. (04) 81283.
Board Members:	Mr. J. Hass, 26 Tel-Maneh, Haifa. Government Employee. Tel. (04) 663403.
	Mrs. B. Cohen, 11 Adam Hacohen, Haifa. Company Director. Tel. (04) 232470.
	Mr. Y. Toren-Hibler, 3 Ehud, Haifa. Tel. (04) 242622.
	Mr. M. Rafalovitz, 8 Hashiloah, Haifa. Director of Girls' School. Tel. (04) 645474.

FINANCIAL INFORMATION

65% of the Society's income comes from grants and projects, 34% from donations, and 1% from membership dues. The Society does not have an annual budget. It is registered as a non-profit Ottoman Association (reg. no. 61/665). Donations in Israel, in the United States, through the American Friends of the Rambam Society, and in the U.K., through the Friends of the Rambam Society, are tax-free (tax nos. not supplied). The Society employs two full-time and three part-time workers in its office, and 14 full-time and 33 part-time workers in the hospital, as well as 15 volunteers for special fund-raising drives.

MEMBERSHIP, SCOPE, AND POLICY

Membership is open to any person above the age of 20 who has submitted an application for membership and been recommended by a member of the Society. There are 250 members in Israel, in one branch, and one branch in the United States, and one in the U.K. Most decisions are made by the Executive Director.

AFFILIATIONS/REFERENCES

The Society is not affiliated with any Israeli political party. It is affiliated with the following organizations:

Operation Wheelchairs Committee, 15 Imperial Court, Prince Albert Road, London N.W. 8, England.

EZRA Association of Israel, P.O.B. 142, Double Bay 2028, Sydney, Australia.

Victorian B'nai B'rith Israel Committee, 99 Hotham St., Victoria 3182, Australia.

Stichting Levi Lassen, Sgravenhage, 40 Cedempte Gracht, Holland.

S.E.D. Sigma Epsillon Delta, c/o Dr. Stephen Bergen, Colonial Woods Drive, West Orange, N.J. 07052, USA.

FUNDING NEEDED

1. To finance the renovation of the Department of Paediatric Surgery (cost $240,000).
2. To finance the renovation of the Department of Neurosurgery (cost $800,000).
3. To finance the completion of an additional floor to the Outpatients Clinic (cost $300,000).

RAMOT SHAPIRA WORLD
YOUTH ACADEMY

רמת שפירא — המרכז החינוכי

Moshav Beit Meir
P.O.B. 7216
Jerusalem
City office: 19 Rambam, Jerusalem
Telephone: (City office) (02) 913291; (Moshav Beit Meir), (02) 668343.
Office hours: 8:00 A.M. to 3:00 P.M.

HISTORY AND DESCRIPTIONS

Ramot Shapira World Youth Academy opened its doors in August 1971
in response to demands of educationists from Israel and the Diaspora
for a school which would offer High School and College youth special
educational programs and courses in the subjects of Israel, Judaism,
leadership, and good citizenship studies. The Academy is located on one
of the highest points in the Judean hills, 18 km. west of Jerusalem at the
foot of Moshav Beit Meir. The Burma Road of Independence War fame
winds through the campus. From the heights of Ramot Shapira many
sites of Biblical panorama are visible such as the Ayalon plain where
Joshua fought and Modiin where the Maccabees re-established Jewish
Independence.

Organizational Structure: The Academy is guided, developed and controlled by its Israel Executive Council, and International Board of
Trustees, headed by a President and managed by a Director, assisted by
an expert educational faculty and administrative staff.

Goals: The Israeli programs, conducted in co-operation with the Ministry of Education and the Ministry of Social Welfare, are geared in the
main to meet educational problems arising from the special situation of
the youth in disadvantaged areas and development towns, where they
often lack proper home motivation, hail from a deprived cultural background, face a disadvantaged social climate and receive a weak school
education.

Services, Activities, and Accomplishments: The following Institutes in the
Academy offer courses to meet the educational and social needs of the
different groups: The Institute of Youth Leadership; The School of
Judaic Studies, the Sephardic Heritage Institute, the Land of Israel
Studies and Field School, and the Higher Judaic Studies Institute.
Among its accomplishments have been to help many thousands of
Israeli youth to strengthen their moral fibre as Israeli citizens and
awareness of the unity and historic continuity of the Jewish people.
Through its program for Diaspora youth the Academy is contributing
to the struggle against assimilation and to the deepening of their Jewish
loyalties.

OFFICERS
Chairman: Rabbi Dr. J. Vainstein
Treasurer: Yitzchak Atzmon
Board Members: M. Barsela, S. Krupnick, Y. Goldshlag,
                   E. Birnbaum, J. Friedman, Dr. M. Shacham,
                   A. Sebag
Director: Chayim Wertheimer

FINANCIAL INFORMATION
70% of the operational budget of the Academy comes from students' fees and the Ministry of Education participation, 30% donations from Friends abroad. For the developmental budget, 75% comes from Friends abroad, and 25% from the Government of Israel and other sources. Last year's annual budget of $310,000 left a deficit of $100,000. The Academy is registered in Jerusalem as a non-profit Ottoman Association (reg. no. 11/1381). Donations are tax-deductible in Israel (no. 535/1344), and the United States (no. 23-7399855), Canada (no. 0476408-21-13) and England (no. 266215). Twenty-seven full-time and 5 part-time workers are employed by the academy.

MEMBERSHIP, SCOPE, AND POLICY
Membership of the Friends' Organizations is open to donors. There are 200 members in Israel and 2,000 abroad in 8 Friends' Organizations. Most decisions are made by the National Board.

AFFILIATIONS/REFERENCES
The Academy is not affiliated with any Israeli political party. It is affiliated with Education and Youth Departments of the World Zionist Organization in New York, Montreal and London, with local Boards of Jewish Education and Synagogue bodies.

FUNDING NEEDED
1. Dormitories for 200 students, classrooms, clinic, library, teachers' and instructors' rooms, gymnasium — estimated cost $2,250,000.
2. Faculty and Staff residences — cost $650,000. The goal of the school is to create for the student a continuous educational experience in which the informal phase of living at Ramot Shapira will also be highly instructive and inspirational. This can only be achieved through an ongoing relationship between students and faculty. Furthermore the Academy is located outside Jerusalem and residential facilities must be provided in order to attract faculty members of the highest calibre. In addition certain administration and technical staff members must necessarily be in permanent residence in such a boarding establishment.
3. Swimming pool, Center for Field School, athletic and soccer field.

RAPE CRISIS CENTER IN TEL AVIV—
ISRAEL FEMINIST MOVEMENT

המרכז לסיוע לקורבנות אונס בת"א, מיסודה של התנועה
הפמיניסטית בישראל

9 Micha Street (P.O.B. 33041)
Tel Aviv
Telephone: (03) 441341, (03) 445678
Office hours: 8:30 A.M. to 1:00 P.M.

HISTORY AND DESCRIPTION

The Rape Crisis Center in Tel Aviv was re-established in January 1980 on the initiative of the Israel Feminist Movement, which operated a Rape Crisis Center for ten months in 1978 but was forced to close it due to lack of funding. The Center is operated by a steering committee, which includes representatives from the Labor and Welfare Ministry, Tel Aviv Municipality, and the organizing committee of the Center (5 women, of which two work half-time as Project Coordinator and assistant coordinator). Another woman works in research dealing with rape and related subjects and is funded by the Jewish Agency. The Rape Crisis Center operates in three major areas: practical help—answering calls from all areas, police stations, hospitals, schools and other institutions, as well as from women who call on their own initiative. More than 100 calls have been received from women for help following a sexual attack. The Center continues to give intensive care to more than half of these women. This work is carried out by volunteers who have received suitable training. Following contacts from the army, universities, various organizations and private people, the Center is offering lectures and talks about subjects connected with rape. However, such information does not always reach the public due to budgetary limitations in printing and distribution. The Center views with utmost importance the changing attitudes and practical care towards rape victims whether with the police, the courts, hospitals, or society as a whole.

Services, Activities, and Accomplishments: In eleven months of operation, the Center received about 120 phone calls about sexual attacks. Half of these people were treated intensively for a long period of time; some for more than half a year. Another 60 women were helped in other areas, such as divorce.

OFFICERS

Director: Esther Eillam, 5 Blum, Ramat Aviv. Sociologist.
                   Tel. (03) 413778.

Treasurer: Sara Sikes, 55 Shen Ein, Givatayim.
                   Tel. (03) 312349.

Board Members: Rina Ben Zvi, 16 Burla, Tel Aviv.
                   Elana Golan, 32 Katzenelson, Givatayim.
                     Music Teacher. Tel. (03) 257763.
                   Goan Yaron, 1 Yosef-Sapir, Kiriat Krinitz.
                     Tel. (03) 756616.

FINANCIAL INFORMATION

Last year's annual budget came from the following sources: membership dues, 3%; local donations, 17%; donations from abroad, 50%; government grants, 20%; local municipality, 10%. No other financial information was supplied. The organization is registered as an Ottoman Association (no. 5983/99). Donations to the organization in Israel are not tax-free. There are two part-time employees and 30 volunteers.

MEMBERSHIP, SCOPE, AND POLICY

Decisions are made by the Organizing Committee. There is one branch in Israel.

AFFILIATIONS/REFERENCES

The organization is not affiliated with any political party in Israel. The following organizations are affiliated with the Center: Women for Women, through P.E.F. Israel Endowment Funds, Inc., 342 Madison Avenue, New York, N.Y. 10173; New Israel Fund, 22 Miller Avenue, Mill Valley, California 94941; and NOW (National Organization of Women), U.S.A.

FUNDING NEEDED

1. Rent and telephone (Hot Line) — $4,000.
2. Salaries — $7,000.
3. Publication of educational material in Hebrew — $2,000.

THE RELIGIOUS CULTURAL CENTER FOR KURDISTAN JEWS IN ISRAEL

מרכז רוחני־דתי ליהודי כורדיסטאן בישראל

25 Hayarkon Street
P.O.B. 6810, Jerusalem
Telephone: (02) 226657
Office hours: afternoon and evening

HISTORY AND DESCRIPTION

In 1973 a religious center was established by the Kurdistan Jewish Community. The motivation was that the Jews of the Kurdistan Community in Israel now dwell in a spiritual wilderness; Kurdistan Jewish youth is slowly abandoning its beautiful heritage of religious customs and traditions. This spiritual desertion has demanded serious thought and action, and after great efforts, the leaders of the Kurdistan Jewish Community have succeeded in establishing the Religious Center, thus preserving and ensuring the continuity and eternity of the sacred values of the Torah.

This Center consists of two main divisions: a post-graduate Rabbinical College, to educate and train rabbis and judges for future positions in the various Sephardic communities in Israel, and afternoon and evening classes for Kurdistan Jewish youth, where the pupils are taught the values and principles of Judaism, Holy Scriptures, Talmud and Jewish law.

The Center also trains young boys for their "bar-mitzvah", and teaches them the laws of tefillin. The Center also holds religious conferences, lectures and debates, and conducts festive communal prayers.

Services, Activities and Accomplishments: The organization's major accomplishments have been a school in the Romema section of Jerusalem with three classes and evening work; 20 students who transferred to a Yeshiva; 50 scholarships which were distributed to students of Yeshivas; and the setting of a cornerstone for a huge building that will serve as the center of the Kurdish people.

OFFICERS

Yitzchak Amedi, 3 Hakishon, Jerusalem.
  Principal of School. Tel. (02) 226657.
Yitzchak Barashi, 25 Hayarkon, Jerusalem.
  Income tax supervisor. Tel. (02) 241523.
Binyamin Barashi, 76 Rashi, Jerusalem.
  Teacher. Tel. (02) 537860.
Moshe Cohen, 4 Sarai Yisrael, Jerusalem.
  Librarian. Tel. (02) 716273.
Meir Levy, 14 Mechalkai Hamayim, Jerusalem.
  Rabbi.
Mualem Eliyahu, Maoz Zyon "A" 104, Jerusalem.
  Rabbi. Tel. (02) 539011.

Ze'ev Zaken, 10 Kovoski, Jerusalem. Clerk.
Hotcha Eliyahu, Yohanan Ben Zakai 57, Jerusalem.
Rabbi. Tel. (02) 635443.
Adika Baruch, Rehov Yafo 52, Jerusalem.
Retired. Tel. (02) 227324.

FINANCIAL INFORMATION

Last year's entire annual budget was supplied from contributions. The budget for last year was $5,000. There was no deficit. The organization is registered as an Ottoman Association (reg. no. 11/2153), and has tax-free status in Israel (tax no. 4504118). There are 7 volunteers who work for the organization.

MEMBERSHIP, SCOPE, AND POLICY

Decisions are made by the Board.

AFFILIATIONS/REFERENCES

The organization is not affiliated with any political party in Israel.

FUNDING NEEDED

1. To build a religious academy (Yeshiva) in areas where there is a large concentration of Kurdish people in Israel in order to train the young as cantors, rabbis, teachers and judges in religious courts.
2. To foster the religious education and to give information and knowledge for improving the religious life of Kurdish Jews.
3. To establish a fund offering scholarships and loans to Kurdish youth so that they will be able to integrate into the rabbinical life in Israel.

RELIGIOUS WOMEN'S UNION

ארגון נשים דתיות

Pevsner 68
Haifa, 33135
Telephone: (04) 667422
Office Hours: There are no fixed office hours; services are available at
any time.

HISTORY AND DESCRIPTION
The Religious Women's Union was founded as a philanthropic society
in Haifa in 1935 by the women of the Ahavat Tora synagogue, immigrants of the German Aliyah.

Goals: The goal of the Religious Women's Union is to give self-help to
new immigrants and residents wherever the need is felt, and to service
the cultural interests of both members and immigrants.

Services, Activities, and Accomplishments: The services provided by the
Union include: the granting of general assistance—both financial and
emotional—to the needy of Haifa; assistance to large families and
one-parent families; the supplying of bedlinen and other household
necessities to needy brides; and the provision of twice-daily kosher meal
service—and thus visits—to cancer patients in the Christian Hospital.
All of these activities are performed on a voluntary basis by the Union's
membership. There are also regular lecture evenings, parties and other
cultural/social events.

OFFICERS
Director: Eva Kahn, Pevsner 68, Haifa.
                    Nurse and Midwife.
                    Tel. (04) 667422.
Treasurer: Chaya Flamm, Pevsner 58, Haifa.
                    Bookkeeper.
Board: Kathe Plessner, Shiloach 17, Haifa.
                    Tel. (04) 665637.
                    Martha Kellerman, Pevsner 17, Haifa.
                    Tel. (04) 661404.
                    Miriam Alperovic, Betar 3, Haifa.
                    Eva Ullmann, Smolenskin 4, Haifa.
                    Tel. (04) 241981.

FINANCIAL INFORMATION
95% of the Religious Women's Union's last annual budget of approximately $4,000 came from donations to the organization; the remaining
5% from membership dues. With little overhead costs, there was no
registered deficit for the last year. The Union is registered with the
Interior Ministry's Haifa District Office as an Ottoman Association
(reg. no. 41114/181). Donations to the organization are tax-free in
Israel (reg. no. 4500048), but not in the United States or any other

foreign country. The Union employs 1 part-time worker; there are also approximately 25 volunteers.

MEMBERSHIP, SCOPE, AND POLICY
One hundred members of the Union constitute its one Haifa branch. Any religious woman of Haifa or vicinity is welcome to join the organization. Decisions are made by an elected executive committee.

AFFILIATIONS/REFERENCES
The Religious Women's Union has no affiliations with any Israeli political party. Internationally, it is recognized by: *Jodiske Kvinders Hjaelpearbejde,* Ole Suhrsgade 14, Kobenhavn, Denmark.

FUNDING NEEDED
In order of priority, the Religious Women's Union lists the following as its most outstanding present funding requirements:
1. The enlargement of its kosher meals service. Estimated cost — $200 per month;
2. The establishment of a family assistance scheme;
3. The establishment and maintenance of summer recreation camps for needy mothers and children.

RESEARCH INSTITUTE OF FAMILY LIFE AND FAMILY LAW IN ISRAEL

המכון לחקר המשפחה ודיני המשפחה בישראל

Mount Zion
Jerusalem
P.O.B. 7479
Telephone: (02) 714602, (02) 665404.
Office Hours: Sunday-Thursday, 9:00 A.M. to 2:00 P.M.

HISTORY AND DESCRIPTION
The Institute was founded in 1970 in Jerusalem, with branches opened in Tel Aviv and Safed.

Organizational Structure: Members at large are accepted on the basis of profession and interests. The Institute is composed of a President and Secretary, in addition to research analysts, sociologists, lawyers and lecturers. Students and clients work together.

Goals: The Institute aims to provide advice in legal, sociological and religious spheres to those with family problems. The organization also works to influence legislature for enactment of laws for the betterment of society, to curtail prejudice against "second Israel" and to make society at large aware of its legal rights.

Services, Activities, and Accomplishments: Monthly lectures are open to the public addressed by judges, lawyers, rabbis, sociologists and scholarly laymen. Books on family topics are published, clients are accepted for individual consultation and are also referred to social organizations, lawyers, and the like. The Institute carries out research on family laws and assists people with family problems and marriage counselling.

OFFICERS
Director: Prof. Avner H. Shaki, 8 Diskin St., Kiryat Wolfson, Jerusalem. Professor, Tel Aviv U. Tel. (02) 665404.

Treasurer: Alphonso J. Saba, 9 Diskin St., Jerusalem. Tel. (02) 630468.

Board Members: Maimon H. Ben-Ami, 42 Uziel St., Jerusalem. Lawyer. Tel. (02) 424387.

David Bergman, Jerusalem. Deputy-Mayor.

Zion Baruch, 15 Ibn Gabirol St., Jerusalem. Constructor. Tel. (02) 222542.

FINANCIAL INFORMATION
90% of the Institute's income is provided by government ministries, with the remainder coming from donations. Last year's budget of $18,150 left the Institute with a deficit of $9,687. It is registered as an Ottoman Association in Jerusalem (reg. no. 11/2615). Donations to the

Institute are tax-free in Israel (reg. no. not supplied) but are not tax-free in the United States. Five part-time and three volunteer workers are employed by the Institute.

MEMBERSHIP, SCOPE, AND POLICY
Seventy members in Israel and twenty members abroad represent the Institute in its three Israeli branches and outside the country as well. Anyone interested in furthering the work of the Institute may join. Decisions are mostly made by the Executive Director.

AFFILIATIONS/REFERENCES
The organization is not affiliated with any political party in Israel. The Institute is also connected with the American Sepharadi Federation (515 Park Avenue, New York, NY) and the United Lubavitcher Organization (770 Eastern Parkway, Brooklyn, NY 11213).

FUNDING NEEDED
1. To enlarge the professional staff; cost, $225,000.
2. For repairs, electrical installment and painting of the Institute's quarters on Mount Zion; cost, $22,000.
3. For expansion of the Family Library; cost, $12,000.

REVACHA—ORGANIZATION FOR FAMILIES BLESSED WITH MANY CHILDREN

"רווחה" אגודה למשפחות ברוכות ילדים

13 Haray Judah Street
Bnei Brak P.O.B. 170, 51101
Telephone: (03) 792093
Office Hours: Sunday, Wednesday; 8:00 A.M. to 4:00 P.M.
Monday, Thursday; 9:00 A.M. to 5:00 P.M.
Tuesday, Friday; 8:00 A.M. to 12:00 NOON.

HISTORY AND DESCRIPTION
REVACHA, a volunteer organization, was established in 1975 for the special purpose of assisting familes who have been blessed with many children.

Organizational Structure: A Board of Directors meets on a bi-monthly basis to discuss and act upon urgent matters. The organization is located in the Neveh Achiezer—Baalei Melacha area of Bnei Brak. This location was chosen due to its proximity to those requiring these services; people coming from such neighborhoods as Kiryat Ono and Ramat Gan, in addition to Bnei Brak.

Goals: The organization works to provide a place where these special familes may purchase their essentials at reduced prices. It is hoped that expansion of the REVACHA store will be possible, since there are many families who have not yet been able to receive aid due to lack of space, equipment and financial resources.

Services, Activities, and Accomplishments: The organization runs a store where these families can purchase food and other essential items at specially reduced prices. When needed, financial assistance as well as scholarships are supplied, so that education will not deprecate. The Minister of Social Betterment has cooperated with the organization so that it is able to provide, at this time, basic minimal assistance and services. Members of the board give freely of their time to assist in the store in every way when and as needed, in addition to the many hours spent in administrative matters. REVACHA started from small rented quarters, with zero capital. Presently the organization has acquired government recognition, membership is still growing, and there is a stock of some funds from individual, tax-free donations. Nonetheless, the number of familes who turn to REVACHA for assistance is growing from day to day; thus, outside help and participation is essential for supporting this program.

OFFICERS
Director: Rabbi Azriel Tzadok, 1 Herzl St., Bnei Brak.
Treasurer: Aaron Drayn, 41 HaCarmel St., Bnei Brak.
                 Supervisor.

Board Members: Dr. Elyakim Asher, 4 Kaplan St., Bnei Brak.
Physicist. Tel. (03) 789658.
Ezra Arusi, 6 Eilat St., Ramat Gan. Accountant.
Tel. (03) 765049.
Joseph Yadai, 37 HaCarmel St., Bnei Brak. Clerk.
Tel. (03) 765049.

FINANCIAL INFORMATION
There are no membership dues for REVACHA; 80% of the organization's budget comes from donations, with the remainder from government assistance. Last year's budget of $120,000 left the organization
with a deficit of $8,000. REVACHA is a non-profit organization and is
registered as an Ottoman Association in Tel-Aviv (reg. no. 6595/99).
REVACHA is officially registered with the Department of Public
Organizations in the Ministry of Welfare, and its activities are under
their constant supervision. In Israel, donations to REVACHA are
tax-free (reg. no. 4505966); but not in the United States. Two full-time
and two part-time workers are employed by the organization, in addition to all the volunteer Board members.

MEMBERSHIP, SCOPE, AND POLICY
Four hundred families constitute the one, main branch of REVACHA.
All families that have four or more children are welcome to join, and no
membership dues are required. Decisions are made mostly by the
National Board.

FUNDING NEEDED
1. To purchase the organization's "own quarters" and a larger area, to
   be able to assist more needy familes.
2. For a clothing department to provide for the "entire family", from
   shoes to underwear to outerwear for men, women and children; cost,
   approx. $40,000.
3. For expansion of services and to be able to provide more household
   goods, bigger and better diversification of food items at specially
   reduced prices; cost, approx. $20,000.

Due to the lack of space, equipment and financial resources needed for
expansion, REVACHA can not honor the requests from many of the
growing number of families turning to the organization for assistance.
Consequently, outside help and participation is now sought and needed
in supporting this program.

R.I.C.H.I.—A COLLEGE FOR RABBIS AND RESEARCH FELLOWS

מכון העם והמדינה — לבירור בעיות חברה לאור ההלכה
בית מדרש לאברכים ורבנים

Mazkeret Batya
Telephone: (054) 50486
Office hours: Sunday-Thursday, 8:30 A.M. to 12:30 P.M.

HISTORY AND DESCRIPTION

RICHI was founded in 1977 on the initiative of Rabbi Ephraim Zalmanovitch, the rabbi of Mazkeret Batya. It is meant to be a literary-religious-educational institute that is to clarify social problems in the light of Jewish laws. It intends to examine contemporary social problems according to Halacha; publish papers, booklets and books on research; apply this research to the everyday life of Jewish society, and lecture to the public on this research.

Goals: The institute hopes to advance Jewish society in Israel, according to Halacha, Jewish religious law, and it will train rabbis and students as Judaica experts for social problems.

Services, Activities, and Accomplishments: The publication of books on alcoholism and drugs, the handling of youth under the influence of narcotics, and responsa on Halacha's answers to social problems.

OFFICERS

Director: Rabbi E. Zalmanovitch, Mazkeret-Batya. Chief Rabbi. Tel. (054) 50486.

FINANCIAL INFORMATION

Twenty percent of last year's annual budget came from donations; eighty percent came from municipalities and government Ministries. Last year's annual budget was $9,500. RICHI is registered as an Ottoman Association (No. 1046-1). Donations are tax-free both in Israel (No. 4504965) and in the United States (no number supplied). There are 12 full-time employees, 10 part-time employees, and 50 volunteers.

MEMBERSHIP, SCOPE, AND POLICY

Most decisions are made by the Executive Director and the National Board. The institution has only one branch in Israel.

AFFILIATIONS/REFERENCES

The organization is not affiliated with any political party in Israel.

FUNDING NEEDED

1. To maintain students, rabbis and scientific experts in Halachic and scientific research, establish a library, and fund projects for developing morals in youth, marital advice, and arbitration courts.
2. The publication of books on Israeli drug abuse.
3. The purchase of a computer, photocopier, and other publication equipment and materials.

THE RIGHT TO LIVE ANTI-ABORTION ORGANIZATION (EFRAT)

האגודה למאבק בהפלות ועידוד הילודה
— הזכות לחיות — אפרת

Zayit Ra'anan 14
Jerusalem (P.O.B. 15004)
Telephone: (02) 817963
Office Hours: Daily 8:00 A.M. to 3:00 P.M.

HISTORY AND DESCRIPTION
The Right to Live Organization was founded in July, 1978 in response to the new 1977 Israeli Abortion Law which legalized most abortions in the country. It is presently located in Jerusalem and surrounding districts only.

Organizational Structure: The organization consists of a president, chairman, secretary, treasurer and several board members. Services are provided by a staff of trained volunteer counsellors.

Goals: The goals of the Right to Live organization are to eliminate all abortions performed against Halacha (Jewish Law), and to promote a growth in the Jewish birth rates in Israel and the Diaspora.

Services, Activities, and Accomplishments: The Right to Live Organization provides an advisory service for women who have physical and/or psychological problems related to their pregnancies. Referrals are also made to doctors and social workers when deemed necessary. The organization attempts to spread anti-abortion information to the general public through the distribution of printed and illustrated materials, plus public lectures on various related topics. The organization also engages in political lobbying in the attempt to change the prevailing Israeli abortion law, and to extract more favorable attitudes from the government and the Jewish Agency regarding an increasing Jewish birth rate, largely through the easing of the burden of housing, education and child allotments to larger families. The Right to Live Organization lists among its major accomplishments the fact that it has taken part in the successful campaign to eliminate the 'social cause' paragraph from the Israeli Abortion Law; it has established a counselling service for pregnant women in the Jerusalem area; and it has published a colored brochure in Hebrew for public education against abortion.

OFFICERS
Director:	Prof. Binyamin Englman, Ben Yehuda 19, Rehovoth. Atomic Physicist. Tel. (054) 74259.
Treasurer:	Yisrael Gellis, Ezrat Torah 23, Jerusalem. Tel. (02) 813683.
Secretary:	Mordechai Blanck, Zayit Raanan, Jerusalem. Talmudic Leader. Tel. (02) 817963.
President:	Sephardic Chief Rabbi Ovadya Yosef, Jerusalem. Tel. (02) 634765.
Board Members:	Dr. Eli Shusshaim, Rynis 6, Jerusalem. General Practitioner. Tel. (02) 522949.

Dr. Chana Kagan, Nochum 14, Bnei Brak.
Pediatrician. Tel. (03) 783264.
Moshe Mann, Even Haozel 7, Jerusalem.
Works for Agudath Yisrael.
Tel. (02) 815791.
Mordechai Arnon, Shaarei Chessed 17,
Jerusalem. Leader in Judaism.
Tel. (02) 669116.

FINANCIAL INFORMATION
100% of the income of the Right to Live Organization comes from donations. There are no membership dues. Last year's budget of $2,240 left the organization with a deficit of $50. The organization is registered with the Jerusalem District Office of the Ministry of the Interior as an Ottoman Association (reg. no. 11/3049), but donations are not tax-free in either Israel or the United States. The Right to Live Organization employs some 50 volunteers.

MEMBERSHIP, SCOPE, AND POLICY
Six Israeli branches of the Right to Live Organization represent some 250 Israeli and 50 foreign members. Decisions are made by the Secretary in consultation with members of the Board. Basic operating decisions are often made by the President and Chairman of the Board. Membership is open to anyone who agrees with the basic aims of the organization.

AFFILIATIONS/REFERENCES
The Right to Live is not affiliated with any Israeli political party. The organization refers to the following international bodies:

The Human Life Center, St. John's University, Collegeville, Minnesota, U.S.A., 56321;

The Value of Life Committee, 637 Cambridge St., Brighton, Massachusetts, U.S.A., 01235;

World Federation of Doctors who Respect Human Life (British Section), 75 St. Mary's Road, Flayton, Merryside, U.K. L36 55R;

Movement per la Vita, Corso dipe denza 24, Milan, Italy;

Emergency Council of Jewish Families, 2 Penn Plaza, Suite 1500, New York, U.S.A., 10001;

Agudath Israel of America, 5 Beckman Street, New York, U.S.A. 10038;

The International Pro-Life Information Centre, 47 Aylesford Street, London, S.W. I, U.K.

FUNDING NEEDED
The Right to Live lists the following as its most pressing funding needs:
1. Nationwide anti-abortion campaign, including posters, literature and advertisements in buses and cinemas. Estimated cost $30,000.
2. The establishment of counselling services in major Israeli centers. Estimated cost $10,000.
3. The provision of economic support to encourage the choice of large families over abortions. Estimated cost $10,000.

RONI (AHARON) SOFFER CHARITY FUND   קרן אהרן סופר ז"ל

14 Marcus Street
Jerusalem
Telephone: (02) 633947
Office hours: 9:00 A.M. to 1:00 P.M.

HISTORY AND DESCRIPTION
The Roni Soffer Charity Fund was established in 1975 in memory of Roni Soffer, who was 23 years old when he died.

Goals: The Fund awards scholarships to needy students, provides for research work in closing the social and educational gap, extends assistance to social welfare cases, and has various other objectives related to youth education.

Services, Activities, and Accomplishments: Utilizing the facilities of the Joseph and Caroline Gruss Community Center, the fund has provided for the following activities during the last five years: a reading room and library for youth; furniture for the synagogue located in the Center; furniture for the Youth Club, including a TV set, stereo and records, and a bar for light drinks and sandwiches. There is a youth club where every evening 60-100 boys gather and benefit from a variety of educational activities as well as a club for a large number of elderly men and women who gather for a cup of tea and occasional lectures. The fund awards a yearly prize to an excellent worker at the Community Center. The fund provides for the above projects according to its ability; the demand is great, but the fund is compelled to limit its help in accordance with its resources.

OFFICERS
Director: Yehezkel Soffer, 14 Marcus, Jerusalem.
       Industrialist. Tel. (02) 633947.
Treasurer: Isaac Bar Moshe, 51 Hapalmach, Jerusalem.
       Commentator. Tel. (02) 631557.
Secretary: Isaac Askenazi, 13 Shimoni, Jerusalem. Asst.
       Br. Mgr., Sonol Oil Co. Tel. (02) 633066.
Members: David Sitton, 9 Itamar Ben Avi, Jerusalem.
       Head, Sephardic Comm. Org. Tel. (02) 632132.
       Hayim Dahan, 11 Strauss, Jerusalem.
       Auditor. Tel. (02) 232097.
       Yehezkel Tweig, 4 Ahad Haam, Jerusalem.
       Br. Mgr. Barclays Bank. Tel. (02) 633493.
       Avraham Soffer, 46-A Tchernikovsky, Jerusalem.
       Clerk. Tel. (02) 636814.
       Arnold Leiblich, 18 Pinski, Haifa.
       Independent. Tel. (04) 84724.
       Mrs. Doris Hay, Shikun Bayit Vegan.

FINANCIAL INFORMATION

Sources of the fund include the monies of the late Roni Soffer, his family, and contributions from various institutions and individuals. Donors have included Mr. Yitzhak Navon, President of Israel, Mr. Teddy Kollek, Mayor of Jerusalem, the Iraqi Organization, the Department for Sephardic Communities in the Jewish Agency, and the Sephardic Community Organization, Jerusalem. The fund is registered as an Ottoman Association (Israel reg. no. 11/2479) and tax-free status has been accorded. The fund is staffed by three volunteers.

MEMBERSHIP, SCOPE, AND POLICY

Anyone who is ready to volunteer and contribute is considered for membership. There are currently thirteen members in one branch and decisions are made by the local board.

AFFILIATIONS/REFERENCES

The fund has no affiliations with political parties in Israel. Abroad, the following individuals know of the work of the fund: Dr. S. Schulzinger, 1235 East 10 St., Brooklyn, N.Y., 11230; Dr. I. Benvenisty, 3725 East 1st St., Los Angeles, CA., 90063; Mr. J. Taylor, 53 Camp Hill Rd., Pomona, N.Y. 10970; Mr. V. Toeg, Hill View Gardens, London NW4, England; S. Levine, 81-06, 190 St., Jamaica, N.Y. 11423.

FUNDING NEEDED

1. Establishment of a Physical Development Hall with appropriate modern equipment: $16,000-$20,000.
2. Extension of individual tuition and purchase of books: $20,000.
3. Equipment for Elderly Club: $16,000. Running the club, $15,000.

ROTARY INTERNATIONAL —
DISTRICT 249 — ISRAEL

רוטרי בינלאומי – אזור 249 – ישראל

Dizengoff 299
P.O. Box 39149
Tel Aviv
Telephone: (03) 454542
Office hours: Sunday to Thursday, 5:00-8:00 P.M.

HISTORY AND DESCRIPTION

Rotary is an international voluntary service organization with 44 clubs in District 249, which includes all the territory of the State of Israel. The International organization was founded in 1905, and the first club in Israel in 1929.

Goals: The objects of Rotary are to encourage and foster the ideal of service as a basis of worthy enterprise. In particular, it strives to develop acquaintance as an opportunity for service; to maintain high ethical standards in business and professions; to lend dignity to each Rotarian's occupation as an opportunity to serve society; to apply the ideal of service by every Rotarian to his personal, business and community life; and to advance international understanding, goodwill and peace through a world fellowship of business and professional men united in the ideal of service.

Services, Activities, and Accomplishments: To date, the Rotary Clubs in Israel have worked to activate the ideals of Rotary in Israeli communities through personal involvement and through the District's Funds. These Funds include the District Relief Fund, which supplies medical equipment, especially artificial kidneys and intensive care equipment, and instruments for public hospitals and ambulatory units.
Scores of artificial kidney and intensive care units have been purchased and installed by Rotary Israel. In addition, Rotary Israel has a District Educational Commemorative Fund, the late M. Greidinger Advanced University Scholarship for Foreign Students, to enable them to study at Israeli academic institutions. Finally, there is the Legal and Social Research Fund, named after the late Professor Ze'ev Zeltzer Commemorative Fund, which grants an award for research at the undergraduate academic level on a legal or social theme connected with the ideals of the Rotary Organization.

OFFICERS

Governor,
District 249:   Andrew S. Kahan, P.O.B. 39149, Tel Aviv.
                   Engineer.
                   Tel. (03) 454542.

Chairman, Dist.
Relief Fund: P.D.G. Avraham Goldwasser, Hanof 6, Savyon.
                   Chemical Engineer. Tel. (03) 803257.

Coordinator,
Treasurer of
Educational Fund: P.D.G. Kenneth K. Greidinger, Hatishbi 98,
Haifa. Co. Director.
Tel. (04) 881267.

Chairman, Legal
& Social
Research Fund: P.D.G. Shlomo Grofman, Kidoshei Kahir 1,
Holon. Financial Director.
Tel. (03) 83028.

FINANCIAL INFORMATION

Organizations provide 100% of Rotary Israel's budget, which last year totalled $21,500. There was no deficit. All 3 Funds are registered as Ottoman, non-profit Associations, but no details are given. Donations in Israel and in the U.S. are stated to be tax-free, but no tax-exemption numbers are given. The organzation is run by 5 volunteer workers.

MEMBERSHIP, SCOPE, AND POLICY

Membership in Israel, in 44 Clubs, numbers 1,600. Total world membership is 875,000 in 19,100 clubs. The various Funds which Rotary Israel operates have no membership. Membership to the Rotary Clubs is based on professional or business activity classification. Decisions on membership are made by the Club Boards.

AFFILIATIONS/REFERENCES

Rotary Israel is affiliated with Rotary International, which has its headquarters at 1600 Ridge Avenue, Evanston, Illinois, 60201, U.S.A. It has no affiliation whatsoever with Israeli political parties.

FUNDING NEEDED

1. For the three District (and not local Club level) Foundations, which have been described in detail in the Services Section, above:
   The District Relief Fund, The Late M. Greidinger District Educational Commemorative Fund - University Scholarship for Foreign Students, and The Late Professor Ze'ev Zeltzer Commemorative Fund: Award for Research at Undergraduate Academic Level on Legal or Social Theme.
2. For the Israel Rotary District's International Service Projects which include the Neve Shalom — Intercommunal Educational Center for Peace and co-existance studies, and the Carmiel International Peace Youth Hostel Project.

SAFED AREA DEVELOPMENT COUNCIL

האגודה לפתוח אזור צפת

P.O. Box 1198, Safed
Telephone: (067) 70748

HISTORY AND DESCRIPTION
The Council, working in cooperation with the city of Safed was established in 1980 by local residents, including many immigrants to Israel from the U.S., Canada, Britain and South Africa.

Goals: The Council's goal is the ordered establishment and expansion of ecologically-sound economic enterprises in the Safed area, in order to improve job opportunities and the general economic climate.

Services, Activities, and Accomplishments: The Council office produces detailed information in English, currently unavailable from any other source, on investment opportunities, employment, and housing in the Safed area, to a steady stream of interested individuals. The Investments Service promotes investment possibilities in business and industry, tourism, and education. The Council encourages personal participation, in expertise and investments, in the restoration and revitalization of the holy city of Safed, once one of the oldest Jewish communities in Israel, and today a struggling development town in a distant corner of the country.

OFFICERS
Director: Mark Olman, P.O.B. 1198, Safed.
                        Public Service.
Treasurer: Robert Lapidus, Sprinzak 166/3, Safed.
                        Community Center Director.
Board Members: Joel Siegel, Sprinzak 165/4, Safed.
                        Project Renewal Director.
                        Eugene Kline, P.O.B. 283, Safed.
                        Retired psychologist.
                        Joseph Heckelman, P.O.B. 1195, Safed.
                        Rabbi.

FINANCIAL INFORMATION
All income has come from loans from members. Last year's budget totalled $500, which was also the amount of the deficit. The Council was registered as a non-profit organization with the Ministry of Interior in 1980, in the same year the Council became an approved project of PEF Israel Endowment Funds, an American Tax-exempt organization. The Council has one full-time employee.

MEMBERSHIP, SCOPE, AND POLICY
Anyone who is a permanent resident of Safed may be a member of the Council. At present, there are 86 members. Decisions are made by the Board.

AFFILIATIONS/REFERENCES

The Council is not affiliated with any political party in Israel. The Director's personal references include Congressman William Lehman, 2440 Rayburn House, Washington, D.C., and Ed Rosenthal Director of Community Relations, Greater Miami Jewish Federation, 4200 Biscayne Blvd., Miami, Fla.

FUNDING NEEDED

1. To produce informational materials: a) Guide to Living in Safed; b) Investment Opportunities prospectus; c) Learning Opportunities prospectus; and d) Tourist Guide to Safed.
2. To cover office operations and provide the following services: a) Jobs and housing information; b) investments casework; and c) correspondence with prospective investors and settlers.
3. Small Business Loan Fund — to help talented local citizens purchase tools and supplies.

Annual budget required is $30,000.

SAMUEL RUBIN CULTURAL CENTER OF MITZPE RAMON

מרכז תרבות ע"ש סמואל רובין, מצפה רמון,

P.O.B. 73, Mitzpe Ramon
Telephone: (057) 88442
Office hours: 8:00 A.M. to 1:00 P.M.
4:00 P.M. to 7:00 P.M.

HISTORY AND DESCRIPTION
The center provides all the cultural life in the town. All activities in Mitzpe Ramon are based in and around the community center.

Goals: The center, dedicated to the needs of the community, is used by the entire community. The center cooperates with other bodies in the community, and attempts to preserve maximum independence through loyalty to the settlement and its elected representatives.

Services, Activities, and Accomplishments: Programs for the community have been developed in numerous areas including recreation, education, and social integration.

OFFICERS
Director: Uzi Hazav, Mitzpe Ramon. Teacher.
Tel. 88278.
Treasurer: Esther Yunger, Mitzpe Ramon. Bookkeeper.
Executive
Committee: Tsvi Hazan, Mitzpe Ramon.
Employee of Magen David Adom.
Tel. 88195.
Tsvi Wolf, Mitzpe Ramon. Clerk.
Yacov Levin, Mitzpe Ramon. Clerk.
Avraham Haklay, Mitzpe Ramon. Clerk.
Tel. 88205.
David Zegen, Mitzpe Ramon. Clerk.

FINANCIAL INFORMATION
50% of the budget is provided by the Regional Council of Mitzpe Ramon; 25% from the Israel Corporation of Community Centers. Membership dues account for 15% of revenues, with donations making up the remaining 10%. Last year's annual budget of $71,428 left the center with a deficit of $12,500. Donations to the center in Israel and in the United States are tax-free (no registration no. or I.R.S. no. supplied). Eight full-time and fourteen part-time workers are employed by the center, as well as twenty volunteers.

MEMBERSHIP, SCOPE, AND POLICY
Membership is open to all who wish to join. Decisions are made by the Board.

AFFILIATIONS/REFERENCES
The center is not affiliated with a political party in Israel. Contact is maintained with Mr. Bob Gummers, Program Director of the Jewish Community Center, Rockford, Illinois.

FUNDING NEEDED
1. To build a second and third floor on the community center.
2. To establish more programs for all age groups.
3. To buy equipment for activities in the center.

SCHOLARSHIP FUND
IN THE NAME OF LEON RECANATI

קרן למתלמדים ע"ש ליאון רקנאטי

38 Yehuda Halevi
Tel Aviv
Telephone: (03) 651066
Office hours: 8 A.M. to 2 P.M.

HISTORY AND DESCRIPTION

The Scholarship Fund was originally established in Salonika (Greece) by Leon Recanati, head of the Jewish community there. Following his immigration to Palestine in 1946, the Fund was also transferred and in 1950 was incorporated in the B'nai Brith Lodge No. 1646, under the name of Rabbi Yehuda Halevi.

Organizational Structure: A committee of elected members of the Lodge, as well as members of the Recanati family, manages the Fund. At the start of every school year, the Fund approaches the various institutions of higher learning in Israel for recommendations of financially needy students studying for their M.A. or Ph.D. The selection made by the university is on the basis of scholastic achievements as well as financial need. The scholarships are awarded during a meeting with Mr. D. Haguel, the Fund manager.

Goals: The Fund wishes to contribute to the ingathering of the various exiles by encouraging young people of the oriental communities in Israel to continue their higher academic studies, and thereby narrow the gap between the Ashkenazi and Oriental communities.

Services, Activities, and Accomplishments: In the academic year 1978-79, the Fund distributed $10,000 to about 70 students, while in the last decade $80,000 has been given to 1600 students. These scholarships provide a moral uplift as well as much-needed assistance toward higher studies.

OFFICERS

Director:	Daniel Haguel, 8 Lessin, Tel Aviv.
Treasurer:	Joseph Dayan, 131/21 Yoseftal, Holon.
Chairman:	Daniel Recanati, Chairman of the Board.
Board:	Itzhak Aboudara, 17 Har Zion, Tel Aviv.
	Haim Nissimov, 40 Frishman, Tel Aviv.
	Avraham Morhaim, 9 Hapalmach, Tel Aviv.
	Haim Cohen, 43 Hazoar, Tel Aviv.
	Albert Ashkenazi, 33A Ha'atzmaut, Bat Yam.
	Elazar Hacohen, 44 Chen, Tel Aviv.
	Moshe Kalaora, 3 Ahuzat Bayit, Tel Aviv.
	Reuben Assa, Assa Pladot Ltd., 3 Ahuzat Bayit, Tel Aviv.

FINANCIAL INFORMATION

Eighty percent of the sources of the fund are donations; twenty percent are repayments by the students. The Fund is a revolving one, free of any interest and linkage, with repayment starting a year after graduation, in small installments. Last year's budget was $10,000. The organization employs one part-time worker. The Fund is registered in the Companies Registrar of the Ministry of Justice (No. 52-002316-9) and donations are tax-free both in Israel and the U.S. (no numbers provided).

MEMBERSHIP, SCOPE, AND POLICY

Any B'nai Brith member can join. Currently there is one branch in Israel. Decisions are made by the managing committee.

AFFILIATIONS/REFERENCES

The Fund has no party affiliations in Israel.

FUNDING NEEDED

To increase the aid to students, to be adjusted to inflation.

SELA YAKOV FUND

סלע יעקב — סיוע ללומדי עבודת-אדמה

c/o R. Kidron, Moshav Magshimim, 56910
Telephone: (03) 914156

HISTORY AND DESCRIPTION
The organization was founded in November, 1978. It is named after the late Mr. Jacob Kidron who was killed in a motor accident in 1977. The main object of the organization is to give scholarships to students studying agriculture at the Hebrew University, Weitzman Institute and other establishments.

OFFICERS
Director: Mrs. Rivke Kidron, Magshimim. Teacher.
Treasurer: Mr. Meir Kidron, Magshimim. Farmer.
Board: Mr. S. Keinan, Magshimim. Farmer.
               Mr. S. Krouthomer, Magshimim. Farmer.
               Mr. H. Noam, 24 Montefiore St. Lawyer.

FINANCIAL INFORMATION
No budget or deficit figures were given, but the organization is registered as an Ottoman Association in Ramle and donations are tax-free in Israel (reg. number not reported). 100% of the organizations' income comes from donations.

MEMBERSHIP, SCOPE, AND POLICY
Anyone approved by the board of directors can join, and as of now there are 10 members in Israel. Most decisions of the organization are made by the Executive Director.

FUNDING NEEDED
Funds are needed for scholarships for students.

SERVICES CENTER FOR THE AGED IN THE VALLEYS

האגודה למען הזקן, מרכז שרותים לקשיש באזורי העמקים

P.O.B. 169
Afula
Telephone: (065) 90016
Office hours: 8:00 A.M. to 4:00 P.M.

HISTORY AND DESCRIPTION

The Services Center for the Aged in the Valleys was established in 1971 by 15 local authorities (8 local councils and 7 regional authorities). The construction of the building in which it is housed commenced in 1972 and the Center began to operate in 1974 as a home for the aged and day-care center.

Organizational Structure: A General Membership Meeting is held at least once a year to make general policy decisions. The Executive Committee represents the association and implements programs and policy.

Goals: To provide personal and medical care and to look after the needs of aged people, especially the veterans in the region of the four valleys: Israel, Beitshean, Zevulun, and Jordan.

Service, Activities, and Accomplishments: The Center has 200 residents in four groups: 25 well-aged people, 75 weak (infirm), 80 in long-term nursing wards and 20 psychogeriatric residents. In addition, the Center provides services and day-care to a group of 15 aged people from the local community. The nursing service has achieved much through the personal touch and friendliness of its personnel.

OFFICERS

Director: Ch. Ream, Beit Shearim, Mayor of
                          Kishon Regional Council.
Board Members: M. Roll, Kibbutz Maagan.
                          Z. Laski, Kibbutz Ein Harod.
                          E. Ovadia, Afula. Mayor of Afula.
                          M. Goldman. Mayor of Kfar Tabor.
                          A. Yarom, Afula.

FINANCIAL INFORMATION

40-45% of the Center's income comes from payment by the residents or their families, 40% from Government offices, and 15-20% from local authorities. Last year's annual budget of $1,200,000 left the Center with a deficit of $10,000. The Center is registered in the North District as a non-profit Ottoman Association (reg. no. 99/37). Details of tax-status for donations not supplied. 95 full-time and 40 part-time workers are employed by the Center, as well as 6-10 volunteers.

MEMBERSHIP, SCOPE, AND POLICY

Membership is open to anyone over 18 who applies in writing and is approved unanimously by members of the Executive Committee. There are 26 members in Israel, in 1 branch. Most decisions are made by the Executive Director.

AFFILIATIONS/REFERENCES

The Center is not affiliated with any Israeli political party.

FUNDING NEEDED

1. To solve the problem of the absence of operating capital.
2. To purchase medical equipment — E.C.G. equipment and a hydraulic bath.
3. To finance activities satisfying the cultural needs of the residents.
4. To purchase teaching aids for the personnel.

SHAAR EPHRAIM AND
BETH REPHAEL YESHIVA

ישיבת שער אפרים ובית רפאל

23 Hapisga Street
P.O.B. 16087
Jerusalem, 91160
Telephone: (02) 272132—415895
Office hours: 9:00 A.M. to 13:00 P.M.

HISTORY AND DESCRIPTION

Shaar Ephraim and Beth Rephael Yeshiva is a new talmudic institute
intended for young gifted yeshiva graduates. It opened in September
1979 and is presently housed in the Sephardic Community Synagoge in
the Shmuel Hanavi Quarter, Eretz Hafetz Street, in Jerusalem.

The Institute is headed and directed by Rabbi Amram Enkaoua, a
graduate of the Mirrer Yeshiva in New York, and by Rabby Meyer
Enkaoua, both descendants of the famous Enkaoua family.

It is a graduate institute of talmudic studies engaging also in publishing
and editing of books and manuscripts of the rabbis of the Enkaoua
family and other rabbis from North Africa.

Yeshiva Shaar Ephraim and Beth Rephael of Jerusalem, was named for
the great Saint Rabbi Ephraim Enkaoua from the city of Tlemcen,
Algeria, who lived about 50 years before the Spanish Inquisition, and
named also for the grand Rabbi Rephael Enkaoua, a descendant of the
Rabbi of Tlemcen, who was chief Rabbi as well as chief justice of the
Rabbinical High court in Rabat, Morocco.

The Yeshiva serves young married scholars who devote their time to all
phases of Torah study and Talmud research. In addition, these scholars
are engaged in the preparation of holy manuscripts of the well-known
rabbis of the famous Enkaoua family.

The Yeshiva plans to publish all the manuscripts of the world renown
Rabbis of the Enkaoua family, which are now in its possession and will
serve as a source of knowledge and information to all. It will reprint
those books which were printed in limited quantities and which are
practically unavailable.

A second phase of the program is for these young scholars to serve as
rabbis, educational leaders and advisors in communities throughout the
world. In doing this they will revive the learning of the saintly rabbis.
The Yeshiva's major accomplishments have been the support of 12
young scholars who study in the Kollel.

OFFICERS

Director: Amram H. Enkaoua, P.O.B. 16087, Jerusalem.
                Rabbi. Tel. (02) 415895.

Board Members: Meyer Enkaoua, P.O.B. 6276, Jerusalem. Teacher.
                Tel. (02) 272132.
                David Amar, Colombia 15/11 Jerusalem. Rabbi.
                Tel. (02) 536675.

Yitzchak Cohen, Shmuel Hanavi 1, Jerusalem.
Rabbi.

David Dahan, Ahinoam 13, Jerusalem. Rabbi.
No telephone.

Shmuel Cohen, Issa Beracha 24, Jerusalem.
House Painting contractor. No telephone.

Jacob Enkaoua, P.O.B. 9440 Jerusalem.
Mechanic. Tel. (02) 417990.

FINANCIAL INFORMATION

All of last year's annual budget came from donations from France, the United States and Canada. Last year's annual budget of $25,000 left a deficit of $5,000. Donations to the Yeshiva are not tax-free. However, an application has been submitted to obtain tax-free status in Israel. The Yeshiva is registered as an Ottoman Association (reg. no. 11/3358). There are no full-time or part-time employees of the Yeshiva, just 3 volunteers.

MEMBERSHIP, SCOPE, AND POLICY

Decisions are made mostly by the Executive Director. There are 25 members in Israel and 15 abroad.

AFFILIATIONS/REFERENCES

The Yeshiva is not affiliated with any political party in Israel. The Yeshiva is in contact with the following: Ohr Joseph Foundation, 110-45 Queens Blvd., Forest Hills, New York; Shearit Israel, 18 West 70 Street, New York, New York; Sam Catton Foundation (no address given); and Rabinat Sepharade du Quebec, Montreal.

FUNDING NEEDED

1. The publication of five books. Estimated cost: $30,000.
2. The granting of annual grants and scholarships for 15 graduates. Estimated cost: $30,000.
3. The purchase of a house or an apartment for an office and study rooms. Estimated cost: $100,000.
4. The purchase of a plot and construction of a building. Estimated cost: $300,000.

SHAARE ZEDEK MEDICAL CENTER

המרכז הרפואי שערי צדק

P.O.B. 293
Jerusalem 91002
Telephone: (02) 555111
Office hours: 8:00 A.M. to 4:00 P.M. (Fridays till 1:00 P.M.)

HISTORY AND DESCRIPTION
In 1873 the first public committee for "Shaare Zedek" was founded in Frankfurt, Germany. Activities started in the clinic which opened in the Old City, and in 1902 the main hospital building opened on Jaffa Road, in West Jerusalem. The School of Registered Nurses opened in 1936. In each of Jerusalem's crises, the hospital was always on call—during epidemics; Arab pogroms; the War of Independence; the Six-Day War and the Yom Kippur War, when the hospital also functioned as a military hospital.

In 1974 the Day Hospital was opened for those who do not require hospitalization. In 1978 an affiliation agreement was signed with the School of Medicine of the Hebrew University. In 1979 the new Medical Center opened opposite Mount Herzl, in order to give the population of Jerusalem and the areas surrounding it comprehensive medical care —hospitalization, clinics and rehabilitation. The new buildings are located on a 14-acre site.

Services, Activities, and Accomplishments: The construction of the Medical Center cost about $54 million. The main hospital building, planned for more than 500 beds, currently contains over 300 beds and 70 baby basinettes. In 1981 a 54-bed chronic care department will be added. Medical facilities include 25 inpatient departments, 33 specialized outpatient clinics, 22 diagnostic institutes and laboratories and 17 other para-medical departments and services, day hospitals, research institute, rehabilitation, auditorium central library and administration.

The Shaare Zedek Medical Center is recognized by the government of Israel, directed by a public committee with members in Israel and abroad, and is supported by, Jewish and non-Jewish, committees and friends in Israel and throughout the world.

The hospital's major accomplishment has been the building of the new and modern comprehensive medical center, which offers a broad range of specialized services, with special emphasis on pediatrics, surgery, geriatrics—hospitalization, clinic and home care.

OFFICERS
Director General: Prof. David M. Maeir, M.D., 36 Ramban, Jerusalem. Tel. (02) 555111.

Associate Director
General-
Administrator: Nachum Pessin, 28 Hidah, Jerusalem.

Deputy Director
General-(Finance): Yechiel Kempner (C.P.A.), 129/18 Sanhedria
                  Murchevet, Jerusalem.
Chairman (Hon.)
Executive Board: Samson Krupnick, 22 Pinsker, Jerusalem.
                  Tel. (02) 635847.
Chairman (Hon.)
Finance
Committee: Dov Genachowski, 6 Magnes Circle, Jerusalem.
                  Tel. (02) 225251.

FINANCIAL INFORMATION

16.75% of last year's annual $17,950,000 operating budget came from
contributions. The deficit was $3,380,000. The source of contributions
were committees and friends in Israel, U.S.A. (No. 98-6001091), Canada
(No. 045455421-08), England (No. 262870), Switzerland, Germany,
Holland (countries where Shaare Zedek has obtained tax deductibility)
and South Africa, Australia, Europe, Central & South America and
other countries. The Medical Center was registered as an Ottoman
Association in 1947 (No. 11/222) and donations are tax deductible (No.
150/352) in Israel.

MEMBERSHIP, SCOPE, AND POLICY

Daily operating decisions are made by the Executive Director. Policy is
determined at an annual international Board meeting. There are also
monthly Executive Board meetings. There are 4,500 members in Israel
and over 100,000 members abroad. The Hospital has fund-raising offices throughout the world. The quota of 850 full-time staff positions is
supplemented by 400 volunteers and 58 girls in National Service. The
School of Nursing has 90 students.

AFFILIATIONS/REFERENCES

The Medical Center is not affiliated with any political party in Israel.
The Medical Center is affiliated with the School of Medicine of the
Hebrew University, Jerusalem. The Medical Center has the following
contacts abroad: Albert Einstein School of Medicine, Yeshiva University, Bronx, New York and The American Committee for Shaare Zedek,
49 West 45th Street, New York, New York 10036.

FUNDING NEEDED

1. The completion of the new Medical Center. Estimated cost — $1
   million.
2. Medical Equipment, $1 million.

SHALSHELET

שלשלת

11/45 Diskin Street
Jerusalem
Telephone: (02) 636413
Office hours: 8:00 A.M. to 12:00 P.M. and 4:00 P.M. to 7:00 P.M.

HISTORY AND DESCRIPTION

Shalshelet was founded in 1980 following a number of propitious events. A survey undertaken in 1977 indicated that numerous social services and funds failed to stem the rising rate of the prison population, delinquency, alcoholism, wife and baby battering, and divorce. An inter-disciplinary professional committee was formed in 1978 to examine these findings, and concluded that these problems stemmed largely from a rejection of their parents' traditional values and practices, and a failure by young people to find satisfactory alternatives. Thus, immediate material and emotional gratification became desirable. This, however, clashed with the economic and defence needs of the young Jewish State and the traditional stability of the Jewish family. Therefore, in January 1980, a committee was formed into a public Ottoman Association, having decided that it was time to intervene in the life cycle in order to prevent symptoms of family breakdown close to the time of marriage. 300 young couples registering for marriage were interviewed in order to understand their needs and to examine how best to improve the situation.

Organizational Structure: Shalshelet has a Board, founder members and friends. The Board's role is to define policy and priorities; to enlist founder members for help in defining projects which can suitably implement policy. Board and founder members act as counsultants to these projects and monitor them, personally carry out some of these projects, and appoint suitable personnel to implement the projects. Friends support Shalshelet by considering goals, funding general and specific projects, general fund-raising, and publicity.

Goals: To restore the status of the Jewish family and community through pre and post-marriage educational programs and a new integrated approach. Shalshelet is developing an integrated approach which combines professional counselling and behavioralistic theories with elements drawn from Jewish values, by working with groups in the general population and with professionals. This new approach has already proved to be of interest to the young couples who have been joining programs. New insights appear to have been gained into their total value system and roles and relationships between themselves within the family, in the community and in Israel.

Shalshelet feels that there is a golden opportunity to reinstate pride in the Jewish family. Its work has shown that it is relatively easy to tap the more spiritual and idealistic values underlying much of the tensions leading to crises—much of which stem from striving for unattainable material goals.

The professional Shalshelet team has found ever-growing interest in its unique approach. This approach is beginning to sensitize both professionals and the community at large to the contribution which Jewish values can make in withstanding today's turbulent society.

The network of baby clinics, prison services and new immigrant groups have requested Shalshelet programs. In particular Shalshelet has started group work with the most vulnerable section of the population, namely Sephardi young couples. Until now the role of the husband and father has been greatly under-rated and neglected in Israel. Social services generally fail to reach men in giving services. Since Shalshelet provides programs for *couples*, it is in the privileged position of being able to attempt to stem problems which later lead to family breakdown.

Services, Activities, and Accomplishments: Shalshelet offers lectures, counselling and seminars to professional and general population; appropriate films, slides and literature, both centrally and in neighborhood community centers, and a central club (a newly-converted shelter) as a safe and neutral base. Opportunities for those of similar and different, cultural, ethnic, socio-economic backgrounds and degrees of religious practice meet at weekend seminars, at homes, at excursions, and at Shabbat lunches. The activities center around Jewish holidays and evening social and cultural events. Professional training of the Shalshelet team in counselling methods integrate with elements drawn from Jewish values.

Shalshelet's major accomplishments until now have been the establishment of the organization; the contacting and motivating of young couples to join groups; weekend seminars in Safad and in the outskirts of Jerusalem; raising the awareness of social service givers regarding the needs of young couples and singles; community discussion groups in community centers and in homes; finding resource people on topics related to Jewish family, e.g. education of the future generation in the light of the past; some fund-raising. Gaining support of Ministry of Welfare and Labor in acceptance of the idea that methods based on traditional Jewish values can help rehabilitate families in distress.

OFFICERS

Director:
Prof. Meir Lowenberg, Bar Ilan Univ. Social worker.
Tel. (03) 920967.

Treasurer:
Harry Sapir, Israel General Bank. Director.
Tel. (02) 665073.

Board Members: Pessy Krausz, M.Sc., 11/45 Diskin St., Jerusalem.
Social Psychologist, project leader.
Tel. (02) 636413.

Dr. Naomi Abramowitz, 4 Keren Hayesod,
Jerusalem. Social Worker.
Tel. (02) 231227.

Rabbi Avraham Druk, 232/13 Dov Gruner,
Talpiot Mizrach.
Community Rabbi.
Tel. (02) 719197.

Mr. Meir Horowitz, 7 Narkiss, Jerusalem. Lawyer.
Tel. (02) 227823.
Mrs. Adina Katzoff, 30 King George, Jerusalem.
Social Worker.
Tel. (02) 221006.
Dr. Daniel Levine, Gesher Educational Affiliates.
Political Scientist.
Tel. (02) 811821.

FINANCIAL INFORMATION

Last year's annual budget came from the following sources: membership dues and donations, 54%; Ministry of Religious Affairs, 9%; Ministry of Education, 9%; Ministry of Social Welfare and Labor, 28%. Last year's annual budget of $5,500 left a deficit of approximately $2,000. Donations to the organization are tax-free in Israel (no number was supplied), and in England (no. 281755). The organization is registered as an Ottoman Association (no. 11/3559). There is one part-time employee plus 18 volunteers; in addition there are 8 professional staff members on an hourly basis.

MEMBERSHIP, SCOPE, AND POLICY

Decisions are made by the national board. There are 15 members in Israel and about 50 in London and an additional 50 in Montreal.

AFFILIATIONS/REFERENCES

The organization is not affiliated with any political party in Israel.

FUNDING NEEDED

1. The decoration and furbishing newly-converted shelter for use as central club-house.
   Estimated cost — $6,000.
2. The provision of suitable and adequate office premises.
   Estimated cost — $10,000 per year.
3. The training and development of professional Shalshelet staff and professional social service givers, such as nurses in mother and baby clinics, community workers, and social workers.
   Estimated cost — $30,000 per year.

SHALVA REST AND CONVALESCENT HOME

שלוה בית החלמה והבראה

1 Mezulot Yam Street
Givataim
Telephone: (03) 317396; (03) 317397
Office hours: 9:00 A.M. to 1:00 P.M. and 4:00 P.M.-6:00 P.M.

HISTORY AND DESCRIPTION

The Shalva Rest and Convalescent Home was founded about 45 years ago on a voluntary basis by a group of people who were sensitive and aware of the distress and difficulties faced by their fellow man. It provides physical assistance and spiritual tranquility to people of limited means. It is run under the auspices of B'nei Brith. The Home serves people of limited means, who are recuperating from surgery and need a period of rest before resuming their normal activities. The services are given on a non-profit basis, and the management performs its duty devotedly and faithfully and is assisted by a polite staff.

The Home is housed in a four storey building, holding 170 beds, cultural hall and a synagogue. It is located in Givataim, near Tel Aviv and is surrounded by lawns, flowers, and trees, in the middle of a park. In order to ease the plight of people of limited means and those who have no means at all, a fund for the needy has recently been established, the fruits of which will be used to finance the rest days of those people. This fund is based on contributions of institutions and friends who are interested in perpetuating their names in the Shalva Home, in honoring the memory of their deceased relatives and in assisting the Home in providing aid to the needy.

The major accomplishment of the organization has been the erection of a four storey building and care for 170 beds, dining rooms, cultural halls and a synagogue.

OFFICERS

Chaim Bar Aba, 62 Galipoli, Tel Aviv.
Retired. Tel. (03) 335497.
Dr. Moshe Salpeter, 11 Megiddo, Tel Aviv.
Economist. Tel. (03) 229645.
Josef Halpern, 12 Baltimore, Tel Aviv.
Businessman. Tel. (03) 454462.
Jesajah Filipson, 12 Josef Elijahu, Tel Aviv.
Retired. Tel. (03) 281626.
Mrs. Gita Flaster, 19 Haroeh, Ramat Gan.
Housewife. Tel. (03) 722126.
Jair Prisant, 62 Galipoli, Tel Aviv.
Functionary. Tel. (03) 339046.
Moshe Kuritz, 9 Hagist, Bnei Brak. Rabbi.
Tel. (03) 791764.

FINANCIAL INFORMATION

20% of last year's annual budget came from donations; the remaining 80% came from an accommodation fee paid by convalescents of social institutions. The budget for last year was $280,000, with a deficit of $2,000. The organization is registered as an Ottoman Association (reg. no. 200/99). Donations to the organization are tax-free, but no tax numbers were supplied. There are 17 full-time and 26 part-time workers employed by the organization, in addition to 7 volunteers.

MEMBERSHIP, SCOPE, AND POLICY

The organization did not supply information regarding membership. Decisions are made by the Board members.

AFFILIATIONS/REFERENCES

The organization is not affiliated with any political party in Israel, and is in contact with the Bnai Brith lodges in Europe and in the U.S.A. However, no specific information was supplied.

FUNDING NEEDED

1. Enlargement of the dining room, kitchen, and supply depot. Estimated cost: $250,000.
2. The renovation of most of the rooms. Estimated cost: $120,000.
3. The construction of an additional two floors to the building. Estimated cost: $200,000.

SHAMIR: ASSOCIATION OF JEWISH PROFESSIONALS FROM THE SOVIET UNION AND EASTERN EUROPE IN ISRAEL

אגודת אקדמאים שומרי מצוות יוצאי רוסיה ומזרח אירופה

6 David Yellin
Jerusalem
Telephone: (02) 223702
Office hours: 9:00 A.M. to 2:00 P.M.

HISTORY AND GOALS

"Shamir" was founded in 1971 to further the Jewish commitment of religious academics immigrating to Israel to help other Soviet Jews with no knowledge of Judaism to learn and practice their heritage which has been outlawed and persecuted in Russia for 60 years. The Association believes that the Jewish exodus from the Soviet Union is only the beginning of the struggle for Jewish revival in its own land; that the aliya of Soviet Jews can only be called successful if it is accompanied by the swift spiritual absorption of the newcomers. A Jew remaining in Russia faces spiritual death; a Jew immigrating to Israel must be able to find spiritual rebirth. No one is better able to assist Soviet immigrants than the people who have stood in their place, who have gone through their trials.

Goals: To bring Soviet Jewry back into the lifestream of Judaism, thus generating genuine national-spiritual motivation to immigrate to Israel and to help revive the over-all religious fibre of the Jewish people.

Services, Activities, and Accomplishments: "Shamir" directs a small staff of teachers, translators and editorial and office workers, It organizes lessons and cultural events at immigration absorption centers and other places in Israel. It also runs an Evening Yeshiva in Jerusalem (where most of the students have already started their Torah education underground in the Soviet Union). The "Shamir" Publishing House provides instructional, cultural and source material for this wide range of adult Jewish re-education. The Association is producing the first Russian translation of the Chumash to be set up in parallel pages of Hebrew and Russian text with Commentaries of Rashi, the Rambam, Ibn Ezra, and others chosen to explain and teach the source of Jewish life and law to both novice and scholar.

OFFICERS

Director: Professor H. Branover, Omer, Beersheva.
                          Professor of Magneto-hydrodynamics.
                          Tel. (057) 61286.
Treasurer: Shalom-Ber Friedman, Jerusalem.
                          Lawyer.
                          Tel. (02) 810135.

Board Members: A. Shif, Shikun Chabad, Lod.
                 Lawyer.
                 Tel. (054) 27224.
                 M. Gorelik, Kiryat Malachi. Architect.
                 R. Petersbursky, Jerusalem.
                 Chemist.
                 Tel. (02) 861353.
                 Z. Wagner, Jerusalem. Economist.
                 A. Godin, Kiryat Sharet, Holon. Lawyer.

FINANCIAL INFORMATION

50% of the Association's income comes from the Jewish Agency, 34% from private donations, 10% from book sales, 6% from the Ministry of Education. Last year's annual budget of approximately $45,000 left the Association with a deficit of $3,600. "Shamir" is registered in Jerusalem as a non-profit Ottoman Association (reg. no. 11/2220). Donations in Israel and the United States are tax-free (Israeli tax no. not supplied, US tax no. 1383331KO M-79-EO-75). 14 full-time and one part-time workers are employed by the Association, as well as a large number of volunteers, including the Chairman.

MEMBERSHIP, SCOPE, AND POLICY

Membership is open to any immigrant from the USSR or Eastern Europe who wants to join. There are 800 members in Israel, in two branches, and one branch abroad. Decisions are made by the National Board.

AFFILIATIONS/REFERENCES

The Association is not affiliated with any Israeli political party. It is cooperating with the following organizations:
National Conference on Soviet Jewry, 11 West 42nd St., Rm. 1864, NYC, NY 10036.
Board of Jewish Education, 426 W. 58th St., NYC, NY 10019.
London Friends of "Shamir", 45 Sheldon Ave., London N 6, England, UK.

FUNDING NEEDED

1. To complete and expand the Association's Basic Jewish library of quality Russian translations of fundamental Jewish texts (Torah with commentaries, Shulchan Aruch, Siddur, the Kuzari and others).
2. To financially rescue the Association's burgeoning Yeshiva and expand it to allow the many additional applicants who want to study but for whom the means is lacking to accept them.
3. To finance the publication of Jewish manuscripts written in the Soviet Union and smuggled out to Israel.

SHARAL —
FURNITURE REPAIR AND RESALE

ש.ר.ל. — שירותים ורהיטים לנזקקים

Hizkiyahu Hamelech 36,
Jerusalem
Telephone: (02) 660221
Office Hours: 8:00 A.M.-2:00 P.M. daily

HISTORY AND DESCRIPTION
In 1977, a special project of the Ministry of Social Affairs funded a number of new programs in two neighborhoods in the southern districts of Jerusalem (Katamon Het-Tet). A special non-profit association was set up to handle the financial aspects of the project, SHARAL — Furniture Repair and Resale.

Organizational Structure: The Board of Directors is composed of a public figure, two employees, a social worker/coordinator of the project, a representative of the Ministry of Labour, and a representative of the Southern Office of the Jerusalem Department of Family Services.

Goals: The goals of SHARAL are to train currently unemployed Jerusalem residents in a profession of light carpentry; to teach them proper work habits; to find jobs in the open market for these workers within a year of their beginning at SHARAL; and to provide good quality, used, fully repaired furniture to neighborhood residents at prices scaled according to their ability to pay.

Services, Activities, and Accomplishments: At present, SHARAL employs 8 men from the neighborhood who had been previously unemployed for 5-10 years, and is training them so they will be able to return to the open job market. A half-time supervisor instructs the workers in how to repair furniture and assists the workers in setting prices, arranging the workshop. The social worker/coordinator recruits the workers, holds weekly group sessions to reinforce good work habits, and irons out personality and group conflicts. On the consumer end of the project, SHARAL picks up furniture, used or repairable, free of charge, for contribution to its workshop/store, and sells the repaired items to the residents of South Jerusalem. The repaired furniture is sold at graduated prices, depending on the ability of the buyer, and recommendation of the Welfare Department of the Jerusalem municipality.

OFFICERS
Director: Ezra Giano, Director of Volunteers, Ministry of Labour. P.O.B. 1260, Jerusalem. Tel. (02) 719081.

Treasurer: Tova Yunai, Amatzia 1, Jerusalem. Teacher. Tel. (02) 668308.

Board Members: Hela Haniv, Hizkiyahu Hamelech, Jerusalem. Social Worker.

Salomon Kadosh, Volunteer.
Batia Erlich. Hizkiyahu Hamelech 36, Jerusalem.
Social Worker.
Tel. (02) 660221.

FINANCIAL INFORMATION

The Ministry of Labour and Social Affairs and the Steering Committee on Project Renewal provides 80% of SHARAL's funds. Another 10% of the organization's income comes from the sale of furniture, and the remaining 10% from donations-in-kind — i.e., contributions of used furniture. Last year's budget totalled $14,180, and a deficit of $9,400 was covered by the Ministry of Labour and Social Affairs. SHARAL is registered as an Ottoman, non-profit Association, but no details are provided. No information is supplied concerning tax-exempt status, either in Israel or the U.S. Eight part-time employees are listed.

MEMBERSHIP, SCOPE, AND POLICY

SHARAL is not a membership organization. Decisions are made on a day-to-day basis by the coordinator/social worker, in conjunction with her supervisor at the City Department of Family Services. Policy decisions are made by the Board of Directors.

AFFILIATIONS/REFERENCES

SHARAL is not affiliated with any Israeli political party. Organizations familiar with SHARAL's work are the Project Renewal Steering Committee, Katamon-Het-Tet Neighborhoods, Block 146, Bar Yochai Street, Jerusalem; and Project Renewal, U.J.A., 1290 Ave. of the Americas, New York (Tel. 212-757-1500).

FUNDING NEEDED

1. For repairing used furniture and for advertising and soliciting more used furniture.
2. For transporting furniture.

SHARVIT HACHESED
CENTRAL HELP ORGANIZATION
שרביט החסד, מפעל מרכזי לסיוע

P.O.B. 5335,
Jerusalem.
Telephone: (02) 286786.
Office Hours: No set hours.

HISTORY AND DESCRIPTION
This organization was founded by a few young men who decided to start
a free-loan fund to help ease the difficult financial situation in Israel.
Assistance is provided both in the form of loans (interest-free and with
easy payments) and donations (to people in need who cannot pay back
the money). Loans are provided primarily to members, but also to
non-members, upon submission of a request from and with the approval
of the Board. The loans are given for the following purposes only: (1)
marriage of the borrower or his child; (2) acquiring or renovating an
apartment which the borrower will live in; (3) establishing a new business; (4) the birth of a child; (5) the bar-mitzvah of the borrower's son.

OFFICERS
Director: Avrohom Mermelstein, Panim Meirot 5, Jerusalem.
                     Head of kollel.
Treasurer: Shmuel Shimon, Tzefania 37, Jerusalem.
                     Yeshiva student.
Board Members: Sholom Philip, Amos 7, Jerusalem.
                     Sholom Markowitz, Tzefania 38, Jerusalem.
                     Chaim Yedvab, Torah Metzion 3, Jerusalem.

FINANCIAL INFORMATION
The members' monthly dues constitute the bulk of the organization's
income (80%), and in turn serve as the capital from which they themselves receive loans as needed. The remaining 20% of the funds come
from donations. Last year's annual budget was $6,000, with no deficit
recorded for this period. Donations to the organization are not tax-free
in the U.S.A. or Israel. The organization is registered as a non-profit
Ottoman Association in the Jerusalem District Office of the Ministry of
the Interior (reg. no. 11/2289). Three volunteers make up the staff of
"Sharvit HaChesed".

MEMBERSHIP, SCOPE AND POLICY
Membership is open to anyone who is Shomer Torah u'Mitzvos, i.e.
Orthodox. Presently, there is 1 branch in Israel with 40 members and no
branches abroad. Decisions are made by the National Board.

AFFILIATIONS/REFERENCES
The organization is not affiliated with any political party in Israel nor
with any group abroad.

THE SHIELD, THE JERUSALEM SOCIETY FOR RETARDED ADULTS

"מגן" האגודה למען המפגר המבוגר בירושלים

4A Lloyd George
Jerusalem
Telephone: (02) 665945
Office hours: 10:00 A.M. to 1:00 P.M.

HISTORY AND DESCRIPTION

The Jerusalem Society for retarded Adults called "The Shield" was formed in 1974 with the active help of its late President, Miss Irene Gaster, who was the pioneer in work for the welfare of the mentally retarded in Palestine and Israel. The Society runs a hostel for severely handicapped retarded adults.

Organizational Structure: There is a Jerusalem Board and an administrative sub-committee.

Goals: To care for multiple handicapped retarded adults whose parents are either no longer alive or are too old, weak and ill to continue to look after their grown-up retarded child.

Services, Activities, and Accomplishments: Many of the 20 wards who have been sent to the Society by the Services for the Mentally Handicapped of the Ministry for Labour and Social Affairs have previously been sent from one institution to another without being able to adjust to their surroundings. There are also quite a number among them with whom the staff of Akim could not cope. The Society has made a great effort to find suitable professionally trained staff who are able to apply the principles of individual and intensive education with the aim of offering a permanent home to those Jerusalemites who were not found to be acceptable to other existing institutions because of their additional handicaps, physical or psychological. For lack of space only 17 out of the 20 are residents at the hostel, three others come in the morning and return in the evening to their families. However, they are all waiting to be accommodated as residents within the hostel. In view of the fact that many of the Society's wards depend on special care (for instance, blind people or those with difficult psychiatric problems) more staff are necessary than is usual in institutions which accept only mentally retarded people without additional problems. The Society's hostel has succeeded in welding 20 mentally retarded adults who joined it as undisciplined individuals into a community, and has developed their potentialities to such an extent that they live a comparatively normal life and enjoy living in a family-like atmosphere.

HON. OFFICERS

Hon. Chairman: Mrs. Eva Michaelis, 6 Shlomo Molcho, Jerusalem.
          Tel. (02) 632148.
Hon. Treasurer: Elisha Miller, 13 Haari, Jerusalem.
          Tel. (02) 637305.

Volunteer
Board Members: Dr. Dux-Citron, 4 Oliphant, Jerusalem.
Retired M.D. Tel. (02) 666446.
Miss Ruth Saenger, 3 Shabazi, Jerusalem.
Psychologist. Tel. (02) 221255.
Mrs. Jacqueline Dan, 59 King George, Jerusalem.
Librarian. Tel. (02) 234497.
Mr. Golan, 6 Klein, Jerusalem. Retired teacher.
Tel. (02) 668932.
Miss Elsa Wieser, 18 Ahad Haam, Jerusalem.
Social Worker. Tel. (02) 638195.
and one representative each from the Ministry of
Social Welfare and the Jerusalem Municipality.
Ex-officio: Educational Director: Kobi Melzer, 235/13 Cottage
Shel Gad, Gilo, Jerusalem. Tel. (02) 671354.
Administrative Director: Joseph Kuriel,
Zangwill 9/51, Kiryat Hayovel, Jerusalem.
Tel. (02) 520907.

FINANCIAL INFORMATION

The Society is registered as a non-profit Ottoman Association in Jerusalem (reg. no. 11/2200). Donations in Israel are tax-free (tax no. 4504248). In the United States the Shield is benefitting from P.E.F. Israel Endowment Funds' services. 10 full-time and 4 part-time workers are employed by the Society. Many volunteers lend a helping hand.

The Society hopes to mobilize sufficient funds to purchase a suitable house. Donations from Israeli friends and from abroad are being used to cover the deficit for the daily work and, when possible, amounts are set aside towards acquiring a new house. Long term planning for the future has become very difficult in view of inflation.

MEMBERSHIP, SCOPE, AND POLICY

The Society is not a membership organization. Anyone interested in furthering the work of the hostel is welcome to do so. The administrative sub-committee makes decisions concerning day-to-day work and the Board decides matters of principle.

AFFILIATIONS/REFERENCES

The Society is not affiliated with any Israeli political party. It is affiliated with the following:

American Joint Distribution Committee, New York.

Gustav Wurzweiler Foundation Inc., 129 East 73rd Street, New York, N.Y. 10021.

P.E.F. Israel Endowment Funds Inc., 342 Madison Avenue, New York, N.Y. 10173.

FUNDING NEEDED

1. To purchase a house to replace existing rented premises for use as hostel (approximate cost $400,000). As it is the Society's principle not to interrupt contact with the families of those who live in the hostel, it was established for those within or not far from Jerusalem.

It is regrettable that many Jerusalemites, for lack of space in town, are being sent to institutions far away from the city, which makes it difficult for the families to keep in contact. It is difficult to find suitable accommodation in town due to the unfortunate attitude of this country's population which is not prepared to accept the disabled in their midst. For this reason and others, it has become increasingly imperative for the Society to acquire a house of its own in non-hostile surroundings.

2. The maintenance money received by the Society from the authorities does not cover actual expenses. Consequently it is necessary to supplement the amount at the Society's disposal for day-to-day running expenses. A deficit of $100 per head per month must be covered. As the Society does not own a car, the $100 include transportation costs to doctors, clinics, etc.

SHIKUD

שקוד — שיקום וביגוד

Eliezer Hagadol 4
Katamon Vav,
Jerusalem

HISTORY AND DESCRIPTION
Formed in the early 1970's as a volunteer effort by residents of the Katamonim neighborhoods in Jerusalem, this project receives contributions of used clothing, sorts them out, and sells them at bargain prices to welfare clients.

Organizational Structure: A board of directors composed of 3 volunteer workers, the project coordinator (a social worker from the Welfare Office), the Director of the Welfare Office, and three public members, meets every two months. The volunteer workers and a volunteer accountant from the neighborhood man the store at regular hours.

Goals: SHIKUD's goals are to provide clean clothes at affordable prices to the poorest sector of the population, and to provide a sense of contribution and self-improvement to the volunteers, who come from the same population as those the project serves.

Services, Activities, and Accomplishments: With money that is accumulated from the sale of clothing, SHIKUD makes wholesale purchases of needed clothing (e.g., at back-to-school time). It has succeeded in organizing the community in a self-help effort, and in meeting the problem of clothing supply for the neediest population in the neighborhood. In addition, the organization has helped enroll volunteers in a night school for adult studies.

OFFICERS
Director: Shula Ankari. Volunteer.
Treasurer: Asher Nigri. Volunteer..
Board Members: Chava Iaari.
Mishelin Traves.
Helen Shriki. Volunteer.
Nourit Papir. Volunteer.
Hela Yaniv, Hizkiyahu Hamelech 36, Jerusalem. Director of local Welfare office. Tel.: (02) 660221.
Shula Fershtman, Hizkiyahu Hamelech 36, Jerusalem. Social worker. Tel.: (02) 660221.
Rachel Stern, Hizkiyahu Hamelech, Jerusalem. Social worker. Tel.: (02) 660221.

FINANCIAL INFORMATION
SHIKUD's entire income comes from fees from the purchase of clothing. Last year's budget was $4,000 with no deficit. The organization is

registered as an Ottoman, non-profit Association, but no details were provided. Donations from Israel and the U.S. are not tax-free. There is one part-time salaried employee and 9 volunteer workers.

MEMBERSHIP, SCOPE, AND POLICY
Membership, which means having the right to purchase regularly from SHIKUD, numbers 2,500. Residents of the Katamon neighborhood are eligible to be members. Decisions of the organization are made, for the most part, by the Director.

AFFILIATIONS/REFERENCES
SHIKUD is not affiliated with any political party in Israel. Organizations abroad familiar with the work of the organization are Cooperation Feminine, Paris, France; Jewish-Danish Friendship Society, Denmark; and Temple Sisterhood, New Jersey.

FUNDING NEEDED
1. To obtain children's clothes—$5,000.
2. To obtain a larger stock of clothing, new and used, for adults of all ages—$4,000.
3. Packages of used clothing should be sent PREPAID and marked "USED CLOTHING", to the SHIKUD office.

SHILO PREGNANCY ADVISORY SERVICE

שילה — שרות יעוץ להכוונה לעניני הריון ומניעה

Bezalel 10
Jerusalem 94591
Telephone: (02) 221057
Office Hours:
Sunday, Tuesday, Wednesday and Thursday, 5:00 P.M.-8:00 P.M.

HISTORY AND DESCRIPTION

The Shilo Pregnancy Advisory Service was established in Jerusalem in October 1976, in response to a perceived unmet need for counseling in cases of unwanted or otherwise psycho-socially problematic pregnancy, contraceptive counseling and contraceptive services.

Organizational Structure: The staff of Shilo, composed of professionals and students from the areas of medicine, psychology, nursing, social work and counseling, works on a voluntary basis. There is an executive board composed of senior members.

Goals: The Shilo Pregnancy Advisory Service lists six basic principles of operation:
— That services should be available to all persons who may benefit from it, although the target populations are the young, the unmarried and those other groups who are not covered by existing services in the community;
— That services should be provided without charge and on a 'walk-in' basis;
— That the staff should operate on an interdisciplinary basis, based on the conception that birth control and unwanted pregnancy have social and psychological, as well as medical, aspects;
— That counseling should be based on the model of a decision-making process;
— That easy access to services should be ensured through the centrality of location (in downtown Jerusalem), and the provision of services in the late afternoon and early evening; and
— That client confidentiality should be assured.

Services, Activities, and Accomplishments: The main services and activities presently performed by Shilo include counseling on both birth control and unwanted pregnancy; the operation by doctors and nurses of a birth control clinic where contraceptives are provided along with instruction on proper use and periodic follow-ups; and a limited 'outreach' program to groups in the community. Shilo lists among its major accomplishments to date the fact that it is the only service presently offering counseling for unwanted pregnancies in Israel, that it has successfully reached its target populations, and that it serves as a model for the reaching and counseling of these populations.

OFFICERS
Board Members: Elizabeth Rothschild, Sderot Herzl 38, Jerusalem.
Social Worker.

Derryl Bloch, Emek Rehaim 51A, Jerusalem.
Nurse.

Chana Kurtzman, Hama'apilim 14, Jerusalem.
Nurse.

Tzippy Lefler, Dorot Rishonim 8, Jerusalem.
Social worker.

Raina Chaimowitz, Bruria 9, Jerusalem.
Counselor.

Ruth Bender, Hashachar 18, Jerusalem.
Social worker.

FINANCIAL INFORMATION
In 1979-1980 expenditures amounted to approximately $8,500. Estimated budget for 1981-1982 is $15,000. The organization is a registered Ottoman non-profit association (reg. no. 11-2652), and is tax-exempt in Israel (no. 4506716).

MEMBERSHIP, SCOPE, AND POLICY
There are at present twenty-six members of the one Jerusalem branch of Shilo. Membership is open to professionals and students from the medical and counseling fields. Policy decisions are made by the Executive Board.

AFFILIATIONS/REFERENCES
Shilo is not affiliated with any Israeli political party. Internationally, it is affiliated with the following organizations.

IPPF—*International Planned Parenthood Federation,*
18-20 Lower Regent Street, London SW1Y 4PW, England
International Clearinghouse on Adolescent Fertility,
c/o *The Population Institute,* 110 Maryland Avenue, N.E., Washington, D.C., 20002
Population Reference Bureau, Inc., 1337 Connecticut Avenue, N.W., Washington, D.C., 20036

FUNDING NEEDED
In order of priority, the Shilo Pregnancy Advisory Service lists the following as its most outstanding funding requirements.
1. Comprehensive sex education training program for staff. Approximate cost—$2,000.
2. Renovation and expansion of gynecological clinic. Approximate cost—$3,000.
3. Additional salary for worker responsible for coordinating community out-reach projects. Annual salary—$4,000.

SOCIETY FOR CRIPPLED CHILDREN—
ALYN אגודה לעזרת ילדים נכים – אלי"ן

Corner Olswanger and Shmaryahu Levin Streets
Kiryat Hayovel
P.O. Box 9117, Jerusalem
Telephone: (02) 412251
Office Hours: Sunday-Thursday 8:000 a.m. to 4:00 p.m.
               Friday   8:00 a.m. to 1:00 p.m.

HISTORY AND DESCRIPTION
The Society for Crippled Children—Alyn—was founded in 1932 by Dr. Henry Keller, an American orthopaedic surgeon. Known originally as the "Palestine Society for Crippled Children", it was set up as a non-profit organization for the treatment of physically handicapped children with no distinciton as to nationality, religion or ethnic background.

Organizational Structure: Activities are supervised by a public committee which elects a Board of Directors.

Goals: As a long-term orthopaedic hospital and rehabilitation center for physically handicapped children, Alyn aims to help each child to reach his own maximum potential. Patients are discharged from Alyn to their own families, or if that is not possible, Alyn tries to assure them proper housing and suitable employment in which they can use the skills learned through Alyn's Vocational Training Program.

Services, Activities, and Accomplishments: In addition to four wards, each with 24 beds, Alyn has Departments for Occupational Therapy, Physiotherapy, Psychology, Social Work, X-ray and a hydrotherapy pool. The out-patient clinics receive over 4000 patient visits annually. There is an elementary school on the premises, and the other children are taken by Alyn ambulances to and from local high schools or vocational training programs. A sheltered workshop as well is on the premises. The children are under psychiatric supervision and there is a special recreation program run by youth counsellors. Alyn has a synagogue that is specially designed for the handicapped.
Alyn is the only long-term orthopaedic hospital and rehabilitation center in Israel caring for physically handicapped children. Until 1951, Alyn was the only out-patient clinic in Jerusalem for these cases. During the polio epidemic in 1951, Alyn became the major center for treatment. In 1971, Alyn moved from its former location, an old Greek monastery in San Simon, to the new premises in Kiryat Yovel, a specially designed and equipped facility for the care of physically handicapped children. Alyn has since become the center for the treatment of children with physical handicaps of all kinds.

OFFICERS
Medical Director: Prof. Gordon Robin, 4 Achad Ha'am, Jerusalem.
          Tel.: (02) 634016.

Adminstrative
Director: Y. Yaniv, Massaryk 6, Jerusalem.
               Tel.: (02) 632275.
Treasurer: A. Kronacher, Abarbanel 23, Jerusalem. Banker.
               Tel.: (02) 669795.
Chairman: Shlomo Choczner, Bustenai 26, Jerusalem.
               Merchant. Tel.: (02) 669076.
Board Members: A. Citron, Alfasi 22, Jerusalem. C.P.A.
               Tel.: (02) 632136.
               Dr. L. Potkaminer, Pinat Hovevei Zion 24,
               Jerusalem. Tel.: (02) 664723.
               R. Berman, Sokolov 3, Jerusalem. Civil Servant.
               Tel.: (02) 633564.
               Y. Boehm, Hatayassim 41, Jerusalem.
               Musiocologist.
               Tel.: (02) 633927.
               Dr. Y. Arnon, Hagai 8, Jerusalem (M.D.).
               Tel.: 525428.
               Mr. Z. Federbush, Tshnernikovsky 3, Jerusalem.
               Special Education Inspector.
               Tel.: (02) 660204.
               Mr. C. Ascheim, P.O.B. 7041, Tel Aviv. C.P.A.
               Tel.: (03) 911055.
               Prof. Myer Makin, Shmaryahu Levin, Jerusalem.
               Head Orthopaedic Dept., Hadassah Hospital.
               M. Levin, Ben Dor 5, Jerusalem. Former
               Director Public Relations Alyn.
               Tel.: (02) 526151.

FINANCIAL INFORMATION

30% of last year's annual budget came from donations and the proceeds of fund-raising; the balance from referral agencies. Last year's annual budget of $1,000,000 left Alyn with a deficit of $13,000. Donations to Alyn are tax-free in the USA (reg. no. 132481), Canada (reg. no. 0530543-11-13), England (reg. no. XD131/63) and Switzerland (no registration number supplied). Donations are not tax-free in Israel. Alyn is registered as an Ottoman Association (Jerusalem, reg. no. 11/666). 170 workers are employed by Alyn as well as approximately 25 volunteers.

AFFILIATIONS/REFERENCES

1. Alyn Society in America: Mrs. Simone Blum, Chairman, 19 West 44th Street, Suite 1418, New York, NY. 11036.
2. Friends of Alyn, London: Mrs. Iris Landau, Chairman, 1 Harford Walk, London N2 OJB.
3. Friends of Alyn, Canada: Mr. Lionel Sharpe, Chairman, 45 St. Clair Avenue West, 13th floor, Toronto, Ont. M4V 1L3.
4. Friends of Alyn, Switzerland: Mrs. Evelyn Blum, Chairman, Rutistrasse 14, Erlenbach 8703.
5. Fredlogans Systerkrets, Sweden: Mrs. Viola Neuman, Chairman, Karlavagen 9, 114 24 Stockholm.

6. Joint Distribution Committee (AJJDC): 60 E. 42 Street, New York, NY. 10017.

Alyn is not affiliated with any political party in Israel.

FUNDING NEEDED
1. To purchase battery-operated wheelchairs and assist in the purchase of cars. A Mobility Fund of about $40,000 would help to meet the direct needs of the young handicapped.
2. To expand the out-patient clinic services. The clinic was originally intended as a small project, but the number of patient visits there has grown from 300 in the first year to 4000 last year. The figure is expected to double in the very near future. At least $60,000 needed in order to enlarge waiting-rooms, doctors' consulting rooms, and X-ray facilities.
3. To help cover the hospital's maintenance costs. The referral agencies which send children to Alyn pay about 70% of the cost of maintaining the child there. The balance, plus funds for improvements and special services, comes from outside assistance. Current inflation makes it necessary to raise the sum of $600,000 this year from overseas contributions in order to meet the needs of Alyn patients.

(SOCIETY FOR) THE BEN GOLAN SCHOLARSHIP MEMORIAL FUND

(אגודה לנהול) קרן מלגות ע"ש בן גולן ז"ל

c/o Glikson
15 Alfasi St.
Jerusalem
Telephone: (02) 635367

c/o Golan
15 Yordei Hasira
Jerusalem
Telephone: (02) 634290

HISTORY AND DESCRIPTION

The Ben Golan Scholarship Memorial Fund was established in 1978 to honor the memory of Ben Golan, of Jerusalem, who fell in the Yom Kippur War at the age of 19. Before joining the army Ben was active in helping disadvantaged youth and worked as a volunteer in the Negev development town of Ofakim.

Organizational Structure: Donations were collected from friends of Ben Golan and from the Golan family to form a capital fund from the income of which the scholarships are awarded. All incidental expenses are paid for by voluntary contributions additional to the capital fund.

Goals: The fund aims to grant annual scholarships to young men and women in difficult economic circumstances from the development towns or needy neighborhoods in the cities who wish to study at university or other insitute of higher learning. Scholarships are awarded upon the recommendations of the deans of the various universities or the principals of pre-academic studies, after interviews by the Committee of the fund. Members of the Committee establish personal contact with the students and follow their progress during the academic year. The award of the first scholarships was reported in *Ha-Aretz*, 10 December, 1979.

Services, Activities, and Accomplishments: Two full university scholarships were awarded for the academic year 1979-80. One was to a first-year student of mathematics at the Hebrew University in Jerusalem. The student had a past record of delinquency but had made great efforts to improve and was recommended by the Principal of the Bet Berl pre-academic study course. The other scholarship was awarded to a second-year student at Ben Gurion University from the development town of Ofakim. He is studying electronic engineering. For the academic year 1980-81 three full scholarships of IS 2,500 each were awarded, to students from Jerusalem, Tel Aviv and Beer Sheba, to study at the respective univesities.

OFFICERS

Hon. Chairman: Moshe Ben Zeev, 2 Mevo Yoram, Jerusalem. Advocate. Tel. (02) 630012.

Hon. Treasurer: Gad Natan, 5 B Alroi, Jerusalem. Statistician. Tel. (02) 662870.

Hon. Secretary: Yvonne Glikson, 15 Alfasi, Jerusalem. Editor.
Tel. (02) 635367.

Members: Yitzhak Tishler, 41 KKL, Jerusalem. Journalist.
Tel. (02) 632824.
Meir Libergal, 9 Haporzim, Jerusalem.
Medical student.
Tel. (02) 638926.
Netta Golan, 114 Zionism, Haifa. Architect.
Roy Golan, 15 Yordei Hasira, Jerusalem.
Student.
Tel. (02) 634290.
Yitzhak Golan, 15 Yordei Hasira, Jerusalem.
Journalist.
Tel. (02) 634290.
Miriam Golan, 15 Yordei Hasira, Jerusalem.
Journalist.
Tel. (02) 634290.

FINANCIAL INFORMATION
Sources of income are solely from donations. The initial capital for 1979-80 amounted to $5,000. The funds are invested in index-linked bonds, and scholarships are awarded from the income. The fund is staffed by volunteers.

MEMBERSHIP, SCOPE, AND POLICY
The criteria for membership state: any person aged 18 or over wishing to serve the aims of the fund in honor of Ben Golan, on acceptance by the Committee. There are ten members in one branch in Israel. Decisions are made by the committee of the society.

AFFILIATIONS/REFERENCES
The fund has no party affiliations in Israel. Abroad, its work is known to the PEF Israel Endowment Funds, Inc., 342 Madison Avenue, New York, N.Y. 10173.

FUNDING NEEDED
Funding is needed to increase the number of scholarships that can be awarded annually, and thus help in the vital task of educating gifted youth in Israel who could otherwise not be able to afford university fees. University fees for 1980-81 were IL 25,000.

SOCIETY FOR THE PREVENTION OF CRUELTY TO ANIMALS IN ISRAEL (I.S.P.C.A.) TEL AVIV-JAFFA AREA

אגודת צער בעלי חיים בישראל, תל-אביב יפו

Salama Road 30, Jaffa-Tel Aviv
Telephone: (03) 827621
Office Hours: Sunday-Thursday, 8:00 A.M. to 4:30 P.M.
Friday, 8:00 A.M. to 2:30 P.M.

HISTORY AND DESCRIPTION
The Society was founded in 1927 during the British Mandate, along the lines of the Royal Society for the Prevention of Cruelty to Animals.

Organizational Structure: The affairs of the society are conducted by a chairwoman, treasurer, and a committee elected at the general meeting. The Society employs a staff for the maintenance of the shelter and conducting its activities.

Goals: To conduct shelters where all strays, injured, sick or unwanted animals are accepted, and where veterinary services are available.
To help insure that anti-cruelty laws are enacted and observed.
To propogate sterilization for animal control and to help educate the public about the need for a humanitarian attitude towards animals.

Services, Activities, and Accomplishments: The Society operates a shelter where on an average 200 animals are housed daily, and which includes an ambulance service, veterinary clinic, and boarding service for short periods of time. They also sterilize animals before sending them to new homes. The Society handles over 13,000 animals annually, sterilizes about 350 animals annually, and places about 800 animals in new homes each year.

OFFICERS
Director: Mrs. H. Friedstein, Hehadarim St. 12, Savyon.
                 Artist. Tel. (03) 753583.
Treasurer: Mrs. G. Blindeman, Hanitzahon St. 151, Tel Aviv.
                 Housewife. Tel. (03) 332429.
Board Members: Mr. M. Otyakar, Hirsheberg St. 18, Tel Aviv.
                 Literary Secretary. Tel. (03) 226127.
                 Mr. Gad Navon, Brodetsky St. 22, Ramat Aviv.
                 Electrician. Tel. (03) 413016.
                 Mrs. Ilana Mashler, Hapardes 11, Tel Aviv.
                 Housewife. Tel. (03) 240459.
                 Mrs. N. Abrahams, Alonim 4, Ramat Ilan.
                 Business. Tel. (03) 758178.
                 Mr. M. Goldschlag, Hehadarim 4, Savyon.
                 PazGas employee. Tel. (03) 755598.
                 Miss Miriam Miruish, Bograshov 23, Tel Aviv.
                 Business. Tel. (03) 289511.

FINANCIAL INFORMATION
Nearly half of the income of the society (49%) is supplied through donations. Kenneling, sales and equipment brings in another 32%, clinic fees 14%, and membership dues 5%. Last year's annual budget was $30,000, leaving no deficit. The Society is an Ottoman Association, number 162/99. Donations are tax-free in Israel (reg. no. not reported). Four full-time and five part-time workers are employed by the organization, as well as one full-time volunteer.

MEMBERSHIP, SCOPE, AND POLICY
The Society's decisions are made by an elected committee, and anyone who pays the membership fee can join. As of now the Society has 538 members in Israel and only one branch.

AFFILIATIONS/REFERENCES
Society for Animal Welfare in Israel—4 North Mews, Northington St. London, WC. England and The World Federation for the Protection of Animals, Dreikonigstrasse 37, CH-8002 Zurich, Switzerland.

FUNDING NEEDED
1. Renovation of the present shelter—$60,000.
2. New ambulance—$10,000.
3. Proper surgery equipment and X-ray unit—$20,000.

SOCIETY FOR THE PREVENTION OF CRUELTY TO ANIMALS IN THE SOUTH OF ISRAEL

האגודה לצער בעלי חיים, באר שבע ודרום ישראל

Alia St. 13/2
Beer Sheva
Telephone: (057) 39405
Office Hours: 8:00 A.M. to 8:00 P.M.

HISTORY AND DESCRIPTION

The Society was established in 1975 as a non-profit Ottoman Association volunteer organization. The facilities are located on the grounds of a school for incorrigible youths in order to help the youths and promote their working with animals. The Society also cooperates with the Municipal Department of Education, a veterinary hospital and doctors.

Organizational Structure: At the founding of the organization, the members elected a Board of Directors, and this pattern is continued, with elections held every year.

Goals: Prevention of cruelty to animals, which is both an educational and social goal, is the basis for the organization. The Society helps the welfare of animals, collects lost and stray animals to feed and care for them, organizes medical help, and also offers help to owners of animals in every aspect.

Services, Activities, and Accomplishments: Aside from the Society's work with disadvantaged youth, it has also obtained the present location and built a line of big kennels.

OFFICERS

Director: D. Shachaf, Hakipod 3, Beer Sheva. Teacher.
              Tel. (057) 37536.
Treasurer: J. Berinsky, Alia 13/2, Beer Sheva. Teacher.
              Tel. (057) 39405.
Board: N. Lebedinsky, Hamesharerim. Chemist.
              Tel. (057) 76970.
              A. Haiman, Atad 55, Beer Sheva. Social Worker.
              Tel. (057) 73046.

FINANCIAL INFORMATION

46% of the Society's income came from donations, followed by 30% for services and 24% from membership dues. Last year's annual budget of $595 left the organization with a deficit of $815. The Society is registered as an Ottoman Association (reg. no. 7867/532) but no information on tax-free status in the United States or abroad was supplied. All six employees of the Society are volunteers.

MEMBERSHIP, SCOPE, AND POLICY
Fifty-two members support the three branches in Israel. Anyone who loves animals and wants to help the organization can become a member. Most decisions are made by the Executive Director.

AFFILIATIONS/REFERENCES
1. L. Richtmann, 34 Bethel St., Ormond 3204, Vic., Australia.
2. S.A.W.I., 4 North Mews, Northington St., London WC, England.

FUNDING NEEDED
1. To establish an operative fund that will give them the ability to grow and maintain the facilities. $20,000.
2. To have a monthly income of $300-$400 to be able to have one full-time employee in the facilities.
3. To have funds for big projects such as building another line or big kennels or building a fully equipped veterinary house on the grounds. $10,000.

THE SOCIETY FOR THE PROTECTION
OF PERSONAL RIGHTS

האגודה לשמירת זכויות הפרט

P.O. Box 46039
Tel Aviv
Telephone: (03) 221721
Office hours: Variable, but answering machine takes messages.

HISTORY AND DESCRIPTION

The Society for the Protection of Personal Rights (SPPR), Israel's first
and only homophile group, was founded in July, 1975, by a group of 12
men and women who shared the goal of improving the situation of
Israel's homosexual minority.

Goals: The objectives of the SPPR are to extend aid and encouragement
to individuals troubled by personal problems and difficulties in adjustment due to sexual orientation; to advise and support those who
encounter difficulties with government bodies and other agencies
merely because they are homosexual; and to raise the consciousness level
of the Society's members, including explanation of aspects of homosexuality and various consequent problems which arise due to misunder-
standing in Israeli society. In addition, the Society strives to create a
healthy social and cultural atmoshpere for its members and to explain
the nature of homosexuality correctly to the general public, thus clarify-
ing erroneous preconceived notions. Another aim of the Society is to
bring about a change in the Israeli criminal code, towards the eventual
goal of decriminalization of homosexuality, although the present stated
policy of the government is not to enforce the law.

Services, Activities, and Accomplishments: The Society undertakes individual counselling to the many people who have turned to it with
personal problems. This is done through correspondence, telephone
conversations, personal interviews and referral to qualified experts in
various fields. In this way, the Society has provided support, advice and
guidance to many homosexual men and women. The SPPR conducts
informational activities, from a "speakers' bureau" which supplies
lecturers and panels on the subject to universities, kibbutzim, and other
institutions, to the initiation of newspaper and magazine articles, radio
programs and a television documentary. A campaign is constantly being
waged to open up the minds of the Israeli public. Cultural activities
which the SPPR runs include classes; monthly Shabbat outings; quiet
club-house evenings with games, library, T.V., conversation; and an
occasional speaker or discussion group. It also has several conscious-
ness-raising groups, as well as a campaign of health education. In
addition, the SPPR, runs a disco coffee-house and holds special social
activities such as the "Aliziada" (gay festival). Special women's activities, such as a social evening of their own, are also run by the Society.
Contacts have been initiated with several government agencies in order

to gain recognition from these bodies, which wield so much influence on the Israeli public. The Society's major accomplishments have been simply beginning and establishing itself in the face of huge internal and external problems. It succeeded in arranging and hosting the 4th International Conference of Gay and Lesbian Jews, held in Israel in the summer of 1979.

This Society is the only one of its kind in Israel to which homosexuals, men and women, may turn for help in understanding and accepting themselves, and thus becoming fulfilled members of society. Similarly, the SPPR is unique in attempting to break down the outdated concepts that homosexuals chose that lifestyle; could change if they wished to; and are sick and depraved.

OFFICERS

Director: Asher Ma'ayan, P.O.B. 16151, T.A. Tour Guide. Tel. (03) 246063.

Board Members: Jon. Danilowitz, Ben Gurion 12, Tel Aviv. Flight Steward. Tel. (03) 236586. Ya'akov Pazi, Cremieux 9, Tel Aviv. Driving Instructor. Tel. (03) 221721. Dov Barkan, Elimelech 12A, Ramat Gan. Advertising Agent. Tel. (03) 723527.

FINANCIAL INFORMATION

Half of the SPPR's funds come from donations, and half from membership dues. Last year's budget was $1500, with no deficit. The Society is registered as an Ottoman, non-profit Association (no number given, Tel Aviv District). Donations in Israel and from the U.S. are not tax-exempt. Six vounteers carry out the work of the Society.

MEMBERSHIP, SCOPE, AND POLICY

There are 130 members in the Israeli branch of the Society. Another 20 people, not living in Israel, have paid special overseas membership dues and are considered "Overseas Members". Membership is open to anyone over 18 who wishes to join, and who has been recommended by a member. Decisions of the Society are made by the Board.

AFFILIATIONS/REFERENCES

The SPPR is not affiliated with any Israeli political party. Organizations which are familiar with the Society's work are Cong. Beth Ahavah, P.O.B. 7566, Philadelphia, Pa. 19101, U.S.A.; Cong. Beth Simchat Torah, P.O.B. 1270, New York, N.Y. 10001, U.S.A.; and the Jewish Gay Group, c/o N. Goldner, 5 St. Mary's Ave., London N3 1SN, England.

FUNDING NEEDED

1. To open a proper office, to purchase needed office equipment and to have a full-time salaried secreatary. Cost: $900 per month.
2. To purchase a property and establish a permanent center for the Society. Cost: $80,000.
3. To continue and extend current operations within the framework of the budget. Cost: from $100-$400 per month.

SOCIETY FOR THE REHABILITATION OF PRISONERS, TEL AVIV

האגודה לשיקום האסיר והעבריין

Melchet 35
Tel Aviv
Telephone: (03) 291406
Office hours: Daily, 8.30 A.M. to 1.30 P.M.; Tuesday, 4.00-6.00 P.M.

HISTORY AND DESCRIPTION
The Society was founded in 1953. The annual General Assembly of the members elects a Committee of eleven, and the Committee in turn elects the President of the Society, the Chairman of the Committee, and an executive body. The General Assembly also elects a control committee.

Goals: The Society seeks to help released prisoners and ex-offenders in their rehabilitation as honorable and helpful members of Israeli society.

Services, Activities and Accomplishments: The organization serves the Tel Aviv region and is affiliated with the League of Societies for the Rehabilitation of Offenders in Israel. Many hundreds of ex-offenders have been rehabilitated as productive members of society through the work of the organization.

OFFICERS
Director: Yohanan Eisenberg, Tel Aviv.
       Ex-police Superintendent.
       Tel. (03) 291406.
Treasurer: Abraham Felman. Accountant.
Board Members: Dr. M. Rubin. Judge.
       Tel. (03) 256090.
       P. Rudick
       Dr. L. Weigeh. Advocate.

FINANCIAL INFORMATION
Last year's annual budget was $16,920. (Information on sources of income not supplied.) Donations in Israel are tax-free (registration number not supplied). The Society is registered as an Ottoman Association (reg. no. 1406/99). Two full-time workers are employed by the Society; the number of volunteers varies from time to time, but there is an active group of about 14 volunteers.

MEMBERSHIP, SCOPE AND POLICY
There are between 75 and 100 members in Tel Aviv, the sole branch of the Society. Membership is open to everyone who is willing to contribute time to helping others. Most decisions are made by the Executive Director.

AFFILIATIONS/REFERENCES
The Society is a member of the International Prisoners' Aid Association

through the League of Societies for the Rehabilitation of Offenders in Israel. The Tel Aviv Society is not affiliated with any political party in Israel.

FUNDING NEEDED
1. To provide housing facilities for ex-prisoners.
2. To provide general and professional education.
3. To pay for after-care.

SOCIETY FOR RESEARCH ON
JEWISH COMMUNITIES
אגודה לחקר תפוצות ישראל

University Campus, Sprinzak Bldg. P.O. Box 7422, Jerusalem
Telephone: (02) 532832
P.O.Box 21650, Tel Aviv 61216
Telephone: (03) 219271
Office Hours: 8:00 A.M.-1:00 P.M.

HISTORY AND DESCRIPTION

The Society was founded in 1957, on the initiative of the late Saul Avigur, with the active involvement of persons in Israel from academic life and government who had occupied themselves in the past with Jewish affairs in the USSR and other Communist countries.

Goals: The Society took upon itself the task of compiling documentary material on East European, and especially Soviet, Jewry, and of conducting research and preparing teaching and informational material on all aspects of Jewish life.

Services, Activities, and Accomplishments: The Jews of Eastern Europe and the USSR were artificially cut off from Jews in the Western world and denied the possibility of a normal communal life. The consequent need to fill the resulting vacuum in their lives underlined the urgency of the projects in which the Society engages. The "Aliyah Library" publishes books in Russian on all aspects of Jewish history and culture, with the aim of bringing Jewish culture to Jews in the USSR and of aiding the acculturation of new immigrants in Israel. To date, 75 books have been published. The Society has published the *Concise Hebrew Encyclopedia* in the Russian language; the first of six projected volumes has appeared, and the second volume is now in press. The Society also maintains a specialized library at the Hebrew University in Jerusalem, containing over 50,000 volumes and more than 100 newspapers and periodicals. The Center for Research and Documentation of East European Jewry (established by the Society in coordination with the Hebrew University) publishes, on a regular basis, a compilation from the Soviet Press of articles relating to Jewish subjects, petitions and letters of Jews in the USSR, and the Jewish Samizdat (i.e., material written by Jews in the USSR and published and circulated unofficially). A total of 150 volumes in these three areas have already been published. The Center also published various studies and bibliographies, and initiates the holding of symposiums on various subjects. At present, it is occupied with an extensive study of Soviet Antisemitism.

OFFICERS

Director:	Zvi Nezer, P.O.B. 7422, Jerusalem.
	Tel. (03) 415690.
Treasurer:	Zvi Ofer, Tel. (03) 219271.
Chairman:	Prof. Shmuel Ettinger, Tel. (02) 632703.

Vice Chairman:	Prof. Chone Shmeruk, Tel. (02) 631358.
Board Members:	Sa. Abramov, Tel. (03) 239587.
	A. Agmon, Tel. (03) 630530.
	Prof. Y. Dinstein, Tel. (03) 410486.
	D. Bartov, Tel. (02) 631893.
	M. Juveeler, Tel. (02) 667780.
	S. Kaminska, Tel. (02) 524235.
	I. Nadel, Tel. (02) 634966.
	A. Rosental, Tel. (02) 418837.
	H. Ben Israel, Tel. (03) 414133.

FINANCIAL INFORMATION

The Society receives all its income from donations. Last year's budget totalled $110,000, and left a deficit of $30,000. The Society is a registered Ottoman, non-profit Association (no. 11/1243, Jerusalem District). Donations in Israel are tax-free, under no. 4501127; donations from the U.S. are not tax-exempt. There are six full-time and 2 part-time employees (most of them new immigrants) who work in research and translation. Professionals work on a volunteer basis for organizational undertakings.

MEMBERSHIP, SCOPE, AND POLICY

At present, the Society numbers 51. Persons involved and interested in the aims of the Society may become members by the decision of the General Assembly. Decisions are made mainly by the Board of Directors.

AFFILIATIONS/REFERENCES

The Society is not affiliated with any Israeli political party. Its references include the National Conference for Soviety Jewry, New York; the New York Conference for Soviety Jewry; the American Jewish Committee; B'nai B'rith International; and the National Jewish Community Relations Advisory Council.

FUNDING NEEDED

1. To publish the Hebrew Encyclopedia: $40,000 per year.
2. For the "Aliyah Library": $50,000 per year.
3. For research on Antisemitism: $20,000 per year.

THE SOCIETY FOR THE "SINGER HOUSE"—THE HOME FOR THE CHILD—KFAR YEHESKEL

האגודה למען "בית זינגר" הבית לילד בכפר יחזקאל

"Singer House"—The Home for the Child
Kfar Yeheskel
Doar Na Hagilboa
The Address of the Society: Haifa 31040
                            P.O.B. 4369
                            Haifa
Telephone: (04) 331770
Office Hours: 8:00 A.M. to 2:00 P.M. (in Kfar Yeheskel,
                Tel. 065-8435)
                5:00 P.M. to 8:00 P.M. (in Haifa)

HISTORY AND DESCRIPTION

The House was established in 1942 by the Singer Family in Haifa, for children of soldiers who volunteered for the British Army and Jewish Brigade. The place in Kfar Yeheskel was selected for security reasons, as the enemy started bombing Haifa. With the establishment of the State of Israel in 1948, when the soldiers came home, the big Aliyah (immigration) began with problematic families, whose children needed shelter in this institution. With full cooperation of the Ministry of Welfare, the children of disordered families or orphans are directed to Kfar Yeheskel. Since then the institution has been called "The Home for the Child". After the death of the Singers in 1976, the name was slightly changed, in commemoration, to "Singer House"—The Home for the Child.

Organizational Structure: The institution in Kfar Yeheskel is administered by a Principal and staff, having close ties with the society's management in Haifa (two members of the Board live in Kfar Yeheskel). In the institution, under boarding-school conditions, about sixty children of both sexes are being educated under full supervision of the Ministry of Welfare (the children are aged six to thirteen). The children go to the regional elementary school together with all children of the area. Children who so require, receive help from the institution with the lectures. Each year a number of children leave Singer House after their Bar-Mitzva or Bat-Mitzva, and enter kibbutzim or go to closed educational institutions within full control of the Minstry of Welfare and continued contact with the Singer House institution.

Goals: The institution strives to create such conditions as to make the children feel at home, when they are compelled by a cruel fate to spend their childhood at Singer House. It is not desirable to increase the institution population beyond sixty children; this way a "home" atmosphere is maintained.

Services, Activities and Accomplishments: The Board members of the Society work as volunteers and take care of the current administration of the House. Maintenance expenses for the children are paid by the Ministry of Welfare, which sometimes does not allocate sufficient funds for current expenses. The management is active in fund-raising for development of the institution, which started its activities at the time of its establishment in an old building, not suitable at all for a home of children.

In the course of the years two dwelling houses have been constructed for the children, as well as a dining room, kitchen and laundry, store-room and partial building for accommodation of the staff. The Society considers its main achievement the education of the children. A great many of them are today good and happy citizens of Israel.

OFFICERS

Director:	J. Weissberger, 22 Hatishbi St., Haifa. Clerk. Tel. (04) 331770.
Treasurer:	M. Weinshal, 4 Brener St., Haifa. Clerk. Tel. (04) 223952.
Secretary:	B. Barkan, 90 Keren Hajeson, Kiryat Bialik. Educator. Tel. (04) 707641.
Board Members:	R. Ariel, Kfar Yeheskel. Farmwoman.
	J. Eshed, Kfar Yeheskel. Farmman.
	R. Kalter, 33 Weizmann St., Kiryat Motzkin. Social Worker. Tel. (04) 713523.
	F. Horowitz, 6 Shivel Israel St., Kiryat Chaim. Supervisor. Tel. (04) 723637.
	B. Yefe-Nof, 10 Jad Charuzim, Jerusalem. State employee. Tel. (02) 719081.

FINANCIAL INFORMATION
Singer House is registered as an Ottoman Association (Haifa district, reg. no. 61/528). 90% of the institution's budget for maintenance of the children comes from the Ministry of Welfare; the remainder of its income is received through donations. Last year's budget of $150,000 left the institution with a deficit of $15,500. Donations to the organization are tax-free both in Israel and the United States (Israel reg. no. 4501936, USA reg. no. not supplied). Fifteen full-time and ten part-time employees work for the institution, as well as ten volunteers.

MEMBERSHIP, SCOPE AND POLICY
The Society is comprised of twenty members and anyone who is willing to contribute by his work for the children is welcome to join. Important decisions are made by the Board and the Director carries them out in close contact with the Principal of the institution.

AFFILIATIONS/REFERENCES
The organization is not affiliated with any political party. The institution is under the full supervision of the Ministry of Labor and Social Affairs. Balance sheets are certified each year by a Public Accountant and there are suitable certifications from the Treasury Ministry as a

public institution; the organization is also included in the list of institutions recognized as public institutions for welfare purposes, which is distributed both in Israel and abroad.

FUNDING NEEDED

1. To build a two-story dwelling house with an overall area of 220 sqm.; estimated cost, $150,000. The building is urgently required for the senior staff, as there is no possibility of renting a house in the village.
2. For heating and cooling in the institution—the entire system is electric; cost, approx. $50,000.
3. To build a cold storage room for food for adequate quantity and period as there is a problem of supply, since the village is situated at a spot almost without regular transport; cost, approx. $25,000.

SOCIETY OF ORPHANAGES, TEL AVIV

אגודת בתי יתומים ויתומות (מיסודו של א.ל. בלובשטין ז"ל),
ת"א

20 Mazeh Street
Tel Aviv
Telephone: (03) 291130
Office Hours: 8:00 A.M. to 3:00 P.M.

HISTORY AND DESCRIPTION
The institution was founded in 1937 by I.L. Bluvstein. At that time there was a small house on Mazeh Street. There are now two buildings; one in Yad-Eliyahu and one in Ramat Gan which house one hundred and twenty boys, and one hundred girls, respectively.

Organizational Structure: The institutions are administered by a voluntary body under the supervision of the Social Welfare Office and Municipality of Tel Aviv-Jaffa.

Goals: The Society hopes to continue its efforts to give children, labelled disadvantaged, a chance to find their place in the world. It aims to change their seemingly negative fate into a positive one, emphasizing that there is no difference between them and other children, and therefore educating them in a regular public school to help bridge the gap. The Society's outlook is towards change and advancement.

Services, Activities, and Accomplishments: The children receive everything at the boarding schools from education with an emphasis on traditional Judaism to workshops consisting of many different areas. They also receive a very warm environment, something that had been lacking up until the time they came to the institution. To encourage the feeling of home and caring, individual attention is given to the children in the classroom as well as out. Movies, sports, etc. are encouraged and monthly birthdays are celebrated.
It is difficult to measure accomplishments in an institution such as this. Nonetheless, they are there along with the pleasure received from children who have graduated and turned into fine upstanding citizens. It's impossible to measure the feeling this produces when invitations to weddings or visits in the office are received.

OFFICERS
President: Chief Rabbi I.I. Frenkel, Tel Aviv.
Vice-Chairman: Mrs. R. Torgownik, 32 Tchernikovsky, Tel Aviv.
Board Members: Yitzhak Diskin, 40 Hen Ave., Tel Aviv.
                       Wine Importer.
                       Tel. (03) 265573.
                    Yehoshua Kahana, 4 Matman, Tel Aviv.
                       Ex-Banker.
                       Tel. (03) 269561.

Israel Rotem, Melchetz St., Tel Aviv.
Economist.
Tel. (03) 614179.

FINANCIAL INFORMATION
The Society is registered as an Ottoman Association (Tel Aviv district, reg. no. 1294).

Government support, which is continuous but includes only the essentials for maintenance, provides 50% of the institution's income. The remainder comes from donations, which are tax-free in Israel (reg. no. 4500108) as well as in the United States (USA no. 986000844). Forty full-time and twenty part-time employees work for the Society, as well as ten volunteers.

MEMBERSHIP, SCOPE, AND POLICY
Decisions are made mostly by the President of the Society. A branch of the Society is located in the United States, in the State of New York.

AFFILIATIONS/REFERENCES
The Society is not affiliated with any political party.
The following individuals abroad are familiar with the Society's work.
1. Rabbi Arthur Schneier, Park East Synagogue, 163 E. 67th St., New York, New York 10021.
2. Mr. Leonard Low, Esq. 10100 Santa Monica Blvd, Suite 2500, Century City, Los Angeles, California 90067.
3. Mr. Paul Beiman, 1455 42nd Ave, San Francisco, California 94122.

FUNDING NEEDED
1. To build a new building. The Municipality of Tel Aviv donated a lot next to the present Boys Home in Yad Eliyahu. Because of the lack of space the institution has had to turn boys away, but now hopes to build new accommodations.
2. For badly-needed repairs in the Girls Home in Ramat Gan, starting from the foundations. From inside to the outside the building needs new installations, reinforcement, and new paint.
3. For general enrichment of the children. Because of the lack of funds the institution is not always able to provide the children with the culture and entertainment that they deserve. It is hoped improvement in this area will be possible, through donations.

SPAFFORD HOUSE

Old City
Jerusalem
P.O.B. 19991
Telephone: (02) 284875
Office Hours: Monday-Friday, 8:00 A.M. to 1:00 P.M.

HISTORY AND DESCRIPTION
Horatio and Anna Spafford came to Jerusalem from Chicago with a small group of friends and settled in a house on the City Wall near the Damascus Gate (now Spafford House). This group came to be known as the American Colony.

Organizational Structure: The mother-child health care center at Spafford House consists of a sick baby clinic, with a pediatrician who sees up to forty patients per morning. Five Israeli specialists volunteer their time on a regular basis for more complicated medical problems. Spafford House is a non-profit organization; a company limited by guarantee and not having a share capital.

Goals: It is the aim of the organization to prevent health problems before they begin through proper nutrition and hygiene and then, if a problem does develop, to treat it immediately. Spafford House also hopes to help with reconciliation, with Jewish doctors and Arab patients getting to know each other, and hopefully learning to live side by side.

Services, Activities and Accomplishments: The well-baby clinic includes regular check-ups and weighing of babies. The Government provides inoculations. Group discussions and individual instruction on proper diet, food preparation, hygiene and child care are included in this program. Visiting nurses follow up clinical treatments and help the families to improve living conditions. The center also operates its own pharmacy, as well as a pre-natal clinic where expectant mothers are given regular examinations and training in proper nutrition practices. As a result of these services, there has been a marked improvement in the health of the children who come to the center.

OFFICERS
Directors: Horatio Vester, American Colony Hotel, Jerusalem. Lawyer. Tel. (02) 282421.
Anna Grace Vester Lind, Spafford House, Jerusalem. Tel. (02) 284875.
Valentine Vester, American Colony Hotel, Jerusalem. Tel. (02) 282421.
Hilda Anne Mathews, Bethlehem.

FINANCIAL INFORMATION

Spafford House is registered as an Israeli tax-exempt company.

70% of the organization's budget is provided by donations from friends and supporters; the remainder comes from the patients who can afford to pay a little. Last year's budget totalled $100,000 and no deficit remained. Spafford House employs fourteen full-time workers, in addition to six volunteers. Donations are not yet tax-free in Israel, but are tax-free in the United States, through Help for Children in the Holy Land (c/o Peter Lind, 2122-112 Avenue, N.E.. Bellevue, Washington, 98004).

MEMBERSHIP, SCOPE, AND POLICY

The three members of the family constitute the organization's membership and decisions are made by these three Directors plus Miss H. Anne Mathews. Spafford House is the only branch of the organization.

AFFILIATIONS/REFERENCES

The organization is not affiliated with any political party in Israel. The following individuals abroad can serve as references:

1. Mr. & Mrs. Lowell Thomas, Hammersley Hill, Pawling, NY 12564, USA.
2. Mr. & Mrs. Peter Lind, Atty., 4550 132nd Avenue, NE Bellevue, Washington 98005, USA.
3. Hon. & Mrs. Evan Wilson, 3145 "O" Street, NW, Washington D.C. 20007, USA.

FUNDING NEEDED

1. To purchase medicines; cost, estimated $27,000 per annum.
2. To pay salaries; cost, $40,000 per annum.
3. To pay utility, fuel and maintenance bills; cost, $10,000 per annum.

STUDENT SCHOLARSHIP FUND IN MEMORY OF SHOSHANA AMIR

קרן מילגות־לימודים ע"ש שושנה אמיר

10 Massaryk St. (College of Administration in Memory of Moshe Sharett)
Jerusalem
Office hours: 5 P.M. to 7 P.M., Sun.-Thurs.

HISTORY AND DESCRIPTION
The Union of Administrative Employees in Israel came to the conclusion that the true key to the improvement of employees' social status depends on achieving a high level of professional skill, which is also necessary for the development of the Israeli economy. Therefore, in 1972, the Union decided to provide advanced studies to its members in their various fields. To that purpose it has provided vocational courses and financial aid to members of low economic means. At first the Fund was established in memory of Moshe Sharett and dedicated to the family members of Israel Defense Forces' invalids. But later, when the Israel Army itself began organizing vocational advanced studies for invalids' family members, the regulations of the Fund were changed so that people of low financial means who were willing to learn any vocation important for the country (e.g. nurses, laboratory assistants, electricians, electronics technicians) could enjoy its aid.

Organizational Structure: The Union of Administrative Employees nominated a Council consisting of the Managing Committee of the College of Adminstration and representatives of public employers. The Council elected the Fund's managing committee, a chairman, secretary, and treasurer. The Fund is run according to a constitution confirmed by the authorities and is also exempted from taxes as a charity institution.

Goals: The aim of the scholarships is to enable those who earn a low salary to advance in their vocation or to study a profession. Students must be at least eighteen years old. Special attention is directed to women in order to enable them to gain a profession and become economically independent. Most of the women who enjoy scholarships are of Islamic countries.

Services, Activities, and Accomplishments: The Fund has succeeded in providing a vocation and a respectable source of income to many non-professionals. Their salary has increased and they have become capable of giving a good education and perhaps even a vocation to their children.

OFFICERS
Director: Izchak Amir, 15 Gat, Jerusalem.
                 Tel.: (02) 524041.
Treasurer: I Amir.
Board: Yakov Manheim, 10 Tomer, Jerusalem.
                 Tel.: (02) 526623.

Zvi Rishpon, 8 Dostai, Jerusalem.
    Tel.: (02) 632939.
Avraham Saban, 97 Herzl, Jerusalem.
    Tel.: (02) 526680.
David Galili, 3 Haran, Jerusalem.
    Tel.: (02) 663182.
Dr. Michael Ziv, 4 Bloch, Kiryat Moshe, Jerusalem.
    Tel.: (02) 523061.
Reuven Sheri, 11 Rashba, Jerusalem.
    Tel.: (02) 632318.
Shlomo Keisar, POB 2209, Jerusalem.
    Tel.: (02) 533734.

FINANCIAL INFORMATION

Sources of income are as follows: 25% from membership dues and the rest from donations from public institutions and workers' committees. All administrative expenses of the fund are covered by the College of Adminstration of Moshe Sharett. The managing committee acts voluntarily. The fund is listed as an Ottoman Association (reg. no. 11/2044) and has tax-free status in Israel only (no. 4503553).

MEMBERSHIP, SCOPE, AND POLICY

Any private individual that donates the equivalent of $100 to the fund is eligible for membership. Members of the board are members of the Managing Committee of the College of Administration who are confirmed by the Central Committee of the Union of Administrative Employees. Decisions of the board are mae by majority of those present. The director has no special prerogatives. There are nine members in one Israeli branch.

AFFILIATIONS/REFERENCES

The Fund is not affiliated with any political party in Israel.

FUNDING NEEDED

According to the constitution, scholarships are given from the interest on the Fund's original endowment. Because of the economic situation, applicants to the fund have increased and so it is necessary to enlarge the fund itself in order to provide more scholarships. Today, the largest amount the fund is able to give is $60, which is very little toward tuition fees which amount to $300-$400 per year.

STUDY OF OUR PEOPLE—INSTITUTE FOR THE STUDY OF THE PSYCHOLOGY OF THE JEWISH PEOPLE IN ISRAEL AND ABROAD

"חקר עמנו" – המכון לחקר הפסיכולוגיה של העם היהודי
בזמננו בארץ והתפוצות

8 Maaleh Hazofim
Ramat Gan—52483
Telephone: (03) 722752
Office hours: 9:00 A.M. to 1:00 P.M. and 5:00 P.M. to 8:00 P.M.

HISTORY AND DESCRIPTION

Founded in Tel Aviv, in 1977, The Lodge of B'nai Brith Tel Aviv "Cheiker Ameinu", is the Institute of Study of the Psychology of the Jewish People.

There are many scientific centers in Israel and abroad for the study of Judaism, study of the Diaspora, and the like. The Study of Our People Institute adds something of its own: the study of the psychology of the Jewish people. This finds expression in the profound study of the special mental traits of the Jewish people; of social-national forms of behavior; of the essence of the Jewish identity—the causes of its shrinking or estrangement from it; of the psychological aspects of the events in the life of the nation in Israel and abroad. The Institute attempts to deal with the national problems from a psychological viewpoint; the aim being to find the way to an original Jewish manner of life, which will aid in preserving the national quality of the nation with respect to spiritual values, in preserving the Jewish speciality as a nation of spiritual power and force that is capable of coping with its difficult problems.

The Institute was founded by volunteers: psychologists, educators, sociologists, writers, historians, and public persons who consider this volunteering as a willing conscription and a national mission.

The Institute suffers from a lack of funds. Hence, for the time being lectures are presented and discussions held on national problems as preparation for research. In addition to lectures on "the Psychology of the Jewish People", lectures are given also in the fields of sociology, literature, or philosophy, which serve as background for psychological analysis.

OFFICERS

Director: Dr. Miriam Reiter-Zedek, 8 Maaleh Hazofim, Ramat Gan. Tel. (03) 722752.

Treasurer: Moshe Zedek, E.E. (address as above). Engineer.

Honorary President: Prof. Arieh Tartakover, 45A King George, Jerusalem. Sociologist. Tel. (02) 224081.

Board Members: Dr. Abraham Elizur, 45 Godenheimer, Tel Aviv. Psychologist. Tel. (03) 459370.

Dr. Moshe Ogein, 1 Hatzanchanim, Azur.
Psychologist. Tel. (03) 801510.
Dr. Alexander Rosenfeld, 47 Bilu, Tel Aviv.
Sociologist. Tel. (03) 233694.
Dr. Abraham Sukenik, 25 Rashi, Ramat Gan.
Educator. Tel. (03) 798367.

Public Relations
Editorial Staff: Zvi Porath-Noy, 38 Bialik, Ramat Gan.
Tel. (03) 771835.

FINANCIAL INFORMATION
Details regarding the sources of income were not indicated. The annual budget for last year was $1200 with a deficit of $850. The organization is registered as an Ottoman Association (no. 7621). Donations to the organization are tax-free both in Israel and the United States, but no tax numbers were supplied. There is one full-time worker, some part-time workers and 17 volunteers.

MEMBERSHIP, SCOPE, AND POLICY
Decisions are made mostly by the National Board. There are 200 members in Israel and 12 abroad. There are no branches in Israel, but there is one in Cape Town, South Africa. Zionists of academic and Jewish education and others who are interested in the study of Jewish national problems who want to contribute their efforts to help the organization are eligible to join.

AFFILIATIONS/REFERENCES
The organization is not affiliated with any political party in Israel. The following are the foreign contacts of the organization: Prof. Israel Singer, World Jewish Congress, 1 Park Avenue, New York, New York 10016; Shlomo Shamir, Director, Histadrut Ivrit of America, 1841 Broadway, New York, New York; Rabbi Simcha Raz, Director, Western Province Zionist Council, P.O.B. 2578, Cape Town, South Africa.

FUNDING NEEDED
1. The establishment of an office and its accessories. Estimated cost: $6000 per annum.
2. The printing and publication of pamphlets and books. Estimated cost: $7000 per annum.
3. Research. Estimated cost: $12,000.

SUCATH DAVID TALMUD TORAH

תלמוד תורה "סוכת דוד"

35 David Yellin Street Jerusalem
Telephone: (02) 228335
Office hours: 8:30 A.M. to 4:00 P.M.

HISTORY AND DESCRIPTION
The organization was founded in 1974 in memory of Rabbi David
Sutton Dabbah. It was started with 15 pupils in very small quarters in
Jerusalem and due to the level of the teaching and the satisfaction of the
parents, the Talmud Torah grew. There are now nearly 300 children
studying in the establishment. A new building was recently purchased.
There are 4 kindergarten classes — 2 classes for 2-3 year olds and 2
classes for 3-4 year olds, as well as 2 preparation classes. There are now 5
primary school classes. Each year one class is added, as well as the
addition of a parallel class starting from the first grade.
The aim is the spreading of Torah in Israel, and the educating of the
younger generation with pedagogical structures applicable to Torah
and Mitzvoth so that they will become scholars.
The major accomplishment of the organization until now has been the
founding of a successful Talmud Torah.

OFFICERS
Director: Menahem Basri.
Treasurer: Yehuda Zaiat.
Board Members: Sasson Basri, Rafael Cohen, Eliyahu Cohen.

FINANCIAL INFORMATION
Last year's annual budget came from the following sources: membership dues, 18%; donations, 28%; other sources, 54%. Last year's annual
budget of $105,000 left a deficit of $55,000. The organization is registerd
as an Ottoman Association (no. 11/2308). Donations to the organization are tax-free both in Israel and the United States, although no tax
numbers were supplied. There are 32 full-time employees.

MEMBERSHIP, SCOPE, AND POLICY
Decisions are made mostly by the Executive Director. There are five
members in Israel. In addition to the one branch in Israel, there is one
branch in Argentina.

AFFILIATIONS/REFERENCES
The organization is not affiliated with any political party in Israel. The
organization is in contact with Sucath David Argentina, Paso 724,
Buenos Aires.

FUNDING NEEDED
1. The financing and support of the Talmud Torah and kindergartens.
2. The establishment of a Yeshiva Ketana and a Kollel for married
   students.
3. The establishment of a girls' schools.

SUPREME COUNCIL (33) OF FREEMASONS IN ISRAEL

המועצה העליונה (33) בבניה החפשית למדינת ישראל

c/o A. Fellman
P.O.Box 53
Tel Aviv
Office hours: Mornings

HISTORY AND DESCRIPTION
This is a friendly and charitable body, with membership limited to Freemasons. International conventions are held every year in a different country, and in 1976 one was held in Jerusalem. The organization gives charity to needy persons and institutions.

OFFICERS
Director: A. Fellman, Rothschild 48, Tel Aviv.
                    C.P. Accountant. Tel. (03) 611992.
Treasurer: J. Jacobi, Nahlat Benjamin 81, Tel Aviv.
                    Merchant. Tel. (03) 623878.

FINANCIAL INFORMATION
50% of the Council's income comes from membership dues, 20% donations and 30% from interest on funds. Last year's annual budget was $2,000, leaving no deficit. The organization is registered in Tel Aviv as an Ottoman Society (registration number 3608/39) and donations in Israel are tax-exempt (no. 4501573). The Council is run only by volunteers.

MEMBERSHIP, SCOPE, AND POLICY
Only distinguished Freemasons can join this organization. There are 28 members in Israel and 1 abroad with 10 branches in Israel. Decisions are made by the Executive Director and at general meetings.

AFFILIATIONS/REFERENCES
All Grand Lodges of Freemasons in 150 countries and all Supreme Councils of Freemasons in 35 countries are inter-affiliated.

FUNDING NEEDED
1. For small institutes.
2. For hospitals.
3. For needy people.

TALMUD TORAH AND YESHIVA TORAT MOSHE

תלמוד תורה וישיבת תורת משה

32 Chaim Ozer Street and
14 Zachariah HaRofe Street
Nahalat Zvi, Jerusalem
Telephone: (02) 282338
Office hours: not listed

HISTORY AND DESCRIPTION
The organization is in existence approximately three years, since 1977, and started rather modestly with Torah lessons. As the idea developed, additional students were attracted, and the Yeshiva recognized the need to expand. At present it operates primarily on a voluntary basis.

Goals: The goals of the organization are to provide spiritual and social guidance to youth from underprivileged backgrounds; to teach Baalei Teshuvah (those who have returned to a traditional life-style) in the spirit of Torah, combined with secular studies; to direct the students to suitable work positions; to provide matchmaking serivces to the students; to provide scholarships and loans to newlyweds and those wishing to continue studying after marriage.

Services, Activities, and Accomplishments: Approximately 20 students learn now at the Yeshiva. Some of the students also work in the morning in jobs which the Yeshiva helped them find. In addition, several students who began their journey back to Torah tradition with the Yeshiva are today learning full-time in other Yeshivot.

OFFICERS
President: Rabbi Ya'akov Joseph, 10 Hanna, Jerusalem.
Director: Rabbi Moshe Ptihi, 14 Zeharia HaRofe, Jerusalem. Rabbi. Tel. (02) 282338.
Treasurer: Joseph Ben Porat, 32 Chaim Ozer, Jerusalem. Store owner.
Board: Rabbi Joseph Haba, 18 Avinadav, Jerusalem. Rabbi. Tel. (02) 289780.

FINANCIAL INFORMATION
All of last year's annual budget came from donations. Last year's annual budget was $20,000, and the deficit was $5,000. The Yeshiva is registered as an Ottoman Association (registration number not supplied). It was not indicated whether or not donations were tax-free, neither in Israel nor in the United States. The Yeshiva operates only with volunteers, approximately ten, and has no paid employees.

MEMBERSHIP, SCOPE, AND POLICY
There are seven members in the one branch in Israel. Most decisions are made by the National Board.

AFFILIATIONS/REFERENCES
The Yeshiva is not affiliated with any political party in Israel. The Yeshiva has no contacts abroad.

FUNDING NEEDED
1. The construction of a building to house students and to provide classroom space, and also to serve as the educational and spiritual center of the organization, open to the general public (with emphasis on youth from lower socioeconomic levels). Estimated cost: $1 million.
2. Meeting the general maintenance expenses (monthly stipend for students, equipment, etc.). Estimated cost: $2,000 per month and increasing rapidly.
3. The establishment of a special fund to help needy students, for newlyweds to assist in setting up homes, and for providing loans. Estimated cost: $20,000.

TALMUD TORAH MORASHA

תלמוד תורה מורשה

21 Ben Zion Street
Kiryat Moshe, Jerusalem
Telephone: (02) 537068
Office hours: 8:30 A.M. to 1:00 P.M.

HISTORY AND DESCRIPTION

Talmud Torah Morasha is an educational institution. Children attend from the age of 3. It was founded by a group of students and graduates of Yeshivat Mercaz Harav Kook in Jerusalem. Talmud Torah "Morasha" presents a new pattern of Jewish national education in guidance from early childhood.

The Talmud Torah is unique in combining within this educational scheme both moral and religious values venerated by the Jewish people, along with a renewed youthful national and spiritual approach of the younger generation living in Eretz Yisrael. The aim of the education is based on Rabbi Kook's ideals: Torah and observance based on great love to the people of Israel, to the Land of Israel and to the State of Israel. It aims to develop a generation of learned scholars — Talmidei Hahamim — who will be totally involved in their communities and who will consider themselves sharing the same problems and needs that are common to the whole population.

The Rabbis who teach in Talmud Torah Morasha are distinguished graduates of Yeshivat Harav Kook, who served in Israel's Defense Forces or in "Hesder" Yeshivot. They have decided to devote their abilities to help shape the developing spiritual and religious basis of these children from their early childhood.

The pattern of schooling adopted is similar to that which was customary in a "cheder", giving special attention to moral values, "Derech Eretz", increasing the desire to learn Torah, and strengthening faith and belief. The educational program is planned for those from the age of three: the first years of education are devoted to Bible and later years are devoted to Talmud. Children of 6-7 years of age (first and second grades) have already completed, several times, the Pentateuch and have read most chapters of the Bible. The success of the Talmud Torah is a result of educating children to the love and study of Torah as a goal in itself. The Yeshiva does not have a system of marks and tests, yet the children dwell on their work much beyond the regular hours of lessons and learn on their own during the afternoon.

OFFICERS

Director: Rabbi Oded Volansky, 20 Ben Zion, Jerusalem. Rabbi. Tel. 532587.

Board Members: Rabbi Jacob Levanon, 13 Givat Shaul, Jerusalem. Tel. 537101.
Rabbi Hillel Plesser, 21 Ben Zion, Jerusalem. Tel. 537068.
Eliezer Sadan, 18 Ben Dor, Jerusalem. Tel. 531618.

FINANCIAL INFORMATION

80% of last year's annual budget came from donations and grants; the remaining 20% came from tuition. Last year's annual budget was $60,000. There was no indication of a deficit. The Yeshiva is registered as an Ottoman Association (No. 11/2747). Donations to the Yeshiva are tax-free in Israel (tax no. 4506465). Donations in the United States are tax-free when made out to Rabbi Kook Universal Yeshiva, Jerusalem (tax no. 13-5562). There are 18 part-time workers employed by the Yeshiva and 10 volunteers.

MEMBERSHIP, SCOPE, AND POLICY

Decisions are made by the national board. Information regarding membership was not supplied.

AFFILIATIONS/REFERENCES

The Yeshiva is not affiliated with any political party in Israel. There are no contacts in the United States or abroad.

FUNDING NEEDED

1. The construction of a suitable building.
2. The funds to cover the annual budget deficit.
3. The purchasing of educational aids.

TECHNION FACULTY WIVES' CLUB
מועדון נשי הסגל בטכניון

Faculty Association, Senate Building
Technion-Israel Institute of Technology
Haifa
Telephone: (04) 292582
Office Hours: 8:00 A.M. to 1:00 P.M.

HISTORY AND DESCRIPTION
Organizational Structure: As its name implies, this is an organization composed of the wives of faculty at the Israel Institute of Technology (Technion) in Haifa. There is a steering committee of 15 members, including a Chairperson.

Goals: The singular goal of the Club is to help in the absorption of new immigrants who have joined the faculty of the Technion, as well as Visiting Professors and Scientists.

Services, Activities, and Accomplishments: The Technion Faculty Wives' Club operates for the most part as a social organization, attempting to fill a possible social/cultural gap in the lives of new immigrant professors and/or visiting scientists. It also offers help to young faculty families and to faculty children serving in Israel's military forces. It therefore sees its major accomplishments as: its being a 24-hour 'open counselling and willing to help institution'; turning foreign visitors into 'Israel's Ambassadors of Good Will'; and, in times of emergency, offering its help and non-financial resources to the Soldier's Welfare Association.

OFFICERS
Chairperson: Sylvia Mizrahi, Technion I.T.T.,
Research Engineer.
Tel. (04) 293076.

Co-chairperson: Edith Katz, 38 Abba Khoushi Ave., Haifa.
Secretary.
Tel. (04) 246356.

Treasurer: Zipora Apeloig, 21 Hapalmach St., Haifa.
Computer Programmer.
Tel. (04) 244919.

Board: Bella Kaplivatzki, 6 A.H. Silver St., Haifa.
Teacher.
Tel. (04) 231539.

Dora Cederbaum, 8 Morad Hazamir, Haifa.
Housewife.
Tel. (04) 245025.

FINANCIAL INFORMATION, MEMBERSHIP, SCOPE, AND POLICY
The Club's last annual budget of $150 was founded totally upon a yearly

allowance from the Technion. Most of the group's activities were in fact based on a voluntary basis, including food served at various parties, and the like. Membership is open to all faculty wives at the Technion, on a voluntary basis. Decisions are made by the Club's steering committee.

FUNDING

Given the nature of its existence and activities, the Club is not in need of financial assistance; although contributions of books — for children and young people in English, and to be sent to Israeli soldiers — would be most appreciated.

THE TEL AVIV-JAFFA COMMON CIRCLE

החוג המשותף תל-אביב יפו

P.O. Box 15049, Tel-Aviv, 61150
Telephone: (03) 942304
Office Hours: 5:30 P.M. to 8:30 P.M. weekdays

HISTORY AND DESCRIPTION
Created by private citizens, the Circle was founded as a place where people could come to freely meet and discuss Jewish and Arab relations.

Organizational Structure: There is no formal membership, and events are open to every citizen 18 years old or more. Elections and decisions are made only by participants with one year seniority, if they attended at least half of the events during the past year.

Goals: The goal of this group is to be all-party, all-denominational, for the normalizing of relations between people of various cultural backgounds.

Services, Activities, and Accomplishments: A permanent framework for the exchange of views is provided for open-minded citizens. Infringement on rights and social hardships are checked up on, lecture evenings and discussions are held relating to Jewish-Arab co-existence or integration, and periodic bulletins are published.

OFFICERS

Director: Chaim Sil, Rishon Le Zion. Production Engineer.
                Tel. (03) 942304.

Treasurer: Eliezer Bor, Tel Aviv. Chemical Supplies.
                Tel. (03) 267161.

Senior
Participants: Ali Yatim, Jaffa. Teacher.
                Tel. (03) 589483.
                Chava Weiss, Natanya. Librarian.
                Tel. (053) 51556.
                Machmood El-Mafra, Kfar Ssulam. Male Nurse.
                Tel. (065) 22078.
                David Ricardo, Rishon Le Zion.
                Spares Manufacturer. Tel. (03) 942819.
                Charbi Nabulsi, Jaffa. Fitter and Welder.
                Machmood Bayadsi, Baka El Garbiye. Accountant.
                Tel. (063) 78694.

FINANCIAL INFORMATION
100% of income is supplied by participants paying for various events and bulletins published. The annual budget was $20 last year, with no deficit because participants pay for all events. The organization is not registered as an Ottoman Association, and donations are not tax-free. The Circle is run only by volunteers.

MEMBERSHIP, SCOPE, AND POLICY
Any citizen over 18 years of age can become a member. As of now 83 participants are registered in Israel and 3 abroad. Decisions of the Circle are made mostly by the Executive Director, after consultation with senior members. There is only one branch in Israel.

AFFILIATIONS/REFERENCES
The American Jewish Committee, Institute of Human Relations, Foreign Affairs Department, New York; University of Wisconsin, Dept. of Political Science; and European Judaism, Palace Court, London, are organizations who know of the organization's work.

FUNDING NEEDED
1. Funds for periodic bulletins (four to six times a year) to publicize events, voice views, and list suggestions.
2. "Letters of Appreciation" to private citizens who did unusual acts to benefit someone of the other ethnic or religious community (Jewish to Arab, or vice versa).
3. Group visits to places of common interest.

TENANT'S PROTECTION SOCIETY

הארגון להגנת הדייר

Jerusalem 5
P.O. Box 4275
Haifa
Telephone: (04) 669312; (04) 244758
Office hours: Monday: 6-8 P.M.; Thursday: 5-7 P.M.

HISTORY AND DESCRIPTION

The Society was established as a voluntary organization for flat (apartment) renters in 1969. The flat-renters represented by the Society occupy flats protected by the law, and all of them have bought the right to rent the flats through the payment of key-money, which amounts to at least two-thirds of the value of a respective flat. The vast majority of the tenants are old-age pensioners (retired persons) whose living is sustained by a low pension from the government.

Goals: One aim of the Society is to protect flat-renters against possible abuse from house-owners. In addition, there is strong pressure in the government, as well as from house-owners to abolish the Law for the Protection of Flat-Renters, and this could mean a disaster to the tenants now covered by the Law. The task of this organization is to fight against such a possibility.

Services, Activities, and Accomplishments: To date, the Society has fought to ensure that the key-money Law has not been revoked and that over the years flat rentals have remained relatively low. It has made sure that every tenant has received legal protection of his rights and has kept tenants informed of their rights. The move to cancel the Protection Law and to raise the rentals of key-money premises (flats and businesses) to an unprecedented level would cause extreme hardship to many tenants. In order to develop and extend the activity of the Society, greater financial support is needed at this time to fight to retain the rights of members and to prevent them from losing the money which they have invested in their key-money premises.

OFFICERS

Director:
T. Wardimon, Kiryat Sefer 25, Haifa.
Public Admin. Tel. (02) 244758.

Treasurer:
A. Porath, Pevsner 10, Haifa.
Accountant. Tel. (04) 674758.

Board Members:
J. Bashan, Gilboa 23, Haifa.
Engineer. Tel. (04) 233224.

M. Kadosh, Ibn Sina 10, Haifa.
Public Official. Tel. (04) 640494.

L. Goldstein, Hasport 4, Haifa.
Graphic Artist. Tel. (04) 83657.

J. Goldler, Disraeli 28, Haifa.
Advocate. Tel. (04) 251646.

A. Harlap, Oren 22, Haifa.
Advocate. Tel. (04) 242203.

FINANCIAL INFORMATION
Membership dues account for 70% of the Society's income; donations provide the other 30%. Last year's budget was $4,000, with a deficit of $1,000. The Society is an Ottoman, non-profit Association (registration no. 61/1118, Haifa District). Donations in Israel are tax-free (no number provided), but contributions from the U.S. are not. Nine volunteers do the work of the Society.

MEMBERSHIP, SCOPE, AND POLICY
There are 10,000 members in the 5 Israeli branches of the Society. Any key-money tenant of flat or business premises or factory can be a member. Decisions are taken by the Board or by the General Meeting of the Society, in which members of the organization take part.

AFFILIATIONS/REFERENCES
The Society is in contact with Tenants' Protection Societies in London, Frankfurt/Main, and Munich, and with other organizations in Western Europe. It is not affiliated with any Israeli political party.

FUNDING NEEDED
1. To finance the public activities of the organization.
2. To maintain the public struggle in order to protect the rights of the tenants.
3. To finance administrative and publicity expenses (such as office maintenance, telephone, post, advertising in press). All workers are voluntary and do not receive salaries.

TENT (HA-OHEL) MOVEMENT FOR NEIGHBORHOOD AND COMMUNITY DEVELOPMENT

תנועת האוהלים

12 Shamai St.
P.O.B. 4123, Jerusalem
Telephone: (02) 249955
Office hours: Sunday through Friday, 9:00 A.M. to 1:00 P.M.

HISTORY AND DESCRIPTION

The Ohel Movement was established in 1973 by a group of young people in the immigrant housing section of the Gonen Tet neighborhood in Jerusalem. This neighborhood has been one of the most problematic residential areas of the city, suffering from a relatively high level of social inequality.

Organizational Structure: In order to cope with local problems, and Ohel Council was established consisting of youngsters who wanted to initiate self-help services in the neighborhood and to upgrade local cultural, social, and physical conditions. Eventually, similar Ohel Councils were established in other poverty areas, and an Urban Board was established as a roof body to coordinate and initiate activities.

Goals, Services, and Activities: The activities of the Movement can be divided into three categories: provision of self-help services such as youth clubs and youth camps, women's clubs, classes for teenagers and adults, protest theatre, and production and consumption cooperatives; exerting pressure on the Establishment in order to promote social change and particularly to upgrade housing conditions (often involving rallies and squattings designed to pressure for change); participation in planning activities initiated by government bodies, including Project Renewal and municipal committees dealing with neighborhood affairs.

Major Accomplishments: The organization claims to have succeeded in lowering the rate of juvenile delinquency, attained more control over the allocation of social services in poverty neighborhoods, and changing the government's attitude toward poverty neighborhoods by making officials more aware of their problems.

OFFICERS

Director: Yamin Swissa, 101/43 Bar Yochai.
Katamon Tet, Jerusalem.
Community worker. Tel. (02) 413602.

Treasurer: Ovadia Eliahu, 47 Bar Yochai, Jerusalem.
Shopkeeper. Tel. (02) 424621.

Board Members: Avner Amiel, 4/25 Ramat Sharett, Jerusalem.
Community worker. Tel. (02) 418833.
Michael Peren, 5 Chel Nashim, Jerusalem.
Community organizer. Tel. (02) 639482.

Azar Cohen, 106/38 Bar Yochai, Jerusalem.
Manager of corporation.
Moshe Salach, 7 Birav, Jerusalem.
Theatre manager. Tel. (02) 244188.
David Cetter, 55 Mehor Chayim, Jerusalem.
Administrator. Tel. (02) 715758.
Avi Elzam, 6/55 Shmuel Hanavi, Jerusalem.
Mechanic. Tel. (02) 281194.
Dr. Shlomo Hasson, 23 Guatamala, Jerusalem.
Tel. (02) 419599.

FINANCIAL INFORMATION

In 1980, the annual budget amounted to $80,000, of which 50 percent came from donations, 40 percent from "Establishment" grants, and 10 percent from membership dues. The organization is registered in Jerusalem as a non-profit association, and donations are tax-deductible (registration and tax numbers were not supplied). There is no tax-deductible status for contributions in the U.S. The Movement employs one full-time and two part-time people, and has 250 volunteers.

MEMBERSHIP, SCOPE AND POLICY

The Tent Movement has 400 members in Israel and 80 abroad, and has seven Israeli branches. Every resident of Israel is entitled to join, and decisions are made by the Ohel neighborhood Councils and the city-wide Urban Board.

AFFILIATIONS/REFERENCES

The organization is not affiliated with any political party in Israel. References abroad include the following:

1. Ohalim France, 14 Rue de la Ferme, Neuilly sur Seine, France (Lydia Chiche).
2. Comite d'Action Pour le Second Israel, 87erd St. Michel, Paris, France (Alexander Bliah, President).
3. Federation Sepharade Mondiale, 78 Rue du Rhone, Geneve, Switzerland.

FUNDING NEEDED

1. For seminars and community theatre to develop local leadership and enhance group solidarity.
2. To develop local enterprises for youngsters and married women who cannot leave the neighborhood.
3. To develop social and cultural activities for the socially deprived population in poverty neighborhoods.
4. For vocational training scholarships for youths of pre- and post-military age, to prevent them from the risk of unemployment after finishing military service.

TESTIMONIUM

עדות

33 Rachel Imenu Street
Jerusalem
Telephone: (02) 663151—8:00 A.M. to 12:00 P.M.
            (02) 631978—4:00 P.M. to 6:00 P.M.

HISTORY AND DESCRIPTION

Testimonium was founded in 1966 as a concert series for works commissioned by local and foreign, Jewish and non-Jewish, composers. It is the brainchild of Recha Freier of Jerusalem, a writer, artist and patron with wide and lively sympathies, and who is still today in her eighties, a woman of remarkable energy and force.

It was Recha Freier's idea in 1966, in collaboration with the composer, Roman Haubenstock-Ramati, to found the Testimonium in Israel, the theme of which was to give expression to the wandering of the Jewish people in the Diaspora and its spiritual creation. The wider implication is interdenominational and international: a breaking down of narrow cultural boundaries, a dialogue between composer and audience that should turn not inward but outward, a place where differing styles and cultures meet.

OFFICERS

Director:	Recha Freier, 33 Rachel Imenu, Jerusalem. Tel. (02) 631978.
Treasurer:	Amos Blitz, 69 Bet Zayit. Tel. (02) 522752.
Board Members:	Prof. Dr. David Flusser, 10 Alkalay, Jerusalem. Tel. (02) 631094.
	Prof. Dr. Edit Gerson-Kiwi, 8 Keren Kayemet, Jerusalem. Tel. (02) 632332.
	Prof. Dan Pagis, 16 Haarazim, Jerusalem. Tel. (02) 531956.
	Prof. Dr. Amnon Shiloah, 10 Hameliz, Jerusalem. Tel. (02) 665474.
	Leo Savir, 10 Metudela, Jerusalem. Tel. (02) 632438.
	Dr. M.M. Spitzer, 14 Hanassi, Jerusalem. Tel. (02) 636332.
	Hanna Meron, 56 Hanassi, Herzlia. Tel. (03) 932304.

FINANCIAL INFORMATION

The sources of Testimonium's budget include the Israel and German governments, subventions, donations, and membership fees. Last year's annual budget of $107,000 left Testimonium with a deficit of $23,800. Donations to the organization in Israel, the United States and England are tax-free (nos. not supplied). In Israel, the organization is an Ottoman Association (no. 11/1410). Two volunteers give of their services for Testimonium.

MEMBERSHIP, SCOPE, AND POLICY
The number of members, both in Israel and abroad, is continually increasing. Anyone over the age of 18 who pays membership fees may join. Decisions are made mostly by the Executive Director and the National Board.

AFFILIATIONS/REFERENCES
Testimonium is politically unaffiliated in Israel. It has contacts with the P.E.F. Israel Endowment Fund in New York City, and with the Ministry of Foreign Affairs in Bonn, Germany, Department for Culture.

FUNDING NEEDED
1. For a "Testimonium-Jerusalem", to be performed in London at St. John's Smith Square. Costs are approximately £1000, of which only £250 has been raised.
2. For Testimonium VI (1982)— one evening at the Jerusalem Theater, and one evening at the Tel Aviv Museum. A play based on the life of the Jewish "Minnesinger" Susskind von Trimberg, music by Mark Kopytman, text by Recha Freier.

THEATRE ARCHIVES AND MUSEUM
ארכיון ומוזיאון לתיאטרון

13 Mesilat Yesharim
P.O.B. 7098
Jerusalem 91070
Telephone: (02) 227566, 669354
Office hours: Monday, Wednesday, Thursday, 9:00 A.M. to 3:00 P.M.

HISTORY AND DESCRIPTION
The first step towards setting up the Theatrical Museum and Archives was the establishment of a public committee composed of leading figures in the theatrical and literary world which set out to secure, in addition to the copious material gathered by "Bamah", the Israeli Theatrical Quarterly, other important theatrical collections. Thus, for example, contact was established with the late Zalman Zilberzweig, a well-known authority on the Yiddish Theatre and author of a many-volumed lexicon of the Jewish theatre, with the view to securing the transfer of his rich archives in Jerusalem. Zilberzweig agreed, and an agreement to that effect was entered into between himself and Mr. Moshe Kol, Israel Minister of Tourism, who heads the public committee. Apart from the large Zilberzweig and "Bamah" collections, which form the basis of the Jerusalem archives, material pours in regularly from actors and producers both in Israel and abroad. Among such material mention should be made of the archives of the late Yitzhak Nozhik, one of the pillars of the now defunct satirical theatre "Hamatate", and of the late Meir Margalit, one of the greatest of Israeli actors who died in 1974 and whose large theatrical collection he bequeathed to the Archives in his lifetime.

Goals: The aim and function of the Theatrical museum and Archives is to enable the Jewish public to learn about their people through the medium of plays written by Jews in Hebrew, Yiddish and other languages. The Jewish Theatre has often served as a focus of activity in many a community. This institution will save from oblivion books, manuscripts and other documents relating to the Jewish Theatre, and record the activities of Jewish actors in theatres the world over. The organization appeals to all people in possession of relevant material to entrust it to the Theatre Archives and Museum in order for it to serve a useful purpose.

Services, Activities, and Accomplishments: The Jerusalem Theatre Museum and Archives was opened to the public in May 1973. It is housed in an eight-room building belonging to the Jerusalem Municipality and which was specially adapted for the purpose. One component of the institution is its library, which includes many a rare, or even unique volume. The other components of the Archives are the thousands of files, including many personal files on producers, actors, playwrights, critics, and theatrical research workers. Generally these files refer to current performances by Israeli theatrical troupes, but they also include files of theatrical material bequeathed to the institution. A

573

sophisticated cross-reference system has been devised by which research workers are directed from one file to another. It is a matter of considerable satisfaction to note that great use is made of the material by students, producers and research workers. The Archives also collects files of clippings from the Israeli and world press of news items and references to theatrical life and activity. An important field of work of the Archives is that of theatrical documentation. Members of the staff interview actors and producers and tape-record their stories. The tape library is constantly growing, and stands at the disposal of theatrical students and research workers. It is hoped that, one day, much of the material thus collected will be published. Already, however, the Museum, in cooperation with "Bamah", is launching a series of bibliographical publications, such as an index to the numerous theatrical periodicals published over the years, in Yiddish and in Hebrew. The Theatre Archives and museum also organizes mobile exhibitions. Major accomplishments of the Theatre Archives and Museum include the accumulation of approximately 5,000 files of plays and personal dossiers (actors, directors, dramatists, set designers, musicians, etc.), and the establishment of a multi-language library for Drama, Theatre and the related Arts.

OFFICERS

Chairman:	Moshe Kol, 10 Jabotinsky, Jerusalem. Politician. Tel. (02) 669788.
Treasurer:	Mordechai Ish-Shalom, 5 Hachotzev, Jerusalem. Banker. Tel. (02) 527305.
Board Members:	Arnon Gafni, 114 Herzl, Jerusalem. Economist. Tel. (02) 528640.
	Avraham Agmon. 14 Simchoni, Jerusalem. Economist. Tel. (02) 634501.
	Shlomo Du-nour, 2 November 29, Jerusalem. Historian. Tel. (02) 631310.
	Yitzchak Tishler, 41 Keren Kayemet, Jerusalem. Journalist. Tel. (02) 632824.
	Yehoshua Yustman, 50 Charlap, Jerusalem. Journalist. Tel. (02) 632959.
	Israel Goor, 45 Berlin, Jerusalem. Editor. Tel. (02) 631940.

FINANCIAL INFORMATION

100% of the Theatre Archives and Museum's income comes from donations. Last year's annual budget of approximately $50,000 left the organization with a deficit of approximately $5,000. It is registered in Jerusalem as a non-profit Ottoman Association (reg. no. 11/2408). Donations in Israel are tax-free (tax no. not supplied). Two full-time and two part-time workers are employed by the organization.

574

MEMBERSHIP, SCOPE, AND POLICY
Membership is open to any interested person who submits a special application. There are 40 members in Israel. Most decisions are made by the Executive Director or the National Board.

AFFILIATIONS/REFERENCES
The organization is not affiliated with any Israeli political party.

FUNDING NEEDED
1. To mount a large exhibition to commemorate 100 years of Jewish Theatre.
2. To finance a bibliographic project.
3. To finance the acquisition of documents and books.

TIFERETH HACARMEL
THE GREAT YESHIVA AND COLLEGE
FOR ADVANCED TORAH STUDIES

ישיבה גדולה ובית מדרש גבוה לתורה — תפארת הכרמל

90 Hatishbi Street
Mount Carmel
Haifa
Telephone: (04) 84044
Office hours: 9:00 A.M. to 1:00 P.M. and 3:00 P.M. to 7:00 P.M.

HISTORY AND DESCRIPTION

The Yeshiva was founded in the year 1961, especially on the historical Mount Carmel, at Hatishbi Street, which symbolizes the glorious past of Haifa during the period of the Prophet Elijah, who sanctified publicly the "Holy Name" by announcing his renowned Declaration: "The Name is the Eternal". The Yeshiva contributes to a certain extent to the reappearance of this glory on Mount Carmel.

It is the continuation of its sister Yeshiva, "Tifereth Israel", in Haifa. It is a special Yeshiva for excellent and outstanding 18-30 year old students from other Yeshivot, both in Israel and abroad. These students who attend the Yeshiva for advanced study in order to perfect and complete their studies in the teaching of Torah, as Rabbis, religious judges and spiritual leaders.

This Yeshiva has founded another separate unit from this Yeshiva for repentant persons who want to find their way back to Judaism.

Services, Activities, and Accomplishments: The absorption, education and training of students, many of whom become rabbis in towns and settlements both in Israel and abroad. This has a great spiritual influence on the surrounding areas.

OFFICERS

Director: Rabbi Raphael Shapira, 37 Pewsner, Haifa. Manager. Tel. (04) 665970.

Treasurer: Zvi Boimel, 100 Hanassi, Haifa. Merchant.

Board Members: Moshe Benyamini, 6 Nahalal, Bat-Galim, Haifa. Yehuda Nierenberg, 37 Pewsner, Haifa. Retired.

FINANCIAL INFORMATION

The sources of last year's annual budget were as follows: membership dues, 3%; donations, 40%; allocations from institutions, 30%; and miscellaneous, 27%. Last year's annual budget was $58,000 and the Yeshiva has a deficit of $5,000. The Yeshiva is registered as an Ottoman Association (reg. no. 61/613). Donations to the Yeshiva are tax-free in both Israel (tax no. 4500152) and the United States (no tax number supplied). Twenty-three full-time workers are employed by the Yeshiva, as well as four volunteers.

MEMBERSHIP, SCOPE, AND POLICY

There are 42 members in Israel and four abroad. A separate branch of the Yeshiva is devoted to studies for repentant sinners. Most decisions are made by the Committee or the Chairman of the Association.

AFFILIATIONS/REFERENCES

The Yeshiva is not affiliated with any political party in Israel.

FUNDING NEEDED

1. The construction of a boarding school dormitory for the young men. Estimated cost: $120,000.
2. The general reconditioning of the central building, the hall of the college and of the classrooms. Estimated cost: $15,000.
3. The construction of housing for the rabbis who teach at the Yeshiva. Cost not estimated.

TIFERET SHLOMO BOYS ORPHANAGE HOME

מוסד ילדים "תפארת שלמה"

19 Rabenu Gershom Street
Jerusalem
P.O.B. 379
Telephone: (02) 282133
Office Hours: All Day

HISTORY AND DESCRIPTION

Tiferet Shlomo Orphanage is a home and shelter for homeless children and children from broken homes, from all parts of the country. The Home includes full dormitory facilities and Talmud Torah and Yeshiva K'tana. Children are accepted from the ages of eight to sixteen.

OFFICERS

Director: I. Bezaleli, 14 Malche Israel St., Jerusalem.
Tel. (02) 284457.

Board Members: N. Namdar
Y. Amar
E. Levy
Y. Eliahu

FINANCIAL INFORMATION

The Orphanage budget is comprised entirely of donations received. Last year's budget totalled $60,000; no deficit was reported. The organization employs seven full-time and six part-time workers. Donations are tax-free in the United States (state I.R.S. no. AU:F:610:SR M-71-EO-249) and in the United Kingdom (reg. no. not supplied); donations are not tax-free in Israel. The organization is registered in Jerusalem as an Ottoman society (no. 11/1565).

AFFILIATIONS/REFERENCES

The Home is not affiliated with any political party in Israel.

FUNDING NEEDED

1. Construction has now begun on a new building, including full dormitory facilities for the boys. More and more such youngsters are being sent for care and it is for this reason mainly that it is necessary to erect a new building. Previous accommodations were much too inadequate, the building was old and the home was forced to place these children in various rented locations as there was no place to house them. The new building will accommodate between seventy and eighty children.

TIKVA

Pua Street 9
Haifa
Telephone: (04) 515978
Office hours: Sunday, Tuesday, Thursday 9:00 P.M. to 12:00 Noon

HISTORY AND DESCRIPTION
Tikva was founded in 1975 by parents of brain-damaged children who wanted to be active in their children's rehabilitation rather than committing them to a new home. In the first instance, this is by means of the American Delacato methods, although Tikva, is also open to other methods.

Goals: A main goal is the development of an Israeli team which can provide parents with year-round treatment for their children more cheaply than the treatment they pay for when the Delacato team is brought to Israel. Tikva also aims to propagate comprehensive information concerning all aspects of brain damage so that it can be diagnosed in its various forms at the earliest possible stage.

Services, Activities, and Accomplishments: In addition to arranging for the Delacato team to visit Israel, Tikva seeks out other methods of treatment, organizes lectures and propagates information concerning them. Tikva also acts as an intermediary in the exchange of various items of equipment required for treatment, and organizes individuals and groups of volunteers to help with the long and tedious treatment programs. Tikva has introduced the use of the Delacato treatment to over 200 families in Israel, and has obtained the official approval of the Ministry of Social Welfare for Delacato as a rehabilitation method. Tikva has succeeded in rehabilitating brain-damaged children and adults (in some of these cases the damage was total) as regards independence in all the requirements of daily life, and gainful employment.

OFFICERS
Director: Ayala Fried, Leon Blum 44, Haifa. Teacher.
                                  Tel. (04) 86632.
Treasurer: A. Bar Niv, Eilat 40, Holon. Accountant.
                                  Tel. (03) 849723.
Board Members: Prof. R. Enis, Asif 1, Haifa. Architect.
                                  Tel. (04) 89676.
                                  E. Barkan, Beit Zayit. Farmer.
                                  Tel. (02) 534211.
                                  R. Fridman, Yeshurun 3, Haifa.
                                  Tel. (04) 88711.

FINANCIAL INFORMATION
90% of last year's annual budget came from membership dues; the balance from the Ministry of Social Welfare. Last year's annual budget

was $50,000; there was no deficit. Donations to Tikva in Israel are tax-free (no registration number supplied). Tikva is registered as an Ottoman Association (Haifa, reg. no. 61/1290). It employs one part-time worker, as well as 500 volunteers.

MEMBERSHIP, SCOPE, AND POLICY
There is one branch in Israel with 180 members. Anyone who needs help and will pay the membership dues can join Tikva. Decisions are made by the National Board. The organization is not affiliated with any political party in Israel. There are no overseas branches.

FUNDING NEEDED
1. To pay three social workers to look after families and give moral and psychological support, to organize and train volunteers, and to maintain contact with the education, health and social services ($30,000).
2. To give financial assistance to those families unable to cover the heavy cost of treatment ($10,500).
3. To establish a lending-library where parents can obtain literature on rehabilitation, as well as educational games and equipment ($20,000).

TORAH B'ZION

תורה בציון

c/o Rabbanit Fanny Kaplan Centre
Rechov Magen Haelef
Shmuel Hanavi Quarter
Jerusalem
Telephone: (02) 289897
Office hours: 8:00 A.M. to 1:00 P.M.; 3:00 P.M.-7:00 P.M.

HISTORY AND DESCRIPTION
Torah B'Zion was founded in 1972 by a group of volunteers led by Rabbi Paul Roitman. It is a continuation of a similar French Movement, Torah V'Zion.

Organizational Structure: At the administrative level is a Board of Directors led by a president. At the core is the principle of regeneration; inspired volunteers work with youth from whom are derived new groups of volunteers. This allows a continued pursuit of the organization's goals.

Goals: The main goal of Torah B'Zion is to rescue children from deprived neighborhoods who might otherwise become "creatures of the street", and to educate them through a special youth movement with religious and national views.

Services, Activities and Accomplishments: Torah B'Zion offers a complementary education to the student's formal education; religious, national, moral and civic. The organization transmits values of Judaism through forums, meetings with children, sports, homework assistance, day camps, excursions, leadership training and youth community training. Through these activities the parents are brought to understand or to "renew aquaintances" with religious and nationalistic social and cultural ideals. The organization's major accomplishment to date has been in the education of the children in the streets, in large part the worst cases. From and original group of 40 students, 25 are now part of a cadre of youth leaders.

OFFICERS

President:	Rabbi Paul Roitman, Eli Cohen 5, Jerusalem. Educator. Tel. (02) 664315.
Treasurer:	Emil B. Dere, Yehuda Bourla 21, Jerusalem. Journalist. Tel. (02) 535730.
Board:	Nathan Samuel, Ein Rogel 16, Jerusalem. Retired. Tel. (02) 712960.
	Helène Samuel, Ein Rogel 16, Jerusalem. Retired. Tel. (02) 712960.
	Raymond Heymann, Mendele 1, Jerusalem. Insurance. Tel. (02) 632878.

Dr. Jacques Bornstein, Rashba 9, Jerusalem.
M.D. Ophthalmologist. Tel. (02) 664733.
Dr. Paul Zilberman, R. Akiva 1613, Jerusalem.
Dentist. Tel. (02) 233220.
Rabbi Robert Dreyfus, Herzog 17, Jerusalem.
Retired Chief Rabbi of Belgium. Tel. (02) 636431.
Leo Adler, Tchernihovsky 25, Jerusalem.
Blueprints. Tel. (02) 638815.

FINANCIAL INFORMATION
Torah B'Zion receives 90% of its income from donations. The remaining 10% comes from "other" sources. To continue current activities an amount of $100,000 is required. The organization is registered in Jerusalem with the Ministry of Interior as an Ottoman Association (reg. no. 11/2368). Donations are tax-free in Israel (reg. no. 4506163) and in the United States, if made through the *Federated Council for Israel Institutions* (I.R.S. no. 94113484300). The organization employs 2 part-time worker and 60 volunteers.

MEMBERSHIP, SCOPE, AND POLICY
Decisions are made by a National Board consisting of a president, treasurer and board members. There are currently "Friends" groups abroad and in Israel who help to support activities.

AFFILIATIONS/REFERENCES
Torah B'Zion is not affiliated with any political parties in Israel. Internationally, it is affiliated with the following institutions:
1. *Consistoire France*, 17 Rue St. Georges, Paris 1X, France.
2. *Torah V'Zion*, 8 Bis Rue de l'Eperon, Paris V1, France.
3. *Federated Council For Israel Institutions*, 38 Park Row, New York, New York, U.S.A.

FUNDING NEEDED
1. To continue present programs and to lengthen the number of hours of children's activities.
2. To enlarge the leadership training programs.
3. To continue winter and summer camp programs.

UNIT FOR CONSULTATION AND INFORMATION ON DEVELOPMENT

מדור ליעוץ ולמידע על התפתחות

4 Wolfson St.
Beersheva
Telephone: (057) 39947 ext. 06, 39
Office hours: Sunday-Thursday, 8:00 A.M. to 12:00 noon
Library hours: Sunday, Tuesday, Thursday, 8:30 A.M. to 3:00 P.M.

HISTORY AND DESCRIPTION
The Unit was established in 1977 as a demonstration project to improve services for persons with mental retardation in the Negev region. Recently the name and focus of the Unit were changed to recognize broader concerns with the problems of persons with developmental disability.

Organizational Structure: The Unit consists of two co-directors who set policy and provide the basic professional input, plus support staff including a librarian, research assistant and library clerk. From 1977 until 1981 this project has been fully supported by the American Friends Service Committee in co-operation with Ben Gurion University. The project is now being devolved, transferred from AFSC's administration to full local responsibility, both adminsitrative and financial.

Goals: Counselling to parents and professionals involved with the problems of persons with developmental disabilities; provision of information and professional literature in the field of programs and services for persons with developmental disabilities; research into problems relating to developmental disabilities; provision of library services for parents and professionals; provision of psychological services to families of and persons with developmental disablities. The Unit has succeeded in establishing a unique library in special education, including professional books, curriculum guides, toys and games. It has also introduced new concepts of ways of relating to and working with persons with developmental disabilities.

Services, Activities, and Accomplishments: The Unit works on a non-fee basis. It does not provide any services that are the responsibility of an existing agency. It works with other agencies to aid them in improving their serivces and with individual families who are seeking to improve their understanding and child-care techniques. The library provides toys, games and books to families. Professional workers may use the toys for reference only. The Unit also seeks to translate and disseminate new materials.

OFFICERS
Chairman: Dr. Philip Reiss, 27/2 Hakotel Hamaaravi,
                      Psychologist.
                      Tel. (057) 39947.

Treasurer:	Mrs. Rosalind Reiss, 27/2 Hacotel Hamaarvi, Psychologist. Tel. (057) 39947.
Secretary:	Ms. Ellen Weissman, 3 Yehuda, Jerusalem, Educator. Tel. (02) 781721.

FINANCIAL INFORMATION

Until 1981 the Unit will be fully supported by the American Friends Service Committee in co-operation with Ben Gurion University. Last year's annual budget was $77,000. Owing to the transfer of administrative and financial responsibility to local authority, a non-profit Ottoman Association has been established (reg. no. 876) through which to seek funding for future operations. It is intended to apply for tax benefits. Two full-time and five part-time workers are employed by the Unit, as well as two volunteers.

AFFILIATIONS/REFERENCES

The Unit is not affiliated with any Israeli political party. It is affiliated with the Ben Gurion University of the Negev, Beersheva, and the American Friends Service Committee, 1501 Cherry St., Phila., Penna.

FUNDING NEEDED

1. To finance development and dissemination of public education materials, to establish increased awareness of the needs of persons with development disabilities (cost — $10,000).
2. To purchase library material, complete cataloging and expand library services (costs — $10,000).
3. To expand consultation services for families and in-service education for professionals (costs $15,000).

UNITED AGED HOME

מושב זקנים המאוחד

Agnon
Katamon
P.O.B. 888
Jerusalem
Telephone: (02) 634024, 666401
Office hours: 8:00 A.M. to 3:00 P.M.

HISTORY AND DESCRIPTION

The United Aged Home was founded 101 years ago in the Old City of Jerusalem and has been situated since 1966 in modern buildings in the San Simon Quarter of Katamon, Jerusalem.

Organizational Structure: Information not supplied other than the fact that the organization is a trusteeship.

Goals: To brighten the lives of its old age inhabitants.

Services, Activities, and Accomplishments: 330 old women and men call the United Aged Home their home, mostly between the ages of 75 and 102 and from the needy strata of the population. 200 of the inhabitants are independent and take their meals in the common dining hall. 125 bedridden cases get full medical and nursing care in the three Hospital departments affiliated to the Home and part of it. The Home's management strives to brighten the lives of its inhabitants by providing social activities, classes in Jewish themes for men and women, handicrafts and tours and visits. The management has put all its efforts into improving the living conditions of its inhabitants. The changes are conspicuous to every visitor who has known the Home for some time. Improvements include all spheres of daily life — food, furniture in the rooms, activities and social life.

OFFICERS

General Manager: Joseph Mayer, Moshav Allon Shvut.
                 Tel. (02) 742993.
Treasurer: Zvi Jacobson, 13 Breuer, Jerusalem.
                 Tel. (02) 414092.
Board Members: Prof. Z. Silberstein. Physician.
                 Dr. J. Kister. Court Justice.
                 Amram Blum. Administrator General.
                 A. Sokolik
                 J. Fogel

FINANCIAL INFORMATION

In the past, 40% of the Home's income came from donations. In 1979, 32% of the annual budget came from donations, 4% from legacies etc., 32% from Government sources, and 32% from payment by residents and/or families of residents. Last year's annual budget of $1,800,000 left a deficit of $50,000. The Home is registered as a non-profit trusteeship. Donations in Israel and the United States are tax-free (tax nos. not supplied). 130 full-time and 40 part-time workers are employed by the Home, as well as 25 volunteers.

MEMBERSHIP, SCOPE, AND POLICY
Decisions are made by the Board of Trustees.

AFFILIATIONS/REFERENCES
The Home is not affiliated with any Israeli political party. It is affiliated with the United Aged Home of Jerusalem, 420 West End Ave., Elizabeth, N.Y.

FUNDING NEEDED
1. To build an additional wing to the hospital department for about forty patients who are able to move about (approximate cost $1,250,000).
2. To purchase equipment for recreational activities in the shelter (cost of furniture and adaptation of the shelter $50,000).
3. To erect storerooms for food and clothes at present stored in insufficient space and unfitting structures (approximate cost $150,000).

THE UNITED CONSERVATORY, YUVAL — RANANIM

הקונסרבטוריון המאוחד "יובל" — רננים

3 Stampfer Street
Netanya 42402
Telephone: (053) 22050, (053) 23650
Office hours: Daily, 4:00 to 6:30 P.M.
Monday and Wednesday, 10:30 A.M. to 12:30 P.M.

HISTORY AND DESCRIPTION
The Conservatory was founded in 1953 by a group of ten music teachers.

Organizational Structure: In addition to the two Directors, who were elected many years ago by the Annual Teachers' Assembly, there exists a Teachers' Board of three, who are jointly responsible for all professional and organizational problems. There is also a Parents' Board and a group of "Friends of the Conservatory".

Services, Activities, and Accomplishments: Apart from instrumental lessons, pupils also receive one or two theoretical lessons a week. Pupils' performances are held every month, and between three and five "learning" concerts are staged for the pupils every season. Examinations for all subjects are held at the end of the year under the jurisdiction of examiners invited from the Tel Aviv Academy of music. Over the past twenty-seven years the Conservatory has promoted musical education in Netanya and its vicinity. Several students have gone on to the Academy of Music and are now artists and teachers.

OFFICERS
Directors: Hanna Barnea, Salomon 14, Netanya. Musician. Tel. (053) 22050.
Ronny Samir, Remes 6, Netanya. Musician. Tel. (053) 23650.
Board Members: Lea Giber, Tel Hai 10, Netanya. Music Teacher.
Seeva Kedar, Hanegev 8, Netanya. Music Teacher.
Members of
Public Board: Reuven Kliegler — Mayor of Netanya.
Meir Bone
Ben-Zion Rubin, M.K.
Hillel Zur
Parents' Board: Zvi Atali
Jona Spiegelmann

FINANCIAL INFORMATION
Last year's annual budget was $45,000, and the Conservatory was left with a deficit of $1000. Due to the Netanya Municipality's extremely

difficult financial state, the Conservatory receives no municipal funding at all. The annual budget is balanced by the teachers' membership fees, which are set at between 11 and 20 percent of the fees they receive for teaching, depending on the number of pupils they each have and the fees paid by these pupils. There were about 330 students last year. Donations to the Conservatory in Israel are tax-free (Israel reg. no. 1326/1). Three part-time workers are employed by the Conservatory.

MEMBERSHIP, SCOPE, AND POLICY
National membership is constituted by thirty-two music teachers, and ten "Friends of the Conservatory". Music teachers with diplomas and new "Friends" may join the Conservatory. Decisions are made by the Executive Directors, the professional Teachers' Board, and the Public Board. The Conservatory has no political affiliation in Israel.

FUNDING NEEDED
1. For the past fifteen years the Conservatory has been located in a rented basement hall in the town center, divided into five rooms and a small office. The monthly rent now reaches $250. The Conservatory ideally needs to own premises of about 250 sq. m. in the basement or ground floor of a building in the town center, which can be divided into seven or eight small classrooms, two larger rooms, an office, and a hall which can seat 130 for concerts. The approximate cost still needed for this is $150,000. Since more than 50 percent of the Conservatory's thirty-two teachers are new immigrants from Russia, absorbed by the Conservatory over the past few years, it is important that teaching facilities be established in the center of town, where all the pupils live.
2. Many of the pupils cannot afford to buy musical instruments. Funds are needed so that the Conservatory can purchase musical instruments which can be loaned to their pupils.
3. The Conservatory needs a good piano for performances ($2000) and a duplicating machine.

VARIETY CLUB OF ISRAEL

מועדון וראייטי בישראל

13 Ranak Street
Tel Aviv 63464
Telephone: (03) 235151
Office hours: Sunday-Thursday, 8:30 A.M. to 2:30 P.M.

HISTORY AND DESCRIPTION

Variety Club of Israel is the Israeli branch of the biggest international charitable organization for needy children, one of fifty-six branches throughout the world. Variety Club was established fifty-four years ago, and its Israeli branch was founded in 1967. Its sole aim is to aid and support needy children, regardless of race, color, or creed. The Club's financial means come entirely from donations, either direct or through the sale of tickets for shows especially organized by Variety for purposes of fund-raising. Each Variety branch is supported by its local community, while the funds of Variety Clubs International go towards charitable causes in countries where there is no branch of the Club.

Services, Activities, and Accomplishments: Variety Club of Israel is active throughout the country, and its activities include help for individual children in need, aid to children's institutions, the support of ambulance fleets serving many children's institutions, the operation of mobile cinemas showing feature films on a daily basis for children unable to attend cinemas, the creation of special playgrounds for handicapped children, the initiation and construction, in cooperation with the Ministry of Health, of Variety centers for child and family developmental habilitation. Accomplishments include the Variety Child Development & Rehabilitation Center in Ashkelon, a playground for disabled children in Haifa, and assistance to over 1500 individual children and youths.

OFFICERS

President: David Shoham, Echad Haam 28, Tel Aviv.
                  Banker.
Treasurer: Shabtai Engel, Rothschild 73, Tel Aviv.
                  Insurance Executive.
Board Members: C.K. Greidinger, POB 1351, Haifa. Businessman.
                  D. Angel, POB 201, Jerusalem. Businessman.
                  A. Ben-Yochanan, Yitzchak Sadeh 34, Tel Aviv.
                  Insurance Executive.
                  S. Zemach, Dizengoff 108, Tel Aviv. Impresario.
                  S. Federman, Dan Hotel, Hayarkon, Tel Aviv.
                  Hotels' Owner.
                  Z. Ghel, Lilienblum 33, Tel Aviv. Businessman.
                  D. Moshevitz, POB 19, Ramat Gan. Businessman.
                  M. Burstyn, Azar 7, Ramat Hasharon.
                  Entertainer, actor.

A. Nathan, POB 4399, Tel Aviv.
Radio Station Owner.
Y. Reccanati, Habankim 3, Haifa. Businessman.

Executive
Director: Mrs. Ora Teveth, Ranak 13, Tel Aviv.

FINANCIAL INFORMATION
The entire balance of last year's annual budget (figure not supplied) came from donations. Variety Club of Israel is a recognized non-profit organization (Israel reg. no. 3830/99), to which donations in Israel, the United States, and Canada, may be made tax-free (Israel: no tax number supplied; USA — through American Friends of the Jerusalem Variety Child and Family Center, Inc., I.R.S. no. 52-1140586; Canada — through the Variety Club of Toronto: no tax number supplied). The Club employs two full-time and two part-time workers, as well as about sixty volunteers.

MEMBERSHIP, SCOPE, AND POLICY
The Club has 110 members in Israel, membership coming mainly from among people affiliated to the world of entertainment. Decisions are made by the National Board.

AFFILIATIONS/REFERENCES
Variety Club of Israel has no affiliations with any of the Israeli political parties. It is in contact with Variety Clubs International, 58 West 58th Street, Suite 230, New York, N.Y. 10019.

FUNDING NEEDED
1. For Variety Jerusalem Center for Child and Family Developmental Habilitation (brochure available on request) — $5 million.
2. For help and support of individuals in need.
3. For ambulances, and a mobile cinema.

WIDOWS SURVIVORS ORGANIZATION
ארגון אלמנות שאירים

P.O. Box 36317
Tel Aviv
Telephone: (03) 399114, (03) 316565
Office Hours: By appointment

HISTORY AND DESCRIPTION

The Widows Survivors Organization was established in 1976 in order to provide services to, and lobby on the behalf of, the wives and children of Israeli men who had died neither through military service nor work-related accidents. 'Widow survivors' include those women whose husbands had died as the result of a variety of diseases (including heart attack and cancer), through road and other accidents, and through suicides and the like. There are approximately 13,000 such widow-survivors, with 35,000 children under the age of 18, presently residing in Israel, and their ranks are increased by some 2,000 each year.

Organizational Structure: The Widows Survivors Organization is a volunteer society divided into six regional 'widow clubs'.

Goals: The organization was established upon the premise that widows of men who had died as the result of non-military and non-work related causes are seriously deprived by the present Israeli legal system of desperately needed financial assistance. The organization argues that despite the fact that their late husbands paid fully into the National Insurance system, widow-survivors receive only 16% of the average salary in the state. Only a small proportion of the widows—about 10%—receive pensions from their late husbands' place of employment, and a large majority—perhaps as much as 75%—were not working when their husbands died, and thus find themselves and their children in desperate situations. In terms of these conditions, the organization pursues three distinct goals. It seeks to: change the law in order to provide the widow-survivors and their children with sufficient income; to establish widow-clubs all over the country which will enable the widows to overcome the social isolation so much a part of a widows' life; and to accommodate the needs of new widows through individual guidance from the more 'experienced' ones.

Services, Activities, and Accomplishments: The Widows Survivors Organization lists among its major accomplishments to date: the incorporation of individual groups of widow survivors into a single strong body; creating feelings of 'self-respect, pride, and hope' for improvement of the present situation for widow-survivors; an increased recognition among the Israeli Establishment and society of the special needs and problems of the widow-survivors; and partial legal improvement of the present situation.

OFFICERS

Director: Ester Rathner, La-Guardia 69, Tel Aviv. Secretary.
Tel. (03) 399114, 824261.

Treasurer: Lea Tirosh, Hashalom 73, Tel Aviv.
Tel. (03) 316565.

Board: Porya Duvdevany.
Tel. (03) 749578.
Devora Dalmedygos, Yod-Alef Bedar 27, Holon.
Tel. (03) 852039, 861510.
Mazal Val, Matalon 92, Tel Aviv.
Tel. (03) 835080, 263119.

FINANCIAL INFORMATION

The Widows Survivors Organization's last annual budget, for the fiscal year ending in April of 1980, stood at approximately $1,100. The organization did not register a deficit for this period. 50% of this budget was achieved through membership dues, 25% from donations; and the remaining 25% from 'other' sources. The organization is registered as an Ottoman Association (reg. no. 6392/99) with the Ministry of the Interior, Tel Aviv District Office. Donations to the organization are tax-free in Israel (reg. no. 450845), but not in the United States. The organization lists as its employees the five volunteer members of the Board.

MEMBERSHIP, SCOPE, AND POLICY

Six branches of the Widows Survivors Organization service an approximate Israeli membership of 1000. Membership is open to all widows and widowers whose husband or wife died not by work accident or in the army. Decisions are made by the Board.

AFFILIATIONS/REFERENCES

The organization has no affiliation with any Israeli political party. Internationally, the organization is recognized by *The New Israel Fund*, 22 Miller Avenue, Mill Valley, California, 94941.

FUNDING NEEDED

In order of priority, the Widows Survivors Organization lists the following as its most pressing requirements.

1. Maintenance of an office with a full-time secretary dealing directly with the needs of members;
2. Establishment of a fund for grants and/or easy-term loans available to members for urgent and necessary needs (i.e., purchasing of refrigerator and washing-machine, dental treatment for parent and/or children, assistance for *modest* bar/bat mitzvahs, etc.);
3. The financing of a variety of activities for widow-survivors, including lectures, trips and parties.

WOLBROM IMMIGRANTS ASSOCIATION IN ISRAEL AND ABROAD

ארגון יוצאי וולברום בישראל ובתפוצות

c/o Mr. Benjamin Katz
192 Arlosorov
Tel Aviv
Telephone: (03) 254966
Office hours: By appointment

HISTORY AND DESCRIPTION
At the end of the Second World War, when the terrible news of the holocaust spread, the Wolbromians in Israel organized quickly. A committee was elected and money raised in order to extend aid to the survivors of the holocaust wherever they were and to those who immigrated to Israel. Later the Association dedicated itself to the work of memorializing and perpetuating the memory of the Wolbromian community.

Goals: To memorialize the holy memory of the Wolbromian community and the martyrs of the Holocaust, and to extend financial help and moral support to the survivors.

Services, Activities, and Accomplishments: A memorial meeting is held at least once a year. A commemorative wood has been planted in the Martyrs Forest, Jerusalem, and a tombstone built in the Chamber of Destruction, on Mount Zion in Jerusalem. The Association has also published a 1,000 page memorial book (500 copies). It brought to Israel the remains of a brothers' mass grave from Wolbrom, the grave of people killed on the "deportation" day of the community of Wolbrom. The remains of the grave were re-interred at the Nachalat Yitzchak cemetery in Tel Aviv and a large, respectable tombstone was erected there.

OFFICERS
Director: Benjamin Katz, 192 Arlosorov, Tel Aviv.
                    Tel. (03) 254966
Treasurer: Dov Fromer
Board Members: Arieh Frenkiel
                    Josef Kornfeld
                    Jacob Welner
                    Naomi Cwajgienbaum
                    Moshe Bydlowski

FINANCIAL INFORMATION
The activities of the Association are financed entirely by membership dues. Last year's annual budget was $400. The Association is registered in Tel Aviv as a non-profit Ottoman Association (reg. no. not supplied).

Donations are not, as yet, tax-free. Seven volunteers are employed by the Association.

MEMBERSHIP, SCOPE, AND POLICY
Membership is open to all Landsmen and their offspring. There are 200 members in Israel, in one branch, and 250 members abroad. Decisions are made by the Executive Director and the Board.

AFFILIATIONS/REFERENCES
The Association is not affiliated with any Israeli political party. It is affiliated with Yad Vashem, Jerusalem, and the Association of Polish Jews in Tel Aviv.

FUNDING NEEDED
1. To help those of the members who are aged, weak and economically underprivileged.
2. To be able to cause the younger generations to become involved and interested in aspects of the holocaust and its consequences.

WOMAN TO WOMAN

אשה – לאשה

P.O. Box 10403, Molcho, 1
Jerusalem
Telephone: Devorah Barkai, (02) 781583;
               Chava Foguel, (02) 634338
Office Hours: Sundays, 9:00 P.M. to 11:00 P.M.

HISTORY AND DESCRIPTION
Woman to Woman—'Isha Le Isha'—was formed in July 1978 as a workgroup of feminist women striving towards the advancement of women, especially battered wives.

Organizational Structure: Meetings of the group are held weekly, and are conducted in a democratic fashion, allowing each person present to express her view and to undertake work and responsibility in accordance with her abilities.

Goals: The group has defined its basic goals as the following: to establish a shelter for battered women, which includes a center to combat violence against women.

Services, Activities, and Accomplishments: Since its formation, Woman to Woman has devoted its full eforts and activities towards the establishment of a shelter for battered women, which, in conjunction with the Municipality of Jerusalem and the Social Services Council, opened in February 1981. The organization lists among its major accomplishments to date the raising of public awareness to the problem of battered women—through seminars, interviews and publications of a pamphlet delineating the problem; fundraising; enlisting the aid of the Jerusalem Municipality in the allotment of a house to be used as a shelter and the assignment of a social worker; and the establishment of ties with various service agencies and interested groups and individuals—including the police, legal aid, vocational training and volunteers.

OFFICERS
Director: Joan Hooper, Shimoni 62, Jerusalem. Translator.
                 Tel. (02) 639740.
Treasurer: Mikhal Zupon, Elroy 5A, Jerusalem.
                 Graphic Designer. Tel. (02) 631969.
Board: Devora Leuchter, Alfasi 35, Jerusalem. Librarian.
                 Tel. (02) 638707.
                 Chava Foguel, Molcho 1, Jerusalem.
                 Physiotherapist. Tel. (02) 634338.
                 Devora Barkai, Korei Hadorot, Jerusalem.
                 Social Worker. Tel. (02) 781583.
                 Barbara Amit, Ein Tzurim 17, Jerusalem.
                 Manager of Daycare Center.
                 Tel. (02) 712365.

Jocelyn Levy, San Simon, Jerusalem.
Director/Coordinator of Shelter for Battered
Wives. Tel. (02) 631218.

FINANCIAL INFORMATION

Last year's budget for Woman to Woman amounted to $8,000. The organization did not register a deficit. 40% of the total income came from donations; the remaining 60% was acquired through grants. Membership dues were negligible. In 1979, Woman to Woman was incorporated as an Ottoman (non-profit) Organization (reg. no. 11/3217) and is registered with the Jerusalem office of the Ministry of the Interior. Donations to the organization are tax-free both in Israel and the United States, although neither an Israeli registration number nor an American I.R.S. number was supplied. There is one part-time employee and the number of volunteers varies, up to ten.

MEMBERSHIP, SCOPE, AND POLICY

Ten Israeli women are involved in the Jerusalem branch of Woman to Woman, with the backing of more than 300 in the Jerusalem area. Any woman who is committed to work with the organization is welcome to join. Decisions are made in a democratic fashion: each person attending a meeting has the right to voice her opinion, and each member has one vote.

AFFILIATIONS/REFERENCES

Woman to Woman has no affiliation with any Israeli political party nor with any foreign organization. Although not formally affiliated with any other women's group in Israel, the nature of Woman to Woman's work is quite similar to other shelters operating in Haifa and Herzlia, and contacts have already been made to establish a cooperative network.

FUNDING NEEDED

In order of priority, Woman to Woman sees the following as its most pressing financial requirements:
1. Funds to cover basic maintenance of the Jerusalem shelter. Estimated 1980/81 costs—$30,000.
2. Salaries for some of the positions presently handled by volunteers. Estimated salary for manager—$4,080.
3. Funds to purchase basic equipment for the shelter, such as a washing machine and stove. Estimated cost—$5,000.

WOMEN'S AID FUND   קרן לעזרת האשה

95 Panorama Rd., Haifa
Telephone: (04) 83817
Office Hours: By Appointment

HISTORY AND DESCRIPTION
The Women's Aid Fund was established in 1977 in order to help advance the status of women and to provide assistance to women in need. It serves as the 'mother organization' to, and is responsible for securing funding for, a variety of women-related projects which it has helped to establish.

Organizational Structure: The Women's Aid Fund is the mother organization, with committee representation from all of its various projects, which are operated on a voluntary basis independently of the Fund.

Goals: The Women's Aid Fund was established as an attempt to fill a vacuum in Israeli society by providing services answering the specific needs and interests of women. In particular, the attempt has been made to raise wife-beating and rape as important social issues, and to make women aware of discrimination and possible avenues for bringing about change.

Services, Activities, and Accomplishments: The projects of the Women's Aid Fund to date include the following:
— Women for Women, a shelter for battered women, established in 1977;
— Woman's Voice, cultural centers for women, including libraries, bookstores, lectures, counseling and courses in basic skills. (Established in Haifa in 1979, Tel Aviv in 1979, Jerusalem in 1980);
— a Legal Aid Bureau, providing counseling and representation in court, with payment according to means (est. 1980);
— a Rape Crisis Center, providing counseling and aid in police and legal proceedings to rape victims (est. 1980);
— the Women's Press (Bat Kol), specializing in materials on the status of women, and *Noga*, A Magazine for Women.
Among its major accomplishments to date, the Women's Aid Fund notes that each of the services it has established has been the first of its kind in Israel. The Fund has therefore succeeded in raising issues heretofore unspoken of — or at least unrepresented — in public, as well as developing ways of dealing with them.

OFFICERS
Director: Marcia Freedman, Panorama 97A, Haifa. Educator.
           Tel. (04) 86449.
Treasurer: Braca Ziv, French 56, Haifa. Contractor.
           Tel. (04) 333829.
Secretary: Judith Hill, Sweden 9, Haifa. Educator.
           Tel. (04) 251010.
Board: Naomi Gondos, Sea 95, Haifa. Lawyer.
           Tel. (04) 82820/641435.

Nurit Gilat, Da Vinci 9, Haifa. Administrator.
    Tel. (04) 231024.
Aliza Finkel, Haviva Reich 59, Haifa.
    Aquatic Engineer. Tel. (04) 234559.
Naomi Shafrir, Galgal 2, Haifa. Bookkeeper.
    Tel. (04) 244289.
Sherry Rabino, Avigail 2, Haifa. Physiotherapist.
    Tel. (04) 243890.

FINANCIAL INFORMATION

In 1980, the annual budget of $25,000 was donated by individuals in the United States and Europe, The New Israel Fund, U.S.-Israel Women to Women, as well as the Israel Ministry of Labor and Social Affairs and the City of Haifa Department of Social Services. There are no membership dues. WAF is a registered non-profit Ottoman Association (reg. no. 61/1339), and is registered with Haifa District of the Ministry of the Interior. Donations to the organization are tax-free both in Israel and the United States, in the latter if made through the P.E.F. Israel Endowments Fund. No Israeli exemption registration number was supplied. The Women's Aid Fund has no paid employees. Its projects are staffed by 3 part-time employees, and volunteers.

MEMBERSHIP, SCOPE, AND POLICY

The Women's Aid Fund has fifteen members on its Board of Directors. It presently has six Israeli projects operating under its auspices. Decisions are made both by the Executive Committee, representing all the projects that the Fund has established, and by the organizers of the individual projects, which operate independently and autonomously of the Fund. Any group working towards the advancement of the status of women or to aid women in need can become a project of the Women's Aid Fund. Representatives of new projects are added to WAF's Board of Directors.

AFFILIATIONS/REFERENCES

The Women's Aid Fund is not associated with any Israeli political party. WAF is known by the following three American organizations:
    P.E.F. Israel Endowments Fund, 342 Madison Avenue, N.Y.C, N.Y.
    U.S.-Israel Women to Women, 156 E. 36th Street, New York, N.Y.
    New Israel Fund, Berkeley, California.

FUNDING NEEDED

In order of priority, the Women's Aid Fund lists the following as its most outstanding funding requirements:

1. The continuance of funding for *Noga*, A Magazine for Women. Estimated cost — $1000 per month, indefinitely.
2. Funding for the establishment of a peer counseling and psychological counseling clinic at the Woman's Voice Center in Jerusalem. Estimated cost — $300 per month, indefinitely.
3. Establishment and maintenance of a General Emergency Fund, to be used for funding conferences, research and assemblies on a variety of related issues, including rape, family violence and women's health. Cost — $10,000.

WOMEN FOR WOMEN

נשים למען נשים

Khouri 20
Haifa
Telephone: (04) 662114
Office Hours: 8:30 A.M.-2:00 P.M.

HISTORY AND DESCRIPTION

Women For Women, founded by five Haifa women in November 1977, opened the first shelter for battered women in Israel. It was established in an attempt to deal directly with the problem of violence in the Israeli family, which, according to a Knesset committee, is a problem which affects ten percent of Israeli women. The Shelter originally opened in a five-room apartment located in a quiet residential area in central Haifa, and in January 1979 moved to a much larger home which provides more comfortable living conditions for battered women and their children. Since its inception, the shelter has given refuge to some 500 women and their children and has given legal and psychological counseling to an additional 200 Haifa-area women. Since January 1980 it has, through an 'out-reach' program, also provided encouragement and counsel to scores of women in development towns.

Organizational Structure: The Shelter is run on a cooperative basis by a team of women. There is no director.

Goals: The purpose of the Shelter is, first, to provide emergency help to women and children who are victims of family violence — a safe place to live temporarily, emotional support and legal aid. The Shelter also is an attempt to change the existing patterns of social service relationships. The onus is upon mutual support and self-help; the guiding principle is to help women to carry out their own decisions. The long-range goals of the Shelter is to bring the problem of family violence to the forefront of public attention, and in so doing, to alter the approach of police, judiciary, and social service agencies to the problem.

Services, Activities, and Accomplishments: The Shelter is usually filled to its capacity of 15 women and their children, or 35-45 people. Upon arrival, women receive any required medical attention, and their children are placed in local schools and kindergartens or attend the nursery school on the premises. Women are also referred to legal aid. Upon request, a staff member accompanies women to the police in order to register a formal assault complaint, to the welfare office, and to hearings in the Rabbinical and civil courts. The staff social worker obtains necessary services from local agencies, including emergency welfare payments, special help for children, psychological counseling and housing aid. The staff provide women with information on legal rights and encourage mutual support and self-help among the residents. The Shelter also provides counseling to women who live at home who request legal and other advice. Besides the operation of the Shelter, the activities

of Women For Women include the following: an Outreach Project in which 'graduates' of the Shelter enter communities with large concentrations of battered women and attempt to raise the issue of family violence and the consciousness of women who suffer from it; the publication, in April 1980, of a *Legal Guide for Women in Family Matters*; a 'graduates' organization for mutual support; and a study group which is investigating working conditions of women in the Haifa area. Among its major accomplishments to date the organization lists the following:
— providing an alternative for battered wives;
— raising public awareness to the problem of family violence;
— improving somewhat judicial and police handling of complaints of family violence (including some stiffer sentences for violent husbands), thereby bringing about recognition of battered women and shelters by social service agencies and courts — both Rabbinical and civil.

OFFICERS

Chairwoman: Barbara Swirski, Shoshanat Hacarmel 90B, Haifa. Sociologist. Tel. (04) 84592.

Treasurer: Joyce Livingston, Louis Pasteur 7A, Haifa. Teacher. Tel. (04) 331537.

Secretary: Pia Tannhauser, Lionel Watson 8A, Haifa. Teacher. Tel. (04) 242188.

Board Members: Eva Elaluf, Habikurim 10, Haifa. Painter. Tel. (04) 87073.
                   Deborah Bernstein, Raziel 6A, Haifa. Lecturer. Tel. (04) 220779.
                   Sarah Erez, Kook 11, Holon. Secretary.
                   Wanda Ben-Aderet, Geula 21, Hod Hasharon. Receptionist.

FINANCIAL INFORMATION

Women For Women's last annual budget totalled $72,000. Grants from the Israeli Ministry of Labor and Social Welfare constituted 55% of the organizations's income; other sources were payments by residents — 25%; and contributions — 20%. The organization's deficit for the last fiscal year was $3,000. Women For Women is registered as an Ottoman Association (no. 61/1469) with the Haifa District Office of the Ministry of the Interior. Donations to the organization are tax-free in both the United States and Israel (Israel reg. no. 4507241; organization is awaiting I.R.S. number). Women For Women employs 6 part-time workers and 40 volunteers.

MEMBERSHIP, SCOPE, AND POLICY

There are 80 members of the single Haifa branch of Women For Women. There are no foreign branches of the organization. The Shelter is run by a team. Decisions concerning policy, finances and/or publications, as well as decisions concerning women staying in the Shelter are made by the staff in weekly staff meetings at which each staff member has one vote. Decisions regarding living arrangements in the Shelter are made by Shelter residents at weekly meetings.

AFFILIATIONS/REFERENCES
Women For Women is not affiliated with any Israeli political party. The organization has relations with the following foreign groups:

National Council of Jewish Women, 15 East 26th Street, New York, N.Y. 10010.

Women To Women, 4 Sniffen Court, New York, New York, 10016.

New Israel Fund, 22 Miller Avenue, Mill Valley, California, 94941.

FUNDING NEEDED
In order of priority, Women For Women lists the following as its most outstanding financial needs.
1. Operating expenses for the Shelter per year: $25,000;
2. The expansion of the staff to include a youth leader for older children and a secretary to free the professional staff of office work: $12,000;
3. The setting-up of a small printing business on the premises to provide occupational training and employment for residents of the Shelter: $30,000.

WOMEN'S LEAGUE FOR ISRAEL, INC.

ליגת נשים למען ישראל

King George 37
Tel Aviv
Telephone: (03) 283195
Office hours: Monday-Thursday, 9:00 A.M. to 5:00 P.M.
           Friday, 9:00 A.M. to 3:00 P.M.

HISTORY AND DESCRIPTION

The Women's League for Israel was established in 1928 in then Mandatory Palestine, in response to the pressing needs of young women
immigrants. The organization continues to respond to these needs by
supporting women's homes and by establishing and helping to maintain
projects for the social, economic and educational welfare of Israeli
youth. The Women's League presently maintains Homes in Jerusalem,
Tel Aviv, Haifa and Nathanya, where young women find a place to live
and receive instruction through vocational training and guidance.

Organizational Structure: The Women's League for Israel is essentially
an American organization, with executive offices in New York City.
Membership is organized into chapters across the United States, with
officers duly elected every two years. There is a single Israeli administrator to represent the League in Israel, and to supervise and implement
policy and programs established by the organization in the United
States. The Israeli representative is also responsible for the Homes,
which are directly supervised by resident staffs.

Goals: The Women's League for Israel was established with the determi-
nation to promote the general well-being of young people in Israel by
furthering the cultural, educational and social conditions in which they
exist. These remain the goals of the present generation of League
members.
The League has an extensive list of goals which it seeks to fulfil in Israel.
Among these are:
— to build and maintain Homes in cities where young people could live;
— to provide support by creating an atmosphere of guidance, warmth,
friendship and help;
— to provide vocational training and placement;
— to support social, cultural and recreational activities in the
community;
— to aid the handicapped through training and to maintain a weaving
workshop for the blind; and
— to aid the Hebrew University through scholarship funding, by creating a chair in sociology and by providing housing, a cafeteria and
a student center.

Services, Activities, and Accomplishments: The services and activities
provided by the Women's League for Israel are wide-ranging. At the
Nathanya center, there is vocational evaluation and training, social

602

service and counseling, special vocational training for the handicapped, a weaving workshop for the blind, and boarding facilities. The centers in Jerusalem, Haifa and Tel Aviv serve as boarding facilities, classrooms (for vocational training, history and culture), as well as meeting places and family counseling centers. Staff from the centers work with city administrators in the attempt to alleviate social problems in the community. The Women's League lists among its major accomplishments to date the establishment of Homes in Jerusalem, Haifa and Tel Aviv, and the vocational training and rehabilitation center in Nathanya; buildings at Hebrew University, including two dormitories at the Givat Ram campus, three dormitories, a cafeteria and a student center at Mt. Scopus; establishment of the Rose Isaacs chair in Sociology, a scholarship and book endowment fund; the creation of a weaving workshop for the blind at Nathanya, and in Jerusalem a library for social workers.

OFFICERS

Israeli Rep.:   Dita Natzor, King George 37, Tel Aviv.
                  Tel. (03) 283195.
U.S. President: Mrs. M. Schwartzman, 115 Central Park West,
                  New York, New York 10023.
                  Tel. (212) 799-4128.
Board Chairman: Mrs. T. Miner, 1050 Park Ave.,
                  New York, N.Y. 10021
                  Tel. (212) 289-6684.
Hon. Pres.:   Mrs. Harry M. Wiles, 2 Warnke Lane,
                  Scarsdale, N.Y. 10583.
                  Tel. (914) GR. 2-4248.

FINANCIAL INFORMATION

For the last year, the Women's League for Israel had a budget totalling $533,108. 7% of this total — $25,000 — was acquired through membership dues, although more than one-half of all membership is Life Members, and thus do not pay annual dues; 9%, or $50,000, came through income from legacies; 32% of the total, or $160,000, came from donations from American chapters, and the remaining $250,000 came as a donation from the New York National Office. The organization did not register a deficit during the last fiscal year. The League is not registered as an Ottoman Association, but is registered in Israel as a 'Foreign Organization' (reg. no. 196). Donations to the League are tax-free both in Israel and in the United States (Israel reg. no. 4500151, I.R.S. no. 86-06288). The League employs 22 full-time and 26 part-time persons in Israel and the United States combined.

MEMBERSHIP, SCOPE, AND POLICY

There are 35 branches of the Women's League in the United States, with a membership of 5,000. There are no Israeli branches. Membership in the League is open to any person who resides in the United States, who subscribes to the purposes of the organization, and pays dues to their respective chapter. Policy decisions for the League are made by the National Board.

AFFILIATIONS/REFERENCES

The Women's League for Israel lists no affiliations with any Israeli political party. Its Israeli office is directly affiliated with its American counterpart, which is located at 1860 Broadway, New York, N.Y., 10023. Tel. (212) 245-8742. The League is also affiliated with a variety of philanthropic organizations, including the *American Zionist Federation,* the *American Friends of the Hebrew University, Hadassah,* the *National Council of Jewish Women,* and the *Jewish Agency.*

FUNDING NEEDED

In order of priority, the Women's League for Israel requires funding for the following projects.

1. Renovation of old building at the Nathanya center;
2. Room to house the Institute for Educational and Social Workers at the Nathanya center. Cost, $175,000;
3. Renovation and repair of Homes in Jerusalem, Haifa and Tel Aviv.

WOMEN'S SOCIAL SERVICE

שרות נשים סוציאלי

Margolin 5
Yad Eliyahu, Tel Aviv
Telephone: (03) 332433, 332012
Office Hours: Daily, 8:00 A.M. to 3:00 P.M.

HISTORY AND DESCRIPTION
The Women's Social Service was first established in 1934 by Mrs. Paula Barth as an attempt to provide for the medical and social needs of elderly new immigrants from Central Europe, and all other members of the general population. These efforts are continued today through a hospital and a variety of old-age homes and community centers located in Tel Aviv, Yad Eliyahu-Tel Aviv and Jerusalem.

Organizational Structure: Although specific information was not available, the Women's Social Service is orgnaized as a corporate structure, with a President (the founder, Mrs. Paula Barth is Honorary President), an Executive Director, and a Board of Directors.

Goals: The goal of the Women's Social Service is to extend the medical and social services of its homes and hospital to the population and to provide home care for all who require it, with regard to the recipients physical or psychological condition.

Services, Activities, And Accomplishments: In terms of its stated goals, the Women's Social Service has established a number of nominal-rent homes for the elderly—Beth Shalom, Beth Achwah and Beth Bracha in Tel Aviv and the Aron Barth Center in Jerusalem. There is also a 'parents home'—Beth Gila—and the Beth Lichtenstaedter Hospital in Yad Eliyahu-Tel Aviv. There is also a central kitchen at the Beth Bracha Center which serves meals and operates a meals-on-wheels program at nominal prices for the needy elderly. To meet the growing needs of the elderly in Israel, the Women's Social Service is endeavouring to enlarge Jerusalem's Aron Barth Center, as well as to build an adjoining neighborhood community center. The W.S.S. includes among its major accomplishments the construction of 474 nominal-rent housing units, the establishment of a hospital for the chronically ill, the establishment of the Beth Gila parents' home, and the maintenance of the kitchen serving meals to the inhabitants and the neighbourhood.

OFFICERS
Director: Moshe Goldstein, Chavakook 16, Ramat Gan.
                  Social Worker. Tel. (03) 742913.
Board President: Gerda Ochs, Emil Zola 2, Tel Aviv. Manager.
                  Tel. (03) 222115.
Board Members: Hadassa Feuchtwanger, Ben-Yehuda 5, Petach
                  Tikva. Educator. Tel. (03) 922562.

Avraham Pressler, Remez 27, Tel Aviv.
Administrator. Tel. (03) 889952.
Elchanan Loeventhal, Ein Vered 3, Tel Aviv.
Manager. Tel. (03) 282155.
Zitta Kober, Rosenbaum 8, Tel Aviv. Secretary.
Tel. (03) 243350.
Malie Spielman, Trumpeldor 26, Tel Aviv.
Social Worker. Tel. (03) 298821.
Leah Nussbaum, Gaza 62, Jerusalem.
Administrator. Tel. (02) 662950.
Shlomo Chaimowitz, Ben-Zvi 52, Ramat Gan.
Director. Tel. (03) 245291.

FINANCIAL INFORMATION

For the fiscal year of 1978, the Women's Social Service had a budget of $2,000,000, with a deficit of $275,000. 20% of the total budget came from donations, while the remaining 80% was acquired through a variety of sources; including nominal rent from the centers, hospital fees, payment for full board at Beth Gila, and so on. Very little income — perhaps .01% — is generated through membership dues. The W.S.S. is an Ottoman Association (reg. no. 2325/99), and is registered with the Ministry of the Interior's Tel Aviv District Office. Donations are tax-free both in Israel and the United States, although neither an Israeli registration number nor an I.R.S. number were supplied. The Women's Social Service employs approximately 150 full-time and 50 part-time employees, as well as perhaps 100 volunteers.

MEMBERSHIP, SCOPE, AND POLICY

There are one hundred members of the one Israeli branch of the Women's Social Service. Anyone interested in the organizations' work and who is willing to support it is welcome to join, although all applications for membership must be approved by the Board of Directors, which makes all executive decisions.

AFFILIATIONS/REFERENCES

The Women's Social Service claims no formal relationship with any Israeli political party, and has an American sister-organization, *The Women's Social Service For Israel, Inc.*, 240 West 98th Street, New York, N.Y., 10025.

THE W.U.J.S. INSTITUTE: INTERNATIONAL GRADUATE CENTRE FOR HEBREW AND JEWISH STUDIES

המכון להכשרה ולקליטת אקדמאים מחו"ל (מכון וג"ס)

The W.U.J.S. Institute
24 Yehuda St.
80 700 Arad
Telephone: (057) 97075, 97446, 97100
Office hours: 8:00 A.M. to 3:30 P.M. (Staff reachable during evenings as well.)

HISTORY AND DESCRIPTION

The Institute was founded in January 1968, initially to deal with some of the needs of the great influx of post-Six Day War volunteers. The first graduating classes (machzorim) were composed entirely of these volunteers. The program then developed a more distinct aliya orientation, as an instrument for integration into Israel for young Jewish academics from abroad. It has continued to function in Arad and has grown up together with the town, with whose citizens it maintains a close relationship.

Organizational Structure: The Institute is governed by a board of governors consisting of government and public officials, as well as private persons. The director implements the decisions of the board.

Goals: The Institute aims to provide as comprehensive an introduction to living and working in Israel as can be compressed into a single year, to an audience of young (21-32) Jews from abroad with either university degrees or vocational training. It hopes in this way to provide its students with a serious Israeli experience and a basis for an informed aliya decision. It further hopes that those of its students who do not decide for aliya will opt for greater commitment and activity in their Jewish communities abroad.

Services, Activities, and Accomplishments: Students commit themselves to a one-year, study/work experience. The first 5½ months are spent in Arad, studying Hebrew intensely, choosing from among a broad array of courses in Jewish/Israel studies, participating in educational tours round the country and in a two-week kibbutz/moshav period, and interacting with the residents of Arad. The Institute assists students in arranging a variety of placements for themselves all over Israel during the second part of the year. This includes regular, salaried employment in the student's profession; volunteer work on a kibbutz or in a development town; further education; professional re-training courses. Students are young (21-32) Jews in possesesion of university degrees or technical/vocational qualifications who are interested in discovering what Israel is all about. Most are single, though married couples without children are equally welcome. Some come with the intention of settling permanently, using the Institute as a stepping-stone in the process. Others come to spend a year learning about Israel and its life, while at the same time enhancing their Jewish awareness. The great majority of students are from English-speaking countries, although efforts are being made to attract participation from Spanish- and French-speaking countries as well. Since 1968 over 3,000 college graduates have passed through the framework of the Institute and have been provided with a basic Jewish/Hebrew/Zionist education and assisted in finding jobs and settling into Israeli society. Of these approximately 1,000 have settled permanently and many of the others are actively involved in both lay and professional levels in all aspects of Jewish communal life in the Diaspora.

OFFICERS

Director:
Baruch Bank, The W.U.J.S. Inst., Arad 80 700
Educational Administrator.
Tel. (057) 97075, 97446.

Board Chairman: Michael Copeland, 21/3 Ben Yair, Arad 80 700
Sthn. Area Dir. Hameshakem. Tel. (057) 90449.

Board Members: Justin Phillips, 34/1 Moav, Arad 80 700
Medical Doctor. Tel. (057) 97048.
Shlomo Dinur, 2 Kaf Tet B'November, Jerusalem.
Teacher and J.A. Official. Tel. (02) 631310.
Moshe Yakir, Aliya Dept., P.O.B. 7384, Jerusalem.
Head of Reg. Desks, Aliya Dept. Tel. (02) 662421.
Shmuel Shinhar, Stu. Auth., 6 Hillel, Jerusalem.
Head, Student Authority. Tel. (02) 242672.
Avraham Shochat, Mo'etza M'Komit, Arad 80 700.
Head, Regional Council (Mo'etza M'Komit).
Tel. (057) 97911.
Tova Povitzer, 26 Barak, Beer Sheva.
Ulpan Supervisor, Ministry of Education.
Tel. (057) 35065.

FINANCIAL INFORMATION

67% of the Institute's income comes from student fees, 25% from the Jewish Agency and 8% from other sources. Last year's annual operating budget of $110,214 left a deficit of $31,746. The Institute is registered in Beer Sheva as a non-profit Ottoman Association (reg. no. 7867/442). Donations in Israel are tax-free (tax no. 4504039) but not in the United States. Eight full-time and eighteen part-time workers are employed by the Institute.

MEMBERSHIP, SCOPE, AND POLICY

Most decisions are made by the Executive Director.

AFFILIATIONS/REFERENCES

The Institute is not affiliated with any Israeli political party.

FUNDING NEEDED

1. To maintain the quality and standards of the basic programme, in the face of astronomically inflating costs a budgetary supplement of $50,000 a year is needed.
2. To construct and equip new buildings and campus for the Institute in Arad and provide facilities such as a synagogue, a large lecture hall, a recreation room, etc.
3. To finance various projects and capital investments: a follow-up project on alumni; the expansion of the Institute's Jewish studies library; the planning of a special symposium on selected topics; the publication of educational material for internal use; the improvement of the Institute's rapidly aging equipment (typewriters, duplicating machine, photocopier, photo-stencil machine, film projector, slide projector, portable tape recorders).

THE YAAKOV MAIMON VOLUNTEERS

מתנדבי יעקב מימון

Keren Kayemeth 21
P.O.B. 7237, Jerusalem
Telephone: (02) 639970
Office hours: By appointment

HISTORY AND DESCRIPTION

The organization was founded in 1977, by friends, colleagues and family members, who wanted to continue the work of the late Yaakov Maimon, who had for over 20 years devoted much time and effort to helping in the absorption of immigrants newly arrived from Europe after the Holocaust and from Arab countries.

Goals: Today, the organization continues to aid in the absorption of immigrants, but has added the goals of bridging the social and cultural gaps between different parts of the nation, and fighting illiteracy.

Services, Activities, and Accomplishments: Volunteers for the organization's activities are recruited from 3 sections of the Israeli population: old-timers who are familiar with Yaakov Maimon's work; high-school and university students, and soldiers, who can contribute a few hours every week; and kibbutz members who want to become involved with problems of immigration and welfare. The volunteers are given training and counselling. Concentrating their activities in the Jerusalem region, they work mainly in helping teach Hebrew to new immigrants, in tutoring children from deprived and underprivileged backgrounds, and in giving English lessons to high-school students in danger of dropping out or failing their matriculation exams. In 1980 the volunteers worked with about 100 families at the Mevasseret Absorption Center. They tutored about 60 children at Maoz-Zion and Mevasseret Yerushalayim, and gave English lessons to 30 more. In addition, the organization has arranged several tours and trips. In these ways, people from different origins and backgrounds have been brought together, decreasing frustration and antagonism, while young people have been trained in good citizenship, making them socially-minded and contributing persons. The organization is presently involved, in collaboration with the World Zionist Organization, the Kibbutz Movement Federation, and government agencies, in developing a 2-year project for Jewish university graduates from abroad, to help with different aspects of community work in development towns and deprived neighborhoods in Israel.

OFFICERS

Director: Joel Dorkam, Kibbutz Palmach Tsuba.
                     Community Worker. Tel. (02) 539494-5.
Treasurer: Dr. Kurt Meyerowitz, Keren Kayemeth 21, Jerusalem.
                     Photographer. Tel. (02) 639970.

Board Members: Chief Justice Moshe Landau,
Elharizi 10, Jerusalem. Judge.
Tel. (02) 632757.
Prof. Elaine Amado, Howewei Zion 18, Jerusalem.
University teacher, Bar-Ilan. Tel. (02) 668067.
Amb. Walter Eitan, Balfour 18, Jerusalem.
Diplomat. Tel. 631268.
Jael Uzay, Ramban 23, Jerusalem. Public servant.
Tel. (02) 634319.
Dr. Shaul Boazson, Ramban 46, Jerusalem. Lawyer.
Tel. (02) 531325.
Dinah Maimon, Kibbutz Zora, D.N. Shimshon.
Teacher. Tel. (02) 911334.

FINANCIAL INFORMATION
Half of the organization's funds come from donations. Another 30% come from the Ministry of Education and 20% from the Jewish Agency and the President's Fund. Last year's budget amounted to $10,000. No deficit developed, since expenses were adjusted to income. Over 90% of the organization's expenses go towards the transportation of the volunteers. The organization is a registered Ottoman, non-profit one (No. 11/2928, Jerusalem District). Donations in Israel are tax-free (no number given), and tax-free contributions from the U.S. are channeled through the Jerusalem Foundation or the P.E.F. Israel Endowment Funds, Inc., 342 Madison Avenue N.Y.C., N.Y. There is no full-time salaried staff, only two very part-time employees. All work is done by the 250 volunteers.

MEMBERSHIP, SCOPE, AND POLICY
All 250 volunteers are considered members, and anyone with motivation can join. The Executive team makes everyday decisions, while major policy decisions are taken by the National Board. A junior advisory Board makes planning decisions.

AFFILIATIONS/REFERENCES
The organization is not affiliated with any Israeli political party. References listed include P.E.F. Israel Endowment Funds Inc., 342 Madison Avenue, N.Y.C., N.Y. U.S.A., and The Gimprich Family Foundation, 60 Washington St., Hartford, Conn. 06106, U.S.A.

FUNDING NEEDED
1. To expand and widen the scope of present activities, deepen training and preparation of volunteers. Cost: $25,000.
2. To open similar activities at other centers. Cost: $50,000.
3. For a 2-year project for visiting Jewish university graduates to do community work (education, health, social work, etc.) in development towns and underprivileged neighborhoods. Cost: $500,000.

YAD AVI SYNAGOGUE ASSOCIATION and KEREN EITAN FREE LOAN FUND

בית־כנסת יד־אבי וגמ"ח קרן איתן

P.O.B. 9592
Kiryat Yovel, Jerusalem
c/o Mr. M. Farkas, Tel. (02) 417245

HISTORY AND DESCRIPTION

The Yad Avi Synagogue Association was established in 1959 by Anglo-Saxon leaders of the community. After the Yom Kippur War, the organization took on the name Yad Avi in memory of a young faithful member who grew up in the community and lost his life in the War.

Goals: The main goal of the organization is to move its center from a shelter to a building, for which the land has already been allocated, and to provide interest-free loans to large families, young couples, new immigrants, and others in need.

Services, Activities, and Accomplishments: Yad Avi gives courses in reading of the Torah and Haftorah, as well as Chazanut. Youths of the community are encouraged to volunteer to lead prayers in daily and Shabbat services. There are also daily lessons of Mishna and Gemara provided for adults. The organization's greatest accomplishment to date is having the Jerusalem Municipality acknowledge the need for a suitable permanent residence for the association and synagogue, and provide a site for such. The loan fund has also helped many people and nearly $8,000 has been distributed to a wide range of needy people.

OFFICERS

Chairman: Mr. M. Farkas, Borochov 53, Jerusalem.
                Tel. (02) 417245.
Treasurer: Mr. Z. Blum, Borochov 49, Jerusalem.
                Tel. (02) 414850.
Secretary: Mr. M. Weiss, Zangwill 9, Jerusalem.
                Tel. (02) 421913.
Volunteer: Mr. S. Grunbaum, Zangwill 9, Jerusalem.
                Tel. (02) 423024.

FINANCIAL INFORMATION

Yad Avi has two sources of income. The largest, accounting for 95% of the income, is derived from membership dues. The remaining 5% is in the form of donations. No annual budget or deficit of the organization was supplied. The organization is registered as an Ottoman Association (reg. no. 11/449/1). The organization does not state if donations to it are tax-free in either Israel or the United States. Yad Avi has no paid employees and lists 7 volunteers.

MEMBERSHIP, SCOPE, AND POLICY

No information was supplied as to the decision-making process of the organization. Anyone is allowed to attend the services of Yad Avi Synagogue and all are eligible to join the Synagogue if they accept the statutes laid down by the Yad Avi Synagogue Association. There are presently 40 families who are members with no members abroad. There is only one branch, in Jerusalem.

AFFILIATIONS/REFERENCES

Yad Avi is not affiliated with any political party in Israel. The Yad Avi Synagogue Association founded the Gemilath Chesed Fund—Keren Eitan.

FUNDING NEEDED

1. To build a worthy synagogue to replace the facilities presently situated in a bomb shelter.
2. The establishment of a religious center for study groups.
3. To greatly expand the Keren Eitan free loan Fund so that many more worthy persons in need of assistance can be helped.

YAD ELIAHU FREE LOAN SOCIETY FOR NEEDY YOUNG COUPLES

גמילות חסד להכנסת כלה יד-אליהו

Head Office:
 Rechov Harav Berlin 2,
 P.O.B. 4092, Jerusalem.
Telephone: (02) 662363.
Office Hours:
 7:00 P.M. to 8:30 P.M.

Branch Office:
 Rechov Bar Ilan 18,
 Jerusalem.
Office Hours:
 11:00 A.M. to 1:00 P.M.

HISTORY AND DESCRIPTION

"Yad Eliahu" was founded in 1963 to help relieve the extreme financial difficulties facing needy brides and young couples about to set up house. The organization provides loans entirely free of interest or linkage, as well as advice for those needing it.

Services, Activities, and Accomplishments: The Society has been able to provide very many young couples with free loans under convenient terms, thus enabling them to buy essentials for the home, and providing them with the means to raise their families. "Yad Eliahu"'s first priority is to increase the size and the number of loans which it grants to those unable to cope with the cost of housing and spiralling inflation. In order to attract contributions toward this purpose, it has established a Charity Fund. This project provides an opportunity for those donors who may wish to establish a special fund in their name or in the name of a departed relative. A contribution of $100 or more is commemorated by a copper plaque inscribed with the name of the donor or relative. Any loans extended from these funds are stamped with the name of the donor or relative.

OFFICERS

Chairman:
 Rabbi Y.Z. Hager, Hagiz 9, Jerusalem.
 Tel.: (02) 245379.

Treasurer:
 Dr. J. Walk, Herzog 5, Jerusalem. Lecturer.
 Tel.: (02) 661342.

Board or
Hanhala
Members:
 Rabbi I.A. Shapira, Aza 21, Jerusalem.
 Teacher. Tel. (02) 665280.
 Rabbi M.P. Gross, Shmuel HaNavi 104/4.
 Mr. M. Bakshi-Doron, Rutenberg 4, Jerusalem.
 Communal worker. Tel.: (02) 662366.
 Mr. E. Zarchi, Palmach 42, Jerusalem. Teacher.
 Tel.: (02) 662779.
 Mr. E. Zipp, Harav Berlin 2, Jerusalem. Secretary
 and Manager. Tel.: (02) 662363.

FINANCIAL INFORMATION
"Yad Eliahu"'s sole source of income is donations. Last year's annual budget was $5,660. There was no deficit, as the organization loans out only funds availabe to it. Donations are tax-free in Israel but not in the U.S.A. (Israeli tax number not supplied). The organization is registered as a non-profit Ottoman Association in the Jerusalem District Office of the Ministry of the Interior (reg. no. 11/1151). All members of the Board work voluntarily. The organization employs a full-time secretary who receives a very small nominal salary.

MEMBERSHIP, SCOPE, AND POLICY
The organization has 2 branches in Israel and none abroad. There is no official membership apart from the Board. Decisions are made at Board meetings, based on the will of the majority.

AFFILIATIONS/REFERENCES
The Society is not affiliated with any political party in Israel nor with any group abroad.

YAD LASHISHA
VOLUNTARY AID SOCIETY

חסד יד לששה (חי"ל) ארגון חסד ועזרה הדדית

P.O.B. 16100
Bayit Vegan, Jerusalem
Telephone: (02) 421425

HISTORY AND DESCRIPTION

"Yad Lashisha" was founded in 1978 as a result of the public's desire to perpetuate the memories of the six young residents of the Bayit Vegan neighborhood of Jerusalem who were killed in the terrorist explosion on the No. 12 bus line in the area.

Organizational Structure: The Society is registered as a non-profit organization. There are 10 main sections, each run by one or more section-heads on a completely voluntary basis. The section-leaders meet from time to time to report on progress and to plan further activities. There is an annual public meeting held on the anniversary of the tragedy.

Goals: The organization aims to promote good neighborliness, friendship and the spirit of voluntary service among the residents of Bayit Vegan. It wishes to foster awareness of other people's needs and to strive to satisfy them, in accordance with the tenets of our Torah.

Services, Activities and Accomplishments: The organization provides a wide range of services to help people in distress and in emergency situations. The major services parallel the 10 main sections referred to above: (1) help for housewives in stressful situations, after childbirth, etc.; (2) hospital visits; (3) visits to the housebound elderly; (4) help with family celebrations; (5) meals-on-wheels, including nutritional advice; (6) welcoming newcomers; (7) a mutual self-help fund; (8) an information center, including emergency car service, kashruth advice, family advice service; (9) educational advice; and (10) Shabbat invitations. The organization also publishes a newsletter promoting these and other activities in the neighborhood.

OFFICERS

Director:	Rabbi A. Carmell, Bayit Vegan 94, J-m. Lecturer. Tel. (02) 420454.
Treasurer:	Rabbi M. Breslauer, HaPisga 61, J-m. Businessman. Tel. (02) 421425.
Gen. Organizer:	Barbara Cowen, Uziel 127, J-m. Tel. (02) 550956.
Board Members:	A. Wormser, Bergman 10, J-m. Tel. (02) 422618. Rabbi A. Posen. Tel. (02) 421457. Rabbi D. Feist, Hida 7, J-m. Tel. (02) 421542. Meira Ben-Yashar. Tel. (02) 424988.

FINANCIAL INFORMATION
Approximately 5% of the organization's income is derived from membership dues; 25% from donations; 65% from grants by the Jerusalem municipality and charitable organizations; and the remaining 5% from (partial) refunds by recipients of services. Annual budget for the current year is $10,000, with an accumulated deficit of $4,200. Tax-free status for donations to the organization in Israel and in the U.S.A. is currently pending. The Society is registered as a non-profit Ottoman Association in the Jerusalem District Office of the Ministry of the Interior (reg. no. 11-3210).

MEMBERSHIP, SCOPE AND POLICY
There is no registered membership. All residents of the Bayit Vegan neighborhood are automatically considered members.

AFFILIATIONS/REFERENCES
The Society is not connected with any political party in Israel. It has been recognized by the Rothschild Foundation abroad.

FUNDING NEEDED
1. To expand the Aid Fund—$20,000.
2. To expand the Helping Hand to Housewives—$15,000.
3. To expand the Meals Service—$15,000.

YAD SARAH ORGANIZATION FOR THE LENDING OF MEDICAL EQUIPMENT AND THE REHABILITATION OF THE SICK

אגודת יד-שרה

P.O.B. 15152
49 Hanevi'im Street
Jerusalem 91 150
Telephone: (02) 244242
Office hours: 24 hours a day

HISTORY AND DESCRIPTION

Seeing the lack in the care and rehabilitation of the sick in the medical-care system in Israel, a group of 13 volunteers decided, in 1976, to establish an organization to loan medical equipment to sick people for emergency home use, to operate a network of volunteers to help care for and rehabilitate the sick in their homes, and to open centers where the sick and/or their families could get medical, psychological and practical guidance and help. From two neighborhood lending branches in Jerusalem, Yad Sarah has expanded to a chain of 22 branches throughout the country.

Organizational Structure: The organization is headed by a Presidium, which is assisted by an executive team that acquires, finances, and maintains equipment.

Goals: (a) Providing vital medical equipment on home loan. (b) Operating volunteers to make home visits and to help with the care and rehabilitation of the sick in their homes. (c) Granting interest-free loans to patients who require permanent use of medical equipment and/or medicines. (d) Establishing centers for the guidance of sick people and/or their families.

Services, Activities, and Accomplishments: Lending medical equipment free of charge, including oxygen tanks, wheelchairs, air pillows and mattresses, walkers, inhalators, crutches, sickbed tables, electric breast pumps, baby scales, hearing aids, orthopedic devices, sphygmomanometers, and more. Operating corps of volunteers to extend practical help and psychological support to the sick in their homes. Granting cash loans to needy and chronically ill persons needing permanent medical equipment. Operating medical guidance centers where doctors, nurses and social workers lecture to patients and their families on relevant problems. Operating a medical-emergency radio-alarm system for bed-ridden and chronically ill patients who have no means of summoning help otherwise.

The organization's major accomplishments until now have been the availability of medical equipment, on loan 24-hours a day from Yad Sarah's 22 branches throughout Israel, which brings great assistance to hundreds of thousands of patients; hundreds of volunteers, visiting the sick in their homes and seeing to their welfare, extending practical help and psychological support to the sick and to their families.

OFFICERS
> Uri Lupoliansky, 108 Sanhedria Hamurhevet, Jerusalem.
> Student.
> > Tel. (02) 813777.
> Gershon Meir, 15 Sorotzkin, Jerusalem. Teacher.
> > Tel. (02) 528827.
> Moshe Haim Gura, 14 Elkana, Jerusalem. Principal.
> > Tel. (02) 813920.
> David Gross, 6 Elisha, Bnei Brak. Student.
> > Tel. (03) 702525.
> Nahman Rosenfeld, 9 Pnina, Jerusalem. Scribe.
> > Tel. (02) 816983.

FINANCIAL INFORMATION
80% of last year's annual budget came from donations; 5% came from other sources, and 15% came from stipends. Last year's annual budget of $100,000 left the organization with a deficit of $30,000. Donations are tax-free in Israel (no. 4505260), and in the United States through P.E.F. The organization is registered as a non-profit Ottoman Association (no. 11/2562). There are 4 full-time and 3 part-time employees, and 350 volunteers.

MEMBERSHIP, SCOPE, AND POLICY
Most decisions are made by the National Board. There are 170 members in Israel, in the 22 branches.

AFFILIATIONS/REFERENCES
The organization is not affiliated with any political party in Israel. The organization is in contact with P.E.F. Israel Endowment Funds, Inc., 342 Madison Avenue, Suite 1010, New York, New York, 10173.

FUNDING NEEDED
1. The establishment of central headquarters to serve as the main office and lending station and to ensure proper management of the organization. Estimated cost—$400,000.
2. The operation of an ambulance that will transport disabled persons requiring ambulatory treatment, serve as a mobile lending station, and transport volunteers to distant locations. Estimated cost —$35,000.
3. The acquisition of additional emergency radio-alarm transmitters to be given to chronically ill persons who might need urgent help suddenly, but who have no other means of summoning it. Estimated cost—$39,500.

YESHIVAT AMALEY TORAH

ישיבת עמלי תורה

Zayit Raanan Street
P.O.B. 6555
Jerusalem
Telephone: (02) 817662
Office hours: 9:00 A.M. to 1:00 P.M.

HISTORY AND DESCRIPTION
The organization was established 8 years ago, in 1972. During this time, several Rabbis have been trained and today serve various communities in Israel, including the Chief Rabbi of Bat Yam. Rabbi Elbas, famous for bringing many Jews back to their heritage, is among the alumni of the Yeshiva.

Goals: The goal of the Yeshiva is to train young men to organize and perform on behalf of our people and our nation, as well as to educate the youth in a true Jewish lifestyle. The Yeshiva encourages them to take an interest in social problems and to set up centers for social activities. These centers will provide an insight and knowledge on how to handle problems of daily life.

Services, Activities, and Accomplishments: The Yeshiva is proud to have produced several "Roshei Yeshiva" (deans), learned rabbis, and top rate educators. They have, in turn, published various works on the Talmud and other sacred volumes.

OFFICERS
Director:	Rabbi Mordechai Eliyahu, 2 Ben Zion, Jerusalem. Member of Jerusalem Rabbinical Court. Tel. 521010.
Treasurer:	Rabbi Ezra Bazri, 24 Imrei Bina, Jerusalem. Rabbinical Court judge.
Board Members:	Rabbi Yitzchak Aynei, 4 Zayit Raanan. Businessman. Tel. (02) 812001.
	Mr. Masod Peretz, 7 Imrei Binah, Jerusalem. Clerk. Tel. (02) 816781.

FINANCIAL INFORMATION
70% of last year's annual budget came from donations, 15% came from membership dues, and the remaining 15% came from Israeli Government allocations. The budget for last year was $27,000, with a deficit $7,500. Donations to the organization are not currently tax-free, but efforts are being made to attain this status. The organization is registered as an Ottoman Association, but the number was not supplied. There are no paid employees, but only five volunteers.

MEMBERSHIP, SCOPE, AND POLICY
Decisions are made by the members of the Board of Directors. There are 15 members in Israel, ten abroad. Plans are under way to open branches abroad.

AFFILIATIONS/REFERENCES
The organization is not affiliated with any political party in Israel.

FUNDING NEEDED
1. Funds are currently needed to purchase land to build permanent housing for the Yeshiva.
2. Funds are also needed to enable the students to continue their studies.
3. The organization would also appreciate funding to print the studies and findings of students' research.

YESHIVAT BETOKHAKHEI YERUSHALAYIM

ישיבת בתוכבי-ירושלים

5 Shoneh Halakhot Street
P.O.B. 14393 Jerusalem
Telephone: (02) 284472
Office hours: 1:00 P.M. to 2:00 P.M.

HISTORY AND DESCRIPTION
The Yeshiva was founded in 1876 by the most illustrious rabbinical leaders of the time, and was destroyed together with the destruction of the Jewish community in the Old City of Jerusalem. Eight years ago, the Yeshiva was reconstructed on its former spot.

Because of its proximity to the Temple Mount, the Yeshiva's Talmud study is focused upon Seder Kodashim, which concerns the Temple service.

Some of the accomplishments of the Yeshiva have been the publication of holy books concerning Seder Kodashim and the partial construction of the present site of the Yeshiva.

OFFICERS
Director: Rabbi M. Zibaled, Jerusalem.
Treasurer: Rabbi A.J. Tversky, Jerusalem.
Board Members: Rabbi A. Nanknsky, Rabbi M. Aviarbach,
                 Rabbi J. Rosental, Rabbi S. Podemsky,
                 Rabbi Z. Perkal, (all Jerusalem).

FINANCIAL INFORMATION
The annual budget for last year was obtained from the following sources: membership dues, 30%; donations, 15%; foundation grant, 10%; and other miscellaneous sources, 45%. The budget for last year was $24,000, with a deficit of $12,000. Donations to the Yeshiva are not tax-free, neither in Israel nor in the United States. It is registered as an Ottoman Association (reg. no. 11/2139). There are five full-time and nine part-time workers employed by the Yeshiva, in addition to three volunteers.

MEMBERSHIP, SCOPE, AND POLICY
There are 50 members in Israel and five abroad. There is only one branch in Israel and none abroad. Decisions are made by the National Board.

AFFILIATIONS/REFERENCES
The Yeshiva is not affiliated with any political party in Israel, and has no contacts abroad.

FUNDING NEEDED
1. Funds for student support.
2. Reconstruction of the present site.
3. Funds for publishing works of the students in Seder Kodashim.

YESHIVAT CHASIDEI BRESLOV—
OR HANE'ELAM

ישיבת חסידי ברסלב — אור הנעלם

Yeshiva: 36 Salant Street, Jerusalem
Telephone: (02) 282578

Office: 36 Salant Street, Jerusalem
Telephone: (02) 812081, (02) 810358, (02) 282578
Office hours: 10:00 A.M. to 1:00 P.M.; 4:00-7:00 P.M.

HISTORY AND DESCRIPTION
The Yeshiva was founded in the Jewish Quarter of the Old City of Jerusalem in 1937. Following the 1948 War of Independence, the Yeshiva moved to the Mea Shearim quarter. In 1953 construction began on the present building.

Organizational Structure: The Yeshiva has a Board of Directors consisting of members from Israel and abroad who meet from time to time to discuss the various needs of the Yeshiva.

Goals: The Yeshiva is divided into several groups: a full-time Rabbinical College to train young men for positions as Rabbis and spiritual leaders, and a half-day program for the many students who hold some other position (i.e., teaching or other work), to enable them to participate in Torah study.

Services, Activities, and Accomplishments: The Yeshiva has established a center of Torah study based on the world-renowned teachings of Rabbi Nachman of Breslov and the dissemination of these teachings.
The Yeshiva has a free-loan fund, a free kitchen, dormitory facilities, and gives aid to needy families. It has embarked on an "Out-Reach" program to attract Jews from all walks of life and to bring them back to the faith. In conjunction with this program the Yeshiva is translating the works of Rabbi Nachman of Breslov into many languages, to attract people to Judaism.
A typesetting school has recently been opened to train students for a profession and to help with the translating and printing of Rabbi Nachman's works.

OFFICERS
Exec. Director   Rabbi E. Rosen, Ein Yaacov 9, Jerusalem.
      Tel. (02) 285959.
Director: Rabbi Chaim Kramer, Ezrat Torah 10, Jerusalem.
      Tel. (02) 812081.
Board Members: Rabbi Kalman Rosen, Ezrat Torah 19, Jerusalem.
      Tel. 810358.
      Rabbi M. Dorfman, Hosea 4, Jerusalem.
      Tel. (02) 289055.

Dr. A. Gross, Sorotzkin 18, Jerusalem. Lawyer.
Tel. (02) 533853.
I. Rosenfeld, Even Ha'Ezer 13, Jerusalem.
Major — Police force.
Tel. (02) 819801.

FINANCIAL INFORMATION

70% of last year's annual budget came from donations, 20% from government sources, and the balance from membership dues. Last year's annual budget of $150,000 left the Yeshiva with a deficit of $20,000. The Yeshiva is registered as a non-profit organization (registration number 11/3256). Donations to Yeshivat Chasidei Breslov in Israel and the United States, Canada, and England are tax-free (Israel: no. 4506778; U.S.A.: no. 11-2524542; Canada: 0547430-09-13; England: 280174). The Yeshiva employs one full-time, three part-time workers, as well as three volunteers.

MEMBERSHIP, SCOPE, AND POLICY

One thousand National members represent the two Israeli branches of the Yeshiva. Membership is open to anyone interested in joining. Decisions are made by the National Board. The Yeshiva also has branches abroad with 250 members.

AFFILIATIONS/REFERENCES

The Yeshiva is not affiliated with any of the political parties in Israel. It is in contact with American Friends of Zvi Latzadik-Breslov, 3100 Brighton 3rd Street, Brooklyn, N.Y. 11235, the Canadian Friends of Chasidei Breslov, 152 Strathearn Road, Toronto, Ontario M6C 1S1, and the Rabbi Nachman of Breslov Charitable Foundation, 21 Brondesbury Park, London NW6, England.

FUNDING NEEDED

1. $500,000 — To translate and print Rabbi Nachman's works in English, French, Russian, Spanish, and German.
2. To supplement this year's annual budget, which is approaching $180,000 with an expected deficit of $50,000 for the coming year.
3. $1 million — For the Building Fund, to enlarge the Yeshiva building.

YESHIVAT DA'AT Z'KAINIM
(YESHIVA FOR RETIRED PERSONS)

ישיבת דעת זקנים

Avissar Street
Beit Yaakov—Mahane Yehuda
P.O.B. 6170
Jerusalem
Telephone: (02) 524063
Office hours: 9:00 A.M. to 1:00 P.M.

HISTORY AND DESCRIPTION
The Yeshivat Da'at Z'kainim was founded in 1965 by the late Rabbi Avraham Adler.
It is headed by a board of directors consisting of at least four members. This body is elected by a meeting of the general membership, which is held at least once every three years. The current chairman of the board is Rabbi David Nesher, the son of the founder.
The Yeshiva attempts to provide an atmosphere in which any observant Jew can engage in the study of Torah. For those who have reached retirement age, there is a stipend to cover their basic needs to subsist. There is also a Free Loan Fund for the needy. The Yeshiva also renders aid to the needy and thirty families in need, receive regular monetary support from the organization.

OFFICERS
Director: Rabbi David Nesher, 14 Nissenbaum, Jerusalem.
                               National Kashrut Supervisor. Tel. (02) 524063.
Treasurer: Meir Nesher, 16 Radak, Jerusalem.
                               Banker. Tel. (02) 636491.
Board Members: Rabbi Jehoshua Zaks, 4 Lunz, Jerusalem. Rabbi.
                               Rabbi Avraham Starisky,
                               18 Mesilat Yesharim, Jerusalem. Retired.
                               Rabbi Yosef Zwebner, 2 Ben Zion, Jerusalem.
                               Administrator. Tel. (02) 524374.

FINANCIAL INFORMATION
The Israeli government provides the major source of funding for the Yeshiva. Last year's budget was $10,000, with a deficit of $1,200. The organization is registered as an Ottoman Association (reg. no. 11/12969). Donations to the Yeshiva are not tax-free, neither in Israel nor in the United States. There are ten volunteers who work for the Yeshiva.

MEMBERSHIP, SCOPE, AND POLICY
There are 50 members in the one Israeli branch. Decisions are made mostly by the Executive Director.

AFFILIATIONS/REFERENCES
The Yeshiva is not affiliated with any political party in Israel and has no foreign contacts.

FUNDING NEEDED
1. Construction of an new study hall. Estimated cost: $110,000.
2. Purchase of a minibus for transportation. Estimated cost: $30,000.
3. Purchase of a library. Estimated cost: $200,000.

YESHIVAT ELON MOREH   ישיבת אלון מורה

Kedumim, Shomron
Telephone: (053) 37849 and (053) 37896
Office hours: 8:00 A.M. to 3:00 P.M.

DESCRIPTION
The founding of Yeshivat Elon Moreh is part of the renewal of Jewish
settlement in Samaria initiated in December 1975. Students from the
Kiryat Arba Yeshiva were among the first pioneers who started the
settlement at Kaddum (now Kedumim). The settlers always regarded
the development of the Yeshiva as an integral part of the development of
Jewish settlement in Samaria. There has always been a realization of the
mutually fruitful influence between the physical act of building a Jewish
home in a new area and the mental effort required to learn and understand the meaning of one's Jewish roots. The original Elon Moreh
group that founded Kedumim continued towards the heart of Samaria—toward Shechem (Nablus). The result was Elon Moreh, another
Jewish settlement. The settlers hope to strengthen Jewish roots in Israel
by physical and spiritual effort.
The growth of the Yeshiva is essential to the growth of Jewish settlement
in Samaria. The standing of Jewish settlement in Judea and Samaria is
vital for the existence of a free and secure Jewish State.
The Yeshiva's main accomplishment is in building its reputation as an
outstanding institution which many youngsters wish to join before and
after army service. Another accomplishment is its contribution to the
shaping up of a strong Jewish settlement in the heart of Samaria.

OFFICERS
Director and
Treasurer: Menachem Felix, Elon Moreh.
                  Tel. (053) 37896.

FINANCIAL INFORMATION
35% of last year's annual budget came from donations; the balance from
the Israeli government and from support by the Kedumim settlement.
Last year's budget was $60,000. The yeshiva is registered as an Ottoman
Association (No. 11/3062). Donations to the yeshiva are tax-free in
Israel (Israel reg. no. 4506937). Three full-time and one part-time
workers are employed by the Council. There are also three full-time and
5-10 part-time volunteers. In addition, salaries are paid to the Head of
the yeshiva, 3 other rabbis, and 10 married students.

MEMBERSHIP, SCOPE, AND POLICY
Most decisions are made by the Executive Director. There are two
branches in Israel—one at Kedumim and the other at Elon Moreh.

627

AFFILIATIONS/REFERENCES
The yeshiva is not affiliated with a political party in Israel. No foreign references were listed.

FUNDING NEEDED
1. To add to the yearly budget for current expenses—$50,000.
2. A Study Hall (Beit Midrash) building—$1,000,000.
3. A dormitory building—$1,000,000.

YESHIVAT HADAROM

ישיבת הדרום

Hagra Street
Rehovot
Telephone: (054) 71067
Office hours: 8:00 A.M. to 5:00 P.M. (until 12:00 P.M. on Fridays)

HISTORY AND DESCRIPTION

Yeshivat Hadarom, founded by the late Rabbi Zvi Yehuda Meltzer soon after the establishment of the State of Israel, is sponsored by the Rabbinical Council of America. Designed to train and prepare educational and spiritual leaders, its program is geared to attract students who have the intellectual capacity to master a concentrated syllabus of advanced Talmudic studies as well as general academic subjects. The junior high school and high school divisions offer programs in humanities and sciences. Extra-curricular activities are also offered. Students generally stay at the dormitory, except for junior high school students who live nearby. Hadarom's Teacher Seminary, Bet Medrash Moreshet Yaakov, was the first Yeshivat Hesder (school in which students combine army service and Jewish studies). Upon completing the Hesder program, the students receive Ministry of Education certificates qualifying them to teach Talmud and other Judaic subjects in the government religious school system. Yeshivat Hadarom instills within its young men a knowledge of Torah, a steadfast devotion to Judaism and its moral values and a love for the Land of Israel. Its graduates assume positions of leadership in the professional, social and spiritual life of their communities.

Services, Activities and Accomplishments: Most graduates of the high school go on the Yeshivot Hesder, and fill teaching and administrative positions in border and development towns as well as in the urban centers of Israel.

OFFICERS

Administrators: Rabbi Moshe Furst, Rehovot.
Tel. (054) 72497.
Yosef Gibraltar, Moshav Hemed.
Tel. (03) 944159.

Chairmen: Rabbi Israel Tabak, Jerusalem. Chairman.
Tel. (02) 420979.
Rabbi M. Solomon, Jerusalem. Hon. Chairman.
Rabbi M. Lewittes, Jerusalem. Hon. Chairman.
Tel. (02) 661795.
Rabbi B. Morgenstern, Jerusalem. Vice-Chairman.
Tel. (02) 638460.
Rabbi Fred Hollander, Jerusalem. Vice-Chairman.
Tel. (02) 810253.
Rabbi Louis Bernstein, New York City. Chairman of Committee in U.S.

Treasurer: Rabbi L. Oschry, Jerusalem.
Tel. (02) 637182.

FINANCIAL INFORMATION
The sources of income for the Yeshiva are as follows: Ministry of Education and Culture, 28%; donations, 15%; Youth Aliyah and Ministry of Social Affairs, 25%; tuition, 12%; Ministry of Religion, 10%; and miscellaneous (JDC-Israel, Rehovot municipality, camps, etc.), 10%. Last year's annual budget of $400,000 left a deficit of $25,000. The Yeshiva is registered as an Ottoman Association (reg. no. 35/1). Donations to the Yeshiva are tax-free in Israel and the United States, but the tax numbers were not supplied. There are 34 full-time and 32 part-time workers employed by the Yeshiva.

MEMBERSHIP, SCOPE, AND POLICY
Policy decisions are made by the Board, implemented by the Director and educational officers. There are about 100 members in Israel.

AFFILIATIONS/REFERENCES
The Yeshiva is not affiliated with any political party in Israel. The Yeshiva is in contact with the following: Rabbinical Council of America, 1250 Broadway, New York, New York 10001; American Friends of Yeshivat Hadarom, 1250 Broadway, New York, New York 10001; and the Canadian Friends of Hadarom Schools, c/o Seymour Brudner, Leo Wynberg and Associates, 1183 Finch Avenue W. Ste 500, Downsview, Ontario, Canada.

FUNDING NEEDED
1. To cover the growing maintenance deficit by obtaining scholarship gifts (Full scholarship $1,000; half scholarship $500).
2. To collect funds to implement much-needed renovations in the dormitory building.
3. To construct a much-needed gymnasium.

YESHIVAT HACHAYIM VEHASHALOM
VE-KOLLEL ATERET MORDECHAI
ישיבת החיים והשלום וכולל עטרת מרדכי

18 Yosef Ben Matityahu
P.O.B. 16144
Jerusalem
Telephone: (02) 286657
Office hours: 9:00 A.M.-1:00 P.M., and 3:00 P.M.-7:00 P.M.

HISTORY AND DESCRIPTION
Yeshivat Hachayim VeHashalom was founded in 1969 by the late Grand Rabbi of Mexico City and Jerusalem, Rabbi Mordechai Attieh, who was a great scholar, community leader, kabbalist and publisher. For the first eleven years it was a part-time kollel, dedicated to the study, elucidation and dissemination of the Kaballah of the holy Rabbi Yitzchak Luria Z"L, a branch of Torah knowledge dealing with the inner meaning of Torah, mitzvot and prayer. In commemoration of the passing of the great rabbi, his son and grandson, reknowned Talmud and Kabballah scholars in their own right, a full-time yeshiva was opened in 1979.

Since the Yom Kippur War, thousands of young Israelis have awakened to the deepest questions of human existence and Jewish Identity. The yeshiva, in the context of a traditional format of Halachah, deep learning of Talmud and love of Israel, is able to support their quest with the insights of the Kabballah. In a short time many students begin to overcome the problems which they had inherited, to live fulfilled, creative, and responsible lives, committed to G-d, Torah, the People of Israel and their Land.

Organizational Structure: The Kollel provides an intense program of study, personal counselling, character development and interpersonal cooperation eight hours a day, and often more. The studies concentrate on Talmud, Jewish Law, character development, and Kabballah.

Goals: To produce well-rounded men who are committed and capable of actualizing their deepest-felt needs to seek G-d, to express their creativity, and to serve the Jewish people in teaching, leadership and service positions.

Services, Activities, and Accomplishments: In addition to study and counselling, the Kollel provides its young men, both singles and married, with monthly stipends. Although these stipends are meager in relation to what they require, they are quite high by standards of what other "ba-alay teshuvah" institutions provide. Very often these stipends determine whether a young man can continue in his studies and personal development.

The Yeshiva has had great success in helping its students, and in training rabbis, teachers and community leaders who are now serving throughout Israel.

OFFICERS

Director:	Rabbi Eliahu Attieh, 77 Bayit Vegan, Jerusalem. Tel. (02) 420553.
Treasurer:	Mr. Shimon Barmatz, Beit Chaninah, Beit Hashiva, Jerusalem.
Board Members:	Rabbi Mantzur Ben Shimon, 47 Bayit Vegan, Jerusalem.
	Rabbi Yitzchak Zafrani, 74 La Guardia, Tel Aviv.
	Mr. Eliahu Arkanzy, Agrippas, Jerusalem.
Honorary Members:	Rabbi Shalom Mashash, Chief Rabbi of Jerusalem.
	Rabbi Mordechai Ben Eliyahu, 45 Kaf Tet B'November, Bat Yam.
	Shaul Batish Halevi, 16 Yosef Hanasi, Jerusalem.

FINANCIAL INFORMATION

All of last year's annual budget came from donations. Last year's annual budget of $25,000 left the Yeshiva with a deficit of $2500. The Yeshiva is registered as an Ottoman Association (No. 11/1467). Donations to the Yeshiva are not tax-free but the Yeshiva is in the process of obtaining this status both in Israel and the United States. There are five full-time employees and one volunteer.

MEMBERSHIP, SCOPE, AND POLICY

Decisions are made by a committee appointed by the Board. There is only one branch of the Yeshiva. The Kollel is open to anyone who wishes to benefit and who is capable of benefitting from its program.

AFFILIATIONS/REFERENCES

The Yeshiva is not affiliated with any political party in Israel. The Yeshiva is in contact with Rabbi Y. Katzin, Sha'arei Tzion congregation in Brooklyn, New York, U.S.A. and with Rodef Tzedek Congregation in Mexico City, Mexico.

FUNDING NEEDED

1. To continue providing stipends, and to increase their amount, and to have the funds to take in more students on this basis.
2. To renovate the building so there will be more room, and to rent apartments for single men.
3. With a view towards expanding the services, it is necessary to have the funds to meet the heavy cost of hiring qualified teachers who are capable of teaching and relating to the young men.

YESHIVAT HAKOTEL

ישיבת הכותל

P.O.B. 603, Jerusalem 91 000
Misgav Ladach Road, The Old City,
Jerusalem
Telephone: (02) 234246, (02) 288175
Office hours: Sunday-Thursday, 8:00 A.M. to 3:00 P.M.
Friday and Erev Yomtov, 8:00 A.M. to 12:30 P.M.

HISTORY AND DESCRIPTION

The Yeshiva was established in July 1967 and was the first institution to return to the Old City of Jerusalem after the Six-Day War. Yeshivat Hakotel is associated with the Merkaz Yeshivot Bnei Akiva network. It offers a post-high-school Yeshivat Hesder, a five-year study program combining Torah study and army service and a five-year post-graduate Kollel program, where students can receive the necessary preparation to become rabbis, teachers, and rabbinic judges for Israel and the Diaspora. Three hundred students currently study at the Yeshiva — 250 from Israel and 50 from abroad.

Organizational Structure: The institution is headed by the Dean of the Yeshiva (Rosh Hayeshiva), and the Dean of the Kollel (Rosh Hakollel). Administrative aspects of the Yeshiva are the responsibility of the Menahel Hayeshiva (Executive Director), a Secretary (Mazkir Hayeshiva) headed by an Assistant Director (Public Relations).

Goals: To educate and inspire the next generation of Jewish youth in the Torah of Israel, with a love and appreciation for the Land of Israel and the Jewish people. To educate scholars who will in turn become religious, educational, and spiritual leaders of the Jewish communities of Israel and abroad. To be in the forefront of the educational leadership in Israel.

Services, Activities, and Accomplishments: Classes and lectures are given for students and for members of the community interested in attending these lectures and classes. A wide range of students is accepted from varying socio-economic backgrounds. The Yeshiva tries to inspire all its students to take their rightful place in working for the Jewish communities of Israel and the Diaspora. A large majority (90%) of the Israeli students receive financial aid, and no student is turned away because of financial considerations. The Yeshiva has produced hundreds of alumni who have taken up leadership positions in the Jewish communities of Israel and the Diaspora, and has become one of the leaders in spearheading the movement of yeshivot hesder in Israel. Yeshivat Hakotel is perhaps best known as the Yeshiva which dances its way to the Kotel every Shabbat and Yomtov evening. This spiritual and emotionally moving event attracts hundreds of friends and tourists every year to the Kotel, who join with Yeshivat Hakotel in prayers. Yeshivat Hakotel still mourns a group of its students who fell during the 1973 Yom Kippur

War. Their memories are perpetuated by appropriate memorials in the Beit Medrash study hall. The Yeshivat Hakotel Beit Medrash study hall is open to the public for daily prayers and studies. Endowment opportunities in the new building of Yeshivat Hakotel are available and the Yeshiva is seeking contributors wishing to perpetuate their name in the Old City of Jerusalem overlooking the Western Wall, the central place of Judaism.

OFFICERS

Rosh Hayeshiva:	Rabbi Yeshayahu Hadari, Jerusalem.
Rosh Hakollel:	Rabbi Yaakov Katz, Jerusalem.
Menahel Hayeshiva:	Rabbi Binyamin Adler, Jerusalem.
Mazkir Hayeshiva:	Elimelech Ben-Pazi, Jerusalem.
Asst. Director (Public Relations):	Dr. F.J. Zisk, Jerusalem. Tel. (02) 234246, or 272271 (Res.)
Chairman of Board:	Kurt Rothschild, Toronto, Canada.
Board Members:	Avraham Diamant, Givatayim.
	Yaakov Drori, Kibbutz Saad.
	Elchanan Loewenthal, Tel Aviv.
	Rabbi Moshe Zvi Neriya, Kfar Haroeh.
	Rabbi Arieh Bina, Jerusalem.
	Rabbi Avraham Zuckerman, Kfar Haroeh.

FINANCIAL INFORMATION

Last year's annual budget of $570,000 left the Yeshiva with an accumulated deficit of $136,500. The Yeshiva is registered as a non-profit organization to which tax-free donations may be made in Israel (Israel Income Tax Exempt No. 4503118); in the United States (American Friends of Yeshivat Hakotel and American Friends of Yeshivot Bnei Akiva are recognized by I.R.S. as exempt organizations); and Canada (Canadian Friends of Yeshivat Hakotel is the recognized exempt organization).

MEMBERSHIP, SCOPE, AND POLICY

The Yeshiva is located in the Old City of Jerusalem, with organized groups of friends and alumni in the United States, Canada, England, Australia. All policy decisions are formulated and approved by the Board of Directors. Other decisions are made by the Rosh Yeshiva, the Rosh Hakollel or the Menahel Hayeshiva.

AFFILIATIONS/REFERENCES

Yeshivat Hakotel is affiliated to the Merkaz Yeshivot Bnei Akiva in Israel. It is in contact with: American Friends of Yeshivat Hakotel, 10 Columbus Circle, NYC 10019; Canadian Friends of Yeshivat Hakotel, 27 Ridgevale, Downsview, Ontario, Canada; American Friends of Yeshivot Bnei Akiva, 39 Broadway, Suite 2709, New York, NY 10006; and any Mizrachi organization worldwide.

FUNDING NEEDED

1. Yeshivat Hakotel is currently building a new educational complex in the Old City of Jerusalem. Dedications of facilities, dormitories, rooms, and courtyards are available.
2. To establish several scholarship plans to support the education and social needs of needy students.
3. To improve the salary levels of the Yeshiva's teachers and the physical conditions of the Yeshiva.

YESHIVAT HAR ETZION

ישיבת הר עציון

8 Alcharizi Street
P.O.B. 7447, Jerusalem
Telephone: (02) 662568
Office hours: 8:00 A.M. to 2:00 P.M.
Campus: Alon Shevut, Gush Etzion
Telephone: (02) 742456

HISTORY AND DESCRIPTION

The Yeshiva was established almost immediately after the Six-Day War in 1967. Located in the Gush Etzion region, south of Jerusalem between Bethlehem and Hebron, the Yeshiva stands near the site where the original Jewish settlers came under fierce attack during Israel's War of Independence.

Services, Activities, and Accomplishments: Yeshivat Har Etzion is a Yeshivat Hesder; the student/soldiers enroll for a four-year course, during which time they complete almost two years of active military service. In fact, after enrolment, the Har Etzion student completes his basic army training before actually entering the Yeshiva. Many of these students become officers in the I.D.F. Twelve students have fallen in battle during and since the Yom Kippur War. A special study room has been dedicated in their memory. Har Etzion comprises a magnificent Beit Medrash, a modern dining hall, and twelve dormitory buildings. Its present student population is 354, from Israel and abroad. Many of the overseas students have decided to remain in Israel. One of the important projects of Yeshivat Har Etzion is the Yaacov Herzog Teachers Training Institute, whose many graduates occupy key teaching positions throughout Israel and abroad. It is the long-range aim of the Institute to produce graduates steeped in traditional learning and possessed of a secular education. The training of Har Etzion stresses Torah learning and full adherence to the tenets of Judaism translated into the modern life of Israel. The Yeshiva has gained special prominence under the leadership of two outstanding scholars, Rabbi Yehuda Amital and Rabbi Aharon Lichtenstein, merging the best traditions of Torah learning in Israel and America with a formidable grasp of the modern world.

OFFICERS

Director:	Benny Brama, Alon Shevut, Gush Etzion.
Treasurer:	Yaakov Drori, Kibbutz Saad.
Board:	Moshe Moskovics, Masuot Yitzchak, Lachish. Government advisor.
	Dr. Meyer Brayer, Shderot Eshkol 46, Jerusalem. Educator.
	Yedaya Hacohen, Ussishkin 39, Jerusalem.
Deans:	Rabbi Yehuda Amital, Shachal 21, Jerusalem.
	Rabbi Aharon Lichtenstein, Yordei Hasira 2, Jerusalem.

FINANCIAL INFORMATION

77% of last year's annual budget came from donations, 15% from government sources, and the balance from tuition fees. Last year's annual budget of $750,000 left the Yeshiva with a deficit of $433,000. The Yeshiva is registered as a non-profit organization (Israel reg. no. 11/1600), to which donations in Israel and the United States may be made tax-free (Israel: no. 4502624; USA: I.R.S. no. 23-722-8230). The Yeshiva employs thirty full-time and twenty part-time workers. Decisions are made by the Yeshiva's Board.

AFFILIATIONS/REFERENCES

The Yeshiva is politically unaffiliated in Israel. It is in contact with the Etzion Foundation, 310 Madison Avenue, Suite 904, New York, N.Y. 10017.

FUNDING NEEDED

1. $1 million—To construct a central library for the entire Gush Etzion region.
2. $600,000—To expand the Yaacov Herzog Teachers Institute.
3. $400,000—To provide additional dormitories.

YESHIVAT HAREI YEHUDA

ישיבת הרי יהודה

Yeshiva: Moshav Beit Meir. Tel. (02) 911423.
City Office: Zvi Kahanna, 68 Rashi, Jerusalem. Tel. (02) 525171.
Office hours: Vary, phone first.

DESCRIPTION
Yeshivat Harei Yehuda is a Yeshiva of higher studies for students aged 15 and above.
Goals: Accepting boys who were not successful in other settings. These youths came to Yeshivat Harei Yehuda and in about a year they became independent in learning, and are inspired to continue learning Torah. The studies include Talmud, Tanach, Bible, and Medrashim, as well as books on ethics, religion, and faith.
Accomplishments: The boys who are learning have been very successful while in their previous surroundings they were not. This inspired them to enjoy learning and to continue independently.

OFFICERS
Director: Rabbi Eliezer Goldshmidt, 1 Panim Meirot, J-m.
Board Members: Rabbi Zvi Kahanna, 68 Rashi, Jerusalem.
                Tel. (02) 525171.
                Yitzchak Arenberg, 18 Sorotzkin, Jerusalem.
                Tel. (02) 528297.

FINANCIAL INFORMATION
Last year's annual budget came from the Israeli government—the Ministry of Religious Affairs and the Ministry of the Interior, as well as from individual donations and from tuition. Information about last year's annual budget and deficit were not given. The Yeshiva is registered as an Ottoman Association, number 11/1239. Donations to the Yeshiva are tax-free in Israel via the Vaad Hayeshivot for Yeshivat Harei Yehuda (number not supplied) and also in the United States via Congregation Minyan Mir in New York City for Yeshivat Harei Yehuda (number not supplied). There are three full-time employees of the Yeshiva.

MEMBERSHIP, SCOPE, AND POLICY
Decisions are made by the Board—Rabbi Zvi Kahanna and Rabbi Y. Arenberg. There are three members in Israel and two abroad.

AFFILIATIONS/REFERENCES
The Yeshiva is not affiliated with a political party in Israel. The Yeshiva is in contact with Congregation Minyan Mir, 5401 16th Avenue, Brooklyn, New York 11204.

FUNDING NEEDED
The most pressing need at present is the cost of maintaining the dormitory for the boys in the Yeshiva.

YESHIVAT HEICHAL HATORAH

ישיבת "היכל התורה"

6-8 Mahari-be-Rav Street
P.O.B. 5167, Mishkenot
Jerusalem
Telephone: (02) 242773
Office hours: 8:00 A.M. to 1:00 P.M.

Services, Activities, and Accomplishments: Yeshivat Heichal Hatorah graduates rabbis and dayanim (religious court judges), and also gives financial support to the new rabbis and their families. It also gives grants to its successful students. The Yeshiva has a Free Loan (Gemilat Chessed) Fund, and is presently trying to raise funds for new premises.

OFFICERS

Director: Rabbi M. Fisher, Haneziv 9, Jerusalem.
Treasurer: Rabbi E. Rabinovitz, Mesilat Yesharim, Jerusalem.
Board Members: Rabbi Dov Rosenkranz, Jerusalem.
Rabbi Aharon Fisher, Bnei Brak.
Rabbi Yosef Zusman, Jerusalem.
Rabbi Shlomo Dugan, Jerusalem.

FINANCIAL INFORMATION

Last year's annual budget of $13,000 (all of which derived from donations) left the Yeshiva with a deficit of $5,000. The Yeshiva is recognized as a non-profit organization (no Israel registration number supplied). Decisions for the Yeshiva are made by the Board. No information was provided concerning tax-exempt status in Israel or abroad.

AFFILIATIONS/REFERENCES

Yeshivat Heichal Hatorah is politically unaffiliated in Israel. It is in contact with the Federated Council of Israel Institutions Inc., 15 Beekman Street, New York, N.Y. 10038.

FUNDING NEEDED

To provide stipends for students.

YESHIVAT OTSAR HAHAIM

ישיבת אוצר החיים

34 Otzer Haim Street
Jerusalem
Telephone: (02) 817073
Office hours: Regular office hours

DESCRIPTION
Yeshivat Otzar Hahaim was founded in 1970 to train teachers, rabbis, and religious court judges for the Sephardic community.
In the ten years that the organization has been in operation, 25 members became religious court judges or teachers for younger students learning in the Higher Yeshivas.

OFFICERS
Director: Asriel Cohen, 10 Imre Baruch, Bnei Brak.
                     Tel. (03) 764734.
Treasurer: Shlomo Cohen, 10 Blau, Jerusalem.
                     Tel. (02) 817073.
Board Member: Haim Eliahou, 19 Yissa Bracha, Jerusalem.

FINANCIAL INFORMATION
The Ministry of Education and Culture funds 25% of the annual budget; the balance comes from other sources. Last year's annual budget of $20,000 left an accumulated deficit of $11,000. The Yeshiva is registered as an Ottoman Association (No. 11/2657). Donations to the Yeshiva are not tax-free, either in Israel or the United States. There are 15 full-time employees and 5 part-time employees of the Yeshiva.

MEMBERSHIP, SCOPE, AND POLICY
Decisions are made by the National Board of the Yeshiva. There is only one branch and 20 members of the Yeshiva.

FUNDING NEEDED
1. The most pressing need is to remove the deficit and to give more support to the students in the future.
2. To build a bigger building in order to attract more students.
3. To open a Torah center for younger pupils.

YESHIVA SHAARE CHAIM ישיבה שערי חיים

7 Sorotzkin Street
P.O.B. 15078
Kiryat Mattersdorf, Jerusalem
Telephone: (02) 523049
Office hours: 9:00 A.M. to 12:00 Noon

HISTORY AND DESCRIPTION

Yeshiva Shaare Chaim was established in the summer of 1978, as a result of a trend of a large group of Yeshiva educators to realize that many students are graduating from Yeshiva high schools with untapped potential. Fired with a desire to continue their Yeshiva studies in the higher yeshivot of Israel, they find themselves unable to cope with the high level of study. Therefore, with the recommendations of some of the greatest Torah authorities in Israel, a select group of Yeshiva graduate students was chosen to form an institution to help prepare these students to enter a higher yeshiva.

Organizational Structure: The Yeshiva is run by a board of four Yeshiva educators who serve as administrators and educators. In addition, there are 3 other teachers and 12 tutors who offer the most personal program available.

Goals: To prepare the Yeshiva high school graduate for the high level of studies at the Yeshiva Gedola.

Services, Activities, and Accomplishments: Classes and tutorials in Talmud, Religious Law, Bible, Philosophy, Jewish Thought, and Jewish Prophets. The major accomplishments are the graduates, most of whom have successfully matriculated into various high quality yeshivas throughout the United States and Israel.

OFFICERS (All board members reside in Jerusalem.)
Board: Rabbi Moshe Lewis, 12 Panim Meirot, Jerusalem.
           Educator. Tel. (02) 533939.
           Rabbi Moshe Finkelstein, 4 Panim Meirot, Jerusalem.
           Educator. Tel. (02) 527972.
           Rabbi David Krohn, 124/5 Maane Simcha, Jerusalem.
           Educator. Tel. (02) 533326.
           Rabbi Eliezer Parkoff, 2 Panim Meirot, Jerusalem.
           Educator.

Advisory
Board: Rabbi Benjamin Krohn, 329 Beach 9th Street,
           Far Rockaway, New York. Rabbi. Tel. 212-337-7030.
           Mr. Meyer C. Parkoff, 385 Donmoor Road, Lawrence,
           New York. Businessman.
           Tel. 516-069-5880.

FINANCIAL INFORMATION
65% of last year's annual budget came from donations, 25% from tuition, and 10% from special fundraising projects. The annual budget for 1980 was $128,000. The Yeshiva is registered as an Ottoman Association (reg. no. 11/3196). Donations to the Yeshiva are tax-free in Israel (no. 4506659). The Yeshiva is in the process of obtaining tax-free status in the United States. There are 4 full-time employees and 10 part-time employees working for the Yeshiva. In addition there are two volunteers.

MEMBERSHIP, SCOPE, AND POLICY
Decisions are made by the Administrative Board. There are seven Israeli members and 2 foreign members of the Yeshiva. The Yeshiva has only one branch.

AFFILIATIONS/REFERENCES
The Yeshiva is not affiliated with any Israeli political party. The Yeshiva is in contact wtih Rabbi Yisroel Plutchok, Yeshiva Derech Chaim, 4907 18th Avenue, Brooklyn, New York 11204 USA.

FUNDING NEEDED
1. To establish scholarship funds for 10 to 15 boys at $3000 per annum, per student. Most of the students are either from poor homes or receive no financial support from their parents.
2. To develop a building fund of $500,000 to $1 million. Shaare Chaim is now temporarily renting study facilities from a neighboring yeshiva and housing students in rented apartments.

YESHIVAT SHAAREI TORAH
IN MEMORY OF THE NETZIV

ישיבת שערי־תורה ע״ש הנצי״ב זצ״ל

12 Mane Street
P.O.B. 1667
Tel Aviv
Telephone: (03) 267357
Office hours: 9:00 A.M. to 6:00 P.M.

DESCRIPTION
This educational institution was established over 90 years ago at Jaffa,
as a stronghold of Torah-Judaism in the city of Tel Aviv. Shaarei Torah
is a religious, educational institution which is one of the oldest in the Tel
Aviv area, and has primarily a Kollel (higher Torah studies department)
for adults. The graduating students have become rabbis, rabbinical
court judges and teachers, both in Israel and abroad.

OFFICERS
Rosh Hayeshiva: Rabbi Zvi Kaplan, Sokolov 18, Bnei Brak.
                  Tel. (03) 786343.
Director: Rabbi Samuel Felman.
Treasurer: Rabbi Ch. G. Landau.
Board Members: Mr. Zalman Shachor.
                  Mr. Pinchas Sheinman.

FINANCIAL INFORMATION
The breakdown of the sources of last year's annual budget were not
supplied. Last year's annual budget of $93,500 left a deficit of $15,000.
The Yeshiva was registered as an Ottoman Association (No. 2722/99)
on January 24, 1962 in Tel Aviv. Donations to the Yeshiva are tax-free
in both Israel (no. 4503076) and the United States (no. AU/F/A18,
BK/EO/64/49). The number of employees was not supplied.

MEMBERSHIP, SCOPE, AND POLICY
The Yeshiva is not affiliated with any political party in Israel.

AFFILIATIONS/REFERENCES
The Yeshiva is in contact with the Union of Orthodox Rabbis, 235 East
Broadway, New York, New York and with Young Israel, West 16th
Street, New York, New York.

FUNDING NEEDED
No specific priorities were listed.

YESHIVA TECHNICUM (TECHNICAL HIGH SCHOOL), KFAR ZVI SITRIN

ישיבה טכניקום — כפר צבי סיטרין

Kfar Sitrin
Hof HaCarmel 30880
Telephone: (04) 942583/4
Office hours: 8:00 A.M. to 4:00 P.M.

HISTORY AND DESCRIPTION

The Yeshiva was founded in 1953 with the help of Mr. Heyman Sitrin in memory of his son, Howard (Zvi), who died at a very young age. He was helped by Minister Pinchas Shapira and Rabbi Dr. I. Sh. Ben Meir who were the Minister and Deputy Minister, respectively, of the Ministry of the Interior. It was first opened as an institution for agricultural education and in 1956 it became a regular Yeshiva.

Organizational Structure: Starting with 20 pupils when the Yeshiva was founded, it now has 450 pupils and has added some valuable courses such as electronics precision control and instrumentation and general and machinery mechanics. Recently a course in naval machinery was added—the only Israeli religious course in this area. The course is designed to train navy officers in the use of this machinery. In 1979 a unique program for dental technicians was added, a profession which is in high demand in Israel. There is a post-high school program for technicians, and a national seminar for professional teachers. The boarding school has six dormitories and many facilities: a synagogue, dining room, first-aid center, sports grounds, sports hall, and a recreational building. The administrative staff, teachers, and youth leaders live in the boarding school together with the pupils.

Services, Activities, and Accomplishments: The Yeshiva has established new workshops, acquired equipment for the different trends, constructed various buildings, including a large building for Navy engines, built a new laboratory for dental technicians, a computer room, an olympic-sized sports hall, and other necessities required for a boarding school.

OFFICERS

Director: Rabbi Aviezer Burstin, Kfar Sitrin.
Author and Educationist.
Tel.: (04) 942584.

Treasurer: Rabbi Josef Shainim, Kiriat Sharet, Tirat HaCarmel, Hof HaCarmel. Town Rabbi.

Chairman: Dr. Yehuda Ben Meir, Simtat Hagivah, Savyon. Knesset Member. Tel.: (03) 752301.

Board of Director: Yeil Salomon, 1821 Broad, Utica, New York, USA 13501.

Rabbi Dr. Vogelman, Kiriat Motzkin.
Israel Grintz, 116 Yafe Nof, Haifa. Banker.
Rabbi Moshe Bernstein, 47 Nachman, Tel Aviv.
Ahron Levi, 53 Haatzmaut, Haifa. Businessman.

FINANCIAL INFORMATION
The Sitrin Family of Utica, U.S.A. were major donors for building and development, and the Education Ministry, the Jewish Agency, The Joint Distribution Committee, the Ministry of Religious Affairs, and the Ministry of Labor and Social Affairs were the sources of last year's budget. Last year's annual budget of $1,000,000 left the Yeshiva with a deficit of $300,000. The Yeshiva is registered as a Public Association, Number 12159. Donations to the Yeshiva in Israel and the United States are tax-free but no numbers were supplied. There are 65 full-time and 45 part-time employees of the Yeshiva.

MEMBERSHIP, SCOPE, AND POLICY
Decisions are made mostly by the Executive Director and by the National Board.

AFFILIATIONS/REFERENCES
The Yeshiva is not affiliated with any political party in Israel, but educates in a national religious spirit. The Yeshiva is in contact with Mr. Y. Salamon, 1821 Broad Street, Utica, New York 13501 USA.

FUNDING NEEDED
1. A new building for the electronics and precision control laboratories to replace the old buildings, at an estimated cost of $240,000.
2. A building with four apartments for additional tutors and youth leaders (to handle the increase in the number of students), at approximately $160,000.
3. A big synagogue, to be used also as a Beit Midrash, for Talmud and Torah studies.
4. Completion and change of equipment for the various educational programs, at an estimated cost of $100,000.

YESHIVAT TIFERETH ISRAEL
TALMUDICAL COLLEGE

ישיבת תפארת ישראל

1 Geulah Street
Haifa
Telephone: (04) 662227
Office hours: 8:00 A.M. to 7:00 P.M.

HISTORY AND DESCRIPTION

The Yeshiva was founded in 1925, by the late Rabbi Dov Meir Robman, of blessed memory. It is the first Yeshiva in this region of Israel.

Adjacent to this Yeshiva are a Talmud Torah and a Heder, where hundreds of pupils are taught and provided with lunch in the Yeshiva's kitchen.

The Yeshiva also has a Mishna association, charity funds, and remembrance funds to perpetuate the names of friends of the Yeshiva.

Over the course of the years thousands of scholars who were educated and trained at the Yeshiva came to occupy important positions in all spheres of life, both in the country and abroad.

The very fact of the existence of this Yeshiva in Haifa has contributed to the advancement and development of the city's religious life.

Services, Activities, and Accomplishments: The education and training of thousands of pupils, many of them poor and orphaned, and the absorption of young refugees, who escaped from the concentration camps in Europe in the 1940's, and of many pupils in the following years who immigrated from all parts of the world.

OFFICERS

Director: Rabbi Raphael Shapira, 37 Pewsner, Haifa. Manager.
               Tel. (04) 665970.
Treasurer: Naftali Herz Boimel, 17 Haneemanim, Haifa.
               Retired.
Board: Yehonatan Neufeld, 28 Nordau, Haifa.
               Tel. (04) 663714.

FINANCIAL INFORMATION

The annual budget for last year was distributed as follows: membership dues, 1%; donations, 45%; collections, 15%; allocations, 24%; and miscellaneous, 15%. Last year's annual budget was $80,000. The deficit was $8,500. The organization is registered as an Ottoman Association (reg. no. 61/173). Donations to the Yeshiva are tax-free in Israel (tax no. 532/455), but not in the United States. There are 36 full-time workers employed by the Yeshiva, as well as seven volunteers.

MEMBERSHIP, SCOPE, AND POLICY

There are 38 members in Israel and none abroad. There is one branch in Israel and none abroad. Decisions are made by the Board.

AFFILIATIONS/REFERENCES

The Yeshiva is not affiliated with any political party in Israel. The Yeshiva has the following contacts in the United States: The Joint Distribution Committee, New York, and the Central Council of Torah Institutions, New York.

FUNDING NEEDED

1. The overhaul and reconditioning of the 40-year old building. Estimated cost: $200,000.
2. The acquisition of new furniture for the classrooms and the boarding school.
   Estimated cost: $15,000.

YISMACH MOSHE
GEMILUT CHASADIM FUND

קרן גמילות חסדים ישמח משה

Joseph ben Matityahu St. 43,
Jerusalem.
Telephone: (02) 272077.
Office Hours: 1:00 P.M. to 3:00 P.M.

HISTORY AND DESCRIPTION
The fund was founded in 1979 in order to help young couples about to
be married. The loans are granted without interest and with very convenient payment terms. The organization also grants loans for medical
and dental treatment, as well as grants to poor people and very large
families. The fund is a non-profit social and volunteer service.

OFFICERS
Director: Rabbi Hanania Wizgan. No address supplied.
                        Rabbi. Tel. (02) 272077.
Treasurer: Rabbi Moshe Cohen. No address supplied.
                        Librarian.
Board or Hanhala
Members: Rabbi Yagel Meir Cohen. No address supplied.
                        Clerk. Tel. (02) 412813.
                    Rabbi Eliahou Azar. No address supplied.
                        Teacher. Tel. (02) 242374.
                    Rabbi Menashe Menahem. No address supplied.
                        Shochet (ritual slaughterer).

FINANCIAL INFORMATION
The organization's income is derived entirely from donations. Last
year's annual budget was $1,500, with no deficit. No information was
supplied regarding tax-free status for donations. The organization is
registered as a non-profit Ottoman Association in the Jerusalem District Office of the Ministry of the Interior (reg. no. 11/3389). The
organization's staff is made up of 5 volunteers.

MEMBERSHIP, SCOPE, AND POLICY
The organization has one branch in Israel and none abroad. There is no
membership as such other than the 5 board members. Decisions are
made mostly by the director and the treasurer.

AFFILIATIONS/REFERENCES
The organization is not affiliated with any political party in Israel nor
with any group abroad.

ZAHAVI—THE ISRAEL ASSOCIATION OF LARGE FAMILIES

תנועת זהבי — האגודה לזכויות המשפחות ברוכות ילדים

10 Shapira Street
P.O.B. 9777
Haifa
Telephone: (04) 666363
Office hours: 9:00 A.M. to 2:00 P.M.

HISTORY AND DESCRIPTION

Zahavi was established in 1972 by the parents of a group of families each having at least four children. It is a grassroots lobby fighting for the rights of large families in Israel, with members coming from the various ethnic, religious, and economic sectors of Israeli society.

Organizational Structure: Each township has a local branch with offi-cers who are elected at a general meeting. Representatives of the branches elect a national Executive Committee which in turn elects the Chairman of the movement. There are more than 20 branches through-out Israel, based on the volunteer work of parents involved in self-help projects and lobbying.

Goals: To assist those parents fulfilling the religious commandment of bearing many children to contribute economically, socially and politi-cally to the State of Israel; to ensure the survival of the Jews in their land; and to create a positive attitude and image in Israel and the world concerning large Jewish families.

There is a trend among certain sectors of Israeli society to stigmatize large families, and to limit family size. They lavish on one or two children all possible material and social benefits. Whereas there are acknowledged advantages to growing up in a large family, raising many children does present problems. In terms of Israel's rapidly spiralling inflation, there have been annual increases in cost of food, clothing, housing and, indeed, all commodities. Today, those wishing to raise many children must consider whether they can shoulder the responsibil-ity. When they do not, the resulting loss of human resources to society is incalculable. When they do, society's gain if often the parents' burden. Zahavi asks for an equal opportunity, for the chance to help themselves. Zahavi does not ask for handouts.

Services and Activities: Zahavi fights cuts in children's allowances; reduced water rates for large families; expanded social security rights for large-family mothers; increases in National Insurance allowances; arranges reduced fees for recreation programs and nursery schools; and elicits some compensation for large families when basic subsidies are cut. It lobbies actively for supportive legislation and is respectfully heard by Knesset members and the media.

Accomplishments: Zahavi has 20,000 registered members in Israel and branches in many Israeli towns. It has been congratulated by the President and Prime Minister of Israel on behalf of its efforts. With only voluntary help it has achieved initial legislation in favor of large families, published a Bulletin of news and information, and has gained press and radio coverage.

The government of Israel has agreed to a major reduction in calculating the water bills for large families as a result of Zahavi's efforts.

It succeeded in having The Large Families Law introduced in the Knesset in 1980, which will spell out for the first time the rights of large families to benefits in housing, income, education, use of public utilities and resources; official recognition of mothers of many children as working mothers with all rights and benefits; increased tax-free child allowances, guaranteed minimum income, reduced utility rates; free or low cost pre-school and other educational services at every level, more quality child-care services; and reduced costs for public transportation and entertainment events.

OFFICERS

Chairman:	Avraham Danino. Social worker educator. Tel. (04) 523711.
Treasurer:	Meir Levi, Moshav Yashresh. Bank Manager.
National Board:	Aharon Ezra, Holon. Tax Consultant. Tel. (03) 621606.
	Dr. Eliezer Jaffe, 37 Gaza, Jerusalem. Professor of Social Work. Tel (02) 637450.
	Dr. Eugene Wiener, 21 Zamenhof, Haifa. Professor of Education. Tel. (04) 24550.
	Yaakov Semadar, Hedera. Accountant. Tel. (053) 26691.
	Yardena Aviram, Jerusalem. Hospital attendant. Tel. (02) 665151.

FINANCIAL INFORMATION

90% of last year's annual budget came from donations, while the remaining 10% came from membership dues. Last year's annual budget was $120,000. There is no deficit. The organization is registered as an Ottoman Association (reg. no. 61/1125). Donations to Zahavi are tax-free in Israel (reg. no. 4503758) and in the United States (reg. no. 23-7447481-N). There are five full-time workers employed by Zahavi in addition to several thousand volunteers.

MEMBERSHIP, SCOPE, AND POLICY

There are 20,000 families in Israel and 500 families abroad who are members. There are 20 branches in Israel and one abroad. Any family (parent) with four or more children can join the organization. Decisions are made by the National and the Executive Director.

AFFILIATIONS/REFERENCES

The organization is not affiliated with any political party in Israel. Zahavi has two contacts abroad. They are: Zahavi-American Office, 2128 Marlindale Road, Cleveland Heights, Ohio 44118 and Max W. Jacobs, 700 Delaware Avenue, Buffalo, New York 14209. Earmarked contributions can be sent through P.E.F. Israel Endowment Fund, New York, N.Y.

FUNDING NEEDED

1. Cooperative enterprise stores—a network of Zahavi stores, which would enable the bulk sale of goods at reduced prices. Cost is estimated at $1.5 million.
2. Furniture Bank—A lending library of children's furniture and household equipment in major urban centers, where good quality used items can be donated and reused by several families in rotation. Estimated cost, $200,000.
3. Legal Aid—The provision, in specific instances, of the best possible legal advice for cases involving legal precedents or class actions on behalf of Zahavi constituents. This project can benefit not only the litigants, but will also help Zahavi in its fight to establish more policies and laws favorable to large families. Estimated cost, $15,000.
4. Scholarship Fund—Tutorial assistance and economic support which would prevent children from large families from dropping out of school.

ZICHRON YOSEF RELIEF FOR B'NEI TORAH

עזרה לבני תורה זכרון יוסף ירושלים

Bergman Street 10, Bayit Vegan, Jerusalem   OR
P.O.B. 16044, Jerusalem.

HISTORY AND DESCRIPTION

The "Zichron Yosef" Relief Fund was founded approximately 30 years ago, in 1950. The organization was established in order to assist needy and poor families in Israel. Funds received are distributed by Rav Joshua Neuwirth, Rabbi of Kol Torah Yeshiva in Jerusalem. The American Friends of "Zichron Yosef" Relief Fund, located in New York City, forward all contributions directly to Israel for distribution here.

Organizational Structure: The organization is managed by a 5-member board located in Jerusalem. Most decisions are made by the Executive Director. Four other board members run the sister organization in New York City. There is no membership as such in either organization.

Services Activities, and Accomplishments: For the past 30 years, the Relief Fund has been providing immediate monetary assistance to the needy for the purchase of food (especially for the holidays). Other services include the distribution of funds to young couples planning marriage, and to families destitute because of illness. As inflation worsens, the number of daily requests is steadily increasing.

OFFICERS

Director: Rabbi Yehoshua Neuwirth, Bergman 10, Jerusalem.
Treasurer: Mr. Naftali Packter, Bait Vegan 105, Jerusalem. Businessman.
Board Members: Mr. Chaim Metzger, Rashdam 3, Jerusalem. Teacher.
Mr. Mordechai Wormser, Neve Ozer 8, Jerusalem.
Mr. Willie Grangewood, HaPisga 54, Jerusalem. Attorney.
In N.Y.C.: Mr. Josef Schuster
Mr. Felix Lehmann
Mr. Theo. M. Levi
Mr. Barry Lichtenstein
P.O.B. 149
Washington Bridge Station
New York, N.Y. 10033

FINANCIAL INFORMATION

Donations and collections are the Relief Fund's sole source of income. Last year's annual budget was $100,000. The organization was short approximately $65,000 in terms of actual requests for assistance which could not be met due to lack of funds. Donations to the Fund in Israel and the United States are tax-free (Israel tax no. 450-3706; U.S.A. no. 23-7396610). The organization is registered as a non-profit Ottoman

Association in the Jerusalem District Office of the Ministry of the Interior (reg. no. 11/1069).
Three volunteers serve the Relief Fund. There is no salaried staff.

AFFILIATIONS/REFERENCES
The American affiliate of the organization in Jerusalem is the American Friends of "Zichron Yosef" Relief Fund, P.O.B. 149, Washington Bridge Station, New York, N.Y. 10033. The organization has no affiliation with any political party in Israel.

ZION ORPHANAGE (BLUMENTHAL)

בית יתומים ציון – בלומנטל, ירושלים

16 Hoshea Street
Geula, Jerusalem
P.O.B. 5017
Telephone: (02) 287491
Office Hours: 8:00 A.M. to 2:00 P.M.

HISTORY AND DESCRIPTION

Founded by the late Rabbi Avraham Blumenthal of Blessed Memory in 1900, the Orphanage has carried on its work through two World Wars as well as the Israeli wars, accepting war orphans and those directly affected by the wars.

Organizational Structure: The Orphanage accepts school-age children who learn at a local school and have their lessons supplemented by tutors in the afternoons. There is a special School Department on the premises for those children unable to follow a normal school education, where they receive individual attention and instruction from specially trained staff. Highly experienced staff at the Orphanage includes social workers, a psychologist, teachers and counselors under the guidance of the Inspector from the Israel Ministry of Education.

Goals: The orphanage aims to educate and bring up the children to become independent individuals who are able to go out into the outside world and function as respectable citizens in normal society.

Services, Activities and Accomplishments: The children eat and sleep at the Orphanage Dormitory and receive the care and attention that children of normal homes receive. There are recreation rooms, a library, a Sports Hall, outdoor playgrounds with suitable play apparatus and a handicraft room, where the children are guided in their activities by experienced staff. The Orphanage has succeeded in bringing up and educating the children in its care—orphans, unwanted children and children from deprived social backgrounds—so that they become independent individuals able to function in normal society. Among the Orphanage graduates are Deans, judges, engineers, accountants, teachers, bookkeepers and professionals, tradesmen and other respectable citizens.

OFFICERS

Director: E. Rakowsky, 16 Hoshea St., Jerusalem. Rabbi. Tel. (02) 287491.

Treasurer: M. Schalpubersky, 24 Malachi St., Jerusalem. Dean. Tel. (02) 286350.

Board Members: Y. Kravitz, Sanhedria, Jerusalem. Dean.
Y. Miletzky, 41 Tzefania St., Jerusalem. Judge.
S. Reichman, 5 Achad Ha'Am, Jerusalem. Rabbi. Tel. (02) 286923.

FINANCIAL INFORMATION

Donations provide 40% of the Orphanage income; 35% comes from the Ministry of Social Welfare (support of children), 15% from membership dues and the remainder from Yahrzheit services (Kaddish, etc). Last year's budget of $200,000 left the Orphanage with a deficit of $35,500. Five full-time and thirty-one part-time staff work for the Orphanage. Donations are tax-free, both in Israel and the United States, as well as England. The organization is registered in Jerusalem as an Ottoman society (no. not reported).

MEMBERSHIP, SCOPE AND POLICY

There are approximately five thousand members in the one Israeli branch of the Zion Orphanage and five thousand more in the two branches abroad. Religious men unaffiliated with any political party and who are experienced in education and do their work as a voluntary service are welcome to join. Day to day decisions are made by the director and more important decisions subject to approval by the Board.

AFFILIATIONS/REFERENCES

The Orphanage is not affiliated with any political party in Israel. Organizations abroad which are familiar with Zion Orphanage are the following: Zion Orphanage Inc. 290 Madison Avenue, New York City, New York (USA); the Federated Council of Israel Institutions; the Rabbinical Council of America; and the Jewish Board of Deputies, South Africa.

FUNDING NEEDED

1. For furniture for the twenty-two bedrooms in the new dormitory wing. Each room requires four beds (total eighty-eight), chairs, tables and closets; cost, $50,000.
2. To purchase equipment for the Sports Hall; cost, $25,000.
3. To replace the old furniture in the old dormitory wing with new, modern furniture; cost, $50,000.

RECOMMENDED READING

Ben, I., *et al* (eds.) (1980). *Who's Who in Israel*,
Bronfman and Cohen Publishers, Tel Aviv.

Bentwich, J. (1965). *Education in Israel*, Jewish Publication Society
of America, Philadelphia.

Chieger, E. (ed.) (1978). *New Dimensions in Rehabilitation*,
Tcherikower Publishers, Tel Aviv.

Cohen, J. (1980). *The New Israel Fund, Progress Report — April, 1980*,
San Francisco.

Curtis, E. and Chertoff, M. (eds.) (1973). *Israel: Social Structure and Change*,
Transaction Books, New Brunswick.

Danino, A. (1978). *The Child Favored Family: Large Families in Israel*,
Zahavi Association, Haifa.

Davies, A.M. and Lockard (eds.) (1980) *Joint (JDC) Israel: Brookdale Institute of
Gerontology and Adult Human Development*, Brookdale Institute, J-m.

Doron, A. (1976). *Cross-National Studies of Social Service Systems — Israel:
The Society Context for Social Welfare*, Division of Research, Ministry of
Labor and Social Affairs, Jerusalem.

Herlitz, E. (1977). "Volunteering in Israel", *Kidma: Israel Journal
of Development*, No. 12, pp. 30-35.

Jaffe, E.D. (1975). "Poverty in the Third Jewish Commonwealth:
Sephardi-Ashkenazi Divisions", *Journal of Jewish Communal Service*,
52:1, pp. 91-99.
— (1979). "Non-Conventional Philanthropy", *Moment*, 4:5, pp. 63-66.
— (1980). *Pleaders and Protestors*, The American Jewish Committee,
New York.
— (1980). "Not Just Charity", *The National Jewish Monthly*,
94:5, pp. 32-33.
— (1982). *Child Welfare in Israel*, Praeger Publishers, New York.
— (1982). *Israelis in Institutions*, Gordon and Breach, New York,
London, and Paris.

Jaffe, R. (1979). "Homemakers for Israeli Families of Retarded Children",
Child Welfare, (June), pp. 403-407.

Jarus, A., *et ai* (eds.) (1970). *Children and Families in Israel*,
Gordon and Breach, New York.

Kramer, R. (1975). *The Voluntary Service Agency in Israel*, Research Series
No. 26, Institute of International Studies, University of California, Berkeley.

Liron, Y. (1973). *Deprivation and the Socio-Economic Gap in Israel*, The Israel
Economist, Jerusalem.

Musher, S. (1981), *PEF Israel Endowment Funds, Inc. — Annual Report*,
New York.

Neipris, J. (1974). *Social Services in Israel*, The American Jewish Committee,
New York.

Rapaport, C., *et al*. (eds.) (1976). *Early Child Care in Israel*, Gordon and Breach,
New York.

Reagles, K.W., *et al* (1974). *Rehabilitation in Israel*, B'nai Brith Career and
Counseling Services, Washington, D.C.

Rosen, H. (1979). *Volunteerism in Israel*, The American Jewish Committee.

Siegel, D. (1981). "Danny Siegel's 1980 Tz'dakah Report", *Moment Magazine*.

Smooha, S. (1978). *Israel: Pluralism and Conflict*, University of
California Press, Berkeley.

Spiro, S. (ed.) (1978). *Programs of Social Work Education in Israel, 1978*, Israel
Association of Schools of Social Work, Tel Aviv University, Tel Aviv.

State of Israel (1981). *Directory of Recognized Agencies, 1981-1983*, Department
of Public Institutions, Ministry of Labor and Social Affairs, Jerusalem.